# Bangkok

Chiang Mai & the Islands
**timeout.com/bangkok**

**Penguin Books**

PENGUIN BOOKS

Published by the Penguin Group
Penguin Books Ltd, 80 Strand, London WC2R ORL, England
Penguin Books USA Inc., 375 Hudson Street, New York, New York 10014, USA
Penguin Books Australia Ltd, 250 Camberwell Road, Camberwell, Victoria 3124, Australia
Penguin Books Canada Ltd, 10 Alcorn Avenue, Toronto, Ontario, Canada M4V 3B2
Penguin Books (NZ) Ltd, cnr Rosedale and Airborne Roads, Albany, Auckland, New Zealand

Penguin Books Ltd, Registered Offices: Harmondsworth, Middlesex, England

First published 2003
10 9 8 7 6 5 4 3 2 1

Colour reprographics by Icon, Crowne House, 56-58 Southwark Street, London SE1 1UN
Printed and bound by Cayfosa-Quebecor, Ctra. de Caldes, Km 3 08 130 Sta, Perpètua de Mogoda, Barcelona, Spain

**Edited and designed by**
**Time Out Guides Limited**
**Universal House**
**251 Tottenham Court Road**
**London W1T 7AB**
**Tel + 44 (0)20 7813 3000**
**Fax + 44 (0)20 7813 6001**
**Email guides@timeout.com**
**www.timeout.com**

## Editorial

**Editor** Philip Cornwel-Smith
**Deputy Editors** Sam Le Quesne, Cath Phillips
**Researcher** Kathareeya Jumroonsiri
**Listings Checker** Chatchai Ngoenprakairat
**Proofreader** Ronnie Haydon
**Indexer** Anna Raikes

**Editorial Director** Peter Fiennes
**Series Editor** Ruth Jarvis
**Deputy Series Editor** Jonathan Cox
**Guides Co-ordinator** Anna Norman

## Design

**Group Art Director** John Oakey
**Art Director** Mandy Martin
**Art Editor** Scott Moore
**Senior Designer** Lucy Grant
**Designer** Sarah Edwards
**Digital Imaging** Dan Conway
**Ad Make-up** Glen Impey
**Picture Editor** Kerri Littlefield
**Deputy Picture Editor** Kit Burnet
**Picture Researcher** Emma Tremett
**Picture Desk Trainee** Bella Wood

## Advertising

**Group Commercial Director** Lesley Gill
**Sales Director** Mark Phillips
**Advertisement Sales (Bangkok)** Jane Bay for
Asia City Publishing Group
**International Sales Manager** Ross Canadé
**Advertising Assistant** Sabrina Ancilleri

## Administration

**Chairman** Tony Elliott
**Chief Operating Officer** Kevin Ellis
**Managing Director** Mike Hardwick
**Group Marketing Director** Christine Cort
**Marketing Manager** Mandy Martinez
**US Publicity & Marketing** Rosella Albanese
**Group General Manager** Nichola Coulthard
**Group Financial Director** Rick Waterlow
**Guides Production Director** Mark Lamond
**Production Controller** Samantha Furniss
**Accountant** Sarah Bostock

## Contributors

**Introduction** Philip Cornwel-Smith. **History** Anon Nakornthab. **Buddhism Today** Mettanando Bhikku, Anon Nakornthab.
**Art & Architecture** Alex Kerr. **Bangkok Today** Philip Cornwel-Smith. **Accommodation** Kelsey Munro, Justin Eeles, Jim
Algie. **Sightseeing** Kathareeya Jumroonsiri. **Phra Nakorn** Steven Pettifor; *Banglamphu* Jim Algie (*Learn to: Massage*
Philip Cornwel-Smith). **Thonburi, River & Canals** Stirling Silliphant (*The mother of all waters* Philip Cornwel-Smith).
**Dusit** Jim Algie. **Chinatown** Jennifer Gampell. **Downtown** Steven Pettifor (*Multiple phantasm* Philip Cornwel-Smith).
**Suburbs** Steven Pettifor. **Restaurants** Rob McKeown, Korakot Punlopruksa, Howard Richardson. **Bars & Pubs** Rob
McKeown, Anon Nakornthab (*Message in a bottle* Howard Richardson). **Markets** Rob McKeown, Korakot Punlopruksa.
**Shops & Services** Anon Nakornthab. **Festivals & Events** Brian Mertens. **Children** Andrea Francis. **Film** Philip Cornwel-
Smith. **Galleries** Phataravadi Phataranavik; *introduction* Philip Cornwel-Smith. **Gay & Lesbian** Robin Newbold. **Mind & Body**
Chamsai Jotisalikorn (*Learn to: Meditate* Philip Cornwel-Smith). **Music** Tim Carr (*High notes* Howard Richardson). **Nightlife**
Sippakorn Suriyakham (*Adult nightlife, The professionals* Thomas Schmid). **Performing Arts** Pichayanund Chindahporn.
**Sport & Fitness** Howard Richardson. **Getting Started** Kathareeya Jumroonsiri. **Central Plains** Thomas Schmid, Scott
Coates, Jonathan Hopfner, Philip Cornwel-Smith. **Eastern Seaboard** Howard Richardson, Philip Cornwel-Smith. **Samui
Archipelago** Terry Blackburn; *Ko Tao* Alyssa Miletti (*Learn to: Dive* Paul Lees). **The Andaman Coast** Alasdair Forbes,
Charlotte Shalgosky. **Chiang Mai** Oliver Hargreave. **Around Chiang Mai** Oliver Hargreave, Philip Cornwel-Smith. **Directory**
Kathareeya Jumroonsiri, Philip Cornwel-Smith.

**Maps** JS Graphics (john@jsgraphics.co.uk). Map data supplied by Bangkok Guide Co Part, 1276 Onnut Soi 34/1, Suan Luang,
Bangkok 10250 (0 2311 1439/www.bangkokguide.homepage.com).

**Photography by** Jonathan Perugia except: page 10 Prommitr Production; page 128 Marcus Goertz; page 254 Paul J Lees; page
158 Nick Nostitz; and page 250 John Everingham. The following images were provided by the featured establishments/artists:
pages 23, 171, 172, 231, 233, 249, 253 and 257. Jonathan Perugia flew between Hua Hin, Samui and Bangkok with
Bangkok Airways (0 2229 3434/www.bangkokair.com) and toured Bangkok canals with Mit Chao Phraya Travel Service
(0 2225 6179).

**The Editor would like to thank** Alex Kerr, Albert Paravi Wongchirachai, Anon Nakornthab, Charlotte Shalgosky, Brian
Mertens, Jason Gagliardi, Anucha Thirakanont, Anan Anpruang, Utopia, Sarah Champion, Bob Halliday, Suchai
Lowhakasamevong, Sumalee Chaitientong, Bill Vaughan, Dr Kanwar Singh, Sanitsuda Ekachai, Jac Vidgen, Norachai
Boonsom, Shane Armstrong, Ronnie Haydon, Simon Coppock, Lily Dunn and all the staff at Time Out Guides.

# Contents

# Introduction

In this era of branding, it's hard to pin down the identity of Bangkok. The city has at least one multiple personality – plus several hidden sides. A crossroads of cultural fusion, but never colonised by the West, Thailand maintains a flair and confidence in its traditions, Buddhist beliefs and the symbols of its independence. Despite modernisation, its capital possesses a contradictory character and a Thai otherness that is palpable yet defies description. Though there's no shortage of clichés and preconceptions to overcome.

Thais call Bangkok Krung Thep, the 'City of Angels', and there are indeed angels in the architecture, its monuments embellished with mythic symbolism. It also resembles its namesake Los Angeles in some ways, with its surface dazzle, diffuse centres amid an ill-defined sprawl, powerful elites, deprived underclass and penchant for fantasy and colour, with an armoury of ready smiles.

'Land of Smiles' – yes, another stereotype that proves disarmingly true. Though, notoriously, there's a different *yim* (smile) for every mood and intention. Charmed, impressed, distressed, nonplussed, furious or even vengeful: just what is that beaming Bangkok grin telling you?

Things rarely go predictably in this culture of indirectness. Here 'yes' might mean 'no' because it's more polite; a misdeed might be done to save face; and efficiency is improved by laughing and nattering and snacking, because 'work' is defined as 'party'. Hence, to get something done, Thais make it fun.

That's not to say it's all the 'tropical paradise' of brochure hyperbole. Amid the glittering temples, poised dancers and intricate offerings, there's a *lot* of concrete. And those smiles mask problems wrought by industrialisation and the consumer boom. Bland suburbs have ballooned faster than the infrastructure, as the already dominant capital has become a magnet for so many upcountry migrants (and illegal immigrants) that no one knows how many people live here. Few cities have transformed as radically in such a short time – so what is its elusive contemporary character?

'Bangkok is like a warm and generous but insecure and overly sensitive young woman,' claims one brand research survey trying to find a common theme among its spicily inviting culture, food and people, and its knee-jerk associations with sex, drugs and pollution. Reinforced by tabloid sensationalism and nudge-nudge innuendo, that sleazy reputation seems passé and unbalanced to residents, who are turning the capital into a cosmopolitan world city that's progressively marginalising its seedier scenes.

So what is the right name for Bangkok's sophisticated reincarnation, with its liberated arts expression, alternative health cachet, international dining and creative new designers? Wags dub it the 'Big Mango' or, less charitably, the 'Big Durian', after the fruit that's at once sublime yet rank. Those brand researchers see the city's prize asset as its people and suggest the 'Big Heart'. That suits the many aficionados of cute, and it does convey how life spills out on to the street, how activity revolves around food and family and sharing. But it's sweeter than a Thai dessert.

No one has come closer to capturing Bangkok's good, bad and downright bizarre than, ironically, the Tourist Authority of Thailand (TAT). Its 'Amazing Thailand' campaign conjures up a kaleidoscope of its artistry, mountains, temples, tribes, fruits, silk, beaches, forests and elephants. To the TAT's surprise, the public then gleefully applied 'amazing' to traffic, to bureaucracy, to unfathomable 'what-was-that?' incidents that crop up constantly. The genius of 'Amazing Bangkok' is that it embraces every extreme and juxtaposition, for the abiding impression visitors get is of sensory overload.

## ABOUT THE TIME OUT CITY GUIDES

The *Time Out Guide to Bangkok, Chiang Mai & the Islands* is one of an expanding series of Time Out City Guides, now numbering nearly 40, produced by the people behind London and New York's successful listings magazines. Our guides are all written and updated by resident experts who have striven to provide you with all the most up-to-date information you'll need to explore the city or read up on its background, whether you're a local or a first-time visitor.

## THE LOWDOWN ON THE LISTINGS

Above all, we've tried to make this book as useful as possible. Addresses, telephone numbers, websites, opening times, admission prices and credit card details are included in our listings. And we've given details where we can of facilities, services and events. However, owners and managers can change their arrangements at any time. In Thailand, the times and dates kept by shops, bars and, in particular, venues and events, can often vary from what's stated. If you're going out of your way to visit a venue, we'd advise you whenever possible to phone for details first. While every effort has been made to ensure the accuracy of the information in this guide, the publishers cannot accept any responsibility for any errors it may contain.

There are two things to remember in Bangkok: everything will inevitably take longer than you expect, and everything will cost more than you expect. The golden rule is to make sure you take a sense of humour with you wherever you go.

## PRICES AND PAYMENT

The prices given in this guide should be treated as guidelines, not gospel. We have listed prices in *baht* (B) throughout, and where relevant in US dollars ($). Hotels, restaurants, bars and shops in major cities widely accept some or all of the following credit cards: American Express (AmEx), Diners Club (DC), MasterCard (MC) and Visa (V). For advice on bargaining, tipping, touts, scams and higher charges for non-Thais, see p53.

## THE LIE OF THE LAND

To make the book (and the city) easier to navigate, we have divided Bangkok into areas, which are reflected in the chapters and headings in our Sightseeing section, starting on p52. Although these areas are a simplification of Bangkok's geography, they follow administrative districts and local terms where possible. The areas are used in addresses throughout the guide and shown on the fully indexed colour maps at the back of the guide, starting on p306.

Distances between sights in Bangkok can be large, and the climate is hot and humid, so many tourists avoid the hassle of the city buses or the difficulties of walking, preferring to take the BTS SkyTrain or to use one of the cheap and plentiful taxis. Though signs in English are a common sight in the capital, addresses nationwide are a minefield of contradictions. Multiple spellings and inconsistent numbering abound. You'll find all relevant orientation guidance on p286.

There is an online version of this guide, as well as weekly events listings for 35 international cities, at **www.timeout.com**

## THAILAND

A third of this guide is devoted to the highlights of Thailand, in the Beyond Bangkok section, starting on p212. It focuses on the northern capital of Chiang Mai, the islands of the south and excursions within easy range of Bangkok, plus ways to explore rural Thailand and nature. We've provided maps for the most important areas within each chapter in the section.

## TELEPHONE NUMBERS

All Thailand's phone numbers now incorporate the former area code in a national system of nine digits plus an initial 0, even when you're phoning from within the same area. If you happen to be referencing an old seven-digit Bangkok number, dial 02 beforehand; for an old six-digit upcountry number start with the old area code. Mobiles are common, with numbers that start 01, 06 or 09; they cost more than land lines for local calls, but are cheaper long-distance. To call Thailand from abroad, dial your international access code, then 66 for Thailand, and omit the initial 0 before the rest of the number.

## ESSENTIAL INFORMATION

For all the practical information you might need for visiting Bangkok, including emergency phone numbers and details of local transport, turn to the Directory chapter, starting on p280.

## MAPS

We've provided map references for most places listed in central Bangkok, indicating the page and grid reference at which an address can be found on our street maps. These are located at the back of the book on pp308-12. There's also a street index, on pp313-4.

## LET US KNOW WHAT YOU THINK

We hope you enjoy the *Time Out Guide to Bangkok, Chiang Mai & the Islands*, and we'd like to know what you think of it. We welcome tips for places to include in future editions and take note of your criticism of our choices. There's a reader's reply card at the back of the book for your feedback – or you can email us at guides@timeout.com.

# Advertisers

We would like to stress that no establishment has been included in this guide because it has advertised in any of our publications and no payment of any kind has influenced any review. The opinions given in this book are those of *Time Out* writers and entirely independent.

# In Context

รัตนโกสินทร์

# History

Thailand's past is a current affair.

History in Thailand is not just about the past; how that past is presented is still front-page news. Issues under debate include how to deal with former enemies in school textbooks and how to acknowledge popular uprisings against dictatorship. While educators try to reconcile events that have happened within living memory, historians are addressing the appropriation of Thai history by an official narrative. The root of *prawat*, the Thai word for history, means 'biography' and, as was once the approach in Europe, Thai history is substantially the biography of kings. However, revisionist academics are broadening 'Thai Studies' to encompass economic, social and geo-political factors.

While historians are split over the origin of the Thai people, adequate records exist to map the history of the Thai domain and the peoples who have occupied it at any given time. Royal chronicles serve as the official record, while historical literature and theses by the indefatigable Prince Damrong, often dubbed the 'father of Thai history', have provided the framework. The most authoritative book on the region's history is *A History of South-east Asia* by the late DGE Hall, professor at the University of London and later Cornell University. (Many of his students gravitated to Cornell and London's School of Oriental and African Studies (SOAS), enlivening debate about the interpretation of history.)

The current monarch, King Bhumibol and Queen Sirikit (*see above*).

An old-school view, exemplified by Cambridge-educated ML Manich Jumsai and two great personalities that preceded him at Oxbridge – King Vajiravudh and his half-brother Prince Chula Chakrabongse – had shaped the history of the Thai nation under a master narrative. But a new generation – chief among them David Wyatt of Cornell and Thongchai Winichakul of the University of Wisconsin at Madison – have advanced an alternative approach beyond the context of nationhood. In *Siam Mapped*, Thongchai literally charts how (before the 19th-century Rattanakosin-era unitary state), the borders, compositions and allegiances of empires, city states and ethnic enclaves in the broad Siamese 'geo-body' were incredibly fluid. So the question is raised: how did Siam start?

## BEGINNINGS TO SUKHOTHAI

When present-day Bangkok was under the sea in the Cretaceous Age, *Siamotyrannus isanensis*, the world's oldest tyrannosaur, roamed the Khorat Plateau to the north-east. On and around that plain the early South-east Asians fashioned some of civilisation's earliest bronze axes and invented the outrigger canoe.

By the time that Prince Sitthatha Gotama (who became the Buddha) was wandering northern India six centuries before Christ, merchants from the subcontinent had established trading posts in Suwannaphum ('Golden Land'), a region close to present-day Bangkok. They traded and intermarried with indigenous inhabitants whose ancestors had thousands of years earlier navigated the sea and crossed land bridges into the South-east Asian peninsula, where they established agricultural communities along the Gulf of Siam. Suwannaphum (a name that has been adopted by tourism promoters and Bangkok's new airport) grew to the extent that, in the third century BC, Emperor Asoka of India, a Buddhist convert, dispatched monks to the 16 points of the compass. Two came to Suwannaphum.

During the Suwannaphum period, Tai clans (the tribal ancestors of contemporary Thais) moved through Yunnan in southern Han-dynasty China, spreading as far as Assam in India and upper Vietnam, where Tai tribes are still found today. Living in stilt houses, they tended rice in water-filled fields using buffaloes, the status symbol of the time. Flanked to the east by powerful Chinese and Vietnamese coastal states, these tattooed clansmen marched their families west and south-west over the following millennia into lowland South-east Asia. Subduing its earlier settlers, they carved a pastoral society out of forest in what is now upper-central Thailand.

From the sixth century, as Suwannaphum faded, Tais cultivated rice along the fringes of Dvaravati, a little-known Therevada Buddhist civilisation. With centres at Suphanburi, Nakhon Pathom and Nakhon Ratchasima (formerly known as Khorat), it spread along trade routes as far as Laos. Southern Thailand was then part of the equally elusive Mahayana Buddhist empire of Srivijaya, centred in Sumatra, with limited traces at Chaiya of its eighth- to 13th-century span. The sole evidence of Dvaravati's name is a clay inscription found near Bangkok. However, its devout Mon population built numerous Buddhist sites, engraving their language on to clay tablets and uncannily lifelike statues.

Still distinct in pockets such as Ko Kred, Phra Pradaeng, Kanchanaburi and Burma's Mon state, the Mons built up Dvaravati over three centuries, only for it to be overrun by ninth-century Khmers under King Jayavoraman II, who had consolidated power around Angkor. By the tenth century, Angkor had placed Khmer nobility to rule over Mons and Tais in settlements such as Sukhothai, Phitsanulok, Phimai, That Phanom and Muang Singh; the Tai long retained the Khmer's Hindu concept of *devaraja*, the divine rule of kings.

Not all of Dvaravati city states were easily conquered. Lavo (present-day Lopburi) remained independent for two more centuries and later defied its Khmer overlords by sending diplomats to China between the early 11th and mid 12th centuries. It had by then become substantially populated by Tais – whom the Khmer referred to as Syam (Sanskrit for 'swarthy'). Angkor's bas reliefs include an 1150 carving of Khmer King Suriyavoraman II reviewing fierce Siamese troops from Lopburi, their commander wielding a bow and arrow atop a war elephant. The seed of Siam was stirring.

By Angkor's decline, following the death of Jayavoraman VII around 1220, Tai clans had blended with the Mon and Khmer in the Chao Phraya basin to form a distinctly Siamese ethnicity. Power now lay further north, with King Mangrai ruling Lanna from Chiang Mai and Tai prince Pha Muang defeating western Khmer outposts and installing himself as King Sri Indraditya of Sukhothai (c1240-70). Meanwhile, the post-Dvaravati Mon empire of Pagan in Burma

> ▶ Many of the places and buildings mentioned here are covered in more detail in other chapters, including **Sightseeing** and **Beyond Bangkok**.

was sacked by the Mongol armies of Kublai Khan, who had displaced China's Sung dynasty. With the two classical empires vanquished, the new Tai kingdoms of Lanna, Sukhothai and Phayao allied in 1287 to ward off Mongol China. In 1301 Mangrai repulsed a Mongol invasion, then Tai troops repeatedly raided China until a truce in 1312, with China accepting elephants in tribute.

The kingdom of Sukhothai, meaning 'Dawn of Happiness', became a force to be reckoned with under Sri Indraditya's son, King Ramkhamhaeng (c1279-98). He'd earned the moniker 'Rama the Bold' when, aged 19, he daringly repulsed an invasion of Tak by the western kingdom of Sot. During his 19-year reign, Sukhothai blossomed into a federation of Buddhist states, including Si Satchanalai and Kamphaengphet. Wielding influence more through *dhammaraja* (Buddhist kingship) than military might, Sukhothai extended its dominion west to the Indian Ocean, east to Lao Vieng Chan (Vientiane) and south to Nakhon Si Thamarat in the Malay peninsula, though skirting the Lopburi-controlled lower plains.

The court lavishly supported a Buddhist revival, visualised through a distinct Sukhothai aesthetic, notable for its stylised forms and the world's first statues of the Buddha walking. In the first Thai script to distinguish tones, Sukhothai left engravings, apparently in the king's own words, attesting to its glory and righteousness. The famous line about abundance – 'fish are in the rivers, rice is in the fields' – is often quoted today by environmental and self-sufficiency advocates. But Sukhothai's moral authority over the Tai plains disintegrated on the death of Ramkhamhaeng.

## THE RISE OF AYUTTHAYA

As Sukhothai swiftly lost its grip up north, the houses of Suphanburi and Lopburi vied for supremacy in the central plains. During an outbreak of cholera, the Lopburi aristocrat U Thong (conveniently wed to a noblewoman from each ruling house), led a fleeing contingent south to a riverine island, where, on the morning of 4 March 1351, a new kingdom was founded: Ayutthaya (named after an ancient city in India, legendary home of Rama). Ascending the throne as King Ramathibodi (1351-69), U Thong sent his relatives to rule Suphanburi and Lopburi (a move that, in the long run, pitted the two dynasties to squabble over Ayutthaya's throne for generations).

The Ayutthaya that U Thong encountered was an international trading centre busy with Chinese and other Asian merchants. As the city grew in importance, the rivermouth

Sukhothai-style Buddha.

trading post of Bang Makok (later shortened to Bangkok) became a strategic gateway. The first of several canals to bypass Bangkok's river meanders was cut in the long reign of King Baromtrailokanart (1448-88). On the west bank, Thonburi was bestowed a fortress just before the first sacking of Ayutthaya by the Burmese in the reign of King Chakkrapat (1548-69).

> **'Ayutthaya prospered in the 17th century to become a great trading hub with a million-strong population, larger than London's.'**

After a spell under King Mahathamaracha (1569-90), Ayutthaya began to reassert its independence through his son, King Naresuan (1590-1605), who'd grown up as a noble hostage at the Burmese court. The turning point was the Battle of Nong Sarai, waged on war elephants, in which Naresuan slew the crown prince of Burma.

Siamese independence restored, Ayutthaya prospered in the 17th century to become a great trading hub with a million-strong population (then larger than London's). Bangkok, a port of duty by the early 17th century, received its first

European ships: Dutch vessels from Java. The English were also trading hereabouts from India, and myriad nations were granted quarters around Ayutthaya. Visiting traders, explorers, writers and engravers attested to the city's gilded opulence and magnificent rituals, such as presentations of white elephants and the royal barge processions that still grace the Chao Phraya river.

Under the diplomatic command of King Narai (1656-88) and Constantine Phaulkon, a Greek adventurer who became his adviser, Ayutthaya's ships were trading alongside those of the Europeans. In 1687, at the invitation of King Narai, King Louis XIV of France dispatched six warships and 500 troops to establish a mission in the southern port of Songkhla. Secretly hoping to control trade and to convert King Narai to Christianity, the French were set on

Bangkok, where General Desfarges ordered his troops to disembark at a fortress.

Siamese xenophobia, exacerbated by an increasing foreign influence in local politics, swept the court as Narai lay dying. A conspiracy of the elite had installed Phra Phetracha, a foster brother of Narai, as regent. After eliminating Narai's heirs, Phetracha ordered that Phaulkon, by now the most powerful minister, should be charged with treason and executed. Following Narai's death, Phetracha (1688-1703) usurped the throne. He then exchanged cannon fire with the French in Bangkok. Although corpses of Siamese troops were displayed on stakes at the fortress, General Desfarges and Phetracha negotiated a truce that hastened the exit of the French.

Siam was effectively closed to *farang* (foreigners) for the next two centuries, though

# Warrior princesses

Thailand has never had a female monarch, but women leaders who have died for the kingdom have gained contemporary resonance through monuments, posters and movies.

### QUEEN SURIYOTHAI

Subject of the recent film *Suriyothai* (pictured), the wife of King Chakkrapat (1548-69) rode a war elephant in raids against Burmese invaders, while wearing the regalia of the Siamese crown prince. In 1548, at the battle at Suphanburi, where her memorial now stands (there's another in Ayutthaya), she

was killed trying to save her husband. Earlier Suriyothai had resisted the scheming of Thao Si Sudachan, a royal concubine of King Chairacha (Chakkrapat's brother), who poisoned the monarch and his heir in a bid to install her lover Khun Worawongsa as king. Instead, the two usurpers were killed and Chakkrapat inherited the throne.

### PHRA SUPHANKALAYA

Daughter of King Mahathamaracha, this enigmatic 16th-century princess was exchanged for her brother Naresuan as

interaction with Asia flourished. Sri Lanka had for centuries been the hub of Buddhism's karmic wheel, from where it was introduced to Thailand in the 13th century via Nakhon Sri Thammarat. In 1751 the Sinhalese asked King Barommakot (1733-58) to help restore Buddhism to Sri Lanka, where it had waned during Portuguese and Dutch rule. In less spiritual matters, Ayutthaya's treasury had swelled through rice exports to China, and the administration of its finances had come to be divided between newly arrived Chinese and descendants of Persians and Indian Brahmans, who had entered service under King Narai – notably the still influential Bunnag family.

During dynastic power struggles over the kingdom's riches, the spectre of a reinvigorated Burmese kingdom arose under King Alongphaya of Angwa. After subduing Mon overlords in

a captive of the Burmese. Legend paints her as a spy for Ayutthaya as her brother fought for Siam's independence. She finally met her death in a vengeful killing when news reached the Burmese court that its crown prince had been slain by Naresuan. A painting of Phra Suphankalaya, commissioned by businesswoman Nalinee Paiboon, has popularised her sacrifice through myriad posters and she is the subject of many shrines (including two in Pai).

### THAO THEPKASATRI AND THAO SISUNTHORN
These southern sisters, known as Lady Muk (widow of the provincial governor) and Madame Chan respectively, led the defence against a Burmese attack on Talang (latter-day Phuket) in the 1785 Nine Armies War. They divided resistance into two camps to repulse the invaders. A statue of the pair is now the island's landmark.

### THAO SURANARI
Laos is currently upset about a new biopic of Grandma Mo, who helped foil the 1826 rebellion by Chao Anuwong of Vientiane after Lao troops had captured Khorat. En route to Vientiane, the mostly female Khorat prisoners paused at Phimai, and Mo engineered the women's wholesale seduction of Anuwong's soldiers, plying them with spirits before dispatching them with makeshift weaponry.

Hongsawadi, then Lanna and the Lao kingdom of Laung Prabang, the Burmese massed a final assault on Ayutthaya in 1765. Following the famously futile resistance by the villagers of Bangrajan, the Burmese besieged the capital in 1766. Famine, disease and fires ensued until the summer of 1767. King Ekatat (1758-67) offered to surrender, but the Burmese declined the offer, penetrated Ayutthaya's walls and systematically reduced the city to a smouldering wreck.

### A NEW DAWN
In October 1767 a fleet commanded by Chaophraya Taksin landed at Thonburi as dawn light bathed Wat Magog (now Wat Arun. the 'Temple of Dawn'). They had escaped from Ayutthaya when an expedition against the Burmese siege had gone awry. After heading south-east and capturing Chantaburi on the Gulf, Taksin's forces doubled back by sea up the Chao Phraya river into a kingdom reduced to anarchy. Instead of returning to Ayutthaya, they started anew at Thonburi.

As newly crowned monarch, Taksin (1767-1782) invited the old nobility from Ayutthaya to help restore order. He advanced north in the following three years to subdue Phimai, where Prince Thepphiphit, King Ekatat's half-brother, had set up court, then to Fang and Phitsanulok, both run by red-robed renegade monks. By annexing Battambang and Siem Reap in the same campaign, Taksin eliminated any threat from Cambodia and reacquired all the territories of Ayutthaya. Even with King Taksin's mastery of war, the campaign required the support of the Teochiu Chinese in strategic trading posts. After all, the new king of Siam was a son of China, a fact not lost on the court's public relations people, who advertised his ancestry in bids to improve trade with the Chinese.

> ### 'Spoils of war included the Emerald Buddha, which remains a symbol of Thai independence.'

Burma, by then embroiled in a war with the Chinese, had largely withdrawn and Lanna became a buffer against further invasions by turning against its oppressor and joining Siam. With the full authority of King Taksin in military endeavours, Chaophraya Chakri and his brother Chaophraya Surasi then moved on Lao, gaining Luang Prabang's submission and cooperation in capturing Vientiane. Surasi returned with spoils of war including the Emerald Buddha, which many cities claim to have possessed. Enshrined in Thonburi, the

The skyline of Rama V's Bangkok is still familiar today.

jadeite statue later became the centrepiece of Wat Phra Kaew in Bangkok, and remains a symbol of Thai independence.

Just as the empire was reconstituted, Taksin's behaviour turned aberrant. Perhaps as a first-generation Siamese reigning before the old nobility of Ayutthaya, Taksin discerned discontent among his subjects, which may have contributed to his new-found religious vision. Beginning around 1779, Taksin arbitrarily lashed out, puzzling visitors and resolving the elite to replace the king for the good of Siam. In April 1782 rebels opposing an avaricious tax official in Ayutthaya were urged to march to Thonburi, remove King Taksin and install Chaophraya Chakri. In keeping with a 15th-century edict that no royal blood should touch the ground, King Taksin the Great was bound in a cloth sack and struck above the neck with a sandalwood club, then secretly buried in the capital he had founded.

## THE RATTANAKOSIN ERA

Chaophraya Chakri returned from quelling a Cambodian revolt to calm Thonburi and assume the throne as King Ramathibodi, aka Rama I (1782-1809), thereby founding the current Chakri dynasty. While keeping Thonburi as a stronghold against attack from the Burmese, the king relocated the palace and government to the river's more defensible east bank at Bangkok. The era of Rattanakosin had begun.

Formed by a girdle of canals, Rattanakosin Island was remodelled after Ayutthaya. Its walls reused bricks from the former capital, a decision that left little to be seen at the original site. Additional canals were dug and what visitors hailed as the 'Venice of the East' soon swelled with craftsmen, merchants, officers and the nobility. Princes and high officials erected stately homes on the central canals. Having been moved out of Rattanakosin, Chinese merchants scrambled for favourable locations along the river, forming Sampaeng (Chinatown) alongside Indian counterparts at Pahurat. Muslims and Catholics settled in communities next to monasteries, notably around Wat Kudee in Thonburi. Bangkok enjoyed its first years as a vibrant, cosmopolitan city.

Rama I drafted the Three Seals Laws, which underpinned judicial decisions for a century, and as Buddhist practice was considered to have slipped, he introduced ecclesiastical laws and sponsored compilation of the Tripidok (Tipitaka) scriptures. To ensure manpower – a lack of which had undermined Ayutthaya – and to prevent private armies being formed by ambitious parties, corvée (forced labour) was introduced. The peasant masses were tattooed with the names of their masters and locality, then required to serve state labour for four months per year.

In the year of his full coronation, 1785, Rama I needed to fend off yet another full-scale attack by Burma, in which 100,000 men in nine

armies invaded from the west, north and south. Though minor skirmishes continued (indeed, until today), this was the last serious challenge from the west. Rama I further secured Siam's borders by imposing authority over the Malay states of Pattani, Kedah, Kelantan and Trengganu, and cementing relationships with Lanna and the Lao states.

Prince Itsarasunthorn, one of Rama I's 40-odd children, succeeded him as Rama II (1809-24) and sired 73 offspring – a testament to the fact that his 15-year reign passed relatively uneventfully. Indeed, the first two Chakri reigns were sufficiently tranquil to entertain a literary revival of sorts, restoring the chronicles and dramatic works lost at Ayutthaya.

Each country's adaptation of the Indian epic *Ramayana* reflects its cultural characteristics. Rama I and his court translated it with a particularly Siamese resonance; its kings are named after the hero, Rama, while monkey general Hanuman brims with fun. The resulting Ramakien verses are depicted in murals around Wat Phra Kaew. Scribes also translated foreign classics, among them the Indonesian narrative *Inao* and the Chinese text on governance and warfare, *Sam Kok* ('Romance of Three Kingdoms'). Rama II, a notable poet, continued to sponsor the cultural renaissance, of which the star was UNESCO-recognised poet Sunthorn Phu.

In the early 1820s Burma's constant will to attack (especially with the compliance of Kedah) was less of a concern than minor tussles with Vietnam for control of Cambodia, which they successfully divided. Siam got Angkor and the Lao territories of Vientiane and Champasak as a barrier between the two powers.

> **'South-east Asian warfare has been as much about populations as territory, with Siam a particularly receptive crossroads of cultures and ethnicities.'**

It was Lao who turned aggressor on the accession of Sing Singhaseni (Rama III, 1824-51). Feeling slighted by the monarch on a visit to Bangkok, Chao Anuwong of Vientiane pushed troops from his city and Champasak as far south as Saraburi in January 1827 in a bid to take Bangkok. But throughout history Lao had never been a match for Siam, and within three months Chaophraya Bodindecha sent the Lao soldiers scattering. The following month Siamese armies sacked Vientiane,

occupied it for several months, then withdrew and, by order of the king, returned to raze Vientiane, leaving only its Buddhist sites. The number of Lao who were brought over the Mekong river to Isaan was so great that today 17 of the 21 million Lao still live in Thailand.

South-east Asian warfare has been as much about populations as territory, resulting in a cultural cross-fertilisation, with Siam a particularly receptive crossroads of cultures and ethnicities. For example, over the centuries, Siamese dance was influenced by performers captured from Angkor, Burma siezed Ayutthayan troupes to enrich its own court arts, and Siam reinvigorated Khmer dance when it regained power over Cambodia through further campaigns by Chaophraya Bodindecha. This reoccupation was partly to save Cambodian Buddhism from the Vietnamese, but the impact was more comprehensive. By Rama III's passing in 1851, Bangkok ran the most extensive Siamese empire ever known.

### EMPIRE-EAT-EMPIRE WORLD

When European nations intensified maritime activities (and imperial intentions) in South-east Asia after the Napoleonic wars, Siam was undoubtedly the region's leading power. The colonial powers of Britain and France had made known their desire for Siamese territories by

**Rama VI** in Lumphini Park. *See p14.*

their encroachment into Burma and Vietnam respectively. King Mongkut (aka Rama IV, 1851-68), who had spent 27 years as a Bhuddist monk, ascended the throne just in time to deal with a right royal headache. In 1855 former Hong Kong governor Sir John Bowring forced the king and his cabinet, led by the powerful Chao Phraya Si Suriyawong, into an unequal agreement that dismantled state monopolies, restricted import and export taxes and limited Siam's judicial power over British subjects. The following decade the French gained control of Siamese Cambodia and began marching up the Mekong river.

> **'Western colonialists claimed to bring civilisation, a pretext undermined by the modernisation of Siam by Rama IV and his son.'**

Siamese attempts to shore up its borders exploded into a full-blown crisis during the reign of King Chulalongkorn (aka Rama V, 1868-1910), when French agents in Laos were expelled and one was killed. French gunboats invaded the Chao Phraya river, forcing Siam to concede Laos and western Cambodia to French Indochina. Britain later received four Malay states after agreeing to relinquish legal jurisdiction over its subjects and to provide a loan for the construction of a railway. Siam lost territories it had annexed or reclaimed over the past century, but remained the only nation in South-east Asia to preserve its independence.

Western colonialists trumpeted the rationale that they brought civilisation, a pretext that was deftly undermined by the modernisation of Siam by Rama IV and his son. Rama IV sponsored the publication of a government gazette, initiated educational reforms and issued laws intended to improve the lives of those bound by slavery or state labour. Foreign tutors, including Anna Leonowens, were hired to oversee the education of the king's children. Anna's famous memoirs are as riddled with innaccuracy and self-aggrandisement as her job application was, hence Thai distaste for the subsequent musical *The King & I* and films that exaggerated her faulty depiction of Rama IV. Rama V continued his father's task by, among other things, establishing the civil service, abolishing slavery and modernising the army.

Rama V was also the first Thai monarch to travel abroad. After visits to British Singapore and Dutch Java in 1871, he changed the dress code and hairstyles of the Siamese court to conform to European trends. Palace design also became influenced by western styles. A number of the king's sons were sent to study in Europe. In 1897 the monarch's visits to the continent proved a crucial influence in the layout of Bangkok, resulting in a grid of formal boulevards leading north to classical and wooden Euro-tropical-style royal residences and landmarks in Suan Dusit.

## BIRTH OF A NATION

In November 1911 Bangkok witnessed the extravagant coronation of King Vajiravudh (aka Rama VI, 1910-25), an event that lasted 13 days and cost the treasury almost ten percent of its budget. Three months later a group of military officers were arrested for conspiring to mount a coup against the king. Absolute monarchy had encountered its first test in modern Siam.

As Bangkok started spreading eastwards, Rama VI donated Lumphini Park as green space, presided over by his statue. The king is also celebrated for his love of drama; he translated classics, acted in plays and installed theatres in his fretworked wooden palaces. Meanwhile, nationalism was on the rise, encouraged by existing trade restrictions imposed by the west and Chinese dominance of the Thai economy. Rama VI's concept of the Thai nation called for a homogenous society rallying under a new flag. The red standard bearing a white elephant was replaced by the current Tong Trai-ron tricolour; red representing *chaat* (nation), white *sasanaa* (religion) and blue *phramaha kasat* (monarchy). A system for Thai surnames was introduced to bolster the concept of the Thai nation, and compulsory education laws were enacted.

The capital then became the stage for a succession of power struggles. On 4 June 1932 a group calling themselves the People's Party – its core being young officials and military officers who had studied in Europe on state scholarships – seized the city in a quiet and bloodless coup that replaced absolute monarchy with a constitutional monarchy and parliament. King Prajadhipok (Rama VII, 1925-35) abdicated while in England three years later, and the cabinet invited his nephew Ananta Mahidol, who was at school in Switzerland, to assume the throne. The schoolboy king (Rama VIII, 1935-46) did not return for another ten years, while the 1932 coup promoters squabbled over control of the country.

A military leader of the coup faction, Luang Phibulsongkram, assumed the post of prime minister. Styling himself on fascist leaders of Europe, the former military instructor

# Court on camera

Thailand's current king and the world's longest reigning monarch, King Bhumibol Adulyadej has a similar constitutional role to Britain's Queen Elizabeth II, but isn't pursued by disrespectful paparazzi. He is revered by all Thais for his moral authority and his tireless efforts to improve the lives of his subjects. Pictures of his thoughtful, bespectacled visage oversee every home, hall and business. Many of these images are also relayed in cinematic collages before every film screening, when the king's anthem is played and all Thais stand in tribute to their sovereign.

Numerous images from the 1960s show the young king at the helm of the various yachts he designed and built. In 1965 he raced the Duke of Edinburgh from Pattaya to Ko Lan, while a famous snapshot shows the king sailing the 11-foot *Vega 1* in a 14-hour solo trip across the Thai Gulf in 1966.

The most photographed royal subject is also an avid lifelong photographer. His mother, known as the 'Princess Mother', gave him a camera when he was eight, and in his teens the prince was a paid staff photographer for the *Standard* newspaper. The early subjects of his portraits were often members of the royal family, and in 2002 Thais enthusiastically bought T-shirts printed with pictures by His Majesty of his pet dog Thong Daeng ('Copper'). His lensmanship is

exhibited in Dusit Park alongside pictures from his boyhood in Switzerland, monkhood and royal ceremonies. He's also a painter, employing modernist styles.

A large archive of images is devoted to the king's love of music. Though his favourite playing style is Dixieland jazz, the 43 songs he has composed are blues-inspired and often heard in public places and concerts. Saxophone and clarinet are his instruments of choice, and he has jammed with jazz greats Benny Goodman, Jack Teagarden, Lionel Hampton and Stan Getz in New York in 1960, as well as with jazz stars visiting Thailand since then. An avid home radio operator, the king also broadcast live jam sessions from the palace in the '60s, often taking phone requests in person.

Also the first monarch to patent an invention (a water aerator), the king keeps up to date with information technology and devotes part of Chitrlada Palace to agro-industrial facilities for his research into improving rice strains, dairy herds and gasohol fuel. He is often pictured poring over graphs and maps, directing royal projects in villages, devising flood prevention strategies and demonstrating weather charts to an audience. In 1995 he appeared on television with satellite charts to counter meteorologists' overstated claims of an approaching typhoon. He was right.

propagated the ideal of the Thai nation, renamed the country Thailand, established paramilitary troops, expanded the military and, with World War II in the Pacific in full swing, ordered the invasion of Laos and Cambodia to reclaim disputed territories. (The debonair soldier also advocated western-style hats and encouraged husbands to kiss their wives on the cheek when leaving the house.) With Japanese forces occupying Thailand in 1942, the Phibulsongkram government declared war on the United States and Great Britain. Regent Pridi Banomyong refused to endorse the declaration, and the Seri Thai ('Free Thai') network of covert operatives was formed to undermine Japanese occupation. Coordinated by Seni Pramoj, the Thai ambassador in Washington, the Seri Thai saved the country from repercussions following the Allies' victory.

As post-war prime minister, Pridi was gearing up to take the country into democratic mode with the introduction of a bicameral

legislature when, in June 1946, King Ananta was found dead in his royal chamber with a gunshot wound to his head. The mysterious circumstances surrounding the king's death have never been made clear. Using the monarch's death as a pretext and branding Pridi a communist, a military faction calling itself the Coup Group seized the government in 1947 and forced Pridi – whom many consider the 'father of Thai democracy' – into permanent exile. In a strange twist, General Phibulsongkram, the man who had declared war on the Allies, returned from retirement in 1948 to head a government that received economic and military assistance from the US.

## POLITICAL UPHEAVALS

For the next quarter-century, military strongmen took turns playing king of the hill while the real monarch, young King Bhumibhol Adulyadej (Rama IX, 1946-present) was confined to ceremonial duties. Bangkok

became the battlefield for a series of coups and countercoups. For three days in February 1949 the capital shut down as the navy and marines unsuccessfully battled the army- and police-led government in a failed attempt to restore Pridi to power. But the army and police were not enough to quell a two-day uprising two years later, when the navy and marines again tried to seize control. The air force settled it by bombing the royal flagship *Sri Ayudhya* in the Chao Phraya river, allowing the captured Phibulsongkram to swim to safety. More than 1,000 soldiers and civilians were killed, and 2,000 wounded. Eight years later, Phibulsongkram's own protégé, General Sarit Thanarat, staged a quick, bloodless night-time coup that drove his mentor into a final exile.

A semblance of order at the expense of democracy buoyed economic fortunes, especially in the increasingly populous capital, while US aid poured in to prevent Thailand becoming the next communist domino. Demand for rice and other commodities to feed the war efforts resulted in the expansion of Bangkok's port. A system of highways and airports sprang up to eclipse the railway networks. With increased electrification, modern consumer goods poured into the country, channelled through new commercial centres in Bangkok. To facilitate modern transportation, the capital's canals were paved over and its tramways dismantled to make way for buses.

As the Vietnam War intensified, Thailand became the strategic centre of US operations. With more than 40,000 US troops stationed in the country in the 1960s, parts of Bangkok,

Pattaya and other cities turned into R&R playgrounds. Music by the Doors and the Rolling Stones blasted from the loudspeakers of hostess bars lining Patpong Road. Sleepy Petchaburi Road reinvented itself as a neon-lit strip of massage parlours and hotels. The capital's population expanded even faster than the national average, as migrants left no-longer-bucolic rural life in search of service and construction jobs. This infrastructure was later reinforced to support a tourist industry that would become the country's biggest earner – though the environment was being degraded at an alarming rate.

Politically, however, the arbitrary abuse of power by the prime minister, Thanom Kittikachorn, and his circle of extended family members proved too much for a new generation of educated Thais raised on Pridi's democratic ideals. On 14 October 1973 more than half a million students, workers and small merchants gathered at Thammasat University to demand the promulgation of the constitution. Protestors and government troops were locked in a stand-off when an unidentified commando unit opened fire. Unprecedented bloodshed ensued and the 'Three Tyrants' – Prime Minister Thanom, his son Colonel Narong Kittikachorn, and Field Marshall Prapas Charusathien, Narong's son-in-law – were forced to leave the country.

After an interval of democracy Thanom returned to Thailand in September 1976 and another protest at Thammasat University quickly snowballed into a mass demonstration. The right wing seized the moment to strike back at the students, who they identified with

# The October generation

The proponents of Thai democracy look to the military crackdowns of 14 October 1973 and 6 October 1976 as historic milestones. These national traumas are slowly and painfully being addressed under the freedom that followed another massacre in May 1992. The 25th anniversary of the 1976 incident provided two ways for Thais to reconcile themselves with what happened.

Bhandit Rittakol's film *Moonhunter* contains emotive scenes of revolt, but is a romanticised chronicle of two real student leaders (Seksan Prasertkul and his partner, Chiranan Pitpreecha), who fled the right-wing backlash to join the jungle insurgency headed by the Communist Party of Thailand. Reintegrated with mainstream society in the 1980s, they now join many from the Tula

(October) generation in positions of seniority in the government, media and institutions. Despite being critically praised, nominated for Cannes and winning best film in Thailand's 2001 Phra Surasavadi Awards, *Moonhunter* drew small audiences. This was perhaps because the film's name was changed to 'October 14: The People's War'.

On the same day that the film was premiered, a memorial was dedicated to the heroes of 14 October 1973 in front of the former headquarters of Colonel Narong Kittikachorn, one of the 'Three Tyrants' that was driven into exile by the students.

A memorial to the 1976 martyrs had earlier been unveiled at Bangkok's Thammasat University, the spiritual home of Thai democratic struggles.

Memories of October 1973.

hotels, business towers and housing estates. Grand shopping malls and giant discotheques sprang up, while factories occupied suburban industrial estates. A network of elevated expressways barely kept pace with Bangkok's legendary traffic, swelled by German cars and the world's second biggest market (after the US) for pick-up trucks. The affluent new middle classes went shopping with a vengeance, showing off imported labels and mobile phones at glittering nightspots. The elite developed a taste for wine, though the tipple of choice remained whisky, especially Johnny Walker Black Label. Students clamoured for the hi-tech trappings and manga taste of Japan – the bubble-era model of what was being dubbed the next Asian economic tiger. Risking fortunes on dubious stocks became the new game in a town where gambling, although illegal, has long been a preoccupation.

> **'In June 1997, the *baht* crashed, dragging the economy down with it. The bubble had vaporised.'**

The party was briefly interrupted when Chatichai and his 'unusually rich' ministers were toppled in a bloodless coup in February 1991 by army and air force officers of the National Peace-Keeping Council (NPKC). Respected former diplomat Anand Panyarachun was installed as interim prime minister to appease the public until a general election in April 1992. When the intended NPKC-backed premier was linked to alleged drug trading, NPKC leader General Suchinda Kraprayoon manoeuvred himself into the prime minister's seat.

This time, the middle classes rallied with students for his removal, led by a popular ex-governor of Bangkok, General Chamlong Srimuang, who was famed for his simple lifestyle and vegetarianism. Protests climaxed in May – known as 'Black May' – when the Democracy Monument near the university became the flashpoint yet again, with dozens of protestors killed (and still unaccounted for). Suchinda was forced to resign and Anand reluctantly agreed to lead for a second interim period. Elections in September brought in a coalition government, with the modest, principled Chuan Leekpai as prime minister. In Bangkok, serious urban planning was undertaken and mass transit schemes finally got under way after decades of false starts.

Order was restored, but influential figures continued to enrich themselves, and the buying

communist China. Shortly after midnight on 6 October the police opened fire on demonstrators, killing hundreds, while quasi-military units took special glee in lynching, beating and even burning some alive. It was a crushing defeat for the students, many of whom joined rural communist insurgents. This brutal suppression left a scar on the national psyche that has yet to heal.

Moderate military rule in the 1980s allowed a degree of political participation and provided some stability. Administrations headed by General Prem Tinsulanond slowly eased the nation into a new rhythm. Media restrictions were relaxed, and insurgents were persuaded to rejoin mainstream society. The groundwork for an elected government was laid and the economy slowly improved, accelerated by the aggressive trade policies of prime minister Chatichai Choonhavan's elected government. His 'buffet cabinet' swelled with industry captains who scrambled for lucrative ministerial portfolios.

**BOOM AND BUST**
Miraculous double-figure economic growth ushered in the 1990s. Farmers and orchard owners on the metropolitan fringes became instant millionaires as developers snapped up land for hundreds of condominiums, luxury

of votes accelerated, prompting anti-corruption clauses in a new liberal constitution that was drafted under Anand and put into effect in 1997. Speculative ventures and market manipulation drove property and share prices to unsustainable levels under the governments of Banharn Silpa-archa and Chavalit Yongchaiyudh. As banks and finance companies gambled on risky loans, foreign debts piled up. Finally, in June 1997, the *baht* crashed, dragging the economy down with it. The construction sector came to a halt, leaving the Bangkok skyline dotted with skeletal concrete eyesores. The bubble had vaporised.

In the aftermath came a period of denial. Many were quick to blame foreign parties, most notably George Soros, who was accused of 'attacking' the *baht*. Nationalists and agitprop performance artists alike heaped scorn on the bailout prescriptions demanded by the IMF (International Monterary Fund); implemented by a second Chuan administration these steadied the economy, but failed to invigorate it. Few were willing to concede that the boom had been one big pyramid scheme.

When recovery didn't occur overnight, practical subsistence was the response, rather than the social upheaval that scuppered Indonesia. Rolex watches were sold by weight in plastic bags at the 'Market for the Former Rich' and corporate art collections were auctioned off. Traffic lessened for several years as vehicles were repossessed. In a land where selling belongings is a loss of face, middlemen surreptitiously traded luxury used goods abroad. For jobless professionals, face-loss gave way to entrepreneurship as car boot sales became an instant, if passing phenomenon.

> **'Rolex watches were sold by weight at the "Market for the Former Rich" and art collections auctioned off.'**

As in Japan, local investment was stifled by the super-rich not being held accountable for their debts. And in a country proud of its independence, nationalist resentment grew against foreign takeovers of faltering firms and competition from multinationals such as Tesco-Lotus hypermarkets. The renewed interest in things Thai dimmed the allure of imported brands, and politicians and marketers were quick to capitalise on this cultural renaissance.

Progressive community and environmental programmes introduced by Bangkok governor Bhichit Rattakul sometimes managed to

# Olives or angels?

Before its 1782 conversion into a capital, Bangkok was known as the 'Village of Plum Olives'. The name stuck with foreigners, who've recently likened it to other orchard produce, dubbing it the Big Mango or, less charitably, the Big Durian, after the city's pungent favourite fruit. Thais call it Krung Thep ('City of Angels'), which is short for the world's longest place name. The name in full – all 64 syllables – is:

Krungthepmahanakornbowornrattanakosin mahintarayutthayamahadilokpopnopparat ratchathaniburiromudomratchanniwet mahasathanamornpimanavatarnsathit sakkhathatthiyavisnukarprasit ('Great city of angels, the supreme repository of divine jewels, the great land unconquerable, the grand and foremost realm, the royal and delightful capital city of the nine noble gems, the highest regal dwelling and grand palace, the divine shelter and living place of the reincarnated spirits').

The name is sometimes shortened to KTM (pronounced Kor Tor Mor), on for example, car number plates.

overcome bureaucratic inertia: dust and litter were reduced, walking street festivals boosted neighbourhoods, and nearly a million trees were planted. Rattakul's successor, the combative veteran politician and TV cook Samak Sundaravej, gained a huge mandate in 2000. While his return to an emphasis on infrastructure, to create a 'looser city' of satellite towns, has yet to yield results, controversy has raged over plans to bury a car park under Sanam Luang and dilute Bhichit's Contemporary Art Museum.

But no one timed it more perfectly than Thailand's richest billionaire, and current prime minister, Thaksin Shinawatra. Under his newly formed Thai Rak Thai ('Thais Love Thais') Party, the telecom tycoon's assembly of political bosses, financial executives, economists and academics swept to the first absolute parliamentary majority in Thai history in 2000. Having escaped conviction in a constitutional court trial, Thaksin has consolidated his power in most national institutions and pledges to transform Thailand through his CEO-style leadership, populist social policies, entrepreneurial reform of the bureaucracy and a new moral order. It remains to be seen how the public will adapt to the model of Singapore.

# Buddhism Today

Thai monk and journalist Mettanando Bhikkhu looks at the effects of modernisation on contemporary Thai Buddhism.

How do the residents of this chaotic capital maintain such light-hearted serenity? The answer, 94 per cent of Thais will tell you, is Buddhism. Calming concepts such as *jai yen* (keep cool) and *mai pen rai* (never mind) derive from their tolerant, non-violent Buddhist philosophy. Increasing numbers of visitors are coming to Thailand to study what seems a particularly relevant way to handle the materialistic nature of modern life.

One of the 20th century's most influential monks, the late Buddhadasa Bhikku, got this message through to stressed-out urbanites via his popular writings on Buddhist economics, environmentalism and the highly accessible meditation techniques that he developed. Buddhadasa Bhikku's **International Dharma Hermitage** (*see p244*) is not only the leading place for foreigners who come to Thailand to study, but has also earned a following among the Thai middle classes and professionals, who come seeking silence and to rediscover mindfulness through simply watching their breath.

This is the wisdom of Siddhartha Gautama, a sixth-century BC Indian prince who only became a Buddha (meaning 'awakened one') after rejecting his privileged upbringing. At first he lived a strict ascetic life, but, finding this unsatisfactory, then used meditation to achieve enlightenment as to the 'Middle Way' between luxury and austerity. Buddhism doesn't require a belief in Buddha as some kind of god; quite the opposite – it's essentially a practical technique to liberate one's self from conditioning, dealing more with the here and now than metaphysical meanderings.

Finding that path has become more challenging to Thais as industrialisation has exposed them to new ideas, activities, possessions and temptations. The past two decades have been the best and worst of times for Thai Buddhism. On the one hand, it has been a period of great spiritual energy, with temples being built, modern Buddhist communities organised, massive social projects undertaken and missions overseas growing. Yet when Buddhism has made the headlines,

# Spirit worship

Although the Buddhist canon rejects the belief in rituals and supernatural power, each Buddhist country's culture is highly superstitious, revealing animist heritage. Most Thais believe in ghosts, omens, magic charms, spirit mediums, astrology, fortune telling and numerology (the number nine is especially lucky). In particular, **amulets** can be blessed by monks to heal the sick, bring fortune, boost sexual charm and protect against injury, particularly for those in dangerous professions. Both sexes may have a wrist bound in sacred thread (*sai sin*), but women are still forbidden physical contact with certain talismans.

Usually worn as a pendant, amulets are most commonly an encased metal or clay Buddha image, while portraits of King Rama V and famous monks are also popular. More exotic charms include cloths inscribed with sacred drawings (*pha yan*), dolls of a beckoning woman (*nang kwak*), carved phalluses (*palad khik*), typically slung round the waist, tiny metal tubes (*ta-krut*), sometimes embedded under the skin, and tattoos of sacred mantras or diagrams, some written invisibly in oil.

Though holy items aren't considered property and may only be 'rented', Thailand is the world's largest market for amulets, with coverage for collectors in every newspaper, and dedicated magazines. Amulet prices are set by quality, popularity, rarity and antiquity, with some exceeding $1 million. Thailand's greatest amulet producer is the heavy-smoking monk, Luang Phor Khoon of Wat Baanrai in Khorat, a lovely character who donates all amulet proceeds to schools, hospitals and charities.

Animist roots also emerge through deity worship. Almost every Thai building plot has a **spirit house** (*sam phra phum*), installed at an auspiciously divined location and time. Resembling a mini-temple on a metre-high pedestal, it shelters the spirit of the land (*phra phum chao thii*), who is appeased with models of servants, elephants and dancers, plus daily offerings. It's believed that each Buddha image and shrine has its own unique personality, and favour is won by offering his favourite food, drinks, habit, mantra and entertainment. Shrines are especially busy the day before lottery numbers are announced.

the news has often been more bad than good. Waves of scandals about dubious fundraising, charismatic sects and monks who are guilty of dabbling in worldly pleasures and sexual impropriety (they are forbidden contact with females) have become a mainstay of the tabloids. Calls for reform also spark controversy. Coupled with a perceptible slipping of adherence to Buddhist practice, particularly in urban areas, this has created what's been described as a crisis of faith. In such circumstances, the *Dharma* (teachings) provides some reassurance, emphasising that everything is subject to change.

### BORN AGAIN (AND AGAIN)

Buddhist theory is big on numerical lists. The Three Marks of Existence (*anicca*,

impermanence of everything; *dukkha*, unsatisfactoriness; and *anatta*, absence of self) describe how everything in mind, body and environment arises and passes away, moment-to-moment. The Four Noble Truths help us see that dissatisfaction is caused by craving (*tanha*); since nothing lasts, craving can never be permanently satisfied. The way to end craving (and hence suffering) is explained in the Noble Eightfold Path and elaborated upon by the Thirty-Seven Factors of Enlightenment. All these labels describe a simple progression in the mind when meditating. And when you apply it to chocolate addiction or seeking the perfect beach, it's quite amazing just how easily the craving fades. Entrenched stuff like lust or anger are a bit tougher.

The ultimate aim is attaining *nirvana*, a final disengaging from the cycle of birth-death-rebirth. One's degree of suffering depends on *karma* (action) earlier in this life or a previous existence. In Buddhism, time is cyclic and endless, unlike the linear, finite human life of monotheistic Judaism, Christianity and Islam. The Buddhist cosmos is eternal and houses innumerable world systems, in which Gautama was the fourth Buddha; Buddhists are still awaiting Lord Metteyya, the future fifth Buddha.

In ancient times, Buddhism in the Thailand region was of the form known as Mahayana, the school prevalent in north Asia that includes numerous *bodhisattva* (enlightened beings delaying *nirvana* in order to help others). Mahayana principles bequeathed customs like the worshipping of statues, though 99 per cent of *Chao Phut* (Thai Buddhists) follow stricter Theravada doctrine – as in Burma, Laos, Cambodia and, notably, Sri Lanka, from where Therevada teaching entered Thailand.

> **'Religion in Thailand still sits on a high social pedestal, alongside monarchy and nation.'**

Reincarnation was part of the Indian belief system at the foundation of Buddhism, but direct Hindu influences are also visible everywhere. The **Erawan Shrine** (*see p93*) in Downtown is the most prominent of the countless shrines in Thailand dedicated to Brahma, while Government ministry logos incorporate the elephant-headed Ganesh; eagle-like Garudas adorn the walls of banks; the city pillar is essentially a phallic Shiva lingam and the *Ramayana* epic permeates all the arts. The Chakri kings (the current line) are considered emanations of Ram, an incarnation of Vishnu, while royal rites are conducted by Brahmin priests.

While imperialism, communism and capitalism have diminished the role of religion (*sasanaa*) in many countries, in Thailand it still sits on a high social pedestal, alongside monarchy (*phra maha kasat*) and nation (*chaat*), and visitors are obliged to show due respect to all three. The current *tong trai-rong* (tricolour) flag signifies royalty (blue), religion (white) and people (red). Therevada Buddhism has been the official religion since the time of the Sukhothai and Lanna kingdoms, and is enshrined in the 1997 constitution – leading many to consider being Thai synonymous with being Buddhist, though the constitution guarantees religious freedom. While there's remarkably little inter-faith conflict, Thai Muslims (who represent around four per cent of the population and are found mainly in the deep south), plus those of south Asian or Middle Eastern origin, are customarily referred to as *khaek* (guests).

## MAKING MERIT

On a practical level, most Thais concern themselves with accruing positive karmic points through *tham boon* (making merit). This encompasses offerings (from standard lotus buds, candle and three incense sticks to elaborate assemblages), donations, charity, depositing food in monks' alms bowls at daybreak and miscellaneous acts of kindness, such as giving to beggars or freeing caged birds. This may also be done on behalf of a deceased relative. A common quip is that you might attain something seemingly unrealisable 'in the afternoon of your next life'.

Making merit by participating in organised Buddhism involves revering the *trirattana* (triple gems): respect the Buddha; study the *Dharma*; and support the *Sangha* (the Order of Disciples, namely the monks). Essentially, the public subsidises Thailand's 270,000 *bhikkhu* (monks) and 90,000 *samaneras* (novices) to live a life of moral example at more than 30,000 *wat* (monasteries), by donating food, clothing and money for necessities like shelter. The core of traditional life, a *wat* is not just a symbolically designed place of worship, meditation and scripture, but may serve as a community centre, orphanage, hospital, hostel, school, market, monastery, playground, crematorium, meeting place, festival site, foundation, museum, theatre, garden and even a zoo.

The strikingly high number of monks is due to the convention that each young man (typically before marriage) becomes a monk for a short period; this is, like conscription, accommodated in job contracts. Considered the most noble way to express gratitude to one's parents, and to generate them great merit, monkhood typically lasts one *phansaa* – the rainy season retreat. Most people believe that men can be ordained and leave up to three times, while a son or grandson may be ordained just for the day on which a deceased parent or grandparent is cremated.

Aside from meditation and scholarship, monks perform ceremonies such as funeral rites and marriage blessings. Senior or famous monks are often requested to anoint a new house or vehicle to provide spiritual protection. It's a life of peace and renunciation, free from harm to fellow beings. Through 227 restrictive precepts (which preclude sexual

activities, soft bedding, entertainment and possession of worldly goods) a Theravadin monk learns to recognise his attachments, and is therefore able to train to relinquish them and free his mind.

Modern lifestyle distractions and compulsions mean that young single men increasingly can't – or won't – find the time; some are ordained for just a week, or maybe never. Hence the calls for the mass-ordination of male high-school or university students during vacations. While some initiates stay on as monks, inspired by their faith, the shortage of those with long-term commitment has caused a sixth of all *wat* to close after being abandoned. The number of monks remaining to propagate the *Dharma* is dropping, while some disreputable types don saffron robes to seek protection from punishment. Some commentators call for tighter screening, others advocate embracing a demonstrably devout sector of society that is currently denied official status: white robed *mae chi* (women who follow a smaller number of precepts).

The order of yellow-robed *bhikkuni* (nuns) was founded by the Buddha, but had faded out long before Buddhism arrived in Thailand. Because the Thai *Sangha* suppresses the ordaining of women, Chatsumarn Kablisingh – ex-professor and daughter of a Buddhist nun ordained in Taiwan – became Dhammananda Samaneri in Sri Lanka in February 2001. Her ordination has intensified what was already a heated, ongoing debate.

### CONTROVERSY AND CHANGE

Within the brotherhood of *bhikkhus*, a succession of scandals has somewhat tarnished public faith, which faltered most noticeably on disclosure that two prominent monks, each with a large following, had had affairs with female followers and patronised prostitutes. One of them, Phra Yantra Amaro, was sentenced to three months' imprisonment for second-degree murder, but managed to slip away to San Diego, where he now leads a Buddhist community. In a still unresolved case, the abbot of Wat Dhammakaya – a temple north of Bangkok Airport with aggressive fundraising tactics, hundreds of thousands of followers and a B500 million *chedi* – was charged with embezzlement.

Both monks and lay people have increasingly called for the strict supervision of the monastic community and, consequently, reform of the *Sangha*, which is largely self-governing and headed by the royally appointed Supreme Patriarch. Administered under semi-democratic structures in 1941, and then placed under a hierarchical bureaucracy by General Sarit Thanarat's dictatorship in 1962, the *Sangha*

is itself subject to *anicca*. Some factions suggest that it might have become overly preoccupied with the ritual and purity of monastic precepts, and as a result, doesn't do enough to help solve social problems.

## 'Ultimately, Therevada Buddhism is about detachment from any craving.'

The state's involvement in education and social matters has deprived *wat* of their social and educative role. A consequence, suggested by the respected monk and scholar Phra Dhammapitaka (PA Payutto), is that some of the *Sangha* have developed a 'habit of idleness', subsisting only on the system of patronage. However, certain monks are far from idle, such as the Buddhadasa disciple Phra Payom Kalyano, an outspoken social activist who has initiated large projects for the poor. In the early 1990s Phra Alongkot converted his *wat* in Saraburi into Thailand's first AIDS hospice, receiving support from the King, the Princess Mother, the WHO and the UN, and he also supports a grass-roots youth network.

Female ordination is supported by a prominent group, Santi Asok, advocating strict precepts of vegetarianism, austerity and sharing of community property. Its founder, Phra Phothirak, a former TV announcer, declared himself independent of the *Sangha* and was arrested, tried and lightly punished in 1988, though the community and its vegetarian restaurants (such as Soi Prasat Court, off Soi Suan Plu) continue. Its most famous adherent is Chamlong Srimuang, a general who was governor of Bangkok, founder of a political party and leader of the anti-dictatorship demonstrations of 1992.

Monks themselves demonstrated in late 2002, when what was popularly referred to as a 'saffron-robed mob' was mobilised to demand, unsuccessfully, that the new Ministry of Religion and Culture be made specifically into a Ministry of Buddhism to oversee ecclesiastical affairs.

Ultimately, though, Therevada Buddhism is about detachment from any craving. It places responsibility on the individual to overcome conditioning, become enlightened and act with compassion. For lay practitioners, Sulak Sivaraksa – Thai Buddhism's sharpest-tongued commentator and a past Nobel Prize nominee for his human rights work – advocates 'engaged Buddhism': active and reflective practice for the benefit of individuals and society.

# Art & Architecture

There's a pattern of individuality in Thai design.

There are some world monuments as beautiful and others more stately or more classically proportioned, but Bangkok's **Grand Palace** has no rival for surreal imagination. Time spent among its façades and pilasters shimmering with inset glass and mirrors, slanting columns that soar to overlapping gables, carved pediments and multi-layered gilded spires, surrounded by doors, windows, walls and corridors that dance with multicoloured paintings and statues of gods, demons and heroes, is a dazzling experience.

The dazzle is not an accident, but an intended effect. It has deep religious and political significance (think: reflection, transience, royal splendour, sudden illumination) and has been refined over centuries through sophisticated techniques. To properly appreciate the palace, and the many other buildings and designs you will see in and around Bangkok, it helps to understand some of the techniques and influences affecting Thai art and architecture.

**DIVINE RULES**

Thai art history is the study of many streams of influence, flowing south from China, west from India and Sri Lanka, north from Java and the Malay peninsula, and east from Cambodia. Thailand resembles Japan in that almost everything of value in its culture can be traced to some outside source, yet the Thais have moulded all these influences into something utterly and distinctively Thai. Copying (and thus honouring) a master has long been the ideal of anonymous Thai artisans, and the aesthetic therefore adapts incrementally.

The earliest layer of Thai art is traceable to the mysterious Neolithic peoples who left behind the patterned Baan Chiang pottery. By the fifth to eighth centuries, the Mon Dvaravati culture combined Theravada Buddhism with animism, giving rise to sacred *sema* (boundary stones) and stone sculpture with amazing realism. The eyes, cheeks and lips of the seated **Mon Buddha** at **Wat Na Phra Men** in Ayutthaya could be those of a

Thai on the streets today – with powerful meditative gravity. Under Khmer sway from the ninth to the 13th centuries, Thailand inherited massive temple complexes, stone satellites of Angkor evoking a Hindu cosmology by way of India and Java.

Khmer temples were microcosms of heaven. Surrounded by moats and sub-temples symbolising the seas and continents of the world, they centred on a scripture vault beneath a *prang* (tower) representing sacred Mount Meru, axis of the universe, and the home of Shiva, represented by a lingam. Such manifestations of gods reinforced the powers of empire and divine kingship.

Although Thailand is devoutly Buddhist, an enduring faith in Hinduism means that spires are capped with Shiva's trident. Pediments and statues feature Vishnu (the creator) mounted on the man-bird Garuda; Indra (King of the Gods) riding the multi-headed elephant Erawan; and popular divinities such as pot-bellied, elephant-headed Ganesha, remover of obstacles, god of the arts (and, indeed, logo of the government's Fine Arts Department). Thailand, it's said, boasts far more Brahma shrines than India. Also from the Khmers came an architectural vocabulary, including the *prang*, multi-stepped altars with redented corners, and relief carvings of intertwining vines and flame motifs.

## TURNING SIAMESE

By the 13th century, Tai tribes had founded the independent kingdoms of Lanna and Sukhothai. Hailing from northern forests, the Tai came from a tradition of wood, not stone. They brought Chinese-influenced house and temple forms, of which the main feature was long sloping roofs.

In the earlier forms – still visible in Lanna – the roofs overlap in layers, sweeping low and wide, almost to the ground. However, at the corners, eaves and ridgelines, they rise again, with devices such as *chofa* (bird-like finials) and *kalae* (Lanna-style criss-cross finials). Their ancient meaning is unclear – the animist roots lie in birds, flames and mythical naga snakes – but their curving, sky-pointing lines are a defining feature of Thai design.

From India, Thais took the traditions of carving the Buddha: the stances and postures, the curly hair, the clinging robe, the halo, the altar and much more. Indian *stupa* (relic towers) evolved into Thai *chedi*, at first modelled after the bell-shaped *dagoba* (the Sri Lankan version of *chedi*). However, the inhabitants of Sukhothai almost immediately produced a trait that could be called 'Thai grace'. They elongated *stupa* to produce an elegant bud-shaped *chedi*. And they

did something unprecedented: they portrayed the Buddha not only sitting or standing, but walking (descending from heaven). In contrast to the solemnity of Khmer art, the walking Buddhas of Sukhothai are flowing, rounded, androgynous, moving so lightly they seem to float.

The process of elongation and 'etherealisation' continued as the centre of power moved progressively south from the 14th century. At Ayutthaya, the Sri Lankan *dagoba* was stretched out so that the spherical base shrank and the upper spire soared, its rings becoming pronounced ribs. The rounded, artichoke-shaped Khmer *prang* lengthened into a lofty corn cob; walls and columns extended, lifting the multi-tiered roofs high into the sky.

Statues acquired crowns and jewellery, while inset glass glowed from elaborately tiered palace walls and roofs. By the 17th century, Ayutthayan art was heavily preoccupied with light: gleam and sparkle was exaggerated by closing what had once been open temple sides (as in the old Lanna temples) and allowing only slits to let in a little air and light. By the Bangkok period, every surface had become encrusted with gilding, filigree and fitted pieces of coloured ceramics and glass.

The final touch came with the influence of the trapezoid. The walls of ancient Tai houses leaned slightly for stability, either outward in the north, or inward in the south. This tapering turned increasingly oblique to create the desired effect of elegance. Doors and windows tilted too. Chests and boxes became trapezoids, and in Ayutthaya the bases of temples and thrones angled in at the sides and swooped low in the middle. This fusion of styles, eras and peoples continues into the modern era (*see p27* **A farang in a Thai hat**), resulting in art that is distinctively Thai.

## WAT: WHERE, WHEN AND WHY?

Whatever its secular roles, even the most humble *wat* (Thai Buddhist temple) is sacred ground, removed from the mundane world by walls beyond an initial gate or even, as at **Wat Phra That Lampang Luang**, a *vieng* (fortified moat). To the Khmer cosmological plan, Thais added *chedi*, and their ancestral rooflines, the eaves chiming with brass bells.

The temple's most important building is the *bot* (or *ubosot*), the ordination hall rarely open to the public and demarcated by eight *bai sema* (boundary stones – and now the Thai

Classic architectural elements (clockwise from top left): a *chofa*; a golden *chedi*; a naga serpent and *modop*; a *bai sema*; Buddha with flame-like *mandorla*; a prang.

Airways logo). Often leaf-shaped, these flat standing monoliths may be sheltered in miniature shrines. Most temples have one or more *vihaan* (assembly halls). Lacking *bai sema*, but resembling *bot* in their decorative gables, crown-like window frames, raised terrace and finialled roofs of green and orange tiles, *vihaan* usually host the principal Buddha image or images and are the place of public worship.

The temple may contain other wood-roofed structures bearing Siamese trademarks. A cubic *mondop* with complex cruciform roof houses a Buddha footprint or scriptures. A *hor trai* (library) is raised on a pedestal or on stilts over water to protect against fire and insects. Sometimes there's a cloister lined with Buddha images – an inner sanctuary removed from the outer world. Inevitably, you'll find *sala*, the elevated open-sided pavilions that are used for anything from resting, eating or meeting to music, dance or massage.

## 'The ubiquitous lotus is the favourite symbol of Buddhism.'

*Chedi* enshrining a relic of the Buddha or a revered person may be the dominant structure. Beside the massive *prang* at **Wat Arun** in Bangkok or recordbreaking **Phra Pathom Chedi** in Nakhon Pathom, the surrounding buildings are merely grace notes.

Inside, complex symbolism is evident in brilliant mural paintings, lacquerwork and wood carvings found on doors, lintels, walls, furniture and ceilings. Attending Hindu gods are lesser spirits, like the half-woman, half-bird Kinnaree, *apsara* (heavenly dancers), *thep* (angels) and the divine serpent Naga. The supreme protector of Buddhism, who must be placated, Naga shelters the Buddha under his multi-headed hood, curves round walls and through decorative panels and slithers along balustrades.

### DECODING BUDDHA IMAGERY

The focus of all this florid decoration is the serene image of Lord Buddha. He sits exalted on a throne built up of complex angles like Khmer temples, or decorated with lotus petals. The ubiquitous lotus, rising from the mud to bloom in purity, is the favourite symbol of Buddhism. Framing the Buddha is the mandorla, a flame-like vortex of light that originated in Buddhism and went west to become the Christian halo.

Buddhist sculpture is very stylised. Initial prohibition of a human likeness left a legacy of abstract representations in Thai *wat* – the wheel of law, the footprint or the bodhi tree (under which Buddha was enlightened). It was

A typical Bangkok blend of old and new.

the ancient Greek-influenced Gandhara sculpture in today's Afghanistan/Pakistan that first gave form to attributes of the Buddha listed in the scriptures, such as curly hair, broad shoulders, eyebrows arching from the nose, the *ushnisa* (bulge atop the head) and so forth. Over time, distinct styles emerged. The *ushnisa* rose to become a flame and then a slender spire. Dvaravati Buddhas feature thick lips, heavy lidded eyes and sweet smiles. Sukhothai statues have rounded, androgynous faces and bodies, with long pointy noses. In affluent Ayutthaya, Buddha images came to be crowned and jewelled, with their elongated faces expressing the hauteur of a powerful court. Bangkok Buddhas (from the 19th-century onwards) could almost be called baroque, with robes and pedestals covered with a profusion of fine detail.

The Buddha appears in a variety of different postures and *mudra* (gestures), conveying philosophical principles to the congregation. Most *wat* contain a series of eight postures denoting each weekday (Wednesday is halved), worshipped according to one's birth date. The most common *mudra* is Bhumisparsa ('calling the earth to witness'), in which the Buddha sits in lotus position, left hand in lap, right fingertips pointing downward to resist the temptations of Mara, the devil. Standing with one or both hands held up, palm frontwards, the Buddha is reassuring or calming; when the thumb and forefinger touch, the Buddha is teaching, or 'turning the wheel of the law'. Each *mudra* relates to an aspect of the Buddha's life, culminating in the 'reclining Buddha', depicting the moment of final release: nirvana.

## ULTERIOR MOTIFS

The roots of Thai design go back thousands of years. Neolithic pottery from Ban Chiang, with its swirls and geometric patterns, bears a distinct resemblance to motifs seen in crafts today. Over the centuries these patterns developed into a language of design, *lai Thai*. These involve the geometrical repetition of certain forms in countless variations, whether in lacquer, *benjarong* (five-colour) ceramics, wood carving, mother-of-pearl inlay or architecture. The *prang* of Wat Arun are, in a sense, one giant *benjarong*.

Most distinctive is *lai kranok* (a twirling flame), traced from 13th-century BC Chinese pottery, as well as the decorative scrolls of Khmer lintels. True to form, the Thais stretched and elaborated *kranok* until they became long, sinewy and pointy. *Kranok* merge with other forms into hybrids; leaves and flowers, even animals and gods flow into rhythms of flame that curl delicately like the fingers of classical dancers. The huge *lai Thai* lexicon also includes *lai bua* (lotus forms), *lai krajang* (pointed leaf forms), interlocking rectangles and diamonds, floral scrolls, vines, hexagons, octagons, roundels, trefoil and quatrefoil lozenges, and 'animal interlace' (snake tails, Naga heads, bird beaks, fishtails and lions). Also, figures of dancers, warriors, Garuda, *thep* (angels), *apsara* (heavenly dancers), cumbersome elephants and the masked pantheon of the *Ramakien* epic are all miraculously rendered fluid.

> **'Painted figures almost always appear in the posed attitudes of dance. By the same token, classical dance is painting come to life.'**

Architecture and crafts merge, with tapering spires, redented corners, incisions and trapezoid lines scaling up or down, so that, for example, lacquer boxes take the shape of altar bases,

# A farang in a Thai hat

One of the most striking buildings in Bangkok's **Grand Palace** is the **Chakri Maha Prasat Throne Hall**, where a Western Renaissance-style structure of marble staircases, arched windows and Corinthian columns is capped by Thai roofs rising to gilded roof finials and three soaring spires. It was built between 1876 and 1882 by King Rama V to designs by John Chinitz, an English architect. Chinitz had planned for a dome, but Chao Phraya Srisuriyawongse, the former regent, convinced the king that Thai roofs were more appropriate. This odd combination was dubbed 'a *farang* in a Thai hat'.

Art critic Apinan Poshyananda sums up the result: 'For many viewers, then and now, the building signifies vulgarity and kitsch, underscoring the mediocrity and banality of a hybrid architectural style created without the pressure of necessity, and unguided by an organic tradition. For others, however, it is the outcome of the cult of innovation and originality which developed during the decades of cross-cultural influence.'

Actually, it is in a continuum of architectural novelties. All Asian cultures experimented with Western modes, but none mixed styles with such breathtaking abandon as the Thais. In 17th-century Ayutthaya and Lopburi Persian windows, Chinese gardens and French mirrored wall panels were in vogue.

Reflecting Rama IV's international outlook, domes and spires coexist in **Phra Nakhon Kiri Palace** in Petchburi, and there are countless examples from the late 19th and early 20th centuries, notably the Gothic interior of Bangkok's **Wat Rachabophit**. The apotheosis was reached at **Bang Pa-In Palace** where Thai, Chinese and Western baroque mingle in a kaleidoscope of periods and styles.

This legacy solidified into bulky Thai-roofed institutions such as the **National Museum** and **National Library**, then diversified into clip-art appendages to ferro-concrete blocks devoid of Thai-ness, whether classical (**Chatpetch Tower**), Gothic (a Soi Suan Plu terrace) or even pharaonic (**Grand Hyatt Erawan Hotel**). The best modern example, the Siam InterContinental Hotel (styled after a royal hat) was demolished in 2002, though Thai accents continue in the gilded peaks of **SCB Park Plaza**, Ratchayothin, and on Sathorn (the cascading sloped walls of **Harindhorn Tower**, the reflecting pools of the **Sukhothai Hotel**, and the trapezoid **Sathorn City Tower** and **Diamond Tower**).

This gleeful mixing is so sustained that the concept of blending itself could be considered innately Thai. Whether you think it kitsch or innovative, globalised Thai architecture has produced some of the world's most quirky and surprising buildings.

*hor trai* (libraries) or lotus buds. In Thai flower arranging, flowers and leaves are folded and threaded into *kranok* and *krajang* shapes that were themselves inspired by flowers and leaves. The effect is of art folded back upon itself, combining complex detail with seamless finishing.

Another strain in Thai design – but less grand than *lai Thai*, which grew out of the courts – is village handicrafts. Handwoven cloth replicates templates unique to each village, most ambitiously in *mudmee* images woven from pre-tie-dyed thread. Simple natural materials – sliced joints of bamboo, slabs of weathered wood, folded bamboo leaves, interwoven reeds – are the theme in much of the nation's new craftwork. Contemporary Thai design is a continuing outgrowth of both classic and rustic traditions, drawing from a well of forms that transcend both elaboration and minimalism.

## 2-D OR NOT 2-D

In Thailand painting is frozen dance. *Thep* and heroes in temple murals bend their fingers, arch their elbows and splay their legs sideways like actors on stage. Whether flying through the air or merely seated quietly at the feet of the Buddha, painted figures almost always appear in the posed attitudes of dance. By the same token, classical dance is painting come to life. Dancers wear costumes and masks inspired by temple murals, and pose in ensembles as if bursting from two dimensions into three.

Thai dance is rooted in ancient India where the core idea was that it was the gods who were doing the dancing. A performer goes through a repertoire of poses and *mudra* that evoke the divine. The courts of Java and Cambodia modified these, with an emphasis on outward curving fingers and heroic stances. Movements in Khon and Lakhon are clearly recognisable from 12th-century bas reliefs at Cambodia's Angkor Wat.

Thais characteristically elongated and elaborated Angkorean dance, adding flames and sparkle. Fingernails (often with extensions) twist backwards at impossible angles; *chadaa* (headdresses) rise into sleek spires like those crowning temples; shoulders curve upwards with miniature finials. Costumes heavy with gold thread and beaded with reflective glass gleam like lavishly decorated temple walls.

To appreciate Thai painting and dance, knowledge of the Indian saga *Ramayana* is essential. Reinterpreted by Thais as the *Ramakien*, it's a colour-coded epic – told in hundreds of episodes – of how the hero, Rama of Ayodhya (coloured green), wins back his wife Sita, who was abducted by Totsakan, the ten-faced ogre of Lanka (red; gold when romantic). Victory is achieved through the help of Rama's brother Laksana (yellow), monkey king Sangkhip (orange), his adopted son Ongkot (blue) and Hanuman (white), the prankish monkey general.

Painting and dance part company, however, when it comes to foreign influence. Classical

# Arts on his sleeve

In the early stages of modern development most East Asian nations have tended to reject their native traditions and embraced all things Western. However, as such nations grow increasingly wealthy and international, there's a point at which they rediscover their past.

The 1997 economic crash spurred just such a renaissance in Thailand, with new talents appearing in every field of the arts. Among them is **Paothong Thongchua**, professor at Thammasat University and scholar of Thai textiles. He also arranges flowers, prepares classic cuisine, guides study tours, produces TV documentaries, consults Hollywood on Thai sets and costume (*Anna & the King*) and, mindful of his years as a model, designs clothing and runs a string of boutiques. Paothong's speciality is to bring all the arts together; he's the impresario of indigenous culture.

At a typical Paothong festival pageants of villagers and classical dancers feature, alongside hill-tribe women weaving and dyeing with natural materials, young traditional musicians, a bewildering variety of flowers arranged in sculptured towers and garlands, shaman dances, hot-air balloons and fireworks. The audience, even casual tourists, is expected to wear authentic costume – available, if you've come unprepared, at booths run by Paothong's weavers.

In Bangkok, these events take on a grand and royal flavour, such as the ceremony that Paothong directed in 2002 at the City Pillar to celebrate Bangkok's 220th anniversary. Complete with palanquins and costumed parades bearing flower offerings from every region, it culminated in ancient Brahman rituals. If there is a Thai renaissance, Paothong is the renaissance man.

Door guardian at **Wat Suwannaram**.

Thai roofs pitch steeper, their end bargeboards reaching sharp peaks, descending in a slight curve to the eaves, where they rise again with *ngao* (a flame-like flick). Plainer houses are thatched with leaves or woven palm; grander roofs are tiled with teak or glazed ceramic. The **Jim Thompson House**, **Wang Suan Pakkard Palace** and **Baan Suan Plu** are prime examples of traditional Thai compounds in Bangkok. Interiors are sparsely furnished for multi-purpose use, *tang* (low seat/bed/table with hoof or claw legs) being a constant, along with triangular *maun khwan* (axe-shaped pillows).

Though an increasingly rare sight, the art of Thai housebuilding is a living art. You can buy a new house in old style in **Ang Thong** province, or even **Chatuchak Market**. Craftsmen carve teak and other hardwoods into pillars, stepped wall-panels, and bargeboards, all in modular units to be reassembled with pegs to enable future moves.

### SHUTTER SPEED

Urban architecture has been dominated by the Chinese shophouse. As in the Peranakan Sino-Malay culture, Sino-Thai *hong taew* (literally, 'row house') are a marriage between the crowded mercantile streets of old Chinese cities – where people lived upstairs and traded downstairs – and colonial Portuguese stone and mortar constructions, with wooden shutters and colonnades. Prime examples adorn **Tha Chang**, **Phuket Town** and **Thanon Charoenrat** in Chiang Mai. Wooden shophouses (well preserved in **Lampang** feature carved panels and lattices, and, when made of masonry, columns, arches and stucco frills. Today's shophouses favour Corinthian columns made of concrete and colonise even country roads.

The earliest Western-style houses were the mansions of nobility and wealthy Chinese merchants, borrowing tropical colonial devices such as porches, decorative vents and verandas lined with wooden shutters. For those with retro taste, Chinatown is a trove of art deco, the **Atlanta Hotel** a 1950s diorama, while Downtown includes modernist whimsy from the 1960s and '70s, such as Silom's **Zuellig Building** and the neighbouring **Dusit Thani Hotel**, the multi-cylinder **Fifty-nine Condo** off Witthayu, and motel-style Sukhumvit inns. Skyscrapers – from the bland to the radical – are a recent trend, and low-rise 'ranch-style' homes in leafy compounds still line many residential *soi*.

dance, centred on the court until very recently, remained conservative (though modern troupes are now reinterpreting it). But painting embraced China and the West with the same gusto as architecture. Painters place Thai temples within natural landscapes resembling Western oil paintings and among figures with dynamic movement, notably at **Wat Suwannaram**. These stand beside Chinese panels depicting fretwork, antiques and bonsai. At its classic highpoint, this resulted in masterpieces, such as the *Ramakien* murals at **Wat Phra Kaew**. Other attempts, as at **Wat Bowoniwet** in Bangkok, result in a bizarre fusion of Thai and western styles that is almost Dali-esque in style. This coded religious heritage remains a vibrant force in contemporary Thai visual arts.

### ABSOLUTELY PREFAB

The archetypal Thai house – made of wood, raised on stilts, with high peaked roofs – belongs to a domestic architectural theme spanning Asia from Indonesia and Indochina through southern China to Japan. Originating in tropical rainforests, the stilts raised homes above flooding, and multiple eaves allowed ventilation while protecting from fierce rain and sun. Not every element, however, is utilitarian. Houses also embody symbolism about earth and heaven, fire and water, and this gave rise to the fish, bird, naga and flame-shaped gables and ridge decorations so prevalent in East Asian dwellings.

The most differentiating Thai characteristics are the elegant rooflines. These vary by region: Lanna roofs are lower, their straight edges sloping to the criss-cross *kalae* finial; central

Many of the buildings mentioned here are covered in more detail in other sections, notably **Sightseeing** and **Beyond Bangkok**.

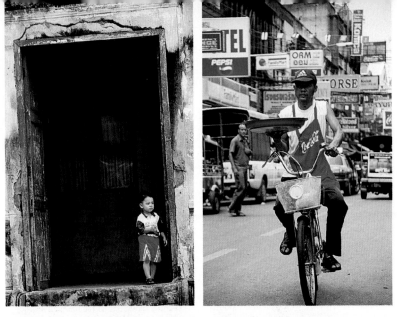

# Bangkok Today

From cosmopolitan chic to a Thai culture revival and a moral crusade, this fascinating capital is at a crossroads.

Bangkok's been on a rollercoaster for the past two decades and every few years it goes over a major bump. It hit two in 1997: the economic crash that later spread throughout Asia, and a reformist new constitution. The impact has been contradictory: globalisation, cosmoplitanism and individualism, coupled with a revival of things Thai and a guardedness about foreign influence.

For many, the crash came not a moment too soon. Much of value in Bangkok was being lost under a pyramid of dubiously financed, often ill-conceived developments. The skyline bristles with hundreds of tall buildings and the city is littered with decaying, unfinished shells. Growth through the early 1990s had mushroomed the middle class into a market for consumer imports, raising concern about values. Bangkok has become a little less polite, while some taboos – notably male/female contact in public – are evaporating. The goldrush of farmers to Bangkok also heralded a breakdown in village life, and with it the extended family and craft industries.

Fortunately, unlike in Indonesia, Thai society proved remarkably resilient. Despite profound hardship and spiralling debts after the crash, villages reabsorbed unemployed Bangkok migrants. Fashion victims adjusted to local labels, and night owls found they didn't need discos designed like a spaceships – Thais can party anywhere.

## FROM FAKING IT TO MAKING IT

After a period of stabilisation, growth is flickering again. Indeed, some allege that those with mega-*baht* simply paused spending their stash for a decent interval. But there's been a sea change in what Bangkok wants. The city has become increasingly cosmopolitan, acquiring more sophisticated shops, venues and entertainments, with a greater awareness of the arts, the environment and its indigenous assets.

When it could no longer afford to be among the world's top three buyers of Black Label whisky, the country had to look at what it had that could be relied upon. It found fruit and herb drinks tastier and healthier than any canned soda; farmhouse recipes that tasted

authentic not processed; rare strains of rice for niche tastes; herbal products that fuelled the new holistic industry; and a wealth of forms and materials ripe for designers. Nowadays foreign buyers scour Chatuchak Weekend Market, not just for antiques and repro, but for new products to export, or even to counterfeit – an ironic reversal of the intellectual property infringements for which Bangkok is infamous.

## 'The market value of Thai goods shot into focus in 2002 when foreigners tried to patent jasmine rice and *tuk-tuks*.'

Consciousness of the market value of what Thais had long taken for granted shot into focus in 2002 when foreigners tried to patent Thai jasmine rice and *tuk-tuks*. It wasn't long before indigenous potential brands were classified as 'Thai Wisdom'. Now local record labels are campaigning against piracy. Thai music might be the next thing to break out globally, though Thai movies only managed that on realising that the world might be interested and putting effort into long-term vision and marketing.

### NEW SOCIAL ORDER

Valuing 'Thai Wisdom' was a campaign promise – along with populist platforms like universal healthcare and farmers' debt moratoriums – that helped elect telecom tycoon Taksin Shinawatra, Thailand's richest man, prime minister in the first poll under the new constitution in 2000. Schemes like 'One Tambon (village), One Product' and the plan to enable smallholders to borrow against 'Thai Wisdom' assets typify efforts by the self-styled CEO of Thailand to turn the whole population into entrepreneurs like himself.

Meanwhile, the country could be left with another credit bubble before fully recovering from the last. Unlike in, say, South Korea, there's been no sacrifice of big fish responsible for the bust. Saving face and the power of corrupt networks means that 'influential' transgressors, the 'unusually rich' or the merely incompetent almost never get punished – they're typically transferred into a vague 'inactive post'.

However, it finally looks as if an accused politician will be tried. Though the constitutional watchdogs face ingrained resistance, ever more scandals are being reported that previously would have gone unexposed. The freewheeling Thai media

has clashed several times with Taksin over questioning the concentration of power, partly resulting from the constitution facilitating stronger government. Taksin stresses that the media – and the parliamentary opposition – should be 'constructive'.

This all feels like the Singaporean/Malaysian model of hi-tech, conservative societies dominated by one party and a charismatic leader. In line with that largely successful template, Taksin's former interior minister, Purachai Piemsomboon, launched a social order campaign. Previous nightlife crackdowns soon eased off, but this one has persisted, with urine tests at bars and nightclubs, curfews of 2am or earlier, limits on the go-go flesh quotient, and even raids on house parties. Nightlife zones are proposed (though astonishingly few in Bangkok) and some provinces are now declared disco-free.

One reason for this crusade is to tackle under-age drinking and drug taking. The amphetamine *ya ba* ('crazy drug') has proved a particular scourge, seared into public consciousness by scenes of drug-crazed people injuring hostages in public sieges. Underlying the campaign is a rearguard action to keep the younger generation from discarding traditional values. No sooner had the authorities gone apoplectic about spaghetti straps revealing teenage shoulders than some Siam Square girls stopped wearing bras altogether. It's a modern dilemma: unconventional youth may be an unavoidable result of current educational reform away from rote learning towards inquisitive thinking. Yet this may also lead to greater appreciation of Thailand's enviable social cohesion.

### PLANNING THROUGH CHAOS

The Singapore path depends on rigid discipline. So far, Bangkok is a byword for unplanned metropolitan sprawl. There's no natural barrier to stop development along new highways paving the city's vast plain, nor to *moo baan* (housing estates) tucked down alleys. One reason for Bangkok's notorious traffic problems is that it has only a fraction of the global norm for road surface. The new mass-transit systems are non-integrated, with separately run underground and overground lines having 'intersections' that don't actually intersect.

Sorting this out has been attempted, but initiatives often founder. If mass transit had started in the 1970s, as planned, the city could have grown around transport nodes rather than suffer infrastructure playing catch-up. The delay was typical of the tendency for new office holders to scupper existing schemes and instead set up their own pet projects. Payback for voter support also means that funding often favours regions at the expense of the capital.

The high-rise skyline of 21st-century Bangkok.

Nevertheless, there is progress. New tunnels now convey anything from wires or water to sewage or subway trains, construction dust has reduced, flood defences are in place, and the sinking of areas because of groundwater pumping is being addressed.

The Bangkok governor, Samak Sundaravej, favours a 'looser' suburban city and mega-projects such as a ring railway, a car park under Sanam Luang and the world's fifth-tallest building – though, by late 2002, none of these had happened. Thailand is among many Asian countries emulating the Japanese focus on construction: of roads, dams and grand urban monuments. Meanwhile, Japan pours money into South-east Asia in the form of 'aid' for vast infrastructure. The resulting boondoggles may or may not bring benefits, but frequently entail destruction of something precious.

### BULLDOZING THE PAST

A typical example is Bangkok's last expanse of boat-accessed canal living at Bang Kruay being carved up by vast highways. That waterworld is an irreplaceable asset for the coming post-industrial era, which will be decentralised, lifestyle-oriented and favour places that take good care of their character, beauty and environment. Bangkok has many such assets (fresh markets, diverse cuisine, tolerance, a vibrant culture and laid-back lifestyle, lush vegetation, houses that suit the tropical climate),

but its bulldozing and standardisation keeps working against those subtle, fragile qualities.

Conservation tends to focus on particular buildings, yet it's often the overall streetscape that buoys the spirits. While much architectural heritage is still disappearing, some buildings are being converted to profitable new uses. This tends to delight foreigners, though Thais often assume ancient houses will be haunted, and Buddhist detachment means Thais cling less to the past.

> **'Bangkok has the potential to be the fulcrum of a region bigger than the EU.'**

Preservation initiatives constantly founder, such as the attempt by the previous Bangkok governor, the eco-aware Bhichit Rattakul, to scale back the jarring signage and wiring that blights Bangkok's streetscape. The wires are slowly being buried, and the city's lack of parkland is being redressed, but residential anger at the butchery of shade-giving trees by utilities reached a crescendo in 2002 when a road planned in Bhichit's scheme to have a million trees was left with a row of denuded trunks.

The difficulty is that Bangkok tries to do too much. It's the focus for virtually every aspect of national life: royalty; government; finance; commerce; tourism; nightlife; shopping; entertainment; manufacturing; the military;

universities; road, rail, port and air transport; historical sights and festivities. Yet, decentralisation is the mantra these days, and even the parliament may move out. Factories and offices are dissipating to the Eastern Seaboard, Chiang Mai, Isaan and growth zones bordering other countries.

## HUB CAPITAL

'Hub' is another buzzword. With its long history as a crossroads of both commerce and culture, Bangkok has the potential to be the fulcrum of a region bigger than the EU. Ayutthaya managed that feat in the 17th century, when its population and wealth matched London's.

With the opening up of formerly closed neighbours, Bangkok will soon be the fulcrum of transcontinental land and rail routes. Huge volumes of freight and people will course through the city from India via Burma and Laos to the coasts of Vietnam and Cambodia; and from Singapore via Malaysia and Burma to China, which is pushing to turn the Mekong river into a hydroelectric facility, to the alarm of downstream countries. A new Bangkok International Airport is being built in the eastern suburbs and the two-century-old idea

of cutting a Kra Canal across the southern isthmus to divert shipping from the Malacca Straits is also being reconsidered.

The wild card in Bangkok's future is China. Thai commerce, diplomacy, tourism and even entertainment are all orienting northwards, keen to benefit from China's market, yet wary of being gutted economically and consigned to being a pleasure zone for Shanghainese nouveau riche and party cadres. Thais are appreciating Chinese fashions, making Sino-Thai fusions, celebrating Chinese festivals and generally sharing its wavelength – in the same deft way that Thailand has repeatedly kept its independence from overarching powers.

Look how Bangkok has dealt with its current encroaching force: tourism. Three decades of relentless hospitality has taken its toll, but the city has also benefited, and not just in a financial sense. In making its amenities more comfortable, cultivating cosmopolitan tastes, rethinking how its culture can be presented and dispatching goodwill worldwide, Bangkok has compromised many things, but not its essence. By embracing every onslaught so warmly, Bangkok remains charmingly, indefinably, steadfastly Thai.

# Indie city

The tenor of our times has swung to the conservative, but two progressive generations are transforming Bangkok. The students who resisted dictatorship in the 1970s are reaching positions of power in government, institutions and commerce, their contemporaries having already radicalised the arts. Meanwhile, a younger, globalised generation, raised under democracy, open to outside influences and often foreign-educated, now wields enormous influence through consumer taste. In a society defined by conformity and consensus, many of these wilful under-30s self-identify as 'indie'.

Their independent taste seeks out underground music, art movies, installations, extreme sports, provocative plays and radical fashion. They communicate these interests in a raft of inventive, often intellectual fanzines and hand-made books, which they sell at impromptu fairs where like minds gather. The indie magazine *a day* was founded through such networks, while the **House of Indies** (*see p187*) isn't just a venue, but an institute for alternative arts like DJing.

What's the indie aspiration? It's partly self-expression, partly to go 'inter' (prosper

overseas) and partly for the sake of discovery itself. Indie Bangkok is like the Bauhaus, the 1960s sexual revolution, psychedelia, punk, postmodernism, the internet and mass consumerism all happening at once, with a strong dose of Japanese 'cute' in the mix.

Establishment smarting at this grassroots individualism surfaced when a regular indie coverstar, **Prabda Yoon**, won the 2002 SEAWrite Award, South-east Asia's top literary prize. There was much blustering that age, experience and tradition should have been rewarded, inferring that youth (late 20s), feverish experimentation and new perspectives were qualities to be overcome, not encouraged. Proving that epics, romances or social critiques aren't the only stuff of literature, Prabda contemplates oddities though abstract, playful language.

The authorities' illegal and groundless investigation of him – along with feisty political commentators like his father, Sutthichai Yoon of the *Nation* newspaper – was a shot across the bows for thinking differently. Still, the genie's out of the bottle. Prabda is an internationally lauded role model for aspiring Thai creatives.

# Accommodation

# Accommodation

From flophouses to penthouses, hotels in Bangkok offer a lot for your *baht*.

When the likes of Josef Conrad and Somerset Maugham were visiting Bangkok a century ago the only place to stay was the **Oriental**. The present-day literati may mouth those same words with a certain hauteur, yet this irreproachable institution – which usually figures in the world's top three in hotel surveys – is only one of many world-class destination hotels. It's not just the grand ones on the river – the **Shangri-La**, **Peninsula** and **Marriott Bangkok Resort** – there are also devotees of the **Regent**, **Grand Hyatt Erawan**, **Sheraton Grande Sukhumvit** and, especially, the minimalist-chic **Sukhothai**. Those who wistfully recall golden ages feel at home in the **Dusit Thani** and **Hilton International**. The ante is being upped further by the opening in early 2003 of the swishly modern **Conrad Bangkok** and the **Davis**, the city's first designer boutique hotel.

## AREAS

The top-end is great value for a single-night splurge of indulgence, but there's an upgrading at the budget end too. Today's travellers seem to be somewhat richer than the penny-pinching backpackers who turned Thanon Khaosan into the world's most famous flophouse alley. Now gap-year lawyers-to-be wheel their backpacks into the lobby of **Buddy Lodge**. This stylish development is forcing an upgrade of rival guesthouses in the whole Banglamphu district and nearby Thanon Si Ayutthaya in Dusit, thus improving the choice for those who wish to stay near the old town in more comfort. It remains the cheapest area to stay (and so unusually intolerant of prostitutes that some have unconscionably banned Thai guests).

Most rooms, however, are to be found downtown, where prices are higher (but still reasonable), services much better, and shopping, dining and nightlife are all present in greater abundance – and all conveniently connected by BTS SkyTrain. Close to the action are bargain enclaves at Soi Ngam Duphli (in South), Kasemsan Soi 1 (Pathumwan) and around Sukhumvit, where mid-range accommodation is thickest. In the latter's Nana area, it's impossible to walk more than a few feet without coming across an Indian-run inn. Chinese hotels offer a faded, no-frills charm in Chinatown, Thanon Samsen (Banglamphu) and the western half of Bangrak.

Further afield, culture buffs might enjoy staying in a Thonburi artist's studio or in a trad teak house on the river in Nonthaburi (Outer North), an area famed for its cooking school.

## ROOMS AND RATES

Single rooms are often spacious enough for two to sleep, and doubles may well have two large beds, so ask to view rooms first. In guesthouses and cheap Chinese hotels, room rates can vary widely between fan-cooled and air-conditioned, en suite or shared bathrooms, and room size. Thanks to Thai communal sleeping habits, some hotels, particularly resorts, have a few huge rooms. At smarter hotels, prices vary greatly between standard, luxury and suites. Bangkok has a habit of snaring visitors long-term or attracting repeat returnees, and monthly room rates can be as low as B10,000, with studios and apartments from B13,000. At the other extreme, notably around Thanons Ratchadaphisek, Phetchburi Tud Mai and Surawong, and Sois Nana and Ngam Duphlee, certain discreet hotels charge by the hour.

We've divided the chapter by area and price category, according to the average cost of a standard double room: **deluxe** (from B5,000), **expensive** (B2,500-B4,999), **moderate** (B1,000-B2,499), **budget** (B500-B1,000) and **cheap** (under B500). Rates are for high season (November to March), and for non-Thais; locals usually pay less. Some hotels list their rates in dollars, but you can pay in *baht*. In the listings of hotel services, UBC is a cable/satellite company offering multiple channels.

## BOOKINGS AND BACKGROUND

Booking in advance is a good idea: traipsing around Bangkok's streets with luggage can be a real drag. Though the better hotels fill up at busy times, you can always find a room in the city, such is the oversupply. Note that rates for upmarket hotels are often higher if you book within Thailand rather than from abroad. But there are always promotions, particularly for business visitors and residents.

Online booking is increasingly popular. The **Thailand Hotels Association** (www.thaihotels.org) offers information and reservations, while other good online booking sites are **www.asia-hotels. com/thailand**, **www.bookingthaihotel. com**, **www.hotelthailand.com**,

Fine ingredients at the **Marriott**. See p38.

**www.sawadee.com** and **www.siam.net**.
For information on youth hostels nationwide,
run to International YHA standards, contact
the **Thai Youth Hostels Association**
(0 2628 7413-5/bangkok@tyha.org).

## Phra Nakorn & Banglamphu

A notorious backpacker enclave since the early
1980s, **Thanon Khaosan** now runs the gamut
from rabbit-hutch guesthouses (imortalised in
*The Beach*) to the opulence of the rebuilt Buddy
Lodge. But as this 'Freak Street' becomes a
cacophonous entertainment and shopping
zone, many travellers are opting for the quieter
confines on **Thanon Rambuttri** behind Wat
Chanasongkhram, and **Thanon Phra Arthit**.
For a more Thai-style neighbourhood, some
prefer the time-worn Chinese hotels huddling
on the side streets off **Thanon Samsen**, or
in and around Dusit.

## Moderate

### Buddy Lodge
*265 Thanon Khaosan, Banglamphu (0 2629 4477/
fax 0 2629 4744/www.buddylodge.com). Bus 39,
59, 60, 201, 503, 511, 512.* **Rooms** 76. **Rates**
standard B2,000; deluxe B2,500. **Credit** MC, V.
**Map** p308 B3.

While its imposing brick façade resembles a town
hall back in the West, the rooms are quite rustic.
They come with gleaming wooden floors, writing
desks, old-style lamps and white wood walls. The
balconies in the deluxe rooms are bigger than the
standard rooms, and make a nice spot for a night-
cap. Try to get a room on the east side, so that you
can catch a glimpse of the Golden Mount, which is
illuminated at night.
**Hotel services** *Air-conditioning. Bar. Coffee shop.
Concierge. Gym. Limousine service. Pool. Restaurant.
Travel agents.* **Room services** *Minibar. Room
service (24hr). Safe. Telephone. Turndown. TV: UBC.*

### The Royal Hotel
*2 Thanon Ratchadamnoen Klang, Phra Nakorn
(0 2222 9111/fax 0 2224 2083). Bus 2, 9, 12, 15,
33, 35, 39, 42, 44, 47, 56, 59, 60, 64, 68, 70, 79,
82, 96, 201, 203.* **Rooms** 300. **Rates** single B1,100;
double B1,600; triple B2,100; suite B4,000. **Credit**
AmEx, MC, V. **Map** p308 B3.
Convenient for the historic sights, the Royal was
doubtless once the pride of the area. These days,
though, it has fallen a little into disrepair but it still
maintains some dignity and character, not to mention offering good-value accommodation. The grand
lobby (which has a bloody history – democracy
demonstrators were once shot here) has been spoiled
by a tacky fountain and a messy coffee shop. Staff
are friendly and helpful.
**Hotel services** *Air-conditioning. Bar. Beauty salon.
Business services. Concierge. Internet access. No-
smoking floors. Parking. Pool. Restaurant.* **Room
services** *Minibar. Room service (24hr). Telephone.
Turndown. TV: UBC.*

## Budget

### D&D Inn
*68-70 Thanon Khaosan, Banglamphu (0 2629 0526-
8/fax 0 2629 0529). Bus 39, 59, 60, 201, 503, 511,
512.* **Rates** single B450; double B600; triple B900.
**No credit cards. Map** p308 B3.
With its big green neon sign and all the funky little
shops and travel agents clustered around the bottom, this hotel is a signpost pointing toward
Khaosan's future: much more mainstream, and a bit
bland. Still, the rooms are clean, if small, and on the
upper floors you can escape the street noise. The
rooftop swimming pool makes for a splendid vantage point. Toss in a comfortable lobby that's a
lively 'chat-room' for travellers from all points of
the compass, and it's a pretty good deal.
**Hotel services** *Air-conditioning. Pool. Travel
agents.* **Room services** *TV.*

## Cheap

### Barn Thai Guesthouse
*27 Trok Mayom, Thanon Chakkraphong,
Banglamphu (0 2281 9041). Bus 30, 32, 33, 64, 65,
506.* **Rooms** 10. **Rates** single B200. **No credit
cards. Map** p308 C4.

To all the visitors who stay at her 80-year-old house in the lane behind Thanon Khaosan, the elderly Thai owner of this charming guesthouse says, 'Call me Grandma'. Her hospitality, near-flawless English and wealth of knowledge about the neighbourhood is part of Barn Thai's allure, but this is also one of the few old wooden homes left that still accepts guests. The rooms are spartan and spotless, and the gleaming bathrooms have western-style toilets. Brightening up the surroundings are flowers, hanging plants and a spirit house, where the guardian deity of the land is supposed to reside. In fact, the only drawback is that it can get a little bit noisy here come nightfall.

### My House
*37 Soi Chanasongkhram, Banglamphu (0 2282 9263/4). Bus 30, 32, 33, 64, 65, 506.* **Rooms** 60. **Rates** double B300-B500. **No credit cards.** **Map** p308 B3.

As the area behind Wat Chanasongkhram becomes a cheap drinking substitute for Khaosan, it's not the tranquil spot it used to be. Fortunately, this well-maintained guesthouse retains an air of quietude. The Thai-style entrance is the most traditional thing about it; the rooms are a touch generic, but clean and comfy. Part of the five-floor guesthouse's enduring popularity is due to the big lounge and restaurant in the front.

**Hotel services** *Air-conditioning. Internet access. Restaurant. Travel agent.*

### Nakorn Pink Hotel
*9/1 Samsen Soi 6 (0 2281 6574/2282 2374/fax 0 2282 3727). Bus 3, 9, 19, 30, 32, 33, 43, 49, 53, 64, 65.* **Rooms** 81. **Rates** double B300-B400; hot water B60. **No credit cards.** **Map** p308 C2.

Of the old Chinese-style hotels off Samsen Road, this place is the pick of the litter. In contrast to the pastel exterior, the rooms are nicely decked out with clunky old wooden furniture and even have small refrigerators. At the mouth of the lane is an excellent seafood restaurant.

**Hotel services** *Air-conditioning. Internet access. Left luggage. Parking.* **Room services** *Refrigerator. Telephone. TV: satellite.*

### Peachy Guesthouse
*10 Thanon Phra Arthit, Banglamphu (0 2281 6471/ 6659). Bus 3, 30, 32, 64, 65, 506.* **Rooms** 57. **Rates** dorm B80; single B100; double B160-B350. **No credit cards.** **Map** p308 B2.

If the tiny rooms in most guesthouses induce claustrophobia, the lodgings in this converted school should help you breathe a little easier. The large double beds and wardrobes, as well as the beer garden/restaurant dotted with plants, make the Peachy the best choice for the thrifty. And the restaurant serves a full breakfast, crêpes, real coffee and Spanish omelettes. Ghost-hunters will thrill to the rumour that it's haunted by the spirits of an old Thai woman and a handyman.

**Hotel services** *Air-conditioning. Internet access. Left luggage. Restaurant. Travel agent.*

City views from the **Peninsula**. *See p39.*

## Thonburi

## Deluxe

### Marriott Bangkok Resort & Spa
*257/1-3 Thanon Charoennakorn (0 2476 0022/ fax 0 2476 1120/www.marriotthotels.com/bkkth). Saphan Taksin BTS then shuttle boat.* **Rooms** 413. **Rates** deluxe $180-$230; suite $260-$1,500. **Credit** AmEx, DC, MC, V. **Map** p310 D7.

Situated quite a way down river, further from the city centre than the other luxury river hotels, the Marriott is an attractive, unpretentious tourist hotel ranged on three sides round a verdant pool area and canal. There are plenty of facilities and dining options (including a great Sunday jazz brunch at Trader Vic's). The attached mall is rather too full of the hotel owner's fast-food franchises (though it has Bangkok's best shop for Thai ethnic music), so shops and nightlife are a bit of a trek away – but that's prized by guests who enjoy the shuttle boats to the BTS/Expressboat stop at Saphan Taksin and River City. For some river romance, take a night cruise on the hotel's luxurious converted rice barge.

**Hotel services** *Air-conditioning. Babysitting. Bars. Beauty salon. Business services. Concierge. Garden. Gym. Internet access. Limousine service. No-smoking floors. Parking. Pool. Restaurants.* **Room services** *Dataport. Kitchenette. Minibar. Room service (24hr). Telephone. Turndown. TV: satellite/UBC.*

## Peninsula

*333 Thanon Charoennakorn (0 2861 2888/fax*
*0 2861 1112/http://fasttrack.bangkok.peninsula.com).*
*Saphan Taksin BTS then shuttle boat.* **Rooms** 370.
**Rates** deluxe $260-$400; suite $980-$2,600. **Credit**
AmEx, DC, MC, V. **Map** p310 D7.

Voted best hotel in Asia by the readers of *Travel &*
*Leisure* in summer 2002, this stylish modern hotel
has rapidly become the hotel of choice for those seeking an alternative to the slightly ageing Oriental
opposite. The interior exudes an effortless sense of
sophistication, with an impressive collection of contemporary Asian art, including works by Thai
artists Natee Utarit and Niti Wattuya. Rooms are
large, well equipped and very modern, and are
blessed with excellent views of the Chao Praya river
and the rooftops of the city stretching out beyond it.
Also, rooms look *at* the more attractive river bank,
rather than from it. The hotel's restaurants, Jester's
(Pacific Rim fusion; *see p106*) and Mei Jiang
(Cantonese; *see p106*), are the city's best practition-
ers of both these styles of cuisine.
**Hotel services** *Air-conditioning. Babysitting. Bars.*
*Beauty salon. Business services. Concierge. Disabled:*
*adapted rooms. Garden. Gym. Internet access.*
*Limousine service. No-smoking floors. Parking. Pool.*
*Restaurants.* **Room services** *Dataport. Kitchenette.*
*Minibar. Room service (24hr). Telephone. Turndown.*
*TV: satellite/UBC.*

## Cheap

### The Artist's Place

*61-3 Soi Tiem Boon Yang, Thanon Krung Thonburi*
*(0 2862 0056/fax 0 2862 0074). Bus 3, 76, 105,*
*111, 505.* **Room** 12. **Rates** single B150-B350; double
B250-B450. **No credit cards.**

Thai artist Charlee Sodprasert has run this guesthouse, gallery and art school for nearly ten years –
it represents a unique opportunity to stay in a
slightly ramshackle but one-of-a-kind suburban
home at rock-bottom prices. Rooms are little more
than a mattress and pillow and the bathroom is
shared, but you're guaranteed an experience not
available anywhere else in Bangkok. There's also a
mini lecture hall where Sodprasert gives art classes,
and a bar where you can bring your own beer
(another welcome money-saving touch for the bud-
get-conscious travellers who stay here). The house
has great character, as does its owner. It's not easy
to find, so ring first and get directions.
**Hotel services** *Air-conditioning. Business services.*
*Coffee shop. Gallery. Internet access. Payphone.*
*TV room.*

## Dusit

A new enclave of budget accommodation
options on **Thanon Si Ayuthaya**, between
the National Library and the river, along with
some internet cafés and travel agencies,
provides an alternative to Banglamphu.

## Moderate

### Royal Princess

*269 Thanon Lan Luang (0 2281 3088/fax 0 2280*
*1314/www.royalprincess.com). Bus 2, 8, 39, 44, 59,*
*60, 79, 157, 503, 511, 512.* **Rooms** 168. **Rates**
superior B2,000-B2,400; deluxe B2,200-B2,600;
suite B4,000-7,000. **Credit** AmEx, DC, MC, V.
**Map** p309 D2.

Part of the Thai Dusit/Princess group, and owned
by one of Thailand's legendarily tough businesswomen, Chanut Piyaoui, this hotel's launching party
was such an emotional affair that she broke down
on the podium mid-speech. A quiet and romantic
boutique hotel and still gleaming after recent renovations, it offers attractive rooms, a large pool and
good service. It's closer to historical Bangkok than
the downtown and entertainment areas, but there's
a free shuttle to MBK and the World Trade Centre
in the day and to Silom/Patpong in the evenings.
**Hotel services** *Air-conditioning. Babysitting. Bar.*
*Business services. Concierge. Garden. Gym. Internet*
*access. Limousine service. No-smoking floors.*
*Parking. Pool. Restaurants.* **Room services**
*Dataport. Minibar. Room service (24hr). Telephone.*
*Turndown. TV: satellite/UBC.*

## Cheap

### Baan Phiman Resort

*123 Samsen Soi 5 (0 2282 5594). Bus 3, 9, 19, 30,*
*32, 33, 43, 49, 53, 64, 65.* **Rooms** 19. **Rates** house
B150; bamboo hut B250; tent B50. **No credit cards.**
**Map** p308 C2.

The slogan for this strange complex of bungalows
and traditional Thai houses is 'the Romance of River
Life'. Nestled in the midst of an old Thai community,
you can choose between a few bungalows right on
the river or small rooms in a house. Other attractions
are the garden and sun deck overlooking the river,
and a very inexpensive restaurant, where a Thai
omelette on rice costs only B10. There are also two
tents, with a mattress, small fan and light.
**Hotel services** *Bar. Business services. Internet*
*access. Payphone. Restaurant. TV room.* **Room**
**services** *Room service (24hr).*

### Sri-Ayuthaya Guesthouse

*23/11 Si Ayutthaya Soi 14 (0 2282 5942/2281*
*6829). Bus 19, 72.* **Rooms** 16. **Rates** double B350-
B450. **No credit cards. Map** p308 C1.

With all sorts of traditional Thai touches, like
wooden angels set in the brick walls, and a downstairs restaurant full of handicrafts, Buddha images
and black and white photos of Bangkok in 1917, this
three-floor guesthouse is one of the classiest acts in
the district. Only two years old, its small rooms are
furnished in rustic style, while the bathrooms have
stone walls outside and saloon-style doors. If you
want cheaper digs, the owner has another guesthouse a little further down the *soi*, where you'll also
find the Backpacker Lodge.

JIM THOMPSON
*The Thai Silk Company*

Hotel services *Air-conditioning. Internet access. Laundry. Payphone. Restaurant.* **Room services** *Room service (24hr).*
**Branch: Tawee Guesthouse** 83 Si Ayutthaya Soi 14, Dusit (0 2280 1447).

## Chinatown

### Moderate

#### Grand China Princess

*215 Thanon Yaowarat (0 2224 9977/fax 0 2224 7999/www.grandchina.com). Bus 1, 4, 25, 35, 40, 73, 507.* **Rooms** 165. **Rates** superior B2,200; deluxe B2,500-B4,000; suite B4,500-B8,000. **Credit** AmEx, DC, MC, V. **Map** p308 C5.
A great base from which to explore Chinatown's many attractions. Rooms are large; some sport huge balconies overlooking the city and the Chao Praya. The top floor has Bangkok's only revolving club lounge, open in the evenings. Facilities are a bit worn and the decor rather thrown together, but it's a good bet if you're after a bit of chaos and character.
Hotel services *Air-conditioning. Bars. Beauty salon. Business services. Concierge. Gym. Internet access. Limousine service. No-smoking floors. Parking. Pool. Restaurants.* **Room services** *Dataport. Minibar. Room service (24hr). Telephone. Turndown. TV: UBC.*

### Budget

#### The China Town Hotel

*526 Thanon Yaowarat (0 2225 0204-6/fax 0 2226 1295/www.chinatownhotel.co.th). Bus 1, 4, 25, 35, 40, 73, 507.* **Rooms** 75. **Rates** mid standard B750; standard B850; executive B950; superior B1,000; deluxe B1,200. **Credit** MC, V. **Map** p308 C5.
If you want to be smack in the middle of Chinatown's main drag and don't mind the noise or the tatty rooms, the China Town Hotel offers cheapish accommodation. However, you could do a lot better for the price. There are no leisure facilities except for the in-house VIP massage service, the TVs in the rooms are small and only tuned to local and Chinese stations, and some of the air-conditioners look rather close to falling off the walls.
Hotel services *Air-conditioning. Bar.* **Room services** *Minibar. Telephone. TV: UBC.*

#### Riverview Guesthouse

*768 Thanon Songwad (0 2235 8501/fax 0 2237 5428). Bus 1, 4, 25, 35, 40, 73, 507.* **Rooms** 45. **Rates** fan room B200-B450; air-con room B690. **Credit** AmEx. **Map** p310 D6.
This guesthouse on the river is very basic, but it's very good value, quiet, clean and friendly, and offers the chance to experience 'old' Bangkok – not least as you try to find it deep in the atmospheric maze of Chinatown alleys. The higher rooms have great views of the river, as does the top-floor restaurant. B690 will get you the largest air-conditioned room with a fridge and TV (local programmes only).

Hotel services *Air-conditioning. Business services. Internet access. Restaurant.* **Room services** *Room service (24hr). Telephone. TV.*

## Bangrak

### Deluxe

#### Dusit Thani

*946 Thanon Rama IV (0 2236 9999/fax 0 2236 6400/www.dusit.com). Saladaeng BTS/Silom subway.* **Rooms** 520. **Rates** superior $190-$260; suite $500-$600. **Credit** AmEx, DC, MC, V. **Map** p311 G6.
A large, established and elegant luxury hotel long favoured by visiting dignitaries and the Thai royal family. Though its geometric 1970s angles attract the hip, interiors are very Thai, with a choice of modern or traditional rooms. The hotel overlooks Lumphini Park and is beside the Silom/Patpong entertainment area, as well as both the subway and BTS. The luxury but good-value Deverana Spa surrounds the waterfall courtyard. The hotel's restaurants were once the best in town, but standards have fallen a little in recent times. The setting, however, remains top-notch and the rooftop Tiara restaurant has fantastic panoramic views of the city.
Hotel services *Air-conditioning. Babysitting. Bars. Beauty salon. Business services. Concierge. Gym. Internet access. Limousine service. No-smoking floors. Parking. Pool. Restaurants.* **Room services** *Minibar. Room service (24hr). Telephone. Turndown. TV: satellite/UBC.*

#### The Oriental

*48 Thanon Charoen Krung Soi 38 (0 2659 9000/fax 0 2659 0000/www.mandarinoriental.com). Saphan Taksin BTS.* **Rooms** 393. **Rates** standard $300; suite $440-$2,200. **Credit** AmEx, DC, MC, V. **Map** p310 D7.
One of the world's greats, this beautiful riverside hotel was designed as a lodge for European traders. The original building was destroyed by fire in 1865, and two Danish naval captains, Jarck and Salje, constructed the hotel in its present position 11 years later. It soon began to attract a more creative and cosmopolitan crowd, and is best known for its long list of literary guests. In 1887 another Dane, HN Anderson, built a new, more luxurious wing now known as the Author's Wing. It's since gone through several owners, including Jim Thompson. A year after its completion, an unknown Joseph Conrad became the first writer to enjoy the Oriental's hospitality, setting a precedent that would be followed by the likes of Somerset Maugham, Noel Coward, Graham Greene, John le Carre and even Barbara Cartland. If you want to experience a piece of living history, the Oriental is still *the* hotel in Bangkok.
Its facilities are magnificent: Le Normandie (*see p109*) is the city's priciest and probably best restaurant; the legendary Bamboo Bar offers some of the best jazz in town; and *khon* dance is staged at the Sala Rim Nam Thai restaurant (*see p203*) across the river, beside the Oriental Spa (*see p182*) and the

Living the high life at the **Sheraton**. *See p45.*

Oriental Cooking School (*see p115* **Learn to: Cook Thai**). A courtesy boat shuttles back and forth to River City and the SkyTrain.

**Hotel services** *Air-conditioning. Babysitting. Bars. Beauty salon. Business services. Concierge. Disabled: adapted rooms. Garden. Gym. Internet access. Limousine service. No-smoking floors. Parking. Pool. Restaurants.* **Room services** *Dataport. Minibar. Room service (24hr). Telephone. Turndown. TV: satellite/UBC.*

### Shangri-La Hotel

*89 Soi Wat Suan Plu, Thanon Charoen Krung (0 2236 7777). Saphan Taksin BTS.* **Rooms** 839. **Rates** deluxe $280-$370; suite $430-$1,700. **Credit** AmEx, DC, MC, V. **Map** p310 D7.

The largest hotel on the river, conveniently located next to a BTS station, is also one of the best. It bears all the hallmarks of the Shangri-La chain: first-rate service, extensive facilities and a wide choice of dining options, including the award-winning Italian restaurant Angelini (*see p107*). The awards don't stop there; since opening it's picked up five pages of accolades. Rooms are a little on the bland side compared to the glitzy lobby, but ongoing renovation is modernising and upgrading facilities. The hotel also offers river cruises on its modern luxury yacht.

**Hotel services** *Air-conditioning. Babysitting. Bars. Beauty salon. Business services. Concierge. Disabled: adapted rooms. Gym. Internet access. Limousine service. No-smoking floors. Parking. Pools. Restaurants.* **Room services** *Dataport. Minibar. Room service (24hr). Safe. Telephone. Turndown. TV: satellite.*

### Sofitel Silom

*188 Thanon Silom (0 2238 1991/fax 0 2238 1999/ www.sofitel.com). Chong Nonsi BTS.* **Rooms** 454. **Rates** classic B7,000-B9,900; suite B12,000-B25,000. **Credit** AmEx, DC, MC, V. **Map** p310 F7.

This large high-rise hotel opened under Sofitel management in mid 2002 after an extensive but not full renovation (it was previously the Monarch Lee Gardens). Positioned at the quieter end of Silom, it breathes class through its contemporary decor, smart furnishings and flamboyant artworks. Check out the lavish top-floor Shanghai restaurant, which has excellent views of the city.

**Hotel services** *Air-conditioning. Babysitting. Bars. Beauty salon. Business services. Concierge. Gym. Internet access. Limousine service. No-smoking floors. Parking. Pool. Restaurants.* **Room services** *Dataport. Minibar. Room service (24hr). Telephone. Turndown. TV: satellite.*

## Expensive

### Tarntawan Place Hotel

*119/5-10 Thanon Surawong (0 2238 2620/fax 0 2238 3228/www.tarntawan.com). Saladaeng BTS/ Silom subway.* **Rooms** 80. **Rates** double B3,000; double suite B4,000; super deluxe B6,000. **Credit** AmEx, DC, MC, V. **Map** p310 F6.

Snuggled in between Surawong and Silom roads, this small hotel is bang in the middle of one of the city's more lively entertainment centres. Those expecting a 'deluxe boutique hotel' will be disappointed – it's small and cosy, but short on in-house

recreational activities. It's ideal as a base from where to enjoy the areas's many nocturnal pleasures and unexpected new friends are not charged.

**Hotel services** *Air-conditioning. Bar. Business services. Internet access. Limousine service. No-smoking floors. Parking. Restaurant.* **Room services** *Minibar. Room service (24hr). Telephone. TV: satellite.*

## Moderate

### La Residence

*173/8-9 Thanon Surawong (0 2266 5400-2/fax 0 2237 9322). Saladaeng BTS/Silom subway.* **Rooms** 26. **Rates** single B950; double B1,400; suite B2,500; studio B2,700. **Credit** AmEx, MC, V. **Map** p310 F6.

Gleaning repeat business from regular visitors, this small modern boutique hotel is out of earshot of Patpong. The decor is tasteful and understated, with each room sporting its own theme and design. It's clean and friendly and fairly good value (breakfast is included). Rooms feature all the necessary mod cons, but there are no leisure facilities on offer except for a small library.

**Hotel services** *Air-conditioning. Business services. Internet access. Limousine service. Parking. Restaurant.* **Room services** *Dataport. Minibar. Room service (24hr). Telephone. Turndown. TV: satellite/UBC.*

## Budget

### Ryn's Café & Bed

*44/16 Soi Convent, Thanon Silom (0 2632 1327/fax 0 2632 1323/www.cafeandbed.com). Saladaeng BTS/Silom subway.* **Rooms** 7. **Rates** single/double B550-B700; family room B950. **Credit** AmEx, MC, V. **Map** p310 F7.

This small inn in the business district offers clean and homely rooms above its disconcertingly good but tiny Swiss restaurant. The owner/chef is an accomplished and experienced cook, and the restaurant is usually busy in the evenings. A great-value hotel, with an intimate B&B feel. Its size means that advance booking is highly recommended.

**Hotel services** *Air-conditioning. Business services. Internet access. Payphone. Restaurant.*

## Pathumwan

## Deluxe

### Conrad Bangkok

*87 Thanon Witthayu (0 2654 1111/www.conrad hotels.com). Ploenchit BTS.* **Rooms** 392. **Rates** $240. **Credit** AmEx, DC, MC, V. **Map** p311 H5.

Scheduled to open in early 2003, this long-awaited business tower has avoided the traditional clichés of Bangkok hotels by dressing its staff in chic uniforms and its rooms in contemporary international design. The accent is modern and modish, especially in its nightclub, 87. The health club is so enormous

it even has a rooftop jogging track. The hotel shares a huge complex with exclusive apartments on one of Bangkok's embassy rows, hi-tech offices and the upmarket All Seasons Retail Centre, which also boasts several fine restaurants.

**Hotel services** *Air-conditioning. Bars. Beauty salon. Business services. Concierge. Gym. Internet access. Limousine service. No-smoking floors. Parking. Pool. Restaurants.* **Room services** *Dataport. Minibar. Room service (24hr). Turndown. TV: satellite/UBC.*

### Grand Hyatt Erawan

*494 Thanon Ratchadamri (0 2254 1234/ www.bangkok.hyatt.com). Chidlom BTS.* **Rooms** 387. **Rates** $280-$1,700. **Credit** AmEx, DC, MC, V. **Map** p311 G5.

The Grand Hyatt has recently undergone extensive refurbishing, with rooms and suites now having a sleek, contemporary aesthetic. The lobby retains its slight feel of classical presumptuousness, but in the new rooms the decor is brown and cream, sleek and modern. The spacious and elaborate marble bathrooms have separate bathtubs. The You & Mee noodle shop in the basement is a locals' favourite.

**Hotel services** *Air-conditioning. Babysitting. Bars. Beauty salon. Business services. Concierge. Disabled: adapted rooms. Garden. Gym. Internet access. Limousine service. No-smoking floors. Parking. Pool. Restaurants.* **Room services** *Dataport. Kitchenette. Minibar. Room service (24hr). Telephone. Turndown. TV: UBC.*

### Hilton International

*2 Thanon Witthayu (0 2253 0123/www.hilton.com). Ploenchit BTS.* **Rooms** 338. **Rates** deluxe $200; executive $230; suite $350-$500; royal suite $1,500; presidential suite $1,500. **Credit** AmEx, DC, MC, V. **Map** p311 H5.

Owned by the formidable businesswoman who heads the Siam Society, the Hilton's glamour is mature, but by no means faded. All rooms have private balconies and hi-tech telecom services, along with gilt bedspreads, deep carpets and thick floral curtains. The best thing is the large, rainforest-like garden, which is overlooked by the big glass lobby and all of the rooms on that particular side of the building. Designed around a freeform swimming pool, a jogging track winds through palms and ponds – this area is big enough to qualify as a real oasis. Oh, and tucked discreetly to one side is the phallus-decked Nai Lert Shrine.

**Hotel services** *Air-conditioning. Babysitting. Bars. Beauty salon. Business services. Concierge. Garden. Gym. Limousine service. No-smoking floors. Parking. Restaurants. Pool.* **Room services** *Minibar. Room service (24hr). Turndown. TV: UBC.*

### Le Royal Meridien Bangkok

*973 Thanon Ploenchit (0 2656 0444/ www.lemeridien-bangkok.com). Chidlom BTS.* **Rooms** 381. **Rates** deluxe $265; executive $320; business $350; ambassador $700; diplomatic $1,200; royal $1,700. **Credit** AmEx, DC, MC, V. **Map** p311 G4.

Built in a tall, glass-sheathed high-rise next door to the ageing Le Meridien President, Le Royal is beautiful, luxurious and extravagant. It's near Chidlom BTS station and adjacent to the glittering new consumer mecca of Gaysorn Plaza. The stylish, modern rooms have expansive city views through broad windows; you might be lucky enough to scoop a special deal of only $160 per night for a deluxe room. The pleasant rooftop pool (37 floors up) has a swim-up bar and small tropical garden, and Espresso offers one of the best Sunday brunch buffets in town. **Hotel services** *Air-conditioning. Babysitting. Bar. Beauty salon. Business service. Concierge. Disabled: adapted rooms. Garden. Gym. Internet access. Limousine service. No-smoking floors. Parking. Pool. Restaurants.* **Room services** *Dataport. Minibar. Room service (24hr). Turndown. TV: UBC.*

### Regent Hotel

*155 Thanon Ratchadamri (0 2254 9999/2251 6127/ www.regenthotel.com). Ratchadamri BTS.* **Rooms** 256. **Rates** superior $280; deluxe $300; suite $380-$600; Rajdamri suite $2,000. **Credit** AmEx, DC, MC, V. **Map** p311 G5.

The Regent has done an excellent job of incorporating Thai handicrafts and design influences (murals, silk, teak) into its furnishings, while still retaining contemporary style and functionality. Rooms are stylish with generous bathrooms and separate dressing areas. The Tony Chi-designed restaurants are impeccable and among the city's best – notably Biscotti (Italian; *see p112*), Madison (grill) and Shintaro (Japanese). There's also the Aqua bar (*see p127*). The small, top-end shopping centre attached to the lobby has a great patisserie. **Hotel services** *Air-conditioning. Babysitting. Bar. Beauty salon. Business services. Concierge. Disabled: adapted rooms. Garden. Gym. Internet access. Limousine service. No-smoking floors. Parking. Pool. Restaurants.* **Room services** *Dataport. Minibar. Room service (24hr). Telephone. Turndown. TV: satellite/UBC.*

## Expensive

### Pathumwan Princess

*444 Thanon Phayathai (0 2216 3700/www. pprincess.com). National Stadium BTS.* **Rooms** 446. **Rates** single B4,100-B4,600; double B4,700-B5,200. **Credit** AmEx, DC, MC, V. **Map** p309 & p310 F5.

Connected to the frenetic MBK mall in the middle of one of Bangkok's biggest shopping areas, the Pathumwan Princess could hardly be described as the place to get away from it all. But with all conceivable facilities and an almost continuously air-conditioned walk to the Siam Discovery Centre, Siam Centre and the SkyTrain, it's certainly convenient. It's a family-friendly hotel (judging by the chaos in the foyer), and even the lowest-priced rooms are generously proportioned and comfortable. Staff are numerous and extremely helpful. The outdoor saltwater pool is a full 25m, beside the superb Olympic Health Club.

**Hotel services** *Air-conditioning. Babysitting. Beauty salon. Business services. Concierge. Gym. Internet access. Limousine service. No-smoking floors. Parking. Pool. Restaurants.* **Room services** *Dataport. Minibar. Room service (24hr). Turndown. TV: satellite/UBC.*

## Budget

### A-1 Inn

*25/13 Soi Kasemsan 1, Thanon Rama I (0 2215 3029). National Stadium BTS.* **Rooms** 20. **Rates** double B480; triple B750. **No credit cards.** **Map** p309 & p310 F4.

Midway down a narrow *soi* opposite MBK mall that is fast converting to a budget guesthouse centre (if the building activity is anything to go by), the A-1 Inn offers basic doubles. These include a colour TV, air-conditioning and a bathroom with hot water showers. It's popular and fills up regularly. **Hotel services** *Air-conditioning. Internet access.* **Room services** *Telephone. TV.*

### Reno Hotel

*40 Soi Kasemsan 1, Thanon Rama I (0 2215 0026/ 7). National Stadium BTS.* **Rooms** 58. **Rates** B780-B1,290. **Credit** MC, V. **Map** p309 & p310 F4.

The Reno has a swish new lobby, and the recent refurbishment of the adjoining Reno Café bodes well for the renovations under way on the guest rooms at time of writing. As they stand, they're big but

Budget chic at the **Atlanta**. *See p46.*

rather musty and stuffy, and certainly not as hip as the café downstairs. Some have private balconies. One to keep an eye on – though the improvements may bump it out of the budget price range.
**Hotel services** *Air-conditioning. Bar. Business service. Limousine service. Parking. Pool. Restaurant. Travel agent.* **Room services** *Minibar. Room service (24hr). Telephone. TV: UBC.*

### White Lodge

*36/8 Soi Kasemsan 1, Thanon Rama I (0 2215 3102). National Stadium BTS.* **Rooms** 30. **Rates** double B400-B500; triple B600. **No credit cards.** **Map** p309 & p310 F4.
With close competition from its budget neighbours, the White Lodge is extremely good value. The rooms are smallish, but clean and functional: all have air-con and a shower/toilet; some have TVs. There is also a tour desk and a solid range of street stall options outside in the *soi*.
**Hotel services** *Air-conditioning. Parking. Restaurant. TV room.* **Room services** *Telephone.*

## Sukhumvit

## Deluxe

### Davis

*88 Sukhumvit Soi 24, Thanon Rama IV end, Sukhumvit (0 2260 8000/davis@saintdavis.com). Phrom Phong BTS then taxi.* **Rooms** 165. **Credit** AmEx, DC, MC, V. **Map** p312 K7.
Bangkok's first *Wallpaper**-style boutique hotel, this postmodern edifice has rooms of radically individual designs and exquisite public areas within an unusual complex. Its ground-level shops are branded Saint Davis. Hidden behind is Baan Davis, an exclusive walled hotel village of new houses in a traditional Thai style. Next door is Camp Davis, a temporary arcade of artfully disguised metal containers housing bars, restaurants and shops around a tent-roofed atrium with a DJ booth. Beside that, another Davis hotel concept is arising. Room rates were unconfirmed at time of writing, but will be in the five-star-and-above range.
**Hotel services** *Air-conditioning. Bar. Business services. Gym. Internet access. Limousine service. No-smoking floors. Parking. Pools. Restaurant.* **Room services** *Dataport. Kitchenette. Minibar. Room service (24hr). Telephone. TV: UBC.*

### Sheraton Grande Sukhumvit

*250 Sukhumvit Soi 12 (0 2653 0333/ www.starwood.com/bangkok). Asok BTS/Sukhumvit subway.* **Rooms** 445. **Rates** deluxe $240; grande deluxe $280; suite $430-$800; royal suite $1,400. **Credit** AmEx, DC, MC, V. **Map** p311 J5.
There's no point even thinking about this one unless you're comfortable haemorrhaging money. As you'd expect, there's fruit, slippers and robes, service is charming and excellent, and the rooms luxuriously finished. The Sheraton does not have a high or low season; rates are the same year round (and corporate rates are considerably cheaper than advertised rates). It's often full with repeat visitors, so booking is essential. The pool is pleasant but surprisingly small, with a spa attached. The impressive restaurants include Basil (contemporary Thai), Rossini (Italian), while the Living Room hosts quality jazz and Riva's is a classy cover band venue.
**Hotel services** *Air-conditioning. Babysitting. Bars. Beauty salon. Business services. Concierge. Disabled: adapted rooms. Garden. Gym. Internet access. Limousine service. No-smoking floors. Parking. Pool. Restaurants.* **Room services** *Dataport. Minibar. Room service (24hr). Telephone. Turndown. TV: satellite/UBC.*

## Moderate

### Majestic Suites

*110-110/1 Thanon Sukhumvit between Sois 4 & 6 (0 2656 8220/fax 0 2656 8201/www.majesticsuites. com). Nana BTS.* **Rooms** 55. **Rates** single B1,165-B1,295; double B1,500-B1,865. **Credit** AmEx, DC, MC, V. **Map** p311 J5.
A small, friendly, Indian-run establishment that's only three years old. The Majestic offers good, air-conditioned, smallish rooms that are nonetheless excellent value for such a central location, especially the extremely comfortable double deluxe room. It's next door to the post office and not far from Nana Plaza. There's no pool but there is a lobby bar, and Majestic Tailors are next door.
**Hotel services** *Air-conditioning. Bar. Business services. Internet access. Limousine service. Restaurant.* **Room services** *Minibar. Room service (24hr). Telephone. TV: UBC.*

### Regency Park Bangkok

*12/3 Sukhumvit Soi 22 (0 2259 7420-39/ www.accorhotels-asia.com). Phrom Phong BTS.* **Rooms** 120. **Rates** superior B1,990; deluxe B2,390; suite B3,800. **Credit** AmEx, DC, MC, V. **Map** p312 K6.
Run by hotel chain Accor, this lovely hotel offers friendly, first-rate service and well-appointed rooms at a fraction of the cost of the bigger luxury hotel brands. Surrounding a leafy central courtyard, all rooms are new, thickly carpeted and have a separate bathtub and shower. The famous *kathoey* Mambo Cabaret and Dubliner pub are a short walk away; it's slightly further to the Emporium shopping centre and Phrom Phong BTS station.
**Hotel services** *Air-conditioning. Babysitting. Bar. Business services. Concierge. Garden. Gym. Internet access. Limousine service. No-smoking floors. Parking. Pool. Restaurant.* **Room services** *Dataport. Minibar. Room service (24hr). Safe. Turndown. TV.*

### Taipan

*25 Sukhumvit Soi 23 (0 2260 9880-98/www. taipanhotel.com). Asok BTS/Sukhumvit subway.* **Rooms** 150. **Rates** standard B2,200; deluxe B2,400; junior suite B6,500. **Credit** AmEx, DC, MC, V. **Map** p312 K6.

A friendly hotel set back from the main road, but close enough to Soi Cowboy and Asok station, the Taipan offers standard and deluxe rooms. The deluxe ones are better value: they're more comfortable, nicely finished and better furnished, and should only cost around B200 extra. Note that reservations are required because they fill up fast. There is a small but unspectacular pool. Breakfast is included in the room price.

**Hotel services** *Air-conditioning. Babysitting. Bar. Beauty salon. Business services. Concierge. Disabled: adapted rooms. Gym. Internet access. Limousine service. No-smoking floors. Parking. Pool. Restaurant.* **Room services** *Dataport. Minibar. Room service (24hr). Telephone. Turndown. TV: UBC.*

# Budget

The small sub-*soi* next to Sukhumvit Soi 11 is crammed with more or less indistinguishable budget accommodation, along with Indian tailors and restaurants predominantly geared to old white males doing the Nana bars. All the inns offer rather dingy, sparse rooms with phones, air-con, cable TV and clean but unexciting en suite bathrooms. The **Bangkok Inn** and **Business Inn** are a couple of the better options.

## Atlanta Hotel

*78 Sukhumvit Soi 2 (0 2252 1650/6069/ www.theatlantahotel.bizland.com). Nana BTS.* **Rooms** 49. **Rates** single B350-B540; double B480-B670. **No credit cards. Map** p311 J5.
Founded in 1952, this one-time beau monde haunt has hosted the likes of Thailand's Princess Mother, Jim Thompson and Scandinavian royalty. Flooding nearly destroyed the hotel in the late 1960s, but thanks to the efforts of Charles Henn, the founder's son, it's currently enjoying a new golden age. It has developed a cult following among a new generation of writers, photographers, producers and other Asia-obsessives. Its concrete exterior may be crumbling and the bathrooms barebones, but its charm lies in a marriage of character and style that owes as much to British manners and Thai-ness as it does to the vintage 1950s deco in the lobby. There's fantastic Thai food, a 24hr pool and traditional Thai dancing on Saturdays – and one night's stay costs the same as brunch at the nearby JW Marriott.

**Hotel services** *Air-conditioning. Garden. Internet access. Payphone. Pool. Restaurant. TV room.*

## Bangkok Inn

*155/12-13 Sukhumvit Soi 11/1 (0 2254 4834-7/ www.bangkok-inn.com). Nana BTS.* **Rooms** 18. **Rates** double B910. **Credit** AmEx, MC, V. **Map** p311 J5.
The Bangkok Inn boasts private safes, but you may have to dodge the condensation leaking from the air-con unit in the ceiling.

**Hotel services** *Air-conditioning.* **Room services** *Minibar. Telephone. TV: satellite.*

## Business Inn

*155/4-5 Sukhumvit Soi 11 (0 2255 7155-8). Nana BTS.* **Rooms** 50. **Rates** double B600. **Credit** AmEx, MC, V. **Map** p311 J5.
The Business Inn distinguishes itself by offering a full travel agency service downstairs, and by being slightly cheaper than its competitors.

**Hotel services** *Air-conditioning.* **Room services** *Minibar. TV: satellite.*

## Honey Hotel

*31 Sukhumvit Soi 19 (0 2253 0646-9). Asok BTS/ Sukhumvit subway.* **Rooms** 75. **Rates** single B750; double B800; deluxe B900; suite B1,200-B1,600. **Credit** MC, V. **Map** p312 K6.
Superbly kitsch, the Honey's long, low, black granite foyer and aqua pool will suit anyone who thinks crimplene and cocktail frankfurters are 'faaabulous!'. Rooms are unglamorous but good value. It retains a slightly musty feel and a cast of ubiquitous middle-aged white men and young Thai girls lounging in the pool area. Tonnes of atmosphere though, and a short walk to Soi Cowboy and Asok station.

**Hotel services** *Air-conditioning. Coffee shop. Restaurant. Pool.* **Room services** *Minibar. TV: UBC.*

## Miami

*2 Sukhumvit Soi 13 (0 2253 0369). Nana BTS.* **Rooms** 100. **Rates** single B400; double B600. **Credit** MC, V. **Map** p311 J5.
Worth it just for its general retro chic, the Miami has certainly seen better days, but still boasts a pale blue pool in the central courtyard. Rooms are plain and old-looking, but large and functional. Friendly *kathoey* staff will cut the rates for weekly or monthly stays, and there are quieter rooms on the non-street side of the hotel. It's very close to the massage joints and souvenir markets lining Sukhumvit Road, and a stone's throw to Nana SkyTrain station. The Miami has a booking desk at Bangkok Airport.

**Hotel services** *Air-conditioning. Pool. Restaurant. Travel agent.* **Room services** *Refrigerator. Room service (24hr). Telephone. TV.*

## The Promenade

*18 Sukhumvit Soi 8 (0 2253 4116/2876/fax 0 2254 7707). Nana BTS.* **Rooms** 44. **Rates** double B900. **Credit** AmEx, MC, V. **Map** p311 J5.
As soon as you head south of Sukhumvit from the glaring red lights of Nana to the even-numbered *soi*, you tend to get better value for your money. Soi 8 is quieter, and in its further reaches much leafier than anything on the north side. The Promenade offers an old-school air of thickly carpeted comfort and brass fixtures in its good en suite doubles.

**Hotel services** *Air-conditioning. Coffee shop.* **Room services** *Telephone. TV: UBC.*

## Suk11 Guesthouse

*1/33 Sukhumvit Soi 11 (0 2253 5927-8/ www.suk11.com). Nana BTS.* **Rooms** 67. **Rates** single B450-B500; double B550-B600; family B800-B1,200. **No credit cards. Map** p311 J5.

Guesthouses are thin on the ground in Sukhumvit, but in the budget accommodation stakes Suk11 is a hands down winner. It spreads out somewhat erratically over four beautifully decorated, old-Thai-style wooden buildings crammed into a sub-*soi* just past Bangkok institution Cheap Charlie's (a great place for reasonably priced drinks). Rooms are smallish, but pleasant, clean and new-looking, and a bed in a dorm is a good option for budget travellers. All rooms have air-con and the price includes breakfast. **Hotel services** *Air-conditioning. Beauty salon. Internet access. Payphone. Restaurant. TV room.*

# North

## Deluxe

### Amari Watergate

*847 Thanon Petchaburi (0 2653 9000/fax 0 2653 9045/www.amari.com). Bus 2, 38, 60, 93, 140, 511, 512.* **Rooms** 563. **Rates** single $184-$199; double $200-$215; suite $256-$272. **Credit** AmEx, DC, MC, V. **Map** p311 G4.

A huge towering hotel in Bangkok's commercial centre. It can feel mall-like due to its size (the escalators don't help), but it seems no expense was spared in providing excellent facilities, including one of the city's best equipped gyms, a large pool and a unique eighth-floor lawn. Rooms are also well equipped and very good value, but the hotel is too large to evoke much atmosphere. Thai on 4 (modern Thai) and Grappino (Italian) are fine restaurants, while the basement restaurant bar Henry J Bean's serves up live music and American favourites.

**Hotel services** *Air-conditioning. Babysitting. Bars. Beauty salon. Business services. Concierge. Disabled: adapted rooms. Gym. Internet access. Limousine service. Parking. Pool. Restaurants.* **Room services** *Dataport. Minibar. Room service (24hr). Telephone. Turndown. TV: UBC.*

## Expensive

### Siam City Hotel

*477 Thanon Si Ayutthaya (0 2247 0120/ www.siamhotels.com). Phayathai BTS.* **Rooms** 500. **Rates** single B3,200; double B3,600; triple B4,400; suite B8,000. **Credit** AmEx, DC, MC, V. **Map** p311 G3.

The Siam City's exterior is a curious blend of art deco and modern glassy architecture, but the interior is more consistent and intimate, and favoured by power-brokers. Tastefully decorated with regional artefacts collected by owner Kamala Sukosol, the lobby is designed like a Victorian conservatory, with an attractive stained-glass dome and a large concrete sculpture depicting the outstanding achievements of four Thai kings. The artistic theme is continued via monthly debates in the Ratanakosin Lounge, and regular music performances, some from Kamala herself. A successful businesswomen, she is Thailand's version of Carmen Miranda, who trills Sinatra stan-

Floral designs and minimalist lines at the **Sukhothai**. *See p48.*

# Hotels

## The best

### For style credibility
**Sukhothai**. *See p48.*

### For retro eccentricity
**Atlanta Hotel**. *See p46.*

### For value
**Pathumwan Princess**. *See p44.*

### For service
**The Oriental**. *See p41.*

### For rooms with a view
**The Peninsula** (*see p39*),
**Banyan Tree Bangkok** (*see p48*) and
**Riverview Guesthouse** (*see p41*).

dards at the drop of a hat. It's a dynasty, in fact; her daughter's big in musicals and her sons started the indie label Bakery and the hit band Pru.
**Hotel services** *Air-conditioning. Bar. Beauty salon. Business services. Disabled: adapted rooms. Gym. Internet access. Limousine service. No-smoking floors. Parking. Pool. Restaurants.* **Room services** *Minibar. Room service (24hr). Turndown. TV: UBC.*

## South

### Deluxe

#### Banyan Tree Bangkok
*21/100 Thanon Sathorn Tai (0 2679 1200/fax 0 2679 1199/www.banyantree.com). Bus 17, 22, 35, 62, 67, 116, 149.* **Rooms** 210. **Rates** premier/deluxe suite $300; spa suite $900; presidential suite $1,300. **Credit** AmEx, DC, MC, V. **Map** p311 G7.
Thai brand Banyan Tree is establishing itself as a leading name in international hotels, with its Phuket operation recently winning an award for the world's best resort. The Bangkok arm is an all-suite luxury hotel in a distinctive, 50-storey, wafer-thin tower with an enormous hole through the middle of it (where you'll find the Banyan Tree Spa; *see p182*). The suites are lovely, and the hotel offers every relaxation service the spoilt international executive could imagine – including six levels of spa facilities, an outdoor 'sky deck', and two pools. Saffron serves contemporary Thai food from the penthouse level, while rooftop al fresco grill Vertigo (Bangkok's highest restaurant) offers astonishing views but indifferent, rapidly cooling food.
**Hotel services** *Air-conditioning. Bars. Beauty salon. Business services. Concierge. Garden. Gym. Internet access. Limousine service. No-smoking floors. Parking. Restaurants. Pools.* **Room services** *Dataport. Minibar. Room services (24hr). Telephone. Turndown. TV: UBC.*

#### Sukhothai
*13/3 Thanon Sathorn Tai (0 2287 0222/ www.sukhothai.com). Bus 17, 22, 35, 62, 67, 116, 149.* **Rooms** 219. **Rates** superior $260; deluxe $310; suite $390-$890; terrace suite $1,600; Sukhothai suite $2,000. **Credit** AmEx, DC, MC, V. **Map** p311 G7.
Designed by Ed Tuttle in a minimalist way to highlight artefacts, with floral designs by Sakul Intakul, this is arguably Bangkok's most beautiful hotel. Set in six acres of gardens modelled on Sukhothai with pools containing brick *chedi*, it's a real retreat. Most rooms look out on the gardens, and it will almost double in size when new villas and a spa are completed. The Thai-style service is unparalleled. Locals relish the food and design at Celadon (Thai; *see p122*), the infamously indulgent Champagne brunch at the Colonnade, and newcomer La Scala (Italian; *see p121*). The health club and pool are free; tennis, squash and massages cost extra. Good deals are offered, especially in the low season.
**Hotel services** *Air-conditioning. Babysitting. Bars. Beauty salon. Business services. Concierge. Disabled: adapted rooms. Garden. Gym. Internet access. Limousine service. No-smoking floors. Parking. Pool. Restaurants.* **Room services** *Dataport. Kitchenette. Minibar. Room service (24hr). Telephone. Turndown. TV: UBC.*

### Moderate

#### Pinnacle Hotel
*17 Soi Ngam Duphli, Thanon Rama IV (0 2287 0111-31/www.pinnaclehotels.com). Bus 14, 47, 74, 109, 507.* **Rooms** 154. **Rates** standard B1,600; junior suite B3,500; deluxe suite B6,000. **Credit** AmEx, DC, MC, V. **Map** p311 H7.
A small hotel that is part of a big chain, with well appointed, comfortable rooms at affordable prices, the Pinnacle has a certain charm but has seen better days. The fading lobby and rather musty corridors are a bit offputting, but the air-conditioned rooms are quite acceptable – particularly if you get the low season rate of B1,500.
**Hotel services** *Air-conditioning. Bars. Business services. Concierge. Disabled: adapted rooms. Gym. Internet access. Limousine service. No-smoking rooms. Parking. Pool. Restaurants.* **Room services** *Dataport. Minibar. Room service (24hr). Telephone. Turndown. TV: satellite/UBC.*

#### YWCA
*13 Thanon Sathorn Tai (0 2679 1280-4/2286 1936/ www.ehotelbooking.com/thailand/bangkok/ywca bangkok). Bus 17, 22, 35, 62, 67, 116, 149.* **Rooms** 40. **Rates** single B750-B1,250; double B1,000-B1,350. **Credit** AmEx, MC, V. **Map** p311 G7.
The YWCA occupies a small, 20-year-old building next to the towering Banyan Tree Bangkok (*see above*). Much of the decor is an institutional grey, and the rooms, though very clean, are uninspiring and not that cheap. Monthly rates are a much better deal: from B9,500 for double occupancy. All rooms have private bathrooms with tubs.

Hotel services *Air-conditioning. Beauty salon. Business service. Internet access. Parking. Restaurant. Travel agent.* Room services *Telephone. TV: satellite.*

## Budget

### Charlie House

*1034/36-37 Soi Saphan Khu, Thanon Rama IV (0 2679 8330/1). Bus 14, 47, 74, 109, 507.* Rooms 17. Rates *single B450-B650; double B540-B750.* No credit cards. Map *p311 H7.*

A budget guesthouse with hotel-level facilities, Charlie also has access to great neighbourhood street food, but you'll need to get a cab or motorcycle to any major tourist destinations or transport hub. Staff are very helpful and friendly; the walls are covered with testimonials from past guests. The great-value rooms, built on funny angles, are small, but clean and well equipped (private bathrooms, air-con, phone and TV). Ministers from Bhutan stay here.
Hotel services *Air-conditioning. Restaurant.* Room services *Room services (24hr). Telephone. TV: satellite.*

### The Malaysia Hotel

*54 Soi Ngam Duphli, Thanon Rama IV (0 2679 7127-36/http://ksc15.th.com/malaysia). Bus 14, 47, 74, 109, 507.* Rooms 120. Rates *single B588-B768; double B688-B868.* Credit *AmEx, DC, MC, V.* Map *p311 H7.*

An old R&R joint, the Malaysia became Bangkok's first real hotel for backpackers in the 1970s, when the neighbourhood became a pre-Khaosan scene – now it's more a hub of sleazy long-stayers. Though far from glamorous, the Malaysia also attracts an assortment of more cultured types who enjoy its frisson, particulary when its coffeeshop becomes a clearing house for people who've been working or partying all night in Patpong. And it offers a lot of services for a budget hotel: rooms have phones, air-con and private bathrooms with hot showers. Step up a notch to the superior room and you'll also get a small fridge, TV and video. Rates are subject to a 10% service charge.
Hotel services *Air-conditioning. Bar. Business service. Internet access. Left luggage. Parking. Pool. Restaurant.* Room services *Minibar. Room service (24hr). Telephone. TV: UBC.*

Step into the 21st century at **Siri Sathorn**. *See p50.*

## Cheap

### Sala Thai Daily Mansion

*15 Soi Sri Bamphen, Thanon Rama IV (0 2287 1436). Bus 17, 22, 35, 62, 67, 116, 149.* **Rooms** 16. **Rates** standard B200; deluxe B300. **No credit cards. Map** p311 H7.

Tucked into the quiet centre of a snail-shaped *soi* off Sri Bamphen, this small guesthouse is eternally popular, especially with journalists and English teachers. Rooms are clean, basic and small, with shared facilities. There is a pleasant communal TV/reading area and a nice rooftop garden, and staff are lovely. Owner Khun Anong may ask you to be a model; she finds *farang* to feature in catalogues and for ad agencies. The neighbourhood is favoured by long-stay visitors, and there are plenty of facilities for budget travellers along Soi Si Bamphen. If – as often happens – Sala Thai is full, other options are nearby, though some of them are sleazy.
**Hotel services** *Payphone. TV room.*

## Suburbs

### Moderate

#### The Thai House

*32/4 Moo 8, Bangmuang, Bangyai, Nonthaburi province (0 2903 9611/fax 0 2903 9354/www.thai house.co.th). Bus 33, 127, 516.* **Open** 9.30am-4.30pm Mon-Sat. Closed Sun. **Rates** single B1,200; double B1,400. **No credit cards.**

One of the few ways to stay in a traditional teak stilt house, this riverside compound is delightfully quiet and as easy on the palate as the eyes, since it also runs day and residential cooking classes (*see p115* **Learn to: Cook Thai**). The panelled rooms are dark, but atmospheric and pleasantly furnished. It's not that far from the centre by expressway.
**Hotel services** *Business services. Internet access. Payphone.*

### Budget

#### Prince

*1573/1 Thanon New Petchburi, North-east (0 2251 6171-6/princehl@asianet.co.th). Bus 11, 58, 60, 72, 93, 99, 113, 512.* **Rooms** 212. **Rates** single B660; double B770. **Credit** AmEx, DC, MC, V.

Quite close to Siam Square and the lower reaches of Sukhumvit but not within a short walk of anything in particular, the Prince is nonetheless a decent budget option. There's a lot of dark wood panelling, but the rooms are clean, pleasant and quite spacious, and the place certainly has character. Rooms all have large fridges, separate bathtubs and many have balconies – though the view isn't anything special.
**Hotel services** *Air-conditioning. Bar. Beauty salon. Business services. Internet access. Limousine service. Pool. Parking. Restaurant. Travel agent.* **Room services** *Refrigerator. Room service (24hr). Telephone. TV: UBC.*

## Serviced apartments

In a welcome expansion of accommodation options, many residential blocks let rooms short-term at very good rates. Hotels are certainly far from happy (in fact, fuming might be a more accurate description) at the competition, but it's not only about price – apartments offer features that hotels can't, while keeping such facilities as a pool, gym and security. In structure, neighbourhood and ambiance they tend to be suited to families, businessmen, self-caterers and the many return visitors wanting to feel at home. Website **www.sabaai.com** allows you to compare apartments and book online.

### Chateau de Bangkok

*29 Ruamrudee Soi 1, Thanon Ploenchit, Pathumwan (0 2651 4400). Ploenchit BTS.* **Rooms** 137. **Rates** (per month) studio junior B39,000; studio superior B50,000; studio deluxe B56,000; junior bedroom B64,000; superior bedroom B67,000; executive bedroom B75,000; deluxe bedroom B81,000. **Credit** AmEx, DC, MC, V. **Map** p311 H5.

On a pleasant residential *soi* close to Ploenchit BTS station, Chateau de Bangkok is a good alternative to the city's deluxe hotels for those who are planning on longer stays. Run by hotel chain Accor, the exterior exudes a slightly scuffed charm, but the interiors are luxurious. Fully furnished, cleaned and serviced daily (including linen and towel changes), all apartments have king-size beds and fully equipped kitchens. All but the smallest studios have jacuzzis. There is a good deli/café off the lobby and the rooftop pool offers good views.
**Apartment services** *Air-conditioning. Bar. Business service. Gym. Laundry. Limousine service. Parking. Pool. Restaurant.* **Room services** *Dataport. Kitchenette. Refrigerator. Telephone. TV: satellite/UBC.*

### Siri Sathorn

*27 Saladaeng Soi 1, Thanon Silom, Bangrak (0 2266 2363). Saladaeng BTS/Silom subway.* **Rooms** 107. **Rates** (per month) classic B68,000; modern B80,000. **Credit** AmEx, DC, MC, V. **Map** p310 E7.

The newly renovated Siri Sathorn is a temple to modern lines, glass art and minimalism. The large rooms are decked out with all the best mod cons (stereo, cable, DVD player), fully equipped kitchens and great designer furniture. Located close to Silom and Sathorn, a five-minute walk from Saladaeng SkyTrain station and Central Department Store, it's an ideal base for long-staying guests with discerning tastes and a high budget. Daily rates are a very reasonable B3,800 for a single.
**Hotel services** *Air-conditioning. Bar. Business services. Concierge. Gym. Internet access. Limousine service. Parking. Pool. Restaurant.* **Room services** *Dataport. Kitchenette. Refrigerator. Telephone. TV: UBC.*

# Sightseeing

## Features

# Introduction

Exploring Krung Thep's treasures is easier than ever – by rail, river or road.

Asked directions to the city centre, Bangkok residents could well reply: 'which centre?' As the capital has grown over two centuries, the centre of gravity has dissipated between districts with different attributes.

History is most palpable in **Phra Nakorn**, the old town of **Rattanakosin Island** and its backpacker enclave **Banglamphu**. The former capital, **Thonburi** (generally indicating the entire west bank of the Chao Phraya river), retains traces of the earlier canal-borne 'Venice of the East' lifestyle. Grandly planned **Dusit** houses the institutions of royalty, government and the military, while chaotic **Chinatown** retains its business might.

West of the railway, the modern Downtown comprises **Bangrak**, the core of finance and nightlife; **Pathumwan**, the shopping nexus; and **Sukhumvit**, an avenue of drinking, dining and entertainment. Speedily linking these parts of Downtown (and most of the hotels), the BTS SkyTrain has also brought distant Chatuchak

Weekend Market into **North Downtown**, and skirts **South Downtown**, a developing area ringed by river commerce.

The suburbs are now quickly reached by expressways, but the SkyTrain is being extended **East** into Samut Prakarn province. The new subway system will imminently open up the **North-east**, a major nightlife zone, and the **Outer North**, encompassing Bangkok Airport and metropolitan parts of Nonthaburi province.

## UPWARDLY MOBILE

Residents used to smile wryly at visitors who attempted to fill their day with sights, shows and supper. Come bedraggled evening, their day had been filled (yet somehow drained), by barely two appointments and horror stories about *rot tit* ('stuck cars'). While traffic still frustrates exploration, the opening of the BTS SkyTrain on 5 December 1999 felt like the end of a war. Excited locals went sightseeing in their own city, because the elevated rails revealed a hidden garden city and lost mansions

---

## The best Places

### For cooling down
Ride a riverboat. *See p53*.

### For 'Venice of the East' remnants
Khlong Om (*see p74*) and the floating markets outside Bangkok (*see p224*).

### For shopping ancient and modern
Chatuchak Weekend Market has everything. See p134 **A day in JJ**.

### For fascinating mayhem
Chinatown (*see p83*) or **Pratunam Market** (*see p134*).

### For quiet, shady relief
Lumphini Park (*see p95*), Dusit Zoo (*see p79*), **Chulalongkorn University** grounds (*see p93*), **Dusit** boulevards (*see p77*) and any *wat* (temple).

### For youth culture
Siam Square and MBK mall (*see p150*) are teen temples. Indie kids hang out at the art bars on **Thanon Phra Arthit** (*see p69*).

### For collecting Thai clichés
Riding a *tuk-tuk* (*see p283*) to **Sampeng Market** for silk (*see p132*), **Silom Village** for dinner dancers (*see p203*), **Lumphini Stadium** for *Muay Thai* boxing (*see p209*), and **Patpong** for anthropology a-go-go (*see p92*).

### For sumptuous former homes
Jim Thompson's House (*see p94*), MR Kukrit's **Heritage House** (*see p98*) or **Suan Pakkard Palace** (*see p97*).

### For daily devotion
Dawn alms-giving to monks (*see p70*), **Erawan Shrine** (*see p93*), spirit houses or amulets (for both, *see p20* **Spirit worship**).

### For the Thai Moulin Rouge
Fong Nam at Tawandaeng. *See p192*.

### For weary or hungover sightseers
Have a herbal sauna followed by a Thai massage. *See chapter* **Mind & Body**.

All aboard the **BTS SkyTrain**, Bangkok's super new elevated railway. *See p52.*

behind the forbidding walls and shophouses. This rollercoaster ride is a tour in itself. The same can be said of the **Expressboats**, which link the BTS to the old town along Bangkok's original highway, the river. The many recently built skyscrapers mean that Bangkok's sprawl over a flat floodplain now bristles with reference points, though zigzagging *soi* and one-way systems can make journeys circuitous. Fortunately, many signs are in English. For information on travel options, *see p282.*

### TIPS FOR TOURISTS

● Treat etiquette and dress codes seriously (*see p286* **Attitude & etiquette**).
● Non-Thais are often charged much more than locals. Argument is futile.
● Many establishments close over Thai and Chinese New Years.
● State museums open early, shut around 4pm and close on Mondays, Tuesdays and holidays. Private museums usually keep office hours daily (including holidays), but may close on Sundays. Many have compulsory tours. Guides without a TAT (Tourist Authority of Thailand) badge may get ejected.
● Temples are usually free, but few *bot* (ordination halls) are viewable. Staff or monks may be willing to open locked attractions.
● English is spoken widely in tourist centres, but given Thai and foreign accents, writing can clarify confusions. Transliterations into English often vary between guides, maps and signs.
● The most photogenic activity (and the best light) is before 10am and after 4pm. Cameras are banned from inside museums, malls and official places, but not most temples. Some places charge a camera fee. Thais (but not Muslims and hill tribes) generally like being snapped, but prefer to be composed, thus spoiling spontaneity. So be sensitive and smile through any awkwardness. Showing people their digital image is an ice-breaker, though you may end up having to send it to them.

'No photo' means just that, though hill tribes may pose for a fee.
● As most shops close late, souvenir hunting can be saved for the evenings (or afternoons in the rainy season).

### TOUTS AND SCAMS

Aside from the pushers of porn, sex shows and massage in Patpong, touts plague major sights and piers. If touts or *tuk-tuk* drivers approach saying 'it's closed today', 'festival across town', 'craft demonstration' or 'one-day tax break', just head straight to the entry desk and prevent them 'guiding' you there.

Touts are paid out of what you are overcharged at the bar or shop they choose (even tour companies get shop commissions). Though touts aren't usually dangerous, food and drink that's offered might be doped. Their patter seems convincing to bargain hunters, particularly when selling genuine but flawed gems without resale value. Ask TAT for reputable gem dealers (*see also p98* **Learn to: Gemology**). It's best to deter touts with a polite *mai ow khrub/kha* (male/female) ('don't want') or *mee laew khrub/kha* (male/female) ('have already'), since they're not evil but opportunists making a living.

## River & canal tours

It is possible to hire a longtail boat, but be sure to go for at least two hours – short tours barely explore canal life and forfeit time at sights better (and more cheaply) seen separately, such as Wat Arun. The principal piers, such as Oriental, Chang and Nonthaburi, are chaotically signed and boat companies' routes vary, priced from B300-B500 for an hour, B700-B750 for 90mins or B900 for two hours. Longer tours may include **Wat Pailom** stork sanctuary, **Ko Kred** and **Wat Chaloem Prakiat; Bang Sai Crafts Centre** and **Bang Pa-in** or **Ayutthaya** (for all, *see p218*).

# Museum island

Instigated in back 1997, the **Krung Rattanakosin Plan** involves 20 projects over two decades that seek to transform Rattanakosin Island into a historical park. This mostly means glorifying old official landmarks by replacing anything around them built later than Rama V's reign with formal gardens – in the name of tourism. While this could open up exciting vistas, particularly along the riverside promenade, Phra Nakorn would be forced to sacrifice much of its own living history and neighbourhood activity.

The herbal apothecaries of the Pra Chan, the wonderfully atmospheric Tha Tien market and various ancient trades that happen to be in more recent buildings would be wiped out. Their communities, intact for generations, would be evicted to faceless suburbs – all so that some older roof peaks would be visible over the treetops. Ironically, one convenience store in an old building will be able to stay, because the committee, in its wisdom, deemed its global chain goods 'serve visitors', reported the *Nation* newspaper.

Most astonishing of all, the National Theatre would be demolished, just to allow views from one side of Wat Bovornsathan Suttavat, which is noted more for its murals than its profile. The adjacent dance school and Thammasat undergraduates have already moved out, though there's no new site for the theatre. Ironically, putting that money into staging Thai dance there every day would fill a definite tourist need, while managing to boost Thai heritage at the same time.

The communities are outraged and academics have hurled accusations that the city's soul is being turned into a theme park. But plans in Bangkok have a habit of not coming to fruition, and the long timescale of the project increases the chances of it being revised or simply forgotten about. What's more, it jars with competing plans, such as turning Thanon Ratchadamnoen into a shopping showcase. Ultimately, though, Thai urban life favours bustling activity at close quarters. Just as in malls and the SkyTrain, these bland expanses, if enacted, would be encroached upon in no time, making the intervening loss all the more tragic.

## Grand Palace & Wat Phra Kaew

*Thanon Na Phra Lan (0 2222 8181). Bus 1, 35, 39, 44, 47, 59, 82, 91, 123, 201.* **Open** 8.30am-3.30pm daily. **Admission** (incl access to Vimanmek Mansion) B200. **No credit cards. Map** p308 B4.

There's no option: you must see this exquisite architectural and spiritual treasure (preferably early on a sunny morning, when it's at its most dazzling). Ignore the gem touts claiming 'it's shut today', and immerse yourself in the palpable dignity of the place (while taking care to observe the stringent dress code: sandals, shorts and bare shoulders are all banned). Nearly 2km (1.5 miles) of pointily crenellated walls enclose what was once a 65-acre (160.5-hectare) self-contained city, comprising ceremonial buildings, royal chambers, servants' quarters, ministerial offices and a small prison. Work began in 1782, and the project was modified by each Chakri king. Designed along the same lines as Chinese imperial structures, Thai palaces have a reception zone, followed by a royal audience zone (the interiors of which are open on National Children's Day; *see p159*). But the general public aren't even permitted to view the exteriors of the inner chambers that lie beyond, where the king's wives used to live. Disused after Rama VI had only one wife, those quarters now house a finishing school for upper-class girls. Since the royals moved to Dusit, the Grand Palace has been used only for certain ceremonies and state visits, but it remains Thailand's proudest and holiest landmark.

Visitors entering Wat Phra Sri Ratttana Sasadaram – better known as Wat Phra Kaew, the temple of the Emerald Buddha (Thailand's most sacred image) – are greeted by a statue of the originator of the ancient art of yoga, Shivaka Kumar Baccha, before being swamped by a kaleidoscope of forms and colours. Modelled on royal chapels in Sukhothai and Ayutthaya, and embellished to an astonishing degree, the temple contains typical monastic structures (minus the traditional living quarters, since there are no resident monks).

The first thing you'll notice is the circular, Lankan-style Phra Si Rattana Chedi, tiled in gold mosaic, which enshrines a piece of the Buddha's breastbone. Adjacent to it on the upper terrace are the Phra Mondop (library of palm-leaf scriptures), a columned cube of green and blue glass mosaic under a tiered spire; and the cruciform, *prang*-roofed Royal Pantheon, where on Chakri Day (*see p159*) the king honours statues of his dynasty. This terrace also features gilded statues of delicate *aponsi* (half-woman, half-lion), with multicoloured guardians supporting a pair of small gold *chedi* to the east. Parallel to the north, Ho Phra Nak (the royal mausoleum) and Hor Phra Monthien Tham (a library) flank porcelain-clad Vihaan Yod and a sandstone model of Angkor Wat in Cambodia (a vassal state when this was carved during the reign of Rama IV).

Along the eastern edge is a collection of eight porcelain-covered pastel *prang* (representing Buddhism's eightfold path). Two stand within a

Serenity is all: **Wat Phra Kaew**.

notch in the cloister, which stretches 2km (1.5 miles), its walls adorned with 178 restored murals lavishly unravelling the entire *Ramakien* (the Thai version of India's *Ramanyana* epic). In the south-east corner is the shrine of the Gandharara Buddha in rain-summoning posture, used in the Royal Ploughing Ceremony (*see p160*). Six pairs of towering stone *yaksha* (demons), also *Ramakien* characters, guard the central *bot*, which is mosaiced in gold and glass and ringed by 112 *garuda* holding naga snakes. From a public altar you enter the muralled interior on your knees, facing a lofty gilded altar topped by the Emerald Buddha. Carved from solid jade, this statue is 66cm (26in) tall and dressed by the king in one of three seasonal robes: cool, hot or rainy. Of mysterious origin, but in late Lanna style, it was discovered in Chiang Rai in 1434 and moved first to Lampang, then Chiang Mai, then Vientiane in Laos, before coming here via Wat Arun in Thonburi.

Visitors can also take advantage of the 12 contemplation *salas*, before entering the palace audience precinct. The halls make for a curious design medley of each Thai period, alongside European classicism, Chinese sculpture and topiary. Visible through railings on the left is the belle époque Borom Phiman Mansion; built in 1903 for the future King Rama VI, it is now a state guest house where Queen Elizabeth II and Bill Clinton have both stayed. Its Sivalai Gardens contain the Phra Buddha Ratana Sathan (Rama IV Chapel).

Next, the Phra Maha Montien Buildings include the Amarin Winitchai Hall, where such esteemed guests as the famous 19th-century ambassador Sir John Bowring were received by the king upon the boat-like Busok Mala throne. The main focus, however, is undoubtedly Chakri Maha Prasat Hall, a celebrated architectural fusion (*see p27* **Farang in a Thai hat**). Beneath its chamber for banquets and state visits is a public Weapons Museum; the top floor houses the ashes of Chakri kings. To its west stand two of the best-proportioned structures in Thailand: the Aphonphimok Pavilion and the cruciform Dusit Throne Hall. The Pavilion was built by Rama IV for changing gowns en route via palanquin

# **Walk 1** Community values

Exploring the fringes of Rattanakosin is like thumbing through a history book. While only a stone's throw from heavily touristed sights, this walk leads through pockets of traditional craft workshops, canal life, intact communities, a Chinese shrine and magnificent royal temples. The best part of a day is needed to do it justice, with refresher stops en route

The best way to get your bearings is to begin at the **Golden Mount** (*see p67*). To avoid a tiring climb, start to the north-west of the mount at Maha Uthit Bridge, famous for its bas reliefs, and head south down **Thanon Boriphat**, a street lined by timber merchants. The first left beyond Thanon Bumrung Muang is **Soi Ban Baat** – known as the **Monk's Bowl Village** – where descendents of Ayutthayan refugees keep alive a Khmer method of beating out alms bowls from eight strips of metal, representing the eight spokes of the Dharma wheel. The community leader's workshop is at 71 Soi Ban Baat (0 2221 4466; open 10am-8pm daily, admission free). When decorated and lacquered the bowls are prized by collectors – despite their function as utensils symbolising non-attachment.

Backtrack a bit and head west along **Thanon Bamrung Muang**, an old elephant trail that was one of the city's first paved streets. Though architecturally unassuming, its shopfronts glow with Buddhist images, regalia and ritual accoutrements. Passing the

**Giant Swing** and **Wat Suthat** (*see p67*), head right along **Thanon Dinso**, past the imposing **City Hall** of the Bangkok Metropolitan Authority. Facing the **Democracy Monument** (pictured), turn left past the Muang Boran bookshop and left again at the **14 October Monument** (*see p65*) into **Thanon Tanao**.

Residents of this street objected to its attractive shophouses being painted for a bar strip that has since disappeared – though there are still some art bars and gay nightclubs one block west via Trok Sake, which runs beside Khlong Theptida. South along Tanao, **Wat Mahanopharam** (0 2224 4675, open temple 8am-5pm daily, *bot* 7am-5pm daily) is a tranquil Rama III-era retreat, where merit-making offerings include *takraw* balls, their tightly woven rattan representing group unity and strength. Further down, and across Tanao is the **Chao Poh Seua Shrine** (0 2224 2110, open 6am-6pm daily), dedicated to the Chinese tiger (*seua*) god. Relocated from Thanon Bamrung Muang, it's guarded by two golden tigers, with vendors selling feline-appeasing offerings like pork, rice and eggs – and the inevitable lottery tickets. Barren couples place sugar tigers here in the hope of pregnancy. Looming ahead on the right is the **Phraeng Sanphasat Palace Gate**, a neo-classical remnant of Prince Sanphasart Supakit's 1901 residence, which was (like many old landmarks) lost in a

to the Throne Hall, which contains the throne of Rama I and is still used for coronation ceremonies and the lying-in-state of royalty. Finally, you come to a cafeteria before reaching the exit, set between neo-classical office buildings.

Allocate at least two hours for a visit, which is made all the more rewarding with a user-friendly audio guide (available in eight languages, for B100 with a passport/credit card deposit) or, better still, a personal guide (B300).

## Sanam Luang & around

A broad field used for anything from royal ceremonies to public recreation, Sanam Luang is ringed by many important institutions. Clockwise up its west side are **Silpakorn University** (*see p61*); the Royal Institute; a Buddhist University at sacred **Wat Mahathat**; **Thammasat University** (for both, *see p62*); the **National Museum** (*see p61*); and the **National Theatre** (*see p202*). To the north

lies the **National Gallery** (in the former Royal Mint; *see p170*), then east are the Royal Hotel; the Mae Toranee Fountain; the City Pillar; **Lak Muang**; and the imposingly classical **Ministry of Defence** (for both, *see p61*).

The Rattanakosin waterfront was once reserved for minor palaces, but these days it's characterised by the charming Phra Chan community between Tha Phra Chan and Tha Chang piers. The shophouses here are bursting with cultural regalia, traditional massage and herbal preparations, alongside outlets catering for the student population, with indie music, concert tickets, obscure videos and artists' materials. **Amulet Alley Market** (*see p132*) spills out of Trok Silpakorn, while fortune-tellers periodically gather on the pedestrianised forecourt of Tha Phra Chan.

Flanked by 33 classically stuccoed shophouses (dating from the fifth reign) on land that once belonged to the poet Sunthorn Phu, Tha Chang's forecourt has also been paved,

fire. A few steps further to the east is narrow **Trok Chang Thong**, a goldsmiths' quarter destroyed by fire (prompting gold diggers to scavenge for treasure) and the former home of wartime dictator Marshal Pibun.

For a fascinating peek into authentic Thai life, nip westwards into **Thanon Phraeng Nara**, the middle lane of **Samphraeng** (three Phraeng streets), where you'll find a (somewhat self-consciously) characterful community. The last remnant of the palace

of Prince Narathip (Rama IV's son) is now a lawyer's office, but the quaintly shuttered shophouses and cottage industries here and around the square on **Thanon Phraeng Poothon**, parallel to the south, offer authentic produce and unadulterated local cuisine for your lunch break. Government workers from nearby offices relish the home-made ice-cream (topped with corn, nuts and red beans) and potions like pig's brain noodles (to improve the intellect).

and vendors of unusual foods shelter under its frangipani trees and in the grim warren of shacks behind the pier where touts flog canal tours. It's named 'Elephant Pier' because the palace pachyderms once bathed here. The landscaped embankment beside the Grand Palace, and its Ratchaworadit Royal Pier and Ratchakitwinitchai Throne Pavilion, are reserved for royal occasions.

## Lak Muang

*Thanon Sanam Chai (0 2222 9876). Bus 1, 2, 3, 6, 9, 25, 32, 33, 39, 43, 44, 60, 91, 506, 507.* **Open** 5.30am-7.30pm daily. **Map** p308 B3/4.

The guardian spirits of a Thai city are said to reside at its foundation pillar and in 1782 Rama I installed this bud-tipped wooden pillar to mark the birth of Bangkok. Essentially, it's a Shiva lingam – the phallic form of the Indian god housed, Khmer-style, in an ornate cruciform tower. It also derives from the Tai tribal adoption of an animistic southern Chinese tradition of placing a phallus in a town crossroads. And Bangkok's laburnum-wood Lak Muang – 274cm/108in above ground, 201cm/79in below – is an infinite crossroads since all metropolitan distances are measured from it. Shellacked and gilded, it's accompanied by the taller Lak Muang of Thonburi, moved here when the former capital joined greater Krung Thep. Spirits of the city and country are embodied in statues housed in a pavilion to the east of this landscaped compound. Those whose wishes have been granted by these spirits pay *likay* performers to perform at a *sala*, as at the Erawan Shrine.

## Ministry of Defence

*Thanon Sanam Chai (0 2226 3814). Bus 1, 3, 6, 9, 15, 19, 25, 30, 32, 33, 39, 43, 44, 47, 53, 59, 201, 203, 507.* **Open** 24hrs daily. **Map** p308 B4.

Splayed before the portico of this elongated 19th-century classical edifice is an open-air Museum of Old Cannons housing 40 guns (all named) dating as far back as Ayutthayan times.

## National Museum

*4 Thanon Na Phra That (0 2224 1333/ www.thailandmuseum.com). Bus 1, 3, 6, 9, 15, 19, 25, 30, 32, 33, 39, 43, 44.* **Open** 9am-4pm Wed-Sun (last entry 3.30pm). **Admission** B20 Thais; B40 foreigners; free 9.30am-noon Wed, Thur. **No credit cards**. **Map** p308 B3.

Boasting the largest museum collection in South-east Asia, the capital's first public museum dates from 1874 and originated as King Rama IV's collection of regalia within the Grand Palace. With branches in various historic sites around the country, it is currently housed in part of the former Wang Na ('front palace') of the 'deputy king', a shortlived office held by Rama IV's brother Phra Pinklao. Most unmissable is the Buddhaisawan Chapel, whose Rattanakosin murals are individually exquisite, while focusing attention on the revered Phra Buddha Sihing (an image thought to date from the 13th century).

Front, left and right are small royal pavilions, including Baan Daeng, an Ayutthayan house with Rattanakosin furnishings and a rare indoor loo. It's behind the Gallery of Thai History, which contains the Ramkhamhaeng Stone, the earliest inscription of tonal Thai lettering. The central audience hall contains rooms of eclectic treasures: old weapons surrounding a life-size model elephant in battle armour in Room 10; intricate wood carvings in Room 13; shadow puppets and *khon* masks in Room 7. Temporary shows occupy the front Throne Hall. Although labelling of the various artefacts lacks context, the museum still provides a good grounding in Thai artistic and cultural history (and its guidebook helps fill in many of the blanks). Contributing to its charm, shaded courtyards enable you to recharge before visiting the modern, two-storey north and south wings.

Beyond the courtyards, a badly lit, ineptly displayed bombardment of religious iconography runs chronologically from Rooms S1-9, spanning Dvaravati and Lopburi periods, continuing (Rooms N1-10) with Sukhothai, Ayutthaya, Lanna and Bangkok styles. But persevere; masterpieces await. Facing the famous Sukhothai-style walking Buddha are arrestingly stylised Hindu bronzes, with a Dvaravati figure and an Ayutthayan Buddha head in the stairwell. Most eye-catching are the gilded funerary chariots from the first Chakri reign. Their sheer teetering scale and glass-inlaid wood carving leaves you speechless. Moving these teak structures is a task that requires 300 men; amazingly, the Pra Maha Pichai Ratcharot chariot was deployed (for King Bhumibol's mother) as recently as 1996.

## Sanam Luang

*Bus 1, 3, 6, 9, 15, 19, 25, 30, 32, 33, 39, 43, 44, 47, 53, 59, 60, 64, 70, 80, 82, 91, 201, 203.* **Map** p308 B3.

Fringed by tamarind trees, this large oval lawn (one of the city's few truly open spaces) is the formal location for constructing pyres for royal cremations. Among the annual ceremonies held here are the bathing of the Phra Buddha Sihing statue at Songkran, the Royal Ploughing Ceremony and the King and Queen's Birthday celebrations (for all, *see chapter* **Festivals & Events**). In decades past, Bangkok's elite came here to partake in horse racing, bird hunting and golf. Until 1982, it hosted the city's famous Weekend Market (now at Chatuchak; *see p134* **A day in JJ**), with produce arriving via Khlong Lord. Current diverse uses include folk entertainments, festivals, concerts and informal recreation, notably kite flying (Feb-April). Plans by the Bangkok governor to dig an underground car park and shopping arcade here have thus far been thwarted by heritage authorities.

## Silpakorn University

*31 Thanon Na Phra Lan (0 2623 6115-21/ www.su.ac.th). Bus 15, 19, 25, 39, 43, 44, 47, 53, 59, 82, 91, 123, 203.* **Open** 8.30am-4.30pm Mon-Fri. **Map** p308 B3/4.

Thailand's oldest and most venerable fine arts educational institution, Silpakorn contains a small museum and a courtyard sculpture dedicated to its founder (Silpa Bhirasri, an Italian commissioned in the 1920s to sculpt landmarks such as the Rama I statue and Democracy Monument). Hosting regular exhibitions, its serene and elegant art gallery was once part of Tha Phra Palace.

### Thammasat University

*2 Thanon Phra Chan (0 2221 6111/www.tu.ac.th). Bus 15, 30, 32, 33, 39, 47, 53, 59, 64, 65, 70, 80, 82, 91, 203, 506.* **Open** *8.30am-4.30pm Mon-Fri.* **Map** *p308 B3.*
The country's second most prestigious university after Chulalongkorn, Thailand's 'knowledge market' was founded in 1932. A statue of its founder, statesman Pridi Bhanomyong, sits in front of its drill bit-shaped tower, near a Chinese stone lion bedecked with animalian offerings. Thammasat students are known for voicing dissent and were the leading demonstrators (and victims) of the democracy protest massacres on 14 October 1973 and 6 October 1976 (*see p16* **The October generation**). Inside the gate on Thanon Deuan Tula are two small memorials, predating Thanon Tanao's 14 October Monument. More recently, protests in 2002 opposed

undergraduates being moved to distant Rangsit campus, leaving a diminished population of post-graduates at this political crucible.

### Wat Mahathat

*3/5 Thanon Maharat (0 2222 6011). Bus 1, 3, 7, 9, 15, 25, 30, 32, 33, 39, 44, 47, 59, 80, 82, 203.* **Open** *7am-8pm daily.* **Map** *p308 B3.*
Less handsome than its neighbours, this large monastic temple is nonetheless important for two reasons. All Thai capitals have ritually required a royal temple of a holy relic (*maha that*), and this is just such a temple (although its interior is off-limits to the public). It is also the first of Thailand's two Buddhist universities. Founded in the 18th century, this is where King Rama IV spent 24 years as a monk before assuming the throne in 1851 (later, Rama V donated a library for the monks here).

This place feels more like a working temple than many Rattanakosin *wats* and runs English-language classes in daily meditation, as well as Dhamma talks and upcountry retreats at the International Buddhist Meditation Centre (*see p181*). From Sanam Luang, you enter through the gates of the imposing, rust-coloured Thawornwatthu Building. Designed by Prince Naris as a royal funerary hall, it's a classic example of East-meets-West architectural fusion.

# **Walk 2** Khlong Lord

Built as a defence for Rattankosin Island, this tree-shaded canal brought produce from the river and Pak Khlong Talad to the Weekend Market when it was at Sanam Luang, and now offers a tranquil setting for a stroll.

Its western side, **Thanon Ratchinee**, starts at Thailand's fanciest drinking fountain. Erected in 1872, it encloses a beautiful sculpture of Mae Phra Thorani, the Earth Goddess, who wrung water from her hair to wash away the demons trying to corrupt the Buddha. Heading south, you pass the Civil Court, the Department of Public Prosecutions and the **Ministry of Defence** (*see p61*). These look across the canal to Thanon Atsadang, where fifth-reign shophouses with crumbling European detailing peddle items like musical instruments, clocks and military uniforms. One of the canal's many interesting bridges is **Charoensri 34 Bridge**, which was named in honour of Rama VI's 34th birthday. Decorated with Thai number fours indicating the year of his reign, the structure was built to withstand an elephant's bulk.

Lining the canal route are timber lamp posts shaped like the original wooden Thonburi city wall pillars. Just beyond, floral

garlands hang from the snout of a gilded **Pig Memorial**, erected in 1913 to honour Rama VI's mother, who was born in the year of the pig. Donations for this monument also paid for **Saphan Pee Goon** ('pig year bridge'), which you can cross to reach the grey, Euro-classical Ministry of Interior on Atsadang and, further south, **Wat Ratchabophit**. On the opposite bank is **Wat Ratchapradit** (for both, *see p64*), which you can dart back over to on **Saphan Hok**, an amalgam of four similar footbridges that used to traverse the canal (it was reconstructed in 1982).

Also on the Ratchanee bank is the gate to **Saranrom Park** (*see p63* – a gay cruising area by night), offering walkers a verdant breather and fruit juice vendors the chance to hawk their wares. A few metres south from here, you can cross back again to Atsadang for some even finer, even more crumbling shophouses, and **Baan Mor Market** (*see p132*), named for its hidden, still used private palace. Finally, grab dinner and a drink at **Café Today** (*see p124*), which faces Saranrom Park – by which time, Thanon Chakphet (running east from the end of Khlong Lord) will be knee-deep in **Pak Khlong Talad Flower Market** (*see p133*).

Home to the Reclining Buddha, **Wat Pho** is the city's oldest temple.

## Wat Pho & around

**Wat Pho**, temple of the Reclining Buddha, is flanked by government ministries and **Saranrom Park** to the east along Thanon Sanam Chai. Near the park is the small 19th-century temple of **Wat Ratchapradit** and, on the other side of Khlong Lord, is the marvellous **Wat Ratchabophit** (for both *see p64*).

Meanwhile, the area around Tha Tien (the pier for ferries to Wat Arun) offers a rare glimpse of how early Bangkok markets were surrounded by shophouses. Dandied up with pillasters, pediments and stucco akin to Tha Chang's, these shophouses still house a working community and are filled with aromas, from herbal apothecaries, dried fish stalls, coffee houses and more. Shockingly, though, these atmospheric retail outlets are under threat – by conservationists (*see p56* **Museum island**).

Thanons Mahathat, Sanam Chai and Ratchinee all converge at the 1914 Phra Ratchawang police station to cross Khlong Lord over the balustraded Charoenrat 31 Bridge. To the east is the gloriously scented flower market **Pak Khlong Talad** (*see p133*).

### Saranrom Park

*Thanon Charoen Krung, at Thanon Rachini (0 2221 0195). Bus 1, 3, 6, 9, 12, 25, 32, 43, 44, 47, 48, 53, 60, 82, 91, 123, 506, 507.* **Open** 5am-9pm daily. **Map** p308 B4.

This picturesque, verdant former garden of Saranrom Palace has been a public domain since the 1960s and, like all Thai parks, is liveliest in early morning or before sunset. Expect loud music as mass aerobics classes step to the beat and joggers thud by the ponds, cherub fountain, Chinese pagoda (at the rear) and central memorial from King Rama V to his wife Queen Sunanda (who drowned in a boating accident in 1880).

### Wat Pho

*2 Thanon Sanam Chai (0 2222 5910). Bus 9, 25, 44, 48, 53, 60, 82, 91, 123, 506, 507, 508, 512.* **Open** 8am-5pm daily. **Admission** B20. **No credit cards. Map** p308 B4.

Spread out behind the Grand Palace, this is Bangkok's oldest and largest temple, formally called Wat Phra Chetuphon. Despite being very touristy, it's mellower than most and rewards casual wandering. Its popular name derives from the 16th-century Wat Photharam, which was rebuilt as part of Rama I's grand Rattanakosin scheme. In one of several restorations, Rama III added its monumental Reclining Buddha in 1832. Rama III also turned Wat Pho into what was dubbed 'Thailand's first university' when he ordered the walls to be inscribed with lessons in astrology, history and literature. It remains to this day a core repository of knowledge on traditional medicine, including meditation and traditional massage (*see p69* **Learn to: Massage**) – perfect for weary sightseers.

Made from brick and gilded plaster, the Reclining Buddha is an awesome 46m (151ft) long and 15m (49ft) high. With pillars of the temple's *vihaan* built around it obscuring a full view, the head and feet capture the photographer's focus. A picture of serenity, this recumbent position illustrates the enlightened Buddha passing into Nirvana. Visitors linger over its large, flat-footed soles, where mother-of-pearl inlay (an early Rattanakosin speciality) depicts 108 auspicious signs. The number 108 recurs in the number of bowls spanning the chapel wall, with a coin dropped in each bringing luck and longevity.

Wat Pho is also a refuge for antique Buddha images rescued by Rama I's brother from Ayutthaya and Sukhothai, with a particularly significant Ayutthayan image residing in the beautiful main *bot*. (The ashes of Rama I were respectfully interred in its pedestal base by Rama IV.) Protecting the inner sanctuary are large pairs of stone guards with Western features. It houses a staggering 99 *chedi* (the number nine is lucky to Thais), the main four being the individually coloured Phra Maha Chedi, signifying the first four reigns. In Rattanakosin style, they resemble a square bell in shape, with indented corners, and are clad in floral ceramics. Two hold the remains of Kings Rama II and III, while another offers the chance for slimmer sightseers to climb inside and enjoy a unique viewpoint. The *kuti* (monks' quarters) are south of Thanon Chetuphon, where the main entrance is less tout-ridden than the gate by the Reclining Buddha.

## Wat Ratchabophit

*2 Thanon Fuang Nakhon (0 2222 3930). Bus 1, 2, 12, 60, 64.* **Open** *Temple* 5am-8pm daily. *Bot* 9-9.30am, 5.30-6pm daily; 8.45am-3.30pm religious holidays. **Map** p308 B4.

With a fruit market to the side and schoolchildren playing in its grounds, this seldom visited but fabulously ornate temple is most lively in late afternoon. Begun in 1869, its structure uniquely encloses the main *chedi* with a circular cloister encased in pastel Chinese porcelain, from which other buildings protrude. The small inner chapel is European in feel thanks to its gothic columns, with intricate mother-of-pearl doors. Outer doors have toy-like soldiers carved into them. The *wat* also has a cemetery for Rama V's family.

## Wat Ratchapradit

*2 Thanon Saran Rom (0 2223 8215). Bus 1, 2, 12, 60, 64.* **Open** *Temple* 9am-5pm daily. *Bot* 9-9.30am, noon-5pm daily; 8am-5pm religious holidays. **Map** p308 B4.

Less grandiose than its neighbours, this pretty little grey marble temple is well preserved, with an inviting, even contemplative atmosphere. Another amalgam of Eastern and Western styles, it was begun in 1864 on what was then a coffee plantation bought for the Thammayut Nikai sect by Rama IV (who is depicted observing a lunar eclipse in the murals focusing on Thai festivals). His ashes are contained under a replica of the Phra Buddha Sihing in a *vihaan* flanked by two *prang*. From behind the temple you can see the elegant Chinese pagoda in adjacent Saranrom Park.

Once the outskirts of the city, this fascinating area was formally planned around the grand boulevard of **Thanon Ratchadamnoen Klang** (meaning 'royal passage'), the eminent

# Tusk force

Nobody ever forgets the sight of an elephant plodding along a busy street at night, flashing its red rear light. Plying downtown Bangkok, the mahouts tout banana and sugar cane to tourists, while superstitious Thais pay to swoop under the elephant's belly for luck.

No such luck for the poor pachyderm. That cute baby Dumbo, away from the protection of its mother, may die. Since the asphalt is only cool enough at night for the elephants' feet, the lights are to stop them being hit by cars, for which drivers are fined a mere B500. Since a tusker's bones won't heal, some have to be put down. In 2000 a cow elephant ate 50 kilos of uncooked rice while being trucked to Bangkok and died after drinking 200 litres of water. Dusit Zoo vet Alongkorn Mahannop, who invariably treats injuries free of charge, estimated in 2000 that 30 elephants roam the inner city, with 20 or so more in the suburbs. At least once a year they're banned from Bangkok, but with aid promises being hollow they return in ever more squalid conditions.

So how could the venerated *chang* – which graced the flag of Siam, carried kings into battle and was in 2002 declared the national animal – be reduced to begging? Two reasons. The 1988 logging ban left most domesticated elephants jobless, particularly in the north.

thoroughfare linking the regal residencies of the Grand Palace and the once rustic Dusit Park. Built around the time of the first cars, this broad, tree-lined mid section (*klang*) is currently a traffic artery flanked by identical rows of sleek 1950s buildings. In 2003 the boulevard will at last come to resemble its model (Paris' Champs-Elysées) when it will be converted into a parade of sophisticated fashion houses, with the existing heavy traffic tidily diverted through an underpass. The handsome avenue is decorated and illuminated with great panache to celebrate royal birthdays.

The avenue contains two constitutional landmarks: the **Democracy Monument**, at the intersection with Thanon Dinso, and the stern, sad **14 October Monument** (*see p65*). The former totem, designed by Italian sculptor Corrado Feroci and dedicated to Thailand's 1932 transition to constitutional monarchy, has a gilded sculpture of the constitution upon

Elephants' ironic involvement in the deforestation of their wooded lowland habitat is especially acute in southern Isaan, where those that visit Bangkok hail from the Kui tribe of Surin, the province that hosts November's **Elephant Round-up Festival**. Each elephant's 125-kilo daily diet costs a fortune to buy, and there's more natural foraging around Rama IX, Ramkhamhaeng and Srinakarin roads than in their village of Baan Ta Klang.

There, the **Jumbo Homecoming Project** (www.taklang.com) aims to bring in tourist income and to help preserve their lore. That

expertise is dying out with the last *mor chang* (elephant shamen) – and the last wild elephants, of which there are 1-1,500 out of a 4-5,000 total. That's down from around 20,000 in the mid 1980s. Organiser Pittiya Homkrailas has also set up a refuge on Ko Chang. Pachyderms are also now on Ko Phuket offering rides to tourists, as they've done for years in northern forest camps. That's not always an answer: those photogenically parading around Ayutthaya in costume are being evicted on spurious charges of damaging ruins and aren't allowed to relocate to the **Elephant Kraal**. So where can the elephants go?

The admirable and innovative, yet cash-strapped **Elephant Conservation Centre** in Lampang (*see p275*), offers refuge to orphans and hospital treatment. It boasts the world's first elephantine sperm bank and mahout school. It's not only wild elephants being threatened by encroachment from loggers and pineapple farmers; their survival in domestication depends on control through quality mahoutship as their wild instincts haven't been bred out. Being a mahout is not just a job but an intimate 4,000-year-old partnership, which is declining even faster now that elephants are a tourist commodity and subject to abuses (including working them longer with amphetamines). Evidently, real effort is required to save this increasingly forlorn symbol of Thailand.

---

a tray surrounded by four vertical wings. A rallying point for demonstrators, it's in a traffic circle ringed by **Sky High** restaurant (*see p105*), **Café Democ** dance bar (*see p195*) and a glaring branch of McDonald's.

South of the two monuments a pleasantly walkable network of streets surrounds the city hall and the **Sao Ching Cha** (Giant Swing) of **Wat Suthat** (*see p67*), one of the country's six principal temples. East of the *wat* is the Brahmin temple of **Devasathan** and lovely **Rommaninat Park** (*see p67*).

Before Phanfa Bridge over Khlong Ong Ang, where Ratchadamnoen bends north towards Dusit, is the cluster of religious buildings known as **Wat Ratchannadda**, including the unique **Loha Prasat** (*see p67*). Nearby is the one-turret **Mahakan Fort**, originally built by Rama I, and on the other side of the bridge, the peaceful **Golden Mount** of **Wat Saket** offers a fine panorama (for both, *see p67*).

## Devasathan
*268 Thanon Dinso (0 2222 6951). Bus 10, 12, 19, 35, 42, 96, 508.* **Open** *Devasathan* 8am-4pm daily. *Chapel* 10am-4pm Thur, Sun. **Map** p308 C4.
This refurbished row of three shrines (to Shiva, Ganesha and Vishnu) was built in 1784 at the same time as the Giant Swing – their interwoven history highlighting the integral Brahmin involvement with Buddhism in royal ritual. There's another smaller shrine to Vishnu to the west of Wat Suthat.

## 14 October Monument
*Thanon Ratchadamnoen Klang, at Thanon Tanao. Bus 2, 9, 12, 15, 33, 35, 39, 42, 44, 47, 56, 59, 60, 64, 68, 70, 79, 82, 96, 201, 203.* **Open** 24hrs daily. **Map** p308 B/C3.
This stark grey granite memorial honours those killed in the 1973 demonstrations against dictatorship (*see p16*). It was erected only as recently as 2002, following many years of denial, evasion and non-investigation by Thailand's powerful elite. The central spire (surrounded by a minimalist

Amsterdam · Andalucia · Bangkok · Barcelona · Berlin · Boston
Brussels · Budapest · Buenos Aires · Chicago · Copenhagen · Dublin
Edinburgh · Florence · Havana · Hong Kong · Istanbul · Las Vegas
Lisbon · London · Los Angeles · Madrid · Miami · Milan
Moscow · Naples · New Orleans · New York · Paris · Patagonia
Prague · Rome · San Francisco · South of France · Stockholm · Sydney
Tokyo · Toronto · Venice · Vienna · Washington, DC

# Time Out City Guides

Available from all good bookshops and at www.timeout.com/shop

Time Out City Guides

www.penguin.com    www.timeout.com

amphitheatre) bears the names of 73 of the victims. Downstairs are an exhibition room, some meeting rooms and a small theatre. Survivors and bereaved families voluntarily maintain the site and are keen to talk about their traumatic experiences.

## Mahakan Fort
*Thanon Maha Chai. Bus 2, 9, 12, 15, 33, 35, 39, 42, 44, 47, 56, 59, 60, 64, 68, 70, 79, 82, 96, 201, 203.* **Closed. Map** p308 C3.

Although Mahakan Fort is closed to the public, it's still worth a visit. Along with the larger Phra Sumen Fort (*see p68*), this white octagonal turret is a surviving example of the 14 watchtowers that once studded the demolished city wall. Built by Rama I with bricks salvaged from Ayutthaya, it has a gate where Thanon Ratchadamnoen passes eastwards. Its cannons were disarmed in 2002, amid concern they might be fired in some terrorist plot. A small lane selling caged doves lies behind the wall, though this characterful neighbourhood is, as we go to press, set to be cleared for a public canalside park.

## Rommaninat Park & Corrections Museum
*Thanon Maha Chai (0 2221 5181). Bus 5, 35, 37, 42, 56, 73, 96.* **Open** *Park* 5am-9pm daily. *Museum* 8.30am-4.30pm Mon-Fri. **Map** p308 C4.

Once the site of Bangkok's prison, this lovely public park numbers ponds, fountains and a large bronze of a conch shell among its attractions. In the cool hours it supports joggers, as well as offering aerobics and weightlifting in an al fresco gym. Housed in the remaining prison buildings, a small penal museum displays instruments of punishment.

## Sao Ching Cha & Wat Suthat
*146 Thanon Bamrung Muang (0 2224 9845/ www.watsuthat.org). Bus 10, 12, 19, 35, 42, 56, 96.* **Open** *Temple* 8.30am-9pm daily. *Swing* 24hrs daily. **Admission** *Temple* B20. **No credit cards**. **Map** p308 C4.

The Giant Swing stands in front of Wat Suthat. A traditional new year event in the Brahmin calendar, symbolising an exploit of the god Shiva, would feature four brave men swinging from this lofty red structure to grab pouches of coins with their mouths. But the swing (first located at the Devasathan) caused such casualties that the rite was banned in the 1930s. The present timber poles were erected in 1919 by the Louis T Leonowens Company in honour of their namesake, the son of Anna Leonowens (the contentious governess of *The King and I*).

Looming behind the swing, Bangkok's tallest *vihaan* houses the 8m (26ft) Phra Sri Sakyamuni Buddha. One of the largest surviving bronzes from Sukhothai, it was ferried all the way south by boat, and its base contains the ashes of King Rama VIII (the older brother of the present king). Begun by Rama I in 1807, the temple took three reigns to complete, and its mesmerising interior was once enriched by murals that are now decaying (despite restoration work in the 1980s). Rama II himself

started the carving of its elaborate teak doors. A Chinese influence comes from the numerous stone statues (found in several Rattanakosin temples), tributes to the king that also served as valuable ballast for rice boats from China.

## Wat Ratchanadda & Loha Prasat
*2 Thanon Maha Chai (0 2224 8807). Bus 2, 9, 12, 15, 33, 35, 39, 42, 44, 47, 56, 59, 60, 64, 68, 70, 79, 82, 96, 201, 203.* **Open** *Temple* 9am-5pm daily. *Bot* 8.30-9am, 4-4.30pm daily; 8.30-10am religious days. **Map** p308 C3.

Unique in Thai spiritual architecture, the step-pyramidal Loha Prasat ('metal palace') is modelled on a Ceylonese metal temple from the third century BC, which was in turn based on an Indian original dating back 2,500 years. Built by Rama III in 1846, it is the only version of this kind of temple still standing. The 37 spires symbolise each of the virtues needed to attain enlightenment. On every level, a labyrinth of passages leads to meditation cells (to which entry is forbidden), with a spiral staircase ascending to interesting rooftop views. In order to reveal the Prasat, the art deco Chalerm Thai Theatre was demolished in the early 1990s amid much public debate. In its place, a park surrounds the Rama III statue and the intricate Mahachesdabodin Royal Pavilion used for official ceremonies. Behind the *wat* is an amulet market.

## Wat Saket & Golden Mount
*344 Thanon Chakkraphatdiphong (0 2621 0576). Bus 8, 15, 37, 38, 47, 49, 169.* **Open** *Temple* 8am-5pm daily. *Golden Mount* 7.30am-5.30pm daily. **Admission** *Golden Mount* B10. **No credit cards**. **Map** p308 C3.

Assembled from canal rubble, the Golden Mount (Phu Khao Thong) was intended by Rama III to be clad as a giant *chedi*. Proving unstable, the rubble was instead reinforced with trees and plants to prevent erosion. Shrines are dotted along the two spiral paths to the summit, where a gilded *chedi* contains Buddha relics from India and Nepal. Its breezy, bell-chiming concrete terrace offers a 360° panorama of both old and modern Bangkok. The terrace is actually part of Wat Saket, which spreads eastward with particularly handsome monks' quarters. With fine murals and a peaceful atmosphere, this *wat* was where the fatalities from various epidemics used to be brought for cremation.

## Banglamphu

Until the late 1990s the Thai press would refer to Bangkok's backpacker central, **Thanon Khao San** ('street of uncooked rice'; *see p68*), as a slum, while the term *farang banglamphu* (a variant of *farang kii nok* – 'birdshit foreigner') became shorthand for the kind of poor, decadent and hygienically challenged hippies who stayed around here. Now the Tourist Authority of Thailand promotes this area, and tourists duly flock here to get photographed with its dreadlocked, batik-trousered residents.

A lot of hot air on **Thanon Khao San**.

With travellers themselves morphing from professional hippies to hip professionals, the area has been revamped with the introduction of flashy hotels, clubs and restaurants. It used to be a semi-scary adventure for moneyed young Thais to go out here, but once that exotic frisson became trendy, a parallel Thai nightlife culture sprung up amid (but largely separate from) the backpacker places. Now there's even a free, monthly magazine for travellers called *FARANG You! You! You!*. Yet Banglamphu has clung steadfastly to its roots. Descendants of palace dancers and artisans still live here and **Banglamphu Market** (*see p133*) remains a labyrinthine local bazaar.

Adding more colour to the area's vibrant multinational community and architectural styles are a load of arty bars on **Thanon Phra Arthit** (*see p69*), where a new riverside park surrounds **Phra Sumen Fort** (*see p68*). From the fort, Thanon Phra Sumen hugs Khlong Banglamphu (a once commercially and defensively important canal dug two centuries ago by Lao prisoners of war); between them ran the former city walls, demolished by Rama V. The diminished hulk of the New World Department Store (closed for infringing height limits) looms over the junction with Thanon Samsen. South from here, on Thana Chakrabong, is **Wat Chana Songkhram** (*see p69*). Heading north, you reach the elevated approach above Thanon Visut Kasat to the new **Rama VIII Bridge** (*see p74*).

Continue eastwards along Thanon Phra Sumen past **Banglamphu Market** and another slab of city wall until you reach **Wat Bowoniwet** (*see p69*) and the surrounding shops specialising in Thai flags and royal imagery. Among the street's many food shops and stalls is the area's most exquisite conversion of a historic mansion, **Baan Bangkok Restaurant & Gallery** (*see p105*), built 150 years ago to face the canal.

Though a slog to reach by road, Banglamphu is easily accessed by Expressboat to Tha Phra Arthit or by canal boat to the Golden Mount.

### Phra Sumen Fort

*Thanon Phra Arthit. Bus 3, 6, 9, 15, 19, 30, 32, 33, 43, 53, 64, 65, 68, 82, 506*. **Open** 5am-10pm daily. **Map** p308 B2.

One of Rama I's 14 octagonal forts, flanked to the east by chunks of the old city wall. Since its restoration in 1999, the fort's whitewashed, cannon-strewn ramparts have formed the centrepiece of a pleasant riverside park, Santichaiprakarn Park – which serves as a venue for college romantics, picnickers, jamming folk musicians, martial artists, jugglers and plain old strollers. On some Sundays, self-consciously 'indie' students sell home-recorded albums, painted cards and handmade books. Intriguingly, the park also caters for the blind with Braille-marked paths and maps of attractions, such as the district's last *lamphu* trees by the water's edge.

### Thanon Khao San

*www.khaosanroad.com. Bus 2, 3, 6, 9, 15, 32, 33, 35, 39, 42, 43, 44, 47, 53, 56, 59, 60, 64, 68, 70, 79, 82, 96, 201, 203, 506*. **Map** p308 B3.

Even before 1997, when Alex Garland's best-selling novel *The Beach* was published (the opening scene unravels in a Khao San guesthouse), this road was the world's most famous haunt for budget travellers. With the addition of a Boots, a 7-Eleven, the luxurious Buddy Lodge (*see p37*), fancy restaurants and bars like Tom Yam Koong and the Club, Khao San is now one of the most expensive pieces of real estate in Bangkok. It's a radical transformation, given the fact that the first guesthouses only opened in 1982 to soak up the human flotsam and jetsam spilling over from the city's bicentennial celebrations around Sanam Luang. Glimpses of the road's past can still be seen in the wooden shophouses just past Khao San Center, and in the beautifully maintained mansion that now houses the Sidewalk Café.

For many young travellers, the road is just one long bucket shop, where they can purchase bus and ferry tickets to the islands, or pick up a plane ticket to Cambodia or Vietnam. It also performs another duty as a kind of bargain basement for discounted clothes, beachwear and sandals. The many second-hand bookshops have the best selection of contemporary fiction in Thailand, with Shaman Books (No.71) stocking the most travel guides and novels. The influx of young Thai artists, who flock here at

night, means there is now a wilder selection of original paintings, T-shirts and jewellery on sale. In the evening, members of the Akha hilltribe walk around in traditional dress hawking silverware.

Since the nationwide 2am closing time has been rigorously enforced, Khao San has ceased to be the party madhouse it once was. But there's still plenty of crazy times to be had in the clubs, such as Gulliver's Traveler's Tavern (across from the police station) and Khao San Center (in the middle of the street). Thai students prefer Suzy Pub, Austin Pub and the Club in the little *sois* off Khao San.

For the less debauched and more studious, some interesting classes are on offer. Near the mouth of Soi Suzy Pub is Pian's (*see p183*), where you can work enjoy Thai, Swedish, herbal and foot massages. From a one-hour introduction (B200) to a 30-hour course (B2,500-B4,000), the classes are cheaper than at Wat Pho. And over in Soi Bowoniwet (between Thanon Tanao and the post office), the Mai Kaidee Restaurant (*see p106*; www.maykaidee.com) holds classes in Thai veggie cuisine (B1,000 per day).

### Thanon Phra Arthit

*Bus 3, 6, 9, 15, 19, 30, 32, 33, 43, 53, 64, 65, 68, 82, 506.* **Map** p308 B2.

A popular hangout of creative students from Silpakorn and Thammasat Universities, this 'little bohemia' of art bars – including Bar Bali (*see p123*), which runs a periodic festival – has come full circle. The area once housed the artisans of court dance and music; their descendants fought (successfully) to preserve the 1925 Khrusapha printing works as an arts centre when Santichai-prakarn Park was being laid out around Phra Sumen Fort. A riverside walkway on stilts leads to the Bangkok Tourist

Bureau headquarters under Phra Pinklao Bridge, passing a seafood restaurant and several mansions.

These include the UNICEF offices in a former home of the queen consort to Rama IV; the home of former prime minister, novelist and culture vulture, Kukrit Pramoj; and the UN-FAO building at Baan Maliwan, where Pridi Bhanomyong lived as regent for Rama VIII and directed the anti-fascist wartime Seri Thai Movement. The classical art-palace Baan Chao Phraya faces art nouveauish Baan Phra Arthit. Built by a finance minister in 1926, it housed the Goethe Institut from 1962 to 1986, then the publishers Manager Group, and now features a swish café.

### Wat Bowoniwet

*248 Thanon Phra Sumen (0 2281 2831-3). Bus 38, 53, 56, 68.* **Open** 8am-5pm daily. **Map** p308 C3.

Home to both the city's second Buddhist university and the Supreme Patriarch (leader) of Thai Buddhism, this temple was founded in 1826 and was the site of Rama IV's and Rama IX's ordinations as monks. Melding Thai and Chinese designs, the main chapel features gilded naga balustrades and windows. It's lovely during Buddhist holidays.

### Wat Chana Songkhram

*77 Thanon Chakrabong (0 2280 4415). Bus 3, 6, 9, 15, 19, 30, 32, 33, 43, 53, 64, 65, 68, 82, 506.* **Open** 6am-6pm daily. **Map** p308 B3.

Originally built in Mon style – because Rama I got many Burmese to lay the groundwork for the fledgling city – this great monastery was renovated and proudly renamed the 'winning the war temple' after the sovereign's brother won an important battle against the Burmese. Most of the 300 monks here study Pali (the ancient Sanskrit derivative of the Buddhist scriptures) at the temple school.

# Learn to Massage

What could make a better souvenir than taking home the ability to massage? It's so appealing, in fact, that classes proliferate in Bangkok. Originating as a physical application of *metta* ('loving kindness'), the ancient massage technique of *nuad paen boran* is still often practised in Buddhist temples. The most important school is at Bangkok's **Wat Pho** (*see p183*), where Rama II retrieved *nuad* knowledge after the fall of Ayutthaya. Its open-air *sala* contains murals of acupressure points on the body's energy meridians. There are 72,000 energy lines in yoga philosophy, which explains why the stretches involved resemble yoga *asanas*. Dotting the courtyards are sculptures of self-healing postures known as 'the hermit's massage'.

Students learn from an *ajaan* (teacher) how to release blocked energy and relax joints,

and maybe advance to identifying and relieving ailments. Originally, massage was preceded by rites, so many masseurs start with a *wai khru* ceremony to honour their teachers and the art's originator – Shivaka Kumar Baccha, the Buddha's physician. This aids mindful awareness and heightens sensitivity to energy flow and ailments. Both giver and receiver should feel equally relaxed.

You can also learn massage at Pian (*see p183*) and outside Bangkok in such places as Samui and Chiang Mai. In Chiang Mai, Chongkol Setthakorn of **International Training Massage** (*see p266*) starts classes with yoga to ensure that the masseurs never strain themselves. He also gets his pupils to practise on each other, which makes his course particularly popular with couples who want to learn together.

# Thonburi, River & Canals

Siam's short-lived capital is a time-capsule of waterborne living.

Sightseeing

Despite its massive size and significance as the post-Ayutthaya capital, Thonburi can't escape being dismissed as the 'other' side of the river, like some oriental south London (one official map even calls this area West Rattanakosin). Even its prime tourist fetcher **Wat Arun** is usually visited on an organised tour. Thonburi's surviving waterborne lifestyle means it is most efficiently, and comfortably, reached by boat, and hence inseparable from the Chao Phraya river (*see p72* **The mother of all waters**).

In the 20th century, *Fang Thon* ('Thonburi side') expanded into a dense mass of roads and low-income housing that contrasts loudly with the stilted, wooden, canalside homes of Bang Khunthien and Bang Kruay. The canal scenes are best viewed at dawn (when monks are peddling for alms) and in the late afternoon. The area's main attractions lie between **Bangkok Noi** and nearly dry **Khlong San**.

## Around Khlong San

Thonburi's two top hotels are both situated far from the area's sights, but are convenient for the Bangrak finance hub. Best reached by ferry, the **Marriott Bangkok Resort** (*see p38*) is like staying upcountry, while the more recent **Peninsula** hotel (*see p39*) soars beside the Oriental Spa, opposite the Oriental hotel. Khlong San district was meant to get a riverside park around a Sofitel hotel, but construction was abandoned in 1996 amid whispers of subsidence. Now the building looms derelict over the commuter-jammed **Khlong San Market** and **Yok Yor Restaurant** (*see p54*) as a testament to developers' hubris.

Thailand's main southbound artery, Phetkasem Highway, starts just east of the equestrian statue of **King Taksin the Great** at the Wong Wien Yai intersection. The statue – brandishing his sword and wearing a conical hat – directs a vehicular armada onwards – though Thonburi's gridlock is among the city's most daunting. The only other sight here is **Wong Wien Yai railway station** where – unbeknown to many Bangkokians – you can catch a train heading

south-west to Mahachai seafood market, where Yaowarat restaurants buy their catch.

A cluster of low-key sights near the mouth of **Khlong Bangkok Yai** makes for a fetching three-hour walking tour – for which you can use signs from the Bangkok Tourist Bureau tour (B100; *see p54*). Tours down Khlong Bangkok Yai often branch off south-west at Wat Paknam where bygone canal life can still be glimpsed along **Khlong Daokhanong**, **Khlong Bangkhuntien** and **Khlong Lart**. Sadly, **Wat Sai Floating Market** is a concrete-and-souvenir shadow of its once prominent role as an aquatic agricultural exchange. The Ayutthayan-era **Wat Sai** (Thanon Thavorn-wattana; 0 2415 7173) is noted for its circular belfry and *kanok* (flame) lacquerwork on the Tamnak Thong monks' quarters.

## Around Khlong Bangkok Yai

Its profile familiar from the TAT logo and B10 coin, the famous temple of **Wat Arun** (*see p71*) is a Thai icon. King Taksin appended it to his new palace **Wang Derm** (now part of the Royal Thai Navy headquarters, and open by appointment only – *see p71*). Walking distance north, **Wat Rakhang** (on Soi Wat Rakhang; open daily 6am-6pm) was restored by Taksin and is famed for its red *hor trai*, comprising three teak scripture halls where Rama I stayed (his ashes are interred here). Taksin replaced the melodious *rakhang* (bell) that he took to Wat Phra Kaew with the five bells that now hang in the belfry beside a perfectly proportioned *prang*.

The temple is best viewed en route to **Patravadi Theatre** (*see p201* **Stage mother**). There you can eat at **Laan Hin Dtaek** café (named after its sledgehammered walls) or on the riverfront at the sister establishments **Patravadi Restaurant** and **Supatra River House** (*see p203*), both run by Patravadi's sister in the house of their late mother, the founder of the Expressboats.

A narrow alley leads through **Prannok Market** to **Siriraj Hospital,** the world's fourth largest, which treats royalty and houses

Bangkok's lifeline, the **Chao Phraya** river.

several gruesome museums (*see below*). Skirting its historic buildings and **Wat Amarin Market** you reach **Bangkok Noi train station**, a Western-style, Rama V-era brick building. It was used by the Japanese in World War II, hence the heavy Allied bombing of Bangkok Noi. Some trains depart from here, and the station also serves as a tourist centre, with a market alongside.

## Siriraj Hospital Museums

*Thanon Phrannok (0 2419 7000). Bus 19, 57, 81, 83, 91, 146, 149.* **Open** *Parasitology & Thai Medicine museums* 9am-4pm Mon-Fri. *Other museums* 8.30am-4.30pm Mon-Fri. **Admission** free. **Map** p308 A3.

The six small museums within Siriraj Hospital are a bizarre testament to the history of medical development. Old-fashioned in design and aimed at students rather than the public, they're definitely not for the squeamish. The **Si Quey Forensic Medicine Museum** (department of forensic medicine, second floor; 0 2419 7000 ext 6547) contains shattered skulls, pickled organs, stillborn babies, crime scene photos and the preserved body of the murderer the museum is named after. The **Congdon Anatomical**

Museum (anatomy department, third floor; 0 2419 7035) displays human organs and bones from embryo to maturity, plus anomalies such as Siamese twins (named after Thai-Chinese conjoined brothers, Chang and Eng, born in 1811). Two floors down, the **Sood Sangvichien Prehistoric Museum & Laboratory** (0 2419 7029) looks at the evolution of humans and other living things. The **Ellis Pathological Museum** (department of pathology, second floor; 0 2411 2005) features diseases at macroscopic and microscopic scale. On the second floor of the parasitology department, the **Parasitology Museum** (0 2419 7000 ext 6488) contains home-lovin' hookworms, whipworms and tapeworms preserved with the organs they've adopted. The **Ouay Ketusingh Museum of History of Thai Medicine** (department of pharmacology, first floor; 0 2411 5026) examines indigenous healing knowledge, and includes mannequins of birth, ageing, sickness and death.

## Wang Derm

*2 Royal Thai Navy Headquarters, Phra Ratcha Wang Derm, Thanon Arun Amarin (0 2475 4117/2466 9355/www.wangdermpalace.com). Bus 19, 57, 81, 83.* **Open** by appointment. **Admission** B50. **No credit cards. Map** p308 A5.

The palace built by King Taksin orginally included Wat Arun, until Rama I reduced the area of the palace grounds. Royals continued to live in Wang Derm, and three kings were born here. Rama V gave the palace to the Thai Navy with instructions to preserve the throne hall and the oldest Chinese-style buildings. A shrine to Taksin features a sword-wielding statue of the king in a century-old *sala* that fuses Thai and Western forms. Both the palace and Wichaiprasit Fort (which still fortifies Khlong Bangkok Yai) display antique ceramics, paintings, old Thai currencies and weaponry.

With Thonburi part of the Krung Rattanakosin Plan it is hoped that Wang Derm can become more accessible to visitors.

## Wat Arun

*34 Thanon Arun Amarin (0 2891 1149/2466 6752/www.watarun.org). Bus 19, 57, 81, 83.* **Open** 7am-6pm daily. **Admission** B20. **No credit cards. Map** p308 A5.

Bangkok's most famous *wat* has been known as the 'Temple of Dawn' ever since Chaopraya Taksin landed by it at sunrise in October 1767. Previously called Wat Magog, this landmark became Wat Jaeng when it was part of Taksin's palace, and then Wat Arunratchawararamat under Rama IV. Much restoration was done under Rama II, who named it Wat Arunratchatharam. Whatever its complex nomenclature, the focus is clear: the 81m-high (266ft) Khmer-style *prang*, with four satellite *prang* at each cardinal corner. These slender 'corncob' spires are inlaid with an eye-popping array of polychromatic ceramic shards. Briefly home to the Emerald Buddha, Wat Arun features a stunning statue pair of mythical *yaksa* (giants), ceramic

**Sightseeing**

gables on its *vihaan* and *bot*, and some 120 Buddha images. These get less overlooked now that climbing the vertiginous *prang* is forbidden after a climber fell off in 1998.

You can visit Wat Arun on a tour, but it's unnecessary: it's a short B2 ferry ride from Tha Tien, where the pier becomes the studenty bar Boh (*see p123*) just as the *wat* is thrown into sunset silhouette. A so-so son et lumière and the fascinatingly retro Wat Arun Festival are intermittent events.

## Khlong Bangkok Noi

A former meander of the Chao Phraya river before a 17th-century shortcut, **Khlong Bangkok Noi** is the capital's most active canal. Now hemmed in by flood barriers, its wooden stilt houses have personal piers where residents hang out. Concrete walkways and

Fantastical, detailed carving at the **Royal Barge Museum**. *See p73*.

# The mother of all waters

Old maps and expeditionary journals call the Chao Phraya river the River Menam – a tautology as *menam* means the 'mother of all waters'. Mythically, it's home to the naga – serpents whose awesome wrath and benevolence determines water's crucial impact on South-east Asian civilisation, from fish, *padi* (rice fields) and transport to flood, drought and ritual.

Draining a basin the size of Britain into an ever-narrowing funnel through Bangkok – its rim embanked and encroached, the disbursing canals plugged by construction – 'the River of Kings' instinctively *wants* to flood. The nourishing inundation of the central plains (though of little use to the concrete conurbation of today) was precious to pre-modern Siamese, whose stilt houses just survive, although dam releases and motorboats have made raft housing uninhabitable. Particularly near Krung Thon Bridge, you can still see nut-profiled teak barges supporting the aquatic lifestyle evocatively painted by Vorasan Suparp.

The river's force is apparent when you're aboard cross-river *kham fahk*. These tubby ferries chug strenuously in looped arcs, wallowing uneasily between the diverse traffic ploughing up- and downstream through ochre eddies, black *khlong* outflows and carpets of water hyacinths (a Brazilian plague

that clogs waterways, but can be woven into furniture). Every vessel imaginable plies the Chao Phraya, from longtails, expressboats and pleasure cruisers to flat-bed canoes, grey police launches and dainty tugs pulling hulking steel barges of rice, cement or other commodities. Though Bangkok now underutilises its previous lifeline, the city was built to face the water – so travelling by river reveals the capital's oldest face, which neglect has helped preserve.

The description below follows 33 kilometres (20.5 miles) of the river from south to north. Check the specific **Sightseeing** chapters for more information on the sights mentioned.

## Pak Nam to Saphan Taksin

**Piers** *S3-S1 & Central. Covered in South and Thonburi chapters.*
Visible from the hill at Ancient City, silt is being deposited at a rate of five metres (16 feet) a year by the river mouth, Pak Nam. The sea, now 30 kilometres (18 miles) south, once started north of Bangkok. The furthest downstream most boat tours go is **Rama IX Bridge**, the suspension span beside the **Thai Farmer's Bank** headquarters. But a hired longtail can zip around the battleships and container behemoths between the vast green forest of trees at **Bang Kra Jao** and the vast grey forest of

hump-back bridges allow for localised walks, but roads are scarce and boating is the norm here. Tours typically take in the **Royal Barge Museum, Wat Suwannaram** (for both, *see below*), **Bang Bu Village**, and fish feeding at **Wat Sisudaram** and **Taling Chan Floating Market**. The market (open 8am-5pm Saturdays and Sundays) is mostly on land rather than on boats, but the food and souvenir vendors occupy a picturesque rural stretch of the canal.

### Royal Barge Museum

*80/1 Rimkhlong Bangkok Noi, Thanon Arun Amarin (0 2424 0004). Bus 19, 57, 79, 81, 124, 503, 509, 511.* **Open** 9am-5pm daily. **Admission** B30; camera B100; video camera B200. **No credit cards. Map** p308 A2.

It's an unforgettable sight to watch dozens of slim, ornate boats carrying the royal family in ancient formation from Vasukri Pier to Wat Arun to present monks' robes in a *kathin* ceremony; an event last held for His Majesty's sixth cycle (72nd) birthday in 1999. Such ceremonies are rare, so visit the Royal Barge Museum to see the barges' astonishing crafts-

manship up close. Eight of the most magnificent vessels are raised in dry berths amid user-friendly displays of regalia, dioramas, barge lore and bilingual description. Most impressive is the king's barge, *Suphannahongse* ('Golden Swan'). Carved from a single log and powered by 50 costumed, chanting oarsmen, the original of this 45.15m (148ft) long, 3.17m (10.5ft) wide vessel was destroyed at Ayutthaya. Rebuilt by Rama I and again by Rama V, its ageing woodwork is no longer risked much afloat. Second in importance is the 54-oar, Rama IV-era *Anantanakaraj*, its bow splayed with a seven-headed naga. The newest, *Narai Song Suban*, with Vishnu riding Garuda at its prow, was built for the king's golden jubilee in 1996. The barges will next process on the king's 60th anniversary in 2006. Appropriately enough, it's best to get to the museum by boat, as it's a long, hot slog from the road via jumbled alleys with scant signage.

### Wat Suwannaram

*33 Thanon Charan Sanit Wong Soi 32 (0 2433 8045). Bus 80, 108, 169, 175, 509, 510.* **Open** 8am-4.30 daily. **Admission** free.

cranes at **Khlong Toey**, Thailand's biggest port. Or you can view the harbour traffic from the wooden decks of **Baan Klang Nam** seafood restaurant (3792/160 Rama III Soi 14). Cruise liners now berth at Laem Chabang (north of Pattaya) or Phuket.

Expressboats do a U-turn at **Wat Ratchasinghkorn**, but it's classier to start the upstream journey from the **Marriott Bangkok Resort** (*see p38*), between **Krung Thep Bridge** and the white portico and campanile of the **First Presbyterian Church**, opposite early godowns (warehouses). The Marriott's free teak shuttleboats and luxury converted barge *Manohra* pass a 19th-century **Protestant Cemetery**, replete with gothic

tombs, beside the **Menam Hotel**. On the western bank, the pointy **Tridhos Marina** condo was designed by Mom Tri Devakul and hosts the **Magic Eyes Chao Phraya Barge Programme** (*see p54*). Thonburi's **Chao Phraya River Cultural Centre** (*see p203*) faces the **Fisheries Organisation**'s market, the **Royal Thai Naval Dockyard** and the ship-shaped *chedi* of **Wat Yannawa**, for which you alight at Central Pier under Saphan Taksin BTS station.

### Oriental Hotel to River City

**Piers** N1-N3. Covered in Bangrak and Thonburi chapters.
The **Shangri-La Hotel** (*see p42*) stands next to the classical edifices of **Assumption** ▶

Art students flock to the *wat*'s classic Ayutthayan *bot* to sketch the Rama III-era murals by Thai artist Thongyu (primarily *jataka* episodes of the Buddha's life). Chinese artist Kong Pae used slim brushes and shadows to accentuate motion. Look out for apocalyptic images of Buddha subduing Mara, and some racy erotic poses.

## Bang Phlad & Bang Kruay

Specific sights taper off north of the **Phra Pinklao Bridge**, where traffic starts its long roll past malls and *mor lam* nightclubs to the Southern Bus Terminal and the elevated expressway west. Expressboats pass the Bang Phlad riverside and the new 2.1-kilometre long (1.3-mile) **Rama VIII Bridge**. Unveiled in 2002, it has eased congestion, not to mention sore eyes, thanks to its beautiful harp-like suspension from a 300-metre high (984-foot), inverted-Y pillar set on the Thonburi side.

Longtail boats follow Khlong Bangkok Noi north through Bang Kruay into Khlong Om, to emerge just north of Nonthaburi. The canalside orchard communities are just about intact, serviced by ancient *wats*, pierside stores and boat vendors selling hot noodles, produce and ice-cream to residents lounging on the flower-decked verandas of their mostly wooden homes.

This idyll is jeopardised by two highways slashed through in 2002 to 'improve' out of existence a lifestyle that will surely become prized. Even those realising its merits are erecting nouveau riche monstrosities that blight the ultra-Siamese canalscape. During recent floods, the area has been callously submerged longer in order to spare Bangkok (and, some suspect, to kill the plantations to facilitate land speculation). Embankments, however, wouldn't just ruin the aesthetics; they would damage the sustaining ecology and prevent small boat travel due to wave buffetting. Will tourist pressure save this time capsule?

## ▶ The mother of all waters (continued)

College, **EAC** (Eastern Asiatic Company) and the **Oriental** hotel (*see p41*) – which runs the **Oriental Spa** (*see p182*) and **Sala Rim Nam** restaurant (*see p203*) on the eastern bank beside the soaring tower of the **Peninsula** hotel (*see p39*). Historic edifices continue with the restored **French Embassy** and mouldering **Customs House**. The latter is set to become a boutique hotel – though fabulous conversions of derelict waterfront gems are continually scuppered by visionless bureaucracy; the green-glass slab of the **Communications Authority Tower** is typical of developments snubbing their location. Beyond the leaf-shaded **Portuguese Embassy** more concrete 'improvement' blights the mouth of Khlong Phadung Krung Kasem, between the overscaled **Royal Orchid Sheraton Hotel** and bland **River City** antiques mall (*see p138*), which serves all river hotel ferries. The saucer-topped tower opposite was a never-finished Sofitel.

### River City to Khlong Bangkok Noi

**Piers** N4-N11. *Covered in Chinatown, Phra Nakorn and Thonburi chapters.*

The dainty **Holy Rosary Church**, the Italianate **Siam Commercial Bank** (Thailand's first bank building) and an ancient Chinese temple precede a shambles of encroachment from Chinatown. So face west to admire the Chinese pagoda and mural-rich temples **Wat Thong Noppakhun** and **Wat Thong Thammachat**. **Phra Pokklao Bridge** forms a double span with the river's first crossing, the obelisked **Rama I Memorial Bridge** (built in 1932). **Pak Khlong Market**'s emptied godowns are named after the mouth of Khlong Lord, beyond which, on Ko Rattanakosin, the exclusive **Ratchinee Girls School** sits in pert Palladian proportion near lantern-towered **Wang Chakrabong**, a graceful aristocratic abode from where Prince Chakraphong's descendent now publishes River Books.

South of Thonburi's Khlong Bangkok Yai, **Santa Cruz Church** and its filigree jetty are flanked by the triple *chedis* of **Wat Prayoonwong** and outsized **Wat Kalayanimit**. The canal's north-bank fortress, **Vichai Prasit**, defends King Taksin's palace, **Wang Derm**, and **Wat Arun**. Facing the latter's crockery-covered *prangs*, **Wat Pho** spires peek above gabled shophouses at **Tha Tien**, where *wai roon* (trendies) frequent **Boh** bar (*see p123*) on the pier, after sunset.

Suddenly, a landscaped esplanade affords clear views of the **Grand Palace** – a vista the Rattanakosin Plan would extend by demolishing much of Phra Chan community, **Thammasat University** (but not its drill-bit dome) and the **National Theatre** (*see p202*),

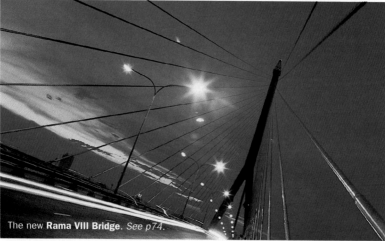

The new **Rama VIII Bridge**. *See p74.*

which rim the river towards **Phra Pinklao Bridge**. The riverscape (and royal barge processions) are best viewed from Thonburi's **Wat Rakhang**, the sister restaurants of **Supatra River House** and **Patravadi Theatre Restaurant** (*see p201*) and **Prannok Market**, **Siriraj Hospital** and the visitor centre at **Bangkok Noi railway station** on the bend of Khlong Bangkok Noi.

### Phra Pinklao Bridge to Nonthaburi

**Piers** *N12-N30. Covered in Thonburi, Dusit and Outer North chapters.*
Under Phra Pinklao Bridge, a stilted walkway starts at the **Bangkok Tourist Bureau HQ** and passes mansions on Thanon Phra Arthit Road on its way to **Santichaiprakarn Park**'s *lamphu* trees and **Phra Sumane Fort**. The classical masterpiece across the river languishes unrestored as **Intara School**. North of Khlong Banglamphu lie numerous Dusit mansions, including the art nouveau **Wang Bangkhunprom**, which influenced the design of **Rama VIII Bridge** to be ingeniously suspended from a single pillar beside the Thonburi **Bangyikhan Distillery** for Mekhong whisky. **Thewes Flower Market** lines the north-west end of Khlong Phadeung Krung Kasem, ahead of the **Royal Barge Dock**; just visible behind the dock is the childhood

home of Queen Sirikit and **Kaloang Home Kitchen** seafood restaurant (*see p107*).
Just beyond the green-shuttered royal pier Tha Vasukri, and **Wat Ratchathiwas**'s wooden *vihaan*, **St Francis Xavier Church** is the focus of a Vietnamese community. Most cruises turn back at the box-girder **Sang Hee (Krung Thon) Bridge**, the illuminated backdrop for **Khanab Nam** restaurant/boat, **River Bar Café** (*see p125*) and the **Royal River Hotel**.
Those chugging further north encounter traditional and commerical activity interspersed with landmarks such as the **Singha** and **Amarit** breweries, **Rama VI Bridge** (carrying the southern railway), the curious-looking **Wat Khien** and **Rama V Bridge**, which opened in 2002.

### Nonthaburi

At the Nonthaburi expressboat terminus, stroll to **Rim Fang** restaurant (235/2 Thanon Pracharat; 0 2525 1742) along the promenade (and impromptu skate park), passing the sublime wooden fretwork of **Nonthaburi Provincial Office**. Hired longtails head back via **Khlong Om** (which loops into Khlong Bangkok Noi) or onward to **Wat Chaloem Prakiat** and **Ko Kred**. You can also take further excursions to **Bang Sai**, **Bang Pa-in** and **Ayutthaya**.

# Walk 3 Old Thonburi

A pleasant stroll away from the river, along winding alleys, allows you to explore two 200-year-old Thonburi communities.

Start at **Wat Kalayanamit**, (371 Soi Wat Kalayanmit, Thanon Thetsaban I; 0 2466 5018; open 8am-5pm daily), near the mouth of Khlong Bangkok Yai. Founded in 1825 by a Chinese nobleman, the temple's hangar-like *vihaan* boasts multi-superlatives: Thailand's highest *chofa* (roof finial), biggest bell and largest indoor sitting Buddha (15 metres/ 49 feet high).

Proceeding to the joss-hazed Chinese shrine of **Kiang An Keng**, you wind through the narrow lanes and wooden houses of the Sino-Portuguese Kudee Jeen community around **Santa Cruz Church & Convent** (112 Thanon Thetsaban Sai I; 0 2466 0347; open 5-8pm Mon-Sat; 9am-8pm Sun). Often rebuilt since King Taksin's time, the current cream-and-pink edifice topped by an octagonal dome dates from 1916. Known as 'Wat Kudee Jeen', it is elegantly simple inside (pictured), with light dappling through circles of stained glass depicting Jesus' life on to a stately marble pulpit under a coffered ceiling in blue and gold. There's a ferry between the church's dainty pier and Tha Rachini.

A culinary legacy survives at **Khanom Farang Kudi Jeen**, a wooden shophouse where pastries of sweetened apple and jujube are baked to the recipes of Portuguese settlers, mercenaries who defended Ayutthaya from Burma. The Persian-descended Bunnag clan, who helped administer Ayutthaya, built **Wat Prayurawongsawat** along Thanon Thetsaban Sai 1. Fenced in English cast-iron, it features Bangkok's first Singh Hon (Sri Lankan-style) *chedi*, while its garden contains an artificial mount studded with Bunnag gravestones, and a pond teeming with turtles.

Turn left and curve round a riverside garden under Memorial Bridge on Thanon Phaya Mai to Thanon Somdet Chaophraya. Take two lefts into Somdet Chaophraya Soi 3 to reach **Somdet Phra Srinagarinda Boromarajajonani Memorial Park** (0 2437 7799; open 6am-6pm daily). Thais are proud that the king's mother, affectionately called Somdet Ya, was born a commoner to goldsmiths and practised nursing. The Princess Mother Memorial Park recreates her girlhood home on land donated by Daeng and Lek Nana, landlords of Sukhumvit's Soi Nana, in 1993.

The king insisted that the existing foliage was kept, and plants frame laterite walls and a sandstone bas-relief depicting Somdet Ya's altruism, while Thonburi and royal family history is documented in the museum (open 9am-4pm daily; admission B30). A gallery holds quarterly exhibitions at the rear, and the park is full of activity on holidays.

Retrace your steps, cross Thanon Somdet Chaophraya and to your right is another Bunnag temple donated to Rama III, **Wat Pichayayatikaram Worawihan**, housing a Sukhothai-era Buddha image from Phitsanulok. Something the Bangkok Tourist Bureau tour omits is that Taksin also allocated land to Muslim defenders of Ayutthaya, whose descendents comprise the Kudee Khao community along Bang Luang Canal. Walk west across thunderous Thanon Prachathipok down the new extension of Thanon Arun Amarin: No.151 is **Bang Luang Mosque**. Though small and whitewashed, it has an elaborate gilded pulpit that uniquely synthesises Buddhist and Islamic motifs.

Head down its old alley entrance to Thanon Thetsaban Sai 3, then turn right to a T-junction. Turn left then right into Itsaraphap Soi 24, then cross Thanon Itsaraphap to Soi 15. At No.539/1 is **Baan Silpa Thai** (0 2465 0420/ 1641 6961; open 8am-8pm daily), where the *khon* masks sold at Chatuchak Weekend Market have been made for two decades. Non-English-speaking Suk Phenphai and Charoen Kitrat may let you try crafting the gilded *Ramayana* characters (on sale for B1,000-B5,000; papier-mâché ones are B100). A portent of such crafts' fate is that Jarin Klinbuppha, the *khlui* (bamboo flute) maker at **Baan Laos** (No. 343; open 8am-11am Mon-Fri), now makes his flutes in plastic.

# Dusit

Bangkok's royal and government quarter is a graceful enclave of shaded boulevards and monumental architecture.

The attractions of this beautiful and uncrowded district are mainly royal, architectural and historic. Flanked by the river and the railway, its main thoroughfare, Thanon Ratchadamnoen Nok, is like a tree trunk, with branches to major institutions and temples and a crown that encompasses the grand headquarters of the monarchy, the government and the military. The leafy enclave of Dusit Park, with its royal villas, harks back to the area's origins as Rama V's country retreat. Even today, Dusit is a popular destination with daytrippers who want to escape the hurly-burly of central Bangkok. Be warned: you'll find vendors and restaurants only at its fringes, so the provision of meals must be strategically planned.

## Ratchadamnoen

Walking up tree-lined Thanon Ratchadamnoen Nok provides a crash course in how Thai design meshed with Western concepts. In the first instance of modern Thai urban planning, Ratchadamnoen's three sections, from the Grand Palace to Dusit Park, were modelled on the Champs-Elysées (seen by Rama V during a trip to Paris). Indeed, this resemblance may become more striking, with plans afoot to turn the middle section (Thanon Ratchadamnoen Klang), into an upmarket fashion strip with an underpass running beneath it. Meanwhile, the more institutional *nok* (outer) arm of the boulevard is focused not on an arch, but on the Italianate marble and copper-domed **Ananta Samakhom Throne Hall**, behind which lies the modernist **Parliament** in democratically horizontal concrete.

Art deco influences are visible in the streamlined brick terraces lining Thanon Ratchadamnoen Klang at the southern end, in **Ratchadamnoen Boxing Stadium** (*see p209*) opposite the Army headquarters, and in the pavilions of **Amporn Gardens**. Now rarely used for expositions, this park forms one side of the broad **Royal Plaza**, which hosts the annual Red Cross Fair. The Plaza is also bordered by the Throne Hall and the former Thai Supreme Command, which has more of a British-style façade and grounds that are now (rather appropriately) used to host the UK-Thai charity event **Ploenchit Fair** (*see p157*). The entire

Ratchadamnoen area is gorgeously illuminated by fairylights for royal anniversaries, such as the king's and queen's birthdays, and processions, including the Songkran Day Parade.

Further down Ratchadamnoen, the Royal Thai Army headquarters (which houses the **Royal Thai Army Museum** – *see p79*) and the **Defence Ministry** are fine examples of the work of 20 Italian architects, who were commissioned in the early 20th century to design grand edifices for the city's institutions. The effortless proportions and pastel paintwork of these buildings were intended to suit Thailand's sunny climate.

Venetian style pervades Government House and Baan Phitsanulok off to the east, while the wooden villas in **Dusit Park** (*see p80*) are 'tropical European' in style – a term greatly preferred to 'colonial' (Thailand avoided colonisation partly by adopting such outward trappings as fretwork verandas and classical porticoes). Rama V was a master diplomat, so it seems appropriate that his home district now hosts the United Nations' Asia-Pacific nerve centre, **UN ESCAP** (*see p79*), in a building that curves around one corner of the double bridge over Khlong Phadung Krung Kasem. Planted with flame trees that flower in summer, this canal bisects Ratchadamnoen Nok.

### Ananta Samakhom Throne Hall

*Thanon Uthong Nai (0 2244 1777/8). Bus 70, 72, 201, 503.* **Open** 8.30am-4.30pm Children's Day (2nd Sat in Jan) only. **Admission** free. **Map** p309 D1.
Though ostensibly built in marble, this symbol of authority was the first Thai building constructed (1908-16) on ferro-concrete pilings, a technique that Rama V saw in Europe. Its awesome cruciform interior – heavily gilded, with mosaic scenes of Chakri reigns I-IV lining the dome – is only open to the public on National Children's Day (*see p159*). The first Thai parliament convened here and it is still used for state occasions.

### Parliament

*Thanon Uthong Nai (0 2244 1000/www.parliament. go.th). Bus 12, 18, 28, 70, 108, 510, 515.* **Open** 8.30am-4.30pm Children's Day (2nd Sat in Jan) only. **Admission** free. **Map** p309 D1.
MPs and senators are still at this building as we go to press, but are due to move to new premises (with pressure for a Siamese design this time) – although there is opposition to the proposed site in Chatuchak.

Wat Benchamabophit. *See p80.*

From the entrance railings along Thanon Uthong Nai you can discern the National Assembly's brutalist yet breezy Brasilia aesthetic, though not Rama VII's signature and handwritten endowment of the first constitution (10 December 1932, Constitution Day), which rests beneath his seated statue at the front. A museum to the monarch is open by appointment.

### Royal Thai Army Museum

*113 Thanon Ratchadamnoen Nok (0 2297 8121/2/ www.rta.mi.th). Bus 70, 72, 201, 503.* **Open** by appointment. **Admission** free. **Map** p308 D2.

Models, weapons, flags, uniforms and insignia dominate this collection housed in the attractive army headquarters and armoury of the Chulachomklao Royal Military Academy.

### UN ESCAP

*United Nations Building, Thanon Ratchadamnoen Nok (0 2288 1234/www.unescap.org). Bus 70, 72, 201, 503.* **Open** 8.30am-4.30pm Mon-Fri.

**Admission** free. **Map** p308 D2.

The function of the UN's Economic and Social Commission for Asia and the Pacific (ESCAP) is to relieve poverty, preserve natural resources and bolster trade, tourism and rural development. Its sweeping green roofs (made up of a million handmade tiles) are an elegant adaptation of the cascading eaves found on Thai temples. The building houses conference facilities, the UN Information service and an academic library (open 11am-4pm Wed-Fri).

## Chitrlada

King Bhumibol and Queen Sirikit have resided at **Chitrlada Palace** for most of the ninth reign, and its broad, tree-shaded gardens are amply protected by a wall, a moat and guardposts. Although the residential and reception quarters are concealed from view, the agro-industrial facilities of the **Royal Projects** (royally sponsored development projects, focusing on such issues as crop sustainability) are just visible along the side facing the horse-racing track of the **Royal Turf Club** (*see p209*). This Western sport was introduced to Siam after Rama V's European tour in 1897, but it was not until his son's reign that the Royal Turf Club was founded. As well as holding biweekly races and four annual derbies, the club also tests and registers the country's thoroughbreds.

Between Chitrlada and Parliament is the popular retreat of **Dusit Zoo**. The canal in front of the zoo leads south past the touristy royal temple of **Wat Benchamabophit** (*see p80*) and thence to **Government House**, with its appropriately Byzantine detailing. Further down Thanon Phitsanulok stands **Baan Phitsanulok**, the prime minister's residence since 1982. Legend has it that this 1925 Venetian Gothic confection is haunted.

### Chitrlada Palace

*Thanon Ratchavithi (0 2280 4199). Bus 18, 28, 108, 125, 510, 515.* **Open** by written appointment only 8.30am-4pm Mon-Fri. **Map** p309 E1.

Once a pastoral retreat where King Rama VI would come to write his theatrical works and books about military history, the former Chitrlada Villa was expanded to form the palace at the behest of Rama VII. As it is now the monarch's permanent residence, access to the palace is restricted and the public is content simply to stroll or jog through its shady perimeter (surrounding a moat dotted with pink lotuses and with fountains at each corner). The area is beautifully illuminated during the periods of the king's and queen's birthdays. But if you are really curious, you can write for an appointment to tour the Royal Projects facilities and displays amid experimental crop fields and dairy pastureland (for enquiries in English, call Maew on 0 2282 7171-4).

### Dusit Zoo

*71 Thanon Rama V (0 2281 2000/www.zoothailand. org). Bus 5, 18, 28, 70, 108, 125, 510, 515.* **Open** 9am-6pm daily. **Admission** B30; B5 concessions. **No credit cards**. **Map** p309 E1.

Bangkok Governor Samak wants to move the state zoological park from its 47-acre site in Rama V's former botanical garden to a location in the suburbs. The plan is to give the zoo a similar amount of space to that enjoyed by the privately run Safari World (*see p163*), while converting its current site into a public park. In a sense, though, Dusit Zoo already functions as a park, with Thai families coming here to relax in their Sunday best surrounded by gardens, mature trees, open-air restaurants (raided by scavenging crows) and a lake, where pedalos brave the spray from a soaring fountain plume. There are even amusement rides and a dinosaur theme park.

As for the animals, they're cramped and forlorn in their concrete habitat (though this is one of Asia's better zoos). There's an assortment of Asiatic jackals, scarlet macaws, white-cheeked gibbons, tigers, golden Thai pythons and pygmy hippos. Along the western side are enclosures for Malayan tapirs and Asiatic elephants (the latter offering rides), and a central aviary containing a wealth of species. But the liveliest areas by far are the lofty octagonal monkey enclosures. Tyres on chains enable some faux-jungle acrobatics by pig-tailed macaques, punk-haired silvered langurs, and banded langurs with black tails three times longer than their bodies. Sadly, anyone who has seen gibbons or orangutans in the wild will probably end up more depressed than impressed by the spectacle.

### Government House

*Thanon Phitsanulok (0 2280 3000/www.thaigov. go.th). Bus 10, 16, 23, 99, 201, 505, 509, 515.* **Open** 8.30am-4.30pm Children's Day (2nd Sat in Jan) only. **Admission** free. **Map** p309 D2.

Built in the sixth reign, Government House's filigree stone frontage is asymmetrically flanked by square and domed circular turrets, with Byzantine-style

*Sightseeing*

frescoes on the main ceilings. Refurbished to host the APEC (Asia-Pacific Economic Corporation) summit in 2003, the building is targeted in most hot seasons (mid February to mid May) by rural demonstrators from the Forum of the Poor, who camp by the adjacent canal to voice grievances about everything from eco woes to corruption.

## Wat Benchamabophit

*69 Thanon Rama V (0 2282 7413). Bus 5, 16, 23, 50, 70, 72, 99, 201, 503, 505, 509.* **Open** 8am-5.30pm daily. **Admission** B20. **No credit cards. Map** p309 D2.

Dubbed the 'marble temple' (it's clad in the Italian cararra stone left over from Ananta Samakhom Throne Hall), this is a particularly well-proportioned melding of Eastern and Western styles. The *bot* (ordination hall) has stained glass windows glittering with jewel-like scenes from Thai mythology. Both the *bot* and cloister were commissioned in 1899 by Rama V, who was a monk in the original Ayutthaya-era temple. The work was carried out by Italian architect Hercules Manfredi, and no major temple has been built in Bangkok since.

In another room are King Chulalongkorn's ashes, along with a replica of Thailand's second most venerated Buddha image (the first being Phra Kaew, the Emerald Buddha): the 14th-century Phra Phutta Chinirat (the haloed Sukhothai-style original is in Wat Phra Si Rattana Mahathat in Pitsanulok province). Lining the cloister are a further 53 famous Buddha images, of every conceivable era, style, *mudra* (gesture) and provenance.

The temple is also a good spot to see Buddhist festivals and morning alms collection (the monks don't perambulate, but receive alms standing on Thanon Nakhon Pathom).

## Samsen

Dusit's northern hinterland is a grid of tree-lined avenues containing the further education facilities of the **Ratchabhat Institute** and the exclusive **Vachirawut School**. Thanon Sukhothai, between Thanons Rama V and Nakhon Ratchasima, has a small northern Thai community where little English is spoken – but say *khao soi* (noodle curry) and you'll get the favourite Lanna lunch dish. Branching off Sukhothai towards filthy Khlong Samsen, Thanon Suphan is a lovely, leaf-dappled street with some open-air food stalls and a sacred *bodhi* tree (the species under which the Buddha found enlightenment) swathed in protective sashes and offerings.

If all this tranquillity leaves you craving a dose of hectic Bangkok, there's always Thanon Samsen. It follows the river north past Samsen railway station, co-op housing and fine art at **Project 304** (*see p170*) and **Numthong Gallery** (*see p172*), and heads south towards Banglamphu. Down Samsen Soi 13 a riverside

Vietnamese community surrounds **St Francis Xavier Church** (*see p82*); nearby is the **Wat Ratchathiwat** monastery (*see p82*). At the **National Library** (*see p81*), an extension of Thanon Sri Ayutthaya leads past the **SEAMEO-SPAFA** activities centre (*see p82*), guesthouses and temples to **Kaloang Home Kitchen** seafood restaurant. Take a breather in the little park on the corner of Uthong Nok Road or in **Thewet Flower Market** (*see p133*).

Finally, tucked behind hideous shophouses on the left of Samsen, is **Wat Indrawihan** (*see p82*), with the pleasingly modernist **Bank**

# Dusit Park

The lush royal estate of Dusit Park, encompassing **Ananta Samakhom Throne Hall** (*see p77*) and **Parliament** (*see p77*), is best known for **Wang Vimanmek** (pictured), the world's largest golden teak building. But there are plenty of other attractions in this canal-laced compound, including diverse museums offering rare insights into royal family members past and present, their interests and their spectacular ceremonies. The compound and court life are explained through continuous audio-visual displays in the **Slide Multivision Hall**.

Completed in 1901, Vimanmek – 'abode of the angels in the clouds' – was home to Rama V for five years. The free, compulsory guided tour (every 30-40 minutes from 9.45am to 3.15pm daily) provides a chance to do some proper snooping; a winding staircase leads to the royal apartment (atop an octagonal tower), where such obscure personal items as a crystal chamber pot and Rama V's wooden wheelchair survive. Downstairs is the Throne Hall, with its four ornate thrones, while sublime panelled corridors connect yet more rooms bristling with antiques. In the lakeside *sala*, dance and martial arts are performed at 10.30am and 2pm, along with fruit carving (free; photography B20).

Other mansions contain carriages, clocks, ritual paraphernalia such as palanquins, and treasures from the prehistoric World Heritage Site of Baan Chiang in Udon Thani province. An **Ancient Cloth Museum** illustrates the diversity, meanings and status-indicators of the patterns in Thai textiles, while upstairs are scenes from Rama V's trips to Europe.

of **Thailand** just opposite. The latter stands in front of **Wang Bangkhunprom** (*see p82*), a former palace best viewed from Rama VIII Bridge (*see p74*).

### National Library

*Tha Wasukri, Thanon Samsen (0 2281 5212/ www.natlib.moe.go.th). Bus 3, 9, 16, 19, 30, 32, 33, 49, 64, 65, 66, 505, 506.* **Open** 9am-7.30pm daily. **Admission** free. **Map** p308 C1.

Incongruous though it may seem in a country where reading is more often than not seen as something of a chore rather than a pleasure, this handsome structure (with its mid 20th-century Thai-style roof and impressive lobby) gets surprisingly crowded.

However, this may, of course, have something to do with all the fashion and soap opera magazines, not to mention amulets, that are stored on the ground floor. On the next level up, books on social sciences share shelf space with those devoted to technology, religion and language (most are written in Thai, but each section also carries a number of English volumes). The third floor is devoted to art, literature and history. In other buildings, you'll find the King Bhumibol Commemorative Library – a tribute to the king's achievements in art and philanthropy – and the Princess Sirindhorn Music Library – which honours the king's second daughter and is devoted to Thai instrumentation.

For her part, Queen Sirikit has been pivotal in preserving the exquisite court arts and other Thai crafts through the Support Foundation at Bang Sai; you can find some of these masterpieces in the **Support Museum**. But wait to buy souvenirs until you reach the **Abhisek Dusit Throne Hall** (a gem of wooden tracery), where the shop is much better value than the souvenir-lined entrance to Vimanmek.

Often missed in the north-eastern corner of the park, the **Chang Ton National Museum** could do with some restoration – echoing the elephant's current sad predicament. Converted from a white elephant stable in 1988, it features a model of the Brahmin ceremony that is held when a prestigious *chang ton* (white elephant) is discovered. Not merely an albino, this elephant (which automatically belongs to the king) must display other distinguishing marks, such as reddish skin and pinkish-white features, including its hair, tail hair, eyes, nails, palate and genitals. What's more, these elephants mustn't labour, so the obligation of caring for one could drain a noble's finances (hence the English phrase 'white elephant', denoting something grand yet impractical). Tusks, ivory regalia and *mahout* charms are displayed alongside details of catching and corralling the beast, and statues of Ganesha, the revered Hindu god of art, knowledge and much else.

Examples of King Rama IX's photography can be found in **King Bhumibol Photographic Museums I and II**. Images of his youth feature in the **Suan Hong Royal Ceremonies Photography Museum**, a gorgeous green wooden mansion. Another fretwork fantasia, **Suan Si Reudu Hall**, has been reconstructed on its original site and displays Golden Jubilee gifts to Rama IX. The filigree **Hor Pavilion** was also moved here in 1998.

### Dusit Park

*16 Thanon Ratchawithi (0 2628 6300-5). Bus 12, 18, 28, 70, 108, 510, 516.* **Open** 9.30am-4pm daily. **Admission** B75 Thais; B100 foreigners; B20 concessions (Thais only); free with stub from Grand Palace B200 ticket. **Map** p309 D1.

### St Frances Xavier Church

*94 Samsen Soi 13 (0 2243 0060-2). Bus 3, 9, 16, 19, 30, 32, 33, 49, 64, 65, 66, 505, 506.* **Services** 6am, 7pm Mon-Sat; 6.30am, 8.30am, 10am, 4pm Sun. **Map** p308 C1.

There's a substantial Vietnamese community in the area surrounding this mid 19th-century church (as evidenced by various cafés dispensing delicacies from Saigon). But beyond the ornate black and gold gates it has a cheery Mediterranean feel, with a dainty shrine of its patron saint on the portico. In the basketball court at the back there's a statue of Christ attempting to heal a kneeling man (though the offerings around it are Buddhist-style jasmine garlands). The adjacent Soi 13 is quite picturesque, and on the north side is the strange, beautifully

# The god king

Thais refer to their kings as *pra jao paan din* ('god of the earth'), because they are seen as reincarnations of Vishnu, and they continue to be revered even after their deaths. King Chulalongkorn (aka Rama V) is particularly highly thought of. As well as abolishing slavery and staving off Western colonialism, he learned about his subjects' concerns by disguising himself as a commoner. In gratitude, his portrait is widely venerated in homes, restaurants and workplaces. On Chulalongkorn Day, 23 October (the anniversary of his death), devotees gather in Royal Plaza at his equestrian statue (a six-metre/20-foot bronze he had cast during a 1907 visit to France). Offerings are also made here on Tuesday and Thursday evenings, asking for luck in business, advice on marital matters or good exam results. The press reported that a gaggle of college girls even brought 999 pink roses to pray for new boyfriends. More common offerings tend to include two of the monarch's favourite things: cognac and cigars.

renovated Pou Pee House, its façade rendered in pink with cherubs, gold fittings and a Greek goddess brandishing a torch on the roof. Masses at the church are held in Thai.

### SEAMEO-SPAFA

*81/1 Thanon Sri Ayutthaya (0 2280 4022-7/ www.seameo-spafa.org). Bus 3, 9, 16, 19, 30, 32, 33, 49, 64, 65, 66, 505, 506.* **Open** 8.30am-4.30pm Mon-Fri. **Admission** free. **Map** p309 E2.

The marathon acronym (South-east Asian Ministers of Education Organisation Regional Centre for Archaeology and Fine Arts) indicates this non-ASEAN (Association of South-east Asian Nations) body's support of cultural heritage. Activities include training, workshops, lectures, academic tours and performances; there are also publications in English and a library.

### Wang Bangkhunprom & Bank of Thailand Museum

*273 Thanon Samsen (0 2283 5286/www.bot.or.th). Bus 3, 9, 16, 19, 30, 32, 33, 49, 64, 65, 66, 505, 506.* **Open** by appointment 9am-4pm Mon-Fri. **Admission** free. **Map** p308 C2.

This Renaissance edifice remained the palace of Prince Baripatra until the end of absolutism in 1932. Now owned by the Bank of Thailand (with a museum to prove it), its baroque and art nouveau touches are still worth a look. But you can't just stroll in off the street – one week's written notice is required. The museum charts Thai monetary evolution from glass beads to notes, via *pot duang*, the embossed 'bullet coins' that were in currency for six centuries from Sukhothai to Rattanakosin.

### Wat Indrawihan

*144 Thanon Visut Kasat (0 2281 1406). Bus 3, 9, 16, 19, 30, 32, 33, 49, 64, 65, 66, 505, 506.* **Open** 6am-6pm daily. **Admission** free. **Map** p308 C2.

Hidden down an alley between grim shophouses, Wat Indrawihan is only really notable for its standing Buddha. Eschewing the usual exquisite proportions, this figure is a lofty 32m (105ft) tall – you can climb to its head for a so-so rooftop panorama – but unfeasibly thin. In fact, it has to be anchored by enormous feet, which are decked in offerings. The adjacent *vihaan* (chapel) poignantly features *benjarong* (five-coloured traditional ceramic) jars of human ashes in its terrace walls.

### Wat Ratchathiwat

*3 Thanon Samsen Soi 9 (0 2243 2125). Bus 3, 9, 16, 19, 30, 32, 33, 49, 64, 65, 66, 505, 506.* **Open** 5am-9pm daily. **Admission** free. **Map** p308 C1.

Restored by Rama IV, this monastery contains two remarkable buildings. The *ubosot* (ordination hall) contains a mural by Italian professor C Rigoli behind a stone façade with Khmer accents by Prince Naris. Prince Naris also restyled the rather Ayutthayan Sala Karnparian, a sublime wooden pavilion with intricate relief panels and complex eaves. It is often compared with Naris' Wat Suwannaram instruction hall in Petchaburi.

# Chinatown

Bangkok's most congested district is a glorious puzzle of bewildering markets, alleys, temples and shrines.

Bangkok may be the capital of Thailand, but it has never been a quintessentially Thai city. It was shaped by the Chinese, both economically and physically, from the earliest shophouses to modern skyscrapers. Many of the city's businesses and almost all its banks (until post-1997 mergers with foreign finance houses) owe their success to the industrious offspring of Chinese labourers who started arriving here in the 18th century.Their political and social influence has never been higher; the government boasts many wealthy Thai-Chinese businessmen – including the prime minister.

Thailand's savvy approach to the rise of China echoes its successful policy toward European colonialism: remain independent through embracing some of its attributes. Things Chinese have become fashionable, cultural exchanges are frequent, Chinese tourists are a huge and growing sector, and an ASEAN-China free trade zone is proposed. Sino-Thai firms are even investing in Shanghai malls. Renewed confidence in Chinese cultural expression is focused on historical Chinatown, with the formerly quiet, family-and-temple-oriented **Chinese New Year** (*see p159*) becoming a state-sponsored street festival, led by the finance minister in Chinese costume.

Chinese were living in Bangkok even before the city existed. Originally invited by King Taksin (himself half Teochew) to augment the workforce, they came by ship from southern China and settled on the opposite bank of the river from the then capital, Thonburi. When King Rama I relocated to the east bank, the Chinese were shifted south of the new city wall in 1782 to a dirt alley called Sampheng. From that nucleus grew today's Chinatown.

The Thai expression 'to travel with a mat and a pot' sums up how little the immigrants brought. Mainly Teochew, with some Hainanese, Cantonese and Hokkien, they worked hard and saved even harder. Soon they were among the wealthiest commoners and generally looked upon favourably by the Thai authorities, though there was a period of nationalist suspicion in the 1920s. King Mongkut (Rama IV, 1851-68) apparently promoted immigration and intermarriage with a view to imbuing his subjects with some of that famous Chinese work ethic. Until polygamy was abolished in the court, wealthy Chinese families offered daughters as consorts, thus entering the blue bloodline.

The original settlers maintained close ties with China, though they had little option but to assimilate after World War II, due to controls on

Catching a nap above busy **Thanon Charoen Krung**.

teaching Chinese languages and on immigration because of fear of communist infiltration. Given the scarcity of ethnic Chinese women, they took Thai wives and surnames (usually long compounds of auspicious words). The Chinese have integrated so well that today it's hard to gauge their magnitude. Some estimate that more than ten per cent of the population and more than half of all Bangkokians have Chinese genes.

Fewer Sino-Thais live in Chinatown nowadays: the wealthier families have moved to suburban mansions, and the ubiquitous shophouses have become offices, warehouses or wholesale shops selling products now rarely made within the community. Yet many commute daily back to an air-conditioned cubicle in the back of their shop to have the final say and issue change on all transactions, overseeing a new migrant staff – from Thailand's north-east.

Until Bangkok sprawled, Chinatown sold goods unavailable elsewhere in the city, and it had Bangkok's first department stores, then convenient for the international traders down Charoen Krung near the Oriental Hotel. While some streets are diverse, others conform to 'one *thanon*, one product' (*see below* **Guns 'n' roses**), which the government made into the 'One Tambon, One Product' policy for villages nationwide (*see p150* **Weaving dreams**). To appreciate the area's dependence on merchants, visit during Chinese New Year, the only time they shut. Chinatown – indeed, Bangkok – suddenly empties.

### GET LOST

Officially bordered by Khlong Phadung Krung Kasem, the river, Khlong Ong Ang and Thanon Charoen Krung, Chinatown spreads west to Khlong Lord and north towards Khlong Mahanak. It can be divided into three swathes parallel to the river: **Thanon Yaowarat** and **Thanon Charoen Krung** are thoroughfares, while the lanes of **Sampeng Lane** and **Thanon Songwat** are better for strolling (*see p86* **Walk 4: Godown town**).

Explore Chinatown logically and you'll miss half the fun and half the sights. It's better to follow your nose (both scents and stenches) down microscopic *trok* (paths) and risk getting lost until a landmark pops up. Confusingly, Chinese street names on rickety signs are giving way to Thai appellations on blue placards, hence fascinating **Soi Issaranuphap** is officially **Soi 16** and **Wanit Soi 1** is actually **Sampeng** (*see p132*), Chinatown's first and foremost market. Once notorious for opium dens, brothels, pawnshops and gambling dens, today it teems with nothing more dangerous than roving snack merchants and motorbikes overloaded with bolts of fabric.

Depending on time – and energy – there are many ways to 'do' Chinatown. You could focus on temples (Buddhist, Taoist, Chinese, Sikh and Chinese). Or markets. Or food (from stalls to fancy restaurants). Or weird juxtapositions: casket makers near chicken hatcheries; mosquito coils beside cock rings. Or crane your neck up at the architecture, notably along Charoen Krung, Songwat and Ratchawong, though there are details to relish on wooden shophouses in offshoots such as Charoen Krung Sois 20 and 23. The classical columns, Sino-Portuguese detailing, sculpted shutters, tiered balconies and bursts of art deco are often partially obscured, but are amazingly free of high-rises. Presumably no one can afford enough land to build them.

All of the above can be found in any given area, so there's no need to rush around. Still, you need a spirit of adventure, a tolerance for heat and crowds, light clothing, comfy shoes, plenty of fluids and the invaluably annotated *Nancy Chandler's Map of Bangkok*. Alternatively, follow two signposted walks from a booth dispensing maps at River City.

# Guns 'n' roses

Need a Beretta, Benelli or Smith & Wesson .38? The strangest of Chinatown's one-product streets has to be the gun shops along **Thanon Burapha** near Charoen Krung. The average tourist probably doesn't have the credentials to buy a firearm (though sleazy *farangs* with bar girls have been spotted in negotiation), but window-shopping is vicariously thrilling.

At the other extreme is flower power. Buying all the B50-bunches of roses you can carry (something Bangkokians do on a post-nightclub detour) wouldn't make a dent in the floralia that floods Thanon Chakphet, where **Pak Khlong Talad** flower market (*see p133*) is at its busiest at night.

Other one-street wonders include herbalists (Thanon Rama IV west of Hualamphong station); stationery (Thanon Chakrawat between Sampeng and Yaowarat); metal cables (Thanon Songwat near Phanu Rangsi); paper funeral offerings (Thanon Phlubphlachai); and even one devoted solely to plastic and jute rice sacks (Thanon Songsawat near Songwat). More culturally interesting, Thanon Plangnam is where you'll find assorted ritual paraphernalia such as masks, swords and tea sets.

## Thanon Yaowarat

For both tourists and locals, Yaowarat is Chinatown – an orientation word for a taxi driver. Today's PR message is that Yaowarat has actually all along been shaped like a dragon, a lucky one, of course, with the creature's eye being Odeon Circle. Hence this traffic island where Yaowarat meets Charoen Krung now hosts the **Soom Pratu Chalerm Prakiat** (Chinese Arch).

Chinatowns all over the world announce their presence with some sort of gate; Bangkok's gate was erected in 1999 to commemorate King Rama IX's 72nd birthday, the illustrious sixth cycle of both Thai and Chinese 12-year calendars. One of the dragon's 'horns', tree-lined Thanon Traimit, is blessed by the solid gold Buddha in **Wat Traimit** (*see p87*), beyond which there are old bamboo stores, where brooms, baskets and utensils are still crafted by hand.

Traffic flows one way east up the dragon's mane (Charoen Krung) and west down its back (Yaowarat), with its forelegs supposedly Thanon Songwat. *Thong* (gold) is a recurrent theme in long, diverse Yaowarat. Just stand at Phadung Dao intersection and be dazzled by the garish red and gold frontages and street signs resembling deco-era cinemas.

Yaowarat is also famed for its restaurants and food stalls, both expensive. After dark it becomes one huge night market of vendors, spreading into Soi Plaeng Nam and Soi Phadung Dao (also called Soi Texas Suki, after an exalted sukiyaki outlet).

For a respite, take Soi Issranuphap to **Talaat Kao** (Old Market, which has been trading every morning for two centuries) and Sampeng Lane, or right through **Talaat Mai** (New Market, a mere century old) to Leng Noi Yee temple. Thanon Ratchawong forms the dragon's hind legs, with the tail (lined with hardware shops) ending at **Merry King Department Store**.

# **Walk 4** Godown town

Chinatown's riverside is still cluttered with godowns (warehouses) that were pivotal to Bangkok's trade. However, weaving through them on its first roads inland, Thanon Songwat and Sampeng Lane, this walk encapsulates this multicultural, multifaceted district perfectly.

Starting as an alley north from River City antiques mall (*see p138*), Wanit Soi 2 passes **Wat Kalawar** (Holy Rosary Church, 0 2266 4849) on the left, a Gothic riverside edifice built in 1787 on land given to the Portuguese for helping to fight the Burmese. On the path joining Soi Charoen Phanit, an ATM stands at the gate of Thailand's first bank building (1904), a classical edifice still part of **Siam Commercial Bank** (0 2237 5000, open 8.30am-3.30pm Mon-Fri). The **Harbour Department** pier faces a famous duck-on-rice restaurant before you enter a maze of lanes coated in oil from engine parts, the trade of this precinct named **Talad Noi** after a cute 'little market' on the right, between Charoen Krung Sois 22 and 20.

Down the left turn opposite, follow signs to the **Riverview Guesthouse** (*see p41*), where the rooftop restaurant offers an amazing panorama. Secreted beyond is the 200-year-old **San Jao Sien Khong** (open 6am-6pm daily). Reputedly the oldest Chinese shrine in Chinatown, it's the only one facing the Chao Phraya river from this bank (a couple of

Gold shops are numerous. Ubiquitous dragons adorn awnings over counters of jewellery, with armed guards highly visible. The most famous gold merchant is **Tang Toh Kang** (345 Wanit Soi 1, 0 2225 2898, plus four branches). Others noted for high gold content include **Hua Seng Heng** (295-7 Thanon Yaowarat, 0 2224 0077) and **Chin Hua Heng** (332-4 Thanon Yaowarat, 0 2225 0202). Yaowarat gold is soft and yellow thanks to its 97.5 per cent purity. It's sold not in ounces, but in *baht* (different from the currency, one *baht* equals 15.2 grammes, subdivided into four *saleung* of 25 *satang*). Gold is viewed as portable (and visible) wealth, and banks and pawnshops post buy/sell rates for those needing cash in a hurry. Traditional pawnshops are also prevalent.

### Wat Traimit

*661 Thanon Charoen Krung (0 2225 9775). Bus 1, 4, 25, 35, 40, 49, 53, 73, 75, 159, 507.* **Open** 8am-5pm daily. **Admission** *Temple* free. *Golden Buddha* B20. **No credit cards. Map** p309 & p310 D8.

In drab surroundings, the world's biggest solid gold Buddha statue has an almost liquid lustre that is arguably less flattering than the gold leaf on its less prestigious counterparts. The Sukothai-era image – 3m (10ft) high and 5.5tonnes (4.9tons) in weight – had been covered by thick stucco to hide it from marauding Burmese and remained unrecognised until 1955, when its shell cracked on being dropped from a crane during its move here.

## Thanon Charoen Krung

Occasionally still called 'New Road' because it was Bangkok's first paved street (1861), Thanon Charoen Krung begins around **Baan Mor Market** (*see p132*) and runs one way south-east before going on a detour at Mitraphan/Songsawat, and re-emerging to skirt the river south through Bangrak until meeting Thanon Rama III.

Its first landmark is **Sala Chalerm Krung** theatre (*see p202*), the last remnant of an

Sightseeing

Chinese pagodas loom on the Thonburi side). During the **Vegetarian Festival** (*see p161*), palm oil replaces engine grease as the lubricant of choice at stalls selling meat and spice-free food to white-clad devotees of Kuan Yin, while the temple plays host to continuous Chinese opera, bygone fairground games and burning incense.

Return via narrow, barely signed Wanit Soi 2 to its end at Soi Phanu Rangsi. Turn right and immediately left on to **Thanon Songwat**, which runs close to the river. Some time-warp alleys lead down to the river between ancient Chinese godowns with deceptively modern frontages, where spice and rice merchants store gunny sacks or display huge grandfather clocks and heavy mother-of-pearl inlaid furniture. When the *soi* becomes one way, gaze up at several beautiful but woefully unrestored Sino-European buildings on the right.

Where Songwat ends at **Thanon Ratchawong**, a famous vendor peddles *khanom jeeb* (Chinese minced pork dumplings) from a huge antique brass steamer in front of the 7-11 shop. Cross Ratchawong and head right (north), then go left at the people-packed crosswalk marking **Sampeng Lane**. Off this chaotic market alley narrow walkways (often obscured by racks of polyester clothes) lead left (south) to unexpected adventures. Sampeng emerges

on to busy **Thanon Chakrawat**. Bear left to a large metal grille (with a 100-year-old Chinese herbalist on one side). This is the entrance to **Wat Chakrawat**, a peaceful temple with two tall *prang*, an artificial hillside housing burial urns and a grotto with a supposed Buddha shadow on one wall. And two ponds of large and languid crocodiles...

Back on Chakrawat, cross the pedestrian bridge just to the south, then turn left a few steps north on to **Soi Bhopit Phimuk**, an alley of shophouses filled with smells of cinnamon, star anise and assorted spices. After crossing tree-lined **Khlong Ong Ang**, suddenly you're not in Chinatown any more, Dorothy. You're facing Little India.

Heading left toward the river, **Thanon Chakkaphet** leads on to Phra Pok Klao bridge, beside the first bridge to span the river, the elegant stone Saphan Phut (Memorial Bridge). It was built in 1932 to honour King Rama I, whose seated statue in a landscaped park commands its approaches. Behind him is the royal temple of **Wat Ratchaburana** (119 Thanon Chakkaphet, 0 2221 9544). Restored since being bombed in World War II, it was built as Wat Liab Jeen in Ayutthayan times by a Chinese trader called Liab. Come nightfall, stalls flood Saphan Phut flea market and **Pak Khlong Talad** flower market (*see p133*) west along Thanon Chakkaphet.

Having a break from the city's bustle.

art-deco chain. With its well-restored wrought-iron detailing and sweeping red-carpeted staircase, it hosts everything from film premieres and festivals to Thai classical dance and Bollywood screenings for the Indian community of Pahurat. Completing this block is **Old Siam Plaza**, a quaint mall of sympathetic design stocking much that you'd find in Chinatown, only in air-conditioned comfort. Don't miss the ground-floor Thai snacks and desserts. Using original recipes and equipment, women in traditional dress create ever-rarer delicacies, such as *khanom krob* (coconut milk batter steamed in tiny cast-iron moulds).

Beyond a block called Wang Burapha after a long-gone palace, stalls clad both sides of Khlong Ong Ang at **Saphan Lek Market** (*see p133*), and **Woeng Nakhon Kasem** (bordered by Thanon Boriphat, Yaowarat, Chakrawat and Charoen Krung) retains its nom de plume 'Thieves' Market', though it's no longer fencing stolen goods. Before **Khlong Thom Market** (*see p132*), change pace south down Thanon Chakrawat to enter **Wat Chai Channa Songkhram** (0 2221 4317), notable both for its Khmer *prang* and its proximity to a night-time dessert vendor on Nakhon Kasem Soi 4 (create your own confection from sweet ingredients in antique copper bowls).

Passing **Leng Noi Yee** temple (*see p89*) are other entrances to Soi Issaranuphap and Talad Mai, before a left turn leads to **Thanon Phlubphlachai**, where dealers in funerary paraphernalia congregate around **Li Thi Miew Temple** (494 Thanon Plabplachai, 0 2221 6985), a small Daoist shrine with a neighbourhood feel. You can see craftspeople making satin banners and complex paper accoutrements – fake money, clothes, houses, cars – all to be burned with the deceased to provide for the soul. Some were doubtless retrieved by the **Poh Teck Tung** foundation nearby (*see p89* **Body snatchers**).

At the bewildering Charoen Krung/Mitraphap/Rama IV junction, head north up Thanon Mitraphap to the 22 July Circle (the date Thailand dispatched forces to help the Allies in World War I). Back southwards, toward Rama IV, Thanon Maitreechit passes the art bar **About Café** (*see p169*) and **San Chao Mae Tubtim**, a joss house where Chinese opera is performed in the **Vegetarian Festival** (*see p161*) in October. North from the circle lies Pomprab, a less congested extension of Chinatown known for its **Talad Fai Chai** (Flashlight Market) running from 5pm on Saturdays until 6pm Sunday around Thanons Luang, Chakrawat, Charoen Krung and Suapa. It's so named because you can't separate the junk from the treasures without a torch.

# Body snatchers

Many Sino-Thais curry favour with the spirits of the dead by offering goods and money at **Poh Teck Tung** (326 Thanon Chao Khamrop, near Thanon Phlubphlachai, 0 2226 4444-8, open 8am-7pm daily), even if the deceased aren't relatives. This unusual Chinatown shrine is home to a charity foundation that organises the collection and burial or cremation of bodies unclaimed at crash scenes. In the early 1990s volunteers from Poh Teck Tung and a rival rescue foundation fought over who got first dibs on the corpses, until they were allocated set zones for their work. Funerary offerings sold outside include elaborate paper models made in the shops opposite, including some of houses more grandiose than the unfortunate crash victims ever inhabited.

Pomprab is bordered by Khlong Mahanak and Khlong Phadung Krung Kasem, a canal lined with flame trees, shophouses and the railway line from Hualumphong station. From here the subway should pass beneath Charoen Krung and the river to Thonburi.

## Leng Noi Yee

*Thanon Charoen Krung, between Thanon Mangkorn & Soi Issaranuphap (0 2237 5000). Bus 1, 16, 35, 36, 75, 93, 162.* **Open** 8.30am-3.30pm Mon-Fri. **Map** p309 & p310 D8.
Set behind an imposing multi-tiered entrance, the 'Dragon Flower Temple', also known as Wat Mangkorn Kamalawat, is Chinatown's biggest. Its courtyard is ringed by several sermon halls filled with statues of Mahayana Buddhist and Taoist deities. Dating from 1871, it takes on a livelier and folksier ambience during the Vegetarian Festival.

## Pahurat

From its inception, Chinatown was divided into specialised trading areas based on ethnicity. The block bordered by Thanon Chakkaphet, ATM Alley, Thanon Triphet and Thanon Pahurat is still Little India. The east side of Chakkaphet is known for its travel agents, seedy cafés blasting Punjabi rock and for the **Royal India** restaurant (*see p107*) on a side alley. Outside its ornately carved door, Indian sweet makers stir huge woks of confectionery. Cross Chakkaphet and turn right at a Chinese temple, passing the dowdy **ATM Department Store** and a vegetarian samosa cart, before darting left into ATM Alley. With its open-air shops selling incense, Indian CDs and DVDs, Ganesh statues, saris, bangles, bindis and spiced *chai* (tea), this funky pedestrian passageway feels more like Mumbai than Bangkok.

The maze-like **Pahurat** cloth market (*see p132*) is similar to Sampeng, except it's in rows under one large roof. Inside (directions are hopeless) looms the yellow onion-domed **Sri Gurunsingh Sabha**, a four-storey Sikh temple (0 2221 1011). The northern perimeter on Thanon Pahurat stocks Thai classical dancers' costumes.

Sightseeing

# Downtown

Sprawling Downtown conceals gems of history and modernism, not to mention the city's best choice of shops, restaurants and entertainment.

Ask a local where Bangkok's Downtown is and their directions will depend on their age and interests. Senior citizens point to the Old Town, whereas youngsters would say Siam Square. Business types proffer Thanons Silom and Sathorn, but bus-riders would indicate the nexus around Victory Monument. And shoppers would advocate Ratchaprasong Intersection, site of the Erawan Shrine and hyped as the city's retail crossroads.

Reinventing itself at speed, the capital keeps shifting its centre of gravity, driven by whim, rivalry, real estate and a legendary resistance to urban planning. Ten years ago Thanon Ratchadaphisek (in the North-east) was going to be the new business district; five years ago Thanon Rama III (South) was touted as the next banking hub. The vaunted 'Bangkok plan', drafted by MIT (Massachusetts Institute of Technology) in 1996, posited the theory that the rail junction at Makkasan swamp (North)

represented the last chance to plan a coherent central business district. The lack of clarity was largely down to the lack of a transport network, and as soon as the BTS SkyTrain imposed a structure, its lines came to define Downtown. And as BTS extensions and the new subway continue to pierce the suburbs, development will increasingly cluster around stations.

The BTS Silom line skirts Lumphini Park and ploughs into **Bangrak**, through its financial and nightlife district to the river and its walkable old international commercial quarter around the Oriental hotel. The BTS lines intersect at **Pathumwan**, scene of intense competition in shopping, fashion, sport and youth culture. Its eastern arm down **Sukhumvit** accesses the area's hotels, restaurants, bars, shops and upmarket residences, and it heads to **North** around the Victory Monument to make Chatuchak Weekend Market suddenly easy to reach. Attractions in Downtown's largely residential **South** are served by both the BTS and the (as we go to press, still to be completed) subway.

It's also possible to tour Downtown the old-fashioned way – by canal boat – since Khlong Saen Saep delineates the north of Pathumwan, Sukhumvit and suburbs to the East, facing North, and suburbs to the North-east. The subway will open up the North-east – making the **Thailand Cultural Centre** (*see p202*) less of a trek. Commuter trains will eventually extend all the way to the Outer North, towards Bangkok Airport and the metropolitan districts of Nonthaburi province, where major expos and concerts draw thousands to Impact Arena.

Downtown is the most convenient place to stay, eat, shop and get things done, but since the features of its skyline and streetscapes are continually appearing, disappearing and mutating, this makes for some fascinating juxtapositions: spiritualism versus materialism, tastefulness fending off vulgarity, extravagance pitted against destitution. Amid the gleaming malls and slums, you find traditional houses, Asian antiquities, tranquil parks and spiritual homes to Buddhism, Hinduism and Christianity – plus the chance to cuddle some snakes.

Admission is free to venues listed below, unless otherwise stated.

## The best Views

### For the highest, furthest panorama
**Baiyoke II Tower** – the sea is (just) visible through its windows. *See p97.*

### For river life
**Rama VIII Bridge** is the city's newest observation deck. *See p74.*

### For eating or swimming in the clouds
**Banyan Tree Bangkok Hotel** has a spa and dining more than 50 storeys up. *See p48.*

### For spiritual highs
The **Golden Mount** *chedi* offers 360° views of old and new. *See p67.*

### For famous landmarks
**Supatra River House** surveys the Rattanakosin riverscape. *See p203.*

### For peering into private places
Jump on the **SkyTrain**, which cruises above wall height. *See p282.*

Hindu stylings at **Maha Uma Devi**.

East along Silom, heritage gets more artificial at **Silom Village**, a theatre, restaurant and shopping arcade rolled into a series of extended wooden houses. A hoard of gem stores entice tourists, with the towering **Jewellery Trade Centre** a testament to Bangkok's status in the global gem trade (*see p98* **Learn to: Gemology**). Beneath it, **Silom Galleria** is yet another art and antique mall.

Beyond the elaborate Hindu **Maha Uma Devi** temple (*see below*) and a dilapidated Chinese cemetery containing mausoleums is Silom's busier eastern end (where thousands of Siberian swallows flock in the trees from October to March). Copping a dropping is, rationalise the Thais, good luck. That could explain the fortunes of businesses around Saladaeng BTS station, which include corporate headquarters with eating and shopping arcades, **Silom Complex** mall, stand-alone shops and restaurants, famous seafood stalls and hotels, including the spired, triangular **Dusit Thani** (*see p41*), which overlooks Lumphini Park.

Bangrak means 'Village of Love' and its district office is besieged by nuptial couples on 14 February. Another kind of love is pursued every day down **Patpong Sois 1** and **2**, the most infamous of Silom's nightlife streets, from which a tourist night market spreads to encompass the bar strips of **Silom Soi 4** (beautiful people), **Silom Soi 2** (gay only) and **Soi Thaniya** (a Little Tokyo of authentic sushi bars and hostess karaoke bars).

Patpong and Thaniya link through to Thanon Surawong, which was Bangkok's tourist hub three decades ago (although it's since gone downhill). Halfway down to the river are the neighbouring **British Club** and **Neilson Hays Library**. Both dating from the early to mid 20th century, they were – and still are – social and cultural focal points for expats. The elegant library oozes charm and good reading, while its circular Rotunda Gallery stages regular exhibitions.

Leading off Silom toward Sathorn are **Soi Saladaeng** (a forked lane of restaurants ending in Surapon Gallery) and leafy **Soi Convent** (another dining parade leading past the Catholic St Joseph's Convent & School to the gothic Anglican Christ Church).

### Maha Uma Devi

*2 Thanon Pan (0 2238 4007)*. **Open** 6am-8pm Mon-Thur, Sat, Sun; 6am-9pm Fri. **Map** p310 E7. Founded in the 1860s by a Tamil community still largely resident hereabouts, this Hindu temple is dubbed Wat Khaek by Thais (*khaek* means 'guest'). It's always buzzing with Thai and Chinese, as well as Indians, making offerings to a small bronze statue of Uma Devi (Shiva's consort), and other images of Vishnu, Buddha and Uma's son, Ganesh. The temple's

## Bangrak

In the mid 19th century a new grid of canals defined the triangular Bangrak district – namely Rama IV, Si Phraya, Surawong, Silom and Sathorn, all subsequently paved as roads – apart from Khlong Sathorn, now reduced to a polluted gutter between thunderous highways. Bisecting them is newly embanked Khlong Chong Nonsi, which features a modern sculpture of a windmill at Thanon Silom (former site of the city's irrigation windmills).

Bangrak's riverside is hugged by Thailand's earliest paved road, Thanon Charoen Krung (aka New Road). The international trading quarter once occupied this stretch between River City antiques mall and Sathorn Bridge. The lanes around the Oriental hotel, the Assumption Cathedral and the Central Post Office retain human-scale appeal (*see p94* **Walk 5: Oriental quarter**) amid antique and craft shops, tailors, travel agents and Indian restaurants. South of a famous pawnshop on the corner of Silom lies a parade of old shophouses and animated **Bangrak Market**.

Sightseeing

multicoloured walls and structures (including a 6m/20ft tower) bristle with devotional sculptures. Rites of self-mortification happen here during the Vegetarian Festival (*see p161*) and the temple observes Diwali (usually in November).

## Patpong

The late Thai-Chinese millionaire Khun Patpongpanit turned a marshy banana plantation into this world-renowned fleshpot. Initially a recreation ground for wealthy locals and airline crews, it went go-go in the late 1960s as American GIs flocked here on R&R from the Vietnam War. Today the lacklustre pole-dancing and oft-raided sex shows provide titillation for tourists seeking to ogle, while outdoor bars on **Patpong Soi 2** tank up lonely booze-hounds. Any remaining frisson is fading through dilution by chainstores and the central **Night Market** (*see p134*).

## Pathumwan

Dug during the early 19th century for commercial and defensive reasons, Khlong Saen Saeb is now filthy, but it still offers glimpses of a bygone canalside life at **Jim Thompson's House Museum** (*see p94*), the former home of the famous American silk merchant. East of Thanon Phayathai the canal passes **Saprathum Palace**. Just visible from

the BTS, this private ochre-coloured edifice was home to the king's late mother, whose funerary tower is kept next door at **Wat Pathumwanaram** (*see p96*). The British, American and Dutch embassies occupy several historic buildings on or around Thanon Witthayu (Wireless Road). Behind the British Embassy and the **Hilton** hotel (*see p43*) on Khlong Saen Saeb, stands the **Nai Lert Shrine** (*see p95*) to phallus worship.

Parallel with the canal to the south, the contiguous avenue of Thanon Rama I and Thanon Ploenchit is hyped as Bangkok's main shopping street. East of the **National Stadium Pathumwan** (*see p207*) are the intricate mazes of boutiques, photo-sticker machines and art cafés at air-conditioned **MBK** (Mahboonkrong Centre; *see p150*) and open-air **Siam Square** where trendy young Thais hang out, often winding up at one of Centrepoint plaza's free gigs (Siam Square Sois 3-4). Chain restaurant pilgrims get their T-shirts at the **Hard Rock Café** (*see p191*).

Across the road, chic rules at the shopping malls of **Siam Discovery** (*see p151*), **Siam Centre** (*see p150*) and **Siam Paragon** (still under construction at time of writing). Around Ratchaprasong is the **World Trade Centre** (**WTC**; *see p151*), a huge faceless chunk of concrete that's enlivened during the cool season by vast competing beer gardens on its forecourt. Across the footbridge are the crafts mall of

**Jim Thompson's House Museum** in all its luxurious glory. *See p94.*

# Multiple phantasm

Spirits are so real to Thais that *phii* (ghosts) are a daily presence filling the pages of comics, newspapers, soap operas and movies – such as the oft-filmed story of Mae Nak Phrakhanong (*see p100* **Wat Maha But**). The shunning of old houses and furniture is a perfectly common occurrence, while buildings sited on former graveyards (Silom Plaza being a notable example) repel customers, and shrines appease danger spots such as Khong Yaek Roy Sop ('hundred corpse bend') on Thanon Kingkaew.

Among the infamous hauntings around the city are Baan Phitsanulok (the avoided prime ministerial residence); Silom's British Club (where herbs placate poltergeists); the First Hotel, following a 1990 fire that engulfed a couple of its floors; the Liberal Arts lift in Thammasat University (where protestors were shot in 1973); and Silpakorn

University's Sala Dtontree (once a palace nursery) and art gallery (above a dungeon), where a pillar is said to weep.

You can even join ghostbusting broadcasts live on the Shock (94FM, midnight Saturdays and Sundays) and see its listeners' ghostly photos in the Shock bar (465 Thanon Kamphaengphet, North, 0 2619 2682, open 6pm-2am daily).

Just don't expect quivering white sheets: Thais are specific about their spooks. Elongated *phii phraet* suffer pin-hole mouths due to greed, elderly *phii bhop* scoff raw chicken entrails, and disembodied *phii kraseu* trail their innards while seeking rotten food, cleaning their mouths on sarongs hung outdoors. But not all are nasty: *phii look krok* is a Casper-esque baby, and *phii dtanee* is a naughty girl living in banana trees, whose name graces the *gluay dtanee* banana.

**Naranyaphand**, the label haven of **Gaysorn Plaza** (*see p150*), the revered **Erawan Shrine** (*see below*) and, facing the restaurant avenue of Soi Lang Suan, the city's best department store, **Central Chidlom** (*see p138*).

Two entire blocks between Thanons Rama I and IV belong to Chulalongkorn University, the most prestigious in the country. The block west of Thanon Phayathai contains **Chulalongkorn Art Centre** (*see p169*) and **Suan Luang Night Market** (*see p135*); east of the road are Chulalongkorn Auditorium and the **Museum of Imaging Technology** (*see below*), with the **Snake Farm** (*see p95*) to the south. East of Thanon Henri Dunant you'll find the **Royal Bangkok Sports Club** (**RBSC**; *see p209*). Founded in 1901, it became *the* recreational spot for well-to-do Thais – and remains a bastion of old money. Serving as Bangkok's only airfield (before, that is, the one at Don Muang), its grounds contain one of the capital's two horse-racing tracks.

East of the green expanse of **Lumphini Park** (*see p95*) the new **Suan Lum Night Bazaar** (*see p135*) encompasses the puppetry at **Joe Louis Theatre** (*see p201*), with *Muay Thai* fights around the corner at **Lumphini Boxing Stadium** (*see p209*).

## Chulalongkorn University & Museum of Imaging Technology

*3rd Floor, Department of Photographic Science, Chulalongkorn University, Thanon Phyathai (0 2218 5583/www.sci.chula.ac.th). Bus 16, 21, 25, 29, 34,*

*36, 40, 47, 50, 93, 113, 159, 163, 501, 502, 529.* **Open** 9.30am-3.30pm Mon-Fri. **Admission** B20 Thais; B100 foreigners; free under-5s. **No credit cards. Map** p309 &p310 F5.

Named after Rama V, this leafy two-block campus has pleasant grounds, with a pond used for Loy Krathong rituals (*see p156*) in November. To the south, the Museum of Imaging Technology is an important archive of photographic development in the kingdom, an art form that has been supported by both Rama V and Rama IX.

### Erawan Shrine

*494 Thanon Ratchadamri (0 2252 8754). Chidlom BTS.* **Open** 6am-10pm daily. **Map** p311 G5.

Dwarfed by and yet dominating a supremely commercial intersection, this landmark exemplifies the Hindu and animist aspects of Thai faith. Swathed in carnation garlands and wooden elephant offerings, a mirror-tiled shelter contains a gilded four-headed image of Brahma (the Hindu god of creation) atop his elephant mount Airavata (aka Erawan). The shrine was erected in 1956 to appease the tree spirits made homeless after timbers were felled during the building of the original Erawan Hotel (on the site of the present Grand Hyatt Erawan). Construction had been dogged by accidents, such as workmen dying and marble lost at sea; the misfortunes ceased after the shrine was built. Thais passing the shrine, even on the SkyTrain or while driving, often *wai* (make a prayer-like gesture with both hands) in respect, while those seeking luck make offerings. Those whose wishes were answered return with more offerings, or else they pay one of the various Thai dancers who are on permanent standby at the shrine to perform.

**Nai Lert Shrine.** *See p95.*

## Jim Thompson's House Museum

*6 Soi Kasemsan 2, Thanon Rama I (0 2216 7368/ www.jimthompsonhouse.com). National Stadium BTS.* **Open** 9am-5.30pm daily (last entry 5pm). **Admission** B100; B50 under-25s; free under-10s. **Credit** AmEx, DC, MC, V. **Map** p310 F4.

The revival in Thai silk production and its international popularity is largely attributable to the vision of Jim Thompson, an American architect who first came to Thailand at the end of World War II as an officer in the OSS (now the CIA). After the war he returned to Bangkok to live, and soon became interested in the disappearing craft of silk weaving and design, then still practised in the Muslim Baan Khrua community facing his home across Khlong Saen Saeb. He quickly spotted the craft's marketing potential, and brilliant hues and shimmering textures became a sartorial trademark of the society figures that Thompson entertained at his remarkable house. Now an impressively run museum, it has proved an influential template for adapting Thai houses to contemporary living. The house has been left much as it was when Thompson mysteriously disappeared in 1967, while walking in Malaysia's Cameron Highlands.

The museum comprises six teak houses, some of which are two centuries old. Found in Ayutthaya province and Baan Khrua, they were transported to this spot in 1959 and reassembled so that the original multi-use rooms could be transformed into a dining room, bedroom, bathroom, air-conditioned study and open-sided drawing room. The guided tour starts and finishes in the lush tropical gardens,

# Walk 5 Oriental quarter

The Bangrak riverside was Bangkok's original international trading centre, home until a few decades ago to foreign banks, businesses and embassies, *godowns* (warehouses), cottage industries, opulent residences and the city's earliest hotels. These lanes wend their tranquil way through historic areas.

Start at **River City** antiques mall (*see p138*). Just beyond the **Royal Orchid Sheraton** hotel is the capital's oldest embassy, the 1820s Portuguese Embassy. The *soi* veers left to **Thanon Charoen Krung**, where you turn right, passing the formidable brown **Central Post Office** that stands on the original site of the British Embassy. Right, down Soi 34, you reach **Wat Muang Khae** past **Harmonique**, the earliest example of a historic shophouse converted into a restaurant. Retracing your steps back to Charoen Krung, continue east past the **Rare Stone Museum** (*see p137*) and take another right into Soi 34.

Passing exquisite timber mansions to the right, and the gate to the recently rebuilt **French Embassy**, head towards the river, where the crumbling classical façades of the **Old Customs House** (used to represent old Hong Kong in Wong Kar Wai's movie *In the Mood for Love*) may still be saved if plans for a boutique hotel on the site come to fruition. Just behind it, a path leads north then west through quaintly carved wooden houses to **Haroon Mosque**, which faces a Muslim cemetery, before circling back south across Soi 36 and past the French Embassy's other wall.

To the left, Soi 38 leads to **OP Place**, another antiques mall in what was an early department store from 1905, and the pleasant **Tongue Tied** Thai restaurant in an old shophouse. One block south, Soi 40 is dubbed 'oriental lane', after the **Oriental** hotel (*see p41*), which was originally accessed from the river. Before reaching it,

where pavilions display Thompson's eclectic and discerning collection of Asian arts and antiquities. Leaving shoes outside (as at any Thai home), you're ushered past Thai, Khmer and Burmese stone and wooden sculptures, rare 19th-century *Jataka* (scripture) paintings, Thai and Chinese ceramics and even two antique chamber pots, among many other treasures. A sympathetically designed annex contains a Jim Thompson Thai Silk shop, a pondside café and an upstairs bar-cum-hall for exhibitions, functions and the Pai Kin Khao cooking school (*see p115* **Learn to: Cook Thai**).

## Lumphini Park

*192 Thanon Rama IV (0 2252 7006). Ratchadamri or Saladaeng BTS/Silom or Lumphini subway.* **Open** 4.30am-9pm daily. **Map** p311 G/H6.
Named after Buddha's birthplace in Nepal, the capital's best, and best-known, green enclave was donated by King Vajiravudh (Rama VI), whose statue dominates the main (south-western) entrance. It's most interesting around dawn and dusk, when its pagoda and lakes (pedalos can be hired) are circled by joggers, its paths become t'ai chi classes and others perform mass aerobics or play acrobatic *takraw*. There are even open-air gyms. Its shaded grounds also refresh lazier souls: there's a restaurant to the north-west, and free concerts bring even more picnickers than usual on Sunday afternoons in the cool season. Under awnings near the school on the north side, you can also get a free haircut from an eager trainee. By night, the perimeter becomes a soliciting ground: women on the east, men on the west.

though, you pass crafts workshops with temple-style roofs and twin timber houses of sublime proportions: first is the former **Commercial Company of Siam**, then the **China House** restaurant (*see p111*). Further down, at Oriental Pier, look north to the Oriental's original river entrance via what is now the Author's Wing. To the south stand the equally imposing Venetian-style **East Asiatic Company** (EAC, built in 1901) and **Chartered Bank**, which has become an annex for Assumption School.

Heading back a little, dart under an archway behind the EAC building into an elegant tree-lined piazza flanked by a Catholic mission, a Catholic centre and the twin towers of red-brick **Assumption Cathedral**. Built in 1910, the cathedral has an impressive marble altar. Via its southern wall Soi 42 leads back to Charoen Krung beside some rickety wooden homes.

Striking stuff: **Snake Farm**.

## Nai Lert Shrine

*Soi Nai Lert, at service entrance of Hilton hotel. Chidlom BTS.* **Open** 24hrs daily. **Map** p311 H5.
Erected to honour the female deity Jao Mae Thapthim, this canalside shrine is decorated with phallic sculptures of every size and shape. Donated by worshippers hoping to become fertile, these red-tipped, anatomically approximate Shiva lingam-style animist totems are planted in the style of a picket fence or else offered on altars, with clusters of gargantuan shafts swathed in sacred ribbons.

## Snake Farm

*Queen Saovabha Memorial Institute, 1871 Thanon Rama IV (0 2252 0161-4/www.redcross.or.th). Saladaeng BTS.* **Open** 8.30am-4.30pm Mon-Fri; 8.30am-noon Sat, Sun. *Demonstrations* 11am, 2.30pm Mon-Fri; 11am Sat, Sun. **Admission** B20 Thais; B70 foreigners. **No credit cards. Map** p310 F6.
Run by the Thai Red Cross, the Queen Saovabha Memorial Institute was opened in 1922. Formerly the Pasteur Institute, it runs research and treatment programmes involving vaccinations, animal bites, snakebites and antivenins extracted from this snake farm (only the second of its kind in the world). It's only worth visiting when the venom is milked, causing spectators in the amphitheatre to squirm in fascinated horror. Thailand has six venomous snake species; the most impressive are the docile but deadly banded krait, with its menacing black and yellow stripes, and the huge king cobra, whose yield of poison could kill 1,000 rabbits. Ther farm also has a python that is fed chicken drumsticks, which

bulge out its belly. Visitors are encouraged to handle the larger serpents and pose for photos. The commentary is only in Thai, but there's an informative booklet in English.

### Wat Pathumwanaram

*969 Thanon Rama I (0 2251 0351). Siam BTS.*
**Open** 8.30am-6pm daily. **Map** p311 G4.
Opposite the Royal Thai Police Headquarters, this historically significant *wat* is under visited considering the quiet, verdant respite it offers shoppers from the surrounding malls. Fronted by a terrapin pond, the temple houses the ashes of Prince Mahidol, father of the present king, Rama IX. In 1996, after the cremation of the king's mother, her ashes and elaborate crematorium were both brought here from Sanam Luang.

## Sukhumvit

Sukhumvit is a testament to just how far and rapidly the metropolis has spread east. When the **Siam Society** (*see p97*) was established on Soi Asoke in 1933, it stood in fields. Today it's suffocated by an incredible number of high-rises. Reaching all the way from Thanon Ploenchit to the Cambodian border, Sukhumvit and its downtown *soi* are tightly packed with luxury condominiums, hotels, shops and fashionable spots to dine, drink and dance. Mostly owned by Thai-Indian Sikhs (whose tailor shops and inns predominate between Sois 3-11), it's also home to other expatriate quarters: Arabs and Africans along Sois 3 and 3/1; Koreans around Sukhumvit

Plaza on Soi 12; and Japanese between Sois 31-53. Westerners are found throughout. There's also Soi 55 (Thonglor), which is an aisle of chintzy wedding plazas, and Soi 33's string of upmarket hostess bars named after Western painters (Dali, Renoir, Van Gogh, Monet).

The Nana area is lined with souvenir stalls, travel agents, massage parlours (both traditional and with extra services) and several salacious nightstrips, which (unlike Patpong) draw in some residents. There are hostess bars everywhere: in the multi-level **Nana Entertainment Plaza** on Soi 4, filling **Clinton Plaza** (near Soi 15), spilling on to the pavement from a maze of open-air 'bar beers' opposite the **Ambassador Hotel**, and lining **Soi Cowboy** (Soi 23). Some are even to be found under the expressway at 'Soi Zero'.

Just before the **Eastern Bus Terminal** is the so-so **Science Museum & Planetarium** (*see p163*), while the **Pridi Bhanomyong Institute** (*see p202*) is on Thonglor. North from the bus station on Soi 63 you can study traditional crafts at **Ban Chang Thai** workshop (*see p97*). East along Thanon Sukhumvit, next to the upmarket **Emporium** shopping centre (*see p149*), is **Benjasiri Park** (*see p97*), while another green lung is set to replace the Thailand Tobacco Monopoly, south of Sukhumvit, where the Bangkok governor wants to erect Bangkok Tower (potentially the world's fifth tallest building) to coincide with the queen's auspicious 72nd birthday in 2004.

Evening traffic streams past the **Victory Monument**. *See p97.*

## Ban Chang Thai

*38 Sukhumvit Soi 63, Ekamai Soi 10 (0 2391 3807/*
*www.baanchangthai.com). Ekamai BTS.* **Open** 9am-
5pm daily. **Map** p312 M6.

Formerly a private residence, this workshop is dedicated to preserving and teaching traditional local
crafts. There are courses on puppet making, painting and an ancient form of *Muay Thai*. Limited
English is spoken, but course prices are a bargain.

## Benjasiri Park

*Thanon Sukhumvit, between Sois 22 & 24 (0 2262*
*0810). Phrom Phong BTS.* **Open** 5am-9pm daily.
**Map** p312 K6.

This compact urban park was opened to celebrate
the present queen's 60th birthday. It is prettied up
with fountains, ponds, Thai pavilions and sculptures by some of Thailand's most celebrated artists.
For exercise, there are basketball and *takraw* courts,
a small skate park and a tiny swimming pool. It
sometimes hosts dance festivals.

## Siam Society & Baan Kamthieng

*131 Sukhumvit Soi 21 (0 2661 6470-77/www.siam-*
*society.org). Asoke BTS/Sukhumvit subway.* **Open**
9am-5pmTue-Sat. **Admission** B100. **No credit**
**cards.** **Map** p312 K5.

Offering a unique insight into northern Lanna culture,
beliefs and lifestyle in Bangkok, Baan Kamthieng is
an ethnological museum in a 150-year-old former
wooden dwelling. Recently updated, it now has multimedia displays, photographs and audio-visual
exhibits on subjects that range from courtship music
and spoken family histories to footage of a spirit
dance and animated instructions on how to build a
Lanna house. Set in a well-tended garden, it's said
to be haunted by the spirits of three women who
were so attached to their home that even death
couldn't evict them. The Siam Society, under royal
patronage, has a library containing rare books on
Thai history, palm-leaf manuscripts and old maps.
There are regular lectures about Thai and Asian
culture, exhibitions, stage performances and study
trips to historic sites.

## North

Hidden amid **Pratunam Market** (*see p134*)
and north of Khlong Saen Saeb stands the
city's tallest structure, **Baiyoke II Tower**
(*see below*), which offers unparalleled views
in this congested locale. Aside from the techie
**Pantip Plaza** mall (west down Thanon
Petchburi; *see p139*) and the **Bangkok Dolls**
museum (*see p162*), most other northward
sights can only be reached on the SkyTrain.
A stop beyond lovely **Suan Pakkard Palace**
(*see below*) is the **Victory Monument**. Erected
in 1941, its bayonet-like obelisk honours those
slain in a brief dispute with France over Laos. It
also commands a chaotic roundabout converged
on by phalanxes of buses.

A short way along Thanon Ratchwithi is the
European-style **Phayathai Palace**, a former
royal getaway of Rama V that has since been
a hotel, a radio broadcasting station and is now
part of King Mongkut Hospital. The SkyTrain
meets the subway at the immense, essential
**Chatuchak Weekend Market** (*see p134*
**A day in JJ**), which is flanked by **Chatuchak
Park** (*see below*), the **Children's Discovery
Museum** (*see p162*) and the quirky bars along
Thanon Kamphaengphet. The neighbouring
Railway Park, meanwhile, may become the new
site of the Thai parliament. One stop further on
the subway is the suburban shopping behemoth
of Central Plaza Lad Prao.

## Baiyoke II Tower

*84th Floor, 22 Thanon Ratchaprarop, in sub-soi*
*north of Indra Regent Hotel. Bus 13, 54, 73, 77,*
*204, 513, 514.* **Open** 10am-10pm daily. **Admission**
B120. **Credit** AmEx, MC, V. **Map** p311 G3/4.

Briefly boasting the world's tallest hotel (now
eclipsed by one in Shanghai), this gaudy, gilded
unfinished tower has a high-speed elevator to an
observation deck on the 84th floor for vertiginous
panoramas of the megalopolis and (supposedly) as
far as the Thai Gulf on a clear day. The views are
just as spectacular by night. There are telescopic
viewfinders, some unexciting displays for tourists
and a bland restaurant.

## Chatuchak Park & Rail Hall of Fame

*Thanon Phahon Yothin (0 2272 4575/1615 5776).*
*Morchit BTS/Morchit subway.* **Open** *Park* 4.30am-
9pm daily. *Hall of Fame* 7am-3pm Sat, Sun.

Offering respite from the Weekend Market mayhem,
this park displays sculptures by artists from the
Association of South-east Asian Nations (ASEAN)
and has gardens with themes, such as herbs or
flowers in literature. The land was once railway
property and a small Rail Hall of Fame houses old
locomotives and various vehicles, including London
taxis and Japanese patrol cars from World War II.
Next door is the small but pretty Queen Sirikit Park,
which has a lotus pond and a botanical garden.

## Suan Pakkard Palace

*352 Thanon Si Ayutthaya (0 2245 4934/www.suan*
*pakkad.com). Phaya Thai BTS.* **Open** 9am-4pm
daily. **Admission** B50 Thais; B100 foreigners.
**No credit cards.** **Map** p311 G3.

Named the 'cabbage patch palace' after the site on
which these five traditional teak houses were assembled in 1952, this delightful museum was preserved
after the death of its owners, Prince and Princess
Chumbhot. Among their accumulated art and antiquities are Khmer Buddha statues, betel nut utensils,
monks' fans, shells, minerals and prehistoric Baan
Chiang pottery. Most exquisite is the Lacquer
Pavilion located beyond a pond in the garden. A
birthday gift from the prince to his wife, this 17th-
to 18th-century Ayutthayan library features some

Sightseeing

astonishing gold and black lacquer scenes from the life of Buddha, the *Ramakien* and Thai life. Within the grounds is the Marasi Gallery, which holds art exhibitions, and the Khon Museum, a tiny multi-media display explaining the classic Thai dramatic art form of *khon* (*see p199*).

## South

Forming the border with Bangrak, Thanon Sathorn evolved either side of a canal dug by Chinese labourers in the late 19th century. As wealthy locals and foreign residents began settling in the neighbourhood, it soon sprouted numerous swanky, European-style wooden mansions. Few have survived, although the splendid century-old Thai-Chinese Chamber of Commerce (built as the Bombay Department Store) has now been preserved as the fashionable **Blue Elephant** Thai restaurant (*see p115* **Learn to: Cook Thai**). Just of Sathorn is also one of Bangkok's best preserved Thai homes, **MR Kukrit Pramoj's Heritage Home** (*see below*). Among today's edifices are the suave **Sukhothai** hotel (*see p48*), the precariously narrow **Thai Wah II Tower** with a hole 50 storeys up, and the quirky **Bank of Asia** headquarters, designed by modernist architect Dr Sumet Jumsai and nicknamed the 'robot building'. Another odd-shaped building is the boat-like **Wat Yannawa** (*see below*) by the Sathorn riverside.

Aside from the work of numerous embassies, foreign governments also promote arts and cinema through the **Goethe Institut** and **Alliance Française** (for both, *see p167*). Superseded by Thanon Khao San, Soi Ngam Duphlee was the original backpackers' flop zone – these days it has become a tad sleazy.

East along Thanon Rama IV and on the way to Khlong Toey, you pass **Plainern Palace**, which is open only on Naris Day (*see p159*). The port district around here is famous for its markets, while its slums are the preoccupation of many aid agencies. The vast loop in the Chao Phraya river bounded by Thanon Rama III is largely industrial, with only **Central Rama III Shopping Centre** and **Tawandaeng German Brewhouse** (*see p192* **Bubbling over**) to divert visitors.

### MR Kukrit Pramoj's Heritage Home

*19 Soi Phra Phinij, Thanon Sathorn Tai (0 2286 8185). Bus 22, 62, 67, 76, 116, 149, 530.* **Open** 10am-5pm Sat, Sun. **Admission** B50; B20 students. **No credit cards. Map** p311 G7.

A charming and politically significant museum, this was once the tasteful, traditional abode of Mom Ratchawong Kukrit, a well-connected politician and cultural preservationist who was briefly prime minister in the turbulent mid 1970s. Known for his writing and promotion of classical Thai drama (*khon*), his former home comprises five teak houses on stilts from the Central Plains. Aside from the antiquities, photographs and memorabilia of a remarkable man, it offers a delightful pond and garden setting in which to relax.

### Wat Yannawa

*1648 Thanon Charoen Krung (0 2211 9317/ www.watyannawa.com). Saphan Taksin BTS.* **Open** *Temple* 5am-10pm daily. *Bot* 8-9am, 5-6pm daily. **Map** p310 D7.

A unique temple, Wat Yannawa actually dates from Ayutthayan times but was restored by Rama I. Rama III later added a building constructed in the form of a Chinese junk (as a tribute to Siam's sea trade), complete with eyes on the prow, twin *chedi* in place of masts, four cannons and a shrine situated on an upper deck.

# Learn to Gemology

Bangkok is the gem capital of the world. While the ruby and sapphire mines around the east coast city of Chanthaburi were the original draw to foreign traders, these days it's Thailand's expertise in heating and cutting (and its access to deposits in Burma and Cambodia) that makes the gem business a top-ten export earner. India and China may have cheaper labour, but they can't compete with Thai-honed beauty. Some of the world's best lapidaries are found in Chanthaburi and in Bangkok, particularly around the area west of Thanon Silom. Because of the diversity and quality of the stones, people come from all over the world to Bangkok to study gemology.

Among many schools, the reputable **Asian Institute of Gemological Sciences** (AIGS, 33rd Floor, Jewellery Trade Centre, 919/1 Thanon Silom, 0 2267 4315-9/www.aigs thailand.com) and the **Gemological Institute America Thailand** (12th Floor, Bisco Tower, 56/12 Thanon Sap, 0 2237 9575-7) offer university-level classes on such topics as crystal structure, geological studies, design, synthetics and ruby grading. To complete a full diploma course takes six to nine months, while short courses teach students the skills and techniques needed to identify and buy genuine gems, and to avoid the fakes that often fool tourists.

# Suburbs

Even though the city is sprawling, there's still space for foraging elephants.

Bangkok's suburbs are evolving much like those of any major city, but at breakneck speed. The SkyTrain was planned in the 1970s to reach the capital's outskirts, but its outlying termini are now essentially downtown. Instead of development following train lines, the infrastructure has played catch-up as flat farmland has been eaten up east, north and west by unplanned condominiums, golf courses, leisure facilities, university campuses, entertainment arenas, some of the world's biggest shopping centres and countless maze-like *moo-baan* (housing estates). The growing middle class, plus workers migrating from downtown and from upcountry, are adopting a suburban lifestyle and suffering traumatic traffic problems and commutes. Though expressways have eased inter-district travel, the subway and its planned extensions are much needed. Canal life may still play a role in much of the peripheries, but, along with local community spirit, it is rapidly disappearing from the Bangkok 'burbs.

## North-east

With the new subway line running the length of Thanon Ratchadaphisek, this fragmented area should at last take off. Its diminishing pockets of marshland still offer foraging for the elephants that wander Bangkok's streets. Intended as a business zone, Ratchada (as the street is known) currently pulsates with a string of huge, flashy, hostess-cum-massage parlours, aimed mainly at Asian business types. Similar outlets dot Thanon Rama IX, while older, rougher saunas dating from Vietnam War R&R days occupy most of Thanon Petchaburi.

Petchaburi's sole pocket of culture is the **Bangkok Playhouse** (*see p202*), though one of Bangkok's best art galleries, **Tadu Contemporary Art** (*see p171*), anchors Royal City Avenue (RCA). Initially a showroom development, RCA has found a niche as a brash, pumping strip of teenybopper nightspots. Ratchada is also a nightlife zone with barn-like discos (known as *theques*) and cavernous beer halls. This long street has an IT mall beside Tesco Lotus supermarket, passes the major venue of the **Thailand Cultural Centre** (*see p202*) and curves west at two interesting modern architectural edifices, the bizarre

**Elephant Building** and the gold-pointed, blue glass towers of **SCB Park Plaza**. Siam Commercial Bank (SCB) runs a **Museum of Thai Banking** in the plaza; it traces the country's banking development since the first bank opened in 1868. At the junction with Thanon Phahon Yothin is the world's largest **IMAX** cinema (*see p167*).

Further out, beyond the anonymous suburbs of Lad Phrao and Ram Indra, lie the family attractions of **Dream World** (*see p162*), **Siam Park**, **Safari World** and **Technopolis Science Museum** (for all, *see p163*), for which a car or taxi is essential.

## East

The SkyTrain terminates at Sukhumvit Soi 77 (Onnut), which has a significant Muslim community, features the ghost-story location **Wat Mahat But** (*see p100*) and eventually leads east to the new **Bangkok International Airport** (Suvarnabhumi Airport), likely to open in 2005. Thanon Sukhumvit dips south along the Chao Phraya estuary, while the Bangna-Trad highway (and the quieter Chonburi elevated expressway above) thunders through golf-strewn, semi-industrial bleakness to the Eastern Seaboard. It passes the impressively hi-tech **Bangkok International Exhibition Centre** (BITEC), **Central City Bangna** shopping plaza, the **Nation Multimedia** tower (designed by Sumet Jumsai to resemble a Braque painting) and the outrageously opulent campus of **ABAC University**.

North from Bangna runs Thanon Si Nakharin, its east side accessing **Rama IX Park** (*see p100*), passing mega malls like Seri Centre and Seacon Square and the **Prasart Museum** (*see below*) before meeting Thanon Ramkhamhaeng. This major artery heading north-east from Petchaburi is packed with malls, shops, markets and bars (including a large gay scene) fuelled by the massive **Ramkhamhaeng University**. Next to the university are the impressive sports facilities of the **National Stadium Hua Mark** (*see p207*).

### Prasart Museum

*9 Krung Thep Kreetha Soi 4A, Thanon Krung Thep Kreetha (0 2379 3601). Bus 93, 145, 207, 519.* **Open** 10am-3pm Mon-Sat. **Admission** 1 person B1,000; 2 people or more B500 per person. **No credit cards.**

Suburban greenery in **Rama IX Royal Park**.

An appointment is required to visit this private collection, though it's hoped it can open as a public museum in the near future. It's worth it to see the replica historic buildings, including a European-style mansion, Khmer shrine and northern and central Thai teak houses, as well as Thai and Chinese temples. There are also antiques and crafts. Collector Prasart Vongsakul's shop in Peninsula Plaza (*see p150*) sells antiques and reproductions of exhibits.

### Rama IX Royal Park
*Sukhumvit Soi 103 (Soi Udomsuk) (0 2328 1385/ www.suanluangrama9.or.th). Bus 133, 145, 206, 207, then motorcycle.* **Open** 5.30am-6.30pm daily. **Admission** 9am-5pm B10; free under-12s.
Although Bangkok has one of the lowest percentages of public green space of any world city, increasing urban parkland is on the agenda. This 81ha (200-acre) space was a major addition in 1987 as a 60th birthday tribute to the king. Centred round a small museum devoted to the monarch, the botanical gardens, large water lily pond, water garden and canal-spanning bridge make for a relaxing break.

### Wat Maha But
*749 Onnut Soi 7 Sukhumvit Soi 77 (0 2311 2183). Onnut BTS.* **Open** 5.30am-10pm daily. **Admission** free.
This nondescript temple is famous for its association with Mae Nak, a young wife who died in childbirth while her conscripted husband was at war. He returned to live with his wife and child, unaware they were both ghosts. Its latest filming as *Nang Nak* was a huge hit and young soldiers visit the shrine in hope of protection. Stalls sell the likes of lavish dresses, wigs and make-up as offerings to appease the spirit of the mother, plus baby clothes and toys for the baby. Skirting the temple, Khlong Prakhanong is a popular bathing and fishing spot for local kids.

## Outer North
A century ago the marshland round **Don Muang** (literally 'highest ground') was stalked by Bangkok's foreign expatriates on excursions to hunt for wild birds. Today, the birds are mostly the metallic variety jetting in and out of **Bangkok International Airport**, Thailand's flying hub since the 1930s, with urban development stretching further north to Rangsit district and beyond. It may (inconveniently) become the domestic airport after the new international airport opens in 2005. Plane spotters with time to kill before flying off will appreciate the nostalgic **Royal Thai Air Force Museum** (*see below*) tucked behind the airport. The **Rangsit Stadium** a few kilometres north of the airport accommodates major sporting events and is the home of the World Muay Thai Council.

East of the airport is Muang Thong Thani, home of a couple of major exhibition centres, where large promotional and international music events take place. The 100 year-old **Khlong Rangsit** alongside Thanon Rangsit-Nakorn Nayok is moored with floating restaurant barges, specialising in a beef noodle dish unique to the area.

### Royal Thai Air Force Museum
*Royal Thai Air Force Base, Thanon Phahon Yothin, behind Bangkok International Airport (0 2534 1575/1764). Bus 34, 39, 114, 185, 356, 503, 520, 522, 523, 543.* **Open** 8.30am-4.30pm daily. **Admission** free. **No credit cards.**
Rarities at this museum include the only Model I Corsaire in existence, one of only two Japanese Tachikawas still left, a Spitfire and Thailand's first completely home-grown aircraft, the Model II Bomber Boripatr.

## Outer West
This area is the gateway to the western provinces, with many tour buses stopping off here before heading further afield to Nakom Pathom and Kanachanburi. Located on the city's edge **Phuttha Monthon** is a huge landscaped Buddhist 'theme' park centred round a 40-metre (131-foot) standing Buddha. The tranquil park has several interesting features pertaining to Buddha's life, including the plethora of historical images contained within the **Lord Buddha Images Museum** (0 2448 1795, admission B100). The park's Utthayan Avenue is probably Thailand's best-dressed street; it's enriched with bridges, fountains, flora and almost a thousand lamp posts each topped by a gilded Thai phoenix.

# Eat, Drink, Shop

# Restaurants

Bangkok's not just complex – it's worth making a meal of.

Food is both the staff of life and life itself in Thailand. It plays leading and supporting roles in events religious, familial, municipal and royal. If 19th-century Paris, by many accounts the root of modern city life, got its creative juice from the interaction of popular arts high and low, then millennial Bangkok does the same with its 24/7 pursuit of flavour and Darwinian drive to snuff out the weak-tasting *ahaan* (food). This may be one of the only cities in the world where you can sit in

front of any random wok-slinger on a corner and eat something to be remembered forever.

Like all social and cultural endeavours, dining is something the Thais have made very much their own by taking the habits and trends or foreign lands – Chinese techniques, Portuguese sweets, London-bred mod-minimalism – and ingredients such as chilli, papaya, tomato, corn and aubergine into their naturally stylish hands and crafting them anew. This holds true whether you are chopsticking noodles in a market or going posh in a five-star hotel restaurant.

If there is one danger to dining in Bangkok, it is that it can be too easy. Don't just settle for any place with English-language menus or air-conditioning. There is a separate (and usually mediocre) realm of eateries that are touristy and baby-food bland. Unless you're determined to eat on a boat (*see p53*) or while watching traditional dance (*see p203*), avoid such places and look instead for queues of Thais, or even expats, and grab a spot. Even if all you can do is point at what's on other tables, you'll eat well.

This is also a thoroughly global city – and a chic one at that. You'll find contemporary Vietnamese food that is better than in Saigon, old-style French food such as pressed duck and boudin, fiery West African stews, Moghul cooking, and even British fry-ups. And you can eat the same food in musty back alleys as you would in *salas* amid lotus ponds and in old wooden mansions on canals. In all cases, the Thai palate can affect the preparation in fascinating ways – Italian food, for example, often has a little chilli and there are fusion dishes using spaghetti as an Asian noodle. After all, Thailand is the original fusion culture.

## WHERE?

The answer: everywhere. There is no hour, alley, market, *soi* or hotel in which a restaurant of some sort can't be found for local cooking. But there are hot zones for trendy places or certain types of food. Soi 36 on Sukhumvit, for example, is well known for Isaan (north-eastern) cooking. The Ekamai and Thonglor areas on the same road are strewn with youthful hotspots in all-white houses and fantastical garden settings. Hotels such as the Regent, the Sukhothai, the Oriental and the Sheraton Grande are all beau monde haunts for dishes both European and Asian. Lang Suan near Lumphini Park is a

## The best Eats

### For one-dish wonders
Kai Thord Soi Polo (*see p113*), Pet Tun Jao Tha (*see p107*), Roti Mataba (*see p105*), Thip Samai (*see p105*) and Xian Dumpling Restaurant (*see p116*).

### For haute Siamese
Celadon. *See p122.*

### For haute Cantonese
Mei Jiang. *See p106.*

### For haute Française
Le Banyan (*see p114*) and Le Normandie (*see p109*).

### For one night in Isaan
Hualumphong Food Station. *See p117.*

### For fearless fusion
Jester's (*see p106*) and Eat Me! (*see p109*).

### For river views and seafood
Kaloang Home Kitchen (*see p107*), River City BBQ (*see p111*) and Supatra River House (*see p203*).

### For garden dining
Ana's Garden. *See p117.*

### For seeing and being seen
Greyhound Café (*see p117*), A Day (*see p111*) and Biscotti (*see p112*).

### For anticipation of greatness
La Scala. *See p121.*

Eat, Drink, Shop

You're in for a treat: colourful, flavoursome Thai cuisine.

restaurant row of sorts, with upmarket Italians and Vietnamese, local seafooders and Chinese restaurants. If you want to go cuisine-specific, there are several tacks to take.

Embassies and national associations, for example, always have nearby outlets akin to staff canteens, whether from India, Burma, France or Indonesia. Little India, near Thanon Pahurat, is peppered with shopfronts with pots aplenty of masala and cases of Punjabi sweets. Ditto Chinatown for dim sum and Cantonese cooking. Expat enclaves include the Korea Town of Sukhumvit Plaza on Soi 12, the Arab/ North African quarter of Sukhumvit Soi 3/1, African trader fuelstops in Pratunam, and Anglo-Irish pub grub on the arteries of Silom and Sukhumvit. In one of the world's best and cheapest cities to eat Japanese, sushi bars, bento lunchboxes and salaryman sake dens abound in Soi Thaniya and Sukhumvit between Sois 23 and 55. The Thai restaurants of note, many dating back to the founding of Bangkok, are studded like cloves around Phra Nakorn, Thonburi and Nonthaburi.

### WHEN?

Thais eat non-stop, but the types of foods available change according to the time of day. Though it's a snacking culture, foods are divided according to when they are served

– *ahaan chao* for the morning, *ahaan thiang* for daytime, *ahaan yen* for the evening and beyond. That's for Thai food, but the omelette-and-burger sets are more traditional in their time-bound nature. Generally speaking, breakfast is taken just after sunrise before the heat becomes insufferable, lunch on the dot at noon, and dinner between 6pm and 8pm. For more global cuisines or fashionable places, add an hour or so to those times.

Reservations are wise, sometimes a must, at hotels and hotspots on Thursdays to Saturdays, and at top hotels for Sunday brunches (whether sumptuous spreads for the chic or clown-and-balloon fare for the kids). Be aware that many places shut on Sundays, holidays are numerous and local kitchens often close by 9pm. Still, late meals and *klub klaem* (drinking nibbles) can be had at most bars or music venues from 7pm until midnight, and they're often high quality (for more information, *see chapter* **Bars**). Turfed out at 2am, clubbers find curry trays lining the exits or grab a hangover-clearing *khao tom* at markets that trade through until dawn (for options, *see chapter* **Markets**).

### TIPPING AND SERVICE

The culture of tipping is a very Western concept that is slowly making its way to Thailand, along with Starbucks and David

Eat, Drink, Shop

Beckham. Restaurants of the international hotel variety will add tax (set to rise to nine or ten per cent) plus a ten per cent service charge to the bill; local places will not. In either case, it is customary to leave small change behind after paying for the meal. This is less a habit than a corollary of the incredible culture of respect and politeness here.

As for service, don't expect the white-gloved variety outside of the Oriental Hotel. In Thailand, things just flow when they're ready. This means that every dish can arrive at once or simply trickles on to the table three or 30 minutes apart. Natural generosity, however, is a part of everyday life, so little touches like complimentary fruit or servers rushing to replace cutlery or to get an extra chair on which to place handbags is absolutely normal.

For each restaurant we've given the average cost of a main course, or equivalent (many restaurants don't really follow the starter/main course/dessert concept). For information on the culture of Thai food and key dishes, *see p118* **Menu & etiquette.**

## Phra Nakorn & Banglamphu

## International

### Baan Phra Arthit Coffee & More
*102/1 Thanon Phra Arthit, Banglamphu (0 2280 7879). Bus 3, 30, 32, 64, 65, 506.* **Open** 11am-10pm Mon-Thur, Sun; 11am-midnight Fri, Sat. **Main courses** B80. **No credit cards**. **Map** p308 B2.
The choice of sandwiches, snacks and cakes is small and only of so-so quality, but there's a good range of juices at this very handsome café in an old building that once housed the Goethe Institut. It's classier than the usual backpacker cafés, and there's a single computer for internet access.

### Chabad
*96 Soi Rambuttri, Thanon Chakkraphong, Banglamphu (0 2282 6388/www.jewishthailand.com). Bus 3, 30, 32, 64, 65, 506.* **Open** 10am-10pm daily. **Main courses** B130. **No credit cards**. **Map** p308 B2.
There are a few Israeli cafés around Banglamphu and a perfectly acceptable street stall selling falafel opposite Gulliver's bar, but Rabbi Nechemya Wilhelm's Chabad offers comfortable, upmarket surroundings without charging much extra for the usual chips and dips. It also has occasional North African dishes, such as Moroccan-style fish.

## Thai

Thai food is mostly horrible around **Thanon Khao San**, but authentic on **Thanon Phra Arthit**. Try also bar **Café Today** (*see p124*).

### Baan Bangkok Bar, Restaurant & Gallery
*591 Thanon Phra Sumen, near Phan Fah bridge, Phra Nakorn (0 2281 6237). Bus 157, 201, 503, 509.* **Open** 5pm-1am daily. **Main courses** B120. **Credit** AmEx, MC, V. **Map** p308 C3.
Pulling off the style-and-sustenance combo isn't easy, but Bangkok Bar does well with its Sino-Portuguese architecture and upbeat vibe. The crowd is diverse: hipsters, *farang*, stewardesses and punk rockers. Diners share plates of sweat-inducing local cooking (try the seafood specials), which somehow seems to result in bigger cocktail orders.

### Ming Lee
*29-30 Thanon Na Phralan, next to Silpakorn University, Phra Nakorn (no phone). Bus 1, 39, 44, 47, 123, 512.* **Open** noon-8pm daily. **Main courses** B75. **No credit cards**. **Map** p308 B4.
Ming Lee represents the Bangkok of old and the classical Thai-Chinese food that is now a rarity. There's a secret-handshake quality to the place, reflected in the hushed response to recipe enquiries and the round table at the centre reserved for older customers. Artists are a mainstay, as are the *mee krob*, *tom kha kai* and the Hainan-influenced dishes.

### Roti Mataba
*136 Thanon Phra Arthit, near Santichaiprakarn Park, Banglamphu (0 2282 2119). Bus 3, 30, 32, 64, 65, 506.* **Open** 7am-9pm Mon-Sat. **Main courses** B60. **No credit cards**. **Map** p308 B2.
The women who run Roti Mataba are experts at patting, flipping, filling and plaiting roti. The eponymous flatbread is available stuffed (with chicken, egg, veggies), drizzled (with sweet milk or honey) or put to work as a dipping implement (alongside curries). Do as the locals do: plunder the array of clove-redolent dishes, such as *kaeng Matsaman*, while people-watching and enjoying the river views.

### Sky High
*14 Thanon Ratchadamnoen Klang, Phra Nakorn (0 2224 1947). Bus 39, 59, 157, 201, 503, 509, 511, 512.* **Open** 8am-2am daily. **Main courses** B150. **Credit** MC, V. **Map** p308 C3.
Sky High's hushed or hurried tones could be coming from local politicians, journalists, poets or simply gossiping friends. This is a seriously Thai place, with lasting popularity, and spot-on cooking of Thai-Chinese staple dishes. The steamed Chinese carp fish head is memorable.

### Thip Samai
*313 Thanon Mahachai, behind the Golden Mount, Phra Nakorn (0 2221 6280). Bus 5, 56.* **Open** 5.30pm-3.30am daily. **Main courses** B45. **No credit cards**. **Map** p308 C2.
*Pad Thai* may be the dish that all visitors know before getting their visa. Thip Samai, known by many in Bangkok as Pad Thai Pratu Pi ('Ghost's Gate Noodles'), is a legend for serving nothing but, in a neon-lit setting. Try the egg-wrapped version and the nutty-sweet coconut juice.

retreat and late-night extension to their romantic aspirations. One of the earliest on the scene when coffee culture hit Bangkok in the late 1990s, Coffee Society has an equally good next-door neighbour in Café Ease. Both provide a fine range of coffees and teas, plus sandwiches, snacks and cakes.

### Eat Me!
*2nd Floor, 1/6 Piphat Soi 2, Thanon Convent (0 2238 0931). Saladaeng BTS/Silom subway.* **Open** 3pm-1am daily. **Main courses** B260. **Credit** AmEx, MC, V. **Map** p310 F7.
Always popular for its interesting fusion menu, newly expanded Eat Me! has evolved into the city's premier art restaurant. The usually quirky, sometimes confrontational canvases provide great conversation pieces and attract a cool clientele, making this as much a hangout as a restaurant. People tend to linger for post-prandial drinks, particularly at weekends, when a small jazz band plays.

### Le Bouchon
*37/17 Patpong Soi 2, Thanon Surawong (0 2234 9109). Saladaeng BTS/Silom subway.* **Open** 11am-11.15pm Mon-Sat; 7-11.15pm Sun. **Main courses** B440. **Credit** AmEx, MC, V. **Map** p310 F6.
Perhaps the most authentic French bistro in town, and consequently the most popular regular dining spot for local Gauls. The very small bar is abuzz with joie de vivre and the glug of Pastis as diners wait to be seated at one of only seven tables. Expect simple but good country cooking.

### Le Normandie
*5th Floor, Oriental Hotel, Charoen Krung Soi 38 (0 2236 0400/www.mandarinoriental.com). Saphan Taksin BTS.* **Open** noon-2.30pm, 7-10.30pm daily. **Main courses** B1,800. **Credit** AmEx, DC, MC, V. **Map** p310 D7.
Bangkok's most famous restaurant is also its most expensive, but it's worth every *baht*. The marmalade interior, dazzling under crystal chandeliers, offers regal European luxury overlooking the river through a full wall of windows. The food offers wonderful combinations of flavours, and is gorgeously presented, while the wine list is monumental in its range of top-quality grape, but also has drinkable possibilities at around B1,700. Feast like a film star on the five-course tasting menu (with different wines for each course), for around $150 a head. A jacket and tie are compulsory for men, and are available at the door if you don't have them with you.

### Zanotti
*1st Floor, Saladaeng Colonnade, 21/2 Soi Saladaeng (0 2636 0002). Saladaeng BTS/Silom subway.* **Open** 11.30am-2pm, 6-10.30pm daily. **Main courses** lunch B370; dinner B800. **Credit** AmEx, DC, MC, V. **Map** p310 F6.
'Exuberance' sums up this restaurant – the jazz music is cranked up high, as is the conversation (the tables are so close you could spoon-feed your neighbours) – and it took Bangkok by storm on opening in late 1998. It's packed with high-fliers at lunch and

A cheeky view of **A Day**. See p111.

dinner, which means the pace is frantic; the waiters a blur in front of the walls of brilliantly coloured paintings. The menu is good, and varied, but the intensity of the operation means that the quality, which can be excellent, sometimes suffers.
**Branch**: Ovvio 1st Floor, Siam Discovery Centre, Thanon Rama I, Pathumwan (0 2658 0111).

## Other Asian

**Soi Thaniya** (with the adjacent malls of **Thaniya Plaza** and **Charn Issara Tower**) is known as Little Tokyo, and is chock-full of good, competitively priced sushi joints. There's a concentration of Indian and Muslim restaurants around **Thanon Charoen Krung**.

### Aoi
*132/10-11 Silom Soi 6 (0 2235 2321/2). Saladaeng BTS/Silom subway.* **Open** 11.30am-2pm, 5.30-10.30pm Mon-Fri; 11am-3pm, 5-10.30pm Sat, Sun. **Main courses** lunch B250; dinner B450. **Credit** AmEx, MC, V. **Map** p310 F7.
The best Japanese restaurant near Little Tokyo is this traditional slate-walled tavern a few blocks to the south. Prices are slightly higher than elsewhere, but the quality is excellent and the interior delightfully individual.
**Branch**: 4th Floor, Emporium, Sukhumvit Soi 24, Sukhumvit (0 2664 8590/2).

*(Eat, Drink, Shop — side tab)*

### Khrua Aroi Aroi

Thanon Pan, opposite Wat Khaek (0 2635 2365).
Surasak BTS. **Open** 9.30am-6.30pm daily. **Main
courses** B40. **No credit cards**. **Map** p310 E7.
Khanom jeen is a quick-fix fave that consists of various
curries spooned over rice noodles and eaten
with cooling, crunchy herbs and vegetables. This
two-level shop – whose name means 'delicious delicious' –
offers an array of tastes, from jungle curries
and chilli dips to coconut milk-rich Muslim varieties
and an archetypal green curry. The Hindu temple
across the street provides wafts of incense, Gaudi-
like tiling and views of multi-headed goddesses.

## Vegetarian

### Khun Churn

64 Saeng Arun Ashram, Sathorn Soi 10 (0 2236
9410). Bus 17, 22, 35, 62, 67, 116, 149. **Open**
9.30am-2.30pm, 4.30-8.30pm daily. Closed 3rd Sat
of the month. **Main courses** B70; Wed buffet B69.
**No credit cards**.
This flower-strewn branch of a Chiang Mai veggie
restaurant, packaged into an airy ashram and yoga
centre, manages to deliver the kind of dynamic Thai
flavours that shouldn't be possible without flesh. It
offers a host of regional specialities, plus vegetal
standards and stir-fries. And it's ludicrously cheap,
with an all-you-can-eat buffet lunch on Wednesdays.

## International

### Auberge DAB

1st Floor, Mercury Tower, 540 Thanon Ploenchit
(0 2658 6222/3). Chidlom BTS. **Open** 11.30am-2pm,
6.30-10.30pm daily. **Main courses** lunch B300; dinner
B800. **Credit** AmEx, DC, MC, V. **Map** p311 H5.
A franchise of the famous Paris seafood restaurant,
with all the food imported. Enjoy huge platters of
crab, lobster and oysters, plus classic meat courses,
amid very luxurious leather seating. It's superb at
best, but unpredictable because of the very high
turnover of chefs.

### Biscotti

1st Floor, The Regent Hotel, 155 Thanon
Ratchadamri (0 2254 9999). Ratchadamri BTS.
**Open** noon-2.30pm, 6-11pm daily. **Main courses**
lunch B350; dinner B550. **Credit** AmEx, DC, MC, V.
**Map** p311 G5.
Politicians, film stars, captains of industry: all dine
in this Tony Chi-designed, thrillingly modern restaurant –
perhaps the only Bangkok restaurant in
people need to be seen. And they're easily spotted in
the huge square room of terracotta and white, dominated
by a large open kitchen. It's absolutely
jammed, lunch and dinner, with devotees of the very
good Italian food.

### Calderazzo

59 Soi Lang Suan, Thanon Ploenchit (0 2252 8108/
9). Chidlom BTS. **Open** 11.30am-2pm, 6pm-midnight
daily. **Main courses** lunch B200; dinner B360.
**Credit** AmEx, DC, MC, V. **Map** p311 H5.
This pleasing contemporary interior has sloping
ceilings and split-level dining areas in restful
creams, resulting in a warm environment to enjoy
the home-style Italian cooking. The food is good,
particularly the own-made pasta, but portions are
small and the desserts disappointing. There's a wide
choice for vegetarians, though.

### Witch's Oyster Bar

20/10-11 Ruamrudee Village, Thanon Ploenchit
(0 2251 9455). Ploenchit BTS. **Open** 11.30am-2pm,
5.30-11pm daily. **Main courses** lunch B270; dinner
B700. **Credit** AmEx, MC, V. **Map** p311 H5.
Alongside imported oysters, the super menu from
Scottish chef John Hogg includes wonderfully rich
chicken livers in puff pastry, several lobster combinations
and Blairgowrie cream, a whisky, cream and
oatmeal dessert. The atmosphere is friendly.

## Other Asian

### Copper Chimney

Le Royal Meridien, President Tower, Thanon
Ploenchit (0 2656 0444). Chidlom BTS. **Open**
11am-11pm Mon-Thur; 11am-11.30pm Fri-Sun.
**Main courses** B230. **Credit** AmEx, DC, MC, V.
**Map** p311 G4.

Hanging on the telephone at **Khrua Aroi Aroi**.

**Calderazzo**, an Italian in Bangkok. *See p112.*

The only Bangkok version of this upmarket Indian franchise has extremely good north Indian curries and the lighter Chinese-Indian fusion cuisine that's extremely popular in Calcutta. A good but very loud band plays in the corner of the room.

### Thang Long
*82/5 Soi Lang Suan, Thanon Ploenchit (0 2251 3504/4491) Chidlom BTS.* **Open** 11am-2pm, 5-11pm daily. **Main courses** lunch B120; dinner B230. **Credit** AmEx, V. **Map** p311 H5.
There's a clean, almost minimalist cool to this restaurant – with rattan, pastels and plants – which makes it very popular with an arty crowd of diners. The Vietnamese food is excellent, but it can get very busy, so book ahead.

## Thai

### Kai Thord Soi Polo
*137/1-2 Soi Polo, Thanon Witthayu (0 2252 2252). Bus 13, 17, 62, 76.* **Open** 7am-7pm daily. **Main courses** B60. **No credit cards. Map** p311 H5.
There's fried chicken and then there's fried chicken from Soi Polo. It strikes the kind of oily, aromatic, crispy, fleshy balance that has won devotion among Thai locals. Owner J-Kee, though a southerner, has four decades of experience cooking the austere yet deeply flavoured foods of north-eastern Isaan. Her beef *tom yum* and fried fermented baby pork ribs proudly represent its earthy and pungent flavours.

### Khrua Nai Baan
*94 Soi Lang Suan, Thanon Ploenchit (0 2252 0069). Chidlom BTS.* **Open** 8am-midnight daily. **Main courses** B170. **Credit** AmEx, MC, V. **Map** p311 H5.
This white wooden house on bopping Lang Suan is a nightly dinner party of sorts, and has a throng of regulars to prove it. The cooking, as clean and endearing as the atmosphere, focuses on seafood –

all taken still breathing from the tanks in front. From Chinese veggies to coconut-creamy *tom yum nam khon*, Isaan-style *jim joom* (herbal soup) and steamed squid in lemon sauce, it's hard to err.

### Le Lys
*75/2 Soi Lang Suan, Thanon Ploenchit (0 2652 2401). Chidlom BTS.* **Open** 11am-11pm daily. **Main courses** B190. **Credit** AmEx, MC, V. **Map** p311 H5.
At Le Lys you'll find a pétanque court in the leafy yard, fine salmon in the Thai *yum* and vintage French wine posters next to Lanna-style textiles on the wall. The French-Thai owners have converted their home in the pursuit of taste and set themselves apart, not with their European-tinged grace, but with their oh-so-Thai menu. Pickled bamboo shoot soup, red curry with duck and lychee, and squid with tamarind sauce lure young and old.

## Vegetarian

### Whole Earth
*71 Sukhumvit Soi 26 (0 2258 4900). Phrom Phong BTS.* **Open** 11.30am-2pm, 5-11pm daily. **Main courses** lunch B140; dinner B270. **Credit** AmEx, MC, V. **Map** p312 K6.
With its Thai-style floor seating at long tables upstairs, this is an ideal venue for party dining. The food is *farang*-friendly (not too hot) vegetable versions of Thai standards.
**Branch**: Soi Lang Suan, Pathumwan (0 2252 5574).

## Sukhumvit

## International

For fusion food, try **Bed Supperclub** (*see p127*); for Anglo-Irish fare there's the **Bull's Head** and the **Londoner** (for both, *see p128*).

Tea shop **China Journal**. *See p115.*

## Bei Otto

*1 Sukhumvit Soi 20 (0 2262 0892). Phrom Phong BTS.* **Open** 9am-1am daily. **Main courses** B400. **Credit** AmEx, DC, MC, V. **Map** p312 K6.

Twenty years ago Otto Duffner set up one of the first German beer houses in Bangkok before branching out on his own. He presents the city's best German food in a pub ambiance, with a more formal restaurant next door and a take-away deli beyond that. Expect good home-made sausages, huge plates of cooked meats and barrel-loads of German beer. Otto also plays accordion when he's in the mood.

## Crepes & Co

*18 Sukhumvit Soi 12 (0 2251 2895). Asoke BTS/ Sukhumvit subway.* **Open** 9am-midnight daily. **Main courses** B300. **Credit** AmEx, DC, MC, V. **Map** p311 J5.

A relaxed, airy restaurant with a North African-style tent ceiling. Large mirrors reflect the long wall of windows overlooking the garden, which also contains a few tables. The crêpes have international fillings alongside the traditional French, and there are frequent promotional menus, particularly from Greece and Morocco. It's handy for the Ministry of Sound, just 100m away.

## Kuppa

*39 Sukhumvit Soi 16 (0 2663 0450). Asoke BTS/ Sukhumvit subway.* **Open** 10.30am-11.30pm daily. **Main courses** B200. **Credit** AmEx, DC, MC, V. **Map** p312 K6.

This huge room of blonde wood and metal, dominated by a giant coffee roaster, is the most modern café in town. It has the scale and feel of a major

international restaurant, but not quite the menu. The comfortable sofas, magazines, art gallery and an occasional (very good) jazz guitarist make it heaven for the thirtysomething fashionable crowd.

## La Piola

*32 Sukhumvit Soi 13 (0 2253 8295). Nana BTS.* **Open** noon-2.30pm, 6-11pm daily. **Main courses** B550. **Credit** MC, V. **Map** p311 J5.

A tiny restaurant set up by Bangkok's premier Italian food importer to try out new produce on local chefs. There's no menu: it serves whatever is available that day, all cooked by the owner's mama. Expect giant plates of cold meats, pizza, pasta, jugs of Chianti and mountains of Italian good cheer. Booking essential.

## Le Banyan

*59 Sukhumvit Soi 8 (0 2253 5556/www.lebanyan. net). Nana BTS.* **Open** 6.30pm-midnight Mon-Sat. **Main courses** B800. **Credit** AmEx, DC, MC, V. **Map** p311 J5.

A traditional, very high-quality French restaurant that understands the theatricality required of fine dining. Many dishes are prepared at the table by the formal but amiable maître d', Bruno Bischoff, or the eccentric chef, Michel Binaux – a charming double act. The speciality is pressed duck, within a menu of superb classic dishes. Situated in an old Thai house, the decor is a little faded at the edges, but this is one of Bangkok's very best restaurants, and a bargain at the price.

## Nasir Al-Masri

*4/6 Sukhumvit Soi 3/1 (0 2253 5582). Nana BTS.* **Open** 24hrs daily. **Main courses** B220. **No credit cards**. **Map** p311 H5.

The highlight of the Arabic and North African restaurants on 'Soi Arab', Nasir the Egyptian has all the ingredients to transport you to downtown Cairo. Outside, men banter in Arabic as they puff on shiny metal and glass *shisha* pipes; inside, beyond the mirror-metal frontage, Islamic motifs and Ramadan lanterns adorn the walls and ceiling. All the food here is good, from kebabs to humous-type dips and the Egyptian national dish, *molokaya*. The only potential downer is the absence of any alcohol.

## New York Steakhouse

*2nd Floor, JW Marriott Hotel, 4 Sukhumvit Soi 2 (0 2656 7700). Ploenchit BTS.* **Open** 6pm-midnight daily. **Main courses** B900. **Credit** AmEx, DC, MC, V. **Map** p311 H5.

A sensation when it opened in early 2001, this restaurant led the new-millennium Bangkok steakhouse boom, and is still unsurpassed for its club-like sophistication. It also has superb seafood in live tanks and the grain-fed US Angus beef is flown in chilled not frozen; the prime cut (served from a silver trolley) is melt-in-the-mouth stunning. The vegetables are disappointing, but this is a carnivore's paradise, after all. There's a large choice of wines by the glass, and 20 Martinis. Booking ahead here is absolutely essential.

### Sign In

*Sukhumvit Soi 24, opposite Impala Hotel (0 2661 0084). Phrom Phong BTS.* **Open** 10.30am-midnight daily. **Main courses** B150. **Credit** MC, V. **Map** p312 K6.

Chef Poh trained at Le Normandie (*see p109*) in the Oriental Hotel, and is a rare example of a Thai who really understands European food. This is his first restaurant, and the food is so good (and cheap) that its popularity will quickly outstrip its six-table capacity. It may well have moved by the time you read this, so look out for the name.

## Other Asian

There's a substantial range of subcontinental curry stops between Nana and the Ambassador Hotel, most prevalent on **Soi 11** and **Soi 11/1**.

Meanwhile, a huge expat population sustains a dizzying variety of Japanese restaurants a little further over on **Sois 23-55**.

### Akbar

*1/4 Sukhumvit Soi 3 (0 2253 3479/2255 6935). Nana BTS.* **Open** 10.30am-1am daily. **Main courses** B200. **Credit** AmEx, DC, MC, V. **Map** p311 J5.

Of all the Indian restaurants around Soi 3, Akbar is the oldest. The interior is a cutesy mish-mash of wooden ornaments, lanterns, coloured glass and Indian fabrics. Unusually for an Indian place it has a few reasonable wines. No smoking upstairs.

### China Journal

*41 Sukhumvit Soi 55 (0 2712 8589). Thonglor BTS.* **Open** 10am-11pm Tue-Sun. **Main courses** B175. **Credit** AmEx, V. **Map** p312 M5.

# Learn to Cook Thai

You can learn to conjure up a curry at one of Bangkok's many cooking schools. Those in hotels veer towards elaborate demonstrations by star chefs that dazzle (but daunt) the observers. Hands-on is best: when selecting a course, ensure you get utensils and time on the range. Some start with a market tour and involve sampling each other's attempts – both amusing and instructive. Fruit and vegetable carving is a frequent element that may thrill dinner party mavens but exasperate purist foodies.

The **Oriental Thai Cooking School** in wooden buildings across the river from the Oriental (see p41) has top-notch demonstrations to cover each style ((9am-noon Mon-Thur, $120 per class). Hands-on instruction is by appointment on Sat or Sun ($150 per class). Another kind of river hotel, in a beautiful traditional compound, **Thai House** (see p50) has residential courses in classic dishes (9.30am-4.30pm Mon-Sat). Choose from one-day (B3,500 excluding room), two-day (B8,950 shared room, B9,550 single), or three-day (B16,650 shared, B18,450 single).

**Blue Elephant**, the Belgium-based international chain of contemporary Thai restaurants, has just converted the century-old Thai-Chinese Chamber of Commerce building into an eclectically styled restaurant (233 Thanon Sathorn Tai, Bangrak, 0 2673 9353/4/www.blueelephant.com, open 11.30am-2.30pm, 6.30pm-midnight daily, main courses B400). Upstairs, a school for its chefs worldwide offers public courses teaching four dishes per day (8.30am-1.30pm daily, B2,800).

**Pai Kin Khao**, publisher of cookbook/CD-Rom *Spice of Life* (0 2652 0082/www.pai-kin-khao.com) runs inspired sessions with prominent chefs every two months at Jim Thompson's House. They cover various cuisines, plus fusion, healthy eating and entertaining. They're also highly social, with wine tastings and a banquet by the chef that friends can join (class B3,750, dinner B1,200-B1,800).

An arty setting for a traditional, Shanghai-style boutique tea shop. The furniture (large Chinese urns and various Asian wooden pieces) is all for sale. The disorienting array of teas from China, Japan and Korea, plus Thailand homebrew, is served in beautifully ornate crockery.

### Joke Club
*155/20-25 Sukhumvit Soi 11 (0 2651 2888/9). Nana BTS.* **Open** 10.30am-2am daily. **Main courses** B70. **Credit** MC, V. **Map** p311 J5.
Wok-bred sizzle and high-rise bustle à la Hong Kong are the order of the day at Joke Club. It's been a scenester since inception, thanks to a swank mix of thoughtful Chinese cookery and modern design – think murals, dark woods, silver detailing. While an in-house singer Bacharachs away, diners feast upon staples like rice noodles, steamed seafood and the namesake rice porridge with all the hot-sour-salty-sweet (and savoury) fixings.

### Kabore
*1st Floor, Sukhumvit Plaza, Sukhumvit Soi 12 (0 2252 5375/5486). Asoke BTS/Sukhumvit subway.* **Open** 9am-10pm daily. **Main courses** B180. **Credit** DC, MC, V. **Map** p311 J5.
Bangkok's Little Seoul is Sukhumvit Plaza, Soi 12, where practically every shop, restaurant and bar caters to Hermit Kingdom expatriates, with more in nearby *soi*. The family-style Kabore is probably the pick of the café-diners, serving a wide range of dishes, including hot and sour soups and the peppery noodle speciality *naingmyon*. Toast the table with the Korean rice whisky *soju*.

### Le Dalat Indochine
*14 Sukhumvit Soi 23 (0 2661 7967/8). Asoke BTS/Sukhumvit subway.* **Open** 11.30am-2.30pm, 5.30-10.30pm daily. **Main courses** lunch B230; dinner B500. **Credit** AmEx, DC, MC, V. **Map** p312 K6.
One of two restaurants in this *soi* owned by the family of the 1930s Saigon socialite Madame Hoa Ly, daughter of the French governor to Indochina at the turn of the 20th century. It oozes class. Downstairs are two dining rooms and a bar, adorned with Asian antiques, while upstairs are more dining rooms and Indochine humour in the collection of penis drawings in the men's toilet. Good specialities, such as prawn on sugar cane, are served with the traditional Vietnamese fresh herb and salad accompaniment. Its more formal branch is also terrific.
**Branch**: **Le Dalat** 47/1 Sukhumvit Soi 23, Sukhumvit (0 2260 1849).

### Rang Mahal
*26th Floor, Rembrandt Hotel, 19 Sukhumvit Soi 18 (0 2261 7100/www.rembrandtbkk.com). Asoke BTS/Sukhumvit subway.* **Open** 11.30am-2.30pm, 6.30-10.30pm daily. **Main courses** B360. **Credit** AmEx, DC, MC, V. **Map** p312 K6.
The superb views above the city and the excellent, rich, north Indian dishes make Rang Mahal worth splashing out on if you want a romantic evening. The interior evokes the Mogul era with lovely, silk

Pure class at **Le Dalat Indochine**.

upholstered sofas and ornate woodwork, while a loud and entertaining Indian band plays in the central area in front of long banquet tables. Good thali and a terrific value Sunday brunch buffet. The air-con is cold, so take a jacket.

### Shin Daikoku
*32/8 Sukhumvit Soi 19 (0 2254 9980-3/ www.shindaikoku.com). Asoke BTS/Sukhumvit subway.* **Open** 11.30am-2pm, 5.30-10pm daily. **Main courses** lunch B250; dinner B500. **Credit** AmEx, DC, MC, V. **Map** p312 J5.
This elegant restaurant is accessed by a Japanese-style wooden bridge leading into an old house. It offers all the usual sushi and sashimi options, plus teppanyaki and matsuzaka beef. Owned by the same people who run the extremely popular and good-value Fuji chain found in malls, Shin Daikoku is the flagship operation, and is something of a favourite for embassy entertaining.
**Branch**: 2nd Floor, Le Royal Meridien Bangkok, Thanon Ploenchit, Sukhumvit (0 2656 0096-8/ www.shindaikoku.com).

### Xian Dumpling Restaurant
*10/3 Sukhumvit Soi 40 (0 2713 5288). Ekkamai BTS.* **Open** 10am-10pm daily. **Main courses** B75. **No credit cards.** **Map** p312 M7.
In the sea of Chinese restaurants the world over, this pocket-sized dumpling outlet in a shadowy yet neon-strewn parking lot off Soi 40 comes across as unique. The hearty Xian food seems to owe as much to Mongolian, Muslim and Silk Road influences as it does to Sino classicism. Think shredded tripe and tofu with chilli oil, stewed aubergine, mutton soup and doughy steamed dumplings in dozens of forms. Pink cloths on the chairs and white-tile wallpaper make for a setting of good-bad taste.

such as *spaghetti pla kem* (stir-fried pasta with Thai anchovies, chilli and garlic), are hard to fault. It's hardly a surprise, then, to find that the core clientele consists of assorted film, media and jetsetting society types.
**Branches**: Central Chidlom, Thanon Ploenchit, Pathumwan (0 2255 6965); U-Chu Liang Building 1, Soi Saladaeng, Bangrak (0 2632 4466); **Nood Food Zen** World Trade Centre, 4/1-2 Thanon Ratchadamri (0 2255 6248).

### Hualumphong Food Station

*92/1 Sukhumvit Soi 34, access signed from Soi 26 (0 2661 3538/www.hualamphongfood.com). Phrom Phong BTS.* **Open** 11am-11pm daily. **Main courses** B175. **Credit** AmEx, DC, MC, V. **Map** p312 K6.
The puzzling name refers to the train station at the centre of not just of a country, but a food culture. Though the menu is wide ranging, it is the bitter-spicy Isaan fare that draws a seemingly endless number of diners. With haunting traditional music and an open-air bamboo hut building, flags waving from the rafters and balconies, it is not hard to to be transported by a meal here.

### Kalapapreuk on First

*1st Floor, Emporium, Sukhumvit Soi 24 (0 2664 8410-2). Phrom Phong BTS.* **Open** 11am-10pm daily. **Main courses** B170. **Credit** AmEx, DC, MC, V. **Map** p312 K6.
Friendly, ever trendy and spacious; that's the Kalapapruek trinity. Cushioned banquettes and wooden lawn benches overlook Benjasiri Park. The menu is strong on regional specialities, such as roti with curry, Chiang Mai's beloved *khao soi*, and *koong foo* (crispy prawn with green mango salad). It's owned by the son of aristocrat Mom Chao Bhisadhet Rachanee, who set up the original Kalapapreuk in Bangrak, where much of the food for the branches is prepared. There's another branch on the fifth floor.
**Branches: Kalapapreuk** Thanon Pramuan, Bangrak (0 2236 4335); **By Kalapapreuk** All Seasons Retail Centre, Thanon Witthayu (0 2685 3860).

### Kannicha

*17 Sukhumvit Soi 11 (0 2651 1573/4). Nana BTS.* **Open** 11am-11pm daily. **Main courses** B220. **Credit** AmEx, MC, V. **Map** p311 J5.
Like all great food countries, Thailand has an enormous repertoire of cooking that was once available only to royalty. Several decades ago these recipes began to trickle to the public's tables – including at Kannicha, with an old wood and glass house down a quiet *soi*. Owner-chef Montri Virojvechapant creates Three Kings rice, salads of rose apple pollens, and chilli dips of symphonic complexity – there's hardly a dish that you'll find elsewhere.

### Khrua Vientiane

*8 Sukhumvit Soi 36 (0 2258 6171). Thonglor BTS.* **Open** noon-11.30pm daily. **Main courses** B100. **Credit** AmEx, MC, V. **Map** p312 L7.

## Thai

### Ana's Garden

*67 Sukhumvit Soi 55 (0 2391 1762). Thonglor BTS.* **Open** 5pm-1am Tue-Sun. **Main courses** B190. **Credit** MC, V. **Map** p312 M6.
Eating in garden settings is a favoured pastime among Thais, but such places can be harder and harder to find when not upcountry. Ana's Garden, in the midst of bustling Thonglor, is a fine example, with its linking wooden decks and lush green garden. Dinner here, whether steak or green curry, can quickly turn into an all-night affair, listening to reggae on the sound system and laughing the night away (so long as the rain stays away).

### Cabbages & Condoms

*10 Sukhumvit Soi 12 (0 2229 4610). Asoke BTS/ Sukhumvit subway.* **Open** 11am-10pm daily. **Main courses** B180. **Credit** AmEx, DC, MC, V. **Map** p311 J5.
Meechai Viravaidhya is known as Mr Condom for his global work on birth control – he more or less put the rubber in the Thai conscience. Safe sex plays a big part in his restaurant, a two-storey building with a rooftop garden, a good-time vibe, wooden furniture and a clear-noodle Condom Salad.

### Greyhound Café

*2nd Floor, Emporium, Sukhumvit Soi 24 (0 2664 8663/2260 7149). Phrom Phong BTS.* **Open** 11am-10pm daily. **Main courses** B200. **Credit** AmEx, DC, MC, V. **Map** p312 K6.
At fashion designer Jitsing Somboon's Greyhound Café, minimalism abounds in the form of white walls, brushed metal, hand-written menus and huge plates. Thai staples, steaks and local fusion conceits,

Eat, Drink, Shop

A block from noisy Sukhumvit, you're practically upcountry in a *soi* that's a trove of Isaan and Lao food. Before you reach similar outlets Bane Lao and Khrua Rommai (the only one without dance shows), this sprawling wooden compound offers seating on a balcony, in cushion-seating *salas* or around an old Banyan tree. *Pong lang* dancers and musicians (7.30-10pm daily) add to what's an enchanting setting. It may be popular with *farang*, but the food's authentic and the ambiance rootsy.

### White Café
*142 Sukhumvit Soi 49 (0 2712 8808). Thonglor BTS.* **Open** 6pm-midnight Mon-Fri; 6pm-1am Sat, Sun. **Main courses** B160. **Credit** MC, V. **Map** p312 L7.

With its serene garden and global grooves, White Café matches retro cool with timeless taste. It evokes both 1980s camp and, in its cuisine, the kind of effortless Thai synergy that produces dishes such as *plan insee kamin* (deep-fried mackerel with turmeric) and *kaeng liang loong* (herbal soup with shrimp). Regulars know to order from the superb selection on the daily menu.

## Vegetarian

### Govinda
*6/5-6 Sukhumvit Soi 22 (0 2663 4970). Phrom Phong BTS.* **Open** 11.30am-3pm, 6pm-midnight Mon, Wed-Sun. **Main courses** B160. **Credit** V. **Map** p312 K6.

Owner Gianni Sotgia hails from Sardinia, and (despite his restaurant's name) the excellent food is all Italian: thin-base pizzas, pastas and risottos, accompanied by own-made bread. The two-level interior is atmospheric, with a winding staircase and upstairs balcony. German beer too.

# Menu & etiquette

It is completely normal for Thais and lovers of things cooked by them to spend hours, days, if not lives in the pursuit of understanding Thai cuisine. Like the culture itself, Thai cooking is a synthetic whole with influences from India, China, Burma, Europe and beyond. There are rural and courtly traditions, dishes reserved for religious purposes and cookbooks written only on the occasion of a death. Thai food can be as simple or as complex as you like, but there are some basics you need to know.

Rice is the foundation upon which most of Thai food rests. With (some) noodle preparations as an exception, rice is eaten with almost every meal or dish. Stir-fries are nestled on top of it, curries are served with it and it is sweetened with coconut milk to make *khanom* (sweets). Everywhere you go there will be *khao plao* on offer: plain white rice. It is also known as *khao suay* – 'beautiful rice'. In northern and Isaan cuisine, as well as desserts, *khao niao* is eaten instead. This is sticky rice, which arrives in small bamboo containers and is eaten with the right hand in the same, or alternate, bites as the food. Should you not like sticky rice, the plain white variety is eaten all over the country.

### ASSEMBLY INSTRUCTIONS
While Thai food is prepared by a cook or chef, it is always assembled by the diner in ways wholly different from in the West. Whether within a single plate of noodles or on a table with enough dishes to feed a football team,

Thai cuisine is balanced naturally between hot, sour, salty and sweet, as well as heavy or light dishes. It's the same penchant for patterns that informs Thai design and textiles. When it comes to sharing meals, Thais don't order in the mine/yours or appetiser/entrée fashion of Europeans. Instead, there is an array of small to medium dishes, soups, curries or fish preparations that are traditionally shared.

The following menu glossary is broken down by category of food and preparation much in the same way that Thais might naturally think about ordering. For example, a curry lush with coconut milk might be accompanied by a sprightly salad to cut the heaviness; a large, somewhat bland steamed fish might be offset with a chilli-strewn vegetable stir-fry, or a big tureen of hot-and-sour soup might be flanked by a stir-fry of meat. Two categories unfamiliar to many foreigners are, in fact, the bedrock of much Thai cooking. They are *yum* – spicy salads, made with hundreds of ingredients, but often having an acid-sweet-spicy balance, most famously in *som tam* (papaya salad) – and *nam prik* – chilli dips that are often based on shrimp paste and can be pungent, spicy or smoky. These two dishes, like plain rice, are tastes Thais keep coming back to for purposes of balance.

### WHAT AND WHERE
It is important to remember that the concept of eating out is very new to Thailand, having become common only in the past few decades. Before that, cooking and eating

# North

## International

There are plenty of African and Muslim cafés and restaurants in **Pratunam Market** (*see p134*) and along **Soi 3/1**.

### The Pickle Factory

*55 Ratchawithi Soi 2 (0 2246 3036). Victory Monument BTS.* **Open** 5pm-1am daily. **Main courses** B200. **No credit cards. Map** p309 E1.
Away from the city bustle down a quiet suburban *soi*, the SkyTrain plus taxi trip is worth it for a laid-back dinner with long-stay American Jeff Fehr. His individually styled pizzas, such as 'alla vodka' and 'Chiang Mai sausage', are the favoured choice, and most people eat them outside by the pool, where they will also probably have a swim. The art deco house and relaxing garden are also the centre of operations for the bakery, which supplies many cafés with New York cheesecake and good key lime pie.

## Thai

Also try **De Bar** and **LarbJazz Café** (for both, *see p129*).

### Hua Plee

*16/74 Wiphawadirangsit Soi 22 (0 2511 1397). Bus 24, 69, 92, 107, 129, 504, 513.* **Open** 4pm-1am daily. **Main courses** B120. **Credit** MC, V.
Hua Plee jogs the memories of Bangkok residents with its old-school looks and quirks. This old house if full of antique fabrics and carvings, toys, bags and boxes. Greenery is everywhere, and the central Thai cooking has the type of oomph and authenticity that only adds to this trip down the local-memory *soi*.

---

were very much confined to the home. So where and when Thais eat – which is pretty much everywhere and always – is a helter-skelter combination of personal urge, modern workday structures and the older cycles of weather and family commitments. Consider: in the Thai language there is no word for lunch or dinner. Rather, there are descriptions of certain foods for certain times of day – morning, midday and night-time – and the vendors change accordingly. Of course, Bangkok is a very modern city and restaurants, while serving all day, tend to cluster business at the traditional mealtimes.

But there are some categories to consider. First, there are *raan ahaan* (food shops), which specialise in one dish, such as *khao man kai* (chicken rice) and tend to open early and close after lunch or in the early evening. Second, and keeping similar hours, are *raan khao kaeng* (curry and rice shops), signposted by a table of silver trays or pots of pre-cooked curries. Third are *raan ahaan tam sang* (food-to-order shops), where you can order from hundreds of dishes to be cooked by memory in the style of that particular place; a sub-category are called *raan khao thom* because the food is served with boiled rice soup.

Restaurants are also classed according to settings that Thais are addicted to, such as restaurants in *baan* (houses) or *suan* (gardens). Then there are *rot khen* (vendor carts) and the many strains of *talaat* (market) running 24 hours a day, seven days a week, 365 days a year.

### TABLE TIPS

Foreigners are often baffled when they can't seem to get chopsticks in Thailand. Thais are confused when *farang* ask for them. So how to eat? The spoon is held in the right hand and the fork in the left. The latter pushes food on to the former and, once you realise that rice will fall through the prongs of a fork, this makes total sense and feels oddly comfortable. Chopsticks are used, but only for noodles and Chinese dishes.

Look out for *Khreung prung* (Thai seasonings), which are carted about in four-bottle holders and include dried chillis, vinegar with chillis, sugar and fish sauce with chillis, and are used for seasoning food to the diner's taste. *Nam jim* (dipping sauces) number in the hundreds and come as flavour partners to seafood, fruit, rice dishes, roast meat and other foods. In all cases there is one goal to Thai cooking: maximum flavour.

### Cooking terms

**neung** steamed; **thord** deep-fried; **phat** stir-fried; **ping** grilled (small or skewered pieces); **phao** grilled (chillis or seafood); **yaang** roasted or grilled (meats and large pieces); **op** baked; **tom** boiled; **tam** pounded; **phet** spicy; **khem** salty; **waan** sweet; **priao** sour; **jeud** bland; **sub** minced; **sod** fresh and uncooked.

### Rice dishes (khao)

**khao plao** plain rice; **khao niao** sticky rice; **khao phat phak** vegetable fried rice; **khao phat kai/muu/neua/phak** (fried rice with ▶

### Mid Night Kai Ton

*Thanon Petchaburi Tut Mai (no phone). Bus 11,
23, 38, 58, 60, 62, 113, 508, 512.* **Open** 7pm-4am
daily. **Main courses** B40. **No credit cards.**
**Map** p309 & 310 F3.

As the name suggests, this is late-night food for the
masses and it comes in the form of *khao man kai.*
It's a classic Hainainese trader dish of chicken-
flavoured rice, steamed chicken and broth offset by
intense hits of ginger and chilli sauce. And quite
understandably, the party-down customer base just
don't seem to be able to get enough of it.

### Tak Sura

*499 Thanon Ratchawithi (0 2245 7274).
Victory Monument BTS.* **Open** 5pm-1am daily.
**Main courses** B100. **No credit cards.**

Tak Sura sits behind a bus stop, an island of a wood-
en house in a sea of concrete buildings. There's a
blurred, smoky quality to the place, which is decked
out in old train benches and Chinese teahouse chairs,
and hasn't changed a bit over the years. One look at
the empty whisky bottles and ravaged plates of
drinking food such as *larb gai* and Thai sausages,
and it becomes obvious that the same can be said
for the eclectic yuppy-student-artist crowd and
chilli-laced local dishes.

## South

### International

### Café Siam

*4 Soi Si Aksorn, Thanon Chueploeng, South (0 2671
0030/1). Bus 17, 22, 35, 62, 67, 116, 149.* **Open**
11.30am-2pm, 6.30pm-midnight daily. **Main
courses** B400. **Credit** AmEx, MC, V.

▶ ## Menu & etiquette (continued)

chicken/pork/beef/vegetables; **khao phat
man koong** shrimp paste fried rice; **khao
yum** southern-style rice salad; **khao kaeng**
curry over rice; **khao mun kai** Hainanese-style
chicken rice; **khao na ped** roast duck rice;
**khao muu daeng** red-roasted pork on rice;
**khao mok kai** Thai-Muslim chicken biryani.

### Noodle dishes (kuaytiao & ba mee)

**Types: ba mee** egg noodles; **kuaytiao**
rice noodles; **sen-lek** narrow; **sen-yai**
wide; **sen-mee** fine; **haeng** dry; **nam** wet.

**Noodles in a bowl: ba mee muu daeng** egg
noodles with red-roasted pork; **kuaytiao look
chin pla** rice noodles with fish balls; **kuaytiao
look chin muu** rice noodles with pork balls;
**khao soi** Chiang Mai-style egg noodles with
chicken curry broth.

**Noodles on a plate: kuaytiao pad thai
sen-lek** stir-fry with prawns, ground peanuts,
tofu, bean sprouts, spring onion and egg;
**kuaytiao pad khee mao** fried rice noodles
with chilli, holy basil and garlic; **pad si-ew
kai sen-yai** fried in black soy sauce with
vegetables and chicken; **kuaytiao rad na
sen-yai** in gravy with vegetables and meat;
**kuaytiao reua** (boat noodles) rice noodles
with dark herbal broth.

### Spicy salads (yum)

**yum tua plu** winged bean salad; **yum
woon sen** glass noodle salad with pork
and shellfish; **yum hua plee** banana blossom
salad; **yum pla dook foo** fluffy fried catfish

A very beautiful old house restored to Indochine elegance with antique and repro furniture, all of which is for sale (the owners have a workshop opposite). The menu consists of reasonable half-French, half-Thai dishes, but nobody minds, because the setting is so luscious. Have a *digestif* upstairs after the meal.

### The Colonnade

*1st Floor, Sukhothai Hotel, 13/3 Thanon Sathorn Tai, South (0 2287 0222). Bus 17, 22, 35, 62, 67, 116, 149.* **Open** 6am-midnight daily. **Main courses** B420. **Credit** AmEx, DC, MC, V. **Map** p311 G7.

In a city that takes Sunday brunch very seriously, this is the queen. You get an extraordinarily luxurious spread, from breakfast cereal through oysters and roasts to a rich display of cheeses, with mountains of seafood, cooked meats and desserts in between. If you really want to show off, go for the Champagne brunch, with an unlimited flow of bubbly. The setting is gorgeous: a high-ceilinged room with a moat outside the window, complete with *stupa*. It's hugely popular, so booking is essential.

### La Scala

*Pool wing, Sukhothai Hotel, 13/3 Thanon Sathorn Tai, South (0 2287 0222). Bus 17, 22, 35, 62, 67, 116, 149.* **Open** 11.30am-2.30pm, 6.30-11.30pm daily. **Main courses** B650. **Credit** AmEx, DC, MC, V. **Map** p311 G7.

Bangkok's classiest opening in ages further ups its already world-class choice of Italian cuisine with reinterpretations of classic components prepared artfully in an unobtrusive open island kitchen by chef Angelo Rittoli. Long lamps and legless solid teak tables seating eight miraculously protrude from walls clad in terracotta and hand-cast bronze strips. Thai materials and eclectic jazz add sensuality to this minimalist, yet sociable showpiece.

---

salad; **yum moo yang** grilled pork salad; **yum som-o** pomelo salad; **yum pla meuk** squid salad; **yum maa-kheua yao** grilled long aubergine salad with minced pork; **som tam** shredded papaya salad; **larb muu/ped/kai** Isaan or northern-style salad with chilli, mint, lime, roasted rice powder, fish sauce and minced pork/duck/chicken; **muu nam tok** Isaan-style salad containing grilled pork and roasted rice powder.

### Stir-fried & fried dishes (phat & thord)

**phat hoey lai nam phrik pao** clams stir-fried with roast chilli paste and holy basil; **kai phat med ma muang** chicken stir-fried with cashew nuts and dried chillis; **muu thord kratiam phrik** Thai pork marinated and fried with garlic and black pepper; **kai phat khing** chicken stir-fried with ginger; **kai phat bai kaphrao** chicken stir-fried with holy basil; **kai thord** deep fried chicken; **neua phat nam-man hoey** beef stir-fried with oyster sauce; **kai phat priao-waan** sweet-and-sour chicken; **puu phat pong karii** crab stir-fried with curry powder and egg.

### Curries (kaeng)

**kaeng khiao-waan** sweet green curry; **kaeng phet** red curry; **kaeng luang** southern-style yellow curry without coconut milk; **kaeng karii** mild yellow curry; **kaeng Matsaman** mild Muslim-style curry with peanuts; **kaeng pa** jungle curry with herbs and ginger without coconut milk; **kaeng panaeng** thick red curry with peanuts; **kaeng tai pla** southern curry with fish stomach; **kaeng som** sour curry not containing coconut milk.

### Clear curries & soups (kaeng jeud & tom)

**kaeng jeud tauhoo/moo sub** 'bland soup' with vegetables and tofu/minced pork; **kaeng liang** aromatic vegetable soup; **tom yum** hot-and-sour soup with kaffir lime and lemon grass; **tom kha** coconut-milk soup made with galangal and kaffir lime; **khao tom** boiled rice soup.

### Chilli dips (nam phrik)

**nam phrik kapi** shrimp paste dip; **nam phrik long reua** shrimp paste and spicy fried fish dip; **nam phrik ong** roast tomato dip with minced pork and lemongrass; **nam phrik nuum** young green chilli dip with roast aubergine; **nam phrik pao** sweet roasted chilli dip with fish sauce.

### Seafood dishes (ahaan talay)

**pla meuk neung manao** steamed squid in lime sauce; **puu op woon sen** crab baked with glass noodles; **hoey malaeng phuu neung** mussels steamed with lemongrass, shallots and kaffir lime; **haey nanng rom** raw oysters with lime, shallots, garlic and cassia; **koong pao** grilled shrimp; **plaa jian** whole fish cooked with ginger, onion and soy; **pla thord kratiam phrik** Thai deep-fried fish with garlic and black pepper; **pla meuk phat phet** squid stir-fried with chilli; **po thaek** a type of hotpot made with mixed seafood.

▶

## Thai

### Celadon
*1st Floor, Sukhothai Hotel, 13/3 Thanon Sathorn Tai, South (0 2287 0222). Bus 17, 22, 35, 62, 67, 116, 149.* **Open** 11.30am-2.30pm, 6.30-10.30pm daily. **Main courses** B280. **Credit** AmEx, DC, MC, V. **Map** p311 G7.

Celadon is something of a rarity: a hotel restaurant serving the kind of fifth-gear cooking that even the discerning locals will grace with their dinner presence. Lotus ponds, bronze vases and Sakul Intakul's floral fantasies give one the feeling of floating, while managing to retain a homely vibe. The *penang* curry, banana flower salad, lotus dumplings and *miang kham* (betel leaf starter) are all can't-miss dishes. Pricing is moderate considering the setting and pedigree of the kitchen.

### Vegetarian

### Anotai
*976/17 Soi Rama IX Hospital, Thanon Rama IX, North-east (0 2641 5366-9). Rama IX subway/bus 137, 168, 179, 517.* **Open** 10am-9.30pm Mon, Tue, Thur-Sun. **Main courses** B110. **No credit cards**. **Map** p312 M3.

A cute modern restaurant with a New Agey atmosphere amid bamboo and natural fabrics, Anotai even has its own yoga school upstairs. As for the food, cheap Thai noodle and rice dishes are offered, as well as Chinese-style mock fish, beef and chicken. And if you aren't hungry enough for all that, there are home-made cakes and herbal teas, too. Of course, you could always work up an appetite upastairs.

---

► ## Menu & etiquette (continued)

### Vegetables (phak)
**pad phak nam phrik pao** stir-fried vegetables with roasted chilli paste; **phak boong fai daeng** stir-fried morning glory with garlic and chilli; **phak kha-na pla khem** Chinese kale with Thai salted fish and garlic; **pad phak nam man hoy** stir-fried vegetables in oyster sauce; **pad ka-na muu krob** Chinese kale with crispy pork; **pad tau-fak-yao nam phrik pao** long beans stir-fried with roast chilli paste; **pad phak ruam-mit** stir-fried mixed vegetables; **pad hed hom** stir-fried mushrooms; **tao hoo trong kreung** tofu in soy gravy with vegetables; **pad phak khee mao** stir-fried vegetables with chilli, holy basil and garlic.

### Sauces & seasoning (nam jim & kreung prung)
**sord phrik Si Racha** sweet chilli sauce; **nam pla** fish sauce; **nam pla phrik** chilli fish sauce; **phrik haeng** dried chilli; **nam tan** sugar; **nam som sai chuu** clear vinegar with chilli; **phak dong** pickled vegetables; **bai horapa** sweet basil; **bai kra prao** holy basil; **ta krai** lemongrass; **phak chee** coriander; **si-ew dum** black soy sauce; **phrik Thai** white pepper; **phrik Thai dum** black pepper; **kratiam** garlic.

### Drinks (deum)
**nam plao** plain water; **nam soda** sparkling water; **nam manao** lime juice; **nam ma phrao** coconut juice; **nam krajeab** roselle flower juice; **nam matoom** bael fruit juice; **nam ta krai** lemongrass juice; **nam ponlamai bun** iced fruit shake; **oh-liang** Chinese iced black coffee; **kafae yen** Thai iced coffee with

condensed milk; **cha dum yen** Thai iced black tea; **cha Thai yen** Thai iced tea with condensed milk; **nam tao hoo** hot soya milk.

### Useful vocabulary
**iik neung** one more; **ah-roi** delicious; **mai phet** non-spicy; **phet nit noi** a bit spicy; **chawp phet phet** very spicy; **kin jeh** vegetarian (without dairy, egg, garlic, onion, celery); **mung sa virat** meat-free (includes dairy, egg); **neua** meat (same word for beef).

# Bars & Pubs

Boozy city, pretty people.

Bangkok is a city of extremes, and one that – despite the zealous enforcing of 2am closing – never really stops partying. What else can be expected from the place that invented Red Bull? Though nightlife zones are mooted, bar strips slip in and out of vogue. Shareholders (often Thai celebrities) invest in venues in emerging locations, invite their friends, get bored with it all and move on to the next up-and-coming neighbourhood. They may leave in their wake a sustainable scene, or (as is often the case) it may just fizzle out. But despite these one-month wonders, Bangkok boasts a host of vibrant bars that cover all points of the price spectrum.

Starting at the bottom, there's your basic streetside drink-up, usually involving big bottles of local beer or whisky. At the opposite extreme are rarefied hotel bars such as the **Sukhothai Hotel Bar** (*see p130*), where you can sip Martinis in distinguished company. But it's the broad swathe of places in between that offer the most fun. Bars can be found everywhere: off dank alleyways in Chinatown; hidden among market stalls; tacked on to shopping centres; teetering over canals on wooden floorboards; even occupying '70s-style homes in suburbia.

Thai drinking habits also follow a pattern (*see p124* **Drinks & etiquette**), typically involving live bands and food, with many bars offering fine menus. This means visitors will find that most shophouse bar-restaurants are pretty much geared up for anything from a short tipple to an extended session. In a city where traffic is bad and nights out typically have a host, bars can have multiple zones (lounge, disco, karaoke, restaurant, band, seasonal beer garden) in what's confusingly called a 'pub'. But, happily for resolutely British pub-goers, there are also plenty of expat watering holes.

## Phra Nakorn & Banglamphu

**Thanon Phra Arthit** is lined with trees and tiny, characterful bars, whose (often intriguing) art displays are perused by a clientele of students, university lecturers, NGO staff, intellectuals and artists. **Thanon Khao San** is a rowdy hive of backpacker video dens with a parallel scene of trendy Thai pubs. **Thanon Tanao**'s former bar strip has now shrunk to a core of gay haunts.

### Bar Bali

*58 Thanon Phra Arthit, Banglamphu (0 2629 0318).*
*Bus 3, 6, 9, 15, 19, 30, 32, 33, 43, 53, 64, 65, 82, 506.* **Open** 6pm-1am daily. **Main courses** B80.
**No credit cards**. **Map** p308 B2.
Like many of the arty single-room bars on riverside Phra Athit, Bali consists of four walls of pictures, as well as the requisite food and cocktails. It's a softly lit space holding no more than 30 people.

### Boh

*230 Tha Tien (Chao Phraya Expressboat Pier),*
*Thanon Maharaj, Phra Nakorn (0 2622 3081).*
*Bus 1, 3, 7, 9, 15, 25, 30, 32, 33, 39, 44, 47, 59,*
*80, 82, 203.* **Open** 6pm-1am daily. **Main courses**
B100. **No credit cards**. **Map** p308 B3.
Like its drinks list of local whisky and mixers, Boh's outdoor setting (bright neon lights and wooden floorboards on the pier) could hardly be described

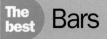

**The best** Bars

**For an arty ambiance**
Pick any bar along **Thanon Phra Arthit**.
*See p123.*

**For bargain booze**
**Mountain Bike**. *See p129.*

**For bohemian abandon**
**Gig Grocery**. *See p128.*

**For discreet chic**
**Nite Syringa**. *See p126.*

**For good beer**
**The Londoner Brew Pub** (*see p128*)
and **Buddy Beer** (*see p124*).

**For meeting expats**
**The Barbican**. *See p125.*

**For a range of drinks**
**Sukhothai Hotel Bar**. *See p130.*

**For spaced-out design**
**Bed Supperclub**. *See p127.*

**For Thai trendies**
**LarbJazz Café**. *See p129.*

**For one last drink**
**Home**. *See p126.*

Eat, Drink, Shop

as classy. But the views are free; and at their most spectacular when the sun sets behind Wat Arun across the river. The clientele of students, artists, gays and workers stay late.

### Buddy Beer

*265 Thanon Khao San, Banglamphu (0 2629 4477/99/www.buddylodge.com). Bus 39, 44, 59, 60, 201, 503, 511, 512.* **Open** 24hrs daily. **Main courses** B90. **No credit cards. Map** p308 B3.

Part of a trendy new boutique hotel, Buddy Beer represents the new face of multicultural Khao San. A service island anchors the bright roomy hall strewn with cushioned wicker chairs, although it's the pool table that is the real centre of attention for the mixed crowd of backpackers and locals. Bavarian pork knuckle and sausages complement imported and domestic beers. The Sidewalk Café (208 Thanon Khao San; 0 2282 5573) in an old house opposite is under the same ownership.

### Café Today

*104-5 Thanon Atsadang, Phra Nakorn (0 2222 5531). Bus 39, 44, 59, 60, 201, 512.* **Open** 6pm-2am daily. **Main courses** B80. **Credit** AmEx, MC, V. **Map** p308 B3.

Owned by former fashion designer Kirati Cholasit, this isolated but well-known bar has attracted fashion and entertainment types since the mid 1990s, and it continues to be a gossip generator for local rags. A square bar-cum-DJ booth dominates the dimly lit dining room.

### Hemlock

*56 Thanon Phra Athit, Banglamphu (0 2282 7507). Bus 3, 30, 32, 53, 65.* **Open** 4pm-midnight Mon-Fri; 5pm-midnight Sat. **Main courses** B90. **No credit cards. Map** p308 B2.

A pioneer of this trendy strip, Hemlock is run by ex-Thammasat students and is set apart by its almost Mediterranean breeziness (think whitewashed walls

# Drinks & etiquette

When Thais go out, it's a party from the start. Groups of six or more tend to settle into one venue, their friends flitting back and forth throughout the night. Though sharing bills is creeping in, it's still pretty much a face thing that the host (often the most senior person or the celebrant at birthday parties) picks up the tab, usually through buying a bottle of whisky. At some suburban venues a bottle of Johnny Walker is the admission price.

This unusual door policy has given rise to a whole ritual, with special furniture to accommodate the bottle, ice bucket, mixing

sodas and lime slices. It's also nigh on impossible to monitor how much you drink, as toasts are legion in communal drinking and drinks are constantly topped up, often by the youngest present, out of respect touching left hand to right elbow. Whatever's left is labelled and stored behind the bar until next time. In fact, it's perfectly normal for the bigger venues to have entire rooms of half-drunk premium whiskies (Chivas Regal and Johnny Walker Red or Black at B800-B2,000 are favoured), along with other, cheaper blends such as Spey Royal (B400-

and a rock-strewn interior). The exhibitions and performances upstairs make it a happening venue, with abundant wines and teas as fuel for the fun, along with Thai food inspired by dishes from old royal literary texts.

### Phranakorn Bar
*58/2 Soi Damnoen Klang Tai, Thanon Ratchadamnoen, Phra Nakorn (0 2622 0282). Bus 39, 59, 60, 201, 503, 511, 512.* **Open** 6pm-1.30am daily. **Main courses** B90. **No credit cards. Map** p308 B3.
A young, creative clientele (and a sprinkling of Khao San escapees) gather on Phranakorn's mellow trellis-and-vines roof terrace for a distant view of the flood-lit Golden Mount and some spicy (to extra hot) Thai food. Artwork is displayed on the third floor (the owner is a photographer), while regulars tend to linger near the second-floor pool table or share some bottles of blended whisky downstairs.

B600) and some local rums such as the Mekhong fire-water (B350) or the mercifully smoother Saeng Som (B350).

Individual bottled beers hold little appeal because Thais like to share, so local brews such as Singha, Chang and licensed Carlsberg and Heineken are mostly seen in huge bottles that get shared between imbibers. Hence the popularity of draught pitchers at the beer gardens that proliferate on every mall or forecourt in the cool season. Beer is often drunk on the rocks.

Cocktails, too, are shared, with the staple Kamikaze coming in a jug. You may even see Saeng Som whisky and Red Bull mixed in a plastic ice bucket and supped through several straws on a dancefloor (a potentially wobbly combination). Rivalling Red Bull in the energy drinks stakes are Shark, M-150 and Carabao Daeng, just launched by rock singer Ad Carabao.

Though drinks lists tend to revolve around whisky, vodka and beer, inroads are being made by wilder cocktails, shots and pre-mixed bottled drinks. Lychee Martinis are also big, as are boozy iced teas and wine, although knowledge of labels and how to serve them is rare.

To absorb all this alcohol, there's a whole repertoire of *kub klaem* (drinking snacks) that includes cashew nuts fried and tossed with touches of chilli and kaffir lime, spicy salads, deep-fried chicken cartilage and grilled meats with chilli dips.

### Suzie Pub
*108-5-9 Soi Rambuttri, Banglamphu (0 2282 4459). Bus 39, 44, 59, 60, 201, 503, 511, 512.* **Open** noon-2am daily. **Main courses** B90. **No credit cards. Map** p308 B2.
This fun alleyway bar – a cross between an American college bar and a dance club – brought Thai nightlife to Khao San. On weekends, young travellers and university students cram into its dark interior to the sound of DJ-spun rock standards, while the laid-back week nights leave elbow room for pool and empty tables for pub dinners.

## Thonburi
There's a very Thai bar strip near Wat Arun at the corner of **Thanon Itsaraphap** and **Thanon Wang Derm.**

### River Bar Café
*405/1 Soi Chao Phraya Siam, Thanon Ratchawithi (0 2879 1748/9). Bus 18, 28, 108, 515.* **Open** 5pm-2am daily. **Main courses** B220. **Credit** AmEx, DC, MC, V.
The glass-encased River Bar Café, tucked away near the Sang Hee Bridge by the muddy waters of Chao Phraya, is one of the few places where it's possible to eat sea-fresh fish in style. The simple preparations (steamed, deep-fried, spicy salads) are pleasingly unfussy and delicious. The terraces and soaring ceilings, done up with modish industrial touches, provide the party setting for an attractive crowd of foreigners and locals.

## Dusit
A knot of bars has opened up amid the **Suan Oi Soi** off Thanon Sukhothai, near Samsen, disrupting this formal district. The most laid-back place choice is **Ad Here**.

## Chinatown
Drink is where you find it in this labyrinth of streets and alleyways. Although, opening nights and trendy parties are often held at **About Café** (*see p169*).

## Bangrak
Bar-restaurants sprinkle Soi Saladaeng and Soi Convent, though cacophonous cul-de-sac **Silom Soi 4** has been trend central since the 1970s, while **Silom Soi 2** is purely gay. Otherwise, there's just sleazy **Soi Patpong** and **Soi Thaniya**'s Little Tokyo.

### The Barbican
*9/4-5 Soi Thaniya (0 2234 3590/www.greatbritish pub.com). Saladaeng BTS/Silom subway.* **Open** 11.30am-2am daily. **Main courses** B200. **Credit** AmEx, DC, MC, V. **Map** p310 F6.

Get ready to party at the **River Bar Café** in Thonburi. *See p125.*

From the same owners as the more rough-hewn Bull's Head (*see p128*), this split-level pub goes against the grain of karaoke and sushi bars on Soi Thaniya, beloved of Japanese expats. Thanks to its modern style – plenty of bright wood and smooth metal – it's a magnet for trendier expats and young westernised Thais. Regular nights with DJs, lucrative prize draws and Premiership screenings feature in the restaurant upstairs.

### Home

*114/14 Silom Soi 4 (0 2238 5257). Saladaeng BTS/ Silom subway.* **Open** 6pm-2am daily. **Main courses** B100. **Credit** V. **Map** p310 F7.

One of the calmest bars on this strip, Home has the de rigueur peoplewatching terrace, but inside there's an air of masculine sophistication in the several floors of dark, comfy leather upholstery, bare wooden floorboards, white walls and moody house music. The bathroom is also much talked about for its expansive jungle leafiness.

### Nite Syringa

*10 Thanon Srivieng (0 2630 3135). Surasak BTS.* **Open** 6pm-1am Mon-Sat. **Credit** AmEx, MC, V. **Map** p310 E7.

Between blaring Silom and Sathorn, this barely converted aristocratic mansion is very much a place apart (look for its tiny sign on the gate lamps). The eclectic taste of its owner, Japanese designer Oguri, reveals itself in the details: Eames-style furniture, Yves Saint Laurent couture, beaded handbags, and knick-knacks from Asia to Zanzibar. Jazzy sounds and subtle lighting provide an atmosphere of confident worldliness that makes for an intriguing night.

### O'Reilly's Irish Pub

*62 Thanon Silom, at Soi Thaniya (0 2632 7515). Saladaeng BTS/Silom subway.* **Open** 11am-2am daily. **Main courses** B300. **Credit** AmEx, DC, MC, V. **Map** p310 F6.

An Irish pub on a Japanese *soi* in the middle of Thailand – welcome to cosmopolitan Bangkok. With its worn floorboards, high stools and tables, and roar of accented English, this is a more rough-and-tumble (and some would argue authentic) antidote for homesickness. Knock back Kilkenny's, munch on fish and chips or simply watch a footie derby. The Thai Chess Club meets upstairs every Friday night.

### Shenanigan's Irish Pub

*1/5-6 Sivadol Building, Soi Convent (0 2266 7160/1/ www.delaney.co.th). Saladaeng BTS/Silom subway.* **Open** 11am-2am daily. **Main courses** B280. **Credit** AmEx, DC, MC, V. **Map** p310 F7.

This smart pub functions as a social embassy for British and Irish expats. Brass detailing, dark mahogany, Irish stew, ales aplenty on tap (Malaysian-brewed Guinness costs B320 a pint), football on the TV and the occasional live jig make it easy to forget you're in Thailand. Presumably, that's precisely the point.

## Pathumwan

One of Bangkok's oldest and calmest bar strips, the west end of **Soi Sarasin** is enjoying a revival. **Siam Square**, on the other hand, acquires and loses nightlife spots as fast as the fashions that flit through its market stalls. And

from November to early February, the mother of all beer gardens fronts the **World Trade Centre**, with three brewers' stages competing for the custom of thousands of revellers.

### Aqua

*Regent Hotel, 155 Thanon Ratchadamri (0 2251 6127 ext 1248/9). Ratchadamri BTS.* **Open** 11am-midnight daily. **Main courses** B180. **Credit** AmEx, DC, MC, V. **Map** p311 G5.

Bangkok's A-list flock to this chic oasis in a hotel courtyard. Wooden rockers and white axe pillows reveal a hint of the sleek, while lush greenery and a pond (and even the odd duck) add a tropical touch. Lean back and sip lemongrass and saké Martinis to live jazz guitar most nights.

### Big Echo

*1st Floor, Kian Gwan Building, 140 Thanon Witthayu (0 2627 3071-4). Bus 13, 17, 50, 62, 76.* **Open** 11am-1am daily. **Credit** AmEx, DC, MC, V. **Map** p311 H5.

Die-hard crooners can pick from a catalogue of more than 30,000 songs (with roughly 40% in English, the rest in Japanese, Chinese and Thai) at this branch of a Japanese chain. There are 40 individual rooms (each holding three to 40), where Japanese and Thai food and international snacks are served.

### Fou Bar

*2nd Floor, 264/4-6 Siam Square Soi 3 (0 2658 4040). Siam BTS.* **Open** 11am-1am daily. **Main courses** B80. **Credit** AmEx, MC, V. **Map** p309 & p310 F4.

Fashion TV plays overhead while customers fight over the candy-coloured couches (most end up settling for simple tables and chairs) at this youthful joint. A small stage hosts bands who blast out pop, rock and punk, much to the delight of the college students supping cocktails and pitchers of beer.

## Sukhumvit

The *soi* leading off this entertainment and expat highway have distinct scenes. **Sois 3-9** lure foreign lotharios to their tacky dens, while **Soi 11** harbours chic destination bars. Connected by the circuitous 'Green Route', **Sois 23-31** form a loop of restlessly trendy ventures, while **Sois 22, 33** and **33/1** are chocka with low-to middle-brow *farang* haunts. **Sois 24** and **26** hold destination discos, facing the posier nightspots of moneyed **Sois 39, 49** and **53**. Soi 55 (**Thonglor**) and Soi 63 (**Ekamai**) bristle with faddish openings and closings; connecting them, Ekamai Soi 22 (**Chamchan**) remains a quirky row of art bars.

### Aise

*33/1 Sukhumvit Soi 31 (0 2662 1177/ www.theaise.com). Asoke BTS/Sukhumvit subway then taxi.* **Open** 6pm-2am Mon-Sat. **Main courses** B100. **Credit** AmEx, DC, MC, V. **Map** p312 K6.

A hip joint, this (pronounced 'I say'), where stylish young things order in casual Thai and gossip in California Valley English. There's a lot of lounging around the strategically lit swimming pool or grooving to the sounds of the DJ in the glass-walled interior. European and US academic holidays are the busiest periods. Expect Western music, Thai food and trendy drinks.

### Bar Baska

*82/38 Ekamai Soi 22 (0 2711 4748/9). Ekamai BTS then taxi.* **Open** 6pm-2am daily. **Main courses** B200. **Credit** AmEx, MC, V.

Across Ekamai from the Soi Chamchan art bars, this retro building has been given a Balinese-style make-over with underlighting, gurgling water and teak decks. The music is hit and miss, but when it's hitting the right note there's a worldly yet tropical formality about the lofty main room. Big groups flock here on weekends.

### Bar-Bu-Ree

*59 Sukhumvit Soi 63 (0 2392 4976-8). Ekkamai BTS then taxi.* **Open** 5.30pm-2am daily. **Main courses** B100. **Credit** AmEx, DC, MC, V. **Map** p312 M7.

Bar-Bu-Ree's expansive layout, complete with car park, is quite a departure from Ekamai's other cramped bars. Well-coiffed finance and fashion types crowd the long bar and tables for post-work tipples. Though the clean interior lines and weighty cocktail list might imply assured poshness, there's also an ostentatious mood to this place.

### Bed Supperclub

*26 Sukhumvit Soi 11 (0 2651 3537/ www.bedsupperclub.com). Nana BTS.* **Open** 8pm-2am daily. **Main courses** B500. **Credit** AmEx, DC, MC, V. **Map** p311 J5.

Celebrities and beautiful people are the target audience of what may be the most ambitious bar in Asia. It's an achingly hip amalgam of futuristic flourishes (spacey oval pods, white mattress, couches, low lighting and staircases leading out to balconies). But aesthetics aside, what are the drinks like? The cocktails are very good (if a little pricey, but then you're paying more for the experience than for the drink itself) and there's also an interesting restaurant, where chef Dan Ivorie (who used to man the hobs at Jester's, *see p106*) conjures fusions as wickedly sharp as the bar's playlist.

### Bourbon Street

*Washington Square, Sukhumvit Soi 22 (0 2259 0328/9). Phrom Phong BTS.* **Open** 7am-1am daily. **Main courses** B320. **Credit** AmEx, DC, MC, V. **Map** p312 K6.

This bar-restaurant, situated in a square of bars and restaurants, is of better quality than most of it neighbours, thanks to its tasty, mainly Cajun and Creole food. Along with blackened chicken and jambalaya, try the crawfish (guaranteed fresh, because the owner farms them upcountry). For dessert, the pecan pie is recommended.

It's all a bit futuristic at **Bed Supperclub**. *See p127.*

### The Bull's Head

*Sukhumvit Soi 33/1 (0 2259 4444/www.great britishpub.com). Phrom Phong BTS.* **Open** 11am-1.30am daily. **Main courses** B300. **Credit** AmEx, DC, MC, V. **Map** p312 K6.

By far the most authentic British pub in Bangkok, this traditional tavern is a wood-and-horse-brass timewarp with past hits on the jukebox, pub grub, games like 'toss the boss' and pop quizzes. An international (mostly British) crowd get stuck into draught Carlsberg and Heineken, mooching up to the second floor every couple of months to check out world-class comics at the Punchline Comedy Club.

### Café 50

*24 Ekamai Soi 21 (0 2381 1773). Ekamai BTS then taxi.* **Open** 5pm-1am Mon-Sat. **Main courses** B100. **Credit** V.

This stalwart art bar pulls off the nifty trick of being a furniture and design shop during the day, then, with the flick of a dimmer switch, morphing into an edgy lounge come nightfall. Its eclectic music and knowingly mismatched Scandinavian furniture appeal to the fashionable arty crowd. Oh, and there's a snooker table too.

### For Hor Kor Dor

*15 Ekamai Soi 4 (0 2391 1326). Ekkamai BTS.* **Open** 6pm-1am Mon-Sat. **Main courses** B120. **Credit** MC, V. **Map** p312 M7.

Redolent of a louche house party, this strangely named bar has space for cars to park on the front lawn next to its laid-back outdoor lounging and dining area. The upper deck of the split-level glassed-in interior hosts rowdy live music, or you can shoot some pool down below. Spicy snacks and bottled alcopops make up the menu.

### Fluid

*57/1 Sukhumvit Soi 53 (0 2662 7738). Thonglor BTS.* **Open** 6pm-2am Tue-Sat. **Main courses** B120. **Credit** AmEx, DC, MC, V. **Map** p312 L7.

Situated behind a buzzing restaurant, this design-conscious bar stimulates its trendy punters with colourful cocktails and a chilled soundtrack courtesy of the resident DJ. On weeknights you pretty much get the run of the L-shaped room with its long bar and sofa lounging area.

### Gig Grocery

*200 Sukhumvit Soi 16 (0 2663 1339). Asoke BTS/ Sukhumvit subway.* **Open** 7pm-1am Mon-Sat. **Main courses** B80. **No credit cards**. **Map** p312 K6.

This peculiar corner bar is a studied blend of kitsch and chic ethnicity, with a knowing atmosphere. Savvy eclectic music and simple drinks also contribute to the laid-back vibe.

### The Londoner Brew Pub

*Basement, UBC II Building, Thanon Sukhumvit, at Soi 33 (0 2261 0238-40). Phrom Phong BTS.* **Open** 9am-1am daily. **Main courses** B150. **Credit** AmEx, DC, MC, V. **Map** p312 K6.

This dim, elongated basement bar attracts suits and tourists with its own-brewed British ale. Loners hug the long bar while Sukhumvit angels perch on stools near the pool table next to the big-screen footie action. Brass rails pen off the dining tables, where generous piles of good old British pub grub are served on heavy oval plates. Live bands also play here from 9.15pm-midnight.

### Love Sick

*159/1 Thonglor Soi 10 (0 2711 4477). Thonglor BTS.* **Open** 6pm-2am daily. **Main courses** B100. **Credit** AmEx, MC, V. **Map** p312 L7.

A novelty pub themed around rejection, betrayal and unrequited love, this glaringly red drinking spot, whose emblem is a bandaged heart, features a crying room, a screaming room and a bottle-throwing pit. There's also karaoke – or you can just weep to live music (7pm-1.30am daily).

### Roots Reggae & World Music Club

*6/7-8 Sukhumvit Soi 26 (0 2259 7002). Phrom Phong BTS.* **Open** 6pm-2am daily. **Main courses** B170. **No credit cards**. **Map** p312 L6.

Bangkok's only all-out reggae bar is a slice of Kingston tucked into a little alcove off Sukhumvit. Expect warm orange lighting, Jamaican rhythms and rum punch cocktails.

## North

West from Chatuchak Weekend Market, **Thanon Kamphaengphet** intersperses fish and plant shops with characterful bars, including **ICQ** (*see p176*) and the **Shock**. Affluent **Soi Aree** (Phahonyothin Soi 7) is dotted with nice neighbourhood bar-restaurants, such as the semi-gay **Aaari Ba Bar** (*see p175*). **Thanon Sutthisan-Winitchai** has a tired parade of differently themed yet somehow identical pubs.

### De Bar

*53/35 Wiphawadirangsit Soi 50 (0 2579 2905). Bus 24, 69, 92, 107, 129, 513.* **Open** 5.30pm-2am daily. **Main courses** B100. **Credit** AmEx, DC, MC, V.

New owners (formerly of Bar-Bu-Ree; *see p127*) have revitalised this low-slung '70s property with the addition of a very Bali-esque courtyard and leather-upholstered vintage furniture. Decent jazz and Latin beats draw everyone from air crews, market vendors and artists to tourists and local celebs.

### LarbJazz Café

*807/1-2 Thanon Khamphaengphet (0 2272 4181). Saphan Kwai BTS/Kamphaengphet subway/bus 38, 104, 134, 136, 183, 512.* **Open** 5pm-1.30am daily. **Main courses** B90. **Credit** MC, V.

Larger than its compact frontage suggests, this busy bar sweeps back and soars up two mezzanines. A glass roof allows for plenty of natural light, but night-time is the right time to come here, when copious cocktails and plates of excellent Thai food are consumed to the sound of dance sets from the DJ.

### Mountain Bike

*275/20-22 Thanon Ratchaprarop (0 2246 3296). Phayathai BTS.* **Open** 5pm-1.30am daily. **Main courses** B100. **No credit cards**. **Map** p311 G3.

Ridiculously low prices and all-you-can-scoop ice cubes are the main draws at this busy, self-service bar. Pick up food at the service counter, mix your own whisky and soda, pay on the spot and leave when you want.

**Branch**: Tiger Mask, 2/11 Soi Rangnam, Thanon Phayathai, North (0 2640 1251).

### Viva

*Chatuchak Weekend Market, Section 26, between Sois 1 & 2, Thanon Phahon Yothin (0 2272 4783). Morchit BTS/Kamphaengphet subway.* **Open** 8am-9pm Fri; 7am-9pm Sat, Sun. **Main courses** B80. **No credit cards**.

A cult among Chatuchak Weekend Market-goers, this two-roomed wooden bolt-hole can transform an afternoon shop into an all-hours drinking session. Many a vulnerable shopper has fallen prey to the enticing whisky bottles that line its shelves, but there are also home-made yoghurt drinks on hand for the more virtuous punters. A relaxed spot, without even an ounce of pretence.

## South

Near Sathorn, residential **Narathiwat Ratchanakharin Soi 15** is sprinkled with charming bar-restaurants that keep the volume down low for the neighbours. Further down the street, **Tawandaeng German Brewhouse** is the city's best microbrewery, and the place to hear bizarre Thai band Fong Nam.

### Monkey Shock 2nd

*17 Narathiwas Ratchanakharin Soi 15 (0 2285 6102). Chong Nonsri BTS.* **Open** 5pm-midnight daily. **Main courses** B140. **Credit** AmEx, MC, V.

Something of a pioneering relic of the 1970s, this lively bar is mobbed with post-work groups on

**Eat, Drink, Shop**

Furniture shop-cum-bar **Café 50**. *See p128.*

weekdays and bevies of boozing students on weekends. Sit outside amid fairy lights and well-worn tables laden with good Thai food. And don't be surprised if an elephant wanders by.
**Branches**: Monkey Shock 3rd 116 Thanon Narathiwas Ratchanakharin, South (0 2287 0957); **Monkey Shock 4th** Thanon Narathiwas Ratchanakharin, between Sois 15 & 17, South (0 2286 5605).

### Sukhothai Hotel Bar
*Sukhothai Hotel, 13/3 Thanon Sathorn Tai (0 2287 0222). Bus 17, 22, 35, 62, 67, 116, 149.* **Open** 4pm-1am daily. **Credit** AmEx, DC, MC, V. **Map** p311 G7.
Dark, moody and striking, this earth- and slate-toned bar lives up to its setting in Bangkok's most sophisticated hotel. The crowd is unsurprisingly elegant and might perhaps have been a little subdued had it not been for the recent addition of a DJ, who has succeeded in creating an agreeably subversive vibe. From an admirably hefty drinks list, the Martinis are among the best in town.

## North-east

Thailand's boom in the early 1990s spawned a litter of monstrous nightspots along **Thanon Ratchadaphisek**, of which some remain, and a kilometre-long crescent of 120-plus bars along

nearby **Royal City Avenue** (RCA), which has now dwindled to nothing more than a stretch of screaming dance outlets.

### Brew Pavilion
*93/3 Thanon Rachadaphisek, near RS Tower (0 2642 2002). Thiem Ruammit subway/bus 73, 136, 137, 185, 206, 514.* **Open** 5pm-2am daily. **Main courses** B180. **Credit** AmEx, DC, MC, V.
Certainly not what you'd expect to find planted in a South-east Asian city, this vast Nashville-esque microbrewery is buckets of fun. It's basically a barn the size of an aircraft hangar, with a floodlit stage and seating for thousands, where musical extravaganzas (disco divas, cover bands and whatnot) take place daily. Alongside the house-brewed lager, there's a menu of more than 400 items of Thai, Japanese and German food.

### Old Leng
*29/78-81 Royal City Avenue (0 2203 0972/3). Bus 11, 58, 60, 72, 93, 99, 113, 512.* **Open** 6pm-2am daily. **Main courses** B80. **Credit** AmEx, MC, V. **Map** p312 L4.
This survivor of the original RCA explosion for once merits the term 'unique' – it looks like a cowboy saloon stranded in ancient China. 'Songs for Life' (Thai blues) fans flock here to hear live bands; smoochers gather on the quieter front deck. Hard-drinking adults make it the most grown-up bar on this otherwise teenybopper strip.

# Message in a bottle

In a daring diplomatic move, Thai wine is to be served to the heads of government due to be present at Bangkok's APEC summit in 2003. This is just part of an ongoing promotion of Siamese vintages, which are seen by the government as something of a lucrative market, with Thai restaurants thriving around the world. In an effort to curb the trade deficit, wine imports (which had increased 400 per cent in the mid 1990s) received heavier duties, while regulations were relaxed to encourage consumption of local wines. Now several Thai wineries open each year.

So how do they taste? By world standards, rather disappointing – although both **Chateau de Loei Chenin Blanc** and **Chatemps** have stood up well in blind tastings. Still, relative to the difficulty of viticulture in this climate, the results are very encouraging. While the wines lack balance, and are often low in acidity, they are nonetheless extremely well made and have good colour. Most vineyards have French or German in-house experts and use the latest technology.

**Domaine St-Lo** – sister property of the Thai-owned Château St-Lo in Saint Émilion – does all its testing at Bordeaux University.

The main hindrance to wine growing is humidity, which along with its associated pests, gives vines a short lifespan. As a result, most vineyards are in the cooler north or in the highlands flanking the central plains. But east of Bangkok, Chatemps has its idiosyncratic 'floating vineyards' – the vines are separated by canals and harvested by boat. They are owned by Chalerm Yoovidhya, famous for that other Thai beverage, Red Bull, and boast unusual grapes: Malaga Blanc and Pok Dum ('Black Queen').

Fruit wines – an illegal moonshine enterprise until a 1998 deregulation – are also a staple at Thai festivals. Hordes of rural producers came out of the woodwork with granny's old-time recipes, from mangosteen to longan. The only problem was, they also used granny's earthenware bottling methods and the new-fangled glass ones had a habit of exploding – most memorably on the Agriculture Minister's desk.

Eat, Drink, Shop

# Markets

From the bazaar to the bizarre, this is a city of stalls, trolleys and fly-pitches.

*Talad* (markets) are the soul of Thailand. They are the tap root of street-level social life and the local economy, and the best way to glimpse life as it has always been. Whether you're eating, shopping or sightseeing, markets are the purest expression of the sensual Thai culture, with their kaleidoscope of scents (jasmine garlands, musty puddles, durian), sounds (yelping hawkers, booming techno), sights (sleeping children, slithering eels), touch (antique silk, fake fur) and tastes (food you'll find nowhere else on earth).

Malls may have been embraced with consumerist fervour, but stall culture still thrives and relentlessly colonises any space. And since the current Bangkok governor reinstated Wednesday vending, trade is thriving every day. Specialist *talad* cater to all tastes, with **Chatuchak Weekend Market** (*see p134* **A day in JJ**) being the one essential smörgåsbord to experience.

Bargaining is still common for goods (but never for cooked food), though you should only push beyond a standard ten to 20 per cent off at tourist traps. Pre-armed with shop prices, you must remain polite and only bid if you are prepared to honour their acceptance of your figure. Asking in Thai can lower the starting price, and walking away from an impasse will usually reveal the 'best price'.

Continuing concerns about cleanliness have started to be addressed through hygiene inspections (look out for green and yellow stickers) and plans for hot-water dishwashers at markets. Even so, it's arguable whether vendor food bought, cooked and consumed within hours is less safe than restaurant fare kept in fridges, though sensitive newbies should avoid the crushed ice.

## Clothes

### Bo Bae
*Soi Rong Muang, Thanon Krung Kasem, near Yotse Bridge, Chinatown.* Bus 53, 110, 204, 511. **Open** 9am-6pm daily. **Map** p309 & p310 4E.
This funky canalside venue specialises in wholesale clothes, with fabrics and designs that range from assembly-line rough to catwalk-worthy. There are separate floors for men, women, children and babies. The outdoors area is also chock-a-block with army surplus equipment, including camping gear and mosquito nets.

### Na Ram
*Thanon Ramkhamhaeng, between Soi 43-53, North-east.* Bus 22, 40, 58, 60, 71, 93, 109, 115, 168, 501, 512. **Open** 4pm-midnight daily.
Stretching miles from the Mall Bangkapi to Ramkhamhaeng University, this bazaar touts fashionable outfits and accessories, vintage shades, fisherman's trousers and even uniforms, all priced for students (who in turn bring their own handmade leather bags and shoes to sell). Snack foods such as *luk chin ping* (grilled meatballs) and *khluay thod* (fried banana) are on hand to energise weary shoppers. It's busiest at night.

### Saphan Phut
*Thanon Triphet, Chinatown.* Bus 6, 8, 53, 60, 73, 82. **Open** 8pm-midnight daily. **Map** p308 4C.
Strung like costume jewellery around Memorial Bridge, this plastic-covered night market brims with vintage clothing, T-shirts, handbags, hats and

**Pak Khlong Talad**, for flowers. *See p133.*

**Charoen Krung** in Chinatown: somewhere here is the hi-fi of your dreams. And a hose.

designer copy perfume. Teenagers swarm, as do Thai designers on the prowl – and it's absurdly cheap. Street food is sold on the periphery.

### Tawanna

*Thanon Lad Phrao, between Makro & Mall Bangkapi, North-east (0 2734 2355/6/7). Bus 8, 44, 92, 137, 145, 502, 514.* **Open** 11am-midnight daily.
Trendy threads from suits to *mor hom* (indigo farmer's shirts) are sold here, alongside an outlet for computers and digital goodies. Food, from grilled meats to curry, satisfies the eclectic, mostly after-dark crowd.

## Crafts & accessories

### Amulet Alley

*Trok Wat Mahathat, Thanon Maharat, Phra Nakhon. Bus 39, 70, 80, 201, 203, 512.* **Open** 9am-6pm daily. **Map** p308 3B.
This speciality market, weaving its way down a lane from Thanon Prachan to the river, is the epitome of old Bangkok with its constant flow of human traffic browsing an array of Buddhist imagery, amulets and medals. Bargaining is a must, and there are old-school food stalls aplenty.

### Pahurat

*Thanon Chakkaphet & Thanon Pahurat, Chinatown. Bus 8, 6, 12, 19, 42, 53.* **Open** 9am-6pm daily. **Map** p308 5C.
The heart of Little India, Pahurat is awash with fabrics and textiles from rainbows of saris to Thai and Chinese silks, synthetics and cottons. Winding alleys are filled with incense sellers, teahouses stocking fine *chai* tea and lassis, food markets, collectives of sewing women, and temples. Bollywood movies and sitars blare, and the onslaught of scents and colours is truly memorable.

### Sampeng

*Soi Wanit 1, Chinatown. Bus 1, 73, 204, 507.* **Open** 9am-6pm daily. **Map** p308 5C.
An epic, bustling alleyway that's crammed with bric-a-brac stalls. Newcomers are advised to tackle it in sections. Out east it's hairclips, earrings, sandals and key rings. Midway you'll find ceramics, monks' bowls, Chinese lanterns, kids' shoes and wrapping paper. Across from Thanon Ratchawong are fabrics, jeans and fatigues, including denim and camouflage. Toward the Mahachai end are blankets, sarongs, buttons and laces. The honking motorbikes, smoky quarters and shouting hawkers come free.

## Electronics

### Baan Mor (aka Lang Krasuang)

*Thanon Baan Mor & Thanon Atsadang, Phra Nakorn. Bus 8, 12, 60, 73.* **Open** 9am-6pm daily. **Map** p308 4B.
This spare-parts paradise clings to the peripheries of Khlong Lord and harbours just about anything for TVs, cable boxes, speakers and audio-visual systems – plus vintage LPs. There's army surplus too (it is behind the Defence Ministry, after all).

### Khlong Thom

*Thanon Mahachak, between Thanon Yaowarat & Thanon Charoen Krung, Chinatown. Bus 1, 8, 48, 49, 73, 507.* **Open** 9am-6pm daily. **Map** p308 4C.

This sprawling area sees foreigners mingling chest-to-shoulder with Thais every day of the week. You'll find assorted engines, wheels, tractor parts, metals and other heavy machinery, plus repair services for CD and DVD players. Various homewares, from hoses to carpentry tools, are also in there somewhere.

### Saphan Lek

*Thanon Boriphat, around Grande Ville Hotel, Chinatown. Bus 1, 8, 12, 43, 73, 507.* **Open** 9am-6pm daily. **Map** p308 4C.

Named after an old iron bridge over Khlong Ong Ang, this meandering alleyway dips four steps below street level. Sidewalk shelves are packed with cameras, toy guns, sunglasses and shoes, while shops stock pricier items such as cellphones, DVD players, digicams and an alphabet soup of entertainment (DVD, VCD, VDO).

### Woeng Nakhon Kasem

*Thanon Chakrawat, at Thanon Charoen Krung, Chinatown. Bus 8, 12, 60, 73.* **Open** 9am-6pm Mon-Sat. **Map** p308 4C.

A charming yet hectic area famous for all things audio – instruments, turntables, high-end stereos – as well as culinary contraptions such as ice-cream makers, mincers, coffee grinders and coconut shredders. Home cooks, DJs, producers and the simply curious mingle.

## Flowers & plants

### Pak Khlong Talad

*Thanon Chakphet, from Memorial Bridge to Khlong Lord, Phra Nakorn. Bus 6, 8, 19, 43, 60, 73, 82.* **Open** 24hrs daily. **Map** p308 5B.

To really grasp the Thai love of flowers, visit this remnant of Bangkok's original fresh market, most spectacular from 10pm until dawn. The scent of jasmine fills the air, orchids in forms unseen by most non-Asians are stacked taller than people, and prayer offerings are strung together with Fabergé delicacy. Go after the bars have closed.

### Thewet

*Thanon Krung Kasem, west of Thanon Samsen, Dusit. Bus 30, 32, 53, 64, 99, 506, 516.* **Open** 9am-6pm daily. **Map** p308 1C.

More neighbourly and less exhaustive than Pak Khlong Talad or Chatuchak, but undeniably pleasant with its potted plants and canal views, Thewet is liveliest by day and picturesque at sunset.

## Fresh food

### Khlong Toei

*Thanon Rama IV, at Thanon Na Ranong, South. Bus 14, 47, 74, 109, 507.* **Open** 6am-dusk daily. **Map** p312 K8.

This area right next to the port offers archetypal regional Thai food, with stallholders shifting vegetables, chickens and rare herbs (it's more wholesale after dusk). The big Lao Market stocks specialities from the north-east, while off-the-back-of-a-boat items at the nearby Penang Market are less prevalent than they used to be.

### Or Tor Kor (OTK)

*Thanon Kamphaengphet, opposite Chatuchak Weekend Market, North (0 274 87799). Saphan Kwai BTS/Kamphaengphet subway/bus 38, 104, 134, 136, 183, 512.* **Open** 6am-6pm daily.

Though it's only just across the bridge away from Chatuchak (*see p134* **A day in JJ**), the Agricultural Market Organisation (OTK) remains a relatively little known centre for some of Thailand's best fruit and veg, prepared foods and sweets. A separate building houses products such as lychee jam and Thai arabica coffee from the Royal Projects.

### Sam Yan

*Thanon Phayathai, at Thanon Rama IV, Pathumwan. Sam Yan subway/bus 25, 29, 34, 40, 73, 502.* **Open** *Market* 6am-6pm daily. *Food market* noon-midnight daily. **Map** p310 F6.

This night-and-day happening encompasses a multi-storey building (the food is on the first floor), a wet market and a rambling spread of street vendors. The products reflect the area's Chinese character, hence the top-grade seafood, unusual stir-fries and other more subtle (sweet and savoury) specialities.

## General markets

### Banglamphu

*Thanon Chakkraphong, Banglamphu. Bus 30, 32, 33, 64, 65, 506.* **Open** 9am-6pm daily. **Map** p308 3B.

This traditional *talad* sprawls in and out of the traffic-heavy *thanon* and quiet *soi* just north of Khao San. Fabrics, satay, wooden crafts, fruits, clothes – the range is enormous.

**Patpong & Silom**, for tit and tat. *See p134.*

**Eat, Drink, Shop**

# A day in JJ

Some 250,000 people a week shop until they drop at **Chatuchak Weekend Market**, a sauna-like labyrinth of 8,000-plus stalls. Long known for the sheer scope of its products from Thailand and further afield, 'JJ' (from the alternative spelling, Jatujak) has recently transcended its Asian knick-knack status to become a hive of young talent trained in Thailand, New York, London and Tokyo. And with its abundance of handicrafts from around the world (Burma and Vietnam to Afghanistan and Tibet), JJ is also a gift-seeker's paradise. You may well need its shipping agents.

To truly 'do' JJ would take several weekends, but despite its apparent random nature there is some method to the madness. Numbered sections, themed and divided by *soi*, are colour-coded on various maps (of which *Nancy Chandler's Map* is the best) and indicated by street signs. Useful landmarks for meeting points are the clock tower and tourist office/bank building (open weekends, with ATMs). Benches and trees provide in-market pitstops, while cafés and toilets dot the edges. Locals visit early to pre-empt the sweaty post-lunch throngs. The following sections tackle the basics.

## Antiques, crafts & furniture

Stalls selling traditional Thai crafts are strewn around the market (especially in sections 1, 24 and 26). Seek out hill-tribe rattanware and loom parts to hang textiles from, plus musical instruments, bamboo boxes and *takraw* balls. In section 1, you'll also find puppets, lacquerware, carvings, bronzes, amulets and Buddhas sourced from Chiang Mai and Burma. Bargain hunters might also want to inspect the Thai silk brought to market on multi-day journeys by Isaan women. You may also see artisans making

pottery or touching up paintings. Wooden furniture can be bought ready to ship or crafted to spec, most cheaply in **Sunday Market** (the other side of Thanon Kamphangphet 2) – a threatened enclave of muddy shacks selling reconditioned teak furniture and architectural salvage, and even whole Thai houses for reassembly. Antiques can be expensive.

## Clothes & accessories

Young designers can be found selling their threads (especially shirts and fabrics) in the second-hand flea market of sections 5-6, bordering Thanon Phahon Yothin. You can also find ethnic and bohemian clobber, hats, handbags and uniforms (from Russian army to Korean boy scout). Bargain hard, though, as T-shirts or jeans can come as cheap as B50. New clothes occupy the eastern half of the central block (sections 10, 12, 14, 16, 18, 20-26; for **Common Tribe**, see p141). Everything goes, including beaded handbags, batik sarongs, fishermen's trousers, leather belts, denim and T-shirts in wild Japanese colours or bearing 'Thainglish' phrases.

## Eating & drinking

As well as being a rootsy market and a major import and export centre, JJ also has a social scene. Cafés and food stalls crop up in all sections, touting authentic samples of regional cuisines and snacks. What's more, a new design awareness is funking up lean-to spaces, coffeehouses and bars such as **Viva** (*see p129*). The latter starts slinging juices in the morning and continues – with roadhouse fervour, good-time tunes, beer and whisky – until 2am. Cute venues amid the fish shops along Thanon Kamphaengphet include **LarbJazz Café** (*see p129*), **ICQ** (*see p176*) and the Shock.

## Pratunam & Nai Lert

*North & south of Phetchaburi Road, west of Thanon Ratchaprarop, North. Bus 13, 54, 73, 77, 204, 513, 514.* **Open** *9am-midnight daily.*

The market stalls at Pratunam (meaning 'Water Gate') burrow around Indra and Bayoke Hotels. This is come-one, come-all shopping, at all times, for textiles, lingerie, ceramics, tourist statues and T-shirts. It's popular with African and Middle Eastern traders, and the food available reflects this. Across Thanon Phetchaburi, the newer, cleaner, tamer Talad Nai Lert reaches back to Khlong Saen Saeb and is more tourist-oriented.

## Night markets

### Patpong & Silom

*Patpong Sois 1 & 2 and Thanon Silom, between Sois 2-8, Bangrak. Saladaeng BTS/Silom subway.* **Open** *8pm-2am daily.* **Map** *p310 F6.*

This double-*soi* red-light strip is becoming a Disneyfied coach party stop, selling a range of tourist tat (the trendier wares are further down Silom). The go-go going guys mingle with shopping families and Thais buying copy watches, fake Levi's or pirate CDs of music, movies, porn and games.

## Home improvements & plants

It's worth exploring the rows of tree-shaded boutiques in sections 2-4, where you'll find Thai designers who rise so quickly their creations may be found in foreign capitals within months. Bordering Thanon Kamphaengphet, look for zinc things, kitsch, 1970s-inspired curtains and clocks (for **Reflections**, *see p145*), *saa* (mulberry) paper lamps, cushion covers and scented candles. The street is lined with cafés, while the inner edge of the road bristles with plants, herbs, seeds and flowers, plus the pots and charms that go with them. There are more interior design goodies in sections 7, 26 and the outer edges of sections 8, 9, 11, 12, 15, 17, 19, 21, 22 and 25, and in **Dream Market** behind the banks. A plant and tree market fills this area from 7am to 6pm on Wednesdays and Thursdays.

## Pets, books & utensils

Cages of kittens and puppies sit alongside containers of reptiles, rare birds and tanks of fish in sections 8, 9, 11, 13, 15 and 17, where there is also a nasty trade in endangered species – although a recent fad for selling hissing cockroaches from Madagascar has been banned. More appealing are the ceramics and kitchenware that are sold along with culinary ingredients in sections 17 and 19; stalls selling new and well-thumbed books and magazines (some decades old) are here Wednesday to Sunday.

## Chatuchak Weekend Market

*Thanon Phahon Yothin, corner of Thanon Kamphaengphet, North (0 2272 4635/6). Morchit or Saphan Khwai BTS/ Kamphaengphet subway.* **Open** 7am-6pm Sat, Sun.

### Suan Luang

*Chulalongkorn Soi 5, Pathumwan. National Stadium BTS then taxi.* **Open** 4pm-2am daily. **Map** p309 & p310 E5.

Amid the ill-lit *soi* behind Chulalongkorn University and the National Stadium, this fluorescent flare of holes-in-the-wall is so hotly contested you're assured a bargain feast. Order from every archetypal market dish, from curry to *kha moo* (stewed pig leg).

### Suan Lum Night Bazaar

*Thanon Witthayu, at Thanon Rama IV, Pathumwan. (0 2252 4776/www.thainightbazaar.com). Lumphini subway/bus 13, 14, 17, 47, 50, 62, 74, 76, 141, 507.* **Open** 3pm-midnight daily. **Map** p311 H7.

Billed as Bangkok's 'first official night bazaar', this concrete-strewn conversion of a one-time cadet school is big and neon-bright, with a Khmer-style fibreglass tourist police station. Situated between Lumphini Park and Lumphini Boxing Stadium, it will be boosted by subway access, but still won't be as convenient as its model in Chiang Mai. Highlights are the Joe Louis Theatre (*see p201*), Sunday lunch pop concerts and dining outlets with wooden walkways and trees. But overall it's characterless and rather forced.

# Shops & Services

From the trendiest looks to the most traditional designs, Bangkok offers shoppers the best of both worlds.

Eat, Drink, Shop

Bangkok excels as a shopping city, not only in the sheer variety of its home-grown products but also as a destination whose myriad malls rival those of Hong Kong or Singapore for global brands – all at competitive prices. Bangkok's notoriety for knock-offs is slowly waning with crackdowns on preventable piracy (though copied CDs proliferate). Attention is now more on Thai craftsmanship, making this a marketplace where the exotic East meets minimalist West, creating an intercultural fusion that is raising the bar on modern oriental style.

## MALL THE MERRIER

More through serendipity than careful city planning, Bangkok has an identifiable retail corridor – and it's increasingly dominated by shopping malls. It consists of three contiguous streets, starting at Pathumwan intersection, where the mammoth **Mahboonkrong (MBK)** centre and low-rise Siam Square vie for the disposable income of *wai roon* (young trendies). Across Thanon Rama I stands the speciality luxury complex **Siam Discovery Centre** and the fashion-oriented **Siam Centre**. In 2007 label hunters will converge on **Siam Paragon**, the Mall Group's B6-billion behemoth currently under construction next door, while arch rival **Central Department Stores** (South-east Asia's biggest retailer) is investing twice that in taking over and renovating the gargantuan **World Trade Centre (WTC)**.

Opposing it across Rajaprasong intersection – and indeed in the mall wars – **Gaysorn Plaza** relaunched amid much hype in 2002. To its north are crafts hangar **Narayanaphand** and discount warehouse **Big C**; just to the south the stately **Peninsula Plaza**. As Thanon Rama I becomes Thanon Ploenchit, you pass **President Arcade** and the **Amarin Plaza**, containing Sogo department store, a pseudo classical pile scheduled for refurbishment, then Central's flagship at Chidlom intersection.

Few contemplate walking the entire two-kilometre (1.25-mile) shopping strip, which extends east from here to the small specialist shops and cafés lining what becomes Thanon Sukhumvit. There are minor malls at **Ploenchit Centre**, **Landmark Plaza**

and **Times Square**, which faces **Robinson**, a mid-range department store chain (also in Central's portfolio) recently reinvented as a classy act (that is, classier than the mushrooming discount outlets). The upmarket **Emporium** complex demarcates the shopping frontier. Between this shopping strip and the suburban hypermarkets and malls (some of the world's biggest), you must navigate a patchwork of mom 'n' pop marts, specialist *soi*, independent stores and the many indigenous markets.

Merchants with a flair for flogging the kingdom's antiques operate shops around Thanon Charoen Krung, between the Oriental and Sheraton riverside hotels. Latching on to that lucrative locale (and along Silom and

## The best Shops

### For reproductions
Triphum. *See p138.*

### For objets d'art
Lotus Arts de Vivre. *See p144.*

### For football obsessives
Star Soccer. *See p154.*

### For inflatable things
Reflections (*see p145*) and Roominteriorproducts (*see p149*).

### For gems without scams
Thaigem.com. *See p144.*

### For Thai fashion
Fly Now and Theatre. For both, *see p140* Cutting ahead.

### For village couture
Mae Fah Luang. *See p140* Cutting ahead.

### For funky Thai products
Coccoon and Panta. For both, *see p147* Designs on fame.

### For anything and everything
Central Chidlom (*see p138*) and Chatuchak Weekend Market (*see p134*).

**Rare Stone Museum** – for all forms of rock formations.

Sukhumvit) are stalls and shophouse vendors dealing in souvenirs that, though tasteful, have all the markings of mass production.

## MODUS SHOPERANDI

With stores open until 8pm or even 10pm, you can easily fit shopping around sightseeing and other activities. Fierce competition means frequent sales, usually at salary time, at the turn of the month. The TAT (Tourist Authority of Thailand) coordinates the biggest mark-downs through the **Thailand Grand Sales** (June-July and December-January). No-frills operators in malls offer seemingly permanent discounts. Several major stores also give instant discounts for tourists, normally five per cent (show your passport) or for certain credit cards. Some services, however, notably travel agents, charge two to five per cent for credit cards. *Baht* is the only currency needed, even if some antiques and hotel rooms are priced in US dollars. The international **Bartercard** cash-free network has many clients in Thailand (0 2237 3666/www.bartercard.com).

Many retailers rely on tourists, and assistants often follow you around. Don't be offended; they're keen to serve, are on commission and save you trips to the till. They'll take your selection with cash (or card) and return from the register with bagged goods, change and receipt stamped with red ink. Otherwise, attempt to say *khor doo dai*

*maii?* ('can I just look please?') or use body language to indicate that you're just looking. A full cash or credit refund is unheard of, but some shops may offer instore credit or a limited exchange deal.

## Antiques & reproductions

### Old Maps & Prints

*4th Floor, River City Complex, Thanon Yotha, Bangrak (0 2237 0077/8). Saphan Taksin BTS then ferry.* **Open** 11am-7pm daily. **Credit** AmEx, MC, V. **Map** p310 D6.
As you might have guessed, this is the outlet for people interested in antique charts and hand-coloured engravings, mainly of Asia.

### OP Place

*301/1 Charoen Krung Soi 38, Bangrak (0 2266 0186-90). Saphan Taksin BTS.* **Open** 7.30am-7.30pm daily. **Map** p310 D7.
This ritzy mall beside the Oriental Hotel is a connoisseur's delight. Galleries include Garuda (religious artefacts and rare objects) and Objects (lingams and antique artists' tools).

### Rare Stone Museum

*1048-54 Charoen Krung Soi 26, Bangrak (0 2236 5666/5655). Bus 1, 16, 36, 75, 93, 162.* **Open** 10am-5.30pm daily. **Credit** AmEx, MC, V. **Map** p310 D7.
As the name suggests, this is the place for truly fantastic rock formations, from fossils, petrified dinosaur eggs and dung to tektite from outer space

(from B50). But owner/collector Khun Banyong quotes a ballpark million *baht* to part with a riverbed stone shaped like the Buddha.

### River City Complex

*River City Complex, 23 Thanon Yotha, Bangrak (0 2237 0077/8). Saphan Taksin BTS then ferry.* **Open** 10am-10pm daily. **Map** p310 D6.
Numerous specialists are to be found here, selling a fabulous range of period pieces, reproductions and antiquities (some, it's alleged, of murky provenance) that would upgrade many a museum. There are also monthly auctions.

### Triphum

*3rd Floor, Gaysorn Plaza, Thanon Ploenchit, Pathumwan (0 2656 1795/6). Chidlom BTS.* **Open** 10am-8pm daily. **Credit** AmEx, DC, MC, V. **Map** p311 H5.
Reproduction mural paintings on tapestries and planks (plus frames and Siamese knick-knacks) are sold here at reasonable prices, considering they're as meticulously crafted as any temple restoration.

## Books & magazines

Stalls on **Thanon Khaosan** sell literary second-hand books, while **Chatuchak Weekend Market** (*see p134*) is unbeatable for back issues, out-of-print finds and discounts.

### Asia Books

*221 Thanon Sukhumvit, between Soi 15 & 17, Sukhumvit (0 2252 7277/www.asiabooks.com). Asoke BTS/Sukhumvit subway.* **Open** 9am-9pm daily. **Credit** AmEx, DC, MC, V. **Map** p311 J5.
Expect a large selection of English-language books published in Asia, plus UK and US bestsellers, lifestyle manuals and coffee-table books on Asian design, cooking and heritage.
**Branches**: in most downtown malls.

### Bookazine

*1st Floor, CP Tower, Thanon Silom, Bangrak (0 2231 0019). Saladaeng BTS/Silom subway.* **Open** 10am-11pm daily. **Credit** AmEx, MC, V. **Map** p310 F7.
The most extensive (and freshest selection) of English-language newspapers and periodicals can be found here, with some popular novels, coffee-table books and a gay section to boot.
**Branches**: 2nd Floor, All Seasons Retail Centre, Thanon Witthayu, Pathumwan (0 2685 3863/4); Nailert Building, Thanon Sukhumvit, at Soi 5, Sukhumvit (0 2655 3834/4); 2nd Floor, Silom Complex, Thanon Silom, Bangrak (0 2231 3153); 286 Thanon Rama I, Pathumwan (0 2255 3778).

### Elite Used Books

*593-5 Thanon Sukhumvit, between Soi 33 & 35, Sukhumvit (0 2258 0221). Phrom Phong BTS.* **Open** 10am-8pm daily. **No credit cards.** **Map** p312 K6.
Elite's several thousand second-hand popular English-language paperbacks are grouped by genre.

Find unusual pieces at **River City Complex**.

### Kinokuniya

*3rd Floor, Emporium, Sukhumvit Soi 24, Sukhumvit (0 2664 8554/www.kinokuniya.com). Phrom Phong BTS.* **Open** 10.30am-9pm daily. **Credit** AmEx, MC, V. **Map** p312 K6.
This Japan-based bookseller has by far the country's biggest and best stock of English-language books and magazines. It's also the best organised: the latest releases and current bestsellers are shelved separately; and there are great ranges of maps, art, poetry and kids' books too. Staff are courteous and well informed.
**Branch**: 6th Floor, Isetan, Thanon Ratchadamri, Pathumwan (0 2255 9834).

### Merman Books

*4th Floor, Silom Complex, Thanon Silom, Bangrak (0 2231 3300). Saladaeng BTS/Silom subway.* **Open** 10.30am-8.30pm daily. **Credit** AmEx, DC, MC, V. **Map** p310 F7.
A small specialist in rare and antiquarian books, Merman also stocks many titles that are just plain old. Out-of-print journals and books on Siamese history are particularly prominent.

## Department stores

### Central Chidlom

*1027 Thanon Ploenchit, Pathumwan (0 2655 7777/ www.central.co.th). Chidlom BTS.* **Open** 10am-9.30pm daily. **Credit** AmEx, DC, MC, V. **Map** p311 H5.

Central's seven-storey flagship store has simply the best product selection and layout in town, and legions of loyal customers. There are extensive ranges of cosmetics, international and domestic fashion labels, leatherware, children's and sporting goods, plus contemporary oriental interior design. B2S meets most book, mag and stationery needs. Micro-shops include Jim Thompson Thai Silk, Starbucks and Tops supermarket.
**Branches**: throughout the city.

### Isetan

*4/1-2 Thanon Ratchadamri, Pathumwan (0 2255 9898/9). Chidlom BTS.* **Open** 10am-9pm daily. **Credit** AmEx, DC, MC, V. **Map** p311 G5.
This upmarket, Japanese-owned store is the focal point for corporate *samurai* and home-makers. Expect imported, conservative attire for men, but some colour and style in womenswear, as well as superior kitchen gear. There's also a first-rate pâtisserie, though it's unnecessarily wasteful in its packaging (buy ten buns, get 11 bags). Greyhound and Jim Thompson Thai Silk have mini-shops within the complex.

### Robinson

*259 Thanon Sukhumvit, between Soi 17 & 19, Sukhumvit (0 2651 1533). Asoke BTS/Sukhumvit subway.* **Open** 10am-10pm daily. **Credit** AmEx, DC, MC, V. **Map** p311 J5.
Not the place for Friday night glad rags, Robinson does, however, stock no-nonsense, useful things (casual, sporty and corporate) at prices that are marginally cheaper than those at Central (*see p138*). Gear tends to the mid-range (more Nike Cortez than Nike Air Max).
**Branches**: throughout the city.

### Zen

*World Trade Centre, 4/1-2 Thanon Ratchadamri, Pathumwan (0 2255 9669). Chidlom BTS.*
**Open** 10am-9pm Mon-Thur, Sun; 10am-10pm Fri, Sat. **Credit** AmEx, DC, MC, V. **Map** p311 G4.
The focus on clothing and accessories makes this Central spin-off a favourite among neophyte professionals and university students, though the home section satisfies more settled types with fad-conscious gifts (and a wrapping service). Young women also flock here for beauty tips dispensed by well-turned-out, lab-coated consultants. Global brands are located on the ground floor; you'll find local apparel on other floors.

## Dry cleaning & repairs

### Novoclean

*Chidlom BTS station (0 2650 4022). Chidlom BTS.* **Open** 6.30am-10pm daily. **Credit** AmEx, DC, MC, V. **Map** p312 K6.
Operated by Novotel Hotel, this dry cleaning and laundry service is ultra convenient.
**Branches**: Saladaeng BTS station (0 2632 6818); Phrom Phong BTS station (0 2663 4635); Thonglor BTS station (0 2714 1906).

## Electronics

For consumer electronics, **PowerBuy** sections in **Central** (*see p138*) and **Zen** department stores (*see above*) offer the latest in personal sound systems, film and digital cameras, PDAs and other tech-gadgets.

### Copperwired Apple Centre

*3rd Floor, Siam Discovery Centre, Thanon Rama I, Pathumwan (0 2658 0447). Siam BTS.* **Open** 10am-8pm daily. **Credit** AmEx, DC, MC, V. **Map** p309 & 310 F4.
For the Mac brigade, this small but well stocked showroom has all the latest Apple models and applications, sold by staff who know their stuff.

### Pantip Plaza

*604/3 Thanon Petchaburi, near the Indonesian Embassy, North (0 2251 9008). Bus 2, 38, 60, 93, 140, 511, 512.* **Open** 9am-9pm daily.
**Map** p311 G4.
A geek's paradise, Pantip is crammed with vendors hawking hardware, applications, games, accessories, entertainment (CDs, DVDs, VCDs) and anything (new or used) that you can plug into your PC. Computers can be bought turnkey, assembled to your specs or upgraded in shops that resemble techno junkyards. Servicing, parts, software for Mac or PC are all offered by knowledgeable staff. Stiff competition means that the latest models are released promptly at slim margins. Manufacturers'

Race along to **Greyhound**. *See p141.*

# Cutting ahead

Bangkok's contemporary fashion scene has been spiced up by a dazzling band of young designers. Stylistically diverse in their approach, all are putting Bangkok on the fashion map; their work is showcased in November's **Elle Bangkok Fashion Week** (*see p156*).

## Act-Cloth

*205/18 Soi Thonglor Square, Sukhumvit Soi 55, Sukhumvit (0 2381 6591). Thonglor BTS.* **Open** 9am-6pm daily. **Credit** AmEx, DC, MC, V. **Map** p312 M5.

Prapakas Angsusingha's distinctly feminine garments neither pander to nor deviate far from trends, striking a fine balance between sweet and sultry.

## Fly Now

*2nd Floor, Gaysorn Plaza, Thanon Ploenchit, Pathumwan (0 2656 1359). Chidlom BTS.* **Open** 10am-9pm daily. **Credit** AmEx, DC, MC, V. **Map** p311 H5.

Established over a decade, Fly Now entered jet-set realms through principal designer Chamnam Pakdisuk, whose voguish, feminine designs twice opened London Fashion Week.

## Kai

*1st Floor, Emporium, Sukhumvit Soi 24, Sukhumvit (0 2664 8000 ext 1533). Phrom Phong BTS.* **Open** 10.30am-10pm Mon-Fri; 10am-10pm Sat, Sun. **Credit** AmEx, DC, MC, V. **Map** p312 K6.

Not yet 30, Japan Fashion Grand Prix 2002 award winner Chatri Teng-Ha is resisting trends and producing bold, daring work for Kai, the doyen of Thai couturiers.

## Mae Fah Luang

*4th Floor, Siam Discovery Centre, Thanon Rama I, Pathumwan (0 2658 0424/www. doitung.org). Siam BTS.* **Open** 11am-8pm daily. **Credit** MC, V. **Map** p309 & 310 F4.

This worthy crafts foundation has wowed catwalks by deviating from conservatism into a stylishly cosmopolitan form, with innovative hand-loomed cottons and linens the key materials.

## Theatre

*2nd Floor, World Trade Centre, Thanon Ratchadamri, Pathumwan (0 2255 9545). Chidlom BTS.* **Open** 11am-8.30pm daily. **Credit** AmEx, MC, V. **Map** p311 G4.

Designer of the year in 2002, Taned Boonprasarn combines hardy fabrics with lace and chiffon. His glamorous gowns and mix-and-matches with frilly details evoke neo-romanticism.

**Branch**: 3rd Floor, Siam Centre, Thanon Rama I, Pathumwan (0 2251 3599).

## Tube

*2nd Floor, Gaysorn Plaza, Thanon Ploenchit, Pathumwan (0 2656 1338). Chidlom BTS.* **Open** 10am-8pm daily. **Credit** AmEx, DC, MC, V. **Map** p311 H5.

Sociable designers Saksit Phisansuphong and Pisit Jongnarangsin have just signed with mainstream Central to promote their avant-garde creations in solid colours. Unusual fabrics and radical profiles forge a wackiness that turns heads.

**Branch**: 3rd Floor, Siam Centre, Thanon Rama I, Pathumwan (0 2658 1108).

warranties normally accompany big-name products, but most shops pride themselves on free post-purchase service. Pirate and unlicensed software keeps reappearing after raids, seemingly without protest from licensed outlets.

## Ploenchit Centre

*2 Sukhumvit Soi 2, Sukhumvit (0 2656 8600). Nana BTS.* **Open** 10am-9pm daily. **Map** p311 J5.

Glaringly bright shops on floors three and four of this otherwise rather dull mall deal in high-end audio components. Some of the best CD players, amps, speakers and cables are sold with a large dose of tech snobbery at the Ploenchit Centre. You'll find that here the measure of a man is his eardrums, and every familiar brand is available to be thrashed in a comparison test with the auditory elite. Bring your favourite CD.

## Fashion

Also *see above* **Cutting ahead**.

## Asian

### Anurak (anr)

*3rd Floor, Siam Centre, Thanon Rama I, Pathumwan (men 0 2252 2762/women 0 2658 1118). Siam BTS.* **Open** 11am-8pm daily. **Credit** AmEx, DC, MC, V. **Map** p309 & 310 F4.

Chic, pared-down designs for men and women line this ultra minimalist shop. Erstwhile publisher Anurak Thangsomboon's signature short-sleeve shirt has been widely imitated.

**Branch**: 2nd Floor, Emporium, Sukhumvit Soi 24, Sukhumvit (0 2664 8473).

Radical design at **Tube**.

Designer Jitsing Somboon (an artist) vamps up formal suit fabrics with bold styling and quirky details.
**Branches**: in most downtown malls.

### Jaspal

*2nd Floor, Siam Centre, Thanon Rama I,*
*Pathumwan (0 2251 5918/www.jaspal.com).*
*Siam BTS.* **Open** 10am-9pm daily. **Credit** AmEx,
DC, MC, V. **Map** p309 & 310 F4.
Local fashion giant Jaspal takes its cues from
Europe, right down to the supermodels on its billboards. The menswear can be a little bit glitzy, but
you can't argue with the quality of the range of
basics in high-tech stretch fabrics.
**Branches**: in most downtown malls.

### Jim Thompson Thai Silk

*9 Thanon Surawong, Bangrak (0 2632 8100-4/*
*www.jimthompson.com). Saladaeng BTS/Silom*
*subway.* **Open** 9am-9pm daily. **Credit** AmEx, DC,
MC, V. **Map** p310 F6.
The Thai silk pioneer has ventured beyond pillowcases, scarves and clubby neck ties into high
fashion, such as Nagara's diaphanous patterned
gowns and lustrous upholstery for Ou Baholydhin's
trendy furniture designs.
**Branches**: 4th Floor, Emporium, Sukhumvit
Soi 24, Sukhumvit (0 2664 8165/6); Ground Floor,
Isetan, Thanon Ratchadamri, North (0 2255 9805).

### Paothong's Collection

*4th Floor, Emporium, Sukhumvit Soi 24,*
*Sukhumvit (0 2664 8000 ext 1554). Phrom*
*Phong BTS.* **Open** 10.30am-10pm Mon-Fri;
10am-10pm Sat, Sun. **Credit** AmEx, DC, MC, V.
**Map** p312 K6.
Designer-cum-historian Paothong Thongchua creates romanticised versions of Thai dress using
native fabrics. They're mainly for women, although,
if he had his way, men would also be wearing
sarongs under robes and scarves.

### Shanghai Tang

*Ground Floor, Emporium, Sukhumvit Soi 24,*
*Sukhumvit (0 2664 8470). Phrom Phong BTS.*
**Open** 10.30am-9pm daily. **Credit** AmEx, DC, MC, V.
**Map** p312 K6.
Though neon-bright chinoiserie has given way to
subtler colours and stylish cuts at David Tang's
boutique, iridescent silk gowns with Chinese fastenings remain hits.
**Branch**: 1st Floor, Regent Hotel, Thanon
Ratchadamri, Pathumwan (0 2250 0758).

### Soda

*3rd Floor, Siam Centre, Thanon Rama I,*
*Pathumwan (men 0 2252 2124/5/women 0 2251*
*4995). Siam BTS.* **Open** 10am-9pm daily. **Credit**
AmEx, MC, V. **Map** p309 & 310 F4.
Soda is a small fashion house that embellishes core
items such as jeans and T-shirts with innovative
sequinned and printed fabrics. The stock-in-trade
here is bold, sexy and diverse styles for the slim.
Another branch called Night & Day (0 2252 2123)
specialises in sleepwear.

### Common Tribe

*Project 24 Soi 2, Chatuchak Weekend Market,*
*Thanon Phahon Yothin, North (no phone).*
*Morchit BTS.* **Open** 10am-6.30pm Sat, Sun.
**No credit cards.**
An oasis of calm in the lively Chatuchak Weekend
Market, Tribe is known for having popularised
handmade leather sandals. Staff wear owner Phi
Oh's trademark pantaloons, jackets and beach tops
in black and white.

### Greyhound

*2nd Floor, Emporium, Sukhumvit Soi 24, Sukhumvit*
*(0 2664 8664). Phrom Phong BTS.* **Open** 10am-9pm
Mon-Fri; 10am-10pm Sat, Sun. **Credit** AmEx, DC,
MC, V. **Map** p312 K6.
This legend among Thai labels offers understated
essentials that work both in and out of the office.

## Outsize

### Browns

*1st Floor, U-Chu-Liang Building, Thanon Rama IV, Bangrak (0 2632 4442). Silom subway/bus 14, 47, 74, 109, 507.* **Open** 10am-8pm daily. **Credit** AmEx, DC, MC, V. **Map** p311 G7.

The outsize skirts, trousers and blouses here (all in light fabrics, with clean prints and patterns) are a godsend to women who find local ranges too small. **Branches**: 1st Floor, Emporium, Sukhumvit Soi 24, Sukhumvit (0 2664 8319); 275 Thonglor Soi 13, Sukhumvit (0 2712 7820).

## Tailors

For tailor-made suits, silk dresses and Thai clothing, *see p144* **Tailor tales**.

### Sequin Queen

*Shop 121-2 Chalerm Larb Market, off Thanon Petchaburi, North (0 2253 1529/ www.sequinqueen.com).* **Open** noon-5pm Mon-Sat. **No credit cards**.

Nothing to wear for Mardi Gras? Pouting designer Khun Tu can run up a subtle little number in chiffon or Lycra, complete with feathered headdresses. All orders are custom-made (for men and women), hand-sewn, and come at bargain prices (given that Tu has won prizes for his outrageous designs). Online ordering.

## Food & drink

**Tops** supermarkets are found at **Central** (*see p138*), while British **Tesco Lotus** and French **Carrefour** hypermarkets face off where Thanon Rama IV meets Sukhumvit Soi 26 (these supermarkets also swamp so many suburbs that they have provoked protests, planning limits and even physical attacks).

### La Boulange

*2-2/1 Soi Convent, Thanon Silom, Bangrak (0 2631 0355). Saladaeng BTS/Silom subway.* **Open** 6am-8.30pm daily. **Credit** AmEx, MC, V. **Map** p310 F7

Owned by ex-hotel manager and chef Michel Meca, this French pavement café sells pastries, sandwiches and authentic loaves (fresh from the oven). Classic snack meals (croque monsieur, salads, quiches) and good coffee are also on offer. **Branches**: throughout the city.

### Ong's Tea

*4th Floor, Siam Discovery Centre, Thanon Rama I, Pathumwan (0 2658 0445). Siam BTS.* **Open** 10am-9pm daily. **Credit** AmEx, MC, V. **Map** p309 & 310 F4.

A table setting allows you to sample the leaves, mostly from China, Japan and Taiwan, surrounded by tea ceremony paraphernalia, from calligraphy and pots to tea-sipping music on CD.

# Shipping

With so much heritage now overseas, national treasures are prohibited from export without a licence from the government's Fine Arts Department. Tight restrictions apply to images of Buddha and cultural artefacts, including reproductions, though they're widely on sale. Most antiques dealers offer to arrange export of goods, but it's best to contact the Office of Archaeology (81/ 1 Thanon Si Ayutthaya, Dusit; 0 2628 5032/2282 2121 ext 306), which handles applications for export licences.

### Bangkok Shipping Agency

*3rd Floor, TSC Building, Ocean Tower 1, 170/7 Thanon New Rajadapisek, Sukhumvit (0 2261 3154). Queen Sirikit National Convention Centre subway/bus 136, 185.* **Open** 8.30am-5pm Mon-Fri. **No credit cards**. **Map** p311 J6.

With its network of shipping operators and 36 years of service, BSA has the resources for customs clearing and freight forwarding, covering both air and sea cargo.

### Sovente

*342/1 Sukhumvit Soi 63 (Ekamai), Sukhumvit (0 2711 7480-4). Ekkamai BTS.* **Open** 10am-10pm daily. **No credit cards**.

This local coffee and tea marketers' outlet serves up fresh brews and sells roasted beans.

### Thaniya Spirit

*62/7 Thanon Thaniya, Bangrak (0 2234 5224). Saladaeng BTS/Silom subway.* **Open** 10am-10pm Mon-Sat; 10am-6pm Sun. **No credit cards**. **Map** p310 F6

Bars and clubs favour this specialist drinks merchant, but it also sells all types of booze.

### Villa Market

*595 Sukhumvit 33/1, Sukhumvit (0 2662 0371-6/ www.villamarket.com). Phrom Phong BTS.* **Open** 24hrs daily. **Credit** AmEx, DC, MC, V. **Map** p312 K6.

This expat haunt is *the* grocer for snacks, junk foods and delicacies from around the world – from cheeses and tortillas to herrings and curry pastes. There's also a decent selection of wines (often discounted) and a community noticeboard. **Branches**: Ploenchit Centre, Sukhumvit Soi 2, Sukhumvit (0 2656 9071-4); Sukhumvit Soi 11, Sukhumvit (0 2253 5528); Sukhumvit Soi 49, Sukhumvit (0 2662 5880-4); Trinity Building, Silom Soi 5, Bangrak (0 2636 6856).

**Eat, Drink, Shop**

O.
V.
Sic
beh
cust
S Br
in ple

**Lotu**
*3rd Flo*
*Bangra*
**Open** 1
**Map** p3
An Asian
rations an

## Tail

Bangkok h
businesses
Chinese sta
Khao San, T
Oriental and
and Sukhumv
a suit or dress
stressful as to
send your mea
to a sweatshop
 Better tailors l
send the pieces
those dubious sa
out a stress-free,
if you map out prec
insist on at least tw
tune, the second to
Needless to say, a s
overnight (in a packa
is unlikely to survive i
 Generally, worthy clo
versed in formalwear, t

# Designs on fame

The cutting edge of Thai product design has been sharpened by incoming global villagers and local talents, many of them architects left jobless by the crash. Variations of new forms range from home furnishings inspired by indigenous elements to objects that transcend cultural constructs. Along with the stalls at **Chatuchak Weekend Market** (see p134), these designers stand out:

## Anyroom

*4th Floor, Siam Discovery Centre, Thanon Rama I, Pathumwan (0 2658 0481/ www.anyroom.com). Siam BTS.* **Open** 10am-9pm daily. **Credit** AmEx, MC, V. **Map** p309 & 310 F4.
Ultra-modernist icons from established names as well as up-and-comers. Those who sip coffee from a Bodum mug while perching on a Verner Panton chair in a room full of Alessi kitchen gear will appreciate the palm-sized ceramic and bronze flower vessels (based on Thai seeds) from designer florist Sakul Intakul, as featured in the new book *Living with Tropical Colours*.

## Cocoon

*3rd Floor, Gaysorn Plaza, Thanon Ploenchit, Pathumwan (0 2656 1006/7). Chidlom BTS.* **Open** 10am-8pm daily. **Credit** AmEx, MC, V. **Map** p311 H5.
The neon-hued silks covering the throw pillows are the most eye-catching of the pan-Asian influences that infuse every item at this much-imitated shop. Stock runs from chopsticks and celadon bowls to incense packs and sofas.
**Branch**: Peninsula Hotel, 333 Thanon Charoen Nakorn, Thonburi (0 2630 7040).

## EGG

*Unit 217, 2nd Floor, CRC Tower, All Seasons Place, Thanon Witthayu, Pathumwan (0 2685 3841/www.eggthai.com). Ploenchit BTS.* **Open** 9am-6pm Mon-Fri. **Credit** MC, V. **Map** p311 H4.
A true proponent of the new Asian style, architect Ekarit Praditsuwana produced Fire+Earth ceramics, then expanded into minimalist furniture with frames made from recycled teak and cushions in natural fibres.
**Branches**: 6th Floor, Central Chidlom, Thanon Ploenchit, Pathumwan (0 2655 7777 ext 3602); 19 Thanon New Rama IX, North-east (0 2300 5131-4).

## Panta

*4th Floor, Siam Discovery Centre, Thanon Rama I, Pathumwan (0 2658 0415). Siam BTS.* **Open** 10am-9pm daily. **Credit** AmEx, DC, MC, V. **Map** p309 & 310 F4.
An artwork in itself, this space showcases distinctly Asian experimental furniture made from natural materials such as wood, tree vines and rattan, with cushions in forest fabrics. The chic geometric designs are minimalist, yet warm and voluminous.

## Propaganda

*4th Floor, Siam Discovery Centre, Thanon Rama I, Pathumwan (0 2658 0430/ www.propagandaonline.com). Siam BTS.* **Open** 10.30am-9pm daily. **Credit** AmEx, DC, MC, V. **Map** p309 & 310 F4.
A cross between Philippe Starck and Damien Hirst, these iconic (and ironic) designer knick-knacks (pictured) that pass for modern art include more than a few salt and pepper shakers, kitchen gear from Alessi and prize-winning accessories, designed in-house, such as illuminated tooth lamps and shark bottle openers.
**Branch**: 4th Floor, Emporium, Sukhumvit Soi 24, Sukhumvit, Sukhumvit (0 2664 8574).

**Eat, Drink, Shop**

**Gaysorn Plaza,** home of swanky labels. *See p150.*

GUCCI

### Roominteriorproducts

*4th Floor, Siam Discovery Centre, Thanon Rama 1, Pathumwan (0 2658 0410/www.roominterior products.com). Siam BTS.* **Open** 11am-8pm Mon-Thur; 11am-9pm Fri-Sun. **Credit** AmEx, DC, MC, V. **Map** p309 & 310 F4

This Australian designer duo sell a rainbow of kitschy props for the modern room, such as folding lawn chairs and beanbags in modern patterns. There's also lots of inflatable plastic stuff.

## Health & beauty

### Chalachol

*1st Floor, Zuellig Building, 1-7 Thanon Silom, Bangrak (0 2238 1123/www.chalachol.com). Saladaeng BTS/Silom subway.* **Open** 11am-8.30pm daily. **Credit** MC, V. **Map** p311 G6.

Somsak Chalachol revolutionised local hairdressing with this chain of unisex designer salons. While your hair is washed, your body gets a massage from a vibrating chair. Cut and blow dry from B350. **Branch:** 205/13-14 Sukhumvit Soi 55 (Thonglor), Sukhumvit (0 2712 6481).

### Completions

*20 Thanon Silom, between Soi 2 & 4, Bangrak (0 2234 3749). Saladaeng BTS/Silom subway.* **Open** 11.30am-5pm Mon, Tue, Thur-Sun. **Credit** MC, V. **Map** p310 F7.

This sparse, long-standing salon's fame skyrocketed when the Prime Minister dropped in for a trim shortly after inauguration. Prices have since gone up, with a cut and blow dry from B1,200 for men, B2,500 for women.

### Oriental Princess

*1st Floor, Isetan, Thanon Ratchadamri, Pathumwan (0 2255 9898/9 ext 3115/www.orientalprincess.com). Chidlom BTS.* **Open** 10am-9pm daily. **Credit** AmEx, DC, MC, V. **Map** p311 G4.

Lipsticks made from cocoa butter and beeswax are typical of the products on sale here. Other examples might be soaps made from orange and avocado, along with similarly herbal-cum-natural skin and hair care potions. **Branch:** 1st Floor, Robinson, Thanon Sukhumvit between Soi 17 & 19, Sukhumvit (0 2651 1557).

## Homewares

### Asian Motifs

*3rd Floor, Gaysorn Plaza, Thanon Ploenchit, Pathumwan (0 2656 1093). Chidlom BTS.* **Open** 9.30am-8pm daily. **Credit** AmEx, MC, V. **Map** p311 H5. The vivid colours of silk lanterns draw attention to this lively shop, which is also noted for unfussy lacquerware, pottery, celadon and Thai silk cushions.

### Ayodhya

*3rd Floor, Gaysorn Plaza, Thanon Ploenchit, Pathumwan (0 2656 1089). Chidlom BTS.* **Open** 10am-8pm daily. **Credit** AmEx, DC, MC, V. **Map** p311 H5.

A pioneer of updating trad Thai products to today's aesthetics, Ayodhya turns out understated and useful items like seats made from tree vines and home-made soaps scented with local flowers.

### Chiiori

*87 Nailert Building, Thanon Sukhumvit between Soi 3 & 5, Sukhumvit (0 2254 4976). Nana BTS.* **Open** 10am-10pm daily. **Credit** AmEx, DC, MC, V. **Map** p311 J5.

*Benjarong* is a five-coloured Thai ceramic with subtle gilding, and a glinting range of it lines the vast window of this top-quality manufacturer. Expect both traditional and modish designs, from lotus-like lidded jars to functioning teapots and dinner sets fit for a state banquet. Chiiori also sells heavier crackle-glazed celadon ceramics in various hues and shapes upstairs.

### NV Aranyik

*3rd Floor, Gaysorn Plaza, Thanon Ploenchit, Pathumwan (0 2656 1081). Chidlom BTS.* **Open** 10am-8pm daily. **Credit** AmEx, MC, V. **Map** p311 H5.

NV Aranyik's much-imitated spoons, forks and knives – with twisted, textured or dimpled metal handles – have made it to the tables of many restaurants around the world during the shop's 25 years in existence. This is simple, elegant cutlery that's worth forking out for.

### Patra

*Ground Floor, Central Rama III, Thanon Rama III, South (0 2673 5640). Bus 14, 205.* **Open** 11am-9pm Mon-Fri; 10am-9pm Sat, Sun. **Credit** AmEx, MC, V.

No self-respecting local hotel would be without a cabinet full of Patra's fine bone china. It stocks trad and trendy sets for both tea-drinking *hi-so* (high-society) patrons and coffee-guzzling fashion and literary circles. This is top-quality gear, which explains why 80% goes for export. Prices are a pleasant surprise.

## Malls

### Emporium

*622 Sukhumvit Soi 24, Sukhumvit (0 2664 8000/ www.emporiumthailand.com). Phrom Phong BTS.* **Open** 10.30am-10pm Mon-Fri; 10am-10pm Sat, Sun. **Map** p312 K6.

A supremely successful mall, Emporium lures *hi-so* Bangkokians and wealthy visitors with European high-fashion houses (Prada, Gucci, Chanel, Hermès, Fendi, for example) and long-established Thai jewellers. Lesser mortals come here for the local and imported fashion outlets, opticians, booksellers, hairstylists, travel agents and interior furnishing shops. Hosting fashion shows, exhibitions, promotions and even concerts, the mall rather plays down its fine Emporium Department Store and its vast (yet crowded) food hall, which stocks specialities from top restaurants.

Eat, Drink, Shop

# Weaving dreams

The government's 'One Tambon, One Product' policy aims to market the myriad village products emanating from Thailand's 7,000-plus *tambons* (sub-districts), with over half being gift items, home decorations, fabrics and handicrafts. Based on a successful Japanese plan, it has earned over B2 billion in two years and made 'indigenous wisdom' more accessible.

Fairs promoting this policy are common, but the official emporium of Thai handicrafts is **Narayanaphand** (pronounced Narai Pun), founded six decades ago with Industry Ministry support. This vast bazaar housing everything – from lacquered bowls and ceramics to wood carving and hand woven fabrics – under one roof feels a bit state-bland, with merchandise mass-produced (albeit by hand).

The laudable directive actually has been pioneered by individuals caring that the crafts retain their associated customs, while earning more for villagers and stemming migration to cities. **Rasi Sayam** has for years kept skills in their locale, while adjusting the designs to modern use. Another pioneer, Pornroj Angsanakul, has applied bygone

expertise in fresh ways, such as his astonishingly lifelike ceramics of monks, or the speciality of his **Tamnan Mingmuang** shop: weaving. His unsurpassed baskets, boxes and handbags aren't limited to wicker or rattan; you'll find wild grass, water hyacinth

## Gaysorn Plaza

*999 Thanon Ploenchit, Pathumwan (0 2656 1516-9). Chidlom BTS.* **Open** 10am-8pm daily. **Map** p311 H5

This swanky corner landmark has had a rather clinical facelift – not unlike some of the shoppers perusing its posh brands (Louis Vuitton, Prada, Hermès), regional fashion houses and contemporary Thai design outlets.

## MBK

*444 Thanon Phayathai, Pathumwan (0 2217 9111/ www.mbk-center.com). National Stadium BTS.* **Open** 10am-9pm daily. **Map** p309 & 310 F4.

It's pointless trying to make sense of the chaotic, overcrowded, boisterous frenzy that makes up this colossal, stacked marketplace. There are well over 1,000 shops and stalls selling everything and anything imaginable: gold, footwear, sausages, dining tables, suitcases, youth fashion and, famously, mobile phones and portable electronics. Specialists in camping gear (*see p154*), cameras (*see p153*) and custom portraits offer possibly the best bargains (and most knowledgeable service) in town – if you can find them. Above this empire's diverse food court are an SF cinema (*see p167*) and Kim Bowl rink (*see p204*). It's next door to Pathumwan Princess hotel (*see p44*).

## Peninsula Plaza

*153 Thanon Ratchadamri, Pathumwan (0 2253 9791). Ratchadamri BTS.* **Open** 10am-8pm daily. **Map** p311 G5.

Flanked by the Regent and Hyatt hotels, this quiet, *faux*-Parisian low-rise is a yellowing throwback to the pre-1997 boom. Still, it attracts those who own at least one two-tone, diamond-encrusted Rolex. It's also popular with shoppers who can differentiate pre-Donnatella from post-Gianni, since it houses the city's flagship Versace store – plus Bangkok's only Loewe. Shop assistants can be patronising if you're anything but a cash millionaire.

## Siam Centre

*989 Thanon Rama I, Pathumwan (0 2658 1000-5/ www.siamcenter.co.th). Siam BTS.* **Open** 10am-9pm daily. **Map** p309 & 310 F4.

Since the Centre opened in 1973 several Thai designers have rolled out their careers here. Although out-muscled by the likes of Starbucks, McDonald's and Levi's, a host of small indie boutiques continue to cater for the trendiest of tastes (and slimmest of frames). CD Warehouse (*see p151*) dominates the top floor, surrounded by sportswear and Gen-X shops for urban skate dudes and surf chicks. It also provides air-conditioning for the teenyboppers and uniformed university students

and ultra-fine *yan lipao* vine with exquisite finishing. His Legend branch sells excellent but more mainstream souvenirs, while his other outlet, Eros, is self-explanatory. The techniques of Siamese arts are applied to the sensual detailing of clay figurines, painted panels and wood carvings.

### Narayanaphand
*127 Thanon Ratchadamri, Pathumwan (0 2252 4670/9). Chidlom BTS.* **Open** 10am-8pm daily. **Credit** AmEx, DC, MC, V. **Map** p311 G5.

### Rasi Sayam
*32 Sukhumvit Soi 23, Sukhumvit (0 2258 4195). Asoke BTS/Sukhumvit subway.* **Open** 9am-5.30pm Mon-Sat. **Credit** AmEx, DC, MC, V. **Map** p312 K5.

### Tamnan Mingmuang
*3rd Floor, Thaniya Plaza, Thanon Silom, Bangrak (0 2231 2120). Saladaeng BTS/ Silom subway.* **Open** 10.30am-8pm daily. **Credit** V. **Map** p310 F6.
**Branches**: (both on same floor) **Eros** (0 2231 2015); **The Legend** (0 2231 2179).

who have spent their afternoons in Siam Square opposite, where youth-oriented stalls deal in cheap (and sometimes chic, but mostly faddish) shirts and skirts copied from Japanese and Korean catalogues.

### Siam Discovery Centre
*989 Thanon Rama I, Pahumwan (0 2658 1000-19/ www.siamcenter.co.th). Siam BTS.* **Open** 10am-9pm daily. **Map** p309 & 310 F4.
The city's alternative luxury mall, this annex to Siam Centre caters for those with money to spend. DKNY, Armani Exchange and Guess? provide the threads, while hairdressing salon Toni & Guy, make-up shop Shu Uemura and salon-spa Leonard Drake provide the finishing touches. There's also a Crabtree & Evelyn for those who want to continue the pampering at home. But the mall's trump card is designer home furnishings by anyroom, Habitat, Panta and roominteriorproducts, among others. The fifth floor is all for kids, while the cacophanous top floor has snack bars and the EGV cinemas (*see p166*).

### World Trade Centre
*4/1-2 Thanon Ratchadamri, Pathumwan (0 2255 9400). Chidlom BTS.* **Open** 10am-9pm daily. **Map** p311 G4.
This dim, cavernous centre's saving grace is its parking lot, which holds 4,000 cars and a convoy of

buses (hence the abundance of package tourists inside). Flanked by Zen and Isetan (for both, *see p139*) department stores, more than 300 shops cater for fashionistas hunting for local labels, as well as those in search of jade, gold, furniture and discount outlets. Major Cineplex (*see p166*) shares the top floors with a bowling alley and ice rink (*see p207*).

## Music

### CD Warehouse
*3rd Floor, Emporium, Sukhumvit Soi 24, Sukhumvit (0 2664 8520-2). Phrom Phong BTS.* **Open** 10am-9.45pm daily. **Credit** AmEx, DC, MC, V. **Map** p312 K6.
Sample the newest tunes at the listening stations of Bangkok's largest and most organised music shop. Shelves of international new releases and seasoned faves run alongside Thai pop, classical, Canto-pop, J-Pop and world music. You'll also find the most commercial film titles on tape or DVD.
**Branches**: 3rd Floor, Siam Centre, Thanon Rama I, Pathumwan (0 2255 2086-8); 7th Floor, World Trade Centre, Thanon Ratchadamri, Pathumwan (0 2255 6552-4).

### Do Re Me
*274 Siam Square, Thanon Rama I, Pathumwan (0 2251 4351). Siam BTS.* **Open** noon-10pm daily. **No credit cards. Map** p309 & 310 F4.
This little shop on Siam Square sells the latest releases (from major and minor labels) at discount prices. There seems to be no attempt to organise the tapes and CDs, so test the owner's incredible memory of what's in stock.

### Music 1
*187 Soi Saladaeng, Thanon Silom, Bangrak (0 2234 1590). Saladaeng BTS/Silom subway.* **Open** 11am-9pm daily. **Credit** AmEx, DC, MC, V. **Map** p311 G7.
Member discounts (together with inspired taste in commercial and alternative music) has fostered a loyal clientele at this tiny outlet. There's a strong emphasis on chillout, mood music, indie (Thai and Brit), Japanese imports, soundtracks and death metal. The inventory also includes 12ins for aspiring and professional DJs, music magazines, world charts and listening stations.

**MBK** – one for shopaholics. *See p150.*

### Siam Dontree

*Royal Garden Plaza, 257/1-3 Thanon Charoen Nakorn, Thonburi (0 2460 2269). Saphan Taksin BTS then shuttle boat.* **Open** noon-9pm daily. **Credit** AmEx, MC, V.

Looking for some Thai music? From *phiphat* to *luuk thuung* and *morlam*, you'll find it here, not to mention instruments and musicians for hire.
**Branches**: Arcade, Le Royal Meridien Hotel, Thanon Ploenchit, Pathumwan (0 1517 7450); 4th Floor, Sogo, Thanon Ploenchit, Pathumwan (0 2255 0782 ext 401).

## Opticians

### Lauderdale

*1st Floor, Siam Discovery Centre, Thanon Rama I, Pathumwan (0 2658 0102/3). Siam BTS.* **Open** 10am-8pm daily. **Credit** AmEx, DC, MC, V. **Map** p309 & 310 F4.

Only the most stylish frames make it to the shelves of this classy (but fairly priced) shop.

### Rajdamri Optical

*2nd Floor, Silom Complex, Thanon Silom, Bangrak (0 2231 3165). Saladaeng BTS/Silom subway.* **Open** 10am-8.30pm daily. **Credit** AmEx, DC, MC, V. **Map** p310 F7.

Run by a couple of trained optometrists, Rajdamri's emphasis is on eye care – so expect frames that are more instruments of sight than fashion statements.

## Pharmacies

### Boots

*1st Floor, Siam Centre, Thanon Rama I, Pathumwan (0 2658 1126). Siam BTS.* **Open** 10am-9pm daily. **Credit** AmEx, MC, V. **Map** p309 & 310 F4.

The UK chemist has dozens of branches nationwide, both in other shops or as stand-alones staffed by a trained pharmacist. Famous brands and good own-brand pharmaceuticals, cosmetics, perfume and beauty care products vie for shelf space.
**Branches**: throughout the city.

## Photography

Photo developers are found on almost every street, supplying snaps in plastic flip books at low rates, sometimes with digital processing or scanning. Professionals process at **IQ Lab** (*see 153*) or get their serious black and white printing done through **Surat Suvanich** (0 1917 8057).

# Go carting

It's hard to walk three steps in Bangkok without coming across one of the city's countless roaming vendors. They bike, push and plant their carts from dusk till dawn, congregating in flocks at markets. Different foods are sold at different times of day (doughnuts after sunrise, grilled seafood after sunset). And with vendors easily accessible and easy on the wallet, you're guaranteed a good feed.

### Coffee & tea

Thais love their caffeine. *Kafae thung* (bag coffee) is strained through a sock-filter, with sweet milk used as a counterpoint to the thick, jet-black liquid. There's also pinkish *cha yen* (Thai iced tea), kiddy favourite Milo (a chocolate drink), *cha dam yen* (black iced tea) and *kafae* (coffee).

### Fruits

Vendors park their carts on street corners, where they peel and cut all the fruit you want for B10-ish a pop. Offerings include green mango, watermelon, papaya, water olive and pineapple. *Prik kap kleua* (a chilli and salt condiment) has just the right kick to counter (and enhance) the natural sweetness.

### Ice-cream

Thailand has its own take on the ice-cream van. Look for silver barrels just higher than the throngs of children that inevitably surround them. Flavours might typically be (sorbet-light) coconut or vanilla, served in a cup or on bread with nuts, lychees, sweet milk and jellies. And yes, the vendors ring a bell.

### Insects

Commanding space on *rot khen* (vendor carts) and now in cans in supermarkets, this protein source has been eaten for years in Isaan as a replacement for scarce meats. Generally speaking, insects are fried and served with chilli dips or salts. Textures of earthworms, scorpions, grasshoppers, spiders, crickets and other *malaeng* (six-legged) and *maeng* (eight or more legs) range from crunchy to mealy; flavours from smoky and earthy to shockingly refreshing. No need for vocab, merely point and smile (just as they will at you when you order).

### Juices

Fresh juices, often as *bun* (shakes) range from *nam som kun* (orange juice) and *nam manao* (lime) to tropical exotica such as

## Camera Collection

*2nd Floor, Thaniya Plaza, Thanon Silom, Bangrak
(0 2231 2730). Saladaeng BTS/Silom subway.*
**Open** 10am-7pm Mon-Sat. **Credit** AmEx, DC, MC,
V. **Map** p310 E7.
An authority catering for professionals across the
region, this cluttered shop is known for its service
and its highly specialised inventory (including classic, rare and large-format cameras). Equipment for
the studio and on-location shooting is also available
for sale or hire.

## Data IT

*Mezzanine, Pantip Plaza, Thanon Petchaburi,
North (0 2252 3466). Bus 2, 38, 60, 93, 140, 511,
512.* **Open** 10.30am-8.30pm daily. **Credit** AmEx,
DC, MC, V.
This IT superstore (within the IT super mall) stocks
a wide range of digital cameras. All brands come
at competitive prices, and all are accompanied by
service warranties.

## Foto File

*1st Floor, MBK Centre, Thanon Phayathai,
Pathumwan (0 2217 9426). National Stadium
BTS.* **Open** 10.30pm-8.30pm daily. **Credit** MC, V.
**Map** p309 & 310 F5.

An extensive stock of the most popular SLR models
and lenses, new and used, make this tiny shop a
favourite among photo enthusiasts and students. It's
also a good place to buy those black and white and
high-speed films you won't find behind the counters
of 7-Eleven. Associate shop SP Camera in
Pathumwan deals only in new equipment.
**Branch: SP Camera** 4th Floor, MBK, 444 Thanon
Phayathai, Pathumwan (0 2611 8062).

## IQ Lab

*ITF Building, 160/5 Thanon Silom, entrance off
Thanon Narathiwat Ratchanakharin, Bangrak
(0 2266 4080/www.iqlab.co.th). Chong Nonsi BTS.*
**Open** 8.30am-6pm Mon-Fri; 8.30am-1pm Sat.
**Credit** AmEx, MC, V.
The only Thai lab trusted by professionals for pro-
cessing, retouching and outputting in all formats, IQ
deals with colour and black and white films.

## Niks Thailand

*166 Silom Soi 12, Bangrak (0 2635 6570). Chong
Nonsi BTS.* **Open** 8.30am-5.30pm Mon-Fri. **Credit**
AmEx, DC, MC, V. **Map** p310 F7.
A mecca for Nikon buffs. Sales, service and a
museum-like collection are all to be found on the
mezzanine level.

rose-apples, baby coconut and custard apple
and, increasingly, vegetables such as carrot.
Watch the stall holder mangle sugar cane into
a juice known as *nam oy* – if you don't want
salt or sugar added, say *mai ow kleua/nam
than* respectively.

### Snacks

Choose from hundreds of user-friendly
variants, including grilled meats on a stick,
such as *moo yaang* (pork), *kai yaang*
(chicken), satay, squid and even *khai ping*
(eggs with black pepper on the side) and
myriad *luk chin ping* (balls of seafood or
meat). Lesser-known are *tod man pla*
(fish cakes), *koong foy thod* (small battered
shrimp) and *salapao* (like doughnuts).
Among the crowd-pleasers are *khluay thord*
(deep-fried bananas) and *roti*, an Indian-style
pancake with banana, egg, chocolate and
other sweet drizzles or stuffings.

### Yum

This mealtime staple of spicy salad also
makes for good snack material. *Yum* is
made to order, with vegetables, mushrooms,
glass noodles and squid as leading players.
Spicy and cooling.

**Eat, Drink, Shop**

# Shoes & leather goods

## Footwork
*2nd Floor, Emporium, Sukhumvit Soi 24, Sukhumvit (0 2664 8375). Phrom Phong BTS.* **Open** 10.30am-9pm Mon-Fri; 10am-9pm Sat, Sun. **Credit** AmEx, DC, MC, V. **Map** p312 K66.
Consistently stylish imports from Europe and South America make Footwork's new shoe deliveries are highly anticipated by both women and men. It's owned by local fashion house Jaspal (*see p141*).
**Branch**: 2nd Floor, World Trade Centre, Thanon Ratchadamri, Pathumwan (0 2255 9547).

## Ragazze
*2nd Floor, Silom Complex, Thanon Silom, Bangrak (0 2231 3190). Saladaeng BTS/Silom subway.* **Open** 11am-8pm daily. **Credit** AmEx, DC, MC, V. **Map** p310 E7.
Employing both leather and lighter materials, this Italian-influenced Thai company's bags, footwear and wallets remain up-to-the-minute stylish.
**Branches**: 1st Floor, Sogo, Thanon Ploenchit, Pathumwan (0 2256 9330); 3rd Floor, Isetan, Thanon Ratchadamri, Pathumwan (0 2255 9898/9 ext 3305); 3rd Floor, MBK, Thanon Phayathai, Pathumwan (0 2217 9364).

## Tango
*2nd Floor, Gaysorn Plaza, Thanon Ploenchit, Pathumwan (0 2656 1047). Chidlom BTS.* **Open** 10.30am-8pm daily. **Credit** AmEx, DC, MC, V. **Map** p311 H5.
Women's shoes and handbags with frilly, playful designs are Tango's signature products. The multi-coloured patchwork, lace trim and embroidery also extend to its range of skirts and blouses.
**Branches**: 3rd Floor, Siam Centre, Thanon Rama I, Pathumwan (0 2252 1773); 2nd Floor, World Trade Centre, Thanon Ratchadamri, Pathumwan (0 2251 2452).

# Sport

No-frills shops touting sportswear and sports equipment flank the National Stadium near MBK. For big-name athletic footwear, **MBK** (*see p150*) and **Siam Centre** (*see p150*) score highly.

## Pro Cam-Fis
*3rd Floor, Emporium, Sukhumvit Soi 24, Sukhumvit (0 2664 8811/2). Phrom Phong BTS.* **Open** 10.30am-8pm Mon-Thur, Sun; 10.30am-8.30pm Fri, Sat. **Credit** AmEx, DC, MC, V. **Map** p312 K6.
It stands for camping and fishing, in case you're wondering. This is the shop for camouflage fans and outdoors' types who can't do without a Maglite torch or a Swiss army knife.

## Sports Revolution
*619-21 Sukhumvit Soi 35, Sukhumvit (0 2204 2588/ 9). Phrom Phong BTS.* **Open** 10am-10pm daily. **Credit** AmEx, MC, V. **Map** p312 K6.

It's not exactly Nike Town, but Sports Revolution pretty much stocks all of this giant sportswear manufacturer's products. To keep abreast of competitors, the store often hands out Nike-brand gifts with purchases.
**Branch**: Siam Square Soi 2, Thanon Rama I, Pathumwan (0 2658 4714).

## Star Soccer
*3rd Floor, Siam Discovery Centre, Thanon Rama I, Pathumwan (0 2658 0375/6). Siam BTS.* **Open** 10am-9pm daily. **Credit** AmEx, DC, MC, V. **Map** p309 & 310 F4.
This is the place to come for footballs, replica kits and memorabilia from world famous clubs and national sides. European and South American colours are prominent, but the main emphasis is on the English scene.

## Super Sport
*Yada Building, Thanon Silom, Bangrak (0 2632 6871). Saladaeng BTS/Silom subway.* **Open** noon-midnight daily. **Credit** AmEx, DC, MC, V. **Map** p310 F6.
As its name suggests, this is Bangkok's largest sports shop, stocking all the major brands – there's even a separate golf section. It also has outlets in Central (*see p138*), Robinson (*see p139*) and Zen (*see p139*), but this is the only dedicated store

## Thaniya Plaza
*52 Thanon Thaniya, Bangrak (0 2231 2244). Saladaeng BTS/Silom subway.* **Open** 10am-10pm daily. **Map** p310 F7.
More than 30 golf shops makes this mall a must for Tiger Woods wannabes. They cater mainly for the influxes of Japanese salary men, hence the preponderance of Nipponese brands such as Yonex (although Callaway and Ping also get competitive discounts of up to 30%).

## Travel Mart
*3rd Floor, MBK, Image Zone, Thanon Rama I, Pathumwan (0 2217 9700 ext 740). National Stadium BTS.* **Open** 11am-8pm daily. **Credit** AmEx, DC, V. **Map** p309 & 310 F4.
Travel Mart is a well stocked shop that's also an authority on camping equipment and adventure sports accessories. Service is knowledgeable and there are obscure spare parts aplenty – goggle strap retainer, anyone?.

# Toys

Most malls have specified activity areas and kids' shops which stock international brands, local Learning Curve educational toys for 0-12s, or Plan Toys' imaginative wooden games. The best outlets are to be found in **Emporium** (*see p149*) and **Siam Discovery Centre** (*see p151*), as well as department stores such as **Central Chidlom** (*see p138*), and **Zen** and **Isetan** (for both, *see p139*) in World Trade Centre.

# Arts & Entertainment

*109, 115, 116, 149.* **Tickets** *Concert* B500. *Open day* free. **No credit cards. Map** p311 J7. **Date** *Concert* 4-9pm 28 Apr. *Open day* 9am-5pm 29 Apr.

Descendants of the polymath Prince Naris (a son of Rama IV and brother of Rama V), who was revered for his arts legacy, commemorate his birth in 1863 by opening up his traditional house. Look around the exhibitions in between the classical Thai performances on 28 April, or all day on 29 April. Other events are held at Silpakorn University, the art school founded with the help of Naris.

### Fringe Festival

*Patravadi Theatre, Thanon Arun Amarin, Thonburi (0 2412 7287/8/www.patravaditheatre.com). Bus 19, 57, 81, 83.* **Map** p308 A3. **Date** Usually Apr-May.

Since 1999 this centrepiece of the performing arts calendar has presented dance, drama and music of East and West, in traditional and modern forms plus myriad fusions. The weekend evening shows are mostly intelligible to non-Thai speakers.

### Demonic

*Thailand Cultural Centre outdoor amphitheatre, Thanon Thiem Ruam Mit, North-east (0 2247 0028/ Lakfa Sarasakul 0 1750 0591). Thiem Ruam Mit subway/bus 73, 136, 137, 185, 206, 514.* **Date** 1st Sat in May.

A biennial bout – next scheduled for 2004 – of death metal, hardcore and other underground music, performed by local bands.

## Rainy season

### Royal Ploughing Ceremony

*Sanam Luang, (Department of Agricultural Extension 0 2579 3926/2940 6050/www.moac.go.th). Bus 1, 3, 6, 9, 15, 19, 25, 30, 32, 33, 39, 43, 44, 47, 53, 59, 60, 64, 70, 80, 82, 91, 201, 203.* **Map** p309 & p310 D4. **Date** Early May.

Farmers from all over Thailand attend these Brahman rites to forecast the year's rainfall and harvest: the official launch of the rice-planting season. A day of Buddhist chanting and the king's blessing of rice seeds is followed, on the second day, by a colourful costumed procession of drummers, Brahmin priests and maidens. A ritual field is ploughed by sacred white oxen, and sown with the blessed rice. Afterwards, farmers rush in to gather the seeds to plant at home for good luck.

### Visakha Bucha

*Nationwide.* **Date** Full moon of 6th lunar month (late May/early June).

Buddhism's holiest date, when Lord Buddha was born, enlightened and died. Devotees make merit by bringing food to monks in the morning. In the evening, temples hold sermons and candle-lit processions. It's also a public holiday, and you'll find that most businesses are closed.

### Fête de la Musique

*Alliance Française 0 2670 4231/www.alliance-francaise.or.th.* **Map** p311 G7. **Date** 3rd Sat in June.

Run simultaneously around the globe, this Franco-backed festival spans multicultural sounds from jazz and pop to classical and ethnic. Venues vary; check the website for details.

### US Independence Day

*US Embassy 0 2205 4623.* **Map** p311 H5. **Date** Sat nearest to 4 July.

A Yankee bash: rhythm 'n' blues bands, a picnic and fireworks, for upwards of 10,000. Check nearer the time for venue details.

### Asanha Bucha & Khao Phansa

*Nationwide.* **Date** Full moon of 8th lunar month (late July/early Aug) & following day.

The anniversary of the Buddha's first sermon after attaining enlightenment is observed with temple rituals. Next day is Khao Phansa (the start of the rainy season) when monks begin 'Buddhist Lent': three months of meditation and prayer while confined within their temples. During this retreat, many youths become a novice, a step to Thai manhood that earns merit for their parents.

### HM The Queen's Birthday

*Nationwide.* **Date** 12 Aug.

Heralding this royal anniversary, which is also Mother's Day, many thousand points of light decorate Thanon Ratchadamnoen and other venues. A glittering spectacle.

### Short Film & Video Festival

*Khun Chalida 0 1615 5137/www.thaifilm.com.* **Date** Mid Aug.

Indie films shine in this festival, which is becoming increasingly international. Screenings (which are free) are held at the Goethe Institut (see p167) and About Café (see p169).

### Chinese Mid-Autumn Festival

*Nationwide.* **Date** Full moon of 10th lunar month (late Sept).

Tiers of tasty mooncakes in restaurants and bakeries around the country herald this ethnic Chinese festival. In 14th-century China, mooncakes conveyed messages among Han Chinese plotting to overthrow the Mongols. Traditionally eaten only after being offered on an altar to Guan Im, the goddess of mercy, the cakes, some are stuffed with pungent durian fruit, are now taken posthaste with tea. The Chinatown Food Festival, held at the same time as the Mid-Autumn Festival, takes over Thanon Yaowarat with hundreds of stalls.

### World Gourmet Festival

*Regent Hotel, 155 Thanon Ratchadamri, Pathumwan (0 2251 6127). Ratchadamri BTS.* **Map** p311 G5. **Date** Mid Sept.

This premium event (launched in 1999) has raised Bangkok's reputation as a hub for fine Western food, which is luckily available at half the Western prices. For ten days, fab meals are prepared by leading foreign chefs, along with cookery classes, demonstrations and wine tastings.

Arts & Entertainment

# Waterworld

Thailand's biggest holiday splash is the Thai lunar New Year, **Songkran**, now fixed at 13-15 April. A Sanskrit term for the sun entering Taurus (at the hottest time of year), Songkran evolved from Indian powder throwing into gentle rituals of reverence and purification – such as sprinkling monks and Buddha images with lustral water to win merit, similar gestures of respect to elders, making sand *chedi* in temples, and a big annual housecleaning.

Today, rites are held for the revered Phra Buddha Sihing image at Sanam Luang, and the Miss Songkran contest is held at Wisut Kasat. In 2002 a spectacular procession down Thanon Ratchadamnoen inaugurated a potential rival to Rio's Mardi Gras, and was also an attempt to counter the aquatic warfare that has come to signify Songkran.

In a mass catharsis of breakneck modernisation, youngsters grab water pistols, buckets and hoses for giddy attacks on pedestrians and each other, day and night. Revellers pack pick-up trucks with barrels of water, sometimes iced or dyed; mixed with talc, it's plastered on to hapless faces. Attempts are made to limit this to the peak areas of Silom between Soi 2 and Patpong, and especially Khao San Road in Banglamphu, where entertainments are staged. The fun is contagious – but wear nothing precious and pack electronics and wallets in plastic.

Much of Bangkok heads upcountry for up to a week, making the city traffic delightfully light. But leaving and returning is an ordeal: 12-hour jams, buses packing passengers into luggage holds, and ghastly road casualties topping 530 dead and 34,000 injured in just six days. Reserve tickets and rooms early if you want to join the celebrated mayhem in Chiang Mai, spiritual home of Songkran.

But there's always a second chance in Thailand: the Mon people celebrate new year a week later, notably at the Phra Padaeng Festival on 20-22 April (0 2463 7800). It's held just south of Bangkok in Phra Padaeng, Samut Prakan and you can expect parades, rites (including courting rituals) and the requisite dousings.

### International Festival of Music & Dance
*Thailand Cultural Centre, Thanon Ratchadaphisek, North-east (International Cultural Promotions 0 2661 6835-7/www.bangkokfestivals.com). Thiem Ruam Mit subway/bus 73, 136, 137, 185, 206, 514.* **Date** Mid Sept-early Oct.
Bangkok's biggest annual arts beanfeast stages world-class performances at Thai middle-class prices. The focus is on opera, ballet and orchestral music, often by east European companies, with leading jazz, world music and dance from elsewhere, plus Thai acts of the same calibre.

### Vertical Marathon
*Banyan Tree Bangkok Hotel, Thai Wah Tower II, 21/100 Thanon Sathorn Tai, South (0 2679 1200). Bus 22, 62, 67, 76, 116, 149, 530.* **Map** p311 G7. **Date** Mid Sept.
There's little challenge in jogging across this super-horizontal city, so why not go up instead? Some 500 contestants pay to sprint up more than 1,000 steps to the top of this 61-storey tower, for charity. Onlookers get to enjoy the food.

### National Art Exhibition
*National Gallery, 4 Thanon Chao Fa, Phra Nakorn (0 2282 2639/40 ext 14 or 17). Bus 3, 6, 9, 32, 33, 39, 43, 53, 64, 65, 506.* **Map** p308 B3. **Date** Sept.
An instant survey of the Thai art scene – though often shunned by the hottest artists. Heavy on neo traditional work, it's an unintentionally nostalgic grab bag of most 20th-century genres. From the mediocre to the brilliant, most works are for sale.

### Vegetarian Festival
*Across Bangkok.* **Date** Early/mid Oct.
Food stalls and restaurants go veggie (look out for yellow pennants) for this ten-day Chinese Buddhist-Taoist period of purging meat and heating foods, though self-mortification is done only by white-clad devotees down south. Chinatown explodes with colour, incense, temple offerings and the strains of Chinese opera, notably in Charoen Krung Soi 20.

### Carlsberg International Rugby Sevens
*Police Stadium, Thanon Wiphawadi Rangsit, North-east (David & Kate Dufall 0 2249 1834/ www.bangkoksevens.com). Bus 29, 504, 510, 513, 538.* **Date** Late Oct.
A three-day regional tournament with competitions for both international and Thai teams. There are divisions for men, women and boys, as well as old boys (over-35s). Plus beer and sandwiches.

### Ok Phansa
*Nationwide.* **Date** Full moon of 11th lunar month (Oct).
The rainy season officially ends, and with it the three months of Buddhist Lent, with *wat* rituals and the shaving of monks' eyebrows and heads. This day is also a public holiday.

**Arts & Entertainment**

# Children

Juniors are treated like VIPs in the city of 'little angels'.

One of the most striking aspects of Thai society is the attitude to children. Thais universally adore kids – to the extent that adults will even give up seats on public transport for youngsters and pet them at any opportunity (which can become quite annoying, especially for small visitors with the novelty of blonde hair). And yet it is equally common to see a mother riding a motorbike with an infant perched on the fuel tank and a toddler clinging to her back, or, indeed, a ten year-old driving a motorbike with no protection at all – both scenarios that seem sharply at odds with the child-loving Thais' otherwise coddling mentality.

This strange dichotomy can be explained by the fact that technological development has sped beyond welfare and education, with the resulting disregard for safety further reinforced by faith in karma. So exercise caution with cheap toys or electrical appliances and when walking hazardous streets, especially with a buggy (baby slings are a much safer bet). But that said, there are many fun things for families to do in Bangkok. **BAMBI** (see p164) is an invaluable resource for getting started.

## Attractions

Sure-fire hits with kids include river and canal tours (see p53) and **Dusit Zoo** (see p79). Otherwise, there are many attractions aimed at families, which while somewhat far away from Bangkok, can be often conveniently paired for day trips. For example, you could visit **Technopolis Science Museum** (see p163) with **Dream World** (see below); **Rose Garden** (see p224) with **Samphran Elephant Ground** (see p223); and the similar wild delights of **Safari World** and **Siam Park** (for both, see p163). Hotel staff will book excursions and **Sunfar Travel** (0 2266 8833) offers a fab Technopolis/ Dream World package (B720-B850 inclusive).

If ice skating appeals in the heat, the **World Trade Centre rink** (see p207) is quietest on weekdays before 4pm. The WTC's seventh floor also has karaoke booths, as do **MBK** shopping mall (see p150) and **Siam Square**, which are geared to teens.

Parks offer runaround and play zones, while most shopping malls and department stores have play areas and rides, as well as kids' shops

– notably **Central Chidlom** (see p138), **Emporium** (see p149), **Siam Discovery Centre** (see p151), and the **World Trade Centre** (see p151).

Booming since the mid 1990s, skateboarding, inline skating, trick-biking and wakeboarding are showcased annually in the **X-Games** in Phuket. But skate parks rarely last long; the one being built as the guide went to press, on Thanon Sathorn Tai facing Thanon Convent, is part of an anti-drugs initiative.

There are family events in August around the **Queen's Birthday** (Thai Mother's Day; see p160) and on **Children's Day** (see p159) in January, when restricted landmarks are open.

### Bangkok Dolls
*85 Soi Mor Leng, Thanon Ratchaprarop, North (0 2245 3008). Bus 14, 38, 62, 77, 513 to Thanon Makkasan then songthaew.* **Open** 8am-5pm Mon-Sat. **Admission** free. **Credit** AmEx, MC, V.
Hidden away in its modest location since the 1950s, this small doll museum and cottage industry is run by Khunying Tongkorn Chandavimol (who has, incidentally, been photographed with the Pope – and is mightily proud of it). The bright displays of ornate costumes and traditional scene (the Ramayana, monks, ethnic groups, stilt houses) have a homespun charm, even if you're not into dolls. Some of the dolls are from further afield, but most were made in the factory (an intriguing process that visitors can observe). Dolls cost from B300 to B5,000.

### Children's Discovery Museum
*Thanon Kamphaengphet 4, Chatuchak, North (0 2615 7333/www.bkkchildrenmuseum.com). Bus 38, 104, 134, 136, 183, 512.* **Open** 9am-5pm Mon-Fri; 10am-6pm Sat, Sun. **Admission** B70; B50 under-15s. **No credit cards**.
A house of fun for kids, the Discovery Museum has lots of experiments and toys, including a percussion music room and a TV/music studio where the young can star in their own action movie or attempt a spot of newsreading. Or visit the animal section, domain of tropical fish, parrots, snakes, reptiles and small fluffy mammals. Bring ear plugs on weekdays, when school parties beef up the decibel levels. Up the road, pleasant Chatuchak Park has a playground and jungle gym and is the home of the Railway Museum (see p163).

### Dream World
*62 Moo 1, Thanon Rangsit-Ongkarak, Thanyaburi, Rangsit, Pathum Thani, North-east (0 2533 1152/ www.dreamworld-th.com). Bus 523, 538, 1155.*

Arts & Entertainment

**Children's Discovery Museum.** See p162.

A broad green area houses the small Railway Museum in a train shed. It displays old locomotives as well as other vehicles, including London taxis and World War II Japanese patrol cars.

### Safari World
*99 Thanon Ramindra km9, Klong Samwa, North-east (0 2518 1000-5/2914 4100-5/www.safariworld. com). Bus 26, 95, 96, 512 to Fashion Island then songthaew.* **Open** *Safari park* 9am-5pm daily. *Marine park* 9am-4pm daily. **Admission** *Safari park* B200; B120 children. *Marine park* B580; B400 children. *Both* B700; B450 children under 140cm/55in. **Credit** MC, V.

You'll need a car (or tour bus) to explore this 150-acre (61-hectare) theme park planted to resemble the African bush, and inhabited by herds of giraffes, zebras, ostriches, rhinos and camels. Unless the kids are squeamish, arrive for the 10am 'feeding show' and watch the big cats tearing into their breakfast. Other shows include Marine Park acrobatics with sea lions and dolphins, boxing bouts between orang-utans, airborne antics by parrots and cockatoos, and various stunts performed by human employees.

### Siam Park
*99 Thanon Seri Thai, Kanna Yaow, North-east (0 2919 7200-5/www.siamparkcity.com) Bus 60, 71, 96, 168, 519.* **Open** 10am-6pm daily. **Admission** B200; B100 children under 140cm/55in. **Credit** AmEx, MC, V.

This place has everything: a zoo, an amusement park and even a water park with slides, a paddling area and waves on an artificial beach.

### Technopolis Science Museum
*Techno Thani, Thanon Rangsit-Nakhonnayok, Klong 5, Klong Luang, Pathum Thani, North-east (0 2577 4172-8/www.nsm.or.th). Bus 1155.* **Open** 9.30am-5pm Tue-Sun. **Admission** B50; B20 under-18s. **No credit cards.**

This truly world-class museum is housed in astonishing steel, glass and fibreglass cubes balanced on their points. You could spend half a day exploring its six floors, the first three of which are best for kids. Interactive installations and exhibitions are explained by English-speaking assistants.

**Open** 10am-5pm Mon-Fri; 10am-7pm Sat, Sun. **Admission** B120; B95 children under 145cm/57in (excl rides); B330 Dream World Visa (incl rides). **Credit** AmEx, MC, V.

All the usual theme park rides and rollercoasters can be found here, including a soaking on the Big Splash. Don't miss Snow Land, a zone of fake fir trees and polar bears, sled rides and freezing artificial snow. For small children there's a petting zoo and Fairy Tale Land's cute characters. The Disneyesque style concedes a few Thai touches, such as elephant rides and Thai massage for some ticklish relaxation.

### Leoland Water Park
*6th Floor, Central City Bangna, 1093 Thanon Bangna-Trad, East (0 2361 0888). Bus 38, 46, 48, 132, 139, 180.* **Open** 11am-6pm Mon-Fri; 10am-7pm Sat, Sun. **Admission** B250; B150 children under 135cm/53in. **Credit** MC, V.

Perfect for humid Bangkok, this huge water park above a mall offers a cooling breeze and great views, not to mention lots of slides, fountains, bubbling pools and sunbeds.

### Planetarium
*928 Thanon Sukhumvit, Sukhumvit (0 2392 5951-5). Ekamai BTS.* **Open** 8.30am-4.30pm Tue-Sun. **Admission** B20; B10 children. **No credit cards.** **Map** p312 M7.

This stargazing centre (aimed mainly at Thais) features projections on its 13m-high (43ft) dome. The attached science museum does little to stimulate interest, with walls of text and no interactivity.

### Railway Museum
*Chatuchak Park, Kamphaengphet 3 Road, Chatuchak, North (Chatuchak Park 0 2272 4575). Morchit BTS/Morchit subway.* **Open** 6am-6pm Sat, Sun. **Admission** free. **No credit cards.**

## Babysitting & childcare

Because expatriates and wealthy Thais often have maids or extended families, so aren't in the market for babysitting agencies, and playgroups are for members only, childminding services are thin on the ground; the best place to seek help with childcare is the support group **BAMBI** (*see p164*), where the staff will know of any services available.

Major hotels that offer childminding services include **Le Royal Meridien Bangkok** (B200, B100 extra child, B200 surcharge after 10pm; *see p43*) and the **Shangri-La Hotel** (B300, B150 extra child; *see p42*).

**Arts & Entertainment**

### BAMBI (Bangkok Mothers & Babies International)

*www.bambi-bangkok.org.*
**Admission** free; voluntary donation.
A non-profit group offering help and information to pregnant women and parents of young children, from education to entertainment and healthcare. The website has details of weekly playgroups and monthly meetings with activities, storytime, songs and spaces for babies and toddlers.

## Eating out

All restaurants welcome kids, so eating out shouldn't be a chore. In fact, Thai dining can be great fun, with shared dishes, keen staff and hands-on grub such as wrap-in-a-leaf *miang* or cook-at-your-table *suki*. Mall restaurant chains have family facilities, but why not try eating on cushion seating at a dance show or aboard a boat? Vendors sell Thai ice-lollies from metal tubes or else scoop ice-cream into bread rolls, and (a favourite among Thai children) serve crushed ice desserts with multicoloured jellies. Major hotels also hold family Sunday brunches with entertainment, including these two:

### Dusit Thani Kids' Club

*Tiara Restaurant, 22nd Floor, Dusit Thani Hotel, Thanon Rama IV, Bangrak (0 2236 0450/ www.dusit.com). Saladaeng BTS/Silom subway.*
**Open** 11.30am-2pm Sun. **Sunday brunch** B600; B375 under-10s. **Credit** AmEx, DC, MC, V.
**Map** p311 G6.
All children receive a free T-shirt and can win prizes by playing games. At 1.15pm there's a magic show.

### Shangri-La Kids' Club

*Coffee Garden, 1st Floor, Shangri-La Hotel, 89 Soi Wat Suan Plu, Thanon Charoen Krung, Bangrak (0 2236 7777/www.shangri-la.com/eng/hotel). Saphan Taksin BTS.* **Open** 11am-2.30pm Sun.
**Sunday brunch** B850; B425 6-12s; free under-6s.
**Credit** AmEx, DC, MC, V. **Map** p310 D7.
The jolly club consists of a buffet with a children's playroom and various entertainers leading the games and performing magic tricks.

# Breaking family Thais?

There's much hand-wringing about child labour in Thailand, though NGOs worry most about exploitative, dangerous or illicit employment, which is far rarer than in neighbouring countries. But insufficient attention is paid to children's rights and needs, though not just those of poor pre-teens selling garlands so that their family can eat. Rich kids can suffer quite different abuse. Mollycoddled, over-indulged and overfed by nannies, servants and short-sighted parents, numerous ten-year-olds haven't learned to tie their own shoelaces (according to teachers), while some don't know how to cross a road safely at 14, because they've always been driven everywhere.

Most child industry occurs within the framework of family businesses such as restaurants or crafts. In this shophouse culture, visible affection, even cossetting, combine with in-at-the-deep-end life lessons in discipline, perseverance, apprenticeship, sharing and social obligation that make for an unselfish character, respect for traditions and elders, and a sense of extended family that reaches beyond blood ties.

Much of Thais' open-hearted sociability is thanks to the collective nature of any activity, from sleeping entwined with others from birth till adulthood, to the lifelong bonds cultivated among student year-groups. While such togetherness was essential in rural contexts, its exaggeration in institutions leads to corruption, violent rivalry between colleges and even coups, with generals still ganging up with classmates to gain advantage.

Reinforcing the hierarchy, pupils pray to teachers in *wai khru* ceremonies at schools, not just to revered experts. Yet because archaic teaching methods are stunting development, those who were educated abroad want the same standards for their own children and are demanding education reform. There is still vast oversubscription by ambitious Thai parents for international schools despite several famous new homegrown ones, such as Dulwich College in Phuket and Harrow School in Bangkok.

While many Thais still live with or near their parents until or even beyond marriage, familial breakdown and domestic violence is rife. Partly because of birth control successes and greater mobility, small, nuclear families are increasing. But without other relatives around, working parents mean latch-key kids are vulnerable to delinquency – or open to non-traditional influences, from materialism, drugs and risqué fashions to previously taboo girl-boy fraternisation. This is one motive behind the 'social order' crackdown. Patronising repression by social dinosaurs or a rearguard action to save an intangible Thainess? It's a dilemma faced by all Thai parents.

# Film

More screens, more festivals, more movies – Thai cinema is booming again.

Thailand is enjoying something of a movie-making renaissance after productions per year (now back above 20) had dwindled into single figures. However, the current output is still only a fraction of that enjoyed during the 1950s, '60s and '70s boom periods, characterised by Burton-Tayloresque romances with Mitr Chaibancha and Petchara Shaowarat, as well as Thai monsters battling in a local version of Ultraman (whose revival is being challenged by the superhero's Japanese originator). Encouragingly, though, this upswing is due to well-made dramas proving more popular than the teen melodramas that had by the mid '90s become monopolistic marketing vehicles for their singer/model/MC stars.

The trigger was Nonzee Nimibutr's retro hoodlum hit *Dang Bireley's and the Young Gangsters*, stylishly set in an imagined 1950s Bangkok. Nimbutr then went on to better his own box office record in 1999 with a sumptuous remake of *Nang Nak* (the perennial Thai ghost story), which netted more than B100 million. Export markets also lapped up *Iron Ladies*, a feel-good biopic by Yongyuth Thongkongkun about Thailand's champion volleyball team turning out to be a clutch of ladyboys. The success of the film recently led to a sequel.

Suddenly in 2001, Siamese cineastes hit the big time, with foreign festivals and art-house cinemas snapping up anything Thai worth projecting. *Tears of the Black Tiger* – a kitsch, colour-saturated homage to 1950s Thai cowboy romps and the pioneering auteurism of Hanuman studio founder Ratana Pestonji – was swooned over in Cannes and London. While sceptics whispered that it was mostly a post-*Crouching Tiger* scramble for things Asian, Oscar hype surrounded the historical epic *Suriyothai* (*see p10* **Warrior princesses**) by Mom Ratchawong Chatri Chalerm Yukol. The socially aware director of *Sia Dai*, Chatri is an aristocrat echoing Thai film's century-old origins as an enthusiasm of King Rama V and Prince Sanbhassatra.

*Suriyothai*'s lavish art direction and plot of revenge and sacrifice appealed to Francis Ford Coppola (a film school pal of Chatri), who re-edited the bloated, confusing tale of Ayutthayan court intrigue. Its B400-B600 million cost was repaid domestically through

dutiful national film-going (including special school trips) and prompted a stream of Burma-bashing yarns such as Thanit Jitnukul's gore-fest *Bangrajan*.

*Suriyothai* set new local standards in ambition, logistics, detail and marketing. Still, local scripting, camerawork and acting can lose impact because of Thai conventions about deference, non-demonstrativeness and appearance, punctuated by mannered outbursts and slapstick humour of *likay* drama lineage (*see p199*) that aren't to all tastes.

## VISION VERSUS VASELINE

The main obstacle to celluloid expression, though, remains censorship. Vaseline may no longer be applied to images involving nipples, but entire scenes (and plot developments) still get excised by the Film Board's moral guardians, who also considered the 1999 movie *Anna and the King* sensitive enough to ban. Nonzee Nimibutr further provoked the board's prudery (and hence public protest against it) with his languid 2001 adaptation of the novel *Jan Dara*, about a boy's sexual awakening at the hands of his stepmother.

There's also talk of reforming the restrictive 1931 Film Act, which was dusted off to harass the indie-inspired **Bangkok Film Festival** (*see p159*). Though far less cosmopolitan than the festivals in Singapore or Korea's Pusan, this annual cinethon has, since its inception in 1998, garnered a passionate youthful following.

Similarly popular is the free annual **Short Film and Video Festival** (mid August; information Khun Chalida 0 1615 5137/ www.thaifilm.com), which is jointly hosted by the **Goethe Institut** (*see p167*) and **About Café** (*see p169*). Indie films shine in this increasingly international festival, with more than 100 Thai screenings over the course of one week and an awards competition.

## GOING INTER

Whatever the growing pains of Thai cinema, at least it is attracting a new audience. Within one short decade, festivals have gone from barely one a year to one a month, with various foreign cultural bodies doing their bit to fill the fixture list – Alliance Française (March), the EU (May), British Council (July) and Japan Cultural Centre (December) – alongside the

Arts & Entertainment

Thai-initiated Short Film Festival (August) and Experimental Film Festival (November). These are typically held at multiplexes, which since 1994 have quadrupled the number of screens in Bangkok. The setting is often super-luxurious, with velvet recliners, tables and waitress service – quite a contrast to the traditional open-air set-ups by touring projectionists, which still feature at fairs, both upcountry and in old Bangkok communities.

With horizons widened, Thai films are now going 'inter' (that is, exporting their cinematic culture). Darling of the festivals abroad is Pen Ek Ratanaruang (director of the black comedy *6ixty-nin9* and folk music drama *Mon Rak Transistor*). While the better Thai movies now earn more abroad than at home, catering to a foreign market had been unimaginable thanks to the language's limitations and the consequent self-defeating omission of subtitles. Nowadays all Thai movies are subtitled and previewed (instead of being rushed to release a week after wrap, as would have been the case in the old days).

The industry is learning to market its assets globally, with leaps in professionalism by two new studios (and potential duopoly): Bangkok Film (which has veered from gritty *Bangkok: Dangerous* to historical *Thawipop*) and GMM Grammy Pictures, which debuts with *February, Beautiful Boxer* and *One Night Husband*. Let's hope that the revival is not a one-night wonder.

To find out film times at the cinemas listed below, check out **www.movieseer.com**.

## First-run cinemas

### EGV

*6th Floor, Siam Discovery Centre, Thanon Rama I, Pathumwan (all branches 0 2812 9999/ www.egv.com). Siam BTS.* **Tickets** B120-B500. **Screens** 10. **Credit** AmEx, DC, MC, V. **Map** p309 & p310 F4.
Great seating and sightlines at all screens, especially the recliners in the exclusive Gold Class theatres (both here and at Seacon Square).
**Branches**: Seacon Square, Thanon Srinakharin, East; Central Pinklao, Thonburi.

### Lido Multiplex

*Siam Square, Thanon Rama I, Pathumwan (0 2252 6498/www.apexsiam-square.com). Siam BTS.* **Tickets** B100. **Screens** 3. **No credit cards**. **Map** p309 & p310 F4.
The Lido offers poorly insulated mini-theatres, but it often has artier programming than elsewhere.

### Major Cineplex

*7th Floor, World Trade Centre, Thanon Ratchadamri, Pathumwan (all branches 0 2511 5555/www.majorcineplex.com). Chidlom BTS.* **Tickets** B120-B300. **Screens** 6. **Credit** AmEx, MC, V. **Map** p311 G4.
An impressive multiplex with unrestrained decor – and 'lovers' seats'.
**Branches**: Ekamai, Sukhumvit; Pinklao, Thonburi; Ratcha Yothin, Thanon Phahon Yothin, North.

### Scala

*Siam Square Soi 1, Pathumwan (0 2251 2861/ www.apexsiam-square.com). Siam BTS.* **Tickets** B120. **Screens** 1. **No credit cards**. **Map** p309 & p310 F4.

# Set peace

Thailand has been the backdrop for so many Hollywood movies that the government is now actively supporting the country's affinity with movie-makers by offering tax breaks. Such film work nurtures both local economies and Thai technical know-how, even when it's not Thailand being depicted – as in 007's rooftop bike chase above the grim shophouses of Chinatown (*Tomorrow Never Dies*) or the decaying stucco of Customs House in Wong Kar Wai's *In the Mood for Love*. Thailand also accounts for 30 per cent of Jackie Chan's $85-million remake of *Around the World in 80 Days*, due for release in 2003.

This is a timely boost, since Thailand is no longer automatically selected for films that might have been shot on location in Vietnam (from *The Deer Hunter* to *Heaven &*

*Earth*) or Cambodia (*The Killing Fields*), now that these formerly closed countries are more relaxed; Cambodia hosted *Tomb Raider* and *Under the Banyan Tree*.

Like many of the resulting movies, though, the impact on the locations isn't always as great as the promise. *The Beach* almost decamped to the Philippines in the face of protests at the temporary transplanting of vegetation to Ko Phi Phi's 'protected' Maya Bay, and a court case was set in motion. The studio minimised the damage, but it was the marketing hype that caused the archetypally 'undiscovered' beach to suffer untold harm from visitors vicariously reliving DiCaprio's quest. It now shares the tourist-trap fate of 'James Bond Island' in Phang Nga Bay, made famous in 1974's *The Man with the Golden Gun*.

Still hand-painting its huge posters, the Scala is one of Bangkok's last old-style, big-screen halls. Its open-air lobby is an art deco treasure.

### SF Cinema City

*7th Floor, Mah Boon Krong Centre, Thanon Rama I, Pathumwan (0 2611 6444/www.sfcinemacity.com). National Stadium BTS.* **Tickets** B100. **Credit** MC, V. **Map** p309 & p310 F4.
A young and funky cinema, with a dramatic foyer. **Branch**: Central Ladprao, Thanon Phahon Yothin, North (0 2927 2111).

### Siam

*Siam Square, Thanon Rama I, Pathumwan (0 2251 1735/www.apexsiam-square.com). Siam BTS.* **Tickets** B120 **Screens** 1. **No credit cards**. **Map** p309 & p310 F4.
An undivided large auditorium with a huge screen, but creaky, unsupportive seats.

### UMG

*31/6-9 Royal City Avenue, Thanon Phetchaburi end, North-east (0 2641 5913/4). Bus 11, 58, 60, 72, 93, 99, 113, 512.* **Tickets** B100-B220. **Screens** 5. **No credit cards. Map** p312 L4.
Plain and functional multiplex in a teen night zone.

### United Artists

*The Emporium, Thanon Sukhumvit, corner of Soi 24, Sukhumvit (0 2664 8711/2/3/4/5/ www.ua-siam.co.th). Phrom Phong BTS.* **Tickets** B120. **Screens** 5. **Credit** AmEx, MC, V. **Map** p312 K6.
Rivalling EGV as the best movie-going experience, UA is comfy, with good services, many festivals and a huge choice of food.

## Repertory & art-house

Weekly screenings of Japanese films at the **Japan Foundation** (*see p173*) are subtitled only in Thai.

### Alliance Française

*29 Thanon Sathorn Tai, South (0 2670 4200/ www.alliance-francaise.or.th). Bus 17, 22, 35, 62, 67, 116, 149.* **Open** 8am-6.30pm Mon-Fri; 8.30am-5pm Sat; 8.30am-12.30am Sun. **Tickets** B40. **No credit cards. Map** p311 G7.
French movies with English subtitles are shown at 7pm on Thursday and 5pm on Saturday. And what was formerly the French Film Festival has now become part of the Bangkok International Film Festival (*see p159*), which takes place in January every year.

### Goethe Institut

*18/1 Goethe Gasse, Soi Atthakarn Prasit, Sathorn Soi 1, South (0 2287 0942/3/4/www.goethe.de/ bangkok). Bus 17, 22, 35, 62, 67, 116, 149.* **Open** 8am-4.30pm daily. **Tickets** B40. **No credit cards. Map** p311 H7.
The Goethe Institut shows German classics from Lang to Wenders, plus *echt* experimental efforts

Painting posters at the **Scala**. *See p166.*

every Saturday at 2pm (free, with English subtitles). The Institut also hosts the annual Short Film and Video Festival every August.

### National Film Archive

*4 Thanon Chao Fa, Phra Nakorn (0 2282 1847). Bus 32, 33, 64.* **Open** 8.30am-4pm Mon-Sat. **Admission** free. **No credit cards. Map** p308 B3.
The main repository and restorer of Thai films throughout its century-long history, the NFA is overseen by devoted archivist Dome Sukwong.

### Sala Chalermkrung

*66 Thanon Charoen Krung, Chinatown (0 2222 1854). Bus 1,25, 48, 507, 508.* **Tickets** B300-B500. **No credit cards. Map** p309 & p310 D5.
An unpredictable mix of arty, mainstream, Bollywood and festival movies, plus live shows, in grand art deco surroundings.

## IMAX

### Krung Thai IMAX Theatre

*Major Cineplex Ratchayothin, Thanon Phahon Yothin, North (0 2511 5595/www.imaxthai.com). Phahon Yothin subway/bus 34, 39, 59, 108, 503, 513.* **Open** 11am-11pm daily. **Tickets** B150. **Screens** 1 IMAX; 13 others. **Credit** AmEx, MC, V.
Long runs of specialist movies, plus some blockbusters, are shown at this 27m by 21m (88.5ft by 69ft) screen – claimed to be the world's largest IMAX cinema. Audiences listen through cordless headsets. There's also a smaller simulator cinema, plus screens showing general release fare.

### Simulator

*Major Cineplex Ekamai, Sukhumvit Soi 61 & 63, Sukhumvit (0 2714 2828). Ekamai BTS.* **Open** 11am-11pm daily. **Tickets** B80; B50 concessions. **No credit cards.**
Swooping, vibrating seats make you think you're experiencing the adventures in the 15-minute films shown on rotation here.
**Branch**: Major Cineplex Ratchyothin, North.

# Galleries

Thai art moves from temple walls to restaurants and malls.

Modern Thai art received unprecedented international exposure in 1998 when Christie's auctioned off the art collections of 56 dissolved finance houses. Bidders were intrigued to find the lots categorised by social rank. Status as a factor in quality is not just a result of Thai deference to age, experience and titles like 'national artist', it also reflects the Asian tradition of the apprentice seeking to emulate the master.

## NEW MURAL ORDER

For centuries, most Thai painting and sculpture took the form of religious illustrations in temples, incrementally changing through each renewal by anonymous craftsmen. Unsurprisingly, many modern canvases possess a muralesque stylisation, with the likes of Pratuang Emjaroen taking Buddhist cosmology into surrealist abstractions, while the paintings of Tawatchai Somkong seem to convey raw thought energy.

It's not all about fine brushwork, though; materials as diverse as clay, handmade paper and gold leaf are employed by contemporary Buddhist painters. Notables include Sompop Budtarad, muralist of London's Thai temple; Panya Vijinthanasarn, who creates fusions of European forms; Preecha Thaothong, specialist in mural depictions; Thawun Praman, who conjures stone carving textures in pop colours; and the northerner Songdej Thipthong, whose worlds within worlds appear in draughtsman-like Buddha footprints. Others, such as Chalood Ninsamer, Damrong Wong-uparaj and Vorasan Suparp, portray ordinary life.

Increasingly, Thai artists have traded anonymity for individualism, breaching conventions by cultivating bohemian appearances and voicing protests (see p170 **Art for life**). Bursting out in the 1970s, Thailand's first superstar artists were Chalermchai Kositpipat, famous for imparting Buddhist scenarios with bright, precise sensuality, and the flamboyant Thawan Dutchanee, whose swirling black visions surge with the shamanistic energies of an oriental Bosch. This led to a critical approach to art in a culture fostering compliments, with academics such as Thanom Chaphakdee leading the way.

## DRAWING FROM OUTSIDE

Thai modern art originated more formally under Corrado Ferroci, an Italian sculptor commissioned to cast monumental bronzes, who subsequently became a Thai national. As Silpa Bhirasri, he founded Silpakorn University, the country's first art school, in 1943, and trained a generation of artists who had a chance to flower before the reactionary dictatorships took hold.

Another crucial seedbed for artistic talent has been the **Goethe Institut** (see p173). For four decades, this German agency has supported nearly every major Thai artist with scholarships and the provision of space to experiment and collaborate with counterparts from abroad (many of whom reunite at its annual **December Art & Fun Fair**). Nowadays, that role is shared with the **Alliance Française** (see p173) and artist-run spaces such as **About Café** (see p169), **Project 304** (see p170) and **Tadu Contemporary Art** (see p171).

This vibrant scene has helped Bangkok become a regional art hub, forcing the new Ministry of Culture and Religion to establish a contemporary art office in 2002. However, since the minister in charge has no arts background and is a champion of 'patriotic art', cultural policy seems likely to emphasise tradition.

Although Bhirasri is still widely venerated, nowadays Thai students are veering towards conceptual art – a field in which the country has attracted global attention, most notably through the work of the late installationist Montien Boonma. Other big names include Nawin Rawanchaikul, who works in Japan and Europe and has created installations in taxis and tuk-tuks, and Rirkrit Tiravanija, who wowed New York and published Ver, a picture-only magazine with interviews on CD. There's also Surasi Kosolwong, whose work frames activity as exhibits; in 2002 he was invited to Germany for the world's first art exposition on shopping.

So who's tipped to be the next big sensation? Perhaps Chatchai Puipia, whose conflicted self-portraits reassess the Siamese smile.

## SPACE: THE FINAL FRONTIER

Where, then, are the best places to see these triumphs of Thai modernism? As with antiques, mostly on private walls. Indeed, future art historians will more than likely find this flourishing era largely absent from the **National Gallery**'s small permanent collection (see p170), while plans for a contemporary

art centre look sure to be thwarted. There is also a grievous lack of arts endowments, with few corporate collections open to the public and a paucity of public art – with the notable exception of Misiem Yipintsoi's bronzes in Benjasiri Park.

Otherwise, it's simply a case of following the free monthly culture map *Art Connection* to lively public openings at the city's few innovative galleries. Or head up to Chiang Mai, home of the Thai 'new wave'. Also, in Bangkok, the spread of art into bars is making celebrities of certain fashionable young artists.

Admission to the spaces and galleries listed below is free unless otherwise stated.

## Exhibition spaces

### About Café/About Studio
*402-8 Thanon Maitri Chit, Promprab Sattrupai, Chinatown (0 2623 1742). Bus 1, 25, 35, 73, 501, 507.* **Open** 7pm-midnight daily. **Map** p309 & p310 D4.

The arrival of the subway is set to make this unique space as convenient as it is hip. At its legendary parties, those in the know fill its floors (and roof) to experience anything from art, film, video, installations and art marts to DJs, live music, dance, poetry, workshops and site-specific happenings. Often all at once. Beer and herbal tea flow in abundance, fuelling the heckling at the Bangkok Poetry readings or the more sedate browsing of the art

library among a jumble of retro furniture. Even the ceiling, floor and toilet become involved in exhibitions that turn every inch – and the street outside – into an art statement. Since 1996 young director Klaomard Yipintsoi has made About a bohemian hub, influencing art cafés, experimental galleries and bars in its resolute quirkiness and affiliations with guest curators (from as far afield as New York's Whitney Museum of American Art). AARA (About Arts Related Activities) also organises workshops, gigs and other weekend events, as well as collaborating online with such famous art groups as Sweden's Superflex. And in August, this venue is also one of the hosts of the annual Short Film & Video Festival (*see p160*).

### Bangkok University Art Gallery
*3rd Floor, Building 9, Kluaynam Thai campus, Thanon Rama IV, Sukhumvit (0 2350 3500/ www.rama9art.org/gallery/bkkuni/index.html). Bus 22, 46, 149, 507.* **Open** 9am-5pm daily.

A small but important whitewashed space run by the faculty, this gallery's multidisciplinary shows tend to be given by lecturers, students and foreign artists in residence.

### Chulalongkorn Art Centre
*7th Floor, Central Library Building, Thanon Phayathai, Chulalongkorn University, Pathumwan (0 2218 2964/5/www.chula.ac.th/arts/index_en.html). Siam BTS.* **Open** *Term-time* 8am-7pm Mon-Fri; 8am-4am Sat. *Vacations* 8am-4am Mon-Fri. **Map** p309 & p310 F5.

Fresh faces at **H Gallery**. *See p172.*

# Art for life

A phrase first coined by assassinated thinker and writer Jit Bhumisak during the 1960s dictatorship, *silapa puer cheewit* ('art for life') has now become the mantra of provocative contemporary artists who are striving to highlight social issues. Their concerns have been voiced in literature, painting, poetry, posters and music (*pleng puer cheewit*, 'songs for life'), while, in the 1990s, performance art protested against further problems such as corruption, consumerism, environmental degradation and globalisation.

The Ukabat ('Fireball') activists led by **Paisan Plienbangchang** and **Vasan Sitthiket** (whose mixed media works thrill with rude panache) are typical of this movement. They work mostly in public spaces, particularly rallies, but their style is more Lennon than Lenin: disturbance-oriented 'happenings', with shouting to music, readings of foul-mouthed poetry, even the odd mock hanging of cabinet look-alike puppets.

Aesthetic wit is more abundant in the work of photographer **Manit Sriwanichpoom**, who was a prominent campaigner against the filming of *The Beach*. Manit raises awareness about exploitation issues at parks, shops and government offices through devices such as 'the Pink Man' – salmon-suited fellow artist **Sompong Thawee** pushing shopping trolleys through national parks, hill tribe villages and touristed temples.

On a more general level, the cancellation of Bangkok's B300-million project for a Metropolitan Contemporary Art Centre at the Pathumwan intersection has caused widespread outrage. Protests, this time in the cause of art itself, are led by AIDs activist and performance artist **Chumphon Apisuk** of Concrete House (57/60 Thanon Tivanond, Nonthaburi, North; 0 2526 8311). Apisuk is also behind **Asiatopia** (*see p157*), the annual Asian performance art festival held in November.

Focusing on social issues through a variety of media, curator Professor Apinan Poshyananda draws on his international reputation to hold at least one solo show a year by a famous foreign artist, and to provide a global springboard for Thais. Notable past exhibitors include Montien Boonma, Navin Rawanchaikul, Manit Sriwanichpoom, Pinaree Sanpitak (explorer of feminine issues) and Chatchai Puipia. This space has also courted controversy through the likes of Vasan Sitthiket, and Yasumasa Morimura and Nobuyashi Araki of Japan.

## Marsi Gallery

*Suan Pakkad Palace, 352 Thanon Sri Ayutthaya, North (0 2245 4934). Phayathai BTS.* **Open** 9pm-4am daily. **Map** p311 G3.

Purpose-built for Thai and international artists in the grounds of an exquisite palace, Marsi hosts open-air performances and workshops.

## National Gallery

*5 Thanon Chao Fa, near Sanam Luang, Phra Nakorn (0 2282 2639). Bus 32, 33, 64.* **Open** 9am-4pm Wed-Sun. **Admission** B10 Thais; B30 foreigners. **Map** p308 B3.

Most local artists dream of exhibiting their work in the high-ceilinged period buildings of this national institution, established in 1977. There is little in the way contemporary art among its smallish permanent collection, which includes work by such notables as late impressionist painter Fua Haripitak, late sculptor Misiem Yipintsoi, late portrait artist Chamrus Khietkong and watercolourist Sawasdi Tantisuk. Shows tend to be of international calibre.

## Project 304

*project304@yahoo.com/www.project304.net.*

Co-founded in 1996 by multimedia artist Kamol Phaosawasdi, Surasi Kosolwong and multidisciplinarian Michael Shaowanasai (founder of the Gay & Lesbian Film Festival; *see p156*), this avant-garde group temporarily moved north in 2002, when its director, Gridthiya Gaweewong, became the first curator-in-residence at Chiang Mai Art Museum (*see p266*). A non-profit organisation nurturing dialogue between artists and with the public, 304 often collaborates with cultural institutes and foreign guest curators. Its shows, installations, performances and experimental film festivals often challenge taboos. Used to mobility, 304 operates in public spaces, assorted venues and cyberspace.

## Si-Am Art Space

*1741-7, Thanon Rama IV, Sukhumvit (0 2221 3841). Bus 22, 46, 149, 507.* **Open** 9am-7pm Mon-Fri; 9am-4am Sat, Sun. **Map** p311 H7.

Opened in 1999 on a small soi between Green Tower and Theptharin Hospital, this artist-run forum for young talent hosts everything from sound installations to abstract painting and mixed media, as well as short courses, lectures, discussions and workshops in all disciplines.

## Silpakorn Art Centre

*Silpakorn University, 31 Thanon Na Phralan, Phra Nakorn (0 2221 3841/www.art-centre.su.ac.th). Bus 1, 39, 44, 47, 123, 512.* **Open** 9am-7pm Mon-Fri; 9am-4pm Sat. Closed during vacations. **Map** p308 B3.

Housed in Tha Phra Palace in Phra Nakorn, the two-storey art centre of Thailand's original art school features exhibitions by students and foreign artists-in-residence, plus ceremonies, forums and training. There are specialist galleries in the faculties of architecture, decorative arts (products and textiles), and painting, sculpture and graphic arts.

### Space Contemporary Art
*582/9 Ekkamai Soi 6, Thanon Sukhumvit, Sukhumvit (0 2711 4427/artspace@thaimail.com). Ekkamai BTS.* **Open** 10am-5pm Mon-Sat. **Map** p312 M7.
Confronting all the senses, Space Contemporary Art is a showcase for nonconformist ideas. It was established by artists in 1999 as an exhibition space for those denied room in stricter and more traditional galleries.

### Tadu Contemporary Art
*Mezzanine, Pavilion Y Building, 31/4 Royal City Avenue, Thanon Petchaburi end, North-East (0 2203 0927-12/www.tadu.net). Rama IX subway/bus 137, 168, 179, 517.* **Open** 9.30am-6.30pm Mon-Sat. **Map** p312 M4.
Founded in 1996 by artists and collectors under director Luckana Kunavichyanont, Tadu presents various visual arts, films and innovative theatre, promoting young Thai artists and educating the public, often in collaborations and with related educational activities.

## Commercial galleries

### Akko Collection House
*919/1 Thanon Sukhumvit, between Sois 49 & 51, Sukhumvit (0 2259 1436). Thonglor BTS.* **Open** 10am-7pm Mon-Sat. **Credit** AmEx, MC, V. **Map** p312 L7.
Japanese dealer Atsuko Susuki Davies sells mostly paintings and prints by Japanese and Thai artists. Names to watch for include feminist woodcut specialist Jarrasri Roopkamdee, radical watercolourist Somboon Phuangdokmai, Ekkachai Luadsoongnoern and Sawai Wongsaprom.

### Bangkok Gallery
*2/5 Sukhumvit Soi 20, Sukhumvit (0 2663 4147). Asok BTS.* **Open** 9am-7pm Mon-Sat. **Credit** DC, MC, V. **Map** p312 K6.
Expect to find erotic paintings, figurative drawings, landscapes and portraits by established names, including the prolific Vasan Sitthiket.

### Carpediem Galleries
*1-1B Ruam Rudi Building, Soi Ruam Rudi, corner of Thanon Ploenchit, Pathumwan (0 2250 0408/ www.carpediemgallery.com). Ploenchit BTS.* **Open** 11am-5pm Mon-Sat. **Credit** AmEx, V. **Map** p311 H5.
Singaporean Delia Oakins has built this tiny gallery into an effective outlet for South-east Asian artists, including Symon and Krijono of Indonesia, Martin

Work by Chatchai Puipia at **Numthong Gallery**. *See p172.*

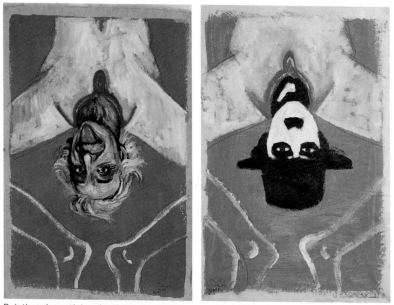

Paintings by acclaimed artist Vasan Sitthiket can be seen in several galleries.

Loh of Singapore and Thai Thawun Pramarn, plus Italian master Luigi Rincicotti. There is more display space down the road (more popular among tourists than purists) in an agreeable Thai restaurant. **Branch**: Baan Khanitha & Gallery, 49 Soi Ruam Rudi, Pathumwan (0 2253 4638/9).

### Gallery 55

*Unit 212, 2nd Floor, All Seasons Place Retail Centre, 87/2 Thanon Witthayu, Pathumwan (0 2685 3877). Ploenchit BTS.* **Open** 10am-10pm daily. **Credit** AmEx, V. **Map** p311 H5.
Experienced dealer Ferdie H Ju schedules mostly abstract and semi-abstract shows by new Thai names and reputable south-east Asians and Europeans. Opening parties are always imaginative.

### H Gallery

*201 Sathorn Soi 12, South (0 1310 4428). Bus 17, 22, 35, 62, 67, 116, 149.* **Open** noon-6pm Thur-Sat; by appointment Mon-Wed, Sun. **No credit cards.** **Map** p310 E7.
Antique wood panelling in this house-cum-gallery contrasts with the fresh, arresting canvases of emergent Thai painters championed by US dealer H Earnest Lee. Lee's fashionable opening parties – here and at art bars such as Eat Me! (*see p109*) – have helped to foster a young middle-class market drawn by its affordable prices and trendy reputation. Names to look out for include Thaweesak 'Lolay' Srithongdee (perverse pop characters), Atjima Jaroenchit (stirring seascapes), Jakkai Siributr (fab fabrics, drab brushwork), Jaruwat Boonwaedlom (fragmented photo-realism), Wuttikorn Kongka (compellingly disturbed figuration) and Jitsing Somboon (fashion portraits).

### Numthong Gallery

*Room 109, Bangkok Co-op Housing Building, opposite Samsen Station, Thanon Toeddamri, Dusit (0 2243 4326/www.rama9art.org/gallery/numthong/index.html). Bus 52, 148.* **Open** 11am-6pm Mon-Sat. **No credit cards.**
Numthong Tang opened this gallery in 1997 to encourage individuality in artists, and his collection of paintings and installations offers a rare marriage of message, imagination and skill. On his roster are masterpieces by artists such as Natee Utarit, Niti Wuttuya, Chatchai Puipia, Kamin Lertchaiprasert, Vasan Sitthiket and Montien Boonma.

### Open Arts Space

*Silom Galleria, 919/1 Thanon Silom, Bangrak (0 2266 4223). Surasak BTS.* **Open** 10am-7pm Mon-Sat. **No credit cards.** **Map** p309 F7.
Off an atrium filled with arts, antique and interior decorating outlets, this café-gallery changes its furnishings to suit the exhibition's theme – going retro for a '50s-style show by Chartchai Puipia, say.

### Sombatpermpoon Gallery

*12 Sukhumvit Soi 1, Sukhumvit (0 2254 6040-5). Ploenchit BTS.* **Open** 9.30am-9pm daily. **Credit** AmEx, DC, MC, V. **Map** p311 H5.

A one-stop shop that sells everything from rare early artworks by masters such as Thawan Dachanee, Pratuang Emcharoen and Angkarn Kalayanapongsa to younger talents' mostly expressionist, figurative and abstract paintings.
**Branch**: Hilton Hotel, Promenade Shopping Arcade, Wireless Road, Pathumwan (0 2252 0377).

## Surapon Gallery

*1st Floor, Tisco Tower, Thanon Sathorn North, Bangrak (0 2638 0033/4). Bus 17, 22, 35, 62, 67, 116, 149.* **Open** 10.30am-6.30pm Mon-Fri; 10.30am-5pm Sat. **Credit** AmEx, MC, V. **Map** p311 G7.
An exclusive gallery with prices to match, Surapon exhibits flawless works by prominent painters who focus on Thai subjects (including dance and Buddhism), such as Prasong Luemuang, Itthipol Thangchalok and Surasit Saokhong.

## Thavibu Gallery

*Suite 308, 3rd Floor, Silom Galleria, Thanon Silom, Bangrak (0 2266 5454/www.thavibu.com). Surasak BTS.* **Open** 11am-7pm Tue-Sun. **Map** p310 E7.
If you don't have time to visit this gallery in person, you can always access its virtual showroom, which presents new exhibitions monthly, with thumbnail archives of established and aspiring artists from Thailand, Vietnam, Burma and Laos. You'll receive your canvas via DHL.

## Cultural institutes

### Alliance Française

*29 Thanon Sathorn Tai, South (0 2670 4200/www.alliance-francaise.or.th). Bus 17, 22, 35, 62, 67, 116, 149.* **Open** 8am-6.30pm Mon-Fri; 8.30am-5pm Sat; 8.30am-12.30pm Sun. **Map** p310 G7.
As well as carrying out its Francophone mission, this state body also stimulates Thai arts by holding exhibitions at indie venues, screening international feature and art films in its refurbished auditorium and supporting major Thai-international collaborations. Run by artist Phiippe Laleu, the Alliance offers Thailand's first internationally recognised visual arts course. There's also a French-language school, a library and a café.

### British Council

*254 Chulalongkorn Soi 64, Pathumwan (0 2652 5480-5/www.britishcouncil.or.th).* **Open** 10am-8pm daily. **Map** p310 F6.
This language school and library brings touring promotions of 'cool Britannia' culture to mostly mall venues, with the likes of artist Damien Hirst, designer Tom Dixon and London-based Thai designer Ou Baholyodhin. It also hosts occasional talks and shows by Thais studying in the UK, as well as running July's British Film Festival.

### Goethe Institut

*18/1 Goethe Gasse, Soi Atthakarn Prasit, Sathorn Soi 1, South (0 2287 0942-4/www.goethe.de/bangkok). Bus 17, 22, 35, 62, 67, 116, 149.* **Open** 8am-4.30pm Mon-Fri. **Map** p311 H7.

This semi-private body offers language classes, and (while tirelessly promoting German art and culture) also has a peerless record for nurturing modern Thai artists. Experimental projects and top-ranking work by German and Thai masters are on show around its charming balcony spaces and venues. The Institute also hosts film festivals and screens edgy German movies (*see p167*). Hungry culture vultures can pick at Thai or Bierkeller fare in the Ratsstuebe restaurant.

### Japan Foundation

*10th Floor, Serm-mit Tower, Sukhumvit Soi 21 (Soi Asoke), Yaek Asok, Sukhumvit (0 2260 8560-4/www.jfbkk.or.th). Asok BTS.* **Open** 9am-7pm Mon-Fri; 9am-5pm Sat. **Map** p312 K6.
A range of Asian artists show here, from masters to children, and the resultant exhibitions encompass everything from wacky installations to an annual show of comics. There are also regular lectures by Japanese artists, curators and cultural experts, plus a Japanese Film Festival and weekly screenings (subtitled in Thai only).

## Art bars

The concept of showing art in social spaces has taken off in a big way since the late 1990s. Many establishments now decorate their walls with beautiful paintings, but among the most impressive are the artist-run **Baan Bangkok**, in a 150 year-old mansion (*see p105*); H Gallery fave **Eat Me!** (*see p109*); the sophisticated **Kuppa** café (*see p114*); the homoerotic **Dick's Café** (*see p177*); the experimental, photographer-run **Phranakorn Bar** (*see p124*); and the **Foreign Correspondents Club of Thailand** in Pathumwan (Penthouse, Maneeya Building, Thanon Ploenchit, 0 2254 8165/www.fccthai.com), which showcases photojournalism monthly.

## Auctions

Art auctions are new to Thailand. The first was the post-crash sale at **Christie's** (0 2652 1097/www.christies.com), when Thai bidders paid over the odds. The London auction house continues to put paintings, prints and jewellery under the hammer every year, with work from Thai masters in the catalogues. **Sotheby's** (0 2286 0788/9/www.sothebys.com), represented by celebrity collector Rika Dila, finds Thai jewellery and fine art by masters and emerging artists for trading abroad, occasionally auctioning jewellery in Bangkok. East Asian antiques attract bids at **Riverside Auction House** in units 459-60 of River City mall (*see p138*) on the first Saturday of each month (1.30pm-4.30pm), with viewing throughout the preceding week.

Arts & Entertainment

# Gay & Lesbian

Boys and girls come out to pay in typically tolerant Thai technicolour.

Not exactly the gay paradise it's often cracked up to be, Thailand is still one of the world's most gay- and lesbian-friendly places. Ironically, some old hands wistfully feel it was more liberated before a Western-style gay movement emerged (*see below* **Siam what I am**). Annual gay parades and periodic protests ruffle a society, which (while tolerant) views sexuality as an innately private matter. Given that homophobic violence is unheard of, gay offspring are rarely shunned by families, and anyone outing a gay would themselves lose face – and instead gain sympathy for the person exposed. Instances of prejudice often betray a Westernised education.

Yet the scene is very visible, from the pole-dancing go-go boys to the Britney/Whitney lip-sync *kathoey* (ladyboy) cabarets. But less discernible than the Lycra-topped disco contingent are the middle-class, confident guppies fresh from the gym or coffee house. Generally, women are less prominent in Thai society, though you can't miss the role-identifying attire of close-cropped *toms* (butch girls) in suits or checked shirts, strolling hand in hand with their glamorous *dees* (from 'la-dies'). Deeming lesbian a term for women who have sex together for male viewing, *tom-dees* socialise at a shifting scene of restaurants and socials run by **Anjaree Group** (*see chapter* **Directory: Gay & lesbian**).

The gay commercial explosion since the 1980s has been huge and venues now outnumber Sydney's. Unsurprisingly, prostitution has flourished and 'money boys' have become a fixture. The trendy gay focus is around Silom Sois 2 and 4 (in Bangrak), the former being solely gay. Venues are also grouped at Trok Sake (Phra Nakorn), Thanon Kamphaengphet (North) and studenty Ramkamphaeng (North-east). Sleazier venues are grouped around Thanon Surawong at Soi Tawan and Soi Duangthawee Plaza (Bangrak), while the Thai-oriented 'boy bars' of Saphan Kwai (North) are declining due to repeated raids (which also affect strips like Suan Saranrom and the stretch between Suan Lumphini and Robinson's Silom). Opulent saunas and discreet massage parlours do a roaring trade. For mainstream ladyboy cabarets, *see p203*. Cruising is everywhere, and in this mood of confidence, Bangkok has stepped fabulously out of the closet.

## RESOURCES

The leading gateway to organising a visit is **www.utopia-asia.com**, which excels at events, insights, contacts, listings and links for gays and lesbians, though **www.dreaded neds.com** has useful listings and forums on gay Thailand.

Free monthly publications with bilingual listings include *Gay Max*, with a *Gay Max Guide Line* map that is smarter but less clear than *Bangkok Variety* and its map, *Gay Guide Bangkok*. Also free from venues, *Thai Guys* is a magazine for locals and visitors, replicated at **www.thaiguys.org**. The book *The Men of Thailand* has invaluable cultural context. It's sold from **Bookazine** (*see p138*), along with the language book/tape *Thai for Gay Tourists*, for phrasing anything from making friends to safe sex and cross-cultural romances.

## Siam what I am

Despite the colourful scene, gay Thais are as *kaeng jai* (reticent) as any compatriot. Until the early 1990s many didn't identify themselves as homosexuals, associating the term with *kathoey* (ladyboys), who were the only role model for effeminate lads. They got married and paid money boys or even kept ladyboys, remaining 'real men' as long as they weren't passive.

While families 'know but don't talk about it', roles are now less defined and many homosexuals aren't shy about parading in the **Bangkok Gay Festival** (www.bangkokgayfestival.com), nor is the public shy about cheering them. The parade was founded in 1999 by Pakorn Pimton, who bravely protested against raids on bars and saunas, and bans on gays on TV. Amid more politicisation, momentum has shifted to the better organised **Bangkok Gay Coalition** (www.bangkokpride.org). This group of gay businessmen, academics and volunteer groups has enlarged **Bangkok Pride** (*see p156*), but made it more Thai in style. After all, gays have historically been a fixture at temple fairs.

Join the friendly atmosphere at **Balcony** and win a prize at happy hour.

The **Long Yang Club** (*see chapter* **Directory: Gay & lesbian**) is the Thai chapter of the international group for gay Asian men and their admirers. Members' only, it provides discreet friendship and support, as well as social events and a newsletter.

### Utopia Tours
*Tarntawan Place Hotel, 119/5-10, Thanon Surawong, Bangrak (0 2238 3227/www.utopia-tours.com). Saladaeng BTS/Silom subway.* **Open** 10am-6pm daily. **Credit** AmEx, MC, V. **Map** p310 F7.
An influential tour company with a famous web portal (www.utopia-asia.com) that has pioneered gay travel in South-east Asia and offers in-depth info and contacts in Bangkok and Thailand. It's resolutely non-sex trade, and its personalised guides are TAT-licensed graduates with specialist knowledge.

## Bars

### Aaari Ba Bar
*36/6 Soi Aree 7, Thanon Phahon Yothin, North (0 2279 7660). Aree BTS.* **Open** 5pm-1am daily. **Credit** AmEx, MC, V.
An intimate gay-owned hangout for those frequenting nearby Chakran, with a limited Thai menu (main courses B80) and inexpensive drinks.

### Balcony
*86-8 Silom Soi 4, Bangrak (0 2235 5891). Saladaeng BTS/Silom subway.* **Open** 5pm-2am daily. **Credit** AmEx, MC, V. **Map** p310 F7.
The terraces of this popular rendezvous are slowly surrounding its arch rival Telephone Pub (*see p176*) opposite. The Balcony is cheap and cheerful (happy hour prize draws, irritatingly friendly staff), and there are even chalkboards in the loos, where profundities are scrawled.

### The Den
*114/10 Silom Soi 4, Bangrak (0 2632 8013/4). Saladaeng BTS/Silom subway.* **Open** 7pm-2am daily. **No credit cards. Map** p310 F7.
Trance and techno are the two flavours of this popular dance bar, and Muscle Marys gather here before heading off to nearby Happen. Both bars are owned by artist Neung, whose gallery of abstract and homoerotic paintings, Art At Play, is a few doors further into Silom Soi 4 (0 1812 0133/www.neungart.com; open 7pm-2am daily).

### E-Male
*62-4 Ramkhamhaeng Soi 24, East (0 2319 6772). Bus 22, 40, 58, 60, 71, 93, 109, 115, 168, 501, 512.* **Open** 8pm-2am daily. **No credit cards.**
In a student area full of bars, saunas and discos between Mall Ramkhamhaeng and Mall Bangkapi, E-Male is probably the best venue for first-time visitors. Shows are held every Wednesday, Friday and Saturday nights.

### The Expresso
*8/6-8 Silom Soi 2, Bangrak (0 2632 7223). Saladaeng BTS/Silom subway.* **Open** 10pm-2am daily. **Credit** AmEx, MC, V. **Map** p310 F7.
Something of a trendsetter when it opened in 2000, the Expresso is a fashionable pre- or post-clubbing lounge that luxuriates in subtle lighting, designer loos and picture windows. The post-club vibe can be flamboyant, to say the least.

### Happen
*8/14 Silom Soi 2, Bangrak (0 2235 2552). Saladaeng BTS/Silom subway.* **Open** 10pm-2am daily. **No credit cards. Map** p310 F7.
A breath of fresh air after the camp goings-on of Soi 2, this bar attracts butch men and their admirers. Dimly lit by illuminated water tanks, it's a starting point for serious clubbers as the DJ spins a heady mix of house, techno and trance.

### I-chub

*2nd Floor, Zarazine, Thanon Sarasin,*
*Pathumwan (0 2650 5598/www.debusen.com/ichub).*
*Ratchadamri BTS/Silom subway.* **Open** 5pm-2am
daily. **Admission** B120. **No credit cards.**
**Map** p311 G6.

A bar that caters to otherwise marginalised chubby
guys and their fans. On offer are karaoke, a small
Thai menu and welcoming service that makes a
point of introducing customers to one another.
Promotions run to free bottles of whisky for four
people exceeding 300kg (660lb).

### JJ Park

*8/3 Silom Soi 2, Bangrak (0 2235 1227). Saladaeng*
*BTS/Silom subway.* **Open** 8pm-2am daily. **Credit**
AmEx, MC, V. **Map** p310 F7.

A long-standing show bar whose loyal customers
are more thirtysomething Thais than fresh faces, JJ
is friendly, warm and often crowded. There's a
nightly cabaret, encompassing lip-sync and real
singers, comedy and talk shows.

### The Mix

*60 Silom, between Soi 2 & 4, Bangrak (0 2238*
*0459). Saladaeng BTS/Silom subway.* **Open** 8pm-
4am daily. **No credit cards. Map** p310 F7.

A stylish new pre-club hangout next to Freeman
offering inexpensive but unspectacular snacks and
a fair range of drinks.Often busy but never crowded.

### Telephone Pub

*114/11-13 Silom Soi 4, Bangrak (0 2234 3279/*
*www.telephonepub.com). Saladaeng BTS/Silom*
*subway.* **Open** 6pm-2am daily. **Credit** AmEx, DC,
MC, V. **Map** p310 F7.

Less raucous but more flirty than Balcony opposite,
Telephone Pub was (in 1987) Bangkok's first Western-
style gay bar and its loyal clientele is constantly
topped up with pretty young things, expats and
tourists. The name comes from the phones that are
used to dial across the dimly lit bar.

## Clubs

### Disco Disco (DD)

*Silom Soi 2, Thanon Silom, Bangrak (0 2266 4029/*
*www.dj-station.com). Saladaeng BTS/Silom subway.*
**Open** 10pm-2am daily. **Credit** AmEx, MC, V.
**Map** p310 F7.

A mini version of DJ Station opposite, DD favours
spiced-up chart hits. Weekend crowds of young
Thais are claustrophobic, but full of potential.

### DJ Station

*Silom Soi 2, Thanon Silom, Bangrak (0 2266 4029/*
*www.dj-station.com). Saladaeng BTS/Silom subway.*
**Open** 10pm-2am daily. **Admission** B100 incl 1
drink Mon-Thur, Sun; B200 incl 2 drinks Fri, Sat.
**Credit** AmEx, MC, V. **Map** p310 F7.

The hub of all-gay Soi 2, this three-floor nightclub
has dominated for a decade and its Puppet String
cabaret has barely changed in that time. There's
little room to dance as it's packed with an up-for-it

Get a bit of knicker at **Freeman**'s cabaret.

throng of local disco bunnies and holidaying *farang.*
It also hosts costume parties, usually for Valentine's,
Halloween, Christmas and the Gay Festival.

### Freeman

*60/18-21 Thanon Silom, in sub-soi opposite Silom*
*Complex, Bangrak (0 2632 8032/3/www.freeman*
*club.com). Saladaeng BTS/Silom subway.* **Open**
10pm-2am daily. **Admission** B150 incl 1 drink Mon-
Thur, Sun; B300 incl 2 drinks Fri, Sat. **Credit** MC, V.
**Map** p310 E7.

A more Thai-oriented club, Freeman differs from DJ
Station in that the midnight cabaret is very professional (headlined by outrageous comic Khun Day).
Many come for the third-floor dark room, where
adventurous types should hang on to their valuables.

### ICQ

*Thanon Kamphaengphet, North (0 2272 4775).*
*Saphan Kwai BTS/Kamphaengphet subway.*
**Open** 6pm-1.30am daily. **Main courses** B80.
**Credit** AmEx.

Now spawning copycat gay venues on this characterful bar strip, ICQ is simple but stylish and *the*
place to come if you're young, gay and Thai. A
candy pressed in your palm means you've been
cruised. It's the bar furthest from Chatuchak Market.

### Saké Coffee Pub

*Soi Damnoen Klang Tai, Thanon Ratchadamnoen,*
*Phra Nakorn (0 2225 6000). Bus 39, 59, 60, 201,*
*503, 511, 512.* **Open** 6pm-2am daily. **Credit** MC, V.
**Map** p308 C3.

This implausibly named venue sees local youths swinging from the rafters, fuelled by a potent mix of Thai whisky and hormones. A bewildering segue of Thai pop and Western hi-NRG makes it impolite not to dance, and a late-night cabaret adds to the disorientation. The crowd eventually flows into TG Street, opposite, a manic disco/karaoke party with pricier drinks but free smiles.
**Branch**: TG Street 60/1 Soi Damnoen Klang Tai, Phra Nakorn (0 2622 1383).

## Restaurants

Venues citywide are gay-friendly, particularly **Café Siam** (*see p120*), **Coffee Society** (*see p107*), **Crepes & Co** (*see p114*), **Eat Me!** (*see p109*), **Sign In** (*see p115*) and **Thang Long** (*see p113*).

### Dick's Café

*894/7-8 Soi Pratuchai, Thanon Silom, Bangrak (0 2637 0078/www.dickscafe.com). Saladaeng BTS/ Silom subway.* **Open** 11am-5am daily. **Main courses** B80. **Credit** MC, V. **Map** p310 F7.
Surrounded by the neon glare and touts of go-go-boy bars in a traffic-free enclave, this spacious restaurant owes much to the movie *Casablanca*. Waiters are dressed in safari khaki, mirrors adorn the walls, and exhibitions by gay artists such as Neung, Symon and Lee Ming Shun are held monthly.

### Sphinx & Pharoah's

*Silom Soi 4, Thanon Silom, Bangrak (0 2234 7249/ www.sphinxpub.com). Saladaeng BTS/Silom subway.* **Open** 5pm-1am Mon-Thur; 5pm-2am Fri; 7pm-2am Sat, Sun. **Main courses** B130. **Credit** AmEx, MC, V. **Map** p310 F7.
Discreetly positioned at the end of Soi 4, this comfortable, sensitively lit restaurant serves the scene's best food. The good value Thai and international menu is famed for its Chiang Mai *larb* and vegetarian *khao soi*. Pharoah's upstairs is an intimate singing lounge and karaoke room. Happy hour runs 5-7.30pm on weekdays.

## Saunas & fitness

### Babylon

*34 Soi Nantha, Sathorn Soi 1, South (0 2679 7984/5/ www.babylonbangkok.com). Lumphini subway/bus 13, 14, 22, 35, 116, 149.* **Open** noon-1am daily. **Admission** B220 Mon-Thur; B250 Fri-Sun. **Credit** DC, MC, V. **Map** p311 H7.
Probably the best gay sauna in the world. A maze of places to find fun includes a fab gym with hunky 'help' in skimpy uniforms. There's a fair-sized pool and even a hotel, Babylon Barracks.

### Ban Thai Sauna

*108 Ratchawithi Soi 6, (0 2245 3946/www.banthai sauna.com). Victory Monument BTS.* **Open** 3pm-2am daily. **Admission** B146. **No credit cards.** **Map** p309 F1.

# Toom raider

Immortalised in a bio-pic and glamorised through a multicultural, pan-sexual pop band, **Parinya Jaroenphon** has turned being a ladyboy boxer into international celebritydom. Not bad for a child of Chiang Mai itineraries, nicknamed **Nong Toom**. Raised to box *Muay Thai* like his devoted father, this girly boy earned a knockout reputation in regional fights. Global headlines and exhibition matches followed a hyped fight at Lumphini Stadium, where more crushing than his two-elbow jab was his kiss for each vanquished foe.

Stardom superseded sparring, though his meek stint in a Bangkok disco cabaret didn't augur well. He did, however, headline the first Bangkok Gay Festival in a dress. Hating terms like *kathoey* and *tuut* (slang from the movie *Tootsie*), this *sao prathet song* ('second kind of woman') was deemed too young at 18 to decide on a sex change. Then suddenly, in 2000, (s)he emerged in a hormone-filled Lycra bustier and tight shorts that announced the snip. No need to change ID; Thai nicknames are unisex.

Toom's misfit credentials proved perfect material for the debut movie *Beautiful Boxer* by Ekachai Uekrongtham, the Singapore-based Thai creator of the hit musical *Chang & Eng*, about the original Siamese twins. Meanwhile, Toom was selected for a UK-based girl band with a difference: Speed Angels was once made up of boys. Trading boxing gloves for nail varnish has served her well, but paparazzi beware: while Toom may be shy, she packs a mighty punch!

A new Thai-style sauna set in a traditional wooden house. Wrap yourself not in a towel but a *pa khao ma*, the traditional male wash cloth.

### The Beach

*306 Soi Panit Anant, Sukhumvit Soi 71, Sukhumvit (0 2392 4783/www.thebeachbkk.com). Bus 35, 71, 501.* **Open** 3pm-2am Mon-Fri; 2pm-2am Sat, Sun. **Admission** B99. **No credit cards.**
This no-frills budget sauna might not match its upmarket rivals, but is so popular with young Thais and some expats that it has diversified into a group. Additions include the Beach Smart Guy, which adds a male beauty parlour to the equation and offers anything from facials and slimming to 'pumper enlarge part' (use your imagination). There's also the Beach Residence, with rooms by the night (from B599) or month (B6,000-B19,000).

Every night's a busy night on Silom Soi 4.

**Branches: The Beach Residence** Soi Chokchai Ruammit, Thanon Wiphawadi-Rangsit, North-east (0 2691 5769-79); **The Beach Smart Guy** Thanon Ramkhamhaeng, East (0 2539 3259/60).

### Chakran
*Soi Aree 4 Tai, Phahon Yothin Soi 7, North (0 2279 1359/5310/www.utopia-asia.com/ chakran). Aree BTS.* **Open** 3pm-midnight Mon-Thur; 2pm-midnight Fri-Sun. **Admission** B200 Mon-Thur; B250 Fri-Sun. **No credit cards**.
Now powering full steam ahead after a 2002 raid, Chakran (meaning unquenched warrior-like desire) rivals Babylon (*see p177*) in design magnificence and otherworldly ambiance. Discreet seating is perched at multiple levels round the Moroccan-style pool and throughout the myriad rooms and restaurant. Chakran is most popular with 'sticky rice' (Asians who like Asians), and is owned by V Club massage parlour round the corner.

### Silom City Fitness
*Thanon Rama IV, Bangrak (0 2636 0667-9/ www.silom-city-fitness.com). Saladaeng BTS/Silom subway.* **Open** 6am-11pm Mon-Fri; 10am-10pm Sat, Sun. **Admission** B220. **Credit** AmEx, DC, MC, V. **Map** p311 G6.
A branch of Sydney's Bayswater Gym, Silom City Fitness is a central, low-cost centre situated next to the Dusit Thani Hotel. The centre draws a mixed but mainly gay following to its good amenities. Lockers are in a former bank safe room.

### Time Health & Spa
*12/25 Thanon Thessaban Songkroh, North (0 2953 9706/www.timehealthandspa.com). Bus 50, 66, 70, 112.* **Open** 10am-midnight daily. **Credit** AmEx, MC, V.
Time Health & Spa offers pampering for poofs with all the understated style of the spa boom. Colourful petal-strewn baths, contemporary Balinese decor, quality treatments – all for a better complexion, healthier body or trimmer figure.

## Tom-dee

A good way to make contact with this elusive community is through the **Anjaree Group**. For over a decade this collective has campaigned for homosexual rights and run social, educational or travel events that welcome visiting women. While Thai speakers predominate and its magazine *AN: Another Way* is aimed at locals, its website – **www.anjaree.org** – has information in English.

Also try **www.lesla.com** (in Thai and English), which hosts regular parties, under the banner of 'the Thai lesbian community', and **www.ellecorner.com**, which has a Thai chat room and buddy board with English posts.

### Dog Days
*100/2-6 Thanon Phra Arthit, Banglamphu (0 2280 6407/2281 4923). Bus 3, 30, 32, 64, 65, 506.* **Open** 10am-3pm, 5pm-1am daily. **Main courses** B80. **No credit cards**. **Map** p308 B2.
This quirky, sassy art-bar has a *tom-dee* following on a very liberal bar strip. There are tables outside and a limited menu of decent Thai food and drink.

### Kitchenette
*1st Floor, Duchess Plaza, Sukhumvit Soi 55, Sukhumvit (0 2381 0861). Thonglor BTS.* **Open** 5pm-1am Mon-Sat. **Main courses** B90. **Credit** V. **Map** p312 M6.
An older *tom-dee* crowd frequents this easygoing café with live folk music on Fridays and Saturdays.

### Vega
*Sukhumvit Soi 39, 50m beyond Soi Phrommit, Sukhumvit (0 2258 8273/2662 6471). Phrom Phong BTS.* **Open** 11am-1am Mon-Sat. **Main courses** B100. **Credit** AmEx, DC, MC, V. **Map** p312 L6.
Owned by a group of *dees* and *toms*, this trendy pub/ restaurant is also a hit with Thai celebrities and see-and-be-seen types. At night there's live music downstairs, while upstairs is the obligatory karaoke.

# Mind & Body

Drawing on Thai healing heritage, Bangkok has become a regional spa hub.

Thailand is the holistic capital of South-east Asia. It hosts an unrivalled number of quality spas, massage houses and healing centres, from budget to luxury, urban to resort. Siam's lone escape from colonisation prevented the dilution of such indigenous healing practices as acupressure, massage, herbal steam, herbal baths, hot compresses, tonics, infusions and meditation. Historical evidence indicates that early Siamese medicine integrated ancient Indian Ayurvedic and Chinese systems, adding local folk remedies and a dose of animism and shamanism. However, its core stems from Ayurvedic teachings brought over by Buddhist missionary monks during the second and third centuries BC.

During the latter half of the 20th century, *ya samoon prai* (traditional medicine) became marginalised by modern allopathic medicine and pharmaceutical monopolies. But a wave of anti-globalisation following the economic crash of 1997 prompted such renewed interest in traditional medicine that degree courses in Thai techniques were introduced in 2001. Assisted by the Institute of Thai Traditional Medicine (0 2965 9825-7/asmunpai@thaipun. com), manufacture of herbal beauty and body treatments is on the increase. Individuals and collectives tout wares at markets and urban fairs, while firms supply health stores and mainstream shops, both in Thailand and abroad.

This means that standards have become an issue, with some labels and catalogues now carrying details in English of their ingredients and supposed efficacy – although this is often of limited use when you're faced with rows of tablets, potions, powders, pastes and essential oils at apothecaries in Phra Chan or Chinatown. Differentiating dosages, allergies, side-effects and even signs of progress all require expert advice, particularly in the case of DIY *ya dong* (herbal aphrodisiac 'whiskies').

### THERE'S THE RUB

The best known Thai therapy is *nuad paen boran* – an ancient form of massage that relieves backaches, headaches, nervous tension and fevers. This is not to be confused with the 'treatments' on offer in seedier parlours advertising simply *nuad* (massage), where the masseuses are nubile and do their job naked, save for a lot of make-up and a little oil. For the real thing, seek out signs offering 'massage for

health' or 'traditional massage', often depicting the body meridian lines or reflexology points.

Unlike Swedish, shiatsu or Balinese styles, Thai massage doesn't use oils (although some spas combine techniques). Divided into the gentler northern and more rigorous southern schools, it instead uses acupressure and stretching techniques. By using body weight through rhythmic rocking, even delicate masseuses pack amazing power through their thumbs, arms, elbows, knees and feet.

Lying on a mattress in a room or cubicle, you remain fully clothed in clean, baggy pyjamas (which are supplied), usually after a foot scrub. Starting with feet and legs, expect to be squeezed, climbed over, walked on, straddled and finally twisted, stretched and flipped backwards. A well-trained masseur should ask if the pressure is too hard or too soft – but do warn them at the outset if you have any back, joint or other pains. Those with heart problems should prevent the

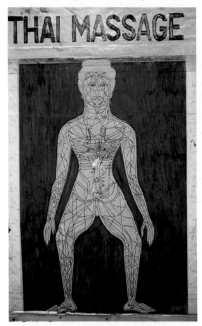

A sign indicating traditional massage.

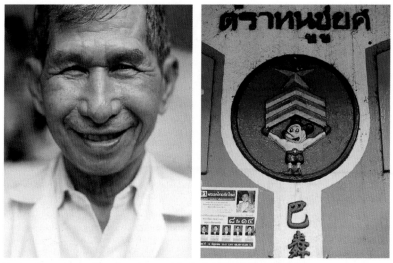

You're guaranteed a friendly welcome at herbalist **Mor Parinya Ya Thai**.

masseur from pausing the blood flow at armpits and groin – an intimate technique (not for prudes) designed to flush stagnant veins. Feedback is also expected, even it it's just *jeb* ('it hurts') or *jakkajee* ('it tickles').

Like all Thais, masseuses may giggle with you, but don't expect any chat. A session should last two hours and, despite occasional pain, it tends to relax you into a snooze. You may find, though, that you ache later in places you didn't ache before – this is due to the release of minute or unconscious tension that has blocked energy flow. Like other purges, *nuad paen boran* dislodges toxins from tissues, which a free cup of herbal tea helps finally to expel. It can take several massages to become limber again, and learning the skill is an investment (although some say addiction to it is damaging).

Most practitioners are women, aged from teens to dotage. Those prioritising healing over relaxation tend to prefer heftier, mature masseuses better able to identify problems and knead stubborn knots. For specific ailments, ask for an *ajaan* (teacher), who are sometimes blind men. Some say the best massages are performed by the sightless, whose heightened sense of touch is honed at special schools. You should tip generously as most masseurs earn only piecemeal rates.

In keeping with the general receptiveness of Thai culture, Bangkok, Chiang Mai and Samui are becoming New Age hubs, with holistic healing centres offering an alternative spectrum of treatments (from aqua therapy and colonics to reiki and Buteyko breathing). Yoga devotees won't be disappointed either. Meanwhile, the Chinese influence, while most noticeable among Chinatown's herbalists and acupuncturists, can also be found in havens such as Lumphini Park, where practitioners of qi gong and t'ai chi can always be found at dawn.

## Holistic healing

### Bahlavi Natural Health Centre

*191-3 Soi Ranong 1, Thanon Rama VI, North (0 2279 5658/www.balavi.co.th). Bus 5, 44, 50, 67, 70.* **Open** *Clinic* 8am-8pm Mon, Wed, Fri; 8am-5pm Tue, Thur, Sat. *Fitness* 8.30am-8pm daily. **Credit** MC, V.

English-speaking Dr Banchob offers colonic irrigation and five-day fasts, supervised by medical doctors, alongside less clinical treatments such as Thai massage, aqua therapy, body treatments and yoga.

### Buteyko Breathing Asia

*0 2253 2614/www.buteykoasia.com.*

Respiratory Health Institute practitioners Jac Vidgen and Chris Drake teach five-day workshops in this Russian breathing technique. Buteyko aims at self-management in reducing dependency medication, improving sports performance and radically improving many conditions, from asthma, allergies and sleep apnoea to stress, obesity and migraine.

### Mor Parinya Ya Thai

*9 Thanon Maharat, Phra Nakorn (0 2222 1555). Bus 6, 39, 47, 53, 59, 508.* **Open** 8am-6pm daily. **No credit cards. Map** p308 B4.

Housed in a typical old apothecary, this outlet offers Thai and Chinese herb preparations, plus various massage treatments (Thai, herbal, acupressure and reflexology). Parinya's recipes for aphrodisiac, herb and alcohol *ya dong* are genuine knee-tremblers. **Branches**: 4 Thanon Maharat, Phra Nakorn (0 2221 8756); 655/13 Thanon Bangkok-Nonthaburi, North (0 2585 4312).

### New Beginnings Holistic Development Centre

*232/15 Sukhumvit Soi 12, Sukhumvit (0 2258 3280/ www.newbeginnings.co.th).* Asoke BTS/Sukhumvit subway. **Open** 10am-5.30pm Mon-Sat. **Credit** AmEx, MC, V. **Map** p311 J5.

New Beginnings is Thailand's first centre to offer the WHO- and UN-acclaimed Art of Living Course, which teaches Sudarshan Kriya breathing techniques. Regular and visiting therapists offer anything from 'cell care therapy', 'emotional freedom technique' and 'ascension energy workshops', to acupuncture, massage, yoga and tarot consultations.

### Suchada Marwah Centre

*Room 1A, Lakeview Apartment, 146 Sukhumvit Soi 16, Sukhumvit (0 2258 1671/www.smc institute.com).* Asoke BTS/Sukhumvit subway. **Open** 9am-7pm Mon-Sat. **Credit** AmEx, MC, V. **Map** p312 K6.

Run by Ayurvedic physician Dr Angelika Hartung, this is Bangkok's first centre to offer instruction (in English) as well as treatment in hard-to-find Ayurvedic techniques, alongside acupressure, reflexology, cranio-sacral therapy and much more. Spa professionals join regular workshops and talks on these therapies. There's also a bookshop. Check the website for more information.

## Meditation

### House of Dhamma Insight Meditation Centre

*26/9 Lad Phrao Soi 15, North-east (0 2511 0439/ www.angelfire.com/al/dhamma/home.html).* Lad Prao subway/bus 8, 44, 73 92, 96, 122, 145, 502, 514, 517, 518, 545. **Open** 10am-5pm Wed-Sun.

Vipassana classes take place on the second and fourth Sundays of each month at the House of Dhamma. Group sessions and retreats of one, four or seven days are also available.

### International Buddhist Meditation Centre (IBMC)

*Room 106, Vipassana Section, Mahachulalongkornrajvidyalaya University, 3 Thanon Maharat, Phra Nakorn (0 2623 6326/ www.mcu.ac.th/IBMC).* Bus 6, 32, 39, 47, 53, 59, 508. **Open** 1-7pm Mon-Sat. **Map** p308 A4.

Thailand's Buddhist university holds the following classes in English: daily meditation at 7-10am, 1-4pm and 6-8pm; a Dhamma talk every second and fourth Saturday from 3-5pm; and upcountry retreats over weekends or five to seven days.

### Wat Mahathat

*3/5 Thanon Maharaj, Phra Nakorn (0 2222 6011).* Bus 6, 32, 39, 47, 53, 59, 508. **Open** 7am-8pm daily. **Map** p308 A3.

Instruction (in English) can be arranged for meditators staying in or outside the crowded dorms here. The daily routine runs from 6.30am-9pm and includes meals and meditation at 7-10am, 1-4pm and 6-9pm daily. Group walking, sitting practice and retreats are also offered.

# Health trips

Not all Thai health tourism is traditional. Another niche caters to Westerners seeking the latest developments in conventional medicine: surgery, gamma-scans and Caesarean sections (the desire for auspicious birth dates make Caesareans the norm in Thailand). Private Thai hospitals offer spacious five-star surroundings, hi-tech facilities and smiley care at up to half international rates. Dental tourism, in particular, benefits from expertise derived from the Thais' notoriously low pain threshold. You've been drilled, capped and root canalled before you feel a thing.

Some specialists say you get what you pay for and cases of misdiagnosis do surface, partly driven by widespread over-prescription (that low pain threshold again). Yet there are some superb hospitals. **Bangkok Hospital**, inventor of the 'motorlance' (two-wheeled ambulance), and **BNH** (Bangkok Nursing Home) have international medical centres, while **Sirirat Hospital** (the world's fourth biggest) treats the Thai royal family. **Bumrungrad Hospital** is not only world-class technically, but room service from restaurants in its opulent atrium includes sushi, Starbucks and McDonald's (maybe not everyone's idea of healthy food).

Thailand is also reputed for plastic surgery (slim noses and eyelid folds carry social cachet), with a specialism in penile reattachment (Lorena Bobbitt's got nothing on cuckolded Thai wives). And there's an informal global network among ladyboys to advise on coming to Thailand to change sex. Born in the wrong body? Avoid the dubious plethora of clinics and consult the **Society of Plastic & Reconstructive Surgeons** at Sirirat Hospital (*see chapter* **Directory: Health**) – and leave a special part of you in Thailand.

Arts & Entertainment

### World Fellowship of Buddhists

*616 Benjasiri Park, Sukhumvit Soi 24, Sukhumvit (0 2661 1284-7/www.wfb-hq.org). Phrom Phong BTS.* **Open** 8.30am-4.30pm Mon-Fri. **Map** p312 K6.
On the first Sunday of each month (2-6pm), English-speaking monks from Wat Pah Nanachart lecture here on meditation.

## Spas

### Banyan Tree Spa

*Banyan Tree Hotel, Thai Wah Tower II, 21/100 Thanon Sathorn Tai, South (0 2679 1054/www. banyantree.com). Bus 22, 62, 67, 76, 116, 149, 530.* **Open** 9am-10pm daily. **Credit** AmEx, DC, MC, V. **Map** p311 G7.
Bangkok's biggest spa (until the neighbouring Sukhothai Hotel's is completed in 2004), the Banyan Tree affords amazing views from every room, though your eyes mostly remain closed. A long, luxurious menu combines Thai, Swedish and Balinese massages, petal-strewn baths and painstakingly developed in-house fusion treatments. Among the pampering packages, the three-hour Royal Banyan leaves you sleeping like a baby. There is also a superb branch in Phuket.

### Being Spa

*88 Sukhumvit Soi 51, Sukhumvit (0 2662 6171/www. beingspa.com). Thonglor BTS then taxi.* **Open** 10am-10pm daily. **Credit** AmEx, MC, V. **Map** p312 L7.
Hotel-quality service elevates this indie spa located in an elegant suburban house. The menu offers eight facials, 16 body scrubs and wraps, nine massages

and ten combinations of the above. A hair and nail salon leaves you looking, and feeling, your best.

### Oriental Spa

*597 Thanon Charoen Nakhon, Thonburi (0 2439 7613/4). Bus 3, 6, 84, 88, 89, 105, 111, 530.* **Open** 7am-10pm daily. **Credit** AmEx, DC, MC, V. **Map** p310 D7.
This pioneer Thai spa remains the grande dame, with top-of-the-range service, ambience and decor. Conceived as a traditional teak house, it faces the Oriental Hotel across the river and is reached via the hotel's ferry. Prices are high and bookings are required – hotel guests get priority in high season.

### Palm Herbal Spa

*103 Sukhumvit Soi 55, Sukhumvit (0 2391 3153/ www.palmherbalspa.co.th). Thonglor BTS.* **Open** 10am-10pm daily. **Credit** AmEx, DC, MC, V. **Map** p312 M7.
You may be greeted by the thumping of mortar and pestle grinding fresh herbs for use in the natural therapy treatments offered at this pleasant house spa. Aside from trad body treatments, there are Thai, Swedish or aromatherapy massages.

### Thai Herbal Spa

*10th Floor, Waterford Diamond Tower, 758 Sukhumvit Soi 30/1, Sukhumvit (0 2261 7829). Phrom Phong BTS.* **Open** 10am-10pm daily. **Credit** MC, V. **Map** p312 L7.
Despite some fancy touches such as jasmine-scented air, this is still just a gym in a condo. Even so, you can expect herbal treatments and exceptional massages. The best are given by its director, Komon Chitprasert, whose training as a traditional healer

# Learn to Meditate

Forget diving and trekking, some visitors come to Thailand to do nothing – or, rather, find nothingness in meditation centres that have been tailored to the needs of English-speaking foreigners. Advice and meditation are available at the **World Fellowship of Buddhists** (*see p182*), **Wat Mahathat** (*see p181*) and the **House of Dhamma** (*see p181*). But while learning amid city conditions instils discipline, a supportive rural retreat is what really helps to forge initial change.

The famous forest monk Buddhadasa Bhikku founded the International Dhamma Hermitage at his southern temple **Wat Suan Mokkh** (*see p244*) as a non-denominational beacon of *anapanasiti* (mindfulness with breathing). There are no eyebrow-shaving strictures and there is equal (segregated) space for women. Retreats over days one to ten of each month feature sitting, walking

and chanting meditation, yoga at sunrise, organic vegetarian food, light chores, dharma talks, abstinence from sex and stimulants, natural hot springs and strict silence. Keeping schtum amid a flood of revelatory thoughts, while hard, aids honest reflection, acceptance of responsibility and control of conditioned habits. And after a regimen of 4am reveille and meals at 8am and noon, you soon emerge physically calmed and mentally sorted. Some meditators transfer to the mid-month ten-day retreats at **Wat Khao Tham Meditation Centre** (*see p240*) on nearby Ko Pha-ngan.

In Chiang Mai, a month-long immersion for 20 hours a day is required at **Wat Ram Poeng**'s English-speaking course (*see p266*), while the less austere can learn about Buddhism and try *anapanasiti* on Sundays at 3pm in **Wat Umong** (*see p261*), which has limited accommodation.

**Ruen Nuad**: yoga classes daily.

and Thai national soccer therapist can release muscle knots, trapped nerves and the occasional repressed emotion.

## Thai massage

**Surawong Plaza** on Thanon Surawong is full of parlours, though prices are twice those in the many good but low-privacy *nuad* houses in **Banglamphu**.

### Arima Onsen
*37/10-14 Soi Surawong Plaza, Thanon Surawong, Bangrak (0 2235 2142/3). Saladaeng BTS/Silom subway.* **Open** 9am-1am daily. **No credit cards.** **Map** p310 F6.
Popular with visiting Japanese, this is a highly professional and hygienic centre for Thai massage, reflexology and *akasuri* back rub. Jacuzzis, steam rooms and Japanese communal showers are also offered, plus VIP rooms, hair and nail care.

### Body Tune
*2nd Floor, Yada Building, 56 Thanon Silom, Bangrak (0 2238 4377/8/www.bodytune.co.th). Saladaeng BTS/Silom subway.* **Open** 10am-11pm daily. **Credit** AmEx, DC, MC, V. **Map** p310 F7.
A swish, modern Thai massage emporium, Body Tune dispenses full-body massage, reflexology and hand massage. It's a white-collar favourite for lunchtime and after-work unwinding.
**Branches**: Sahai Place Building, 49 Sukhumvit Soi 24, Sukhumvit (0 2661 0076/7).

### Foundation for Employment of the Blind
*2218/86 Thanon Chan, South (0 2678 0763-8/ www.fepblind.ksc.net.th). Bus 22, 62.* **Open** 9am-8pm daily. **No credit cards.**
For over a decade the Foundation has furthered careers in body work for the sightless, whose touch skills are legendary. Massage (traditional and herbal) and reflexology are offered.

### Pian
*108/15-16 Thanon Khao San, Banglamphu (0 2629 0924). Bus 3, 9, 15, 19, 32, 53, 65, 506.* **Open** 8am-12.30am daily. **No credit cards.** **Map** p308 B3.
Intense competition keeps prices low and quality high in Banglamphu's cramped open parlours. Pian is the best of the bunch, with men and women giving reflexology and traditional massage and (rather public) Swedish oil massage or herbal massage. There's an attached beauty parlour and certificated teaching courses (in English) are also available.
**Branch**: Lane between Soi Rambuttri & Thanon Phra Arthit, Banglamphu.

### Ruen Nuad: Massage & Yoga
*2nd Floor, 42 Thanon Convent, Bangrak (0 2632 2663). Saladaeng BTS/Silom subway.* **Open** 10am-10pm daily. **Credit** AmEx, MC, V. **Map** p310 F7.
This picturesque wooden house behind Khao Kup Kaeng restaurant offers Thai, aromatherapy and herbal massages with classy attention to detail. There are also daily yoga classes.

### Wat Pho
*2 Thanon Sanamchai, Phra Nakorn (0 2221 2974). Bus 1, 3, 6, 47, 48, 53, 508.* **Open** 8.30am-4pm daily. **No credit cards.** **Map** p308 B4.
Thailand's most famous massage and reflexology school. You can have a massage or just see the origins of the southern massage technique depicted in murals, as well as the traditional medicine pavilions beside the *chedi* (relic towers) of Rama II and Rama III. Classes and massages are given in public view at open-sided *salas* near the eastern gate from 9am to 6pm daily.

## Yoga

See also restaurant **Anotai** (*p122*).

### Yoga Elements Studio
*Suite 401, Kijpanich Building, 2-18 Thanon Surawong, Bangrak (0 2634 3095/www.yoga elements.com). Saladaeng BTS/Silom subway.* **Open** 1-8pm daily. **No credit cards.** **Map** p310 F6.
Thailand's only Western-style yoga studio (and the first to teach Vinyasa yoga, as well as Ashtanga and Tibetan styles), Yoga Elements is directed by US yogi Adrian Cox, who studied at India's Bihar Yoga University. Hourly classes take place daily in Thai and English; monthly workshops on topics such as meditation, Sanskrit, *pranayama* and *kirtan* are given by visiting lamas and swamis.

# Music

From folk to classical, indie to T-Pop, protest rock to *rap Thai*, Bangkok is a barely explored mine of music.

'Asian composers attempting to copy Michael Jackson's music are not really so much different from young Western musicians looking to the Balinese gamelan for the way out of their artistic dilemma'. So said Bruce Gaston, US composer and leader of *phiphat* orchestra/rock band Fong Nam, in 1996. He has a point.

In 1992 Jackson played Bangkok, followed by Danish band Michael Learns to Rock in 1993. In 2002 Bangkok hosted Roger Waters, Deep Purple and the Pet Shop Boys. As quality gigs by international names are few, the Thais have had to go it alone. And have they. There's a common misconception among tourists that there's no actual music scene in Bangkok – as they might have concluded in the Seattle of 1990, the London of 1966 or the Soweto of 1980. In actuality, Thailand lives for *pleng* (songs). Perhaps it's in emulation of the king, a jazz musician and composer. Thais seem to crave music as they do rice – and they have as many alluring ways of serving it. But it's all sung in the native tongue and, for the uninitiated, hard to figure out. So you may as well hide out in tourist bars and hear 'Hotel California' one more time. Or wait for *morlam* to be served up on a platter by Messrs Sting, Simon, Byrne & Albarn, then buy its pirate version off the stalls.

Or you can choose to see and hear the music hybrid of the future. Hail a cab; the radio's tuned to Luuk Thuung 90 FM. Marvel at the sideways logic of *luuk thuung* and *morlam*, its techno beats and brass blasts and worldlywise female raps. Roll down the window to hear that blind busker's plaintive *khaen* (mouth organ), watch the hip hop boys bust out the breaks to new rap act Thaitanium, see those schoolgirls wafting towards the free T-Pop concert in the park, or join the masses disposing of their salary on the first Saturday night of each month – and get ready to, as the Thais say, rock.

Admission to venues listed below is free unless otherwise stated, and most provide food.

## Classical

### Thai

The Chao Phraya river at sunset can mean sensory overload, but try to listen past the combustible cacophony and you may catch the delicate shimmer of tiny metal mallets on tuned cymbals. It might be an evening festival at Wat Arun (if you're lucky) or a *phiphat wong* (Thai classical orchestra) soundchecking for a riverside hotel's cultural evening. Perhaps your only chance to hear the indigenous classical music of Siam, such evenings open with a standardised, competent medley of classical snippets before the ensemble is put to service as accompaniment to dance.

But you'd be better off sneaking into the recital hall of a university music department, or the practice sessions at **Siam Dontree** shop (*see p152*) or **Luang Pradit Phairoh Foundation**. There students still eagerly study the *cha-ke* (three-string banjo), *khlue* (flute), *khim* (dulcimer), *ree chava* (woodwind), *saw sam sei* and *saeng* (the string section of a *phiphat* orchestra), cymbals, gongs, cymbal-phones and *ranat* (gong-rimbas) – but on graduation they all seem to work for the Tourism Authority of Thailand's hotel outreach programme. That's an exaggeration (barely), but there's no equivalent to the New York Philharmonic, or even regular *phiphat* concerts. Still, there are festivals and, at least once a month, a superlative concert at the **Queen Sirikit National Convention Centre** or the **Thailand Cultural Centre** (*see p202*), often presided over, or participated in, by royalty.

Tickets are elusive, but try to get hold of one, because *phiphat* music is fascinating. Organised horizontally (not harmonically in the Western sense), it builds simple motifs, mainly in pentatonic mode, which move not melodically, but simultaneously forward and backward, creating layers of contrast through repetition. The music may seem dense, but it has a pulse and it breathes. Break those hotel medleys apart and you'll find symphony-sized structures: *ruang* (based on ancient melodies), *thao* (sonatas of flowing augmentation and diminuation) and *tap* (operatic and theatre suites).

### Luang Pradit Phairoh Foundation

*47 Thanon Setsiri, Dusit (0 2279 1509/ www.thaikids.com). Bus 44, 67.*
The *1 Giant Leap* project recorded its Thai elements at this *phiphat* music school, where you can witness (even join in) practice sessions (9am-3pm Saturdays and Sundays). The school gives a performance on the first Sunday in August; the venue varies.

Elvis lives on in Bangkok, at various venues, including **Radio City**. *See p191*.

## Western

Paradoxically, there is an abundance of
Western classical performances – by the
**Bangkok Symphony Orchestra** (BSO),
multiple chamber groups and, most
interestingly, the new **Bangkok Opera**.
The BSO (0 2256 9935-7/www.bangkok
symphony.com) has monthly concerts at
the **Regent Hotel** (*see p44*) and offers free
open-air concerts in the cool season (*see p159*
**Music in the Park**). Other venues include
the **Alliance Française** and the **Goethe
Institut** (for both, *see p167*).

### Bangkok Opera

*55 Sukhumvit Soi 69, Sukhumvit (0 2391 0245/
www.bangkokopera.com). Phra Kanong BTS.*
**Tickets** house concerts B300; other venues B500-
B2,000. **No credit cards.**
Bangkok Opera is the brainchild of international bon
vivant, Somtow Sucharitkul (aka SP Somtow). Born
in Thailand and schooled at Eton, he began as a pre-
cocious avant-gardist putting on experimental festivals in the early 1980s before exiling himself to
Los Angeles for 15 years, where he became a screen-
writer and novelist. He announced his return with
a splash: a royal commission, the *Mahajanaka
Symphony*, based on the king's translations of this
most holy of Buddhist scriptures. Emboldened, he
rallied support for his dream project, the Bangkok
Opera, and wrote the first Thai opera, *Madana*,
based on a Hindu folk legend. Then he decided to
build an opera house (still in progress). Now he's

writing a new opera a year, commissioning other
Thai composers and staging monthly recitals. He
also founded the Bangkok Sinfonietta (with Mifa
Music Academy), which debuted in late 2002 with
the premiere of the first symphony by Trisdee na
Phattalung. And, fingers crossed, soon *phiphat*.

## Dontree nanachat

A range of clubs feature *dontree nanachat*
(global roots music), with **T-Bone** – Bangkok's
best freeform ska-reggae-worldbeat implosion –
raising the roof (solid teak) off **Saxophone
Pub** every Sunday at midnight since the
millennium. Vocalist/guitarist Gop, all husky
rasp and flapping dreads, leads lead guitarist
Golf (the Keith to Gop's Mick) and keyboardists
Nuong and Pae, plus turntable-ist Puk, bassist
Nor, tribal drummer Lek and percussionist
extraordinaire Num. They shift seamlessly from
ska to samba back to ska over to reggae up to
*tropicalista* around the bend to Senegal stomp
and home – phew! – to a ska outro. T-Bone
members also provide percussion at dance gigs,
often on weekends at **Tapas** (*see p196*).

**BAT: Bangkok Assault Team** are a
mobile dub/hip hop/tribal party unit with DJs
O-Fay and Buddha, along with live MCs and
percussionists; they do a show every Sunday
night (11pm-2am) at **Q Bar** (*see p195*). And
although the Latin boom has largely faded
away, look out for gigs by the excellent Chilean
**Silva Brothers**.

**Arts & Entertainment**

# Buffalo stance

**Ad Carabao** is the most prolific, prodigious and, possibly, profligate musician/artist/personality in Thailand. Period. A slight, humble man in his late forties, he resembles Carlos Santana or Willie Nelson – wispy moustache, long, stringy hair wrapped in a bandana, and a uniform of T-shirts, jeans and sneakers. He's been on the scene – often been the scene – since the late 1970s in the *pleng puer cheewit* band, **Carabao**. Like their forebears and folkier rivals, Caravan, Carabao formed as a rock expression of solidarity with 'the peasants' during the fight against dictatorship. Exiled to the Philippines, the band adopted Tagalog slang for 'water buffalo' as its name and learned to rock with a vengeance hitherto unknown in Thailand.

Carabao has since put out a dozen classic albums – notably *Made in Thailand*, *Welcome to Thailand* and the recent score for the movie *Bangrajan*. In the 1990s Carabao dissolved, or rather evolved, into a part-time project. Continuing with rock sidemen on electric guitars, bass, keyboards, percussion and ethnic instruments, Ad Carabao channels not only Nelson and Santana, but Bob Dylan, Bruce Springsteen and Neil Young – oh, and a 1,000 years of Thai folk.

But music ain't the half of it. Through his lyrics (always in Thai), Ad acts as a cultural conscience, whether berating the military,

## Arabian Night

*Ground Floor, Grace Hotel, 12 Sukhumvit Soi 3, Sukhumvit (0 2253 0651-75/www.gracehotel.th.com). Nana BTS.* **Open** (except Ramadan) 10pm-2am daily. *Shows* midnight-2am daily. **Credit** AmEx, DC, MC, V. **Map** p311 J5.

An awesome Arabic band blasts souk rhythms to mesmeric singers in a vast, ornate interior. Belly dancers shimmy on tables under a shower of notes peeled off by men who dance like dervishes.

## Saxophone Pub & Restaurant

*3/8 Thanon Phayathai, south-east side of Victory Monument, North (0 2246 5472). Victory Monument BTS.* **Open** 6pm-1.45am daily. *Shows* 9pm-1.45am daily. **Credit** AmEx, DC, MC, V.

Any night can be fun at this knocked-through, two-storey log and beam sculpture, a kind of trompe l'oeil hunting lodge, but Sunday belongs to T-Bone. The other regulars lay down roots, rock, reggae, jazz and blues, all of them competent, some even excellent ensembles. And the sound system excels – a rarity.

## Señor Pico

*1st Floor, Rembrandt Hotel, 19 Sukhumvit Soi 18, Sukhumvit (0 2261 7100/www.rembrandtbkk.com). Asoke BTS/Sukhumvit Subway.* **Open** 5pm-1am daily. *Shows* 7.30-11.15pm Tue-Thur, Sun; 8pm-midnight Fri-Sat. **Credit** AmEx, DC, MC, V. **Map** p312 K6.

A favourite venue for party groups, this Cal-Mex restaurant also has good Latin bands, usually from Cuba or Colombia.

## Siam Diary

*14/10 Soi Saladaeng 1, Thanon Rama IV end, Bangrak (0 2633 8348). Lumphini subway/bus 14, 17, 47, 50, 115.* **Open** 5pm-1am Mon-Sat. *Shows* 7-10pm Tue-Thur; 7pm-midnight Fri. **Credit** AmEx, MC, V. **Map** p310 F6.

Formerly the Front Page (which has moved nearby) this galleried, timber-lined pub heaves to live bands. Reggae and rock play on Fridays and Saturdays.

## Glaung sayree

Don't let all the uniforms fool you, Siam Square is Bangkok's crossroads of hip. Of alternative. Of indie (or *glaung sayree*, literally 'independent drum'). Packs of university-uniformed individuals rush into the Japanese CD store at Soi 5, because nothing's hipper than all things J-Pop. Others weave between the coin-op karaoke booths, alternative art spaces and coffee shops above the Lido Theatre, then cut

belittling sex tourists or lambasting shallow materialists. He's had multiple attempts on his life, for such minor indiscretions as shouting out names of generals involved in teak smuggling during a live televised concert. Lest you suspect him to be sanctimonious, check out his odes to toking, rocking, loving and cock fighting.

In 2002 he was everywhere: acting as a taxi driver on a TV drama; advertising Beer Chang during World Cup broadcasts; protesting the 2am bar crackdown's effect on a million livelihoods in his hit 'Purachai Curfew'; launching his own energy drink, Carabao Daeng (Red Buffalo); releasing a CD, DVD and book championing Shan independence from Burma; appearing at an anti-piracy rally with the prime minister; and organising a benefit for the rural poor featuring a reunion of his band with special guest Steven Seagal.

What Fela Anikulapo Kuti was to Nigeria, Bob Marley to Jamaica, Caetano Veloso to Brazil, Bono to the MTV nation, Ad Carabao was, and is, to Thailand. But for the language disconnect, he'd be an international superstar.

through the alley to **New DJ Siam** (292/16 Siam Square Soi 4; 0 2251 2513), a hole in the wall that stocks the best mix of international alternatives: New York hip-hop, California alt-metal and British house. There's also a whole wall of Thai CDs, ranging from Grammy stable's T-Pop to the new Thai underground, via the pioneering indie label Bakery.

From 1994 until 2000 Bakery was almost alone in discovering and developing alternative talent, from **Modern Dog** (a Chili Peppers/ Rage Against the Machine proto rap-rock quartet) to **Orn Aree** (Thailand's PJ Harvey *and* Sinead O'Connor); from **Rik** (a black mass enchantress) to **Joey Boy** (for years the sole proponent of *rap Thai*).

Bakery was founded by Kamol 'Suki' Sukosol, a great A&R man who witnessed 'alternative' as a student in New York. What he lacked in airtime or distribution, Suki and his brother made up for with extravagant live shows, videos and edgy packaging never before seen in Bangkok. Then, while the brothers were forming their own band, PRU (a moody quartet in the mode of Roxy Music), the dam burst.

Now dozens of little labels – Hua Lampong Riddim (with their genius act Photo Sticker Machine), Genie, Small Room, Junkfood, Free/Airport, NYU Club, Genie, Lucky Café and Panda – each have one or two artists recording and pressing their own CDs. You can hear them on **104.5 Fat Radio** (7.30-10.30pm Sun), which sponsors the annual **Fat Festival** (*see p156*) with some 40 indie bands.

**Centrepoint Plaza** (Siam Sois 3 and 4, 0 2252 1754-6), **Suan Lum Night Bazaar** (*see p135*) and other informal spaces get really crowded for free weekly afternoon gigs that mix T-Pop with *glaung sayree*. However, beyond one-off, irregular events at indie venues such as **About Café** (*see p169*), **Phranakorn Bar** (*see p125*) or **Café Democ** (*see p195*), there are nowhere near enough venues for alt rock, let alone *rap Thai*.

### House of Indies

*Prasanmit Plaza Building, 45 Sukhumvit Soi 23, Sukhumvit (0 2664 0399/www.houseofindies.com). Asok BTS/Sukhumvit subway.* **Open** 9.30am-6.30pm Mon-Sat. *Shows* 4-8pm Sat, Sun. **Map** p312 K5.
Call to find out who's playing at parties in the live space of this label and school for alt arts like DJ-ing, or at venues like Café Democ.

### Immortal Bar

*1st Floor, Bayon Building, 249 Thanon Khaosan, Banglamphu (0 1750 0591). Bus 39, 59, 60, 157, 201, 503, 509.* **Open** *DJs* 6pm-2am Mon, Sun. *Hip hop* 6pm-2am Tue-Sat. **No credit cards.** **Map** p308 B3.
As dilapidated and charming as NY's CBGBs or the Garage in London, this totemic space shakes with punk rock to speed metal. It's mostly DJs, but there are some band nights.

### Overtone

*21/4 Zone B, Royal City Avenue, Thanon Rama IX end, North-east (0 2203 0423-5/www.prartmusic.com). Bus 137, 168, 179, 517.* **Open** 8.30pm-1am Sat. *Shows* 9pm-1am Sat. **Admission** B150. **No credit cards.** **Map** p312 L3.
Session players cram this tiny club to air their own compositions (a rarity) on a great sound system (another rarity).

### Luuk grung (aka T-Pop)

Thanon Ratchadaphisek is the land of the super-discos and beer pavilions. Goliaths of the 1980s and '90s, such as NASA and Phoebus, crashed with the economy, but spawned more modest monstrosities – **Hollywood**, **Dance Fever** (for both, *see p197*), the **Brew Pavilion**, plus Sukhumvit's **Coliseum Brew Arena** – each of which could hold a measly 2,000 punters, every night.

Lively **Saxophone**. *See p186.*

Hollywood is a disco, but it's also a show bar. The dancefloor is a field of tiny, circular tables, piled with ice buckets, whisky bottles, mixers and bowls of fried chicken. Each table is circled by six or so twentysomething Thais in crisp white shirts (the men) or little black dresses. And they're all in full force *sanuk* mode: laughing, drinking, flirting, dancing and singing, in unison, to T-Pop (Thai pop music).

Thai multimedia entertainment giant Grammy (plus RS Promotions) controls nearly all of the T-Pop scene. Since conglomerating the fledgling groups of 1980s *string* pop (early T-Pop; it was awful), the company has built a Motown/Brill Building monopoly of songwriters, session musicians, producers, manufacturers, retailers and radio/TV/movie outlets, creating a dynasty of *luuk grung* ('city kids') popstars. By the mid 1990s, the best, most beautiful, most malleable stars, as decreed by fickle teens, were *luuk khrung* (half-Thai, half-*farang*). But then singers began to exercise their rights as artists. Even Grammy reluctantly accepted that, amid the cookie-cutter pop-fluff, wonderful aberrations could emerge. For every Nicole, Kathariya, Nat or Mai, there's now a **Palmy**, the Belgian Thai hippy chick, who combines the Cranberries with Kylie; or a **Panadda**, who's all poetry and pathos; or a

**Bua Chompoo**, Thailand's answer to Japan's Hikaru Utada. Then there's Amita 'Tata' Young, who left Grammy for emerging rival BEC Tero, wresting contractual liberty to shift from puppy-love Barbie doll to hip hop vamp.

**Tata Young** mesmerises and polarises Thais the way Britney Spears does Americans. Even those who openly hate her – for recording with US producers, for dating UK footballers or for posing in a monk's robe for a fashion spread – secretly love her increasingly funky hits. Tata's new (and old) videos play nonstop at Hollywood until midnight, when the crowd out-sings the variety showband covering Tata, Palmy and Chompoo.

The boys of T-Pop aren't as important or as liberated as the girls, but acts do break out. In the 1990s it was the Hall & Oates-does-Devo duo **Assanee and Wasan**, and **Thongchai 'Bird' McIntyre**, the fiftysomething part-Cliff, part-Elton, part-Bowie perennial. Today's heroes are **Loso** (as opposed to jet-setting *hi-so*, geddit?), a Bon Jovi-cum-U2 singing the sweetest ballads then rocking through protests like 'Mai Bai Pantip', along the lines of a Thai 'I Don't Want to Go to Chelsea'.

### Debut Café

*Queen Sirikit National Convention Centre, 60 Thanon New Ratchadaphisek, Sukhumvit (0 2229 3399/www.debutcafe.com). Queen Sirikit subway/ bus 136, 185.* **Open** 11am-1am daily. **Credit** AmEx, DC, MC, V. **Map** p311 J7.
Grammy bands in rep every night except Sunday, with room for 1,000 to eat. On Sundays (from 9pm to midnight), it becomes the airport executive lounge version of a Songs for Life venue, being the only fixed gig for SFL giants Pongsit Khampee and Caravan's Surachai. Show times vary.

### Imageries by the Glass

*2 Sukumvit Soi 24, Sukhumvit (0 2261 0426). Phrom Phong BTS.* **Shows** 9pm-1.30am daily. **Credit** AmEx, DC, MC, V. **Map** p312 K6.
Bangkok's answer to New York's Bottom Line or London's Ronnie Scott's for live *luuk grung*, started by Grammy session musicians.

## Luuk thuung & morlam

You may choose to miss reggae in Bangkok, but would anyone ignore reggae in Kingston? Samba in Rio? Blues in Chicago? *Luuk thuung* or *morlam* in Bangkok?

A plaintive country music, *luuk thuung* ('child of the rice field') conquered the capital in the late 1980s, mostly through its own Patsy Kline, **Pohm Phuang Duangjian** (who died, aged 31, in 1992). She blew the style wide open with her perfect pitch (emotional and musical), encyclopedic memory for every song she'd ever heard (she was illiterate), and her showmanship.

*Luuk thuung* concerts took on the spectacle of Superbowl half-time shows, with choruses of dancing girls, orchestras and a cavalcade of stars leading up to her entrance.

Attention grew again after the crash of 1997, with a heady flow of one-hit-wonder waiters and 'real people', from which emerged **Jintara Poonlap** and **Siriporn Amphaipong**. Jintara, the genre's Dolly Parton, is the sassy, sultry home-wrecker with a tiger's purr, a kitten's growl and a heartbreaker's shattered heart just looking for some relief. Siriporn has a sandpaper sob so sorrowful, so desperate, so eloquent, resistance is futile. Her *morlam* – a close associate of *luuk thuung* – feels like Aretha's soul or Loretta Lynn's country.

At any venue (and weekend midnights at **Rama IX Café**; *see p203*) you might catch hit-makers Lam Yai, Joy Apaporn, Pamela or (if you're lucky) Jintara or Siriporn, or maybe the blonde *luuk thuung* stars – Jonas (Swedish) and Kristy (English). For the weirdest, wildest ride at the fair, head into Thonburi to **Isaan Therd Terng**, where a cool 1,000 people gather for upcountry fun and hot Isaan food.

*Morlam* (literally 'doctor dance') began as church music, the way soul began as gospel. It starts with a long chanted overture – the original rap – over church-organ chords played on the Isaan pipe, the *khaen*. A flurry of guitar arpeggios announces the singer, dressed like a *phra ek* (lead actor) in a costume influenced by the court of Siam and the court of the Jackson 5.

To epitomise the male ideal (based on the princes from Buddhist scripture or the Hindu man-god Krishna), these 'rock idols' plaster on more make-up than a Kiss/Poison double-bill. As they sing (a mix of sweet crooning and plaintive sad warbling) the hits of the day in the dress of a century past (or a century hence), yours will be the only dry eye – unless you speak Lao. All *morlam* is sung in that north-east folk dialect and was – until a couple of years ago – quite distinctive from *luuk thuung*. But the two forms have virtually merged and singers flip easily from Lao to central Thai.

Countering each *phra ek* with witty, catchy half-rap, half-torch tunes, come the *nang ek* (female leads), dressed as if for the Miss Khorat Pageant. Mannered as a Bollywood heroine, they flirt and taunt with clipped little-girl coos swirling over mandolin-style guitar, circular-breathing saxophonics and chase-scene brass blasts. It seems she loves the guy until she unleashes the best, most accusatory use of the universal syllables of disgust ('eee-uuu') since a frog got thrown into the sixth-grade girls' toilet.

### Champ Isaan

*44/31 Sukhumvit Soi 105 (Soi La Salle), East (0 2744 4329). Bus 2, 23, 45, 116, 142, 365, 507, 508, 511, 513, 536, 545.* **Open & shows** 7.30pm-2am daily. **No credit cards.**

For purists. Slightly rickety, but this is *morlam* as band music, mixed with *pleng puer cheewit* in a true Isaan neighbourhood.

Experience *morlam* in all its glory at **Isaan Tawandaeng**. See p190.

Arts & Entertainment

### Genting Plaza

*461/127-9 Thanon Somdet Phra Pinklao, Thonburi (0 2433 5246-9). Bus 11, 57, 146, 149, 201, 503, 509.* **Open & shows** 8pm-2am daily. **Credit** MC, V. **Map** p308 A2.

Genting Plaza is similar to Isaan Therd Terng, with full *morlam likay* (*see p199*) shows on the 15th and last days of the month.

### Isaan 19

*2nd Floor, Country Road II, Sukhmvit Soi 19, Sukhumvit (Country Road II 0 2253 2500). Asoke BTS/Sukhumvit subway.* **Open** 5pm-2am daily. **Credit** AmEx, MC, V. **Map** p311 J5.

Off-duty construction workers compete in a star search every night at this churning venue, where crooners in bright jackets take turns.

### Isaan Tawandaeng

*484 Thanon Pattanakarn, east of Khlong Tan intersection, East (0 2717 2321-3). Bus 11, 92, 133, 206, 517.* **Open** 6pm-2am daily. **Shows** 8.30pm-2am daily. **Credit** AmEx, MC, V.

A diverse roster of shows crowd the stage of this *morlam* barn, from dancing girl revues to formation crooners in Day-Glo tuxedoes.

### Isaan Therd Terng

*104 Thanon Somdet Phra Pinklao, near Pata Pinklao, Thonburi (0 2883 4434/1278 2967). Bus 11, 57, 146, 149, 201, 503, 509, 511.* **Open** 8pm-2am daily. **Shows** 9.30pm-2am daily. **Credit** V. **Map** p308 A2.

Not geared to tourists (the fact that the signs are in Thai is something of a clue), this *morlam* showcase features wild costumes most nights, with full-scale *likay* (*see p199*) productions on the first and 15th of each month. Mingle with off-duty cops, construction workers, taxi drivers and bar girls.

## Pleng puer cheewit

**Tawandaeng Saad Saengdeuan** is one of a chain of barn-like bars associated with Thailand's musical legend, Ad Carabao (*see p186* **Buffalo stance**) and *pleng puer cheewit*. Meaning 'Songs for Life' this is the bluesy, socially conscious folk rock of the 'October generation'. There are hundreds of *pleng puer cheewit* clubs, often resembling the set for *Rawhide*, with many being full-on stateside country & western venues, complete with log walls and apache headdresses. Primetime is midnight. Food is fiery Isaan. Beer is cheap. Whisky is sold by the bottle. A night out for four costs less than B1,000. In utter contrast, pastel **Debut Café** (*see p188*) hosts the SFL greats **Pongsit Khampui** and Caravan's **Surachai** on Sundays.

### Baan Mai Daeng Saad Saengdeuan

*24 Yasoob Soi 2, Thanon Viphavadi Rangsit, North-east (0 2691 5347). Bus 24, 69, 92, 107,*

*129, 513.* **Open** 6pm-2am daily. *Shows* 7.45pm-2am daily. **Credit** AmEx, MC, V.

A veritable shrine to '70s struggle, with photos of demos, portraits of Marx and Confederate flags. Plus voices that can slice your heart.

### Baan Sato

*2578/9 Sukhumvit Soi 70, East (0 2744 8908). Bus 2, 23, 38, 45, 46, 48, 116, 132, 507, 508, 511, 513, 545.* **Open** 6pm-2am daily. *Shows* 9pm-1am daily. **No credit cards.**

The place for southern-style *pleng puer cheewit*. Imagine the bar where the Blues Brothers had to play behind chicken wire. Three bands jam wildly for locals, bikers and aficionados.

### Loong Kee Mao

*74/1 Sukhumvit Soi 72/1, East (0 2398 6601/6929). Bus 2, 23, 38, 45, 46, 48, 116, 132, 507, 508, 511, 513, 545.* **Open** 2pm-2am daily. *Shows* 8.30pm-2am daily. **No credit cards.**

All wagon wheels and raw wood, with neon signs in Thai leading behind a 'short-time' hotel then upstairs, 'Drunken Uncle' is wild. Swastikas face off against Union Jacks, and next to the stage are giant buffalo skulls with fairylights in their eye sockets.

### Raintree Pub & Restaurant

*116/64 Soi Rang Nam, Thanon Phayathai, North (0 2245 7230). Victory Monument BTS.* **Open** 6pm-2am daily. *Shows* 8.30pm-2am daily. **Credit** V.

Despite the C&W motifs, this stalwart feels more like a little blues bar.

### Tawandaeng Saad Saengdeuan

*855/5 Thanon Pattanakarn, just east of Khlong Tan intersection, East (0 2717 2108/9). Bus 11, 92, 133, 206, 517.* **Open** 7pm-1.30am daily. *Shows* 7.30pm-1.30am daily. **Credit** MC, V.

In case you're wondering, the name means 'Scattered Moonlight at Sunset'.

**Branch: Baan Fa Daeng Saad Saengdeuan** 2 Soi Lumsalee, Thanon Si Nakharin, East (0 2379 5021).

## Rock cover bands

Since the mid 1980s many hotels have sought to build a pseudo-sophisticated, mirror-walled, mirror-balled disco lounge. They open with a splash as *hi-so* elites come to be seen, luring the yuppies, who attract the *farang* – and there goes the neighbourhood. Out come the freelance artists of the *demi-monde* and – voila! – throbbing pick-up joints. But the band plays on. And there's no shortage of bands: bizarre cover bands, made up of Thais, Westerners and a lot of Filipinos, reprising international rock and pop faves past and present. There are even tribute acts, like the Elvis and Tom Jones of **Radio City**, and the Better, clones of the Beatles who play Thursdays to Saturdays at **O'Reilly's** (*see p126*). Venues are numerous; here are some of the best.

# High notes

Jazz holds a special place in Thailand. This is largely due to King Bhumibol's involvement with the genre over several decades. An accomplished saxophonist and composer, King Bhumibol has played with legendary figures such as Benny Goodman and Duke Ellington. Visiting jazz luminaries still get invited to jam at the palace and several concerts are arranged around the King's Birthday (5 December).

Quality jazz venues are changeable, but the **Living Room**, which has a lounge bar feel, attracts the best players, notably twice-yearly residencies by Scotty Wright and ex-Ramsey Lewis bass player Eldee Young. The Oriental's low-ceilinged **Bamboo Bar** is a cool cocktail lounge straight out of the 1940s with a long jazz pedigree. Expect black American women singers (Cheryl Hayes, Monica Crosby) backed by a good house band.

In addition to the hotels, the long-time favourite is the earthy, clubby **Brown Sugar**, where Thais and expats reel out a less commercial blend of often inspired playing. Many of them join the Bangkok Big Band, a 20-piece that gigs sporadically, usually at the **Londoner** pub (*see p128*) and **Sundowner**. Jazz jams also feature amid the blues at **Saxophone Pub** (*see p186*).

## Bamboo Bar

*Oriental Hotel, 48 Charoen Krung Soi 38, Bangrak (0 2236 0400). Saphan Taksin BTS.* **Open** 11am-1am daily. *Shows* 10pm-1am daily. **Credit** AmEx, DC, MC, V. **Map** p310 D7.

## Brown Sugar

*231/20 Thanon Sarasin, Ratchadamri end, Pathumwan (0 2250 1825-6). Ratchadamri BTS.* **Open** 6pm-2am daily. *Shows* 9pm-1.30am daily. **Credit** AmEx, MC, V. **Map** p311 G6.

## Living Room

*1st Floor, Sheraton Grande Hotel, 205 Thanon Sukhumvit, Sukhumvit (0 2653 0282). Asoke BTS/Sukhumvit subway.* **Shows** 9pm-midnight Mon-Thur, Sun; 9pm-12.30am Fri, Sat. **Credit** AmEx, DC, MC, V. **Map** p311 J6.

## Sundowner

*1st Floor, Imperial Queen's Park Hotel, Sukhumvit Soi 22, Sukhumvit (0 2261 9000). Phrom Phong BTS.* **Open** 5pm-1am daily. *Shows* 9pm-1am daily. *Big Band show* every 3rd Sun of the month. **Credit** AmEx, DC, MC, V. **Map** p312 K6.

## Log Cabin

*40/5-6 Thonglor Soi 18, Sukhumvit Soi 55, Sukhumvit (0 2714 8614). Thonglor BTS.* **Open** 11am-1.30am daily. **Credit** AmEx, DC, MC, V. **Map** p312 M6.
Country and western from Bangkok city, housed in a log cabin built with half a forest.

## Hard Rock Café

*424/3-6 Siam Square Soi 11, Pathumwan (0 2254 0830/www.hardrockcafe.co.th). Siam BTS.* **Open** 11am-2am daily. *Shows* 10.45pm-1.30am daily. **Credit** AmEx, DC, MC, V. **Map** p309 & p310 F4.
It fits the global formula, with George Harrison dominating its memorabilia. Look for good Filipino alt-metal band Energize.

## The Metal Zone

*82/3 Soi Lang Suan, Pathumwan (0 2255 1913). Ratchadamri BTS.* **Open** 9pm-2am daily. *Shows* 11.15pm-2am daily. **Admission** 1 drink (from B155). **No credit cards. Map** p311 G5.
A dragon rears off the frontage, beyond which tables of solidified chainlink cluster on a metal grate floor. The music takes in Priest and the Scorpions, with a little Deep Purple for variety, by way of Tornado, Angel and HeadBanger.

## Radio City

*76/1-3 Patpong Soi 1, Bangrak (0 2266 4567) Saladaeng BTS/Silom subway.* **Open** 6pm-2am daily. *Shows* 10-11pm, 1-2am Mon-Sat; 10pm-2am Sun. **Credit** MC, V. **Map** p310 E7.
Merging with Patpong's crowds, the audience laps up impersonators of Elvis (11pm daily except Sundays) and Tom Jones (midnight). Any knicker-throwing is optional. Upstairs you'll find Lucifer's disco (*see p197*).

## Riva's

*1st Floor, Sheraton Grande Hotel, 205 Thanon Sukhumvit, Sukhumvit (0 2653 0333/www.luxury collection.com/grandesukhumvit). Asoke BTS/Sukhumvit subway.* **Open** 5pm-2am daily. *Shows* 10pm-1am daily. **Credit** AmEx, DC, MC, V. **Map** p311 J6.
It looks classy, but the gulf between the diners near the curvaceous bronze bar and the distant stage is hard to bridge for import bands like Tall Beat.

## Rock Pub

*93/26 Hollywood Street Centre, Thanon Phyathai, Pathumwan (0 2208 9664). Ratchatewi BTS.* **Shows** 9pm-2am daily. **No credit cards. Map** p309 & p310 F3.

Arts & Entertainment

You enter via the mouth of an Angkor version of the talking tree from *The Wizard of Oz*, to shake your thing to heavy metal ranging from the Scorpions to Judas Priest.

### Spasso

*1st Floor, Grand Hyatt Erawan Hotel, 494 Thanon Ratchadamri, Pathumwan (0 2254 1234). Ratchadamri or Chidlom BTS.* **Open** noon-2.30pm, 6pm-2am daily. *Shows* 10pm-2am daily. **Credit** AmEx, DC, MC, V. **Map** p311 G5.

If you've ever wondered how to get diners (eating generic Italian meals and good pizzas) bopping to black/white US pop-soul showbands with names like Shades, Spasso provides the template.

### Witch's Tavern

*306/1 Sukhumvit Soi 55 (Thonglor), Sukhumvit (0 2391 9791/www.witch-tavern.com). Thonglor BTS.* **Open** 5pm-1.30am daily. *House band* 9.30pm-1.30am Mon-Thur; 10pm-1.30am Fri-Sat. *Jazz* 8-10pm Fri-Sat; 7pm-1.15am Sun. **Credit** AmEx, MC, V. **Map** p312 M5.

Soft rock gangs up with smooth jazz at the Witch's Tavern, killing you softly in this freehouse with English country motifs.

# Bubbling over

And now, the culmination. In one band. The melting pot of all Thai musics – *pleng puer cheewit, luuk thuung, morlam, phiphat* and cheesy covers – can be caught in the mind spasm of one man: **Bruce Gaston**, the US composer who leads the *phiphat* orchestra-cum-rock band, **Fong Nam**.

A 1970s' New York avant-garde peer of Philip Glass, Steve Reich and Laurie Anderson, Gaston was known as a lover of chance music as pioneered by John Cage. One day he was performing at New York's Kitchen, the next he was in Thailand 'on a mission'. Whatever the apocryphal stories, he came to study, and master, Thai music.

In the early 1980s he joined the premier *phiphat* ensemble, Fong Nam ('bubbles'), founded by the greatest *ranat* master, Boomyong Ketkhong. Over the next 20 years Gaston transcribed centuries' worth of ancient texts and whispers into both Thai and Western notation, and Fong Nam recorded them. After Boomyong retired, Fong Nam became the instrument for Gaston's compositions. And they're good. So good he's played for the king and is known by nearly every Thai as *ajahn* (professor) Bruce. In 1999 he took to gigging nightly at the cavernous **Tawandaeng German Brewhouse**.

A rock band buckles on to the *phiphat* orchestra, singers and flory-dory girls appear and – lights, gamelan, action – the mercurial multimedia extravaganza explodes: films, fireworks, dancing waters, dancing girls, shadow puppets, ladyboys, a repertoire from Herbie Hancock's 'Watermelon Man' to Led Zepplin's 'Black Dog' by way of Carabao's 'Made in Thailand'. Then Gaston in drag singing a 50-year-old *luuk thuung* chestnut, followed by an Elvis medley, sax pieces by the king, the latest *luuk khrung* sensations, culminating in a full double-orchestra version

of the Thai disco smash that'll take over once the band departs. It's Sgt Hanuman's Lonely Hearts Club *phiphat wong* and he wants you all to sing along.

### Tawandaeng German Brewhouse

*462/61 Thanon Narathiwat Ratchanakharin, at Thanon Rama III, South (0 2678 1114-5). Bus 77, 162.* **Open** 4pm-2am daily. *Shows* 8.30pm-1.45am Mon-Sat. **Credit** AmEx, MC, V.

A vast *rong beer* (microbrewery) with galleries swung out from under a barrel-like dome. There's room for 1,600 diners necking Thai food and German beer. Fong Nam plays each Wednesday, but bands vary nightly.

# Nightlife

Crossing through the rebirth of DJ-spinning, early clubbing and cop dodging.

DJs first surfaced in Bangkok during the 1970s disco era, but were soon displaced by a pub scene of comfortable seating, chit chat, *kup klaem* (drinking snacks) and covers from Filipino bands – or karaoke. Even the mega-discos of Thanon Ratchadaphisek lost their dancefloors to tall round tables and high stools around which clubbers jiggled. This was partly because few dancing licences were available, and venues were raided simply because customers moved to the music. Although these elements persist today, Bangkok's nightlife is going through a transition, making it a more vibrant, experimental and unpredictable scene.

Since house music raves started in 1994 – spawning one-off or short-lived party venues in odd places (car parks, warehouses, hotel ballrooms, the karaoke atrium of a hospital) – Western-style dance music has penetrated the masses from the top, concurrently with indie rock, the internet and alternative media in general. A liberal new generation of rich kids educated abroad has imported its experience of DJ-ing from London, Sydney or America's East Coast to the Bangkok club scene. DJ schools have started to pop up, notably at **House of Indies** (*see p187*). Spinmeisters to look out for include DJs **Spydamonkee**, **Dragon**, **Joeki**, **Nutek**, **Tul** (Toon) and **Seed** (founder of Thailand's first indie music magazine), plus prominent *farang* DJs **Billy V** and **Ofay 1**.

Nightclubs have tended to have a permanent turntable crew and occasional party nights that have welcomed a pool of talent (Paul Oakenfold has played here annually for a decade, mainly at **Narcissus**; *see p198*). This has enabled venues to differentiate between nights of the week, starting with the opening of **Q Bar** (*see p195*), at the start of the new millennium, which brings in famous DJs from overseas and exemplifies the popular 'dance bar' format. The same now goes for **Faith Club** (*see p197*), **Café Democ** (*see p195*) and the UK-derived titan **Ministry of Sound** (*see p197*).

But the effort, energy and investment put into these clubs often goes to waste, due to zealous enforcement of the 2am closing time in the government's Social Order Policy – which cites drug taking and under-age drinking as its reasons, but generally takes a dim view of youthful behaviour outside traditional norms. During crackdowns in 2001-2 many

venues had to close early, and police ID checks and urine tests have been imposed on entire clubs, whether populated by businessmen, high society or celebrities such as rapper Joey Boy. Police are trailed by reporters and even people testing negative to drug tests have had their faces splashed across newspapers and on TV. It's estimated a million workers' incomes have been affected by the crackdown and there's a vociferous lobby of venue owners pleading for their businesses' survival. Nightlife zoning has been proposed for enclaves where clubs can stay open until 4am, with licences progressively being denied (and revoked) outside. While practicable if managed reasonably, zoning is stifling many existing venues. Only Silom, RCA and Ratchadaphisek have so far got zones, leaving myriad bar strips, especially the entertainment hub of Sukhumvit, in limbo.

Crackdowns have come and gone before, and venues open and close with bewildering speed, but Thais have a way of finding fun wherever

Karaoke is a perennial nightlife fave.

they go. The full moon party, an all-nighter on Ko Pha-ngan (*see p237* **Moon dance**) was once way ahead of Bangkok musically, spawning related venues in Silom Soi 4 and Thanon Khao San. Now the party traffic is more the other way, with Bangkok DJs joining international names at a variety of beach scenes, notably on Ko Samet (*see p232*), Ko Samui (*see p235*) and Krabi (*see p254*).

Currently clubbers are meeting early, around 9.30pm to 10.30pm, though the vibe doesn't kick in until around 11.30pm. Food is available in most places. And, unless otherwise stated in the listings, admission is free to the venues listed below.

## Adult nightlife

For decades visitors have been ushered – by tourist magazines, tour guides, hotel concierges, guidebooks (including official ones), and not least by sensationalist reportage and word of mouth – to Bangkok's 'other' nightlife scene. In a word, **Patpong**. Hoary anecdotes, exaggerated boasts, nudge-nudge jokes and *One Night in Bangkok* song lyrics have pumped up the 'sexotic' reputation of this fleshpot – though the rather unerotic reality suffers from premature expectation.

Patpong, a hangover of the Vietnam War, seems like a relic of an era when entertainment options were more limited. The go-go bars are now being marginalised in both physical space

and perception by increasing sophistication among residents, visitors and venues. Their menus of bizarre sex acts are brandished by touts specifically at tourists (the Thai sex industry is quite different – *see p196* **The professionals**). Even stalwarts of family values and the politically correct seem compelled to view such a licentious novelty – which can also be found at Nana Entertainment Plaza, Clinton Plaza and Soi Cowboy on Sukhumvit.

Hence the curious fuel the cycle as much as the sex tourists and the simply lonely buying drinks to gain the company of dancers (who are numbered, as pointing is considered rude). Some then pay the 'bar fine' (B200-B500) to take the prostitute (for a negotiated tip) to a room upstairs, a hotel, a weekend in Pattaya or maybe – so the bar girl/boy hopes – a new life abroad. Many end up playing off multiple sugar daddies in different countries.

The sex industry has other guises. Open-air 'bar beer' zones (as at Patpong Soi 2, Sukhumvit 'Soi Zero' and facing the Ambassador Hotel on Sukhumvit) cater mainly for Westerners. Asian businessmen favour plusher, sometimes more discreet karaoke bars (those in Soi Thaniya are just for Japanese), cocktail lounges (Sukhumvit Soi 33 is lined with them), 'no-hands' restaurants (where you are fed, and so forth, by hosts/hostesses) and massage parlours, which litter Thanons Phetchaburi and Ratchadaphisek. Some exclusive members' clubs bask in gratuitous opulence.

Sophisticated New York-style **Q Bar**. *See p195*.

## The best Nightspots

### For Thai DJs
Café Democ. *See p195.*

### For a full-on rave
Ministry of Sound. *See p197.*

### For New York chic
Q Bar. *See p195.*

### For arty parties
The opening nights at **About Café**.
*See p169.*

### For houseparty grooves
Tapas. *See p196.*

The government's Social Order Policy has intermittently made go-go dancers don skimpy clothing, and has periodically tamed the shows – which are typically held upstairs, so that there's time to respond to occasional police raids. Complaints about inflated bar bills (and even drinks laced with sedatives) are rarer now, and many bars post fixed prices. But those exploring the scene should be alert to touts, scams, their valuables and dubious scenarios.

## Dance bars

### Absolute Bangkok
*23/51 Zone F, Royal City Avenue, Thanon Petchaburi end, North-east (0 2203 0669). Bus 11, 58, 60, 72, 93, 99, 113, 512.* **Open** 6pm-2am daily. **Credit** MC, V. **Map** p312 M4.
One of the best dance bars outside Downtown, this three-level joint is a more hip version of Bangkok Bar. The leather seats and spacious tables just exude comfort, and there's a big pool table on the top floor. Music ranges from acid jazz to house and hip hop. Keep an eye out for events organised by MTV, and various DJ parties.

### Bangkok Bar
*149 Thanon Rambuttri, Banglamphu (0 2629 4443/ www.bangkokbar.cjb.net). Bus 3, 6, 9, 15, 30, 32, 33, 43, 53, 64, 65, 68, 82, 506.* **Open** 6pm-2am daily. **Credit** MC, V. **Map** p308 B3.
The tiny shophouse interior of this bar exudes Thainess. While it's popular with tourists looking out for the exotic, Bangkok Bar is also frequented by locals. Dark wood and giant candles dominate the place, and there's a large dancefloor. Join the crowds on the weekend for pop, dance and house music, and enjoy a Sawasdee cocktail or two. Not to be confused with Bangkok Bar in Ekkamai Soi 63 or Baan Bangkok Restaurant & Bar (*see p105*), although they're also good venues.

### Café Democ
*78 Thanon Ratchadamnoen, near Democracy Monument, Phra Nakorn (0 2622 2571). Bus 39, 59, 60, 201, 503, 511, 512.* **Open** 4pm-2am Tue-Sun. **No credit cards.** **Map** p308 D3.
Known for giving birth to local young DJs like Spydamonkee, Dome and Circle, Café Democ also welcomes guest spinners from other countries. Parties start at 10.30pm on Wednesday, Thursday and Sunday, while the music ranges from hip hop and house to drum 'n' bass and tribal. If you find yourself in need of a breather, the mezzanine level has a homely feel with comfortable couches and photographs of retro Bangkok.

### Q Bar
*34 Sukhumvit Soi 11, on sub-soi towards Soi 3, Sukhumvit (0 2252 3274/www.qbarbangkok.com). Nana BTS.* **Open** 8pm-2am daily. **Admission** B500 (incl 2 drinks) Fri, Sat. **Credit** AmEx, MC, V. **Map** p311 J4.
This exclusive club is a reincarnation of a Saigon venue of the same name, praised by *Newsweek* and others as the 'world's best bar'. Owner David Jacobson, with associate Andrew Clark, has forged a New York-style bar with padded pillars, a chillout balcony, a back-lit silhouette wall, podium dancers and clever use of lighting. It also has the best range of drinks in town, professional bar staff, its own merchandise and record label, and diverse music (from chillout to house, with hip hop on Sundays). You might even get to see international celebs such as Michelle Yeoh, Oliver Stone and Matt Dillon at one of its regular party nights.

### Skunk
*1/1 Ekkamai Soi 2, Sukhumvit Soi 63, Sukhumvit (0 2390 0495). Ekkamai BTS.* **Open** 6pm-2am daily. **No credit cards.** **Map** p312 M7.
Packed at weekends, Skunk is guaranteed to pour out the best of progressive house and drum 'n' bass. Occupying just one narrow shophouse, it's not a place to sit and chill, but to dance like there's no tomorrow. For a more relaxing time, go early or during the week. Skunk is a crash pad for youngsters and creative types.

### Speed
*80 Silom Soi 4, Bangrak (0 9890 8441). Saladaeng BTS/Silom subway.* **Open** 9.30pm-2am Wed, Thur, Sun; 8.30pm-2am Fri, Sat. **Admission** *Top-floor hip hop* B100 (incl 1 drink). **No credit cards.** **Map** p310 F7.
A tiny, long-standing venue in the still-relevant original nightlife *soi*, Speed attracts a younger crowd than Tapas opposite. It's nothing more than a square room with graffiti all over the walls, where youngsters dance to any music that is playing – usually a mix of techno and pop dance, with the top-floor hip hop sweatbox popular among black Americans. On a bad day, you might encounter girls and their gay friends choreographing to *YMCA*. No fancy cocktails here, just standards and beers.

# The professionals

Long-suppressed aspects of the flesh trade are sparking a debate about sexual roles in Thailand. Of the 10.13 million tourists who visited Thailand in 2001, 60 per cent were male. That surplus of males may have various reasons, but evidently includes substantial numbers of sex tourists. It's not hard to spot the Western and north Asian males milling about the seedier nightlife zones of Bangkok, Pattaya and Patong (on Phuket), or the southern city of Had Yai's throngs of weekending Malaysian men.

It's also hard to miss the suppliers (male, female and ladyboy) in an industry of diverse sexual services, with prostitutes in Thailand totalling between 200,000 (police figures, 1991) and two million (Centre for the Protection of Children's Rights). Even vaguer are the numbers working here from Burma, Cambodia, China, Vietnam or Russia.

Highlighted by the recent arrest of 'America's Most Wanted' paedophile Eric Rosser (ex-pianist at Bangkok's Oriental hotel) is the number of under-age prostitutes. The Department of Public Welfare estimates 12,000 to 18,000; anti-child prostitution agency ECPAT claims 200,000 (both sets of figures from 1997), some notoriously sold or deceived into sexual slavery (in Thailand or trafficked abroad). While bonded brothels (where prostitutes are treated like slaves) are a problem upcountry rather than in tourist areas, say reports, the undoubted element of Western exploitation has been widely exposed, though less publicised aspects of this complex social issue have now hit the news too.

In 2002 a Thai senator was prosecuted for sex with three girls below the 'statutory rape' age of 15 (the age of consent is 18), under a 1995 law that toughened penalties for procurers and brothel operators, but decriminalised prostitution itself in an effort to manage the problem. Some say child prostitution has since declined, others claim it has been driven underground. This unprecedented conviction joined headlines about upper-class Thai women hiring gigolos, and editorials fretting over surveys of how many middle-class students are selling their bodies to afford luxuries, drugs, nightlife and mobile phones. A procurer-turned-activist at a Chiang Mai rehabilitation centre claims that half the male students he knows do this (*The Nation*, 2002). A similar motivation drives some rural women to sacrifice status in order to gain economic freedom and mobility out of poverty and social conditioning.

Some 95 per cent of prostitutes cater to a local clientele, and one in four Thai males admits to patronising them regularly (*Bangkok Post*, 2001), most discreetly via restaurants or escorts. Paying to lose one's virginity is common, though declining due to relaxation of courting traditions. Many older Asians believe that deflowering virgins boosts their longevity and libido – and assume that young girls are clean of STDs or HIV. Such beliefs are common among north Asian businessmen; for many, group massage parlour visits are as conventional as golf meetings.

The trade is too lucrative for it to be easily reformed, with another structural resistance being that it's a distortion of historic Thai polygamy. Promiscuous men often take *mia noi* (illegal minor wives), a practice some claim strengthens potentially incompatible marriages. But male sexual impunity is also being contested over workplace harassment, paternity responsibility and more libertarian sex education. Having overcome taboos through successful family planning and anti-AIDS campaigns in the 1980s and '90s, Thailand is openly engaging in a mature national debate about the role of sex in its rapidly changing society.

## Tapas

*114/17 Silom Soi 4, Bangrak (0 2234 4737/ www.tapas-café.com). Saladaeng BTS/Silom subway.* **Open** 5.30pm-2am daily. **Admission** *Upstairs lounge* B200. **Credit** AmEx, DC, MC, V. **Map** p310 F7.

A veteran from the original house boom, Tapas has yet to find a worthy adversary. The Spanish influence and intimate house party terrain keeps the party-goers moving their feet. Sexy house tunes are spun by San Francisco DJ Emmanuel, often accompanied by percussionists or an MC (11pm-2am Wednesday, Friday and Saturday). Frequented by the beautiful people (both Thai and *farang*), this is a place to be seen – whether out front, inside or upstairs in the members' bar.

## Nightclubs

### Concept CM2

*Basement, Novotel Bangkok, Siam Square Soi 6, Pathumwan (0 2255 6888). Siam BTS.* **Open** 9.30pm-2am daily. *Bands* 10pm-1.15am daily.

Kitsch rules at **Narcissus**. *See p198.*

**Admission** (incl free drink worth B150) B200.
**Credit** AmEx, DC, MC, V. **Map** p309 & 310 F4.
Probably the leading hotel nightclub, this low-ceilinged complex has themed zones around the stage and dancefloor, with an Italian restaurant and karaoke (over 100,000 songs in six languages). It also imports live bands, such as Big Noise and Ghetto Tea Party. Its newish DJ-driven venue, the Boom Room, spins trance, hip hop and progressive house from 10.30pm nightly.

### Dance Fever
*76/2 Thanon Ratchadaphisek, between Sois 6 & 8, North-east (0 2247 4295). Thiem Ruam-mit subway/bus 73, 136, 137, 185, 206, 514.* **Open** 6pm-2am daily. *Shows* 10.30pm-1am daily. **Credit** AmEx, DC, MC, V.
A formula disco barn for young Thais to enthuse over mostly Thai songs amid a forest of tiny tables. Many of the hits are played live, sometimes by famous bands. Order beer or whisky.

### Faith Club
*96/4-5 Sukhumvit Soi 23, Sukhumvit (0 2261 3007/ 4446). Asoke BTS/Sukhumvit subway then taxi.* **Open** 6.30pm-2am daily. **Credit** AmEx, DC, MC, V. **Map** p312 K5.
Residing in a small *soi*, this London-inspired club is managed by club lovers, who you're sure to meet on the dancefloor on any given night. The decor retains

its edge, despite one premature renovation, with black furniture and raw cement walls, floor and bar counter. Music-wise, there's something for everyone.

### Hollywood
*72/1 Thanon Ratchadaphisek, between Sois 6 & 8, North-east (0 2246 4311-3). Thiem Ruam-mit subway/bus 73, 136, 137, 185, 206, 514.* **Open** 8pm-2am daily. *Bands* 10pm-2am daily. **Credit** MC, V.
Next door to Dance Fever and not much different; it's also presents live *luuk grung* (*see p187*).

### ID4
*3rd Floor, Thonburi Free Style, Thanon Ladya, Thonburi (0 2437 0274-7). Bus 3, 42, 43, 84, 88, 89, 105, 111, 120, 149, 164, 505, 530.* **Open** 8.30pm-2am daily. **Credit** AmEx, MC, V.
Not exactly a tourist hangout, this club in the suburbs has a local charm with an accent on fun. As with many no-music-policy clubs, techno and house are sonic highlights by default. Built like a ware-house, it's comfortable even when packed.

### Lava
*Basement, Bayon Building, 249 Thanon Khao San, Banglamphu (0 2281 6565). Bus 39, 59, 60, 157, 201, 503, 509.* **Open** 8pm-2am daily. **No credit cards. Map** p308 B3.
This place has changed hands so many times, but the decor remains much the same: raw concrete, metallic stools and glass tables. And a sound system just good enough considering what's playing (techno and dance). It draws more young locals than backpackers despite the neighbourhood.

### Lucifer
*3rd Floor, Radio City, 76/1-3 Patpong Soi 1, Bangrak (0 2266 4567). Saladaeng BTS/Silom subway.* **Admission** B120 Fri, Sat. **Credit** MC, V. **Map** p310 F6.
Here, devil-uniformed attendants welcome you to a satanically decorated nightclub that's changed many times. This incarnation, with very loud trance, is popular with young tourists and expats. It's in a B500,000 complex that incorporates Radio City (*see p191*) situated below, Muzzik Café opposite, and Lucile & Krazy Cat.

### Lucile & Krazy Kat
*29/53-64 Zone C, Royal City Avenue, Thanon Rama IX end, North-east (0 2203 0240-2). Rama IX subway/bus 137, 168, 179, 517.* **Open** *Lucile* 10pm-2am daily. *Krazy Kat* 7pm-2am daily. **Admission** *Lucile* (incl 1 drink) B150. *Krazy Kat* free. **Credit** AmEx, MC, V. **Map** p312 L3.
While the twee Krazy Kat attracts a young crowd, Lucile feels more like a nightclub. Behind the ordinary exterior is a cave-like venue with a big dancefloor where trance reigns, spun by big-name local DJs on a state-of-the-art sound system.

### Ministry of Sound
*2 Sukhumvit Soi 12, Sukhumvit (0 2229 5850-3). Asoke BTS/Sukhumvit subway.* **Open** 10pm-2am

**Ministry of Sound**: welcome to the biggest club in Bangkok. *See p197.*

Wed-Sun. **Admission** B300 (incl 2 drinks) Wed, Thur, Sun; B500 (incl 3 drinks) Fri, Sat. **Credit** AmEx, MC, V. **Map** p311 J5.

Still the biggest club in town (in both capacity and ego), the UK-derived Ministry took Bangkok by storm in 2001 with its global high-profile DJ parties, launch events and fashion shows. It may have mellowed somewhat since, but heart-palpitatingly loud blasts of trance and progressive house and its huge dance capacity still command attention, as do its podium dancers. The VIP balcony decor doesn't match the membership fees, but rumour has it that Kylie Minogue moved her derrière here last year.

### Narcissus

*112 Sukhumvit Soi 23, Sukhumvit (0 2258 4805/ 2549). Asoke BTS/Sukhumvit subway then taxi.* **Open** 9pm-2am daily. **Admission** B300 (incl 2 drinks) Mon, Tue, Thur, Sun; B500 (incl 3 drinks) Wed, Fri, Sat. **Credit** AmEx, DC, MC, V. **Map** p312 K5.

Once attracting the beautiful crowd, this temple to classic kitsch has reduced its glam factor, but a decade of consistent quality means business remains good. The ostentatious relaxation area in front of the ladies' rooms isn't quite the Spanish Steps, but offers many vantage points for viewing. Music is house and trance. Tourists won't feel intimidated.

### Route 66

*Royal City Avenue Zone B, 29/33-48 Thanon Rama IX side, North-east (0 2203 0407/8/www.route66 dancepub.com). Rama IX subway/bus 137, 168, 179, 517.* **Open** 7am-2am daily. **Credit** AmEx, DC, MC, V. **Map** p312 L3.

A few blocks from Absolute Bangkok, this ever-expanding bar-disco caters for youngsters of all classes. DJs spin a varied mix of music to keep the crowd going crazy.

### Twenty Pub

*Chao Phraya Park Hotel, 247 Thanon Ratchadaphisek, North-east (0 2693 8022-5). Bus 73, 136, 137, 185, 206, 514.* **Open** 9.30pm-2am daily. **Credit** AmEx, MC, V.

Formerly called Phuture, this disco (and sometime concert venue) is great for people-watching. Most of the clubbers are students and rough suburban types armed with cash. The DJs here don't impose a style, but will play anything to keep people dancing.

# Performing Arts

With performance woven into its cultural fabric, all Thailand's a stage.

In Thailand, where wedding processions dance, sacred ceremonies unfold in dramatic rites and boxing matches begin with a balletic ritual, where aesthetic presentation is imperative and grace a virtue, performance is a philosophy of life. Theatre arts exist in ceremony, the royal tradition and daily life – belonging to both a sacred sphere and common conventions.

In the most classical form, *Khon*, performers must undergo years of codified training, whereas pure wit may suffice for a *talok* (comedy) star. Thai thespians to this day believe they must be taken over by their characters' souls to truly deliver a great performance. Traditionally, before every production, from grand *Khon* and *Lakhon* productions to fairground *Likay* entertainments, the cast and crew would convene for a *wai khru* (ritual of respect to their teachers and the art's original master). Conversely, performance often serves as sacred offerings — the **Erawan Shrine** (*see p93*) and **Lak Muang** (*see p61*) host examples of this.

The government's department of fine arts remains a fortress of traditional forms and home to virtuoso masters recognised with the highest title, National Artist. Since Thai theatre's modernisation during King Rama VI's reign, however, the department has inclined towards Western styles.

Today, when contemporary forms emerge, they usually follow commercial, mainstream formulas. Popular plays, musicals and other conventional dance-dramas have their fans, but offer little room for creative innovation. Lack of funding can be blamed for a rather apathetic arts scene; commercial presentations and trade events often enjoy bigger budgets than typical theatre productions. However, the gradual emergence of fresh talent, interdisciplinary dialogue and the use of unconventional venues means that all is not lost for contemporary Thai performance.

One of the most memorable ways to see puppetry, Chinese opera and *khon chuk rok* dance-drama comes in early November with the **Wat Arun Traditional Arts Festival** (0 2559 0505 ext 257-9/www.watarunfestival. com). It's held at the famous Thonburi temple (*see p71*). Synopses of performances are given in English, and food is exchanged for old Siamese bullet coins.

## Traditional forms

### Khon

This intricate and venerated genre, historically performed only before royalty, remains infrequently seen. Highly trained masked performers dance the *Ramakien* epic, in which protagonist Phra Ram and his monkey army led by Hanuman ultimately defeats ten-headed giant Tosakan and wins back his beautiful wife Sita. A complete *khon* rendition of *Ramakien* would take weeks, but today's abridged version is adequately delivered in a couple of hours.

From an early age, dancers are trained in character styles based mostly on body type: Phra the lanky, graceful male, Nang the coy leading lady, Ling the comical, acrobatic monkey or Yak the powerful, robust giant. Each character executes distinctive steps and movements, startling contemporary audiences with warlike 'lifts', Totskan's jolting jumps and Hanuman's gymnastic stunts and monkey twitch. Choreographic clarity and symbolism, the dancers' poise, elaborate costumes and live music eliminate the need for stage design, except in rare *khon chuk rok*, when peformers fly on wires before a tableau. There's a **Khon Museum** at Suan Pakkard Palace (*see p98*).

### Lakhon

*Lakhon* (drama) has two principal threads. *Lakhon nok* typically features *Jataka* tales (Buddha's past worldly lives), with rousing action and melodramatic plots. The more refined court recital *lakhon nai* belongs to the inner royal sanctum. In meticulously tuned choreography that emphasises emotion, dancers convey the romance and tragedy of such literary masterpieces as *Inao*, *Unarut* and *Ramakien*. Today, *lakhon* most commonly signifies TV melodrama, whose plots and exaggerated acting identify more closely with *lakhon nok* and its successor, *likay*.

### Likay

This once ubiquitous musical theatre satisfies all appetites with its blend of action, fantasy, tragedy and romance, in diverse storylines, from folk fables to episodes of literary

**Joe Louis Theatre.** See p201.

masterpieces. High-pitched resonant singing, extravagant costumes, and expressive choreography characterise this popular folk derivative of *lakhon nok* and Malay traditions. Also distinctive is its *ohk kaek* prologue – a solo burlesque of an Indian or south Asian.

From famous companies to struggling temple fair players, *likay* has steadily declined, with many emerging talents having sought stardom though *luuk thuung* or *morlam* music instead (*see p188*). You may catch it at festivals and **Lak Muang** (*see p61*).

## Manohra

Representing the behaviour of a mythical bird, this southern art form with Malay associations is now focused around a master from Songkhla, who teaches and performs in Bangkok. Shimmying in a beaded, multicoloured costume, with a buffalo horn tail, the dancer twirls brass nail extensions with speed and complexity. After duelling with a masked hunter to rhythmic percussion, the bird survives to dance another day. Devotees hope this rare dance genre keeps going in similar style.

## Nang & Hun puppetry

Shadow puppetry with its roots in a southern folk tradition employs elaborately stencilled and dyed *nang* (animal hide) characters and a backlit screen – which led to *nang* becoming the Thai term for cinema. Conceived during the Ayutthaya era, *nang yai* showcases two-metre-tall (six-foot) puppets with no moving parts held on sticks by visible dancing puppeteers. The less formal and very popular *nang talung*, which uses puppets with hinged, moving parts, has more movement, percussive music and sometimes satirical comedy or singing from the multi-skilled *talung* (narrator/puppeteer).

The ingenious manipulation of dancing *hun* (marionettes), once a disappearing art, is now resurfacing at festivals. Puppeteers of *hun luang* (royal puppets, as seen in the National Museum) can engineer the delicate *jeeb* finger gesture, by dint of ringed strings and poles. Worked with sticks by three visible dancers, the uncannily lifelike *hun lakorn lek* (small dancer puppets) has a surviving lineage through the **Joe Louis Theatre** (*see p201*).

## Companies

### Bangkok Community Theatre
*www.bct-th.org.*
Run by volunteers, this company's members are Thai and expat actors, choreographers, directors and technicians. Newcomers are welcomed to meetings on the first Thursday of every month at the British Club (0 2234 0247). Professional standards are maintained when reviving Broadway/West End productions at the Bangkok Playhouse.

### Bangkok Opera
*0 2391 0245/www.bangkokopera.com.*
Thailand's first Western classical opera company was founded by SP Somtow after the 2000 premiere of the first Thai opera, *Madana*. Featuring Thai and international opera stars in its four annual programmes and international co-productions, the non-profit company stages European classics and aims to premiere one new 'Thai' opera per year, starting with the ghost story *Mae Nak* (in late 2002). The Bangkok Symphony Orchestra, Meefa Orchestra and Rangsit Philharmonic regularly take the pit in performances at the Thailand Cultural Centre.

### Company of Performing Artists
*Dance Centre, Soi Klang Racquet Club, Sukhumvit Soi 49/9, Sukhumvit (0 2712 8323/www.dance-centre.com). Thonglor BTS.* **Open** 10am-6pm Mon-Fri; 10am-5pm Sat. **Tickets** B500-B1,200. **No credit cards. Map** p312 L5.
Run by Vararom Pachimsawat, CPA stages fusions of classical ballet, *khon*, other Thai forms, contemporary dance and even Japanese *butoh*. Venues vary from malls and parks to the Thailand Cultural Centre.

## Joe Louis Theatre

*Suan Lum Night Bazaar, 1875 Thanon Rama IV,
Pathumwan (0 2252 9683/4). Lumphini subway/
bus 14, 17, 47, 50, 115.* **Open** 9.30am-9.30pm
Mon-Fri; 1-9.30pm Sat, Sun. *Shows* 7.30-8.45pm,
9.30-10.45pm daily. **Tickets** B600; B300 concessions.
**Credit** DC, MC, V. **Map** p311 H7.

The beautiful 70cm-high (28in) marionettes of the
world's last *hun lakhon lek* troupe come dynamic-
ally and uncannily to life with much humour
and charm. Each puppet requires three performers
to manoeuvre it, using sticks. Despite the loss
of his original puppets in a fire, Joe Louis (aka
Sakorn Yangkiawsod, National Artist) started
again from scratch and trained up an enthusastic
new generation of youthful performers.

The theatre's move to this easily accessible location in Pathumwan should help it to build upon its
mushrooming success and growing international
acclaim. The company's progressive attitude and a
policy of collaborating with other theatrical disciplines have given new cultural relevance to this once
endangered art form.

Lack of publicity and sensible scheduling
deprives traditional Thai performance of a
potentially greater audience. Visitors are often
surprised that neither the National Theatre
nor Thai theatre companies do much to promote
national art forms. Enthusiasts must rely
on luck, careful timing or insider knowledge
to experience authentic performance at
elite gatherings or festivals. Others are left
with 'greatest hits' excerpts churned out
disinterestedly to diners at theatre-restaurants.

The **Joe Louis Theatre** (*see left*) has proved
how, with cultivation and marketing, Thailand
could enjoy a performance scene as thriving as
Bali's – and secure its dramatic arts beyond the
lifetimes of surviving masters. There are too few
expert dancers around, and they are kept busy
on foreign tours and official shows. There is
hope, though, for Thai performing arts, since
the culture ministry was founded in 2002.

# Stage mother

Thailand's foremost diva, **Patravadi
Meechudhon**, transformed her riverside
family compound into the open-air Patravadi
Theatre in 1992. Now with a tent-like roof
and a studio annex, this celebrated space
for independent theatre arts and dance
offers diverse programmes and events.
A sanctuary from Bangkok's bedlam, the
building, a mix of modern industrial, ethnic
Thai and natural rustic, is a cross between
a 1970s' artists' compound, a Thai academy
and a contemporary art gallery.

Many of Patravadi's original productions,
fusing Thai and Western forms, have
toured internationally. The *Rai Pratraitpidok*
contemporary adaptation of Buddhist
scripture has become a local favourite.
Collaborations, such as with the Joe Louis
Theatre and with disabled children, help
expand the possibilities for dramatic arts.
Independent companies also perform here,
especially during the annual **Bangkok
Fringe Festival** (*see p160*) in April/May.
The Patravadi Awards reward talents in
all artistic genres.

Renaissance woman Patravadi's job titles
are many: actor, teacher, dancer, producer,
director and writer. This leading lady is
the grande dame of contemporary Thai
drama. Patravadi ensures her influence
lives on through classes and workshops.
Her students range from acclaimed dancers

to TV actors and *luuk thung* singers. Resident
choreographer Manop Meejamras is one
of Thailand's few pioneers of contemporary
dance and movement.

### Patravadi Theatre

*69/1 Soi Wat Rakang, Thanon Arun Amarin,
Thonburi (0 2412 7287/8/www.patravadi
theatre.com). Bus 19, 57, 81, 83/ferry
from Tha Chang to Tha Wat Rakhang.*
**Open** 9am-5pm daily. *Shows* usually 7-9pm
Fri-Sun during seasons. **Tickets** B300-B800.
**Credit** AmEx, V. **Map** p308 A3.

**Arts & Entertainment**

# Sport & Fitness

Box, ride or putt your way around town.

Rarely seen running, Thais are understandably languid in the heat, but at dawn and dusk young and old tap shuttlecocks or rattan *takraw* balls around open ground, jog in parks or imitate David Beckham (though never while wearing a sarong).

During the 2002 World Cup Thailand drew global headlines, not just for rampant illicit gambling but for its worship of the English Premiership. Major Premiership matches are relayed on huge screens and loyalty is divided in June when top European sides play Thailand's national team – which is coached by Peter Withe (who scored the 1982 European Cup final winner for Aston Villa). The team also contests the King's Cup each February with three invited countries. But Thailand's own Premier League is lacking in quality, despite some skilful players, such as national team captain Kiatisak 'Zico' Senamuang and juniors on UK scholarships, including Teerathep 'Leesaw' Winothai, currently at Crystal Palace. Astonishingly, Thailand beat Spain to finish fourth at the Beach Soccer World Cup in 2002, possibly thanks to *takraw* skills.

Golf became massive in Thailand after the euphoria of discovering that Tiger Woods was half Thai. Locals now accept that he has little interest in his mother's homeland, and consider him arrogant for not accepting an honorary degree. But, happily, there are homegrown golfers to cheer along, such as Thongchai Jaidee and twins Aree and Naree Song Wongluekiet (although the latter have now taken their father's Korean nationality).

Tennis is the new pet sport thanks to Tammy Tanasugarn and Paradorn Srichaphan. Meanwhile, Chanya 'Cherry' Srifuengfung is making her name in equestrianism, and pop star Jetrin 'Jay' Wattanasin has been a world champion jetskier. But the kingdom's sporting pride hinges on boxing. And not just in *Muay Thai* (kick boxing); its two Olympic gold medallists in conventional boxing – Somluck Khamsing in 1996 and Wicharn Ponrid in 2000 – were rightly fêted.

Various traditional Thai sports are practised throughout the city, as well as during the annual **Traditional Thai Games & Sports Festival** (*see p159*), which is held at Sanam Luang around March; every other year it also includes the **International Kite Festival**.

## Active sports/fitness

### Bowling

Bowling is a popular pastime and most malls have top-floor alleys. You should book ahead for weekends.

#### Brunswick
*5th Floor, Central Pinklao, Thanon Barom Ratchachonnani, Thonburi (0 2884 8452-4/ www.brunswicksiam.com). Bus 11, 57, 146, 149, 201, 503.* **Open** 10.30am-1am Mon-Fri; 10am-1am Sat, Sun. **Rates** B70-B80. **Credit** AmEx, MC, V.
A modern bowling alley with fluorescent-hued 'Cosmic' disco bowling on weekend evenings.
**Branches**: RCA Plaza, Thanon Petchaburi, North (0 2641 5870-3); Seacon Square, Thanon Sri Nakharin, East (0 2721 8310-4).

#### Kim Bowl
*7th Floor, Mahboonkrong (MBK) Centre, Thanon Phayathai, Pathumwan (0 2611 7171-4). National Stadium BTS.* **Open** 10am-1am Mon-Thur; 10am-2am Fri-Sun. **Rates** B70-B90. **Credit** MC, V. **Map** p309 & p310 F5.
A snazzy bowling alley with equipment hire and weekend disco bowling.

### Chess & Go

Ubiquitous games of Thai chess (which has slightly simpler rules and uses Siamese-style pieces) can be seen in parks and at roadsides, but for international rules, the **Thailand Chess Club** meets upstairs at O'Reilly's (*see p126*), where blitz games are faster than the drinking. Serious contests take place every Friday. The subtle territorial game of Go, which came from China via Japan, is hugely popular; contact the **Thai Go Association** (0 2677 1628/9) for details.

### Diving

#### Planet Scuba
*5th Floor, Soi Klang Racquet Club, Sukhumvit Soi 49/9, Sukhumvit (0 2712 8188/www.thewildplanet. com). Thonglor BTS.* **Open** *Training* 10am-6pm daily. **Rates** B8,000-B12,500. **Credit** AmEx, DC, MC, V. **Map** p312 L5.
Start your PADI certification in town and complete it qualifying at sea during one of the regular diving trips. For more details, *see p242* **Learn to: Dive**.

**Lumphini Park** doubles as an open-air sports centre. *See p206.*

## Football

If you want to join in a casual game, call the **British Club** (0 2234 0247).

### New International School of Thailand (NIST)

*Sukhumvit Soi 15, Sukhumvit (0 2651 2065). Asoke BTS/Sukhumvit subway.* **Open** 6-10pm Mon-Fri; 10am-10pm Sat, Sun. **Rates** *Pitches* B2,400 10am-6pm; B2,800 6-10pm. **No credit cards. Map** p311 J5.
Covered all-weather pitches for five-a-side matches.

## Golf

Well-appointed golf courses surround Bangkok, Chiang Mai, Chiang Rai, Kanchanaburi, Khao Yai, Pattaya and Phuket (you'll need a car or taxi). Many are designed by star names, such as Player, Nicklaus and others, and the bargain green fees have Japanese visitors flying in to play and still saving money. You should tip caddies B100.

### Bangkok Golf Club

*99 Thanon Tiwanon, Pathum Thani province (0 2501 2828/www.golf.th.com).* **Open** 6am-midnight daily. **Rates** *18 holes* B1,600 Mon-Fri; B2,600 Sat, Sun. *Caddy* B210. **Credit** AmEx, DC, MC, V.
Nine interesting par-three holes, each designed after a world-famous hole. The club is 20 minutes from town by expressway.

### Bangsai Country Club

*Thanon Thangluang (Route 3111), Ayutthaya province (0 3537 1494/5/6/7).* **Open** 7am-4pm Mon-Fri; 6.30am-3pm Sat, Sun. **Rates** *18 holes* B320 Mon-Fri; B580 Sat, Sun. *Caddy* B200. **Credit** MC, V.
Popular, challenging course with well-tended greens.

# Learn to Muay Thai

Fit visitors are increasingly taking up *Muay Thai* – reputedly the world's most violent martial art, allowing everything except headbutting. It's possible to live and train in gyms, such as **Fairtex**, designed for dollar-paying visitors, or to slum it – literally – at the temporary gyms that are set up to train deprived kids in the Klong Toey docklands. Khao San backpackers head for **Sor Worapin**.

The first move to learn is the round kick to the body: your shin against the padded trainer. After several days of this, the nerve ends in your legs die and the hairs fall out – useful for when you start hitting real (harder) body parts as you move up to sparring.

Trainers put you through the paces of their fitness regimens and will even train you until they think you're ready to fight at one of the many minor stadiums. Some overseas fighters have followed this path to become world champions, and the World Muay Thai Championships are no longer dominated by Thais. In fact, the sport has been scheduled for demonstration status at the 2004 Olympics.

In recent years women have also started trading kicks and elbow blows, enraging traditionalists. Although trained for defence centuries ago, women haven't been allowed in the ring because it was believed they would offend the ring spirits to whom all boxers pay homage in the *wai khru* ceremony before each bout (this is a tradition that foreign fighters must also observe, insists the World Muay Thai Council; 0 2280 7251/2).

This clean, sensitive image is at odds with the professional code, which is plagued by under-age boxing and accusations of drugging fighters to benefit gamblers. New laws banning match-fixing and under-15s are rarely enforced. Boys (mostly from impoverished Isaan) still begin as young as seven at *ngan wat* (temple fairs), from where scouts bring prodigies to the capital. At B500 a fight, with five fights a month, many become the family breadwinner.

### Fairtex

*99/5 Soi Boonthamanusorn, Thanon Theparak, Samut Prakarn (0 2385 5148/9/ www.fairtexbkk.com). Bus 2, 144, 511, 513 to Imperial World Samrong then songthaew.* **Open** 6-8.30am, 4-6.30pm daily. **Rates** $15 per day; $150-$200 per wk. **Credit** MC, V.
A *Muay Thai* camp with upmarket facilities, in an out-of-town garden setting.

### Pudthaisawan Sword Fighting Institute

*5/1 Thanon Petcha Kasem, Nongkaem, Thonburi (0 2421 1906). Bus 80, 163.* **Open** 9am-3pm Mon-Tue, Thur-Sun. **Rates** B300 per hr; courses B3,500-B35,000. **No credit cards**.

## No 1 Driving Range

*19/7 Thanon Pracha Utith, North-east (0 2935 6270).* **Open** 10am-1am daily. **Rates** B100 per 4 trays 10.30am-1.30pm, 10.30pm-1am; B35 per tray 1.30pm-10.30pm. **No credit cards**.
This driving range offers top-class nets, with landscaped holes, bunkers and water hazards, plus a bar, Japanese restaurant and coaching.

### Royal Thai Army Golf Club

*459 Thanon Ramindra, North-east (0 2521 1530/ www.rta.mi.th/armygolf). Bus 26, 512.* **Open** 5am-6pm daily. **Rates** *18 holes* B900 Mon-Fri; B1,200 Sat, Sun. *Caddy* B200. **No credit cards**.
There are two fine, good-value courses here, close to town by expressway.

## Gyms & sports centres

**Lumphini Park** in Pathumwan is not just a major green space, but a casual sports venue. People jog and powerwalk the paths, dunk basketballs, tap *takraw* balls or pump (and pose) in open-air gyms, most sensibly at dawn and dusk. Thousands greet sunrise by practising martial arts or playing Thai chess or Chinese chequers. The same is true (to a lesser extent) of **Saranrom Park** and **Benjasiri Park**. Some hotel health clubs also have day rates. For good value, there's also **Silom City Fitness** (*see p178*).

### California Fitness

*Liberty Square, Thanon Silom, Bangrak (0 2631 1122/www.calfitnesscenters.com). Saladaeng BTS/ Silom subway.* **Open** 6am-midnight Mon-Sat; 8am-10pm Sun. **Rates** B1,000 per day. **Credit** AmEx, DC, MC, V. **Map** p310 F7.
A multi-floor, all-hours gym with immodest window walls, hi-tech machines, loud music, huge classes and a hard-sell attitude – but no swimming pool. It's part of a global chain.

### Fitness First

*4th Floor, Landmark Plaza, Landmark Hotel, Thanon Sukhumvit, Sukhumvit (0 2653 2424). Nana*

Arts & Entertainment

Along with how to wield swords and pikes (one in each hand!), Thais and non-Thais can learn *Muay Thai* and the Thai stick martial art *krabi-krabong*. Visitors can view apprentices in action. Steven Segal pays his respects here, and the *wai khru* ceremony is held on 5 May.

### Sor Worapin

*Thanon Chakraphong, Banglamphu (0 2282 3551). Bus 3, 30, 32, 64, 65, 506.* **Open** *7.30-9.30am, 3-6pm daily.* **Rates** B500 per day; B2,000 per wk; B6,000 per mth. **No credit cards.** **Map** p308 B3.

Formerly called Jitti's Gym, Sor Worapin has one ring and basic lodging at the end of a small *soi*. Expect lots of backpackers.

*BTS.* **Open** 6am-10pm daily. **Rates** B428 per day; B2,000 per mth (min 3 mths). **Credit** AmEx, DC, MC, V. **Map** p311 J5.

A well-equipped UK rival chain to California Fitness. It's a less hyper place, but also lacks a swimming pool.

### National Stadium Hua Mark

*Thanon Ramkhamhaeng, Hua Mark, East (0 2318 0940/1). Bus 22, 40, 58, 60, 71, 93, 109, 115, 168, 501, 512.* **Open** *Gym* 7am-9pm Tue-Fri; 10am-9pm Sat, Sun. *Pool* 6am-8pm Tue-Fri. **Rates** *Gym* B15; B375 per yr (gym plus any 2 sports). *Pool* B30 6am-6pm Tue-Fri; B50 6pm-8pm Tue-Fri. **No credit cards.**

The indoor stadium, velodrome, Ratchamangala Stadium and other facilities were used for the 2002 Asian Games.

### National Stadium Pathumwan

*Thanon Rama I, Pathumwan (0 2214 0120/ www.krompala2.com). National Stadium BTS.* **Open** *Gym* 8.30am-7.30pm Mon-Fri. *Pool* 4.30-6.30pm Tue-Fri; 9.30-noon, 1-6pm Sat, Sun. *Tennis*

6am-9pm daily. **Admission** *Gym* B10. *Pool* B30; B20 concessions. *Tennis* B30 per hr 6am-6pm; B50 per hr 6-9pm. **No credit cards. Map** p309 & 310 F4.

This stadium hosts Premier League soccer matches, and also offers two gyms, a 50m laned pool and ten tennis courts. It's flanked by sports shops. Annual rates are also available.

### Soi Klang Racquet Club

*Sukhumvit Soi 49/9, Sukhumvit (0 2712 80101/ 2/3/4/www.rqclub.com). Thonglor BTS.* **Open** 7am-10.30pm daily. **Rates** B360 per day Mon-Fri; B450 per day Sat, Sun; B8,000 per yr. **No credit cards. Map** p312 L5.

A smart sports centre with tennis, squash, badminton and basketball courts, plus snooker, swimming, gym and a branch of Dance Centre (0 2712 8323/www.dance-centre.com).

## Horse riding

There are also options outside Bangkok: namely in **Hua Hin** and **Pattaya**.

### Garden City Polo Club

*Thanon Bangna-Trad, Samut Prakarn province (0 2707 1534/5/6/7/8).* **Open** 9am-11am, 2.30-4.30pm Tue-Sun. **Rates** B800 per hr, B700 per hr concessions Tue-Fri; B200 per hr, B800 per hr concessions Sat, Sun. **No credit cards.**

This residential country club has excellent facilities, but is more than an hour from town (with no public transport). Jumping and dressage take place in a small ring. Coaching is also available; call for details.

## Ice skating

### World Trade Centre

*8th Floor, 4 Thanon Ratchadamri, Pathumwan (0 2255 9400). Chidlom BTS.* **Open** 10am-8.30pm Mon-Fri; 10am-2.45pm, 3.30-8.30pm Sat, Sun. **Admission** B130. **Credit** MC, V. **Map** p312 G5.

The WTC rink's fine facilities and equipment for hire, along with good European coaches and low prices, draw kids of ambitious foreign parents.

## Martial arts

You can also direct your energy in disciplines like t'ai chi at **Lumphini Park** from 4.30am to 8am daily or in *krabi-krabong*, the Thai stick martial art, at the **Pudthaisawan Sword Fighting Institute** (*see p206* **Learn to: Muay Thai**).

### SMAC

*1st Floor, Q House Building, Sukhumvit Soi 66, Sukhumvit (0 2264 2202-3). Asoke BTS/Sukhumvit subway.* **Open** 6.30am-10pm Mon-Fri; 9am-6pm Sat, Sun. **Rates** B200 per day; B1,500 per mth. **Credit** MC, V. **Map** p312 K5.

This modern facility offers many disciplines, as well as self-defence classes for women.

*Arts & Entertainment*

# The best Pools

### For lap swimming
The laned, saline expanses at **Pathumwan Princess**. *See p44.*

### For showing your strokes
... and togs. It must be the **Sukhothai** hotel's natty natatorium. *See p48.*

### For paddling with a panorama
Riverscape and skyscraper skyline meet at the **Peninsula** hotel's string of canalside dips. *See p39.*

### For tropical island fantasies
The amorphous jungle lagoon at the **Hilton International**. *See p43.*

### For urban seaside *sanuk*
**Siam Park**'s artificial streams, falls, waves, flumes and cement beach. *See p163.*

## Running

For scenic runs with Thais, contact **Jog & Joy** (0 2741 1900/www.jogandjoy.com).

### Hash House Harriers
*www.bangkokhhh.com.* **Runs** *Mixed* 5-6.30pm Mon, Wed, Sat. *Men only* 5-6.30pm Sun.
This social club of mad dogs and Englishmen runs around in the sun then gets pissed. Hash House Bikers do likewise, but with bicycles. Silly names are compulsory.

## Sepak Takraw

An acrobatic game in which players knock a woven rattan ball over a net, volleyball style. In a rarer variant, players tap the ball through a high hoop. But *takraw* is losing ground to soccer, despite Thai victories in both the men's and women's 2002 World Takraw Cup. There are nets in parks and at the two **National Stadiums** (*see p207*).

## Snooker

Many of Bangkok's numerous snooker dens are noted for iniquity, gambling and dodgy customers, though they generally have decent tables, straight cues and cheap, late-night beers.

### Pro Q Snooker
*5th Floor, Charn Issara Tower I, Thanon Rama IV, Bangrak (0 2234 0011). Saladaeng BTS/Silom subway.* **Open** 9am-2am daily. **Rates** B120 per hr. **No credit cards. Map** p311 G6.

Pro Q in Bangrak is one of the respectable snooker parlours, with 11 tables to choose from.

## Swimming

Crawl to hotels or the **YMCA**. Otherwise, the **National Stadium Pathumwan** has a 50-metre pool with lanes (*see p207*). *See also left* **The best: Pools.**

### Barracuda Club
*Soi Pipat, Thanon Silom, Bangrak (0 2237 5090). Saladaeng BTS/Silom subway.* **Open** 6am-8pm Mon-Fri; 7am-8pm Sat; 10am-7pm Sun. **Rates** B200 per day; B1,800 per mth; B1,000 per mth concessions. **Credit** V. **Map** p310 F7.
The nicely named Barracuda is a centrally located single pool with good facilities.

### Thai-Japan Centre
*Thanon Wiphawadiragsit, North-east (0 2245 3360). Bus 24, 69, 92.* **Open** 10.30am-9pm daily. **Rates** B15; B40 per yr. **No credit cards.**
An excellent pool that even has starting blocks for wannabe Thorpedos.

## Tennis

You'll mostly find hard courts with ball boys, racquet hire and coaching; contact the **Lawn Tennis Association of Thailand** (0 2504 4381/2) for details of facilities. There are also courts for hire at the **National Stadium Pathumwan** and **Soi Klang Raquet Club** (for both, *see p207*).

### Central Tennis Court
*Thanon Sathorn Soi 1, Bangrak (0 2213 1909). Bus 17, 22, 35, 62, 67, 116, 149.* **Open** 6am-10pm daily. **Rates** B100 per hr 10am-2pm; B120 per hr 6am-10am, 2-6pm; B200 per hr 6-10pm. **No credit cards. Map** p310 F7.

Siamese fighting fish.

Five good hard courts, with coaching, racquet hire and a semi open-air Thai cafeteria. It gets crowded during the cooler hours, so book ahead.

## Spectator sports

### Boxing (Western)

At any moment, Thailand is likely to have a good few pro world champions. World title bouts often take place in upcountry venues; for more information, contact the **Thai Boxing Association** (0 2280 7251/2).

### Cock fighting

Battling birds with heel spurs is bloody and illegal, but nonetheless common in villages on Bangkok's outskirts (where indiscretions are legion despite having referees and 'cock doctors'). Breeding is a serious business – witness Kamnan Vichien's Fighting Cock Farm (3 Moo 9, Thanon Suan Samphan, Nong Chok, East, 0 2543 1425) – and combat cocks are sold cagily at Chatuchak Weekend Market (*see p134*), though less openly than pirated goods.

### Fish fighting

Contests between iridescent male *pla kad* (Siamese fighting fish) are unlawful, yet happen on weekends in Chatuchak Market. You may overhear word around the shops in Section 9, or in the adjacent Sunday market.

### Football

Check with the **Football Association of Thailand** (0 2216 4579/www.thaifootball.com) for info on league and international games.

### Horse racing

One of two sports where gambling is legal (*Muay Thai* is the other). Wise punters delay betting until they see a horse's odds moving just after the due start times; the 'off' can be ten minutes late. Illegal gambling is rife, but there's always a great atmosphere – it's one of the few areas where rich and poor fraternise.

#### Royal Bangkok Sports Club (RBSC)
*1 Thanon Henri Dunant, Pathumwan (0 2255 1420/ 1/2/3/4/5).* Bus 16, 21, 45, 141. **Races** noon-6pm 2nd & 4th Sun of the mth. **Admission** B50-B100. **No credit cards. Map** p311 G5.
A venerable, century-old club with wide-ranging facilities, whose members basically either own or run the country. Members only, except during races.

#### Royal Turf Club
*183 Thanon Phitsanulok, Dusit (0 2628 1810/1/2/ 3/4/5).* Bus 201, 509. **Races** 11am-6pm 1st & 3rd Sun of the mth. **Admission** B50-B100. **No credit cards. Map** p309 E2.
A tight track visible from the Dusit traffic jams.

### Motor sports

North of Pattaya, **Bira International Speedway** (Highway 36, km14; office 0 2971 6450/www.grandprixgroup.com) is Thailand's principal motorsport circuit. Open 9am-5pm daily, it also has a museum about Prince Bira.

### Muay Thai

Indigenous kick boxing is a compelling, if gruesome spectacle, with the pugilists and crowd whipped up by ever more fervent music. Equally fascinating are the wildly gesticulating gamblers – the sport is exempt from gambling bans, along with horse racing and legal lotteries. Top pro fights are held at **Lumphini** and **Ratchadamnoen Stadiums**, each offfering similarly basic facilities and equipment shops. Ticket prices are inflated for foreigners, who wisely favour the ringside seats. To learn the art yourself, *see p206* **Learn to: Muay Thai**.

#### Lumphini Stadium
*Thanon Rama IV, beside Suan Lum Night Bazaar, Pathumwan (0 2251 4303). Lumphini subway/ bus 14, 47, 74, 109, 507.* **Open** 6.30-10.30pm Tue, Fri; 5-8pm Sat; 8.30pm-midnight Sun. **Tickets** B500 3rd class; B800 2nd class; B1,500 ringside. **No credit cards. Map** p311 H7.

#### Ratchadamnoen Stadium
*1 Thanon Ratchadamnoen Nok, Phra Nakorn (0 2281 4205).* Bus 157, 201, 503, 509. **Open** 6-10.30pm Mon, Wed, Sun; 5-10.30pm Sat. **Tickets** B500 3rd class; B800 2nd class; B1,500 ringside. **No credit cards. Map** p308 B3.

**Arts & Entertainment**

# Beyond Bangkok

# Getting Started

Touring Thailand made easy.

Most visitors to Bangkok also travel elsewhere in Thailand – not surprisingly, since the country (the size of France and shaped like an elephant's head) is justly famed for its natural and cultural diversity. More than ten million tourists a year enjoy its beaches, mountains, jungles, reefs, heritage and ethnic cultures. But it's possible to escape the crowds, since there's always another island to hop to, village to visit or specialist tour to suit your interests.

Travelling is fairly easy on an improving infrastructure, although chasing information and adhering to schedules can be challenging. Destinations close to Bangkok can be visited as day trips or en route to elsewhere. Longer hops, preferably by plane or sleeper train, are required to reach the south or north.

North of Bangkok, the fertile **Central Plains** are dotted with the ancient Thai cities of **Ayutthaya**, **Lopburi** and **Sukhothai**. To the west lie the national parks and 'Death Railway' of **Kanchanaburi**, the palaces of **Phetchburi** and the upper Gulf of Thailand resorts of **Hua Hin** and **Cha-am**. The **Eastern Seaboard** has become industrially crucial, but is most visited for its beach resorts, from poorly planned **Pattaya** and beach party isle **Ko Samet** to the currently developing **Ko Chang**.

To the south, the lower Gulf of Thailand is dominated by the **Samui Archipelago**, comprising laid-back resort island **Ko Samui**, backpacker rave retreat **Ko Pha-ngan** and divers' delight **Ko Tao**. On the other side of the peninsula, the **Andaman Coast** contains the world-famous resort island of **Phuket** and emerging beach idylls **Krabi** and **Ko Lanta**,

as well as remoter adventure playgrounds such as **Ko Tarutao**. In the north, **Chiang Mai** has retained much of its distinctive charm while expanding into a centre of commerce, slick design and New Age spirituality. Around Chiang Mai it's easy to tour the north Thailand, from **Lampang** and the **Mae Hong Son Loop** to **Chiang Rai** and the **Golden Triangle**.

Naturally, there's more of Thailand to experience between and beyond these particular highlights. The tour companies listed in this chapter can help you explore the western border, deep south, far north and north-east (Isaan) and even the country's greater Mekong neighbours: Cambodia, Laos, Vietnam, Burma and Yunnan, China.

The **Tourism Authority of Thailand** (TAT; 0 2250 5500) offers a wealth of impressive information that is available online (www.tat.or.th), and may be accessed from its variable offices in major centres. Tour agencies often have more accommodation and activity options. Public transport isn't very integrated or savvy, so maps and timetables for trains and buses aren't always decipherable, or even followed. But travelling among Thais is usually a more interesting experience than sticking with other tourists, particularly on trains.

## Travelling around Thailand

### By air

Well served by US airstrips left over from the Vietnam War, Thailand's skies have recently bloomed with several domestic rivals

**Beyond Bangkok**

## The best National parks

Whatever your interest, there's a park to suit:

**For tropical rainforest**
Khao Sok. *See p252.*

**For temperate rainforest**
Doi Inthanon. *See p274.*

**For marine life**
The **Similan Islands**. *See p252.*

**For wetlands**
Khao Sam Roi Yot. *See p228.*

**For pristine islands**
Ko Taruatao (*see p256*) and **Ang Thong** (*see p244*).

**For wildlife**
Khao Yai (*see p216* **Wild at heart**) and **Kaeng Krachan** (*see 228*).

to **Thai Airways** (reservations 0 2628 2000/
www.thaiairways.com). **Bangkok Airways**
(reservations 0 2265 5555/www.bangkokair.
com), has built private stunning airports at
Sukhothai, Samui and Trad, uses new ones at
Hua Hin and Krabi and has won awards for
networking the heritage honeypots of east Asia.
For other airlines, *see p281*.

## By bus & minibus

*Rot tour* (inter-provincial buses) are the
mainstay of ordinary Thais and often sell out,
so it's best to book ahead through travel agents,
hotels or bus terminals. Buses without air-con
can be gruelling and cramped; *rot air* (air-
conditioned buses) may be roomier, particularly
the VIP buses serving food and drink, though
overnighting by road is draining as drivers can
be reckless. Be alert to the security of your bags
and valuables. Website www.transport.co.th
provides information on all bus terminals.

Hiring a minibus with a driver is a great
solution for self-guided trips (B1,500-B1,800
per day trip, overnight around B2,000 per day),
from car rental firms (*see p284*) and travel
agents. Minibuses run regularly for upcountry
destinations, calling in particular at
Banglamphu and Soi Ngam Duphlee.

### Eastern Bus Terminal

*300 Thanon Sukhumvit, near Soi 42, Sukhumvit
(0 2391 8097). Ekamai BTS.* **Open** 6am-midnight
daily. **No credit cards. Map** p312 M7/8.
This station is commonly known as Ekkamai.

### Northern & North-eastern
### Bus Terminal

*999 Thanon Kamphaeng Phet 2, North (0 2936
2852-66). Bus 3, 49, 77, 104, 122, 134, 136,
138, 139, 157, 512, 517, 523.* **Open** 24hrs daily.
**Credit** MC, V.
Often called Morchit, this station also serves the
central region.

### Southern Bus Terminal

*147 Thanon Boromratchachonnani, Thonburi
(0 2435 5605). Bus 19, 28, 30, 40, 57, 66, 123,
503, 507, 511, 516.* **Open** 4am-1am daily.
**Credit** V.
Sometimes nicknamed Sai Tai Mai, buses from here
also serve the west.

## By car

Regional highways are often better surfaced
than city roads, with plentiful food, toilet and
fuel stops, but unpredictable road users. Roads
are numbered according to the size: single-digit
arteries, two-digit highways, three-digit main
roads and four-digit minor roads. Exiting
Bangkok is quickest via elevated expressways

to Chonburi (east), Bang Pa-In (north) and
Taling Chan–Nakhon Chaisri (west).

*See p284* for car rental agencies, or try
**Krungthai Car Rent** (0 2291 8888/
www.krungthai.co.th) or **Lumpini Car Rent**
(0 2255 1966-8). For route advice, contact the
**Department of Highways** (0 2245 5277/
www.doh.motc.go.th). The **Transportation
Safety Centre** (0 2280 8000/hotline 1356)
and **Highway Police** (hotline 1193) can assist
with road-related problems.

## By train

The century-old **State Railway of Thailand**
(0 2621 8701/2220 4567/www.srt.or.th) runs
lines north, north-east, east, west and south,
mostly from Bangkok's Italianate
**Hualumpong station** (*see p283*). Trains are
slow but entertaining, good value and more
scenic and roomier than buses or planes.
Express trains have second-class fan or air-
conditioned seats that fold into beds; some
have first-class air-con private cabins. Stopping
trains have third-class wooden benches with
fans. Long-distance and sleeper services leave
mainly in the late afternoon. Seats do sell out,
but you can book three to 60 days ahead by
phone or at stations.

The State Railway also runs train tours
every Saturday, Sunday and on public holidays
(usually 6.30am-7.50pm). Tours include
Damnoen Saduak floating market; River Kwai
and rafting; and Cha-am, Hua Hin and Suan
Son beaches. On Thai Railway Day (26 Mar),
King Chulalongkorn Day (23 Oct) and the
King's Birthday (5 Dec), a steam train leaves
Hualumpong station at 8am to Ayutthaya
(B100 return). Tour company **Real Asia** (*see
p54*) also runs train-based tours.

### Eastern & Oriental Express

*0 2267 4670/www.orient-express.com.*
**Credit** AmEx, DC, MC, V.
Asia's retro luxury train runs to and from Bangkok
and Singapore twice a month, in both directions.
The trip takes three days, stopping at Kanchanaburi
and Butterworth (in Malaysia), with an extension
to Chiang Mai in the north.

## Specialist tours

Most Bangkok tour agencies also go upcountry.
Among the bigger companies, **Diethelm
Travel** (0 2255 9150-70/www.diethelm-
travel.com) and **Asian Trails** (0 2658 6080-9/
www.asiantrails.com) have discerning
packages. The **Siam Society** (*see p97*)
runs study trips with experts to cultural and
archeological sites (often getting privileged
access). Spas, meditation retreats and massage

An alternative travel option: slow but stately.

courses (for all, *see chapter* **Mind & Body**) are New Age temptations, while agro-tourism encompasses farms, plantations, Royal Projects and village homestays.

### Asia Voyages
*0 2256 7168/9/www.asiavoyagesonline.com.*
**Credit** AmEx, MC, V.
This French-run pioneer of comfy rooms in hill-tribe villages offers combinations of treks, cycling, elephant riding, rafting and cooking classes, linking nights in charming Lisu Lodge, rustic Lahu Outpost and tranquil Lanna Farm. It also runs Mekong river trips into Laos, and the sumptuous Mekhala cruise from Bangkok to Ayutthaya, which includes an overnight mooring near Bang Pa-In.

### Bike & Travel
*0 2990 0274/www.cyclingthailand.com.*
**No credit cards.**
Cycling and canoe tour packages all over Thailand, tailored to different fitness levels. Also hires and sells gear, bikes and Mad River canoes.

### Circle of Asia
*0 2650 8655/www.circleofasia.com.* **Credit** AmEx, DC, MC, V.
A Thai-based web counselling service, with cultural expertise, for visitors to Thailand or Indochina.

### Royal Thai Army Tourism
*0 2297 5904/www.rta.mi.th.*
Much pristine land is in military camps, and is now open to the public for hardy treks, obstacle courses and tower jumps, plus riding, sharpshooting and the generals' favourite: golf. Chulachomklao Royal Military Academy, near Khao Yai (0 3739 3010-4 ext 62960/1/www.crma.ac.th) offers biking, canoeing, hiking, camping and climbing.

## Eco tours

A much-hijacked term, so check the **Thailand Eco-Tourism & Adventure Travel Association** (www.thaieco-adventure.org). The following have good reputations, as do kayak explorers **Sea Canoe** (*see p252*).

### Bird Conservation Society of Thailand
*0 2943 5965/www.bcst.org.* **No credit cards**.
Runs field trips, the Thai Birdwatching Festival (Oct) as part of Japan's World Bird Count, and the Thailand Bird Race (Dec; *see p157*).

### Friends of Nature
*0 2642 4426/7/www.friendsofnature93.com).*
**Credit** AmEx, DC, MC, V.
Activities in natural, historical and cultural sites for different age or interest groups, including bird-watching, snorkelling, rafting, waterfalls, trekking and elephant rides.

### Lost Horizons
*0 2860 3963/www.losthorizonsasia.com.*
Eco-minded adventure tourism, from nature and culture to rafting, diving and trekking, plus turtle conservation volunteering.

### Nature Trails
*0 2735 0644/www.naturetrailsthailand.com.*
**No credit cards.**
Weekend birdwatching trips led by Kamol Komolphalin, bilingual ornithologist and illustrator of *A Guide to the Birds of Thailand*.

### REST
*0 2938 7007/www.ecotour.in.th.* **No credit cards**.
Responsible Ecological Social Tours runs sensitive village homestays to learn about life in communities in the north and south.

### Wild Watch Thailand
*0 1821 2575/www.wildwatchthailand.com.*
**Credit** MC, V.
A variety of field trips led by a UK naturalist and a US wildlife biologist, from 'comfy camping' to hands-on research. Donates 5% to rural projects.

**Beyond Bangkok**

# Wild at heart

Though Thailand has lost most of its formerly massive forest cover to logging, agriculture, mining and other 'development', the country protects an impressive 38 million *rai* (23,475 square miles) in a growing roster of 110 national parks, plus wildlife sanctuaries. Each accessible park is detailed, with accommodation, on **www.thaiparks123.com**.

Several are marine parks offering great diving and kayak exploration, despite some damage from fishing, tourism and climate phenomena, and the loss of fish-spawning mangroves to prawn farms. Also encroached upon, wetlands offer rewards for birdspotters, though most visitors want to explore the remaining intact jungle. Tropical rainforest in the south gives way to animal-rich, semi-evergreen forests and then deciduous monsoon forest further north. The favourite all-rounder is **Khao Yai National Park**.

Thais are becoming more environmentally aware, though, to be frank, trippers on public holidays heedlessly pollute waterfalls, mountains and beauty spots with noise, litter and golf balls in pursuit of *sanuk*. Worse, hunting persists: to supply illegal wildlife restaurants for largely north-east Asian custom, and for species smuggling that flouts the CITES convention. Logging was banned in 1988 after deforestation caused fatal landslides, though recent floods signal threats to watershed cover from illegal logging, and from slash'n'burn agriculture by the northern hill tribes.

The underfunded parks have increased their fees to B200 for a foreigner, though their future rests on three gambles taken in 2002. A controversial Community Forest Act allows 'sustainable' human presence in wildernesses, to preserve traditional lifestyles and support medicinal forest resources. The government also ordered national parks to become 'profit centres' and decreed that **Ko Chang** (*see p234*) will become an eco-friendly 'new Phuket'. Much that has been heroically preserved is being bet at one go. But, on past record, will nature win?

## Khao Yai National Park

*Khao Yai Visitor Centre, Thanon Thanarat km37, Amphoe Muang, Nakorn Nayok province (0 3731 9002). Via Friendship Highway (route 2), Saraburi & Pak Chong to Thanon Thanarat.* **Open** 8.30am-4.30pm daily. **Admission** Thais B20; foreigners B200.

Thailand's first national park (founded in 1962), and its second largest (2,168 square kilometres/837 square miles) is also the most visited, being just 200 kilometres (124 miles) from Bangkok. Straddling four provinces on the threshold of the Khorat Plateau, this mostly old-growth tropical rainforest is some 400 metres (1,312 feet) above sea level. Warm clothing is necessary if you want to trek its myriad trails, particularly in the most popular cool season when you get the best of its many *namtok* (waterfalls).

The waterfalls feature on most of the 12 trails from the visitor centre. The highest and biggest is **Namtok Haew Narok**, with three levels totalling 150 metres (492 feet), while **Namtok Heo Suwat** (filmed in *The Beach*) has a swimmable pool. Two days' hiking and jungle camping is required to see the most stunning, **Namtok Wang Heo**. Around 50 metres (164 feet) wide, its abundant flora and fauna include gibbons, hornbills, tigers, loris, deer, clouded leopards and Thailand's biggest wild herd of elephants. The animals congregate at water sources more in the hot season, and dissipate during the wet, when trekking is more treacherous and leech-prone.

Information and hiking permits are available from the entry gates and the visitor centre, where there's rudimentary accommodation and cheap food. Rangers run truck-borne **Night Safaris** (B300), with variable results, and accompany all tours, of which the most reputable is **Wildlife Safari** (0 4431 2922; B1,150 per day and a half).

The park is surrounded by golf courses and resorts that offer restaurants and tours. Most luxurious is **Juldis Khao Yai Resort** (54 Thanon Thanarat km17, Pakchong, 0 4429 7297/www.khaoyai.com, main courses B130, rates B2,420-B7,865). **Khao Yai Garden Lodge** (135/1 Thanon Thanarat km7, Pakchong, 0 4436 5178/www.khaoyai-garden-lodge.com, main courses B80, rates B100-B1,800) has a diversity of rooms and good tours. **Cabbages & Condoms Resort** (98 Moo 6, Phaya Yen, Pak Chong, 0 3622 7065, main courses B100, rates B2,000-B5,000) offers the non-profit development agency's fine Thai food and tours that explore jungle and rural lifestyles. Cheaper is the **Jungle House** (21/5 Thanon Thanarat km19.5, Pakchong, 0 4429 7307, main courses B70, rates B450-B800).

# Central Plains

A heartland of ancient kingdoms, floating market values and right royal resorts.

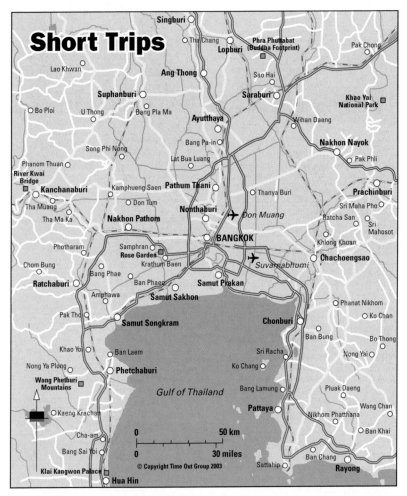

**Short Trips**

The Chao Phraya river valley, one of the world's grain baskets, has supported the Thai kingdoms of **Sukhothai** and **Ayutthaya**, as well as ancient Mon centres like **Lopburi** and **Nakhon Pathom**. To the north-east stand impressive Khmer citadels at **Phimai** and **Phanom Rung**. Remnants of the primeval rainforest are accessible in **Khao Yai** (*see p216* **Wild at heart**) and **Kanchanaburi** province, where the 'Death Railway' was carved along the River Kwai. The Thai resort industry began on the **Upper Gulf Coast**, with royal retreats at **Petchaburi**, **Cha-am** and **Hua Hin**. All these lie within a day's, or overnight, reach of Bangkok.

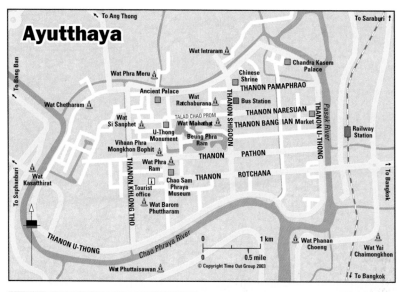

Map caption / labels:

Ayutthaya

To Ang Thong
To Saraburi

To Bang Ban
Wat Intraram

Chandra Kasem Palace

Wat Phra Meru
Chinese Shrine

Ancient Palace
THANON PAMAPHRAO

Wat Chetharam
Wat Ratchaburana

Bus Station

THANON SHIGOON
THANON NARESUAN

Wat Si Sanphet
TALAD CHAO PROM
Wat Mahathat
THANON BANG IAN Market

To Bang Ban

Pasak River

THANON U-THONG
Railway Station

U-Thong Monument
Beung Phra Ram

Vihaan Phra Mongkhon Bophit
THANON
PATHON

Wat Phra Ram
THANON

To Suphanburi

THANON KHLONG THO
Chao Sam Phraya Museum
THANON
ROTCHANA

Wat Kasatthirat
Tourist office
Wat Barom Phuttharam

To Bangkok

THANON U-THONG
Chao Phraya River

0        1 km
0     0.5 mile
© Copyright Time Out Group 2003

Wat Phanan Choeng
Wat Yai Chaimongkhon

Wat Phuttaisawan
To Bangkok

# Ancient Cities

Heading upstream, preferably by riverboat, you can retrace the development of Thai civilisation. Within day-trip range are the Mon islet of **Ko Kred**, the 19th-century **Bang Pa-in** summer palace and the ruined Siamese capital of **Ayutthaya**. Rarely visited gems include **Lopburi**, key to several empires over 16 centuries, and the north-eastern Khmer sanctuaries of **Phimai** and **Phanom Rung**.

## Upriver to Bang Pa-in

North of Nonthaburi Expressboat Pier you can reach Ko Kred on longtails or boat tours from Bangkok, while day trips to Bang Sai, Bang Pa-In and Ayutthaya usually combine boat, minibus or train (*see p220* **Boat trips**).

On the west bank, **Wat Chaloem Prakiat** in Nonthaburi was founded by Rama III in memory of his mother. Next door, **Chalerm Kanchanaphisek Park** is culturally themed, with *salas* on stilts, canals, orchards and a planned library and exhibition space.

A rural, car-free islet, **Ko Kred** is renowned for the carved Mon ceramics at its north-eastern settlement. Facing the mainland's Pakkred ferry pier, **Wat Poramai** has a stunning Buddha image, a museum and two Mon-style *chedi*, one slipping into the river. Under the queen's patronage, rare crafts like nielloware, *yan lipao*

weaving and iridescent beetle jewellery have been saved through training to diversify farmers' incomes at **Bang Sai Folk Arts & Crafts Centre** (0 35366 252-4/www. bangsaiarts.com, admission B100), 51 kilometres (32 miles) from Bangkok.

About 53 kilometres (33 miles) from Bangkok, **Bang Pa-In** summer palace (0 3526 1673-82/ www.palaces.thai.net, B100) has been a retreat from realpolitik since 1632. Named after a drowned princess and transformed by Rama V in 1872, the island looks extraordinary. Flanked by ponds, topiary and lawns it's a collage of baroque, Gothic and Chinese styles. The dazzling Chinese **Wehat Chamrun Palace** contrasts with the simple **Wat Nivet Dhammaparvat**, near a pier where longtail boats can be hired for a scenic 45-minute trip to Ayutthaya. Tour parties engulf Bang Pa-in before having lunch in Ayutthaya, so try to visit later.

## Ayutthaya

This UNESCO World Heritage Site is an essential visit. Not only are the former capital's remains impressive, but its fall is a cataclysm that still reverberates, as in recent films about resisting Burma. With its 400 temples razed and 90 per cent of its people gone, the scorched red-brick ruins were abandoned (and much looted) until Prime Minister Phibun tidied it into a showpiece in the 1950s. He cleared the vast city walls for a ring road, but during excavations

Beyond Bangkok

royal regalia was stolen from the frescoed crypt of **Wat Ratchaburana** and **Wat Mahathat**. Remnants of the gilded cache – plus marvellous statuary – are displayed at **Chao Sam Phraya Museum** (108/16 Thanon Rotchana, 0 3524 1587, closed Mon, Tue, admission B30). Other treasures occupy the fretworked galleries of **Chandra Kasem Palace Museum** (Thanon U-Thong, 0 3525 1586, closed Mon, Tue, B30).

There's minimal material to help you explore the **Phra Nakhon Si Ayutthaya Historical Park** (0 3524 2284, open 8.30am-5pm daily, admission B30 each site). Overnighting ensures quiet, cool sightseeing before the hordes descend after 11am. Specialist interest visits can be arranged by **Classic Tour** (0 3524 4978/1832 4849). The excellent, concrete-clad Japanese-funded **Historical Study Centre** (Thanon Rotchana, 0 3524 5123-4, admission B100) should not be missed.

Ko Ayutthaya – formed by the Lopburi, Pasak and Chao Phraya rivers and a canal – has the **Trimuk Pavilion**, rebuilt by Rama V for ceremonies. Only foundations indicate the presence of the Grand Palace, though the three *chedi* (built in 1492) of its temple, **Wat Si Sanphet**, remain. The vast, vine-clad, roofless Buddha image of **Vihaan Phra Mongkhon Bophit** next door was revamped in 1975. Beyond the market and the majestic teak 1894 **Khun Phaen's Residence**, you can get elephant rides (ten minutes for B200). Opposite is **Beung Phra Ram**, a park of lily ponds and

a lone *prang*. Behind it, **Wat Mahathat** was, as in each Thai royal city, the ritual centre housing a Buddha relic. Cameras love its root-encased Buddha head.

Outer-bank remains include the unmissable **Wat Phramane** (Thanon U-Thong, 0 3525 1992, B10), the only surviving original temple. To the north-east the restored **Elephant Kraal** was where wild pachyderms were trained. East on Highway 3058, **Wat Maheyong** retains stucco elephants around a Sri Lankan-style *chedi*, while a Ceylonese sect-built **Wat Yai Chaimongkhon** boasts a 60-metre (197-foot) bell *chedi*, a reclining Buddha and a shrine to toys. Dominating a south-western meander, the immaculate five-*prang* **Wat Chaiwattanaram** hosts boat races at Loy Krathong in November. To the less accessible south, King U-Thong stayed at the cloistered **Wat Phuttaisawan** before developing Ayutthaya. Fine murals line its ancient Somdet Phra Phutthakhosachan residence. On the journey there, you will pass the restored **St Joseph's Church** in the old French settlement. The first of many foreign quarters was the Portuguese, around the restored San Petro's Church on the west bank of the river.

If you're after crafts, there's *khon* (*see p199*) mask maker **ML Punsawat Sooksawasdi** (95/1 Thanon U-thong, 0 3524 1574) and the teak house carpenters based in **Baan Pahan**, which is a 13-kilometre (eight-mile) journey north on Highway 32.

The extraordinary **Wat Mahathat**, the ritual centre of Ayutthaya.

# Boat trips

Most tour agents run boat trips beyond Bangkok. Those listed below all call at Bang Pa-in.

The **Chao Phraya Expressboat** tour (0 2623 6001-3) runs 8am-6pm every Sunday (one way B250, round trip B350) via Bang Sai, and either Wat Pailom (Nov-June) or Wat Chalermphrakiat (July-Oct). The **Mit Chao Phraya** tour (0 2225 6179) at 8am-5.30pm every Sunday (B350) calls at Bang Sai and Wat Pailom. The **Manohra** (0 2476 0021-2/www.manohracruises.com) berths at Bang Pa-in overnight, returning the next day at 4pm.

Many tours include Ayutthaya as well. **Si Phraya Boat Trip & Travel** (0 2235 3108) runs a day trip (7.45am-5pm daily, B1,600) by bus to Bang Pa-in then by boat to Ayutthaya and a cruise aboard the Pearl of Siam back to Bangkok. **River Sun Cruise** (0 2266 9125-6/www.riversuncruise.com) goes by coach from the River City complex to Bang Pa-in, then to Ayutthaya, cruising back to Bangkok onboard a two-deck air-conditioned boat carrying 150. The trip costs B1,600 including lunch; book one day ahead.

**Asia Voyages**' exquisitely converted Mekhala teak barge (0 2256 7168-9/www.mekhalacruise.com) offers two overnight trips, each costing around B7,200. Passengers cruise upstream from 2.30pm, berth at rural Wat Kai Tia, walk to Bang Pa-in, take a longtail boat to Ayutthaya for lunch and a tour, then return by minibus to Bangkok. Otherwise, you could catch a bus at 8am to Ayutthaya, then after lunch go to Bang Pa-in by longtail, cruise to Wat Kai Tai for a candlelit dinner and sleep, and return by boat to Bangkok by 11am.

## Where to stay & eat

**Baan Khun Phra** (48 Thanon U-Thong, 0 3524 1978, rates B150-B350) is a wooden garden enclave near Chao Phrom market's food stalls. An ex-teacher runs **PS Guest House** (23/1 Thanon Chakrapat, 0 3524 2394, rates B120-B300) and offers the doubly attractive prospect of a warm welcome and some tasty home cooking. Riverside dining at **Ruen Rub Rong** (13/1-2 Thanon U-Thong, 0 3524 3090, main courses B150-B200) also includes the possibility of dinner cruises.

The riverbank to the north passes the wooden **Ayothaya Riverside Inn** (0 2585 6001, rates B400-B1,000) and continues through Wat Kasatrathirat to two good Thai restaurants overlooking the river. **Baan Watcharachai** (0 3532 1333, main courses B50-B140) has plush, Thai-style buildings in a garden setting, plus a river terrace and a boat for dining afloat. Next door is the subtly rustic **Perb Phitsadang** (0 1823 9334, main courses B80-B250).

## Getting there & around

### By boat

For river cruises from Bangkok, see *left* **Boat trips**.

### By bus

Buses from Bangkok's Northern Bus Terminal leave every 20mins 5.20am-8pm daily (B34). Trip takes 90mins.

### By car

Ayutthaya is 72km (43 miles) north via Highways 31, 1, 32 and 309; the Bang Pa-in expressway, then Highway 9, are a shortcut to Highway 32. Journey takes 90mins.

### By train

Trains leave 4.20am-11.10pm daily from Bangkok's Hualumphong station (B12-B20, 90 mins), also calling at Bang Pa-in.

### Getting around

In Ayutthaya, you can rent the Benjarong rice barge (0 3521 1036) or hire longtail boats at piers by Chandra Kasem Museum or Wat Phanan Choeng. You can hire bicycles from the tourist police (B50 per day) or near the train station (B30 per day).

## Resources

### Tourist information

*TAT, 108/22 Thanon Si Sanphet, Ayutthaya (0 3524 6076/7)* **Open** 8.30am-4.30pm daily.

## Lopburi

A stopover rather than a day trip, Lopburi satisfies connoisseurs of walkable historic towns, and is famed among Thais for its feral urban monkeys. Settled in prehistory and the semi-capital of several empires, it was Luvo (a Mon Dvaravati centre) from the sixth to tenth centuries. The triple-towered **Phra Prang Sam Yod** (admission B30), also on Thanon Vichayen, originally venerated the Bhrama-Shiva-Vishnu trinity, though now two Buddhist images are resident – along with a colony of mischievous, mangy macaques. They're thanked for bringing prosperity at a **Monkey Buffet** in late November.

The great Khmer leader King Narai the Great made Lopburi his second capital, its conch-shell island shape echoing Ayutthaya's. His era is evoked at the **King Narai Fair** in February, with costumed parades with elephants, a *son et lumière*, stalls and traditional arts. His palace, **Phra Narai Ratchanivet** (1665-77), is an early fusion of Thai, Khmer and classical French forms, with Persian pointed windows and niches. In the first instance of Thais presenting a Westernised face to ensure independence, he decorated it with carpets, mirrors and gilt. Yet behind the inner palace walls, Thai style prevailed in halls now housing the **Somdet Phra Narai National Museum** (Thanon Sorasak, 0 3641 1458/www.thailandmuseum.com, grounds open daily, museum closed Mon, Tue, admission B30).

Constantine Phaulkon, a Greek adventurer who under King Narai rose higher than any *farang* (foreigner) to the jealously coveted position of Vichayen (chief minister), had a mansion in the town: **Baan Vichayen** (Thanon Vichayen, admission B30). Narai died in Lopburi in 1688, and Phaulkon was executed by the next monarch, King Phetracha, who sealed Siam's borders. Lopburi dropped off the radar until Siam again looked outward under Rama IV; in 1856 he restored the palace for court use as a precautionary measure against marauding colonialists.

After World War I, the nondescript modern city east of the railway became a garrison town, and several barracks now offer tourists pistol-packing, skydiving, climbing and canoeing – details from **Somdet Phra Narai Military Camp** (Thanon Narai Maharaj, 0 3641 2192). Lopburi may again become a sort of capital if the province hosts the decentralised parliament at **Pasak Chonlasith Dam**, a forested weekending area, which you can visit on train tours from Hualumphong station (Sat, Sun and holidays, 8.05-11.10am, return 2-6pm, B200).

## Where to stay & eat

**Nett Hotel** (17/1-2 Thanon Ratchadamnoen Soi 2, 0 3641 1738, rates B160-B400) is the best of a drab range in the old town. **Lopburi Inn Resort** (144 Thanon Phahon Yothin, 0 3661 4790-2, rates B1,200-B1,600) is comfier, but in the new town. There are Thai, Chinese and breakfast eats along Thanon Na Phra Karn, and market stalls on Thanon Ratchadamnoen. The best restaurant is **White House Garden** (18 Thanon Phraya Kumjud, 0 3641 3085, main courses B40-B120). Facing the north-west corner of Wat Mahathat, **Chan Jao** (0 3661 7174, main courses B80) is a pub-restaurant.

## Getting there

### By bus
Buses leave every 30mins from Bangkok's Northern Bus Terminal (5am-8pm daily; B91). Trip takes 3hrs; on arrival get a *songthaew* 2km west to the old town.

### By car
Lopburi is 153km (95 miles) north of Bangkok on Highway 1. The older, slower Route 347 from Ayutthaya is more scenic.

### By train
Many visitors take a morning train from Bangkok's Hualumphong station (3hr trip, B28-B64), then in the evening rejoin multi-class sleeper trains heading north to Chiang Mai.

## Resources

### Tourist information
*TAT, north side of Wat Mahathat (0 3642 2768/9).* **Open** 8.30am-4.30pm daily.

## Sukhothai

Established in 1238, this first coherent Thai kingdom lasted until the mid 15th century; today just 25,000 inhabitants live mostly in New Sukhothai, 12 kilometres (seven miles) west of **Sukhothai Historical Park**. It took $10 million and ten years (1978-87) to turn the

Lopburi's **Phra Prang Sam Yod**. *See p220.*

**Phra Narai Ratchanivet** palace. *See p221.*

100 historical sites in these 45 square kilometres (17 square miles) into a UNESCO World Heritage Site. Surrounded by three walls and two moats, the main compound contains 21 sites and four large ponds. Its trees are a refuge for birds, as hunting has always been forbidden.

If you want to visit five or more sites, first get a full-access pass (B150) at the gate (Thanon Jarot Withithong, 0 5569 7310, open 6am-6pm daily). Start at **Ramkamhaeng National Museum** (0 5561 2167/www.thailandmuseum. com, closed Mon, Tue, B30) to grasp the history and stylised design trademarks such as the lotus-bud *chedi*, walking buddha image, tilde-shaped fingers, reflecting pools and stucco elephants protruding from walls. Amid original artefacts is a replica of the **Ramkamhaeng Stone** inscription. The stone was found just east of **Wat Mahathat**, the city's spiritual centre. Flanked by standing Buddhas, its central lotus-bud *chedi* is ringed by a frieze of circumambulating disciples and towers over 200 smaller *chedi* containing nobles' ashes.

Triple-*prang* **Wat Sri Sawai** probably predates the Siamese settlement. Made from laterite (a porous soil), it contains Hindu and Buddhist images. In one of the most beautiful settings, **Wat Sra Sri** sits on two connected islands in a flower-strewn moat, with two more Ceylonese *chedi* and a walking Buddha. The second-ranking temple, the moated **Wat Phra Phai Luang**, just north of the city wall, has three *prang* and multiple Buddha images. For quiet reflection, head a couple of kilometres south of the walls to tree-shaded **Wat Ton Jan**, **Wat Wihan Thong** and **Wat Chetuphon**.

Sukhothai is also the spiritual home of the **Loy Krathong** festival in November, when it gets pretty crowded.

## Around Sukhothai

Nearly 70 kilometres (43 miles) north from Sukhothai, **Si Satchanalai-Chalieng Historical Park** (0 5567 9211, open 8am-5pm daily, admission B40) is also a World Heritage Site, and is ringed by a wide moat by the Yom river. Traditionally governed by the crown prince of Sukhothai, this satellite city quickly followed Suhothai's absorption by Ayutthaya in 1438, forming the frontier to the Lanna kingdom. Dating mainly from the 13th century, its ruins are generally more intact but less restored than those at Sukhothai.

**Wat Chang Lom** was the centre, built by King Ramkamhaeng in the late 13th century. Other fruitful stops within the walls are **Wat Khao Phanom Phloeng**, **Wat Nang Phaya** and **Wat Chedi Jet Thaew**, which offers seven photogenic rows of *chedis*. A kilometre east at Chalieng are the laterite **Wat Chao Chan** and, surrounded by river meanders, **Wat Phra Si Ratana Mahathat**.

Extending into the Ayutthaya period, the **Sawankhalok Kilns** two kilometres upriver at Ban Ko Noi exported Sangkhalok ceramics (often glazed with greyish or greenish celadon) as far as Japan and Indonesia, as explained at the **Sangkhalok Kiln Preservation Centre** (B30). Original figures, bowls and pots, plus anthropological artefacts, are displayed in the **Sangkhalok Museum** on Highway 101 (0 5561 4333-5, admission B100). The heavy stoneware, notable for its blue fish motif, is still made; try **Anajak Poh Ku Sangkhalok** (1/29 Thanon Charodvitthitong, Old Sukhothai, 0 5569 7380).

## Where to stay & eat

Right by the Historical Park, **Vitoon Guest House** on Thanon Charodvithitong (0 5569 7054, rates B200-B500) is bland, clean, rents bikes and runs a crafts tour. **Thai Village Hotel** (214 Thanon Charodvithitong, 0 5569 7020-3, rates B600-B1,000) has teak houses in a canalside garden and a good restaurant known for its snakehead fish curry.

Choice, amenities and transportation are all better in New Sukhothai, where **Lotus Village** (170 Thanon Ratchathani, 0 5562 1484/1463/ www.lotus-village.com, rates B680-B1,130) has converted teak rice barns around a lotus pond, and runs tours. **No 4 Guesthouse** (140/4 Soi Mae Rampan, off Thanon Charodvithitong, 0 5561 0165, rates B150-B180) offers Bali-style rattan bungalows and cooking classes.

Beyond Bangkok

**Dream Café** (86/1 Thanon Singhawat, 0 5561 2081, main courses B70-B250) is tastefully decorated, with a diverse bilingual menu, while **Kuaytieaw Thai Jay Hae** (6/10 Thanon Charodvithitong, 0 5561 1901, main courses B15-B25) specialises in noodle dishes. The **Night Market** is on Thanon Ramkhamhaeng.

The only resort at Si Satchanalai is **Wang Yom Resort** (78/2 Thanon Kaengluang, 0 5563 1380, 0 9539 9045, rates B800-B1,200), which also serves food.

## Getting there & around

### By air
Bangkok Airways has daily flights (70mins, return B4,290) from Bangkok to Sukhothai Airport.

### By bus
Buses from Bangkok's Northern Bus Terminal leave hourly (7am-4pm) and then every 30mins (8-10.50pm) daily to New Sukhothai (Thanon Bypass, 0 5561 4529). Fare is B256; journey takes 6hrs.

### By car
Sukhothai is 427km (265 miles) north of Bangkok. Take Highways 1, 32 and 117 to Phitsanulok, then Highway 12.

### By train
A sprinter train (reservations 0 2220 4444/www.srt. motc.go.th) leaves from Hualumphong station at 9.30am daily arriving at Phitsanulok, 58km (36 miles) south-east of Sukhothai at 4.15pm; fare is B372. Then catch a bus from Phitsanulok bus station (0 5524 2430) to Sukhothai. There are also overnight trains to Chiang Mai via Phitsanulok.

### Getting around
Buses and *songthaew* ply the roads to the historical parks. Cars are allowed into the parks (B50), but bicycles are the best way around the ruins; they can be hired near the park gate for B50 per day.

## Resources

### Tourist Information
*TAT, 209/7-8 Surasi Trade Centre, Thanon Boromtrilokanat, Phitsanulok (0 5525 2742/3).* **Open** 8.30am-4.30pm daily.

## Khmer citadels

The ancient Khmer empire's northern outposts in southern Isaan explain a major aspect of Thai heritage, embodying Hindu cosmology in laterite and stucco sanctuaries. At Songkran in mid April, the rising sun beams through the 15 doors of **Prasat Hin Khao Phnom Rung** (0 4463 1746, admission B40), located south off Highway 24, 115 kilometres (70 miles) east of Khorat. A 40-metre (130-foot) processional way and three

Naga bridges lead up a towering volcanic plug to this astonishing tenth- to 13th-century recreation of Shiva's domain on Mount Kailash.

Meticulously restored, **Prasat Hin Phimai** (0 4447 1568, B40), 60 kilometres (37 miles) north-east of Khorat, was built a millennium ago to face Angkor. Alongside *Ramayana* scenes, the carved sandstone lintels reflect its 12th century conversion into a Mahayan Buddhist temple, and a Naga-sheltered Buddha sits beneath the rounded central *prang* within square galleries. Other carvings are displayed at the nearby **Phimai National Museum** (Thanon Tasongkran, closed Mon, Tue, B30).

Both sites are easiest visited from **Khorat** (aka Nakhon Ratchasima), which is 259 kilometres (162 miles) from Bangkok on Highway 2. It's a modernised ancient city famous for the **Thao Suranari Statue** (*see p10* **Warrior princesses**) at its moat's western gate, the focus of a fair in late March. Shops along Thanon Chumphon sell Isaan silk, while Dan Khwian (15km south on Highway 224) produces unique ceramics.

If you decide you want to stay overnight, the **Royal Princess** (1137 Thanon Sura Narai, 0 4425 6629-35/www.royalprincess.com, rates B2,000-B12,000) has the poshest rooms, while **Doctor's Guest House** (78 Thanon Sub Siri Soi 4, 0 4425 5846, rates B180-B350) is simple by comparison (but characterful nevertheless). **Old Phimai Guesthouse** (off Thanon Chomsudasadet, Phimai, 0 4447 1918, rates B80-B350) is unusually good.

Air Andaman flies daily except Sunday from Bangkok to Khorat Airport (0 4425 7211-3), and there are nine trains daily from Bangkok, (B90-B295); the journey takes four to five hours.

# West to Kanchanaburi

## Day trips & canal life

Taking Route 4 (Thanon Phetkasem) from Bangkok, you pass **Samphran Elephant Ground & Crocodile Farm** (km30 Thanon Phetkasem, Samphran, 0 2429 0361/2/www. elephantshow.com). A popular country fun park with elephant rides, its packed programme of tourist-pleasers includes croc wrestling and feeding, log hauling and *Suriyothai*-style costumed battle re-enactments. Every year, on 1 May, it hosts the **Jumbo Queen** contest for women weighing more than 80 kilos (176 pounds) who display 'the grace of an elephant' (*see p158* **Crowning glory**).

Nearby is the **Rose Garden Aprime Resort** (km32 Thanon Phetkasem, 0 3432 2544-7/www.rose-garden.com), a landscaped magnet overlooking the Tha Chin river for passive, snap-happy tour groups. It offers elephant rides, a golf course, traditional dance, a bland hotel (rates B2,500-B25,000) and bland Thai food. Trips down the river take in Don Wai market, Wat Rai King, orchards, a fish sanctuary and stilt houses.

Many trips west of Bangkok start with a visit to **Damnoen Saduak Floating Market** in Ratchaburi province (Moo 9, Tambon Damnoen Saduak, 0 3224 1204), which offers the fullest experience of the old riverine Thai lifestyle. The market is best seen between dawn and 9am, when the tour buses unload, and it's over by late morning. While most of the paddle traders dress traditionally and carry authentic cargo such as fruit, produce and food – notably *kwaytiao reua* (boat noodles) – some pester you with souvenir trinkets, and the canals through orchards and between stilt houses are flanked by ugly souvenir displays. Touring in a boat (wildly negotiable; try around B500) is probably cheaper from the central concrete market.

However, the provinces of Samut Sakhon, Samut Songkram, Ratchaburi and Nakhon Pathom are laced with canal communities, some holding floating markets on auspicious days, though English skills are limited. **Lam Phya Floating Market** (Wat Lam Phya, Lam Phya, Bang Lane, Nakhon Pathom province, 0 3439 1985, open Sat, Sun only) has been made more accessible to visitors, but a more authentically preserved one is at **Amphawa** (at Wat Amphawan, 6am-8am daily); 60 kilometres (37 miles) from Bangkok on Highway 35, it's served by trains from Wongwien Yai station.

The equally scenic **Tha Kha Floating Market** (0 3476 6208, 7am-noon Sat, Sun and 2nd, 7th & 12th days of waxing and waning moons) is part of itineraries from the new **Baan Tai Had Resort** (1 Moo 2, Thanon Wat Phuang Malai-Wat Tai Had, 0 3476 7220-4). It runs dinner cruises to view fireflies and hires out kayaks to explore the canals' human and animal life at your own pace.

Homestays in Amphawa's stilt houses include: **Baan Song Thai Plai Pong Pang** (contact Nimit Intaluang on 0 3473 2428, rates B400), **Baan Tha Kha** (contact Thaweep Chuathai or Jaroon Chuathai on 0 3476 6170/ 6123, rates B350), and **Homestay Baan Hua Had** (contact Thong-yip Keawninkul on 0 3473 5073, rates B350).

Samut Songkram is also the birthplace of 'poet king' Rama II. His literary achievements are celebrated in an eponymous museum in **King Buddhalertla Napalai Memorial Park** (Highway 325, open 9am-6pm daily, B20), which stages authentic *khon* during its fair in early February.

The **River Kwai Pandaw** (with ten teak cabins sleeping up to 20) offers a seven-day, six-night cruise through Samut Songkram, Ratchaburi and Kanchanaburi waterways, with excursions to markets, boat builders, temples, historical sites, Khmer ruins, waterfalls, war cemeteries, hot springs and the bridge on the River Kwai. For more details, contact **Asian Trails** (15th Floor, Mercury Tower, 540 Thanon Ploenchit, Pathumwan, 0 2658 6080-9/ www.asiantrails.com).

## Nakhon Pathom

Possibly the oldest city in the country, and the original entry point of Buddhism to Thailand, this provincial capital 56 kilometres (35 miles) west of Bangkok was a Mon centre two millennia ago. From the train or Highway 4 you can't miss **Phra Pathom Chedi** (0 3424 2143/3425 7629), reputedly the world's tallest stupa at 120 metres (414 feet). Its ochre-coloured bell-shape derives from the 1853 cladding of a Khmer *prang* that encased the original Mon stupa. A mural showing these layers and a model of the *prang*, plus a reclining Buddha

Crumbling temple in **Ayutthaya**. *See p218.*

and a circular cloister, is one of the terrace attractions. **Phra Pathom Chedi National Museum** (0 3427 0300, closed Mon, Tue, admission B30) contains some Dvaravati archaeological treasures. The many artefacts in the free **Phra Pathom Museum** (closed Mon, Tue) are less well organised.

Just west sprawls **Sanam Chan Palace** (6 Thanon Rajamankha Nai, near Silapakorn University, 0 3424 2649/3425 5099, closed Mon-Wed, B50). Set in leafy grounds, it's a collection of exquisite wooden residences in Thai, tropical European and chateau styles built by Rama VI, including a *wat*-like theatre.

## Getting there & around

### By bus
Buses leave daily from the Southern Bus Terminal to Samut Songkram (every 30mins, 5am-9pm, B42) and Nakhon Pathom (every 30mins, 4am-10pm, B34).

### By train
To Nakhon Pathom, nine trains (every class) leave 7.45am-10.50pm daily from Hualumphong station (B20-B40), while four 3rd-class trains run daily from Thonburi station (B22). To Samut Songkram, 3rd-class trains leave hourly 5.30am-8.10pm daily from Wongwian Yai station (B10).

## Resources

### Tourist information
*TAT, 310/2 Thanon Saeng Chuto, Kanchanburi (0 3451 1200).* **Open** 8.30am-4.30pm daily.

## Kanchanaburi Town

Kanchanburi, Thailand's fourth-largest province, has crystal waterfalls hidden in tropical forests, vast national parks and cave-riddled karst ridges along the border with Burma. Rivers meander through fertile valleys dotted with traditional villages of naturalised Mon, Karen and ethnic Burmese.

The main base for exploring Kan'buri (as locals call it) is the fairly pleasant provincial capital of **Kanchanburi**, 129 kilometres (81 miles) from Bangkok. Its claim to fame is as the location of the infamous **Bridge on the River Kwai** (four kilometres/2.5 miles north of today's bridge), part of the World War II 'Death Railway' commissioned by the Japanese army to supply its campaign against the British in Burma. An estimated 18,000 POWs and 90,000 Asian slave labourers perished during the bridge's construction. Their remains are in various nearby cemeteries.

The prisoners' story is conveyed through reconstructions at the **Jeath War Museum**, (admission B30) beside Wat Chai Chumpon on

# Royal retreats

The striking Phetchaburi and Prachuap Khiri Khan coastlines have long been preferred destinations for royal summer retreats. And the best known is **Phra Ratchawang Klai Kangwon** ('Far from Worries Palace') in Hua Hin, an eclectic art nouveau-influenced compound closed to tourists while the king is in residence (which is often).

There are no such restrictions on browsing Rama VI's restored **Phra Ratchaniwet Marukhathayawan** ten kilometres (six miles) south of Cha-am (Rama VI Army Camp, 0 3250 8033, open 8am-5pm daily, admission B90). A lattice of tropical European-style teak buildings connected by intricate covered walkways, it's scented by frangipani trees and displays great craftsmanship and flair. Two pavilions jut into the sea and a viewing gallery surrounds an open-sided theatre.

Phetchaburi's older royal properties include the remnants of an 1860 palace built by Rama IV crowning **Khao Wang** (Thanon Phetkasem, at Thanon Bandai-it, 0 3242 5600, open 8.30am-4.30pm daily, admission B40). There's a faded grandeur about its temples, chedis, royal residences, official halls and forts, constructed in an intriguing blend of neo-classical and Thai styles, many with curvaceous Chinese roofs. Just outside town, **Phra Ratchawang Ban Peun** (121 Thanon Ratchadamnoen, 0 3242 8506-10 ext 50225, open 8am-5pm daily, admission B50) was constructed for Rama V in the early 1900s by German architects. It contains some beautifully preserved murals and classic glazed tile work, making another Thai-Western architectural fusion.

Thanon Pak Praek, while another **War Museum** next to the current rail bridge (at the north end of Thanon Maenam Kwae) has interesting but often kitsch displays. The rail bridge crosses the Kwae Yai (larger tributary), converging in town with the Kwae Noi (smaller tributary) to form the Maeklong river, where myriad double-decker disco boats are moored by day and a wire-operated ferry operates.

A couple of kilometres past Chung Kai, **Wat Tham Khao Poon** is perched on a hill commanding fine views over the Kwae Noi,

from which it can be reached by hired longtail. The *wat* has a cave containing several large halls and passageways. The annual ten-day **River Kwai Bridge Week** at the end of November focuses on a sound and light show.

## Around Kanchanaburi

About 15 kilometres (9.5 miles) south, near Tha Muang village, **Wat Tham Khao Noi** and **Wat Tham Seua** straddle a rocky outcrop overlooking lush green rice paddies. The temples are not interconnected, and require separate steep ascents.

Some 65 kilometres (35 miles) from Kanchanaburi, Route 3199 leads to the nine-tier waterfalls in **Erawan National Park** (0 3457 4234), which gets very crowded at weekends, and to **Srinagarind National Park**, which contains a reservoir behind a hydroelectric dam. Both charge for entry.

Because the Death Railway was mostly dismantled after the war, the line ends at Nam Tok (daily trains from Kanchanaburi trace the scenic Kwae Noi valley over many rickety viaducts in a 90-minute journey). The **Sai Yok Noi** waterfall at km46 on Highway 323 is busy with picnickers, but far inferior to the cascade at **Sai Yok Yai National Park** (km82, 0 3451 6163-4, admission B200 ), which plunges into the muddy Kwae Noi. The toughest rail cutting was the mostly hand-chiselled **Hellfire Pass**, which took such a human toll that Australia funded the impressive **Hellfire Pass Memorial & Museum** (km64-5, 0 1754 2098/1210 3306) and brings survivors here every November along a 4.5-kilometre (3-mile) jungle walk. At km105-6, there are signs to **Hin Dat Hot Springs**, with Japanese-built sulphurous hot baths next to a brook for cooling off. From here, a poor dirt road leads eight kilometres (five miles) to the marvellous, multi-tiered **Phra That Waterfall**.

Also on Highway 323, 147 kilometres (90 miles) from Kanchanaburi, **Thong Pha Phum** has a Wild West feel with its single main road, but apart from a huge Buddha image there's little to do. Monkeys greet visitors and beg for food at the imposing **Vajiralongkorn Dam** six kilometres (3.5 miles) north. The dam holds back the vast **Khao Laem** reservoir, its western shore spotted with resorts (many on rafts) that attract anglers and those seeking quiet. Skirting the flooded valley like a riviera corniche, Highway 323 winds on another 73 kilometres (47 miles) to **Sangkhlaburi**. The last major town before Burma, it's ringed by mountains and settled mainly by Karen and Mon. Its awesomely tall wooden bridge was badly damaged by flood a few years back.

About 20 kilometres (12.5 miles) on lies **Three Pagodas Pass**, an old Burmese invasion route and now a godforsaken marketplace with a trio of tiny *chedi* and a lot of shoddily made teak furniture.

## Where to stay & eat

In Kanchanaburi Town, a good selection of hotels and guesthouses cluster on Thanons Song Kwae and Maenam Kwae, many with raft rooms, the province's hotel niche. Several bars and floating restaurants are moored along Thanon Song Kwae, most with good food and sunset views. **Sam's Place** (7/3 Thanon Song Kwae, 0 3451 3971/www.samsguesthouse.com, rates B150-B350) offers garden bungalows or comfortable bamboo rafts. It has two nearby branches. For more upmarket lodgings, head upstream to the well-equipped **Felix River Kwai** next to the River Kwae road bridge (Tha Makham, 0 3451 5061/www.felixriver kwai.co.th, rates B3,000-B20,000).

More remote and enchanting is **Jungle Rafts** (www.junglerafts.com, rate B1300) in a gorge below Sai Yok Yai, an ecotourism pioneer from 1976. Priding itself on a lack of electricity, it has great food, massages, elephants and dancing by oil lamp from the adjacent Mon village, where tours offer a fascinating insight into this ancient ethnic group's culture and plight. It is reached only by boat upstream from its sister **River Kwai Resotel** (0 2642 5497/www.riverkwaifloatel.com, rates B2,000-B3,400) with cottages, orchards and a cave in its grounds. Arrange transport via the office.

## Getting there

### By bus
Buses to Kanchanaburi leave from Bangkok's Southern Bus Terminal every 20mins (5am-10.30pm daily, B79). Provincial buses are scarce.

### By car
Kanchanaburi is 128km (80 miles) from Bangkok via Route 4 (or join Route 4 from Route 338) to Nakhon Pathom, then Route 323. Journey takes about 2hrs.

### By train
Trains leave daily to Kanchanaburi from Thonburi and Hualumphong stations. Rail tours (6.30am Sat, Sun) include the Bridge, Muang Singh, Erawan and Srinagarind National Parks, Sangkhlaburi and Three Pagodas Pass (tour info 0 2225 6964 ext 5217).

## Resources

### Tourist information
*TAT, 310/2 Thanon Saeng Chuto, Kanchanburi (0 3451 1200).* **Open** 8.30am-4.30pm daily.

Palace on the hill at **Khao Wang**.

# Upper Gulf Coast

Thanon Petkasem (Route 3) leads south to
the historic city of **Phetchaburi**, the Thai-style
resort of **Cha-am** and the royal seaside retreat
of **Hua Hin**, all favourite weekending spots of
well-to-do Bangkokians.

## Phetchaburi

Often bypassed by travellers, this provincial
capital – also called Phetburi – is 123 kilometres
(77 miles) from Bangkok. It boasts fine temple
architecture and a unique palace of Rama IV
on **Khao Wang**, a hill to the west of town (*see
p225* **Royal retreats**). Equally interesting
are the imposing Khmer-style towers of **Wat
Kamphaeng Laeng** on Thanon Prasong and
the murals of **Wat Ko Kaew Sutharam**,
off Thanon Panichjaroen near the Phetchaburi
river. Thais also associate the town, however,
with its bargain-priced hitmen and its
toothsome sweets. For the full range (of the
latter), from chews and coconut slices to
wafers and candied seafood, try **Nanthawan**
(607 Thanon Phetkasem, off Thanon Bandai-it,
0 3240 2468).

### Where to stay & eat

Many of the budget hotels seem to double as
small-scale brothels. Safer bets, both on Thanon
Phetkasem, are the **Phetkasem Hotel**

(No.86/1, 0 3242 5581, rates B200-B500), which
is fairly clean, and the decidedly more upmarket
**Royal Diamond** (No.555, 0 3241 1062, rates
B800-B1500). There are few dining options,
but the **Night Market** on Thanon Surinleuchai
hawks local delicacies such as *khanom maw
kaeng* (mung bean, egg and coconut milk
pudding) among Thai and Chinese standards.
**Rabieng** restaurant, part of Rabieng
Guesthouse on the west river bank off Thanon
Chisa-in, has the broadest Thai menu.

## Cha-am

This seaside town 45 kilometres (28 miles)
south of Phetchaburi is less than scenic and the
beach is increasingly polluted, but there are few
better places to observe Thais in holiday mode.
Extended families rest under awnings on
deckchairs, munching snacks, sweets and
whisky, rising occasionally to wade in the sea
fully clothed, lark on rubber rings, ride tandems
or find fun wherever they look. The concrete
shophouse blocks behind the casuarina-shaded
promenade lack appeal, but ten kilometres
(six miles) south stands **Phra Ratchaniwet
Marukhathayawan** summer palace (*see p225*
**Royal retreats**)

### Where to stay & eat

Strung mainly down the long straight beach
south to Hua Hin, Cha-am's 'nicer' hotels are
often condominium-style blocks. Exceptions
include the **Dusit Resort & Polo Club** (1349
Thanon Phetkasem, 0 3252 0009/www.dusit.
com, rates B9,500-B25,900), commanding a
pristine beachfront north of town, and the
**Regent Cha-am Beach Resort** (849/21
Thanon Phetkasem, 0 3245 1240-9/www.regent-
chaam.com, rates B4,400-B21,000), a vast five-
storey property in lush gardens. For
inexpensive but well-appointed cottages near
the beach, try **Paradise Bungalows** (223-9/13
Thanon Ruamchit, 0 3247 1072, rates B800-
B1,200) or **Santsuk Bungalows & Beach
Resort** (263/3 Thanon Ruamchit, 0 3247 1212,
rates B1,500-B3,500).

    **Poom Restaurant** (274/1 Thanon Ruamchit,
0 3247 1036, main courses B70-B250), is so
popular for beachfront seafood that booking
is essential, particularly at weekends. For
Western food, **Cha-am Steakhouse** (Cha-am
Avenue, corner of Thanon Ruamchit, 0 3247
1871, main courses B200), and **Capone's
Pizza & Pasta**, three doors up, are both
acceptable, if pricey. Nightlife options are
limited to casual pubs such as **Lodge Bar**
(274/19 Thanon Ruamchit, 0 3247 0362) and
**Max** (222/57-9 Thanon Ruamchit, 0 3243 4096).

**Beyond Bangkok**

# Hua Hin

This small Gulf town would have little to distinguish it from any other fishing village in Prachuap Khiri Khan province had King Rama VI not built his summer palace here in 1926. Its royal legacy and the town's proximity to Bangkok have made it an enduring beach destination, which suffers less from frenetic development, pollution, prostitution and con artists than do Patong and Pattaya.

Hua Hin's five kilometres (three miles) of beaches are its biggest draw, though the often-murky water and jellyfish (numerous during monsoons) deter swimmers. Weekends can get overcrowded, compounded by vendors hawking everything from pony rides to corn on the cob around the Thanon Damnoen Kasem beach. So strike south to the beach fronting the Sofitel and beyond to the relatively tranquil sands of **Had Khao Takiap** (with its temple and standing Buddha on the rocks) and **Khao Tao**. The new **Hua Hin Butterfly Garden** opposite (2/95-96 Thanon Phetkasem, 0 3251 2642, admission B150) is a delight. The quaint half-timbered railway station provides a great photo opportunity.

**Khao Takiab**, a hill overlooking Takiab beach four kilometres (2.5 miles) outside Hua Hin, offers sweeping views from an unexceptional temple. Far better is **Khao Sam Roi Yot National Park** (0 3261 9078, admission B200), a fast 58 kilometres (36 miles) to the south. Named '300 peaks', the park features broken-tooth karsts soaring out of wetlands ideal for sea-kayaking and has a diverse bird population. More arduous exploration awaits at the World Heritage rainforest of **Kaeng Krachan National Park** to the north-west (0 3245 9291, admission B200).

## Where to eat & drink

Hua Hin is justifiably famous for its seafood, best sampled in the restaurants around the fishing pier on the north end of Thanon Naresdamri. The best is **Chao Ley** (No.15, 0 3251 3436, main courses B60-B300), built on piers over the ocean. For cheaper seafood, visit the evening vendors at the rambling outdoor **Chatchai Market** off Thanon Denchanuchit. Thanon Punsuk and Thanon Damnoen Kasem have Italian restaurants, while **Buffalo Bill's Steak & Grill** (13 Thanon Damnoen Kasem, 0 3253 2727, main courses B100-B400) isn't as rough-hewn as it sounds.

Hua Hin's bars and pubs are mostly humble open-air affairs parallel to the carnival-like beach on Thanon Naresdamri. The current hotspot is the mammoth **Hua Hin Brewing Company** attached to the **Hilton Hotel** (33 Thanon Naresdamri, 0 3251 2888, main courses B100-B250). A short hop down the road, **Blue Elephant** is popular for its cheap, wide-ranging drinks list. Sois north off Naresdamri are choked with beer bars populated by working girls; an exception is the friendly **Takeang Pub** on Soi Bintaban, which is a rustic country and western bar offering live folk music.

## Where to stay

Hua Hin has some of the world's most exclusive resort spas. **Chiva Som International Health Resort** (73/4 Thanon Phet Kasem, 0 3253 6536/www.chivasom.com, rates $315-$1,000), attracts celebrities with its upscale, traditional villas and strict holistic treatments, while the new **Evason Hua Hin** (9 Thanon Khao Ka Loak, Paknampran, 0 3263 2111/ www.evasonhuahin.com, rates B5,750-B16,000) is a tastefully minimalist beachfront property. Or there's the village-like **Anantara Resort & Spa** (43/1 Thanon Phet Kasem, 0 3252 0250-6/www.anantara.com, rates $165-$630) and the classy **Sofitel Central Hua Hin Resort** (1 Thanon Damnoen Kasem, 0 3251 2021-38/ www.sofitel.com, rates B7,239-B33,000).

If you're on a budget, **Ban Somboon** (13/4 Soi Kasemsamphan, Thanon Damnoen Kasem, 0 3251 1538, rates B550-B800) is a Thai home with cosy rooms, art and antiques.

## Getting there

### By air

Bangkok Airways flies daily from Bangkok to Hua Hin in the morning, returning early evening. Return fare is B3,300; flight takes 40mins.

### By bus

Air-con buses leave frequently from Bangkok's Southern Bus Terminal to Phetchaburi (B90), Cha-am (B113) and Hua Hin (B128). The trip takes 2-3hrs.

### By car

Hua Hin is 280km (174 miles) south on Highway 35 via Samut Sakhon and Samut Songkram. Turn left to Thanon Phetkasem (Highway 4) to Phetchaburi. The journey takes 2.5-3.5hrs.

### By train

Trains leave Bangkok's Hualumphong station for Phetchaburi and Hua Hin 12 times daily, taking 3-5hrs (B44-B280). Trains for Cha-am leave twice daily.

## Resources

### Tourist information

*TAT, 500/51 Thanon Phetkasem, Cha-am (0 3247 1005/6).* **Open** 8.30am-4.30pm daily.

Beyond Bangkok

# Eastern Seaboard

This is the closest coast to Bangkok, offering beach raves, sex-on-sea and deluxe desert islands.

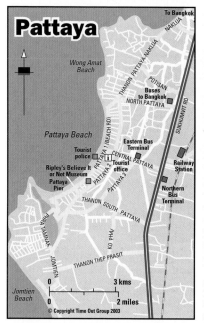

## Pattaya

Welcome to a laboratory of tourism. Thailand's unplanned first resort, **Pattaya**, is slowly cleaning up its sleazy, reckless reputation, while **Ko Samet**'s national park is now manageably encroached by beach party bungalows, and pristine **Ko Chang** has been earmarked for a classier, eco-friendly land-grab.

### Samut Prakarn & Chonburi

There are some worthwhile diversions in the coastal provinces, which could be visited en route to the beach or on a day trip. **Samut Prakarn Crocodile Farm** (555 Thanon Thai Baan, 0 2703 5144-8, admission B300) claims to be the world's biggest croc farm. It's got 100,000 of the critters, including the near-extinct Siamese species and the world's longest crocodile at six metres (20 feet). Hourly shows feature wrestling, head-in-jaws and similar touristy faves, plus elephant shows and rides, and an audio-visual dinosaur display.

More subtly superlative is **Muang Boran** (Sukhumvit Sai Kao km33, Bangpu Mai, 0 2323 9253, admission B50). One visionary created this under-visited, open-air architectural museum, reconstructing salvaged masterpieces and scale versions of landmarks in a park shaped like Thailand. It's a relaxing place, but vast and without public transport, so go by car or on a tour. If you want seafront seafood, a favourite spot nearby is **Sala Suk Jai** (Sukhumvit Sai Kao km36, Bangpu Mai, 0 2323 9911, main courses B70-B200).

Just beyond **Chonburi** town (and its extensive speciality market along Route 3) is **Bang Saen**. Sixty kilometres (37 miles) south-east of Bangkok, it's the closest resort to the capital and an insight into Thai seaside culture. To prevent suntanning, the sand is covered by awnings over rows of deckchairs that face tables strewn with grilled chicken, *somtam* (spicy papaya salad) and whisky. In the late afternoon, daytrippers swim fully clothed or lark on inner tubes or boat-towed 'inflatable bananas'. North of the promenade in the fishing harbour is a seafood restaurant on stilts.

More rewarding than overnighting here (though you could try **Bang Saen Beach Resort**, 4-4/48 Bang Saen Sai Song Soi 14, 0 3838 1675, rates B500-B2,500) are the pierside guesthouses down route 3 at **Si Racha**. Most notable is **Siri Wattana** (35 Chermchomphol Soi 8, 0 3831 1037, rates B160-B300), which is flanked by seafood restaurants. Si Racha, home of *nam phrik Si Racha* spicy sauce, is noted for the **Sriracha Tiger Zoo** nine kilometres (5.5 miles) to the south (0 3829 6556/ www.tigerzoo.com, admission B300).

### Pattaya

Pattaya has been a mass-touristed resort with a reputation for raunch ever since the Vietnam War, when it became an R&R playground for US troops. Uneven efforts to clean up both its pollution and highly visible sex trade (both straight and gay) have left it a place of crude contrasts. Its once idyllic bay has a corniche of dingy concrete. Its sewage is now processed, but few swim off Pattaya beach. There are watersports and attractions for families and couples, who often add the go-go bars to their must-see lists.

Beyond Bangkok

Along Beach Road, middle-aged men in singlets pose with bikes, babes and Ray-Bans, as if in a counterfeit Elmore Leonard novel. Leading inland to Thanon Pattaya 2, some 20 *soi* feature open-air bars, where mainly Western men chat to waitresses and freelancing hookers over cheap beer. Pattayaland Sois 1, 2 and 3 host the most massage parlours and go-go bars, with short-stay rooms upstairs. Many visitors stay and open businesses, hence the pubs with names such as Rosie O'Grady's, Scot's Bar and Pat's Pies.

Around town, menus are in English, German, Arabic and Russian, but activities associated with prostitution – paedophilia, murder, extortion – come in those languages too, causing visa-on-arrival rights to cease for several nationalities. The *Pattaya Mail* luridly reports such incidents, though mainstream tourists face little risk.

Strangely, Pattaya has a certain charm, perhaps because there's little of the ugly atmosphere or apparent danger associated with such scenes elsewhere. Moreover, it is morphing into a dormitory hub for the corporatising Eastern Seaboard. Malls, cinemas and international schools have moved in, hotels have upgraded and 15 golf courses have opened. Still, with most residents coming from elsewhere, there's little non-artificial culture. Proposals to open Thailand's first legal casino here carry risks, but Las Vegas is a model of how such places might be reformed.

South around the headland, the longer, wilder and cleaner beach of **Jomtien** has sparser boutique resorts and delectable seafood, and seems to be avoiding some of the mistakes that Pattaya has made.

## Sightseeing

Almost a museum of itself, **Ripley's Believe It or Not** (Royal Garden Plaza, Thanon Pattaya 2, 0 3871 0294-8, admission B320) showcases replicas of freakish things. **Nong Nooch Tropical Gardens** (Thanon Sukhumvit, Sattaheep, 0 3870 9358-62, admission B80) offers cultural and elephant shows (9.45am, 10.30am, 3pm, 3.45pm daily, B300) and mini zoos where hornbills fly around to classical music. You can also overnight here; bungalows cost B1,600. **Wanasin Farm** (Thanon Pornprapanimit, 0 3842 8055/ www.wanasinfarm.com, Thais B80, foreigners B250) runs interactive cultural shows amid lakeside stilt houses.

Still unfinished after 20 years, the **Sanctuary of Truth** (206/2 Naklua Soi 12, 0 3822 5407, admission B500) is a truly fantastical carved wood temple, which,

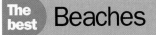

# The best Beaches

**For squeakily fine sand**
Had Sai Kaew on Ko Samet. *See p232.*

**For watersports**
Ao Patong on Ko Phuket. *See p246.*

**For scenery**
Had Phra Nang on Krabi. *See p254.*

**For solitude**
Tarutao archipelago. *See p256.*

**For Robinson Crusoe luxury**
Maiton Island, in Phang-nga. *See p252.*

**For partying**
Had Rin (*see p240*) on Ko Pha-ngan; Ao Tonsai (*see p255*) on Krabi; and Ao Wong Deuan (*see p232*) on Ko Samet.

curiously, hosts a dolphin show. You can even swim with the flippered mammals, so take your cossie. More temples (Chinese, Khmer and Thai) contain exhibitions at **Wat Yarn Sang Warraram** (999 Thanon Sukhumvit, 0 3823 8369), where a huge gold Buddha has been lasered into a cliff.

Watersports and fishing trips are widespread in Pattaya and Jomtien. The **Blue Lagoon Watersports Club** (23/4 Na Jomtien Soi 14, 0 3825 5115/6) offers a private beach, kayaks, windsurfing and (uniquely) kite surfing. Island reefs, wrecks and instruction are the diving draws for **Aquanauts** (437/17 Thanon Beach Soi 6, 0 3836 1724) and **Mermaids** (75/122-5 Thanon Jomtien Beach, 0 3823 2219/20). **Gulf Charters Thailand** (Ocean Marina Yacht Club, Jomtien, 0 2641 8679) rents yachts.

There are thrills aplenty at **Bungee Jump & Paintball Park** (248/10 Thanon Thepprasit, 0 3830 0608), **Pattaya Kart Speedway** (248/2 Thanon Thepprasit, 0 3842 2044) and **Siam Air Sports** in Si Racha (0 3848 2628), where parachuting costs B6,500. Among several good-value golf courses, **Phoenix Golf Club** (Thanon Sukhumvit km158, 0 3823 9391-8, rates B800 Mon-Fri, B1,500 Sat, Sun) is nearby and has sea views.

## Where to eat & drink

Pattaya town has few streetfood options, though the Royal Garden Plaza mall (Thanon Pattaya 2) has a food court. Amid de-spiced Thai, fast food and so-so Euro fodder, some restaurants stand out. **Sugar Hut** (391/18

Thanon Thappaya, 0 3836 4186) serves Thai for a price (main courses B200) with optional floor seating, while great, cheap Isaan cuisine is on offer at **Jeh Wah** (Thanon Pattaya 3, main courses B50) and **Sri Isaan** (opposite the Ambassador Hotel, Thanon Sukhumvit, Jomtien, main courses B50). **Ali Baba** (1/13-14 Thanon Pattaya Klang, 0 3842 9262, main courses B120-B280) has decent Indian food, but slow service in an Aladdin's cave-style interior.

Pattaya's classiest eatery is **Bruno's** in North Pattaya (463/77 Sri Nakorn Centre, 0 3836 1073, main courses B400), with a fine European menu and service engendering a formal ambience. **Casa Pascal** (485/4 Moo 10, Thanon Pattaya 2, 0 3872 3660, main courses B230-B690) serves French food in a beautiful Euro-Thai setting, with desserts to return for.

Hospitable **Mahasejthi Seafood** (79/56 Thanon Jomtien Beach, 0 3823 2929, main courses B250) has a clear view of the sea, and food live from tanks. Best of South Pattaya's Middle Eastern cafés, **Abu Saed** (363/13 Soi Saen Sanran, 0 3871 0277, main courses B120) is known for its royal couscous. A bargain Swiss-French menu with a touch of fusion (and good mussels) is available at **Paradise Café & Grill** (215/62-3 Thanon Pattaya 2, 0 3872 3177, main courses B220).

Most drinking and nightlife options revolve around the hundreds of beer bars, which vary little. Among the pubs, **Shenanigans** (Marriott Pattaya Resort, Thanon Pattaya 2, 0 3871 0641-3, main courses B250) offers Irish food, Guinness and bands. **Blues Factory** (Soi Lucky Star, Walking Street) has good live R&B from 9.30pm daily; bands also play at Thai disco **Excite** (Thanon Pattaya 3, at Soi Chaiyapoon). **Tiffany's** (464 Thanon Pattaya 2, 0 3842 1700-5, admission from B400) is the best of the three Las Vegas-style ladyboy cabarets.

## Gay & lesbian

Pattayaland Soi 3 is 'Boys' Town'. Amid go-go and massage outlets are classier bars in gay hotels, such as the **Café Royale Hotel, Bar & Restaurant** (0 3842 3515, main courses BB220-B340, rates B1,000-B2,800) and **Ambiance Hotel** (0 3842 4099, main courses B250, rates B1,100-B2,500). The swish **ICON** (146/8-9 Thappraya Soi 1, 0 3825 0300, main courses B200, rates B1,700-B3,000) stages a Chippendales-type show.

The gay beach is a few hundred metres north of the Royal Jomtien Resort. The **Pattaya Gay Festival** (www.pattayagayfestival.com) is held in late November.

## Where to stay

The best upmarket option, **Royal Cliff Beach Resort** (353 Thanon Phra Tamnuk, 0 3825 0421-40, rates B6,500-B65,500) has four hotels, 11 restaurants, a conference centre and bay views from the rooms and spa. **Sugar Hut** (rates B8,500-B14,200 – *see p230*) offers gorgeous stilt bungalows, while music memorabilia and a climbing wall adorn the **Hard Rock Hotel** (429 Thanon Beach, 0 3842 8755-9, rates from $95). Horse riding and an oriental teahouse are the attractions at spacious **Horseshoe Point** (Thanon Siam Country Club, 0 3873 5050, rates $89-$120).

Set in gardens on a virtually private beach, the new **Cabbages & Condoms Resort & Restaurant** (366/11 Phra Tamnak Soi 4, 0 3825 0035, rates from B2,500) is good value and provides a condom under your pillow. Knobbly rubbers are provided in the minibars at **Penthouse** (Pattayaland Soi 2, 0 3842 9639, rates from $15), where Elvis-style boudoirs secrete a raunchy DVD library and go-go poles for private dancers.

Budget rooms are rare, but the **J House** guesthouse (595/2-3 Thanon Beach, 0 3842 0852) is moderately priced (rates B550-B650) and overlooks the sea. For gay hotels, *see above* **Gay & lesbian**.

Lovely **Cabbages & Condoms** in Pattaya.

**Beyond Bangkok**

## Getting there & around

### By air

Bangkok Airways (0 2265 5555/www.bangkokair.
com) and charters fly to nearby Utapao Airport
(0 3824 5194/5). From Bangkok Airport it's 2.5hrs
by limo or taxi.

### By bus

Air-con buses leave every 30mins from Bangkok's
Eastern Bus Terminal (5am-10pm), and Northern Bus
Terminal (5am-7pm). Journey takes about 3hrs.

### By car

It's a 2hr drive from Bangkok via elevated highway 7
(Bangna–Chonburi Expressway). Car rental outfit
Budget (0 2203 0250/www.budget.co.th) has drop-offs
in Pattaya if you don't need a car every day. A taxi
from Bangkok costs around B800.

### Getting around

The centre is walkable, or you can flag down a
*songthaew* anywhere (B10 downtown, up to B30
outskirts). Motorcycles (from B150) and jeeps/cars
(from B800) are easy to hire.

## Resources

### Hospital

*Bangkok Pattaya Hospital, 301 Thanon Sukhumvit,
Naklua (0 3842 7751-3).*

### Money & internet access

Banks, ATMs and exchange booths are plentiful, as
are places providing internet access.

### Post office

*183/23 Thanon Beach (0 3841 4316).*

### Tourist information

*TAT, 609 Thanon Phra Tamnak (0 3842 8750).*
**Open** 8.30am-4.30pm daily.
Also check out www.pattaya.com.

### Tourist police

*Thanon Pattaya 2 (0 3842 9371).*

## Ko Samet

Among weekending Bangkokians, the more
conservative head for Hua Hin, while the
sparkier, younger set hold parties on Ko Samet.
The easiest tropical isle to get to, it's a fairly
workable combination of convenience and
conservation, being a national park (0 3865
3034, admission B200).

Boats from Baan Phe dock at **Na Dan** at
the hilt of what resembles a Malay kris dagger,
with a scalloped blade of fine beaches down
its east side, backed by a sliver of intensive
construction and the protected interior slopes
of mixed forest. While smart new resorts are
forcing bamboo shacks and concrete bunkers
to upgrade, the avoidance of planning has left

# The poet's tale

A mermaid statue at Ao Hin Kok on Ko
Samet marks the setting for the signature
tale by Thailand's UNESCO-honoured poet
**Sunthorn Phu** (1787-1855). Falling in and
out of favour during the second and third
Chakri reigns, he also fell in and out of
love affairs, prompting the verse-story
*Phra Aphai Manee*; it tells the tale of a
dashing prince who fell for a mermaid, was
seduced by a giantess and experienced
countless rollicking romances. With a
distinctive human touch, it's one of the
few epics to rival the *Ramakien*'s literary
sway in Thailand. Bronzes of Sunthorn
and his characters dot the site of his
father's home, some 20 kilometres
(12.5 miles) east of Baan Phe at Bam
Klam, near Klaeng. A festival is held here
on his birthday (26 June) featuring
puppetry, recitals and folk entertainment.

the shabbier bungalows light on amenities and
aesthetics, with rumbling generators, tenuous
phone connections and water delivered by boat.

Such eyesores get less dense as the coccyx-
bruising road judders south from the squeaky
clean **Had Sai Kaew** via **Ao Hin Kok**,
**Ao Phai** and **Ao Tubtim** (with a short walk
to rocky cove **Ao Nuan**). A path through
dingy **Ao Cho** or the precipitous road reaches
**Ao Wong Deuan**, a busy arc bisected by
a pier. Boulder strewn **Ao Thian** is a short
hike further. The remote, upmarket resorts
that dot the north, west and southern tip have
their own ferries.

Aside from the jetskis, inflatable banana
rides and coach parties in matching hats on Had
Sai Kaew, mellow lazing about is only disturbed
by beach massages. There are also tours to
snorkel, dive or fish the clear waters, which
develop surf in the rains, when the island is
relatively dry and easy to visit. By night, it
turns into a laid-back party scene.

## Where to stay, eat & drink

The dauntingly painted cement **Naga** (Ao Hin
Khok, 0 3864 4035/1353 2575, rates B200-B700)
has the cheapest rooms, but is most prized for
its bakery and coconut grove bar (main courses
B80-B210). The nightlife is groovier on Ao Phai,
where **Silver Sand** (Ao Phai, 0 1218 5195)
hosts a beachside disco with cocktails served
in plastic ice buckets. Its topless gigolo fire
jugglers are rather keen on teaching Western

women their swinging techniques… Out of earshot to the south are the timber lodges of **Samet Villa** (Ao Phai, 0 3864 4094, rates B600-B1,000) and gay-friendly **Tubtim Resort** (Ao Tubtim, 0 3864 4025-7, rates B500-B1,200), which serves great seafood (main courses B60-B200) on the beach.

Ao Wong Deuan still suffers dowdy resorts and daytrippers, but also hosts raves with Bangkok and foreign DJs. On the northern rocks, **Oasis** bar (0 1847 9507, main courses B70-B150) is a private spot to chat and bop. **Bay Watch** (0 1826 7834) is the liveliest bar amid the central clamour of seafood restaurants, while a suavely minimalist dance room opens on to the terrace of **Taleburé Bed & Bar** (0 1762 3548/1862 9402, main courses B250), where retro-chic garden bungalows (rates B700-B1,400) have stunning views but poor service.

Ao Thien is developing fast, with Balinese bathrooms added to **Sang Thien** (0 1218 6934, rates B1,200-B2,000), eccentric shoreline huts at **Lung Dum** (Noppadol, 0 1458 8430, rates B300-B700) and the rustic, Wild West-themed hangout of **Apache Garden View Restaurant** (Oud, 0 1452 9472, main courses B80-B150, rates B300-B700).

The best food is found north-west of Na Dan at **Moo Ban Talay** (Ao Noi Na, 0 3861 6788/1838 8682/www.moobantalay.com, main courses B250-B375). Its spa and sleek minimalist villas with roofless bathrooms (rates B5,000-B8,000) face Baan Phe across a shallow gritty beach. Isolated on the west, humid Ao Phrao shelters the snazzily

romantic **Ao Phrao Resort** (0 364 4101-5/www.aopraoresort.com, main courses B100-B380, rates B2,300-B10,300).

## Getting there

### By car
Baan Phe is 200km (124 miles) from Bangkok on Route 3 (cutting a corner on Route 36); journey takes 3.5hrs. Park at the piers.

### By bus
Air-con buses leave Bangkok's Eastern Bus Terminal direct to Baan Phe (hourly, 5am-9pm daily) or fast to Rayong (hourly, 4.30am-10pm daily); from Rayong bus station (0 3861 1006) it's a 20mins *songthaew* ride. Get return bus tickets before boarding the ferry. Rooms can be scarce on Ko Samet after noon, and boats rarely run after dark.

### By boat
Ferries to Na Dan (B100 return; journey 30-40mins), depart Baan Phe bus station pier and Saphan Nuan Thip pier 500m into town (hourly 8am-5pm Nov-Feb, otherwise 2-hourly, but they wait to get 20 people). Fewer ferries serve Wong Deuan (45mins). Pricey speedboats (0 3865 1999) go direct to beaches.

## Resources

### Hospital
*Rayong Hospital (0 3861 1104); Phe Health Centre (0 3865 2613).*

### Money & internet access
There are ATMs in Baan Phe, but a poor exchange rate on Ko Samet. Phones and internet access are very expensive from shops and resorts on Samet.

Exercising to the sound of the sea.

**Beyond Bangkok**

## Tourist information

You'll find minimal maps, leaflets and touts at piers. Website www.kohsamet.com is worth a look.

## Tourist police

*0 3865 1669/hotline 1155.*

# Ko Chang

A national park of 46 islands bordering Cambodia includes Ko Chang (Elephant Island), Thailand's second largest island, with 30 by eight kilometres (19 by five miles) of rainforest. Since 2002, when Prime Minister Thaksin Shinawatra proclaimed that the island should become the 'next Phuket', it's been lurching upmarket in a clash between frenzied tourism development and the eco-sensitivity. While the supposedly unintrusive infrastructure is being noisily constructed, tranquillity is at a premium and the tenure of many resorts, shops and services is uncertain. Trucks shake the lone road that's being built around a mountainous interior containing three waterfalls and a 740-metre (2,428-foot) peak.

But there's enough beauty-with-amenities to warrant the 300-kilometre (186-mile) trip from Bangkok. Admission to the park (0 3953 8100) costs B200 for foreigners, B20 for Thais. You get to Ko Chang via the provincial capitals of Chanthaburi (Thailand's gem centre for 500 years) and Trad; the main port, Laem Ngop, is 17 kilometres (10.5 miles) from Trad.

The activity is centred on its north-west, where **Had Sai Khao**, a 25-minute *songthaew* ride from Tha Dan Kao pier, is thronged (at the moment) with backpacker-style places. Among jungle trek operators are basic bungalow set-up **Rock Sand** (Had Sai Khao, 0 1863 7611, rates B400-B600). The reefs are reasonable and diving is possible from August to May with **Eco Divers** (0 1863 7314).

Elephants aren't indigenous to the island, which is named after a pachyderm-shaped southern headland, though it has a refuge, open to visitors, at **Baan Kwan Chang** (Ko Chang Elephant Camp, 22/4 Had Khlong Son). You'll need a four-wheel drive to get there.

## Where to stay & eat

Rooms at Had Sai Khao are mainly guesthouse style or beachside, such as **Cookie Bungalow** (0 1861 4227, rates B1,500), which has fresh seafood barbecues. **Banpu Koh Chang Hotel** (0 1863 7314, rates B2,500-B6,500) is more upmarket. German-run **Baan Nuna** (no phone) on southern Had Sai Khao serves decent pizzas and Thai fare to the accompaniment of 1960s/70s rock. South on Ao Klong Prao,

**Koh Chang Resort** (0 3953 8055, rates B1,900-B2,800) is feverishly expanding, so it might be quieter around the bay at **Klong Prao Resort** (0 3959 7216/1830 0126, rates B1,500-B3,000), built on a lagoon. Both have private beaches. In a sign of things to come, the northernmost bay is home to Chang's first luxury villas at **Aiyapura Resort & Spa** (Ao Klong Son, 0 3952 1656-60, rates B7,200-B26,000), while **Boutique Resort & Health Spa** (Ao Klong Phrao, 09-938 6403, rates B2,000) offers treatments in stylish wooden *salas*. In the south-east, accommodation is advertised at several houses in Bang Bao, a fishing village perched on stilts over the sea, where the seafood is certainly fresh.

The adventurous can head south to islands that are accessible only in dry season. There's more white sand on Ko Mak; the **Ko Mak Resort** (0 3959 7296, rates B350-B850) has the best bungalows. Large, exquisite Ko Kood already has exclusive set-ups, such as **Ko Kood Island Resort** (Ao Yai Klerd, 0 2332 8502, rates B4,350-B3,550).

## Getting there

### By air

Bangkok Airways' Trad Airport is scheduled to open in March 2003.

### By bus & car

Buses to Trad depart almost hourly from Bangkok's Eastern Bus Terminal, and three times daily from the Northern Bus Terminal (journey takes 5-6hrs); then take a *songthaew* to the pier. By car, take route 3 to Trad, then road 3148 to Laem Ngop, then a ferry. On Ko Chang, *songthaews* and easily hired motorbikes are the norm.

### By boat

Hourly ferries to Tha Dan Kao leave Laem Ngop 7am-5.30pm daily in the high season; trip takes 1hr. Ferries to Ko Mak (3hrs) leave at 3pm daily Nov-Apr, returning at 8am.

## Resources

### Hospital

*Trad Hospital (0 3951 1040/1).* There are also clinics on Ko Chang.

### Money & internet access

There are ATMs in Trad and Laem Ngop, but a poor exchange rate on Had Sai Khao. Phones and internet access are pricey from Had Sai Khao resorts/shops.

### Tourist information

*TAT, Laem Ngop (0 3959 7259/60).* **Open** 8.30am-4.30pm daily. Also check out www.kohchang.com.

### Tourist police

*0 39511 035/hotline 1155.*

# Samui Archipelago

There's a Gulf between these diverse tropical islands.

The 80 islands off the Thai Gulf coast of Surat Thani province, 650 kilometres (403 miles) south of Bangkok, have a different character to those in the slightly more crystal Andaman Sea. A mellow charm pervades its main three inhabited islands: **Ko Samui**, with its mix of unhurried sun-worshippers, partying types and New Age vibes; the rugged hedonistic backpacker frontier of **Ko Pha-ngan** with its full moon parties; and the remote divers' domain of **Ko Tao**.

## Ko Samui

With smart hotels, gourmet restaurants, luxury spas, second homes and the continual presence of New Age pilgrims, Samui is more cosmopolitan than Phuket, yet it hasn't forgotten its roots. While the jet set could dispose of $500 a night in a palatial villa on a virtually private beach, backpackers – who pioneered travel here in the 1970s and '80s – can still find beach huts for under B300.

The local infrastructure reflects this demographic, from a Tesco Lotus hypermarket and a British pie maker to plans for an airport in the south to receive national carrier Thai Airways. Yet from the lush forests of the mountainous interior to its rugged capes and sweeping beaches, Samui's primordial beauty remains its greatest asset.

The area of **Nathon** around the ferry port is Samui's commerical and official hub, with many Hainan-influenced teak shophouses, a bustling market and a diversity of delicious hawker food. Heading north at **Ban Bang Makham** is the main stadium for buffalo fighting (Samui's indigenous sport), where events – advertised on trucks – take place at 5.30pm, usually during festivals.

The sea along the **North Coast** is a little murkier than in the east, but it remains calm throughout the year. The good-value, well-spaced accommodation along this coast appeals to backpackers and long-termers. An attractive fishing community compensates for **Had Maenam**'s less appealing beach, while **Had Bophut** is easily Samui's most charming village – quaint old shophouses overlook its beach, many converted into guesthouses, restaurants and shops. Further east and home to the 12-metre-high (39-foot) landmark statue in Wat Phra Yai, **Big Buddha Beach** (Had Bangrak) has the edge over the rest for eating, drinking and watersports. There's not much nightlife in the north outside Bophut, though on full moon night the coast reverberates with the sound of revellers being ferried to and from Ko Pha-ngan (*see p237* **Moon dance**).

Hugging a picturesque crescent of fine sand, swimmable waters and arching palms, **Chaweng** is either party central or a vaguely sleazy lesson in over-development to be avoided. Both views are valid, but in among all the dross and congestion, you'll find some fine restaurants and funky bars. There's even secluded beachside accommodation – you just have to look hard to find it. Chaweng is also home to Samui's main Thai boxing stadium (Lagoon Road, 9pm-1am Mon & Fri, B500).

Over a ridge with giddying northwards views (near Beverly Hills Café), yawns **Ao Lamai**. Coral-strewn and shallow in the north (with independent resorts), the bay's southern end is stunning, with crystal waters and sand-studded granite boulders, including **Hin Tin** and **Hin Yai**. Just one kilometre south on Thanon 4169 (the island's ring road), these headland rocks resemble male and female genitalia, spawning crowds and souvenir stalls. Mid-bay, **Lamai** town is a mess and perhaps best viewed from the precipitous **Overlap Stone** (3 kilometres/two miles south on 4169). The centre is dominated by prostitute-filled bars (much more so than Chaweng) and mediocre restaurants.

While the south's barely disturbed beaches – especially around **Lipa Noi** and **Laem Set** – are as good as the far busier northern ones, you can also head down Thanon 4170 for surprising vistas of rolling fields, terraced rice paddies, water buffalo and intriguing **Wat Khunaram** (Thanon 4169, east of Hua Thanon) – where fans of esoterica might be interested to see the displayed body of marathon-meditating monk Luang Pho Dang. **Uncle Nim's Waterfall & Magic Garden**, an extraordinary sculpture park based on Buddhist scriptures, is also worth a look. At Ban Saket, turn inland off 4169 on to an asphalt road, then hang a right a kilometre before the end (ask for Nam Tok Ta Nim). The mountain views are equally impressive.

### ACTIVITIES

Samui's fine diving and snorkelling reefs (best from May to October), suffered coral bleaching in the 1997 El Niño. They're recovering well,

**Had Bophut** – Samui's most appealing village. *See p235.*

but generally speaking the further offshore the reef, the more likely it is to be teeming with life. Sites include Sail Rock's famous natural chimney, and Chumphon Pinnacles' whale shark habitat. **Easy Divers** (0 7741 3373) and **Samui International Dive School** (0 7742 2386) both have branches all over the island. For low-volume advantages, try the **Dive Shop** (Beach Road, Chaweng, 0 7723 0232) or **Discovery Dive** (Amari Palm Reef Resort, Chaweng, 0 7741 3196). Other watersports, from windsurfing and parasailing to the selfish indulgences of jet-skis and 'banana floats', are most prevalent at Bangrak and Chaweng.

'Ride with photo ops' would be a more accurate term than 'elephant trekking' for numerous tours, though it's a leisurely if jerky way to explore the interior. **Living Thailand** (Ban Nok Sai, 0 7741 8680/1) and **Island Safari** (Chaweng, 0 7723 0567) are both professional (from B300 for 15 minutes). Meanwhile, foodies can learn Thai cooking at **SITCA** (Chaweng, opposite Central, 0 7741 3172/www.sitca.net) for B895.

## Where to eat

Offering the best coffee in town, **About Arts & Crafts** on the seafront south of Nathon Pier (0 1499 9353, open 9am-5pm daily, main courses B80-B120) is a shop serving excellent vegetarian breakfasts, muffins and health shakes, though the **Spa Resort**'s veggie menu is incomparable (*see p240* **In the fast lane**). For New York deli-style eating, **Angela's Bakery & Café** (Thanon 4169, Maenam, 0 7742 7396, 8.30am-7.30pm daily, main courses B100-B150) impresses with fresh breads, cakes, pies, salads and sandwiches. A chilled atmosphere, funky decor and an eclectic menu rule at **Eddy's** (Zazan Resort entrance, Thanon 4169, Bophut, 0 7724 5127, main courses B60-B120), taking in multiple influences (notably Middle Eastern) with bargain set lunches.

Cheap and cheerful curry house **Shabash** (Thanon 4169, Bangrak, 0 7724 5035, noon-10pm daily, main courses B80-B150) spans Indonesian, Indian, Singaporean and kosher food. Service is slow, but on the whole the grub's worth waiting for. Expect low-key alfresco dining with a dash of Gallic élan (and prices to match) at the **Mangrove** (Thanon Airport, Big Buddha, 0 7742 7584, 11.30am-late daily, closed last three days of the month, main courses B250-B350).

Among hotel selections, fine French and Asian fusion cuisine is balanced by a superb wine list, excellent service and a romantic beachside setting at **Poppies** (Beach Road, South Chaweng, 0 7742 2419, noon-midnight

# Moon dance

Many visitors still come to the archipelago for one thing only: Full Moon Inc. Every month some 8,000-10,000 people flock to the hard trance on **Had Rin East** at the world's biggest beach party. Most stay on Ko Pha-ngan, but many also come over in speedboats from northern Samui, straining accommodation on both isles.

Officials always step up efforts to suppress drug use by deploying increasingly well-disguised undercover officers, occasionally with DEA or Interpol. But none of this seems to reduce substance abuse, and stories of dodgy drugs abound. Be warned: the Burmese-produced, super-addictive amphetamine *ya ba* (sold as pink pills) is more like crack than speed, and can be psychologically dangerous.

Not wanting to risk having too little of a good thing, the beach party scene now includes **Black Moon** (Had Rin and Rocky Bay, near Chong Mon on Samui), **Ritual Beach** and **Freedom Beach** (both Rocky Bay) and **Half Moon** (Ko Som, off Big Buddha Beach on Samui). None of the Samui parties have Had Rin's captive audience, so it's easy to grab cheap (sometimes free) *songthaews* there and back. Smaller parties also rock **Krabi** (*see p254*).

Since the parties are one of the few remaining options for legally having a good time beyond 2am, they're too economically important to stop. So in a 2002 compromise, the Had Rin party moved one night away from sacred Buddhist full moons. Check schedules online (*see p243* **Tourist information**).

daily, main courses B250-B350). There's also good but pricey Thai food and unobtrusive live music most nights. Sumptuous, expensive bungalows nestle in its tropical garden. Intricately presented, delicately spiced Royal Thai cuisine, brought by fawning waitresses, prevails at **Sala Thai** at **Santiburi Dusit Resort** (Thanon 4169, Maenam, 0 7742 5031, 6pm-midnight daily, main courses B200-B300). A well-considered vegetarian selection, great wines and herb ice-creams are further highlights at this, one of Samui's smartest resorts.

**Central Samui Beach Resort** (Beach Road, Chaweng 0 7723 0500, 6-10.30pm daily, main courses B200-B300) is a behemoth housing

a warren of well-maintained, mostly charmless rooms (B5,500-B24,000) and top-level dining: immaculate Japanese fare is offered at authentically formal **Hagi**, while the Modern European menu by Fabian Strutz at **Palm Grove** excels in imaginative flavour combos.

## Where to drink

Capturing the original backpacker spirit, **Dragon Bay** in the middle of Chaweng beach (open 5pm-2am daily) is a mat-and-cushion operation on the sand, with a mellow mood and an ambient playlist. **Barefoot Bar** (Chaweng, near Central Samui Resort, 0 9878 4640, 6pm-2am daily) offers authentic cocktails, good tunes, a relaxed vibe, friendly management and no bar girls: a unique combination on Beach Road.

The music tends towards banging house and trance at **Gecko Village** (Bophut, 0 7724 5553/4, 10am-2am daily), where the high decibels are a warm-up for big beach parties. Families, couples and fans of TV sport prefer **Tropical Murphy's** (opposite McDonald's, Central Chaweng, 0 7741 3614/5, 9am-2am daily). Its bustle and size create an authentic Irish pub feel.

## Nightlife

Samui's weekly Glastonbury, the **Secret Garden Festival** (Big Buddha Beach, 4-10pm Sun) has offered a family-friendly mix of food, drink, stalls and live Thai and Western rock since 1992, attracting the occasional big name. Every August, Bophut's **Fisherman's Village Festival** is similar. Chaweng's three big clubs (all free) – **Green Mango** (Beach Road, 0 7742 2148), **Full Circle** (Beach Road, 0 7741 3061) and the **Reggae Pub** (Chaweng Lagoon, 0 7742 2322) draw large crowds nightly. Full Circle is streets ahead of the other two (both pick-up joints that play awful Euro house) and has a large Thai following, which moves on to dark and half-moon parties (*see p237* **Moon dance**). **Christy's Cabaret** (Beach Road, Chaweng, 0 1788 1057, free) parades miming ladyboys nightly at 11pm.

## Shopping

Most of Samui's shops and stalls are to be found among Chaweng's array of tailors, carving shops and places selling copied CDs, DVDs and games. You'll find similar stuff in Lamai and (cheapest of all) in Nathon. **Thai Craft Village** (opposite Samui Seafood, Chaweng, 0 7741 3221, 10am-10pm daily) is a good one-stop emporium. The **Farn Shop** (beside Wat Phra Yai, Bangrak, 0 7724 5245, 10am-6pm daily) has imaginative handmade silverware and jewellery. **Sawang Optical** (opposite Boots, Chaweng, 0 7742 0230, 11am-9.30pm Mon-Sat) bulges with cheap designer glasses and shades, while **Nathon Books** (Pier Road, Nathon, 10am-7pm daily) has the best selection of second-hand books. **Travel Solutions** (Chaweng Beach, 0 7723 0203, 10am-9pm daily) is a friendly, efficient, British-run agent offering worldwide ticketing, Samui activities and accommodation. There are banks with ATMs in Nathon, Chaweng and Lamai.

## Where to stay

The best five-star option is **Tongsai Bay** (Choeng Mon, 0 7742 5015/www.tongsaibay. co.th, rates B10,000-B30,000), on a near private beach, with most rooms having a sea view and all boasting bathtubs on their balconies. Its hillside cottages have the best vistas, while the hotel rooms are a bit poky and the palatial villas pricey. By contrast, **Muang Kulay Pan** (Beach Road, Chaweng, 0 7723 0850/ www.sawadee.com/samui/kulaypan, rates B3,400-B7,000) blends Javanese, southern Thai and Japanese influences in minimalist rooms to stunning effect. The expansive garden and communal areas are dotted with bonsai plants and objets d'art, and there's an impressive black-tiled pool.

The achingly hip beachside bungalows of **Long Island Resort** (Thanon 4169, north of Lamai, 0 7742 4202, rates B700-B3,500) tend to attract Thai and international media types and celebrities. Its beachside superior rooms are worth the higher rates; there's also a decent pool and attached spa. **Baan Taling Ngam** is the focal resort in the quiet east (0 7742 3019/www.lemeridien-kohsamui.com, rates $430-$830) offering reliable Le Meridien luxury. **Zen Holiday Villas** (Thanon 4169, Bang Po, 0 9866 1085/www.zenholidayvillas.com, rates B4,000-B15,000) rents short- and long-term villas.

A notch cheaper, the **Lodge** (Bophut Village, 0 7742 5337, rates B1,200-B1,500) is a classy beachside boutique hotel. Its immaculate hardwood rooms all have fans and air-conditioning, sea views, balconies and TVs. There's no restaurant, but the beach bar serves decent snacks. The brick, earth-toned Mediterranean-style bungalows of **Zazen** (Thanon 4169, Bophut, 0 7742 5177/ www.samuizazen.com, rates B900-B3,000) are good value, given the decent pool, quality international restaurant, small spa, sun decks and innovative shaded alcoves on the beach.

Commanding the island's best panorama, **Jungle Club** (Thanon 4169, South Chaweng, 01 894 2327/www.thejungleclub.net, rates B350-B700) is a very chilled, peaceful bungalow set-

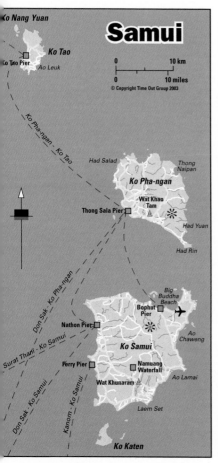

Other options include **Poppies** (bungalow rates B6,300-B8,100), **Santiburi Dusit Resort** ($450-$990) and **Central Samui Beach Resort** (B5,500-B24,000); for all, *see p237* **Where to eat**.

## Resources

The best of Samui's free publications, full of hotel, dining and activity options, *Samui Guide* is still as ad-driven as its rivals *Samui Dining Guide, Samui Spa Guide* and *Samui Director*. Useful websites include www.on-samui.com and www.samuiguide.com.

### Hospitals
*Bandon Hospital, Thanon 4169 (0 7724 5236-9).* High prices.
*Samui International Hospital, Beach Road, North Chaweng (0 7742 2272).*

### Immigration office
*0 7742 1069.*

### Post office
*Seaside Road, Nathon.* **Open** 8.30am-4.30pm Mon-Fri; 9am-noon Sat, Sun.

### Tourist information
*Thanon Thaweeradphakdee, Nathon (0 7742 0504/ tatsamui@samart.com).*

### Tourist police
*Thanon Thaweeratphakdee, Nathon (0 7742 1281).*

## Getting there & around

### By air
Samui International Airport is owned by Bangkok Airways (www.bangkokair.com), charging B400 departure tax. Flights leave 12 times a day to and from Bangkok (70mins) ,as well as to Phuket, Chiang Mai and U-Tapao (Pattaya). Flying Thai Airways from Bangkok to Surat Thani and getting a shuttle bus to the ferry saves about B1,500, but adds 3hrs each way.

### By bus or train
Buses (B380-B660) hurtle through the night from Bangkok's Southern Terminal to Surat Thani. Several daily trains from Bangkok's Hualumphong Station stop at Surat Thani (sleepers B578-B1,119).

### By ferry
Between 4-6 ferries a day make the 2hr trip from Surat Thani to Samui (Seatran Ferry, 0 7727 5060/1/2, every 2hrs 5.30am-7pm daily, B150). Car ferries at Don Sak run 5am-7pm daily, but to avoid 2-3hr queues, arrive by 8am. Contact Racha Ferry (0 7747 1151/2/3, hourly, B64) or Seatran Ferry (0 7747 1173, hourly, B80).

### Getting around
Thailand's third largest island, Samui is 21km (13 miles) wide and 25km (15.5 miles) long, and its ring road, Thanon 4169, takes 50mins by car,

up, but an arduous slog uphill (use the free airport pick-up). Basic and without fan or air-conditioning – not needed at this altitude – it also has a good French/Thai restaurant and is scheduled (by mid 2003) to get a pool.

Budgetwise, **Shambala** (Had Bangrak, 0 7742 5330/www.samui-shambala.com, rates B400-B800) is run by friendly English couple Jules and Jessica – a great source of local info and Thai staple dishes. Its simple, well-spaced fan bungalows (some with hot water) are in a mature shoreside garden. Handy for town, **Nathon Residence** (Thanon Taweeratpakdee, Nathon, 0 7723 6081, rates B500-B600) has clean, spacious doubles and twins – all with TV and air-con, some with hot water – and a very cheap restaurant.

**Beyond Bangkok**

90mins by motorbike. Cars are easily hired and much safer than mopeds (Samui's narrow, hilly and often sandy roads have Thailand's highest accident rate). Garishly painted *songthaews* can be flagged down anywhere and act as cheap buses by day (B20-B70) and taxis by night (up to B300; cheaper if people are already aboard). Motorcycle taxis are quick and negotiable (Airport to Chaweng B100). Yellow metered taxis are a rip-off, their drivers often demanding unreasonable, unmetered fees.

## Ko Pha-ngan

Only an hour by ferry from Samui, Pha-ngan is ten years behind, slightly less beautiful and noticeably friendlier than its neighbour. Famous for **Had Rin**'s full moon parties (*see p237* **Moon dance**), it attracts a fascinating blend of backpackers, entrepreneurs, dreamers and wasters to its smaller, craggier, often reef-laden bays. Local Thais have adapted well, although coconuts and fishing remain village mainstays. Electricity is not always constant and the roads are sometimes too bumpy even for motorbikes – longtail boats and hiking are often necessary to cover the island's mountainous terrain.

The new international ferry port is at the commercial centre, **Thong Sala**, which has little to recommend it beyond the convenience of an ATM. At Ban Tai, a few kilometres east, is **Wat Khao Tham Meditation Centre**. Its regular Vipassana retreats can

be booked by writing to PO Box 18, Ko Pha-ngan, Surat Thani 84280, after first consulting www.watkowtahm.org.

The other ferry dock, **Had Rin West**, is rocky and shallow outside its shipping channel, and lies back to back with the headland's better beach, **Had Rin East**. Home of the full moon raves, this strand would be good for swimming and snorkelling if it weren't for the perpetual longtail traffic. If you're staying hereabouts – Had Rin has the lion's share of Pha-ngan's nightlife options and good restaurants – it's worth walking to the near pristine **Had Leela**.

A short B40 boat ride from Had Rin is **Had Yuan**, with fine, clean white sand and excellent swimming. The next (rather pebbly) bay, **Had Tien**, is home to the **Sanctuary Spa & Wellness Centre** (*see p240* **In the fast lane**) – take a B60 boat from Had Rin or make the 60- to 90-minute walk if the seas are rough.

Flanked by Thaan Prawet and Wung Thong falls, the double bay of **Thong Naipan** in the north-east was favoured by Rama V and is great for snorkelling. Access by boat is preferable to the muddy, potholed track from Thong Sala. Boats also run to the very special **Had Kuat** (Bottle Beach), reached faster from Ao Cha Lok Lum. This cup-like bay has a major fishing village, a steep (but worth it) viewpoint and a better road from Thong Sala. In the north-west, **Had Salad** is very, very relaxed even by Pha-ngan's soporific standards.

# In the fast lane

Offering everything from colonic irrigation, tropical enzyme wraps and sea salt scrubs to yoga and meditation, as well as acupuncture, reiki, chi kung and t'ai chi, Samui is at the forefront of the world spa boom. In fact, the Thai massage scene is so competitive it's rumoured that therapists' fingers get broken for switching parlours.

First on the scene in 1992 was the **Spa Resort** in Lamai (0 7723 0855/ www.spasamui.com, open 10am-9pm daily). Although this beach facility is grubbier than the branch in the hills, it has an outstanding vegetarian menu. For purist colonic fasting, **Samui Dharma Healing Centre** (Sawai Home Bungalows, Lipa Noi, 0 7723 4170/ www.dharmahealing.com) is run according to strict Buddhist principles.

For more orthodox pampering (facials, wraps, massages and whatnot), **Santiburi Spa** at the Santiburi Dusit Resort (Maenam,

0 7742 5031, 9am-10pm daily) sets the benchmark, though it isn't cheap (B1,500-B2,500 per treatment). Also recommended in this category are the **Imperial Spa** (Imperial Boathouse Resort, Choeng Mon, 0 7742 5041, 10am-10pm daily) and **Tamarind Retreat** (Lamai, 0 7742 4221/ www.tamarindretreat.com). Among the freelance yoga teachers, Jo Grant can be contacted at her stone and crystal shop, **Inner Guidance** (Bophut Village, 0 9867 7725/innerguidance@hotmail.com).

Over on Ko Pha-ngan, the palatial **Sanctuary Spa & Wellness Centre** (sanct_spa@ kohphangan.com/www.sanctuaryfasting.com, treatments B80-B2,000) has sea views from hillside suites and a fine seafood and vegetarian restaurant, with separate centres for fasters and for upmarket spa treatments (far cheaper than on Samui: B300-B1,000 each). B80 dorm beds come with chores.

**Chaweng** beach:
not just for parties.

## Where to eat & stay

If you must stay in Thong Sala, the **Asia Hotel** (0 7723 8607, rates B350-B700) has cramped but clean air-conditioned rooms, while the portside **Yellow Café** (open 7am-10pm daily) is a good spot for a sandwich while waiting for your boat.

Due to Had Rin's preponderance of backpacker bungalows, decent rooms are scarce. **Suncliffe** (0 7737 5134, rates B250-B1,500) and **Seabreeze** (0 7737 5162, rates B300-B1,000) have more spacious bungalows in the hills above. Dining here is surprisingly cosmopolitan, with high-quality Italian, the **Shell** (Had Rin Lake, 0 7737 5149, 10am-11pm daily, main courses B150-B200); Indian, **Om Ganesh** (Main Road, 0 7737 5123, 9am-3.30pm, 5-11pm daily, main courses B60-B100); and Spanish, **Bamboozle** (Main Road, 0 9587 0142, noon-11pm daily, main courses B80-B120). For fry-ups, burgers and beers, the **Outback Bar** (Main Road, 0 7737 5126, main courses B100-B150) is well away from the pounding bass of the beach bars. **Niras Bakery** (Crossroads, 6am-2am daily) is good for breakfast or lunch.

Pha-ngan's only three-star hotel, **Panviman Resort** (0 7723 8543/www.panviman.com, rates B950-B3,500) is perhaps overpriced, but its Mediterranean-style brick cottages have huge balconies commanding fine sea views, plus good international food. Further down the beach, which is family-oriented and has excellent snorkelling, **Tongtapan Resort**

(0 7723 8538/tongtapan@yahoo.com, rates B300-B700) is built on and around a series of huge boulders, like many Samui venues. The friendly staff can help organise treks and trips.

On Had Yuan beach, there are stilt bungalows at **Big Blue Bungalows** (0 1270 1537/bigb@ksc.th.com, rates B350-B900). The VIP bungalows sleep up to six and there's a restaurant. For the **Sanctuary** on Had Tien, *see p240* **In the fast lane**. On Had Salad, **Salad Hut** (salad_hut@hotmail.com, rates B300-B600) has simple wooden fan bungalows and cushions, mats and hammocks to enhance the chilled atmosphere. Overlooking Had Yao to the west, **Tantawan Bungalows** (0 1229 4804, rates B250-B400) has passable fan bungalows and shared bathrooms, but amazing views, superb Thai/French cuisine and Pha-ngan's best pool.

## Nightlife

Full moon is not the only excuse for Had Rin's bar strip to party. **Harmony**, behind Bamboozle restaurant (9pm-2am Mon, Wed, Fri), and **Backyard**, on the road to Had Leela, (9pm-2am Tue, Thur, Sun, full moon 9am-2am) play uplifting trance and hard trance respectively to packed dance floors.

## Resources

### Banks

Thong Sala's main street banks have ATMs; Had Rin crossroads' ATM is often empty.

**Beyond Bangkok**

The ferry to **Ko Tao** at **Had Bophut**. *See p243.*

# **Learn to** Dive

Thousands choose Thailand for their first dive, and taking the plunge in its constantly warm waters couldn't be simpler, with world-class schools and qualified independent instructors from myriad countries. It's a close-knit scene with socialising fostered by 'dive buddy' bonding.

Preliminary pool teaching in Bangkok is conveniently completed at **Pattaya** (*see p229*), where there are diveable wrecks, while, further east, **Ko Chang** has a skeleton operation from October to May. But you're better off training on either the southern coast, where the reefs teem with life (despite some damage from dynamite fishing and reckless touching of coral). Though the Gulf waters are shallower, fringing reefs, submerged pinnacles and sheer underwater walls can be quickly accessed (best from May to early October). **Ko Tao** has it all, particularly for learners, with diverse courses, good value for money and an almost year-round season. It's reached from Chumphon, Ko Pha-ngan and Ko Samui, which all have dive companies – the latter's is the most established.

In the Andaman Sea visibility can top 35metres (115 feet). **Ko Phuket** (*see p245*) boasts more dive and training facilities than the rest of Thailand combined. From there, live-aboard trips for the experienced take in the pristine **Similan Islands** (*see p252*), **Ko Surin**, **Richlieu Rock** and even the **Burma Banks**, with sightings of whale sharks. **Krabi** (*see p254*) and **Ko Phi Phi** (*see p253*) have many dive operators, though the few at **Khao Lak** (*see p252*) and **Ko Lanta** (*see p256*) in Trang (refuge of the dugong) tend to open only in the Andaman high season (October to May).

Whether PADI, NAUI, British Sub-Aqua Club or another standard, the training options are similar: uncertified Discover Scuba introduction; three- to four-day Open Water/Novice Diver; Advanced/Sports Diver, adding navigation, night diving and photography; Rescue Diver; and the first pro level, Dive Master. Shop around and beware of 'bargains'. PADI 5 Star schools must utilise the full programme, while others should provide sufficient materials in (not too large) classes. Sticking with one tutor improves comprehension and trust – also an issue regarding students you'll 'buddy' with.

All you'll need is swimwear, waterproof sunscreen, a T-shirt and two passport photos. For reef reference, check *Thai Diver* magazine. Worried about claustrophobia? Don't; diving is like suspension in infinite space and so visually wondrous the main concern is usually the temptation to stay down too long.

**Beyond Bangkok**

## Hospitals

*Koh Phangan Hospital, 6km (4 miles) north of Thong Sala (0 7737 7034).*

## Post office

*East of Thong Sala, toward Had Rin.* **Open** 8.30am-noon, 1-4.30pm Mon-Fri.

## Tourist information

Try www.hadrin.com, www.kohphangan.com and www.thaisite.com/fullmoonparty

# Getting there & around

You can only get to Pha-ngan by boat. Ferries run from Don Sak or Surat Thani to Thong Sala (5-6 times a day, 4-6hrs) and Nathon (Samui) to Thong Sala (3 a day, 70mins). A catamaran runs between Maenam or Big Buddha and Thong Sala (2 a day, 45mins) – check changing times with local agents. Three reliable ferries a day run from Big Buddha to Had Rin (10.30pm, 1pm, 4pm; return 9.30am, 11.40am, 2.30pm; 50mins) and a daily longtail from Maenam stops at all beaches between Had Rin and Thong Naipan (noon, returns from Thong Naipan at 8am). Speedboats to Samui from Had Rin cost B4,000.

## Getting around

Travelling around is time-consuming, so it's best to choose a beach and stay there. *Songthaews* run regularly to all accessible beaches from Had Rin and Thong Sala (B50-B80) when a ferry docks, otherwise once or twice a day, and at bar closing in Had Rin. It's also possible to charter a boat: Had Rin to Thong Sala B200, Thong Sala to Thong Naipan B800. Several east and north coast beaches are only accessible by boat. Longtail taxis run from Had Rin East for short trips (B60 in the day to Had Tien, B300 at night), longer charters are exorbitantly priced (B1,000 to Thong Naipan). On dry land, even the paved roads can be terrifying slaloms with frequent dead man's bends; unpaved ones are rutted tracks, so motorbike hire (in Had Rin and Thong Sala) is dodgy, though it's dirt-biker heaven.

# Ko Tao

Still home to sea turtles, **Ko Tao** (Turtle Island) resembles a turtle swimming south towards Ko Pha-ngan (40 kilometres/25 miles away) and Ko Samui (60 kilometres/37 miles). It consists mostly of dense jungle bordered by rocky bays; on the western side is a long strip of beach facing **Ko Nang Yuan**, three islets connected by a unique 'Mercedes tristar' of pristine sandbars.

Because Ko Tao is a diver's mecca, you can feel seriously out of place if you're not here to strap on an air tank – but there are alternatives. With everyone diving all day, there's hardly anyone on the island's 11 beaches. For gorgeous sand, head to **Ao Leuk** in the south-east or **Jansom Bay** and **June Juea** in the south-west. Snorkelling equipment can be rented at **Black Tip Diving & Water Sports** (Ao Tanote, 0 7745 6488/9/www. blacktip-diving-kohtao.com), which also has the greatest variety of kayaks, bubble boards, wakeboards, waterskis and banana boats.

Longtail boats on **Had Sairee** beach do day trips (B1,000-B1,500); locals recommend driver No.29, Khun Yut. Alternatively, **Two View** healing centre, 700 metres off Main Road, past Moonlight Bungalows (0 9970 2515/ www.geocities.com/twoview2000, closed Oct-Nov) offers everything from yoga and aromatherapy to past-life readings.

### ACTIVITIES

Among the 24 dive sites, averaging 40 metres (131 feet) in depth, **Chumphon Pinnacles** and **Green Rock** are known for their swim-throughs, **White Rock** for its night diving, **Nang Yuan Pinnacle** has a cave and **Shark Island** is particularly diverse. Shallow water training is best at **Ao Leuk**, **Mango Bay** and the **Coral Gardens**. Barrel sponges, whip coral, gorgonian sea fans, barracudas, groupers, snappers and leopard

**Beyond Bangkok**

and whale sharks are commonly seen, alongside the rarer manta rays, sting rays and whales.

Over 20 resorts cater to every level of diving experience, notably **Bans Diving Resort** (Had Sairee, 0 7745 6061/2/3/4), **Buddha View Dive Resort** (Chalok Baan Kao, 0 7745 6074/5), **Scuba Junction** (Had Sairee, 0 7745 6013/www.scuba-junction.com) and **Planet Scuba** (Mae Had pier, 0 7745 6110/ www.planet-scuba.net). Generally, diving conditions are best from late May to early October (when visibility is up to 30 metres/ 98 feet), and possible most of the year (except during the November monsoon).

## Where to eat & stay

The charming **New Heaven Bakery** (Sairee Village & Thian Og, 0 7745 6462, main courses B50) has cinnamon rolls, bagels and the best coffee. Italians swear by the own-made pasta and pizza at **La Matta** (Main Road, Mae Had, 0 1229 4718, main courses B150). **Suthep Lounge Bar & Restaurant** (Sairee Village, 0 7745 6270, main courses B150) is famed for its steaks, Bailey's cheesecake and large portions. You can also indulge your sweet tooth with crème caramel or nougat glacé at **Farango** (Main Road, Mae Had, 0 7745 6205, main course B150).

As for accommodation, it's a case of dive or be damned. Most resorts offer lodging only to divers, especially in high season. Basic bungalows go for B400 a night. **Viewpoint Bungalows** (Chalok Baan Kao, 0 7745 6131, rates B250-B1,200) has good sunsets. The bungalows at **Koh Tao Palace Hotel & Resort** (Baan Had Sairee, 0 7745 6250, rates B1,500) are an unusual cross between an igloo and a Mexican haçienda. The pleasant **Baan Charm Churee** (Jansom Bay, 0 7745 6393/4/ www.koh-tao-resort.com, rates B2,700-B7,700) offers wood-and-wicker rooms on a stunning private beach. **Nang Yuan Island Dive Resort** (0 7745 6088/90/91/www. nangyuan.com, rates B1,500-B4,500) is the islet's sole, beautiful venue.

## Nightlife

Groups who dive together, drink together – most head to the alternating beach parties on Sairee and Mae Had. It may be a meat market, but the island's oldest venue, **AC Bar** (Beach Road, south Had Sairee, 0 7745 6197), goes strong on Sundays, Tuesdays and Thursdays. Otherwise, there are tiki torches, sand sculptures and giant swings on Wednesdays and Saturdays at **In Touch** (south Had Sairee, 0 7722 2723/0 1229 4814). Friday nights are shared by **Dry Bar** (north Had Sairee, a

favourite with a gnarled live tree for a bar, and the more upmarket **Whitening Bar** (Mae Had beach, 0 7745 6199). The latest opening is **Venus Park** (between Had Sai Daeng & Rock Resort, Chalok Baan Kao, www.venuspark.org), a massive dance venue in the jungle, though the busiest bar is **Seamonkey's** (Mae Had).

## Resources

### Tourist information

*TAT, 5 Talad Mai Road, Bandon, Surat Thani (0 7728 8818/9).*
Also visit www.kohtaoonline.com.

### Tourist police

*Hotline 1155.*

## Getting there

### By boat

Boats to Mae Had run twice daily from Ko Samui (1.5-3hrs, B300-B550), Ko Pha-ngan (1-3hrs, B150-B350), Chumphon (2-5hrs, B200-B450) and Surat Thani (6-9hrs, B495). Contact Songserm Travel (172 Khao San Road, Bangkok, 0 2280 7897; Ko Tao, 0 7745 6274). Boats may not run in poor weather, especially Nov-Dec.

### By bus

Combination bus/boat tickets are offered by any Bangkok travel agent. Buses leave Khao San Road for Chumphon at around 6pm and boats arrive at around 9am on Tao.

## Around Samui

The setting for the 'perfect island' in the novel *The Beach*, **Ang Thong Marine National Park** is a stunning sprinkling of 41 sheer, karst islets, fringed with wildlife-rich jungle. They're best explored by sea kayak: try the award-winning pioneers **Sea Canoe** (Lamai, 0 7723 0484/www.seacanoe.net) or **Blue Stars Kayaking** (Beach Road, Chaweng, 0 7741 3231). Many of the evocatively shaped outcrops have collapsed sea caves, including the 'golden bowl' lake in Ko Mae Ko, after which the park is named. Near the park heaquarters on Wo Wua Talab is a stunning viewpoint.

**Chaiya**, 50 kilometres (31 miles) north of Surat Thani (it has a railway station), dates from the seventh-century Srivijaya empire (as witnessed by the square, multi-spired *chedi* of Wat Phra Boromathat). Further south on Thanon 41, **Wat Suan Mokkh International Dharma Hermitage** (0 7743 1596/www.suanmokkh.org), base of the late thinker Buddhadasa Bhikku, holds meditation retreats during the first ten days of each month (*see p182* **Learn to: Meditate**).

# The Andaman Coast

Beach paradises come in many guises, from posh Phuket to craggy Tarutao.
Dive straight in.

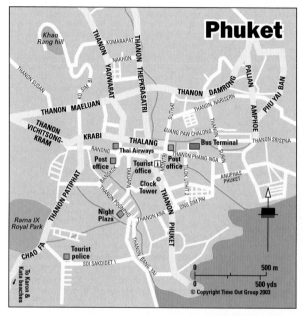

With planning negligible, national park regulations ineffective and 'influential people' riding roughshod over sustainable limits, inappropriate development blights beaches and beauty spots. Most suffer traffic, shops, guesthouses, nightly video shows and pestering vendors. The flipside is that most amenities are available; though patience is required, it's easy to find whatever you need, from email and ticketing to sports gear and book exchanges.

Resorts tend to have restaurants of varying quality (go where the Thais eat), open from breakfast till mid-evening, while bar-oriented places hum until 2am. On remote islands food is rarely of great quality, choice or value, since everything must be shipped in. The savvy stock up at markets for snacks, film, batteries, toiletries and medication. Some even take better-filtered water than the islands sell.

Bordering the Indian Ocean, the Andaman Sea coast is garlanded with, in travel agents' parlance, 'tropical paradises' of varying quality, from jetsetters' retreats to concrete resorts with thumping bars, full of gap-year Eurotrash and ageing Aussie beachniks. Beach bungalows with basic facilities predominate on the remoter islands. **Ko Phuket** and **Ko Phi Phi**, with their mouthwash-green waters, are Thailand's most glamorous destinations, thanks to DiCaprio's cinematic dud *The Beach* and TV's reality show *Survivor*, both shot around the Andaman area.

Thai tour operators have cashed in on Leo fever, so Phuket and Phi Phi become even more choked in high season (Nov-April), though some operations shut during the rough Indian Ocean monsoon (May-Oct). Both are scenically spectacular and fun-filled, but perhaps as a result, the least idyllic. To sample truly paradisical crystal waters and unspoilt beaches, visit **Ko Tarutao**, **Krabi** or **Khao Lak**.

## Ko Phuket

Scallop-edged Ko Phuket, Thailand's largest island at 49 kilometres by 27 kilometres (30 miles by 17 miles), has been a powerful tourist magnet since the 1970s. Known for centuries by mariners and traders for its tin deposits, a 19th-century tin rush turned Phuket Town into the island's hub, brought thousands of Chinese settlers and, on its decline, left the rainforested, copper-hued hills scarred. Phuket (from *bukit*, Malay for 'hill') now mines an even richer seam of tourism. Tranquil fishing villages have been turned into smart resorts

Beyond Bangkok

or ramshackle shanties with myriad polyglot operators offering diving and yachting trips and so-called 'eco-adventures'.

## Sightseeing

In the high season, thousands flock into busy Phuket International Airport near the island's northern link to the mainland, Sarasin Bridge. Though the 11-kilometre (seven-mile) **Mai Khao** beach nearby now has a major resort – a **JW Marriott** (0 7633 8000, rates $580-$3,900) – most tour buses head south down the hilly Highway 402, passing huge rubber plantations and bypassing the western shores of Hat Nai Yang, part of **Sirinat National Park**. At a busy intersection 20 kilometres (12 miles) further on, the **Heroines' Monument** recalls two young women who helped repel the Burmese in 1785 (*see p10* **Warrior princesses**).

Westward, the narrower road leads to relatively quiet **Kamala** and **Surin** beaches, where some of the ritziest hotels, apartments and timeshares have been built. The hotels, lagoons and golf courses clustered around the upmarket **Phuket Laguna** complex (or, more correctly, Ao Bang Thao) are rehabilitated open-cast mines. Shaded Kamala beach (with a great swimming spot at Laem Singh), was a sleepy Muslim area now transformed by the **Phuket FantaSea** extravaganza. From the steep descent into Patong, skeletal concrete shells mark doomed condominiums built by greedy developers.

**Patong**, a once sleepy Muslim village in a perfect, hill-ringed crescent bay, has become party central for those in search of 'va va voom' vacations. Running sewage, ineffectual rubbish disposal and potholes are a by-product of its fast, haphazard growth. Prostitutes hang out on crowded bar strip **Soi Bangla**, with its gem stores, stray dogs and souvenir stalls selling fake brand goods. Touts pester mercilessly, some offering, illegally, the chance to pet a python, or have your photo taken with young gibbons or sea-eagles – all protected species. Gorgeous *kathoeys* frequent the nightclubs, while the gay community thrives around the **Paradise Complex**. The state anti-vice drive has tamed the 'shows', whatever their sexuality, and forced closing at 2am.

The more developed lower west coast arguably has the best beaches – except in the monsoon, when big 'dumpers' and deadly Langkawi Express rips claim swimmers' lives. Such natural forces carved out the deep sandy bays of **Karon** and **Kata** south on winding Highway 4233. The road, with its high-speed *tuk-tuks* and racing teen-bikers, spoils longer, noisier, shadeless Karon beach, which has

cheaper room rates. Separated by a headland and the snorkellers' favourite islet of **Ko Pu**, **Kata Yai** is prettier, family-friendly and hosts September's windsurfing championships.

There are stunning views north from beyond here, and particularly at the southernmost tip, **Laem Phrom Thep Cape**, which is crowded at sunset. East round the cape, **Nai Harn** has an impressively undeveloped beach. Yachties and yuppies head for the **Le Royal Meridien Phuket Yacht Club,** which is more a luxury resort and spa than a functioning marina.

From the Heroines' Monument crossroads, madcap traffic continues south to **Ban Kathu**. The area's history is uncovered in the Mining Museum at **Ban Kathu Heritage Centre** (Ban Kathu School, 0 7632 1035, open 8.30am-4pm daily). West lies Patong, while south-east is the provincial capital, **Phuket Town**, which retains its tin baron architecture (*see p248* **Florid fusion**). On top of **Khao Rang** hill a small, shady park is dedicated to a 19th-century governor and philanthropist. To the south you can locate **Saphan Hin**'s new **Mangrove Walk** (open 6am-7pm daily), a short meander through the threatened muddy environment crucial to sealife.

## Tours & activities

Several companies run 4WD tours through the interior's twisting jungle roads to rubber plantations. There are also farm visits to coconut, cashew nut and banana producers. Elephant treks are mostly short bush rambles; others combine that with a sea canoe paddle through mangroves. Bring plenty of water, a T-shirt and sunscreen, and check low tides to avoid being stranded.

Full-day eco-tours (B1,500-B2,000 including lunch and transfers) are run by **Siam Safari** (45 Thanon Chao Fa West, Chalong, 0 7628 0116), **Phuket Union Travel** (64/23 Thanon Chao Fa West, Chalong, 0 7622 5522/33) or **Asian Premier Holidays** (74/90 Poonphon Night Plaza, Thanon Poonphon, Phuket Town, 0 7624 6260). Mountain bike specialists include **Bike Tours** (10/195 Thanon Kwang, Phuket Town, 0 7626 3575/1797 6540).

Phuket is Thailand's diving headquarters, with more than 50 companies of varying quality (*see p242* **Learn to: Dive**) and a recompression chamber in Patong. Among the best are **White & Blue Dive Club** (0 7628 1007/8), **Dive Master** (0 7629 2402/3), **Scuba Cat** (0 7629 3121) and **South-east Asia Liveaboards** (0 7634 0406). Golf is a major diversion, notably at **Blue Canyon Country Club** (165 Thanon Thepkasatri, Had Nai Yang,

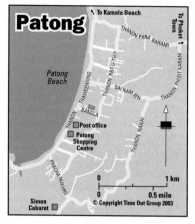

**Patong**

To Kamala Beach
To Phuket Town
THANON PHRA BARAMI
THANON RAT-U-THIT
THANON PHIST KARANI
Patong Beach
THANON THAWEEWONG
SAI NAM JEN
SOI BANGLA
THANON NANAI
Post office
Patong Shopping Centre
PRACHA NUK HRO
Simon Cabaret

0   1 km
0   0.5 mile
© Copyright Time Out Group 2003

0 7632 7440) and **Phuket Golf & Country Club** (80/1 Thanon Wichirtsongkram, 0 7632 1038-41/www.phuket countryclub.com).

Thailand's only regular gay day trip (to Ko Khai, on Thursdays, B1,500), is run by **Connect Restaurant & Guesthouse** (125/8-9 Thanon Rat-u-Thit 200 Pii, Patong, 0 7629 4195/www.beachpatong.com/connect).

## Where to eat & drink

There's an *oliang* (Chinese coffee) culture here, especially over morning dim sum, *pa tong goh* (Chinese doughnuts) or *tao sor* (stuffed Chinese buns) in Phuket Town holes-in-the-wall or Patong's Soi Sainamyen stalls. In Phuket town, try **Khoo Khwan** (Thanon Phuket, near Thanon Kra) or **Boonrat** (Thanon Dilok Uthit 1, near Methee). **Somchit** and **Ton Pho**, both on Thanon Phuket, by the clocktower, are good lunch spots for Hokkien noodles, served *chek* (dry) or with *sapam* (soup).

Other, often incendiary, southern dishes include *tom som phak*, *oa tao* (fried oyster with egg and bean sprouts) and *kaeng tai pla* (curry with fish stomach).

## Restaurants

Overlooking town and sea, Phuket Town's Khao Rang hill boasts **Phuket View** (87/12 Thanon Ko Sim Bi, 0 7621 6865, open 11am-11.30pm daily, main courses B230) and **Thungka** (0 7621 1500) for authentic fare. Down below, there's **Tamachart** (Soi Puton, 0 7622 4287, open 10.30am-midnight daily, main courses B200) with a model railway through its quirky jungle decor; **Baan Sapam** (22/16 Thanon Thepkrasatri, 0 7623 9033, main

courses B67); and stalls at **Talad Kaset** on Thanon Dilok Uthit, behind Robinson's department store.

Also in Phuket Town, **Chez Serge** (64/3-4 Thanon Rassada, 0 1754 1584, open 11am-2pm, 5.30-11.30pm daily, main courses B400) is frequented by royalty, partly because owner Serge Consani ran a top French restaurant in Bangkok. There are also two good Italian options. **La Gaetana** (352 Thanon Phuket, 0 7625 0523, open 11.30am-2pm, 6-10pm daily in high season, main courses B460) has probably the friendliest host in town, Gianni, known for doling out free 'Vitamin C' (limoncello), while **Salvatore's** (15 Thanon Rassada, 0 7622 5958, open noon-3pm, 6-11pm daily, main courses B400) is a favourite with influential Thais and *farang*.

Resort restaurants vary massively, and it's tough to find undiluted Thai or southern dishes – though you could try **Patong Night Market** on Thanon Ratcha Uthit. Come dusk, Patong's fairy-lit northern seafront is one long iced seafood display. The delicacies come fresh from tanks at **It's Alive!** (3/1 Thanon Had Patong, 0 7634 2908, open 11am-11pm daily, main courses B400). The island's top dining is found on the northern bluff overlooking Patong at **Baan Rim Pa** (223 Thanon Phrabaramee, 0 7634 0789, open noon-11pm daily, main courses B1,300). Jumbo prawns stand out on the fine Thai and international menu of **On The Rocks** (Marina Phuket Resort, 47 Thanon Karon, Karon, 0 7633 0625, open 8am-11pm daily, main courses B430).

## Bars & pubs

In Phuket Town, bright colours, fun decor and a Thai/expat mix suit the funk, soul and R&B sounds at **Gitano** (Thanon Ong Sim Pai, 0 7622 5797, open 4pm-midnight Mon, Wed-Sun). The new owners have Thai distribution rights for a Swedish herbal aphrodisiac, a key ingredient in the bar's Love Volcano cocktail. Expats gather for live bands at **Timber Hut** (118/1 Thanon Yaowarat, 0 7621 1839, open 8pm-2am daily), while you'll find loud music and trendy Thai regulars at the starkly black and white **GorTorMor** (Thanon Chana Charoen, 0 1370 5114, open 7pm-2am daily).

Events, posted on www.the-green-man.net, are legion at the **Green Man** on the road from Chalong to Kata (82/15 Thanon Pratak, Rawai, 0 7628 0757/1445/52, open 10.30am-2am daily). It looks like an English pub with a backdrop of rubber trees and tourist-toting elephants; inside there's good food, pricey Irish beer and even pub quizzes. In Patong, **Molly Malone's** (94/1 Thanon Thaweewong, 0 7629 2771, open

**Beyond Bangkok**

11am-2am daily) is an Irish pub, run by the owners of **Scruffy Murphy's** at the beach end of Soi Bangla. People-watching is the activity at **Tai Pan** near the end of Soi Bangla (Thanon Rat-u-Thit 200 Pii, 0 7629 2587).

**Bluefin Tavern** (Thanon Taina, Kata, 0 7633 0856, open noon-11pm daily) is a bit of an institution, and a haunt of old-hand expats. Rock 'n' roll, burgers and Mexican nosh are all on the menu.

## Nightlife

The best nightclub, Shark, was closed in the crackdown, leaving just the **Banana Pub & Disco** (124 Thanon Thaweewong, Patong, 0 7634 0306) alongside Thai-style clubs, notably the **Beach** (Royal Paradise Hotel, 135/23 Thanon Rat-u-thit 200 Pii, 0 7634 0666).

**Phuket FantaSea** on Kamala beach (0 7638 5000/www.phuket-fantasea.com, open 5.30-11.30pm daily) is a themed collection of shops containing the 4,000-seat Golden Kinnaree restaurant and the 3,000-seat Palace of the Elephants theatre, which features an award-winning, all-singing, all-dancing spectacle with acrobats, pyrotechnics and magic (show B1,000, B1,500 with supper). More outrageous costumes can be admired at **Simon Cabaret** in Patong (8 Thanon Sirirach, 0 7634 2114) with stunning ladyboys entertaining a 600-seat theatre packed with tourists.

A more conventional cultural evening at **Thainaan Restaurant** (16 Thanon Vichitsongkram, Phuket Town, 0 7622 6164-7) includes a B1,300 dinner at 6pm in traditional surroundings, a movie about southern Thai culture and live Thai dances from the Srivijaya period (850-1450).

## Shopping

Souvenir-hunting is an evening entertainment at resorts, especially Patong, though pushy touts can take the fun out of stall perusal or selecting a tailor. Pearls are sold prominently in Patong and Rawai; genuine pearls are rougher than the coated cultured variety. **Mook Ko Kaew** (41/6-7 Thanon Vichitsongkram, 0 7622 2563/4, open 8am-7pm daily) sells both kinds, plus tin-derived pewter ware.

The **Robinson's** department store on Thanon Ong Sim Pai in Phuket Town sells genuine, inexpensive brands. The market beside it is known for southern nibbles. **Chai Batik House** (22/8 Thanon Chao Fa, Phuket Town, 0 1978 9249) is the place for indigenous hand-painted batik. If you're into art, exhibitions are held periodically at the **Loft** (36 Thanon Talang, Phuket Town,

# Florid fusion

Cruise travellers from Singapore via Melaka and Penang to Phuket are retracing ancient maritime links in commerce and culture between these Melacca Straits settlements. **Phuket Town** also shares their distinctive Sino-Portuguese architecture. Dubbed 'Shophouse Rafflesia', it takes the long, narrow Chinese row house with its inner courtyard and adds Greco-Roman columns, decorative tiles and calligraphy, gilded window surrounds, 'lucky' motifs, shuttered balconies and wide colonnades.

A conservation area now includes the exuberant examples around **Thanon Yaowarat** and its crossroads: **Thanon Krabi/Thanon Thalang** and **Thanon Deebuk**. The last two are also linked by the quaintly ramshackle former red-light district of **Soi Rommanee**. Many of the houses and shops still belong to their original families, while others are being converted into bars, boutiques and galleries. Historical walks take place during the Phuket Heritage Festival (0 7621 2314) in late December. The Provincial Hall (15 Thanon Narisorn, 0 7635 4875, open 8.30am-9.30pm Mon-Fri), which is also in this fusion style, exhibits early photographs of the island.

0 7625 8160, open 10am-7pm Mon-Sat) and at **Mom Tri's Boathouse** (*see p251*), which hosts book launches and author talks at its Chao Phraya River Club Art Gallery.

## Arts & entertainment

### Festivals

Opening the high season, **Phuket Vegetarian Festival** is held on the first nine days of the ninth lunar month (October). It's followed by the **Patong Carnival** (1 Nov), whose street parades and entertainment are an overture to the week-long **Phuket International Seafood Festival**. The **Phuket Laguna Triathlon** precedes international yachties blowing in for **King's Cup Regatta** races in early December, while the **Old Phuket Festival** falls around late December. February is the time for the **Phuket Gay Festival** (www.gayphuket.com). In March, there's art and music at the **Baan Kata Art Festival** at Mom Tri's Boathouse, and heroines are

honoured at the **Tao Tepkrasattri-Tao Srisunthorn Fair** (*see p10* **Warrior princesses**). After convoying down from Bangkok, Harley fans rev up in Patong for **Phuket Bike Week** around **Songkran** (Thai New Year) in mid April. April also sees the **Sea Turtle Release Fair** on Had Mai Khao, Ao Bang Thao.

## Gay & lesbian

Thanks to tolerance, *sanuk* and the 'pink *baht*' tourist sector, February's Phuket Gay Festival (*see p248*) can parade down Patong's Thanon Thaweewong and up Soi Bangla to the phallic **Paradise Complex** and its gay bars and clubs. Extravagant midnight shows at the **Boat Bar Disco** (125/20 Thanon Rat-u-thit, 0 7634 1237) are unmissable. Other options in this zone are **Tangmo** (0 7634 0478), also with cabaret, **My Way** (0 1978 4172) with elaborate shows, and **Uncle Charlie's** spiffy new premises (0 7634 2865). Quieter drinks are available at **James Dean Guest House** (Rat-u-thit Soi 5, 0 7634 4215, rates from B600).

Gay visitors often stay in Patong at **Club Bamboo** (47 Thanon Nanai, 0 7634 5345, rates from B1,200), the Thai-style **Icon** (47/1 Thanon Nanai, 0 7629 6735/www.iconasia.com, rates B2,500-B4,500), **Thara Patong Beach Resort** (170 Thanon Thaweewong, 0 7634 0135, rates from B2,500) or the **Beach Resort Hotel** (37 Thanon Thaweewong, 0 7634 0544).

Among gay-friendly restaurants, **Sea Hag** (89/128 Soi Permpong, Soi Wattana Clinic, Patong, 0 7634 1111, open noon-11.30pm daily, main courses B460) draws a Thai/expat/tourist mix. Even better Thai food comes with music at the offbeat **Kah Jok See** (26 Thanon Takuapa, Phuket Town, 0 7621 7903, open 6.30-11pm daily, main courses B400).

## Mind & body

The wellness culture that has seized Samui is just emerging in Phuket. You can be pampered amid beautiful surroundings or enjoy herbal saunas, traditional massage and facials at budget parlours. Roving beach masseuses offer a rub on your sunburn for around B200.

The spa at top-class resort **Banyan Tree Phuket** (see *p250*) has created its own treatments, from one-hour wraps (from $75) to all-day pampering. The jungly **Hideaway Spa** (382/33 Thanon Srisoonthorn, Cherng Talay, 0 7627 1549) adapts ancient recipes to use in its herbal steam rooms. Thai massage (B300 per hour) is also on offer at the new **Royal Spa** (Boat Lagoon Marina, 22/1 Thanon Thepkrassatri, Ko Kaew, 0 7627 3394).

## Where to stay

Phuket has some 500 properties across all price ranges, easily booked via www.phuket.com. Hotels and guesthouses are often full from

Enjoy upmarket lodgings and arts events at **Mom Tri's Boathouse**. See *p251*.

Beyond Bangkok

mid October to Songkran in mid April; discounts are possible at other times.

At the top end, **Banyan Tree Phuket** (Laguna Phuket, 0 7632 4374, rates $420-$2,200) has tasteful villas close to the sea and the **Laguna Phuket Golf Club** (34 Thanon Srisoontorn, 0 7632 4350, rates $800-$2,500). It, and the other Laguna Phuket luxury resorts, are bookable at www.lagunaphuket.com. Even classier are the hillside bungalow resort of **Chedi Phuket** (Ao Surin, 0 7632 4017-20, rates $160-$780) and the sublimely minimalist, Thai-style pavilions and private villas at **Amanpuri** (Ao Surin, 0 7632 4333/www. amanresorts.com, rates $500-$6,000).

Kamala beach has some cheaper options. **Taeng Yai** guesthouse (73/98 Soi Java, 0 7638 5256, rates B500-B800) is three minutes from the beach, while **Malinee House** (75/4 Thanon

Rim Had, 0 7638 5094, rates B600-B900) has a strong backpacker following and offers tours.

In Patong, **Club Andaman Beach Resort** (2 Thanon Had Patong, 0 7634 0350, rates B2,900-B6,500) is set in enormous gardens close to the nightlife, whereas the only beachfront option is the charmingly verdant **Impiana Phuket Cabana** (94 Thanon Thaweewong, 0 7634 0138/www.impiana.com, rates B8,156-B9,686). Set back from the noisy road and bar strip, the **Holiday Inn** (52 Thanon Thaweewong, 0 7634 0608, rates B2,900-B7,500) has a new second wing.

**Thara Patong Beach Resort** (see p249) is a pleasant mid-range central option. **Sansabai Bungalows** (171/21 Soi Saen Sabai, Patong, 0 7634 2948/ www.phuket-sansabai. com, rates B500-B1,400) are convenient and pleasantly situated.

# Vegetarian kebabs

Horrifying the nut-cutlet set, **Phuket Vegetarian Festival**, held during the first nine days of the ninth lunar month (usually October), features human kebabs. Buddhist devotees skewer their cheeks, tongues and some other parts with inanimate objects, from pineapple stalks and saw blades to (amazingly) bicycle frames.

This provides a hideously compulsive sight at the street parades between shrines in Phuket Town and Kathu, which are always

accompanied by a fusillade of firecrackers. Dressed in white for the duration of the festival, devotees abstain from sex, stimulants and avoid meat and 'heating' vegetables, such as onion and garlic. Stalls flying yellow pennants offer *ahahn jeh* (vegetarian food). Come evening, these entranced 'mediums' climb razor blade ladders and walk across coals without injury. Similar events happen in Trang and Krabi, usually at around the same time.

**Le Meridien Phuket** (Ao Karon Noi, 0 7634 0480-5/www.lemeridien-phuket.com) is concrete and vast, but has a good cooking school, huge pools, umpteen activities and effectively sole use of stunning 'Relax Bay'. Its launch cruises out of **Le Royal Meridien Phuket Yacht Club** (Ao Nai Harn, 0 7638 1156-63/www.phuket-yachtclub.com, rates $530-$1,500), secreted into a vertiginous cliff.

On Karon, **Casa Brazil** (9 Luang Pho Chuan Soi 2, 0 7639 6317/www.phuket homestay.com, rates B1,000-B1,400) has designer adobe rooms with air-con, while there's a lot for your *baht* (including a pool) at **Little Mermaid**'s guesthouse and bungalow (197 Thanon Taina, Karon, 0 7633 0730, B365-B1,800). The self-catering apartments at **Central Waterfront Suites** (35 Thanon Patak, 0 7639 6767-9/ www.central hotelsresorts.com, rates B6,000-B8,000) overlook Karon beach.

Between Karon and Kata, **Mom Tri's Boathouse** (182 Thanon Kok Tanoad, 0 7633 0015-7/www.theboathousephuket.com, rates B8,500-B19,00) is the flagship of award-winning Phuket tourism pioneer and architect Mom Tri Devakul. In Kata Yai, **Peach Hill Hotel & Resort** (13 Thanon Karon, 0 7633 0520/1, rates B1,400-B2,500) is set in hillside gardens; more gardens and sea views are available at **Flamingo** (5/19 Thanon Patak, 0 7633 0776, rates B800-B1,200).

In Phuket Town, **Royal Phuket City Hotel** (154 Thanon Phang-nga, 0 7623 3333, rates B3,050-B3,408) has a popular fitness centre. The venerable **On On Hotel** (19 Thanon Phang-nga, 0 7622 5740-1, rates B200-B400) oozes period charm. Not far south, **Hostelling International Phuket** near Wat Chalong (73/11 Thanon Chaofa, 0 7628 1335/0103/ www.phukethostel.com, rates B180-B350) maintains YHA standards.

Most spartan is the free lodging in Khao Phra Thaew National Park, east of Talang, at the **Royal Forestry Guesthouse** (254 Thanon Thepkasatri, 0 7631 1998). Coastal nature lovers need to reserve the huts (sleeping up to four) at **Sirinart Marine National Park** (89/1 Had Nai Yang, 0 7632 8226, rates B300-B600). A group room (sleeping up to 20) is B3,000, and there's also a campsite.

For gay-friendly accommodation, *see p249* **Gay & lesbian**.

# Getting there & around

## By air

Many companies fly from Bangkok to Phuket International Airport (0 7632 7230). Thai Airways has more than a dozen flights a day; Phuket Airlines

has flights Mon, Wed, Fri-Sun; and Bangkok Airways flies four times a day from Bangkok and twice a day from Ko Samui. Foreign charters and some flag carriers also land at Phuket.

## By bus

Buses run overnight from Bangkok's Southern Bus Terminal; cheap but exhausting. There are also bus connections from other tourist centres in Thailand, including local centres such as Surat Thani, Trang, Satun and Had Yai. Or try Phuket companies Transport Co (0 7621 1480) and Phuket Travel Service (0 7622 2107). There are bus links to Surat Thani station, the nearest rail link to Phuket.

## Getting around

Though cross-island routes are half decent, driving can be deadly, with hairpin bends, gear-crunching gradients and general recklessness behind the wheel. *Songthaews* provide a lackadaisical transport system; otherwise, it's *tuk-tuks* or motorbike taxis. Bargain hard. As on many get-rich-quick islands, 'influential people' operate with impunity, especially among Patong's ruffian *tuk-tuk* and longtail boat cartels – don't mess with them. Phuket Town's small taxi-meter company (0 7623 2157) won't pick up in Patong for this reason.

# Resources

## Hospitals

*Bangkok Phuket Hospital, Thanon Yaowaraj, Phuket Town (0 7625 4421).*

*Phuket International Hospital, Thanon Chalermprakiet Ror 9, Phuket Town (0 7624 9400).*

## Internet cafés

There are plenty of places to get online. Here are some options:

**Friendship Beach** *Thanon Viset, Rawai (0 7628 8996).*

**In Touch World Wide** *Patong Tower Shopping Complex, 114/2 Thanon Thaweewong, Patong (0 7634 0024).*

**The Surfing Eagle** *98/15 Thanon Patak, Kata (0 7633 3105).*

**The Tavern** *64/3-4 Thanon Rassada, Soi Shopping Centre, Phuket Town (0 7622 3569).*

## Post offices

*Thanon Montri, Phuket Town (0 7621 6951/1020).*
*Thanon Thaweewong, Patong (0 7634 0365).*

## Tourist information

*TAT, 73-5 Thanon Phuket, Phuket Town (0 7621 2213/www.phukettourism.org).* **Open** 8.30am-4.30pm daily.

Look out for local English-language newspaper *Phuket Gazette* (www.phuketgazette.net). Websites www.phuket.com and www.hoteltravel.com are both travel booking sites with info on Phuket. Good maps and info comes via www.phuket-maps.com.

## Tourist police

*100/31-2 Thanon Chalermprakiet Ror 9, Phuket Town (0 7635 5015/hotline 1155).*

# Around Ko Phuket

## Ao Phang-nga

Sheltered by Phuket, this vast bay is famed for its stunning limestone karst pinnacles soaring from the water and topped by jungle. Tours run by countless agencies leave from north-east Phuket or the north of Ao Phang-nga National Marine Park. Most take in **Ko Tapu**, which has been branded 'James Bond Island' because it was the location for 1975's *The Man with The Golden Gun*. Stretching down the centre of the bay are **Ko Yao Yai** and **Ko Yao Noi**, sparsely inhabited by an almost exclusively Muslim community. Homestays (B300 a night, including three meals) are offered; they're an ideal way to get away from the crowds (and the booze; most families ask that you don't bring alcohol) and learn more about a way of life that's all but disappeared on Phuket. Contact the Ko Yao Or Bor Tor local council (0 7659 7122) for details. Regular longtail boat services leave from the pier at Baan Bang Pae.

Further south, **Ko Rang Yai** has one of the bay's most beautiful beaches, fringing a day resort with an outdoor restaurant and activities such as kayaking, windsurfing, mountain biking and trekking. There are no bedrooms, though tents are allowed. In contrast, **Maiton** island (0 7621 4954-8/ www.maitonisland.com) is given over to one resort of upmarket villas (beach, hillside or terrace, rates from B7,000).

**Sea Canoe** (0 7621 2252/2172/www.sea canoe.net) offers tours to collapsed sea caves (*hong*) hidden among the bay's karst islets, while educating visitors in respecting the fragile ecosystem. In fact, the company was set up by John 'Caveman' Grey after he chanced upon these humid caves, accessible only at low tide by canoeing through tunnels. The tours reveal secret beaches, emerald swimming holes and overgrown cliffs. Other tour operators have cashed in on this tourist brochure wet dream, but not all are as responsible or ecologically sensitive as Sea Canoe – which also explores the mangroves and karsts of Krabi, Khao Sok National Park, Ko Tarutao, Samui's Ang Thong archipelago and Vietnam's Halong Bay.

## Khao Sok

**Khao Sok National Park** (0 7739 5025) is on the mountain ridge between the east and west coasts of the peninsula, 160 kilometres (100 miles) from Phuket. Its geology is similar to that of Ao Phang-nga, with karst outcrops rearing up out of the forest, and out of the waters of Chiow Lan reservoir at its heart. Organised treks are the best way to visit it.

**Asian Adventures** (0 7634 1799), **Sea Canoe** (*see above*) and **Trekking Thai Ecotour** (0 1762 1898/2448 5464) run eco tours that include elephant trekking, canoeing and river rafting. You overnight in tree houses or floating bungalows. Treks usually start at dawn (before the heat) and can be fairly rugged (insect repellent and anti-leech bags are essential). But it's worth the discomfort for the scenery, wildlife and the sheer fun of gliding down a river in an inner tube.

## Khao Lak

Thailand's answer to Australia's Cape Tribulation – where rainforest tumbles steeply down to pristine beaches on a turquoise sea – this emerging destination 50 kilometres (31 miles) north of Phuket has so far resisted girlie bars, karaoke dens and jetskis. It has eight beaches, with facilities.

The more upmarket resorts – **Khao Lak Resort** (0 7642 0060) and **Khao Lak Palm Beach Resort** (0 7642 0060/3) – are around **Nang Tong**. Bang Niang has a good selection of cheaper bungalows; try **Bang Niang Beach Resort** (0 7642 0171/5) or **Amsterdam Resort** (0 7642 0634). Further north, the beautiful **Similana Resort** (4/7 Moo 1, Kuk-kak, Takuapa, 0 7642 0166/7), sweeps down a tousled hillside to its own beach. The lower, stilted bungalows are set in mangroves. Ulli makes fab pizzas at the **Khao Lak Restaurant** (0 7642 0273) near Nang Tong beach, and there's good Thai fare at **Baan Suan** (0 1894 0703).

Diving trips are easy to arrange, especially to the Similans, leaving from **Tab Lamu**. Try **Kon Tiki Khao Lak** (0 7642 0208) or **Sea Dragon** (0 7642 0420). For jungle trips, on foot or by elephant, call **Khao Lak Guide** (0 7642 0177) or **Asian Adventures** (0 7634 1799).

## Similan Islands

About 90 kilometres (60 miles) north-west of Phuket, these nine uninhabited islands are among the world's top ten dive sites. Rounded slabs of grey granite with powdery white beaches, the islands attract hikers and beach lovers, but the vast majority are divers or snorkellers seeking its underwater wonders: fantastic visibility, rich coral gardens and a huge variety of fish, including whale sharks. As there's only basic lodging on two of the islands (they're a national park; 0 7659 5045) and no public transport, most visitors stay on yachts belonging to Phuket dive companies. The Similans are off-limits during the monsoon season (mid May-Nov/Dec).

Paddle among the mangroves with eco-tour outfit **Sea Canoe**. See p252.

## Ko Phi Phi

Equidistant from Phuket, Krabi and Ko Lanta is the mini archipelago of Ko Phi Phi. The karst scenery is breathtaking, but has been blighted by unsustainable development since the early 1980s, when the first tourist bungalows arrived. **Ao Maya** bay on **Ko Phi Phi Le** is where the DiCaprio flick *The Beach* was filmed; legal wrangles about transportation of vegetation still plague Fox Studios. The film's worst impact is the sightseeing traffic from Phuket.

The ecology is most overwhelmed on inhabited **Ko Phi Phi Don**. Its twin ridges of sheer limestone are joined by a coconut-fringed sand spit, creating two awesome bays. **Ao Loh Dalum** is shallower with trace sediment, while amid the yachts and speedboats at postcard-perfect **Ao Ton Sai**, a pier offloads shipfuls of wannasees into a maze of guesthouses, shops, services and restaurants. Officially part of Krabi province and a national park, Phi Phi is effectively autonomous, leading to insufficient infrastructure, freshwater depletion and poor disposal of refuse and sewage.

Boat trips circumnavigate Phi Phi's impenetrable coastal cliffs, taking in Phi Phi Le's **Viking Cave**. Guides show how the highly prized swallows' nests (used for the Cantonese delicacy bird's nest soup), are collected at dizzying heights. A 30-minute hike uphill from **Pee Pee Viewpoint Resort** (0 7562 2351) on the east side of Ao Loh Dalum affords wonderful views. The sunset is also fab from **Ao Yongkasem**. **Had Yao** is the best beach, but therefore busy.

Divers (including many beginners; see p242 **Learn to: Dive**) go further afield in longtails. Among the reputable companies are **Moskito Diving** (0 7561 2092), **Phi Phi Scuba** (0 7561 2665), **Island Divers** (0 7562 0800) and **White & Blue Dive Club** (0 7562 0589).

## Where to eat & drink

The beachside **Tonsai Seafood** at Phi Phi Banyan Villa is a bargain, with dinner averaging B200. **Le Grand Bleu** on Ao Ton Sai is not much more expensive (main courses B230) and is known for its mussels. The **Reggae Disco Bar** in Ton Sai mixes, bizarrely, good music with a Thai boxing show. Tranny-fans can see the hugely popular ladyboy show at **Apache**, or head for the more intimate **Jungle Bar**, a good spot at sunset.

## Where to stay

At the northernmost tip of Phi Phi Don, the **Holiday Inn** (Laem Thong Beach, 0 7562 1334, rates B2,900-B6,400) has pricey chalets in a quiet garden setting and romantic dinners at **Tai Rom Prao** (open 7-10am, 11am-3pm, 7-9.30pm daily, main courses B500). It's a boat ride to everything else.

Close to the nightlife, **Phi Phi Cabana** (Ton Sai Village, 0 7561 2132/www.phiphi cabana-hotel.com, bungalow with fan B1,050-B2,200) has a superb cliffside location. Between 24 and 31 December, guests at these hotels must pay for compulsory festive suppers.

Among the Ton Sai conurbation, **Chong Khao** (24 Ao Dalum, 0 1894 8786, rates B300-B1,200) is relatively quiet, with basic to middling bungalows, while **PP Princess** (0 7562 2079/www.ppprincess.com) has stylish timber bungalows. On Had Yao, **Maphrao** (7 Ao Nang, 0 7562 2486, rates B200-B1,000) is more secluded than **Paradise Pearl**, where the huts are better appointed (0 7562 2100).

Spectacular, idyllic **Krabi**.

## Getting there & around

### By boat

Regular ferries to Phi Phi Don depart from Phuket, Krabi and Ko Lanta. It's best to turn up at least 30mins before the scheduled departure, earlier on holidays and in high season. Comfier services from Phuket are provided by Seatran (0 7621 9391/2/ www.seatranferry.com, B750 single) and Andaman Wavemaster (0 7623 2095, B660 single). Both leave at 8.30am and return at 2.30pm.

Services are basic from Krabi Town: PP Family (0 7561 2463, B250 single) has a 10.30am and 2.30pm service, leaving Phi Phi at 9am and 1pm. Ao Nang Travel (0 7563 7152/3) leaves Ao Nang at 8.30am via West Rai Leh, returning the same way at 3.30pm (B300 single). A daily service from Ko Lanta leaves Ban Sala Dan at 8.30am, returning at 2pm (B250 single).

### Getting around

Longtails are the only public transport, and can be hired for beach-to-beach runs.

## Resources

### Tourist information

Check out websites www.phi-phi.com and http://krabi.sawadee.com/phiphi.htm.

Along with Trang province to the south, Krabi is at the forefront of efforts to develop more eco-friendly tourism. Until Krabi's airport opened in 2001 to domestic and international traffic, it had been favoured by those prepared to slog the nearly 1,000 kilometres (622 miles) from Bangkok. The province's draw is its karst scenery, beaches, diving sites, islands and caves. Overland travellers are dumped in **Krabi Town** – and get out fast – there's little but a pier, guesthouses and urban amenities, though the **Andaman Festival**'s folk entertainments in the week before Loy Krathong (late Oct/early Nov) are worth seeing.

**Ao Nang** maintains a laid-back feel despite its fast-growing resorts, dive shops, restaurants and tour agencies. It faces a long, handsome cliff, but the daily destination is **Laem Phra Nang** (Princess Cape), the triple-beach headland behind it, which is only accessible via boat. Longtails pull into the fine sands of **Had Railay West**, a coconut-studded sand spit sitting back to back with the murkier, mangrove-dotted crescent of **Had Railay East**. A lane skirts Rayavadee Resort (ducking through caves under stalactites) to **Had Phra Nang**, where a glorious panorama of cliffs, offshore islets and cascading greenery suggests paradise on earth. At the beach's eastern end, legend avers that the cathedral-sized cavern **Tham Phra Nang** was a refuge of a Hindu princess, who the Rayavadee honour with a flame-lit ceremony every full moon night. Along the connecting path are washrooms and a *sala* from where the fit can pull themselves up knotted ropes to a viewpoint and then abseil down to **Sa Phra Nang Lake**.

Between Krabi Town and Laem Phra Nang, **Susaan Hoi** is a 40 million-year-old fossil shell beach. The mainland has limited activity options, though **Chan Phen Travel** (145 Thanon Utarakit, Krabi Town, 0 7561 2004) is known for its eco-trails and sea canoes, which operate up the estuaries from Ao Nang.

Numerous water-based activities on offer include sea kayaking, and Railay is also is an international rock climbing centre (*see p255* **Learn to: Climb**). Tiny travel offices offer internet hook-ups, money changing, massage, book swaps, basic supplies and private boat trips. Ao Nang is home to **Sea Canoe** (0 7569 5387) and dive centres offering day and live-aboard trips. Scuba outfits include **Aqua Vision** (0 7563 7415), **Phra Nang Divers** (0 7563 7064) and **Reef Watch** (0 7563 2650).

Few islands around Krabi allow overnight stays, but boatmen can be hired if you want to visit the desert isles of **Ko Poda** and

Ko Kai. **Ko Hong** is a seemingly impenetrable fortress out at sea, at the heart of which lies a delightful lagoon. Boats from Krabi Town serve tranquil **Ko Jam**.

## Where to stay & eat

Krabi Town has limited mid-range options, but you could stay (like DiCaprio did) at the (sort of) luxury **Krabi Maritime Park & Spa Hotel** north of town (off Thanon Utrakit, 0 7562 0028/ www.maritimeparkandspa.com, rates B4,000-B30,000). Cost-cutters mostly scour Thanon Chaofa flophouses, though **Star Guest House** (72 Thanon Khong Kha, 0 7563 0234, rates B100-B250) has shady traditional architecture and a riverside view. Great food is served at **May & Mark** (6 Thanon Ruen Rudee) or from stalls at Chao Fa Pier's night market.

The sublime **Rayavadee Resort** (0 7562 0740-3/www.rayavadee.com, rates B17,000-B37,000) has full sports facilities and a new spa. Waste water is treated through special lagoons, where mighty carp thrive on the five-star flushing. **Sand Sea** (39 Had Railay West,

0 7562 2609, rates B2,000-B3,200, **Railay Bay Resort** (0 7562 2571/2, rates B750-B1,600) and **Railay Village** (0 7562 2578, rates B800-B2,000) have a range of pleasant bungalows. All also have beach restaurants. **Coco's** (0 1228 4258, main courses B100) serves decent Thai food in a bosky setting.

## Nightlife

Krabi is refreshingly sleepy: Railay's beachfront bars favour chilled sounds over techno and fire-juggling. The grooviest scene is at **Bobo's** and **Sunset Bar**, both on Railay West. The clientele is more sophisticated than at your average beach resort, with a trippy scene at **Freedom Bar** (Ao Tonsai, www.tonsaibeach party.com). It has so-so rooms (B350), but a circular dance *sala* pulsates to psychedelic, progressive, acid and Goa-trance at all-night parties every two weeks, with lamp sculptures and pyrotechnics on its rather gritty beach. Check the website for the latest schedule.

## Getting there

### By air
Thai Airways, PB Air and Phuket Air offer frequent daily flights from Bangkok to Krabi Airport (0 7563 6541/2).

### By boat
PP Family (0 7561 2463) runs boats from Phuket and Phi Phi to Krabi and Railay, and from Hua Hin pier south of Krabi Town to Ko Lanta. Ferries are sparse in low season. Laem Phra Nang is reached only by boat; it takes around 30mins from Krabi Town pier, plus waiting time for the longtails to fill up.

Be warned that longtail boats are great in smooth seas, but perilous when the water turns choppy; people have ended up adrift between Krabi and Phi Phi without life jackets. In such conditions, take a dual-motor speedboat.

### By road
Krabi Town is just off Thanon Phetkasem (Route 4). Cars, motorcycles and minivans can easily be hired in town, Ao Nang or Krabi Airport; try Krabi Thaimit (177 Thanon Utrakit, Krabi Town, 0 7563 2054/www.asiatravel.com/thailand/krabicarrent). There's no rail link to Krabi, but buses and minibuses connect to Surat Thani, Thung Song (Cha Mai) and Trang train stations.

## Resources

### Hospital
*Krabi Hospital, 325 Thanon Utrakit, Krabi Town (0 7561 1226).*

### Money
There are banks, exchanges and ATMs in Krabi Town and Ao Nang, but not on Laem Phra Nang.

# Learn to Climb

Climbers, novice and pro, flock from around the world to Krabi's cliffs to tackle its steep inclines and eroded overhangs. Almost 500 routes are plotted, named and ranked in difficulty, some 300 with supporting hooks embedded in the rockface. The craze has spawned myriad small climbing outfits at Ao Nang and Railay beaches. Promoted via websites and often with just a mobile phone contact (not always answered), they also play hard in après-climb parties. Not all companies will last – shop around to find the one with whom you feel happy to risk your life. Route maps have been written by **King Climbers** (Ao Nang 0 7563 9125; Railay East 0 7576 4035); other notables are **Krabi Rock Climbing** (Railay 0 1676 0642) and **Tex Rock** (Thanon Kong Plalung, Krabi Town, 0 7652 2491/mobile 01 1891 1528; Railay East 0 1607 4882).

Most outfits rent equipment and offer insurance (though it's a long way to the nearest hospital). A half-day climb with safety gear and an instructor costs around B800; a full day is B1,500, and a three-day course B5,000. Take water with you. All play stops during the slippery wet season.

### Post office

*Thanon Montri, Krabi Town.* With poste restante.

### Tourist information

*Krabi Tourism Centre, Thanon Utrakit, Krabi Town (0 7562 2163/4).*
Also check out websites http://krabi.sawadee.com and www.railay.com.

### Tourist police

*Hotline 1155.*

## Ko Lanta

Inhabited mostly by Muslim Thais and *chao lay* (sea gypsies), the island of Ko Lanta resembles Thailand as it was 30 years ago, with few sealed roads, no mobile phone reception and an erratic electricity supply. Many places close during the rains. The National Marine Park, in which the island lies, is rich in dive sites, including **Ko Rok** and **Ko Kradan,** and stunning karst outcrops like **Ko Mook**. Boat and kayak trips to the caves and mangroves of the island's east coast operate out of **Ban Sala Dan**, the backpacker hub on the northern tip.

The century-old town of **Lanta** on the east coast consists of a few wooden shophouses and a shabby pier. Its *chao lay* hold full moon festivals each June and November, when they launch paper boats to honour the sea gods. Some tours visit **Sangka-u** to observe Muslim village life, others take in **Tham Mai Kaew** bat cave and the seasonal waterfall behind Ao Khlong Jaak, just north of **Ko Lanta National Park** (0 7562 9018/9) at the southernmost tip. **Had Khlong Dao** and **Ao Phrae-Ae** (also called Long Beach) in the north-west are the busiest stretches, dense with cheap bungalows, lively bars, internet cafés and suchlike. As the roads deteriorate southwards, through **Had Khlong Khoang**, **Had Khlong Nin** and **Ao Kantieng**, accommodation tends to be either quiet, classy resorts for well-heeled Bangkok escapees, or ramshackle concrete chalets and bamboo huts huddling on rocky beaches.

### Where to stay & eat

The newest and finest digs are at the **Pimalai Resort** (0 7562 9054/7/Bangkok office 0 2320 5500/www.pimalai.com) on the superb Ba Kan Tiang beach, providing thatched villas, mountain bikes and kayaks, spa treatments and spectacular sunsets over Ko Ha from its bar and restaurant. Not far away, **Sri Lanta** (Bangkok office 0 2204 2458/www.srilanta.com) is a more Zen-chic resort with similar facilities, but it's less pricey and more laid-back. Rustic pit-stop **Same Same But Different** (south of Ba Kan Tiang) is a hippyish beach hangout.

Veggie fare is served at **Sanctuary** (Hat Khlong Dao, closed mid May to mid Oct). Nearby **Diamond Sand** serves Thai food.

## Getting there & around

### By boat

Private and public ferries for Ban Sala Dan leave from Ban Hua Hin pier south of Krabi Town year round (PP Family, Thanon Khong Kha, Krabi Town, 0 7561 2463). Private speedboats (booked via deluxe hotels, B1,200 one way), use the same pier, with hotel minibus transfers to/from Krabi Airport. Direct boats from Ban Sala Dan leave for Krabi Town (10am and 1pm, returning 10.30am and 1.30pm Nov-Apr).

### By road

Public buses from Krabi Town (11am and 1pm, returning 7.30am, 8am and 12.30pm) take 90mins to Ko Lanta Yai. Pick-ups can be arranged in advance from bungalows in Ban Sala Dan, or from tour agents countrywide. Turning off Route 4206 at Baan Huai Hin, Ko Lanta Yai is reached via ferries from barely inhabited Ko Lanta Noi.

### Getting around

The hilly central terrain is good for motorbikes (easily hired) and hiking, though when the clay roads get slippery in the rains, a 4WD is safer.

## Resources

### Hospital

*Ko Lanta Hospital, 118 Thanon Sanga-ou, Ban Sala Dan (0 7569 7100).*

### Post office

South of Lanta town (0 7569 7068).

### Tourist information

Website www.ko-lanta.com is a useful source.

### Tourist police

*Hotline 1155.*

## Tarutao archipelago

Comprising 50 islands hugging the sea border with Malaysia, the barely visited **Tarutao National Park** (open Nov-May) is clustered around **Ko Tarutao**, 22 kilometres (14 miles) offshore, and the **Adang-Rawi** island group 40 kilometres (25 miles) further out.

The eponymous main island is 25 kilometres (15.5 miles) long, covered with untouched hardwood forests and extensive mangrove swamps. Almost inaccessible, it was used for the reality TV show *Survivor* in 2002 and, more interestingly, as a political penitentiary in 1938. During World War II some prisoners took to piracy; their story is told in *The Pirates of Tarutao* by Thai politician Pongpol Adireksarn (aka Paul Adirex). Prison ruins remain, along

**Ko Tarutao**: welcome to paradise.

with feral descendants of farm animals. Wildlife-watchers come for hornbills, loris, monitor lizards, reticulated pythons and tiger-striped fish-hunting cats. Crocodile Cave lies in the estuary of **Ao Pante**, in the north of the island, where there's a beach with basic huts run by the national park (0 7478 3485), which can also organise treks.

Outward boats usually lunch at Ao Pante, pause at isolated **Ko Kai**, view the bouncing (sacred) pebbles of **Ko Hin Ngam** and offer snorkelling at **Ko Yang**. There's another park office on **Ko Adang** (0 7472 9002), also offering treks, huts and a restaurant. Above the park headquarters, a cliffside viewpoint overlooks **Ko Lipay**, with a reasonable beach facing Ko Kra and an idyllic crescent at **Had Pattaya**, both with good snorkelling and kayaks for hire.

Phuket-based **Sea Canoe** (*see p252*) operates four-day kayaking trips to Tarutao for $550; **PaddleAsia** (0 7624 0893) does six-day ones for $925. There's good diving at Christmas Tree Rock, Stingray City and Stonehenge, though intermittently in a short season; try **White & Blue Dive Club** (*see p246*) on Phuket or **Sabye Sports** (0 7473 4104/1897 8725/www.sabye-sports.com) on Lipay.

## Where to stay & eat

National park accommodation includes huts, campsite and rental tents (B100) on Tarutao; on Ko Adang there are three-room bungalows (B1,000) and huts sleeping four with a shared bathroom (B100). On Ko Lipay, private resorts include **Pattaya Seafood**, which has rooms at around B200-B600 per night and probably the park's best food. There are thatched cottages at **Lee Pae Resort** (0 7472 4336, rates B500-B600) and **Andaman Resort** (0 7472 9200, rates B300). Simple food can be bought at the park's café and shop (in season) on Adang. Those staying in park huts should bring their own provisions.

## Getting there

### By boat

Wassana Travel & Tour (0 7472 2143) runs ferries from Pak Bara pier on the mainland (0 7478 3368/ 1609 2604) at 10am and 2pm Dec-May; otherwise it's by charter only. The pier is 45km (28 miles) north-east of Satun town, reached by bus (2hrs) from Had Yai. Boats call daily at the north of Ko Tarutao (B300 return), taking much of the day to moor in the strait between Ko Adang and Ko Lipay (B800 return). Passengers are taken off by longtail boats. Pak Bara's several tour companies include Adang Sea Tour (0 7478 3368/1609 2604).

## Resources

### Medical centre

*Ko Tarutao National Park, Pak Bara (0 7478 3485).*

### Tourist police

*Hotline 1155.*

# Chiang Mai

Thailand's temperate second city remains culturally distinctive.

'It is entirely your fault you have tarried there so long,' wrote a director of the British East India Company to his agent, Thomas Samuel, who had been sent to Chiang Mai to trade in cloth in 1613. He enjoyed its charms too long, being carted off to his death in Pegu as a prisoner following the Burmese re-invasion of the city in 1615.

Contemporary travellers tend to linger in the capital of the north too, many becoming expats in a city that is human in scale and close to nature, yet equipped with modern amenities. It's not all temples and treks; recent years have seen a surge in New Age activities, a modern art movement, the development of handicrafts into contemporary design, and an upsurge of pride in local culture. Chiang Mai is the hub for visiting the northern Thailand, but there's plenty to keep you in this highly liveable town.

## HISTORY

The region's aboriginal inhabitants were Lawa, who were supplanted by the northern branch of the Mon's Dvaravati civilisation at Haripunchai (now Lamphun) around the ninth century. Migration by Tai tribes created an early manifestation of what is now Thai culture on a southern branch of the Silk Route. A Tai chief called Mangrai, threatened by the Mongols, established Chiang Mai as the capital of Lanna ('kingdom of a million rice fields') in 1296.

Though Buddhist scholarship thrived in Lanna, and political sway was to extend far beyond today's national borders, internal dissension and repeated wars against Ayutthaya weakened the kingdom, which easily succumbed to the Burmese in 1558. The city's remote mountainous location, some three weeks' journey up the Chao Phraya river, ensured relative autonomy under the Burmese, with only two brief Siamese incursions. Chao Kawila, aided by Siamese forces, recaptured Chiang Mai in 1774, only for the city to be abandoned until 1796, when Kawila re-established it as a vassal to Bangkok. This relative autonomy lasted until 1897, when, faced by British and French colonials, King Rama V took over administration of the northern provinces.

The charms that seduced Samuel became marketable to tourists after the journey time from Bangkok was slashed by the opening of the 700-kilometre (435-mile) railway line in 1921. Early promotions touted Chiang Mai as an exotic mountain outpost, graced by women with pale, sweet features and by the flowers of its temperate climate (it can get downright cold on winter nights). And so it was until the fight against communism and drugs from the Golden Triangle in the 1950s and '60s brought commercial development that has since swamped the city's gentle temple character, with concrete and cars replacing wooden buildings and carts.

The cultural and educational centre for the entire north, Chiang Mai is also a trading centre, with the valley's economy founded on agriculture, crafts and industry, with electronics and global clothing brands drawn by local handiwork flair. Flash floods are a recent result of dam building and deforestation, partly due to the slash-and-burn agriculture of hill tribes. With fires lit to prepare fields for ploughing, smoke becomes a severe haze at the hottest time (February to May).

Life on the move in Chiang Mai.

Though considered large by provincial Thai standards, Chiang Mai's conurbation is only 166 square kilometres/64 square miles) in size (Bangkok is almost ten times bigger, covering 1,565 square kilometres/604 square miles). There are 267,254 registered residents, though the true figure could be twice that.

## Sightseeing

### The Old City

The old city is contained within a moat almost two kilometres square; the brick walls have largely disappeared and the five gates are 1960s reconstructions, but the corner bastions are much as Chao Kawila rebuilt them after 1796. Originally laid out by Mangrai, the moat conserves some bygone atmosphere, while the main streets are less interesting than the lanes that once linked villages to temples and markets. It's best to explore on foot or by bike.

Halfway along Thanon Moon Muang, **Thaphae Gate** forecourt is used to stage anything from *takraw* games to the beauty contests of Songkran and Loi Krathong. Northward, the road passes **Sompet Market**, where lanes are thick with guesthouses, before reaching **Chaeng Si Phum**, the auspicious north-east bastion. An old town walk could divert across the moat to charming **Wat Pa Pao**, built by Shan timber workers in the late 19th century. West of Sompet Market, **Wat Chiang Man** stands on the same spot as Mangrai's first encampment. A 14th-century *chedi* with supporting elephants stands behind two Lanna *vihaan*, the northerly one (open 8am-5pm daily) housing two revered images.

The former 'navel of the city' is found at the southern end of Thanon Inthawarorot, where two old *chedi* and a shelter housing Buddha images are all that remain of a temple. The nearby plaza contains the **Three Kings Monument**, which depicts Mangrai and the kings of neighbouring Phayao and Sukhothai discussing the city layout. Dignitaries pay respects here every 12 April to celebrate the city's founding. Looming behind, the old provincial hall (built in 1924) now houses the **Chiang Mai Art & Culture Museum** (Thanon Prapokklao, 0 5321 7793, open 8.30am-5pm Tue-Sun, foreigners B90) containing audio-visual displays, models and regalia.

A few steps east of Thanon Prapokklao into Thanon Ratchadamnoen stand two buildings of former *chao* (chiefs). They now house the **Lanna Architecture Centre** (open 9am-4pm Mon-Fri) and the numismatic collection of the **Treasury Pavilion** (0 5322 4237/8, open 9am-noon, 1-3pm Mon-Sat). South down Prapokklao,

# Lanna revival

The current resurgence of northern Thai culture comes after a lengthy suppression that began after the Shan rebellion of 1902. Compulsory education used the language of central Thailand, and school history books ignored Lanna. Bangkok culture became so dominant that *khon meuang* (people of the city states) were ashamed to speak their dialect, *phasaa meuang*.

In the late 1980s opposition to further high-rise development in Chiang Mai culminated in citizens publicly performing a cursing ritual by burning chilli and salt together with the names of those responsible. By coincidence or not, the then governor of Chiang Mai died in the Lauda Air crash of 1991. However, despite opposition by a vociferous minority spearheaded by academics, Bangkok-style development continues, with flyovers built during the premiership of Thaksin, a son of Chiang Mai.

In the free-speech atmosphere following the 1997 constitution, *phasaa meuang* is frequently heard on local FM radio, and magazine *Northern Thai Citizen* publishes criticism. *Khon meuang* say they have no ambition beyond wanting a say in decisions affecting them.

Meanwhile, Lanna culture has been officially supported to encourage tourism, and officials wear local costume on Fridays. A more spontaneous reawakening of traditions is evident in the young people taking up northern music and organising fairs promoting local arts, food and clothing.

**Wat Phan Tao** has a large wooden *vihaan* reconstituted from a *chao* reception hall, with notable carvings above the door. The adjacent **Wat Chedi Luang** contains a colossal old stupa toppled by a 1545 earthquake. In its cruciform *vihaan*, the city pillar is the focus of prayers for prosperity in the Inthakhin Festival (in the sixth lunar month).

Of the old city's 36 temples, perhaps the most significant is **Wat Phra Singh** at the west end of Thanon Ratchadamnoen. Its Vihaan Lai Kham displays classic Lanna architecture, and houses the revered Phra Phuttha Singh Buddha image and early 19th century murals. Don't miss its elaborately decorated wooden *bot* and the finest *hor trai* (raised scripture library) in the north.

**Beyond Bangkok**

**Chiang Mai**

© Copyright Time Out Group 2003

0 _____ 1000 m

0 _____ 1000 yds

## Commercial district & river

The commercial centre of Chinatown is located between the moat and the Ping, a tributary of the Chao Phraya river. Gold shops cluster around Kaad Luang at the eastern end of Thanon Chang Moi, with two Chinese shrines near the **Postal Museum** (Thanon Praisani, open 9am-4pm Tue-Sun). Walking is the only practical way to visit the Chinese, Indian and Thai merchants located in the various markets, shops and alleys.

A few wooden buildings along Thanon Thaphae and Thanon Loi Kroh hint at the area's old character, and both streets house interesting temples, as well as shops, restaurants and bars (especially on Sundays, when Thanon Thaphae becomes a walking street). A couple of hundred metres to the south, on Charoen Prathet Soi 1, is **Baan Haw**, an ancient settlement of Muslim Yunnanese traders that is still great for inexpensive halal food. Nearby is the sprawling **Night Bazaar**.

The first Chinese settled on the east bank in **Ban Tha Chang** (Thanon Charoenrat); its less commercial location saved its wooden buildings, which are now chic boutiques, pubs and restaurants. Artefacts of the area feature in the museum (usually open 10am-noon, 2-4pm daily) at **Wat Ketkaram**, where the *chedi* is crooked because it was considered rude to point it at heaven. Much of the riverfront to the north has been taken over by pub-restaurants and a riverside walk.

Downstream from Saphan Nawarat the city's first wooden church (now part of the Chiang Mai Christian School) dominates the land where Presbyterian missionary John McGilvary was first allowed to settle in 1867. Missionaries still persist in the north.

Four kilometres (2.5 miles) further south is **Wiang Kum Kam** (near the east bank, just south of the innermost ring road 1141); the site contains the ruins of a city that predated Chiang Mai and thrived until the 17th century.

**Beyond Bangkok**

## West & north Chiang Mai

West from Suan Dok Gate along Thanon Suthep lies **Wat Suan Dok**, a fortified monastery containing a mass of *chedi* serving as reliquaries for Chiang Mai royalty. The Prachao Kan Teu, a seated bronze image cast in 1504, is housed in the smaller *vihaan*. Five exemplary Lanna buildings have been reconstructed by the **Centre for Promotion of Arts & Culture** (0 5394 3628). Beyond the irrigation canal a lane heads south half a kilometre to tranquil **Wat Umong**. A forest temple shaped by Buddhadhasa Bhikkhu, it features tunnels as meditation cells beneath a round *chedi*.

From **Chaeng Hua Lin** bastion, Thanon Huai Kaew starts by **Kat Suan Kaew**, a seven-floor labyrinth of shopping and entertainment. A north turn on the Chiang Mai–Lampang Superhighway 11 leads to **Wat Chet Yot**, which mimics designs from Pagan and Bodhgaya and was built by King Tilokarat for the eighth Buddhist Council in 1477. North along the same road, the Thai-style edifice of **Chiang Mai National Museum** (0 5322 1308, open 9am-4pm Wed-Sun, admission B30) surveys the region's history and has a collection of religious objects. North of town at **Suan Luang Ror IX** (Ratchamankha Park), the **Tribal Museum** (0 5321 0872, open 9am-4pm daily) is part of the university's **Tribal Research Institute** (0 5322 2494, open 8.30am-noon, 1-4.30pm daily).

Continuing on Thanon Huai Kaew, student hangouts herald **Chiang Mai University**, before passing **Chiang Mai Zoo** (0 5322 1179, open 8am-5pm, admission B30), which features big enclosures over a couple of hundred acres, including a fine walk-in aviary. Though a controversial cable car is proposed, it's another nine kilometres (5.5 miles) up the 1,685-metre high (5,530-foot) mountain to **Wat Phrathat Doi Suthep**. The temple is a pilgrimage site for Thais, who come to circumambulate the golden stupa – a marvel of proportion and delicacy – and look over the city. A funicular railway saves the 300-step climb. It's a short walk to the headquarters of the particularly bio-diverse **Doi Suthep-Pui National Park** and then down to **Monthatharn Falls** (check the status of the trail before you set off).

## Tours & activities

Companies offering tours by van can hardly be avoided downtown. Standouts include mountain biking outfit **Click & Travel** (0 5320 1194/www.clickandtravelonline.com) and **Chiang Mai Green Alternative Tours** (0 5324 7374), which offers cultural and nature tours, birdwatching, mountain biking, rafting, hill-tribe studies, organic agro-tours, elephant conservation and trekking. **Thai Adventure Rafting** (0 5327 7178/www.activethailand.com)

Monks tuck into a feast at **Wat Suan Dok**.

**Beyond Bangkok**

Sample street food after dark at the **Anusarn Night Bazaar**.

gets you though white water professionally. For aerial adventure, try **Oriental Balloon Flights** (0 5339 8609) or **Chiang Mai Sky Adventure Club** (0 5386 8460): its microlight/paragliding flights cost B1,200-B2,200 for 15-30 minutes. For trekking, *see p277* **Hit the trek**.

**Chiang Mai Land Sports Club** (0 5327 2821) has a pool, tennis and aerobics open to non-members. Golfing visitors can tackle **Green Valley Country Club** (0 5329 8220-3, closed Tue), **Chiang Mai-Lamphun Golf Club** (0 5388 0880-4) or **Royal Chiang Mai Golf Club** (0 5384 9301-6).

## Where to eat & drink

Along with *nam phrik* (spicy dips with steamed or fresh vegetables), the watery northern curries, which don't use coconut milk – such as *kaeng no mai* (with bamboo shoots) and *kaeng khae* (veg with meat) – flavour the staples of glutinous rice or wet white noodles. Other dishes are Burmese-influenced, such as the oily pork curry *hang leh*. Most restaurants serve only a few northern Thai dishes, and visitors tend to get their first taste at a *khantok* dinner and dance show. Dining and drinking is inexpensive, and most venues combine the two.

Street stalls offer authentic cuisine, such as *naem* (fermented pork sausage), *sai ua* (spicy sausage) and *laab* (spicy ground meat), but the daunted can sample a more sanitised experience at **Anusarn Night Bazaar** (between Thanon Chang Khlan and Thanon Charoen Prathet south of the Night Bazaar proper), and in restaurants along the main access road through the market.

Aside from hotel and guesthouse coffee shops (purveying the ubiquitous shakes and banana pancakes), Chiang Mai has a wealth of acceptable international restaurants, mainly in the **Thaphae** and **Night Bazaar** districts.

## Restaurants

### Gallery Bar & Restaurant

*25-9 Thanon Charoenrat (0 5324 8601).*
**Open** noon-midnight daily. **Main courses** B120.
**Credit** AmEx, DC, MC, V.
Built on a foundation of huge logs, the front godown of this century-old mercantile premises is now a gallery. The charming riverside wooden dining area is quiet and shady, while the quality of the central/northern dishes varies from good to merely OK.

### Hong Tauw

*95/17-8 Thanon Nimmanhaemin (0 5321 8333).*
**Open** 11am-10pm daily. **Main courses** B90.
**Credit** AmEx, MC, V.
Green shutters and trim contrast with the dark wooden chairs, cabinets and wall clocks in this stylish and comfy air-conditioned shophouse. You'll find central Thai dishes with a few Lanna staples.

### Huen Penn

*112 Thanon Ratchamankha (0 5327 7103).* **Open** 8am-3pm, 5-9.30pm daily. **Main courses** B30-B50.
**No credit cards**.
Packed at lunch, this leading northern Thai restaurant displays its specialities in the main dining area, beneath a sheltered terrace surrounding an air-conditioned room. Banana flower and pork rib curry star on the larger menu at dinner, when food is also served in a small wooden house.

### Just One

*16/1 Thanon Huai Kaew (0 5389 2123).*
**Open** 10am-midnight daily. **Main courses** B75.
**No credit cards**.
Most people dine outside here, where wooden walkways above a lotus pond link decks containing romantically lit tables. It's a branch of Bangkok restaurant Soi Ngam Dupli.

### Khao Soi Lamduan Faham

*352/22 Thanon Charoenrat (0 5324 3519).*
**Open** 8am-4pm daily. **Main courses** B30.
**No credit cards**.
One of several similar places serving the Burmese-influenced lunch staple *khao soi* (mild curry soup with dry and wet wheat noodles, and chicken or beef) plus other daytime classics.

### La Gondola

*Rimping Condominium, 201/6 Thanon Charoenrat (0 5330 6483).* **Open** 11am-midnight daily.
**Main courses** B160. **Credit** AmEx, DC, MC, V.
Facing a high-rise reviled for its impact on the Chang Mai skyline, this glasshouse of a restaurant with lawn tables overlooking the river serves some of the city's best Italian food.

### Tha Nam Restaurant & Guest House

*43/3 Mu 2, Thanon Chang Khlan (0 5328 2988).*
**Open** 8am-11pm daily. **Main courses** B85.
**Credit** AmEx, DC, MC, V.
Enjoy northern and central dishes accompanied by classical Lanna music while sitting around a rocky pool terrace by the river or in an open-sided wooden house. One wing has guest rooms (B400, air-con).

### Whole Earth

*88 Thanon Sidonchai (0 5328 21463).* **Open** 11am-10pm daily. **Main courses** B135. **No credit cards**.
No shoes are permitted in the air-conditioned plank and bamboo dining room. Ostensibly vegetarian, it also offers Thai, Western and Indian meat dishes. There are intimate tables on a terrace.

## Bars & pubs

Bars where food is not the focus are in zones where residents can bar hop without having to find a new parking space. Travellers mix with young Thais at small bars along eastern **Thanon Rathwithi**, with other local spots along **Thanon Nimmanhaemin** near Soi 17 and in **Chiang Mai Land**, linking Thanon Om Muang and Thanon Chang Khlan.
Where food combines with live music you've got a 'pub'. They're found all over Chiang Mai, but the best are beside the river, especially on **Thanon Charoenrat**.

### Brasserie Bar & Restaurant

*37 Thanon Charoenrat (0 5324 1665).* **Open** 5pm-2am daily. **Main courses** B90. **Credit** V.

Strong drinks complement the chords of virtuoso R&B guitarist Tuk as he wows the Western/Thai crowd in this bohemian bar. On the river terraces, the Thai food is good and the folk music quieter.

### Cottage

*27 Thanon Chiang Mai-Lamphun (0 5330 2225).*
**Open** 6pm-2am daily. **Main courses** B110.
**Credit** MC, V.
A ten-piece band plays under the extended roof of an old wooden house, prompting dancing between the tables to jazz-rock and Latin.

### Huan Sontharee

*46 Thanon Wang Sing Kham (0 5325 2445).*
**Open** 4pm-1am daily. **Main courses** B100.
**Credit** AmEx, DC, MC, V.
Northern folk classics by famed singer Sontharee Wechanon filter down from the covered upstairs wooden terrace to the riverside terrace, where diners feast on northern and central fare.

### Mau Dok Mai (Drunken Flower)

*295/1 Nimmanhaemin Soi 1 (0 5321 2081).*
**Open** 6pm-1am daily. **Main courses** B70.
**No credit cards**.
Selections from a large CD collection don't dampen the intimate vibe at the wooden garden tables or inside this converted home full of retro bric-a-brac.

### Riverside Bar & Restaurant

*9/11 Thanon Charoenrat (0 5324 3239).*
**Open** 10am-1.30am daily. **Main courses** B100.
**Credit** AmEx, MC, V.
An early presence on the river means this institution has one of the best locations. There's a long, low terrace below the open main wooden buildings, from where two bands blare (sometimes including Lanna tribal rocker Todd 'Thongdee' Levelle). It's one of the best places for trying three-chilli specials, such as 'golden needle mushroom salad'.

### Sax Bar

*35/2 Thanon Moon Muang (0 5322 1140).*
**Open** 6pm-2am daily. **No credit cards**.
Artist Rudi's imaginative interpretation of shop-house design and the DJ's extensive range of music make this an essential bar stop.

### Warm Up

*60 Thanon Na Wat Ket (no phone).* **Open** 6.30pm-1am daily. **Main courses** B80. **No credit cards**.
Thai rock blares over the jostling ground-floor tables of this wooden house, but it fades into the background at the rear, where mixed twentysomethings socialise. Bands play at 9pm.

## Nightlife

A once notorious red-light district that straddled the ancient Kamphaeng Din ramparts has been all but replaced by food shops, bars and traditional massage parlours. Bars with girls serve foreigners until late at the west end of **Loi**

**Kroh,** but it doesn't attempt to match Bangkok or Pattaya in the play-and-pay scene. A dozen more bars at the **Bar Beer Centre** (Thanon Moon Muang, open 6pm-2am daily) feature Thai boxing bouts around 11pm every night; foreigners who challenge locals usually lose.

### Space Bubble Discotheque

*Pornping Tower Hotel, 46-8 Thanon Charoen Prathet (0 5327 0099).* **Open** 9pm-2am daily. **Admission** B100 incl 1 drink. **Credit** AmEx, DC, MC, V.
The last remaining popular disco gets packed with ravers, bar-girls and tourists gyrating to the smoky thud of techno.

## Performing arts

Coachloads eat northern food while watching classical dancing at a dozen *khantok* dinner shows. Set menus of around six dishes always include *nam phrik ong* dip, *kaeng hang lae* (pork curry of Burmese origin) and fried chicken, eaten on axe pillows at low tables. Food is less of a differential than location, price and show. Among the grandest, **Khum Kantoke** (Chiang Mai Business Park, 0 5330 4121/2, set menu B290) has a show at 7.45-9pm; after 9.30pm you can continue at the adjacent **Plubpla Thai** restaurant until midnight. The more authentic **Old Chiang Mai Cultural Centre** (185/3 Thanon Wualai, 0 5327 5097, show 8-9.30pm, set menu B270) has northern Thai dancing with dinner, plus hill-tribe dances later.

### Kawila Boxing Stadium

*Camp Kawila, Thanon Kong Sai (0 5320 1899 ext 101).* **Shows** 9.30pm-midnight Fri (except Buddhist holidays). **Admission** B300.
The only serious *Muay Thai* (Thai kick-boxing) ring. There are also bouts for tourists at Galare 2 Food Centre (Night Bazaar) and the Bar Beer Centre (Thanon Moon Muang).

### Lanna Folk Puppets

*Centre for Promotion of Arts & Culture, Thanon Chonlaprathan (0 5389 2450).* **Shows** *Oct-Apr* 6.30pm Fri, Sat or by arrangement. **Admission** B200.
Modern interpretations of folk stories using bilingual puppets are presented at this quaint open-air theatre next to the Art Museum.

## Shopping

Chiang Mai is famous for handicrafts, and virtually everything produced hereabouts is found around within walking distance of the **Night Bazaar** on Thanon Chang Khlan (open late afternoon-11pm daily). Its two floors of swish galleries and simple stalls sell everything from woodcarvings to portraits. **Chiang Inn Plaza** is more relaxed and upmarket. Haggling's the norm, especially at street stalls.

The atmosphere and prices are cheaper in the galleries of **Kat Luang** and on nearby Thanon Khuangmen. On Thanon Thaphae, **Lost Heavens** (No.234, 0 5321 5557, open 9.30am-6pm daily) stocks tribal and primitive art, while **Living Space** (No.267-8, 0 5387 4299, open 9am-8pm Mon-Sat) does modern lacquerware. Cottons, hill-tribe fabrics and basketry are sold at **Par Ker Yaw** (180-4 Thanon Loi Khroh, 0 5327 5491, open 8.30am-7pm Mon-Sat).

**Baan Tha Chang** arcade on Thanon Charoenrat is crammed with chic outlets with matching prices. Nearby **Paothong's Private Collection** (No.66, 0 5330 2072, open 10am-10pm daily) specialises in fine Asian clothing, in a wooden house stylishly converted by Paothong Thongchua. **Oriental Style** (No.36, 0 5324 5724, open 8.30am-11pm daily) features both a furniture showroom and a restaurant in the city's best surviving late 19th-century mercantile building.

On the eastern highway Thanon San Kamphaeng there are upwards of 30 workshop-cum-showrooms, including **P Collection** (2 Mu 1, 0 5324 0222-5, open 8am-5.30pm daily) for lacquerware, and **Baan Celadon** (7 Mu 3, 0 5333 8288, open 8.30am-5.30pm daily) for ceramics. **Piankusol** (56 Mu 3, San Klang, 0 5333 8040-6, open 8am-6pm daily) is one of several silk shops on the same street. **Preservation House,** 300 metres north up a side road near km8 (29/3 Baan Ton Pao, 0 5333 9196, open 8am-5pm daily), sells the *saa* paper speciality of Baan Ton Pao village. In the umbrella village of Bo Sang, cameras snap at hand-painted brolly production in the **Umbrella Making Centre** (111/2 Bo Sang, 0 5333 8324, open 8am-5pm daily).

South of the old city, **Ngern Chiang Mai** (37-9 Thanon Wualai, 0 5327 5105, open 8am-6pm daily) sells traditional Chiang Mai silver, while silverworking and panel beating can be seen down Wualai Soi 3 and at Wat Si Suphan. Ceramic, art and furniture shops dot the road that leads 20 kilometres (12.5 miles) south to **Baan Thawai,** the hub of Thai woodcarving. Among hundreds of smaller shops are several purpose-built timber emporia, including **Yuthana House** (131 Mu 2, 0 5344 1570, open 8am-5pm daily).

In west Chiang Mai, **Kad Suan Kaew** mall includes a Central Department Store (open 10am-9pm daily) and Kaad Muang (zone A, ground floor), where small retailers sell local products. Several upmarket shops are located at the east end of Thanon Nimmanhaemin around Soi 1: **Gong Dee** (Nimmanhaemin Soi 1, 0 5322 2230, open 10am-7pm daily) has a gallery and studio selling locally designed artefacts and artworks, and **Sipsong Panna** (95/19 Thanon

**Gong Dee** offers an upmarket selection of local handicrafts and art. *See p264.*

Nimmanhaemin, 0 5321 6096, open 9.30am-5.30pm daily) specialises in antique silver. For reading matter, **Suriwong Book Centre** (54/1-5 Thanon Sridonchai, 0 5328 1052-5, open 8am-7.30pm Mon-Sat, 8am-12.30pm Sun) has the biggest range, while the **Lost Bookshop** (34/3 Thanon Ratchamankha, no phone, open 9am-2pm, 5-8pm daily) is first among many second-hand stockists.

## Arts & entertainment

### Festivals & events

Festivals are a chance to hear northern music, which differs considerably from central music, with deep gongs, booming *klong yao* (long drums), wispy *khlui* (bamboo flutes) and shimmering stringed instruments including the *pin-pia*, in which a coconut shell resonates against a bare chest. Northern music can be as infectiously rhythmic as Isaan *mor lam*, and the churning *sor* genre features a yodel-like male/female rap that's quite saucy.

#### Cool season

The cool season kicks off with a uniquely charming version of **Loy Krathong** (in Nov; *see p156*). There's boat racing during the day; at dusk homes are decorated with lanterns and, on all three festival nights, competitively decorated floats laden with young women in costume parade down Thanon Thaphae. Locals don't only float candle-lit *krathongs* on the river, but launch huge flame-heated paper balloons into the sky. Fireworks can turn the river area into a war zone.

Every two years, the **Chiang Mai Social Installation** (Nov-Jan) brings art closer to everyday life through fascinating multidisciplinary works in parks, temples, canals and pavements. The Art &

Culture Museum (*see p259*) will probably host the biennial **Experimental Film Festival** in Dec 2003 (usually held in Bangkok). The **Food Festival** (mid Dec) and **Winter Fair** (30 Dec-8 Jan) have both mushroomed into raucous commercial events. Two crafts promotions, **Bo Sang Umbrella Festival** (3rd weekend of Jan) and the **Ban Thawai Woodcarving Fair** (last weekend of Jan) are followed by the **Flower Festival** (morning of 1st Sat in Feb), when a colourful parade of floats laden with blooms and beauty queens parades down Thanon Thaphae Road and the southern moat road.

#### Hot season

Increasingly an expression of Lanna culture, the **Chiang Mai Arts & Culture Festival** (30 Mar-9 Apr) features performances and shows at the Art Museum, Three Kings Monument and other venues. It coincides with **Poy Sang Long** at Wat Pa Pao (1st week of Apr), when decadently glammed-up Shan boys are fêted and held on the shoulders of dancers before being ordained into saffron robes.

The Thai new year of **Songkran** (lasting 3-7 days around Apr 13-15) is most associated with Chiang Mai, where the Burmese-influenced water throwing festivities arose. The moats become gridlocked with pick-up trucks carrying revellers and drums filled with moat water and factory-sized blocks of ice. Devotees take time off to bathe elders' hands, make merit in temples in the early morning and throw lustral water on the Phra Singh Buddha image as it's paraded from Nawarat Bridge to Wat Phra Singh on the afternoon of the 13th. A second, lesser parade by officials to pay respect to the governor is on the 15th. Otherwise, wear old clothes, tote a spray gun and unleash your inner child.

### Film

For Hollywood blockbusters and Thai movies in high-standard theatres, **Vista** offers seven screens at Kad Suan Kaew mall (fifth floor, 0 5389 4415) and two at 12 Thanon Huai Kaew

(0 5340 4374). Tickets cost B70-B90. At seven-screener **Major Cineplex** (fourth floor, Central Airport Plaza, 0 5328 3939), tickets are B70-B120. The **Alliance Française** (Thanon Charoen Prathet, 0 5327 5277) shows French films with English subtitles monthly. Some guesthouses screen new releases on video nightly.

## Galleries

Many contemporary Thai artists are northerners or have studios in the area. The **Chiang Mai University Contemporary Art Museum** (Thanon Nimmanhaemin, 0 5394 4833, open 9.30am-5pm Tue-Sun) is a centre for Lanna culture and Thai modern art. It has monthly exhibitions and regular evening events curated by Gritthiya Gaweewong of Bangkok's Project 304. **Gong Dee** (*see p264*) also holds shows.

## Gay & lesbian

If you're looking for tour guides who are gay (no sex tourists), **Utopia Tours** (*see p175*) is very reputable. Licensed guide **Khun Tan** (0 1716 2485) and *tuk-tuk* driver **Khun Sukit** (0 1796 4415) also offer tours.

The social order clampdown in the PM's home town has driven student activity into internet chat rooms, and unsettled the substantial scene (check out www.pinkmaps. com/Chiang_Mai_ Text.html). Though rent-a-boys (mostly hill-tribe) are said to be less visible, they find their clients, while the bars mostly have hosts.

**Adam's Apple** (132/46-7 Soi Wiangbua, Thanon Chotana, 0 5322 0380/1, open 9.30pm-1.30am daily) has a regular following and a kitschy show at 11pm, while the **Lotus Garden** bar beer opposite is more congenial for a drink. At **Circle Pub** (161/7-8 Soi Arawan, Thanon Chang Phuak, 0 5321 4996, open 9pm-1am daily) there are shows at 10pm and 11.30pm Mon-Thur, 11pm Fri-Sun; they combine fashion and *kathoey* lip-synching.

### House of Male

*19 Sirimangkhlachan Soi 3 (0 5389 4133/ www.houseofmale.com).* **Open** noon-midnight daily. **Admission** B130. **Credit** AmEx, V.
This stylish wooden house has a clean sauna, gym, pool, lounge and candlelit nooks.

## Mind & body

Chiang Mai has long been a place where teachers of esoteric traditions have passed on skills, with many visiting just to take courses in the gentler northern Thai massage. This is often combined with herbal saunas, and there are parlours citywide. Buddhist instruction is given in English at **Wat Umong** (3pm Sun), and

foreigners can study meditation at **Wat Ram Poeng** (0 5381 0197), though its public sessions (4am-10pm daily) are not formally structured.

Fliers in guesthouses show the city has also become a magnet for alternative medicine, New Age therapists, pampering spas and health food outlets. Also common downtown are cooking schools and courses in handicraft production; the two are combined at **Mae Sa Valley Craft Village** (Mae Sa Valley Resort, 0 5329 0051), where it costs B600-B1,200 for a two-hour course (including meal, materials and 45-minute transfer to/from city hotels).

### Baan Thai Cooking School

*11 Thanon Ratchadamnoen Soi 5 (0 5335 7339/ www.cookinthai.com).* **Open** 9am-4pm daily. **No credit cards.**
Three-day courses (B700 per day) in a wooden house. Courses typically start at a market, with hands-on practice and sampling of each concoction.

### Ban Sabai

*17/7 Thanon Charoen Prathet (0 5328 5204-6/ www.ban-sabai.com).* **Open** noon-midnight. **Credit** AmEx, DC, MC, V.
This stylish spa is pricey (B900 for a massage) compared to nearby traditional massage parlours. Also facials, reflexology, aromatherapy and herbal steam.

### International Training Massage (Institute of Thai Massage)

*17/7 Thanon Morakot (0 5321 8632/www.infothai. com/itm).* **Credit** AmEx, MC, V.
Four five-day certificated courses (from basic to advanced therapeutic; B2,250-B5,000) are taught in a double air-conditioned shophouse under experienced Chongkol (John) Setthakorn. There's also a teacher-training course, and massages.

### Padma Aroma Spa

*204-6 Thanon Charoen Rat (0 5324 8358).* **Open** 10am-8pm daily. **Credit** (above B3,000 only) AmEx.
Built in a compound containing two wooden houses, this boutique spa has a pleasing Lanna feel. Treatments (B650-B6,000) include herbal and oil massages and herbal steam rooms.

### Old Medicine Hospital

*238/8 Thanon Wualai, opposite Old Chiang Mai Cultural Centre (0 5327 5085/office 0 5320 1663).* **Open** 9am-4pm daily. **No credit cards.**
In a newish air-con building you can take ten-day classes (starting on the first and third Monday of the month; B4,000) in the theory and practice of northern traditional massage, ending in certificated exams. Massages cost B200-B400 for 90-180 minutes.

## Where to stay

Several upmarket hotels are found near the **Night Bazaar**. There's more variety in the cheaper price range, in more ambient locations,

even in the busy east moat area. Rates listed below are for a double room; high season is from November to mid April.

## Amari Rincome

*1 Thanon Nimmanhaemin (0 5322 1044/rincome@ amari.com).* **Rates** $90-$120. **Credit** AmEx, DC, MC, V.

A well run hotel with wood tracery and panelling. The quieter deluxe rooms overlook the garden, tennis court and one of two pools. The La Gritta Italian restaurant (11.30am-2pm, 4.30-10pm daily) is reasonable. Transport is provided to the Night Bazaar.

## Galare Guest House

*7 Soi 2 Thanon Charoenprathet (0 5381 8887/ www.galare.com).* **Rates** B720-B860. **Credit** MC, V.

This central low-rise hotel has no pool, but a garden, dining hall overlooking the river and rooms with air-con, fan, cable TV and minibar.

## Lai Thai Guest House

*111/4-5 Thanon Kotchasan (0 5327 1725/ www.laithai.com).* **Rates** B390-B660. **Credit** AmEx, MC, V.

Beige paint, wooden carvings and fretwork lend character to the two main buildings overlooking a pool. A quieter extension has a garden. Most of the 105 air-con rooms are en suite and have cable TV.

The **Baan Thai Cooking School**. *See p266.*

## Namkhong Guest House

*55-7/1 Thaphae Soi 3 (0 5327 5556/npanada@ hotmail.com).* **Rates** B150-B250. **Credit** MC, V.

Signs say no escort girls are allowed into the plain, functional air-con and fan rooms (all en suite with hot water), but rivals nearby might be more tolerant. Cable TV lounge and internet room.

## Royal Princess

*112 Thanon Chang Khlan (0 5328 1033-43/rpc@ dusit.com).* **Rates** B3,200-B3,500. **Credit** AmEx, DC, MC, V.

The chic lobby mixes oriental and Western styling, while restful colours and wooden platform beds make the deluxe rooms appealing. There's a pool and gym. It's close to the action, but you can also dine at the Garden Café, restaurants Jasmine (Chinese) and Miyuki (Japanese) or use the 24-hour room service.

## SK House

*30 Moon Muang Soi 9 (0 5341 8396).* **Rates** B400-B800. **Credit** AmEx, DC, MC, V.

Formerly a so-so guesthouse amid several around Si Phum Corner, the upgraded SK House has an air-con building with Lanna-style door paintings. Rooms are en suite, but have fans. There are nightly videos, a fair-sized pool and internet access.

## Smile House

*2 Ratchamankha Soi 2 (0 5320 8661-3/ smile208@loxinfo.co.th).* **Rates** B150-B400. **No credit cards.**

A wooden house with a balcony over a small garden houses five fan rooms sharing three bathrooms. There are also fan and air-con rooms in the row buildings in this convenient compound.

## Suan Doi House

*38/3 Soi Charntrasup, Thanon Huai Kaew (0 5322 1869).* **Rates** B950-B1,400. **Credit** MC, V.

You'll find aged minah birds shrieking in Thai amid the foliage-festooned low-rise buildings. Beads and mobiles obscure the walkways to small, but adequate air-con rooms, Le Gong Gum Vietnamese restaurant and a *sala*-cum-library.

## Suriwongse Hotel

*110 Thanon Chang Khlan (0 5327 0051/ suriwongse_htl_cnx@hotmail.com).* **Rates** B2,600-B2,800. **Credit** AmEx, DC, MC, V.

The comfy deluxe rooms have a Lanna feel; the ones in the old wing overlooking the Night Bazaar are bigger. Le Bistrot serves French fare, while Fueng Fah offers Euro-Thai dishes. There's a small pool.

## Tamarind Village

*50/1 Thanon Ratchadamnoen (0 5341 8898/9/ www.tamarindvillage.com).* **Rates** B4,000-B6,000. **Credit** AmEx, DC, MC, V.

Chiang Mai's only international-class boutique hotel, with 40 elegant, minimalist rooms built in local style around large trees. The greenery means

Paradise at **Tamarind Village**. *See p267.*

mosquitoes buzz you in the early morning and evening as they head to the open-sided dining *sala* overlooking the sizeable pool. Book in advance.

### Top North Hotel

*41 Thanon Moon Muang (0 5327 9623-5/topnorth @hotmail.com).* **Rates** B400-B900. **Credit** MC, V.
Empty for years, this great-value hotel has now been refurbished. If it's full, the Top North Guest House on Moon Muang Soi 2 has a similar pool, but less attractive rooms.

### The White House

*12 Soi Thanon Ratchadamnoen (0 5335 7130).* **Rates** B250-B350. **No credit cards.**
The best in a zone of comparable guesthouses. The 21 fan and six air-con rooms with TV have tiled floors and hot water. The dining area overlooks a garden. Thai owner Joe speaks English and runs tours that include his Siam Kitchen Cooking School.

## Getting there & around

### By air

Thai Airways (240 Thanon Prapokklao, 0 5321 1044-7/24hr hotline 0 2628 2000) has at least 10 flights a day (6.30am-10.45pm) to/from Bangkok and Chiang Mai. A limousine service from the Chiang Mai terminal's north end takes you anywhere downtown for B100. Bangkok Airways (0 5328 1519) has daily direct flights to Bangkok, Sukhothai and Jinghong.

### By train

Perhaps the nicest way to reach Chiang Mai is by sleeper train from Bangkok's Hualamphong station; it reaches the most scenic stretch of the route at

dawn. The Diesel Express (reclining seats only) is fastest (11hrs 35mins), departing Bangkok 7.25pm, returning 8.10pm. The slower Express departs Bangkok 6pm, 7.40pm, returning 4.25pm, 6pm. The Rapid service is slowest (14hrs 20mins), departing Bangkok 6.40am, 3pm, 10pm, returning 6.25am, 3.45pm, 9.30pm.

### By bus

There are long-distance bus and minibus connections nationwide to Chiang Mai; contact any travel agent. A famous Bangkok operator to Chiang Mai is Nakhonchai Air (27 Thanon Wiphawadirangsit 19, North, 0 2936 0800/www.nca.co.th). Bangkok to Chian Mai takes 8hrs.

Long-distance buses to northern destinations run frequently from Arcade bus station (off Thanon Kaew Nawarat) by day, while evening VIP luxury coaches head across country. Local buses north on highway 107 depart from No.1 bus station on Thanon Chang Phuak.

### Getting around

The most convenient way to get around Chiang Mai is by bicycle (from B30 per day) or motorbike (Honda moped from B120 per 24hrs); both are easily hired along Thanon Moon Muang. For reliable Hondas and 250cc dirt bikes, try Goodwill Motorcycles (26/1 Chang Moi Soi 2, 0 5325 1186). Helmets are a legal requirement. As well as taxis and local buses, you can use *tuk-tuks* (from B20) or flag down red *songthaew*, which have a mystifying repertoire of routes varying according to passenger demand (B10 in downtown).

For car hire, try Budget (1 800 283438/www. budget.co.th). Its cheapest vehicle costs B990 per 24hrs; self-drive tour information is also offered. North Wheels (0 5341 8233/4/www.northwheels.com, cheapest car B600 per 24hrs) can also supply drivers (B300-B500 plus full board per day).

## Resources

### Hospital

*Chiang Mai Ram Hospital, 8 Thanon Bunruangrit (0 5322 4861).* Offers efficient private care.

### Post offices

Thanon Praisani and Thanon Prapokklao offer regular services; those at 402 Thanon Charoen Muang and Thanon Samlan also have international telephones until 6pm. All are open 8.30am-4.30pm Mon-Fri; 9am-noon Sat.

### Tourist information

*Tourism Authority of Thailand (TAT), 105/1 Thanon Chiang Mai-Lamphun (0 5324 8604).* **Open** 8.30am-4.30pm daily.
Free magazines with maps are widespread. For maps with good detail, look for Nancy Chandler's *Map of Chiang Mai* and Oliver Hargreave's *Exploring Chiang Mai: City, Valley & Mountains.* Also check out www.chiangmaicitylife.com.

### Tourist police

*75 Thanon Chiang Mai-Lamphun (hotline 1155).*

# Around Chiang Mai

Mountains, treks and hill tribes – the north combines natural and ethnic diversity.

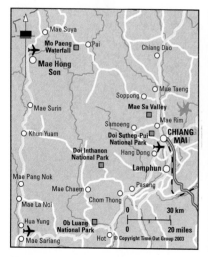

The colourful minority peoples and the mythical aura of the Golden Triangle have, since the 1960s, lured many tourists to northern Thailand. Each province is defined by fertile valleys ringed by mountains and, given the multiple indigenous and migratory peoples, both lowlands and highlands possess an ethnic and cultural diversity that's unmatched elsewhere in Thailand – or, indeed, in most other countries.

The landscape is so beautiful and so varied that areas containing many of the sights, waterfalls and tribal villages mentioned below have been declared national parks. The **Mae Hong Son Loop** is the best all-round sampler and features the highlights of languid Pai, remote Mae Hong Son and the towering Doi Inthanon peak. The north's second city, **Lampang**'s major attractions are still under visited, while **Chiang Rai** and the **Golden Triangle** maintain a frontier feel, joining Chiang Saen and Doi Tung at the triangular border with Laos and Burma.

Visitors to this area, particularly those interested in trekking (see p277 **Hit the trek**), are likely to come into contact with the many colourful tribes in the surrounding hill villages, including the Shan, Lua, Akha, Karen, Lisu, Lahu, Meo and Haw peoples.

## GETTING THERE AND ESSENTIALS

There's an airport at Lampang (0 5422 6347), with two flights a day to/from Bangkok. Trains from Bangkok (journey 11 hours) run six times a day to Lampang station (0 5421 7024), a kilometre south-west of town, near the bus station. Thai Air flies four times a day to/from Chiang Rai Airport (0 5371 1179). Air-con buses leave every 30 minutes 7am-8pm daily from Bangkok's Northern Bus Terminal.

Buses regularly ply the highways (from Chiang Mai's Arcade bus station for Pai, Mae Hong Son via Mae Sariang, Chiang Rai, Mae Sai, the Golden Triangle and Chiang Khong), with *songthaew* for local hops. Organised treks into the hills are simpler (via minibus or *songthaew*), though the north rewards touring by motorcycle or car (readily hireable, self-drive or with driver, for B1,500-B2,000 per day). Rent 4WDs or dirt bikes to explore the side roads. *B&B's Thailand North* road map is the best overall, but others are also sold in Chiang Mai and Chiang Rai.

For tourist information, **TAT** in Chiang Mai (105/1 Thanon Chiang Mai-Lamphun, 0 5324 8604) also covers Mae Hong Son province. TAT in Chiang Rai (448/16 Thanon Singkhlai, 0 5371 7433) covers the north's eastern provinces. Both are open 8.30am-4.30pm daily. Banks, ATMs and money exchange are available in main towns, plus Pai, Mae-Ai (ten kilometres/six miles from Thaton), Fang and Chiang Saen. The tourist police hotline is 1155.

## Mae Hong Son Loop

Sheer cliffs, caves and sunken valleys make this one of Thailand's most impressive routes. Anticlockwise on Highways 1095 and 108 with overnight stops at Pai, Mae Hong Son and Mae Sariang (it's about a half-day drive between each), the loop is almost 600 kilometres (372 miles). A shorter 520-kilometre (323-mile) route now cuts east from Khun Yuam (Highway 1263) to Mae Na Chon, then south to Mae Chaem before climbing over the shoulder of Doi Inthanon to the Ping Valley at Chom Thong, taking in Lamphun before returning to Chiang Mai.

The rolling green hills...

## Mae Sa to Pai

Some 17 kilometres (10.5 miles) north of Chiang Mai on Highway 1095, take a detour to the left on Highway 1096 to reach the Mae Sa Valley, which actually forms a day-trip loop via Highway 1296 back to Chiang Mai or continues to Pai via Samoeng and Wat Chan for 4WDs in dry season only. The several waterfalls that culminate in **Mae Sa Falls** (in Doi Suthep-Pui National Park) are flanked by resorts with gardens and restaurants. Most impressive of all is the state-run **Queen Sirikhit Botanic Garden** (Highway 1096 km12, 0 5329 8171, 8am-5pm, admission B20), which harbours nature trails, a glasshouse and a botanical museum within its 2,600 acres (6,420 hectares). **Pong Yaeng Elephant Camp** (Highway 1096 km18, 0 5321 5943) offers shows (9.15am & 10.15am, B100) and rides (until 3pm, B1,000 per hour) with good views.

Back on Highway 1095, the main route passes **Mok Fa Falls** (near km23 in Doi Suthep-Pui National Park) before climbing through narrow upland valleys and crossing a scenic 1,350-metre (4,429-foot) pass. **Pong Duet Hot Springs** (six kilometres/four miles on a side road north from near km42, and a viewpoint east over Nam Mae Taeng Valley (turning six kilometres/four miles north from km65), are found around Lisu and Hmong villages within **Huai Nam Dang National Park**.

## Where to eat & stay

One of the world's best hotels, **Regent Resort Chiang Mai & Lanna Spa** (Thanon Mae Rim-Samoeng Sai Kao km7, Mae Rim, 0 5329 8181/www.regenthotels.com, rates $400-$500) offers all-suite, contemporary Lanna-style luxury overlooking working rice terraces (run by the hotel), with a modern cooking school and shuttles to Chiang Mai. Also very pretty are the bungalows with views at **Pong Yaeng Garden Resort** (Thanon Mae Rim-Samoeng Sai Kao km14, Mae Sa, 0 5387 9151/2, rates B1,500-B2,000). **Samoeng Resort** (79 Moo 2, Samoeng, 0 5348 7074, rates B800-B1,200) offers creature comforts in cabins but less impressive facilities. **Mokfa Resort** (1095 km17, 0 5330 6287, rates B250-B350) has simple huts, and there are noodle shops in nearby villages. Cheap local restaurants (with English menus) are scattered throughout Mae Sa Valley.

## Pai

Throughout the 1990s, this tranquil overnight stop boomed into a charming destination for Bangkokians seeking activity amid tranquility. Its teak houses have been converted into coffee shops and cottage industries like the ethno-chic **Elite Galerie** (Thanon Rangsiyanon, 0 5369 9775) or **Mit Thai Art Shop** (Thanon Chaisongkram). More than 70 guesthouses are

... and hungry elephants of **Mae Hong Son**.

dotted about the valley, most tempting guests not just with views, comforts or a river frontage, but with such idiosyncratic activities as the study of batik or art (at **Crafty House**, Baan Mae Yen, 0 1769 0142, course B600 per four hours) or pressure points (at **Pai Traditional Thai Massage**, 68/3 Thanon Tessabarn 1, 0 5369 9121/1288 6497, course B2,000 per three days).

Nature provides the other attractions, with **Tha Pai Hot Spring** and **Pai Gorge** east and west of the river crossing eight kilometres (five miles) south. Beyond the rice terraces, wooded hills shelter tribal villages and waterfalls. **Pai Mountain Bike on Tour** (0 5369 9384/1952 8102, B80 per day) provides pedal power; **Pai Enduro Team** (0 5369 9395) organises trail-biking through the jungle; and **Back-Trax** takes care of the trekking (0 5369 9739, B500) – all are on Thanon Chaisongkram. **Thai Adventure Rafting** (13 Thanon Rangsiyanon, 0 5369 9111/www.active thailand.com/rafting; B1,800 per two days) runs the rapids.

Overlooking the valley from the east, dizzyingly designed **Wat Mae Yen** has a shrine to Princess Suphankalaya (*see p10* **Warrior princesses**), and is on the route west to swimmable **Mo Paeng** waterfall. Ethnic costumes are also seen in town, which is mostly Shan, with many Karen, Lisu, Lahu, Meo and Haw Chinese Muslims, who wrangle over the level of nightlife.

## Where to eat & drink

Tiny Pai boasts French, Japanese, Chinese, vegetarian, Muslim, Irish, modern European, Thai and Shan cuisine, but still the most popular joint is **All About Coffee** (100 Thanon Chaisongkram, 0 5369 9429, main courses B70), which is arguably Thailand's best coffee house. **Lek's Pause Café** (no phone) on the opposite corner does French, international and Thai food, while there's more espresso plus teas and salads at the **Sunflower** (Thanon Chaisongkram, near Wat Pha Kham).

Pai also has superb bread (available at the Muslim stall facing Thanon Rungsiyanon market) and good vegetarian grub (**Thai Yai**, Thanon Rangsiyanon, 0 5369 9093, main courses B70). **Monkey Magic** on the *soi* off Thanon Khetklang near Wat Luang serves sushi to the sound of mellow reggae. But Pai is mainly an early-to-bed town, with **Be-bop** (99 Thanon Chaisongkram, 0 5369 9024, live blues jams 9pm-11pm) the pick of the nightspots.

## Where to stay

In town, the upmarket river tree houses of **Rim Pai Cottage** (17 Thanon Chaisongkram, 0 5369 9133, rates B800-B1,400) rival the big, comfy wooden rooms of **Ever Green Guest House** (220 Thanon Wanchalerm 18, 0 5369 9882, rates B200).

Uphill to the east, **Pairadise** (second left before Baan Mae Yen, 0 9838 7521/ www.pairadise.com, rates B350-B450) has fine views and snuggly blankets to keep you warm at night. **I'm Fine Garden** (0 9857 2519, rates B250-B350) has quirky, clean chalets between Baan Huai Pu and Baan Wiang Nua, where **Sipsongpanna** (60 Baan Wiang Nua, 0 17351 786/1884 1124, rates B500-B700) enchants with huts on the river's edge and popular classes in art and cooking (B600 per day).

Six kilometres (four miles) south, the bungalows and tents in manicured **Thapai Spa Camping** (84-84/1 Mae Hee, 0 5369 9695/ 9851 8362, rates B600-B800) have smart thermal pools for both sexes.

## Resources

### Information

Hand-drawn maps abound *(Sipsongpanna* is the most detailed). *A Study of Pai* by Bongpoun Arunleurd outlines the culture. Internet terminals are plentiful.

### Police

On Thanon Rungsiyanon, south of the market.

### Post office

On Thanon Khetkalang.

Traditional Akha tribe crafts.

## Mae Hong Son & around

At **Tham Lot** cave (8am-5.30pm, lamp and guide B100), eight kilometres (five miles) up a side road north from Soppong (Highway 1095 km141, two kilometres/one mile west of Pang Mapha), guides lead rafts across the river flowing through the 200-metre (61-foot) cave. More caves can be explored by going to Mae La Na on Highway 1226 and requesting guides in the market. Amid this spectacular karst scenery, dirt roads pass though Shan and Karen valley villages and elevated Lahu and Lisu villages.

**Mae Hong Son** is a Shan town in a valley just large enough to accommodate an airstrip for jets from Chiang Mai. Overlooked from the **Wat Phrathat Doi Kong Mu** viewpoint, Nong Jong Kham lake has a picturesque backdrop of the stupas and filigreed roofs of **Wat Jong Kham** and **Wat Jong Klang**. The dual-temple compound houses large Shan-style wooden *vihaans* – one of which contains a small museum (8am-6pm, free), where carvings and pictures illustrate the *Vessantara Jataka* (stories of the Buddha's past lives). In a third hall is a large white Shan Buddha image from 1933.

Apart from its perennial shroud of mists (rainy season, winter morning dew and summer smoke), Mae Hong Son is known for **Poi San Long** in March – a colourful ordination ceremony for Shan boys. Also Buddhist, **Jong Para Festival** falls three days before the 11th full moon (in October).

Companies such as **TN Tour** (107/17 Thanon Khunlumpraphat, 0 5361 3454) run tours and treks in the surrounding mountains. Signs tout 'long necks' and 'big ears' half-day excursions to one of three refugee villages of Padaung (long-neck Karen), whose women's collarbones are depressed by heavy metal coils, and Kayah, whose women's ear lobes are expanded by rings. One village, Ban Huai Phu Kaeng, is only accessible by boat from Ban Huai Dua (8am-5pm daily, B500). The pricey entrance fee (B250) suggests exploitation, but actually it goes towards helping the refugees.

## Where to eat & stay

Two rustic bases for exploring Pang Mapha are **Cave Lodge** (15 Moo 1, Pang Mapha, nearly a kilometre from Tham Lot, rates B100-B700) and **Wilderness Lodge** (Highway 1095 km166, rates B60-B80). **Little Eden Guest House** (195 Moo 1, Soppong, 0 5361 7054/www. littleeden-guest house.com, rates B350) has nicer cabins and organises treks.

Mae Hong Son's best dining and lodging is close to Nong Jong Kham lake. **Fern Restaurant** (87 Thanon Khunlumpraphat, 0 5361 1374,

Having a laugh in **Wat Jong Klang**. *See p272.*

main courses B84) is excellent and its **Fern Resort** (via the restaurant or 0 5361 3585, rates B950-B1,500) is in a pretty spot south of town. Both tone down spices for foreign palates. **Thip Restaurant** (23/1 Thanon Praditjongkham, 0 5362 0553, main courses B75) and the same owner's **Lake Side Bar**, which has live music, are the only places directly viewing the lake.

**Piya Guest House** (1/1 Khumlumpraphat Soi 3, 0 5361 1260, rates B600) has central bungalows in a garden. **Mae Hong Son Hill Resort** (No.106/2, 0 5361 2475, rates B500-B600) has wooden bungalows a few hundred metres further south. **Phen Phon Guest House** (16/1 Phadung Muai To, 0 5361 1577, rates B250) has rooms a short walk from the lake and nightspots on Thanon Phadung Muai To.

The posh **Imperial Tara Mae Hong Son** (Tambon Pang Mu, 0 5361 1021-25/www.imperialhotels.com, rates B2,884-B3,296) is in wooded grounds to the southern edge of town, while **Rim Nam Klang Doi Resort** (108 Ban Huai Deua, 0 5361 2142, rates B500-B700) is one of several wooden bungalow resorts in scenic locations along the Pai river.

## Mae Sariang & Inthanon

Highway 108 passes south through **Khun Yuam** – a short parade of shops with a small museum (8am-5pm, free) at its northern end exhibiting artefacts from the Japanese occupation in World War II.

Those with their own vehicle can cut east to Mae Chaem on Highway 1263. After 12 kilometres (seven miles), a side road climbs north on a panoramic route that passes stunning sunflower fields – packed with Thai tourists for the two to three weeks of peak blooming (during late November) – and ending at the awesome **Mae Surin Falls** (in Mae Nam Surin National Park). Highway 1263 climbs east over Hmong-cultivated high country, before descending south from Mae Na Chon into the Nam Mae Chaem valley to join Highway 1088 heading south to **Mae Chaem** – a quiet, traditional town noted for the weaving in the villages to its south. Narrow Highway 1192 winds up to a junction with Highway 1009: here you can either turn left to the summit of Doi Inthanon or right to Chom Thong in the Ping Valley.

From Khun Yuam, public buses wind south down Highway 108 via Mae La Noi to **Mae Sariang**, an old Yuam River trading town in deep Karen country (their shy married women are easily identified by blue or black blouses and hand-woven red tube skirts). Heading east on Highway 108, you pass another turning north to Mae Chaem (on Highway 1088) just before **Ob Luang National Park**, which contains a small, scenic gorge. The road is then fast via Hot to Chom Thong.

Just north of Chom Thong, Highway 1009 soars west to the summit of **Doi Inthanon**, Thailand's highest mountain at 2,590 metres

Among the hill tribes in the region are the Karen (*left*) and Kayah.

(8,500 feet), passing **Mae Klang Falls** and **Vachirathan Falls** into the country's only temperate rainforest. At any time, you can take the short Ang Kha boardwalk trail amid the lofty, fern-draped trees at the summit, though clouds may close in around you.

But the four-kilometre Kiw Mae Pan trail (km42, open November to April) to the western ridge requires permission from **Doi Inthanon National Park** HQ (near km31).

Before getting to Chiang Mai, divert to **Lamphun** – a moated city where **Haripunchai National Museum** (Thanon Inthayanongyot, admission B30) takes its ancient Mon name. Founded by a Mon Dvaravati queen, whose dynasty was replaced by King Mangrai in 1281, **Wat Chamadevi** houses the only intact Dvaravati structures: two *chedi* with trademark niches. A pinnacle of Lanna style, **Wat Phrathat Haripunchai** has a museum of Lanna Buddha images, a large *vihaan* containing the Phra Chao Thongtip Buddha, a four-in-one Buddha footprint in a *sala*, and a *vihaan* with striking 1950s' murals of hell. Its gilded, Lankan-style *chedi* is bathed during festivities on the sixth full moon.

Lamphun is well worth visiting on a day trip from Chiang Mai (reached via an avenue of lofty *yang* trees).

## Where to eat & stay

**Ban Farang Guest House** (Khun Yuam, 0 5362 2086, rates B200-B300) is about the only accommodation north of Mae Sariang, where **Riverside Guest House** (Thanon Laeng Phanit, 0 5368 1188, rates B350) lies on the river's east bank. **Mit A Ree Guest House** (24 Thanon Wiangmai, 0 5368 1109, rates B600-B1,200) has snug bungalows behind a so-so hotel. **Renu** (174/2 Thanon Wiangmai, 0 5368 1171, main courses B75), has slightly better food than **Inthra** opposite. In Mae Chaem, food is basic and accommodation lies off the road to Doi Inthanon: a couple of kilometres out, **Pongsara Resort** (Chang Deung, 0 5348 5011, rates B300) has new bungalows beside **Lai Hin Restaurant** (main courses B80). Another kilometre on, **Navasoung Resort** (Thapha, 0 5382 8477, rates B600) is a bit smarter.

# Lampang

Despite multiple charms – most famously its kitsch pony carriages (B300 per hour) – Lampang remains an under-visited city. Supplies of teak (long since logged out) once floated down the River Wang, which is now no more than a dammed trickle between denuded

embankments. Still, some timber wealth remains visible along **Talad Kao**, where rustically galleried teak shophouses and Burmese-style mansions sport fantastical fretwork – a reminder of what Chiang Mai once looked like.

At the riverside **Wat Sri Rong Muang** (on Thanon Takrao Noi, west of the clocktower), coloured glass and intricately cascading eaves enshrine broad-faced Mandalay-style Buddhas. Intricate **Wat Sri Chum** (on Thanon Sri Chum) was recarved by the Burmese after a fire, while on the north bank site of the original Haripunchai (Dvaravati) town, **Wat Phra Kaew Don Tao** (Thanon Phra Kaew, B20) housed the Emerald Buddha from 1436-68. Legend hints it was swapped with the Phra Kaeo Don Tao image that now draws pilgrims to **Wat Prathat Lampang Luang**. A so-so museum shows mainly Burmese wood carving, but through this suburb of wooden houses you can see better teakwork at **Baan Sao Nak** (Multi Pillar House, 6 Thanon Ratwattana, 10am-5pm daily, B30), also displaying lacquerware and Lampang's naïve painted ceramics. On the north-west edge of town, **Lampang Medicinal Plants Conservation Assembly** (177 Thanon Kwanmuang, 0 5435 0787) offers all things herbal (baths B150, scrub B200 and sauna B80) plus massage (B150 per hour), with the shop explaining its products' efficacy in English.

### Where to eat & stay

Cosy wooden rooms at **Riverside Guesthouse** (286 Thanon Talad Kao, 0 5422 7005, rates B300-B350) are wonderfully serene and characterful (with good food). A few doors east, **Heuan Boonma** (no phone, rates B150) occupies a stunning Lanna house, with modern rooms behind. Further along, **Heuan Chom Wang** (276 Thanon Talad Kao, 0 5422 2845, main courses B90) serves authentic local dishes in a wooden sala bedecked with jars of floating flowers. At the cement embankment, **Baan Rim Nam** (the Riverside, 328 Thanon Tipchang, 0 5422 1861, main courses B80) has a broader menu and live music in a multi-level wooden compound.

### Around Lampang

Head 37 kilometres (23 miles) west on Highway 11 to the **Thai Elephant Conservation Centre** (328 Thanon Tha Ma-O, 0 5422 8108, admission B50), where you can witness the elephants bathing in the lake before their show (10-11am & 11am-noon daily plus 1.30-2.30pm Sat, Sun). If you're arriving by bus, you'll need to hire a *songthaew*, as it's a couple of kilometres from a stop on any Lampang–Chiang Mai route. Returning on Highway 11, don't miss the exotic forest products, spear foundry and cute local ceramics at **Thung Kwian Market** (21 kilometres/13 miles west of Lampang).

Turn south at Hang Chart for the north's most revered and beautiful temple, **Wat Phra That Lampang Luang**. Dating from Haripunchai times, this rare intact *wiang* (fortified temple) has moated walls punctuated by a magnificent (and much-copied) gate. The eaves of the main wooden *vihaan* sweep low, harbouring exquisite carving, a pulpit and *ku* (gilded tower). Behind it looms the definitive Lanna *chedi*. Its aged copper patina is also viewable through a camera obscura in a nearby building. Beyond the weathered cloister, ancient banyan trees are propped up by long wooden crutches signed by merit-makers, beside the *viharn* securing the prized **Phra Don Tao**, a Buddha made of green jasper.

The easiest route here from Lampang is to get a direct *songthaew* from the Thai Farmer's Bank on Thanon Robwiang (B30).

### Resources

#### Post office
On Thanon Thipchang, east of the market.

#### Tourist information
*Lampang Tourism Centre, Thanon Boonyawat (0 5421 8823).* Open 8.30am-4.30pm Mon-Fri. Non-TAT tourist information.

# Chiang Rai & the Golden Triangle

Associated back in the 1960s with the Chinese Kuomintang, who were dealing opium and heroin to finance the fight against communism, and nowadays with the Red Wa, who are said to be flooding the country with *ya ba* (methamphetamines), the Golden Triangle conjures up images of mystery and intrigue. But these days, despite battles between the Shan State Army and the Wa/Burmese forces, the only impact on tourists is periodic border closures at Mae Sai, near Doi Tung's royal projects. Chiang Rai province still lures many travellers looking to raft on the Kok river or visit ancient Chiang Saen on the Mekong river.

### Around Fang

The most interesting route to Chiang Rai is the indirect Highway 107, skirting Thailand's third highest peak, **Doi Luang Chiang Dao**

**Beyond Bangkok**

(2,175 metres/7,136 feet), then tracing the Nam Fang valley. A steep road ascending a ridge along the Burmese border goes to **Doi Ang Khang**, where Yunnanese Chinese, Lahu and Palaung villages are close to a government agricultural station growing temperate fruits.

Fang town is less interesting than **Ban Thaton**, a large village base for treks and trips down the Kok river, a Mekong tributary (12.30pm daily for Chiang Rai, 0 5337 3224, B250 per person; charters 7am-3pm, B1,600). Ten stops include three with guesthouses.

## Where to eat & stay

In Fang, good food can be found at **Khu Charoenchai Restaurant** (6 Thanon Chotana, 0 5345 1215, main courses B75), but it's more preferable to stay in Thaton's pleasing riverside lodges and guesthouses. **Thaton River View Resort** (302 Ban Thaton, 0 5337 3173-5, rates B1,330) has the nicest cabins and the best food. **Tip's Traveller House** (1/7 Thanon Tha Phae, 0 5345 9312) organises rafting tours, as does **Mae Kok River Village** (84 Tambon Thaton, 0 5345 9328/9/www.trackofthe tiger.com, rates B3,500).

Hikers of Chiang Dao's striking terrain get basic digs at **Malee's Nature Lovers Resort** (Chiang Dao, 0 1961 8387, rates B250), while further north on Highway 1178, **Rim Doi Resort** has pleasant terrace dining and rooms (Ngai, 0 5337 5028-9, rates, B200-B350). Upmarket chalets run by the Amari hotel chain at **Ang Khang Nature Resort** (1/1 Ban Khum, 0 5345 0110, rates B3,130-B4,500) are ideal for nature trails and hill villages.

## Chiang Rai

Founded by King Mangrai in 1262, this bland town on the Kok river has two hills, with **Wat Phrathat Doi Chom Thong** on top of the western one. But **Wat Phra Kaew** (Thanon Trairat) is the leading temple in town, and is reputedly where the Emerald Buddha was found encased in stucco – a jade replica donated by Canada and carved in China can now be seen in its westernmost *vihaan*. A large temple museum was due to open as we went to press. Also under construction is the phantasmagorically embellished *vihaan* of Wat Rong Khun (in Pa-or-donchai) by Buddhist artist Chalernchai Kositphipat.

The **Hill Tribe Museum & Handicraft Shop** (620/1 Thanon Thanalai, 0 5371 9167, B50) also runs treks. **Oup Kham Museum** (Thanon Na Khai, 0 5371 3349, B100) displays artefacts of Lanna nobility.

Chiang Rai's stunning **Wat Phra Kaew**.

## Where to eat & stay

Most places of interest can be found within walking distance of the clock tower intersection on Thanon Banphaprakan. Pubs and bars line Thanon Chet Yot south from the clock. There's more open-air dining and drinking around the night bazaar close to the bus station off Thanon Ratanaket. **Muang Thong Phattakan** (Thanon Phahonyothin, near Wiang Inn, 0 5371 1162, main courses B60) is a bracingly authentic Chinese-Thai *khao tom* (boiled rice soup) shop. Grander **Salung Kham** (No.834/3-4, 0 5371 7192, main courses B98) dispenses grilled meats and northern dishes.

As for accommodation, the **Wiang Inn** (893 Thanon Phahonyothin, 0 5371 1533, rates B1,600-B2,000) is functionally pleasant, while **Golden Triangle Inn** (No.590, 0 5371 1339 rates B500-B600) is a quiet, leafy compound. This is not a budget town but **Chian House** (172 Thanon Ko Loi, 0 5371 3388, rates B200-B400) has large rooms and a small pool on a quiet island suburb. You need transport to enjoy the Thai design and gardens of **Rimkok Resort** (6 Thanon Chiang Rai-Thaton, 0 5371 6445, rates B2,477) across the river, or the remote 'luxury bamboo' **Phu Chaisai Resort & Spa** (26 kilometres/16 miles north of

Chiang Rai, 0 5391 8333/www.phu-chaisai.com, rates B4,000-B15,000). It offers hilltop views from the baths in its love-nest villas.

## Resources

### Hospital
*Overbrook Hospital, Thanon Singhaklai, opposite Wat Phra Kaew (0 5391 0100).*

### Post office
On Thanon Uttarakit.

## Mae Sai & around

The town centre is divided by a highway ending at the narrow bridge into Tachileik in Shan State, Burma. Mae Sai offers little that's respectable apart from views at Wat Phrathat Doi Wao, myriad jade workshops and some river guesthouses. Shops and stalls selling tapestries, puppets, cheroots and other Burmese goods fill the market by the checkpoint, which you may cross for $5 (if open) into greener (but grimmer ) Tachilek, with its new Rangoon-style *chedi* and rare animal parts brazenly on sale.

Several kilometres south on Highway 1, a turning west leads to the deep cave complex of

**Tham Luang**. A little to the north (km886), a road west leads to a narrow cobbled lane that climbs through the Akha village of Ban Pha Mi, joining a security road along the border. Ascending spectacularly to the summit of Doi Chang Mup (1,509 metres/4,950 feet), it passes an arboretum. On a nearby eyrie overlooking the valley is the sacred **Wat Phrathat Doi Tung**.

This area is supervised by the Mae Fah Luang Foundation, responsible for reforestation, local hill tribe welfare (Akha, Lahu) and now catwalk fashion (*see p140* **Cutting ahead**). You can visit what are probably Thailand's finest ornamental grounds at **Mae Fah Luang Palace & Gardens** (palace 8am-5pm, B70; garden 8am-6pm, B50; both B100). Take a Chiang Rai–Mae Sai bus and alight at Pa Sang for a *songthaew* ride up the mountain on Highway 1149.

## Where to eat & stay

**Mae Sai Guest House** (6898 Thanon Wiangpakkam, 0 5373 2021, rates B200-B400) is the nicest, though not the cheapest, of the bungalows overlooking the narrow Nam Ruak, a short walk west of the Burma bridge. For mountain air but institutional ambience, Mae

# Hit the trek

Most visitors to the north take some kind of trek or 'soft adventure' – with typical components being hiking, bamboo rafting, elephant riding and visiting hill tribes (some people stay in village homes for up to a week). It can be fascinating (if voyeuristic), but 30 years of cut-rate trekking and the desire to see authentic (poor) villages has done little to help the hill tribes.

Eco-tourism is touted as a remedy, although many of the countless operators in Chiang Mai, Pai, Mae Hong Son, Thaton and Chiang Rai pay lip-service to its principles. When choosing, check your specific guide's knowledge of tribal ways and language.

A positive force is the **Population & Community Development Association** (PDA), which is formalising arrangements with a B40 fee to enter the Akha village of **Ban Lorcha** (Highway 1089 km53, 20 kilometres/12.5 miles north of Ban Thaton). Entrance is during the day, 8am-5pm. The money goes into funds for village development and to replicate the project elsewhere. There are signs in the village instructing visitors to ask permission (through gestures) before taking

photographs and to desist if refused. Similarly, ask before entering houses, don't step on the doorsill (home of house spirits) and remove shoes if the floor is raised. Changing clothes, showing nudity or public intimacy are deemed offensive. And even if beer and liquor are sold, drinking it only emphasises the gap with villagers who can't afford it. Handing out gifts or money encourages begging, so it's best if the guide distributes such items fairly.

**Mae Hong Son Guest House** (295 Thanon Makasanti, Mae Hong Son, 0 5361 2510, rates B600-B900) liaises with a co-operative of freelance guides committed to community-based tourism. **PDA Tour** (620/25 Thanon Thanalai, Chiang Rai, 0 5374 0088, B2,500-B4,800) hires Akha and Lisu guides and supports responsible projects like Ban Lorcha. Book well ahead for specialised eco-trekking with **Natural Focus** (129/1 Thanon Pa-Ngiw, Chiang Rai, 0 5371 5696). When trekking, warm clothing, torch, insect repellent, toiletries, towel, a water bottle and supportive footwear are musts – oh, and maybe bring a sleeping bag.

**Beyond Bangkok**

The stunning scenery of the infamous **Golden Triangle**.

Fah Luang-run **Ban Ton Nam 31** (0 5376 7003, rates B2,500) has rooms in low buildings in the woods below the Royal Villa, while its restaurant (open 7am-8pm daily) is in the building facing the entrance to the gardens.

## The Golden Triangle

Near **Wat Prathat Phukao**, a hill overshadows the confluence of the Ruak and Mekong rivers, forming the Thai–Lao–Burma borders. The spectacle is only slightly marred by a casino-hotel in Burma (banned in Thailand, casinos proliferate around the Cambodian and Burmese checkpoints). The single street of Sop Ruak below consists of shophouses and one-storey restaurants. Touts hawk short boat trips and tourists snap each other at gateways announcing 'the Golden Triangle'. The small **House of Opium** museum (B20) in mid Sop Ruak will be upstaged in 2003 by the huge, ambitious **Hall of Opium** (opposite Baan Boran Hotel in Golden Triangle Park, 0 5378 4062, admission B20), which traces every aspect of drug use worldwide over 5,000 years.

Just down the Mekong, **Chiang Saen** is sleepily set amid the ruins of a greater past. The town has been boosted by river trade with China (which is prompting potentially disastrous blasting of rapids to ease navigation) and by evenings the promenade is packed with noodle stalls, as trucks wait to unload preserved fruits, rubber and cement for export upstream. Between a tourism booth and the massive **Wat Chedi Luang**, **Chiang Saen National Museum** (Thanon Phahonyothin, 0 5377 7102, open Wednesday to Sunday, B30) displays artefacts plucked from the many ruins

– of which **Wat Pa Sak** (B30), set in a teak forest outside the west wall, is a lone *stupa* in good condition.

The road from Mae Sai via Sop Ruak and Chiang Saen to Chiang Khong is only served by *songthaew*, but boats run from Chiang Saen to Chiang Khong (two hours, B2,000 one-way; to Sop Ruak and back B1,600). Facing the tiny Lao provincial capital of Huai Xai, **Chiang Khong** is a vibrant border crossing for travellers into northern Laos or downriver to Luang Prabang. Restaurants and bars occupy wooden buildings at the northern end of the main street.

## Where to eat & stay

**Baan Boran** (north-western Sop Ruak, 0 5378 4084, rates $150-$180) has stylish Thai-influenced facilities with distant views over the Golden Triangle. **Mekong Balcony** (Highway 1290 km30, half a kilometre south of Sop Ruak, 0 5378 4333, rates B500) has a restaurant (main courses B90) and split-bamboo huts on the river. In Chiang Saen, **Gin's Guest House** (Thanon Rim Khong, 0 5365 0847, rates B150-B400) has huts in a shady garden north of the old walls, but bird-watchers and those wanting to be amid the promenade night market may prefer to seek out 'Jungle Jim' at his **Chiang Saen Guest House** (Thanon Chiang Saen-Sop Ruak, rates B200). **Chiang Saen River Hill Hotel** on the second road back from river, south of the old town (0 5365 0826-9, rates B1,300-B1,800) is clean if bland. In Chiang Khong, **Bamboo Riverside Guest House** (Highway 1020, just south of the ferry, 0 5379 1629, rates B150-B250) and **Ban Tammila** (113 Thanon Sukhaphiban, 0 5379 1234, rates B250-B350) are among several pleasant river lodgings.

# Directory

# Directory

## Getting Around

Bangkok is not an easy city to get around. In rush hours (7am-9am, 4-8pm, and around lunchtime and school closing) you can waste literally hours. It gets much worse in the rainy season, school terms and around holiday weekends. So it pays to travel during quieter hours and to use the extensive expressways to reach the ever-expanding suburbs. Within downtown, the BTS SkyTrain has revolutionised transportation, and will be enhanced by the subway in late 2003. The BTS connects most of the hotel, shopping, restaurant and nightlife districts (and some sights), and it also links to much of the old town via the Expressboats. River travel becomes addictive to visitors, who relish the speed, cooling breezes and exhilaration of the Thai waterworld. Canal commuting is another (cramped) option for crossing long distances quickly.

Hiring a car within Bangkok is quixotic. If you really must command four wheels, hire a car with a driver for little more expense. The bus service, though reputedly the world's biggest, is defiantly non-tourist-friendly. Bangkok's famous *tuk-tuk* might look funky, but it can't weave far through jams, is open to fumes and rain and is not as good value as the more plentiful taxi-meters. Motorcycle taxis are nippy for heading down side streets and will get you across town on time (minus your kneecaps, breath and several years of your life thanks to the cavalier risks they take). A note to cyclists:

Bangkok is flat and has canals, but this is no Amsterdam. Walking, though immensely interesting, can be a stressful, wearisome challenge.

### NAVIGATION

Physically moving around is a challenge; navigation is quite another problem. A lot of signs are bilingual and English is widely spoken, but confusion between Thai and foreign accents, and frequent lack of knowledge about destinations, means that hotels are used to writing directions in Thai. Transliterations from Thai to English often vary between guides, maps and signs. Many Bangkok streets look alike and building numbers often aren't contiguous.

If lost, seek directions through body language and key words rather than abstract phrasing. Map reading involves entering a whole new head-space; Thais simply don't conceptualise their surroundings through the kind of cartographic systems that westerners are used to. One-way systems are common and shortcuts can seem strange, but may be following traffic radio advice. One reason for the proliferation of mobile phones in Bangkok is for locating people you're trying to meet. Getting a pre-paid SIM card for a foreign-registered *meur teur* ('hand carry') is now legal and particularly useful for calling someone bilingual to help translate. Half of all Bangkok calls must be to say 'I'll be late'. Accordingly, transport schedules adopt rubber time.

## Arriving & leaving

### By air

**Bangkok International Airport**, 27 kilometres (17 miles) north of downtown, is known by its slightly elevated location, Don Muang (literally, 'highest ground'). You can whizz there by road in under 30 minutes if you're near an expressway ramp, double that in rush hours.

Planned for four decades, the **New Bangkok International Airport (Suvarnabhumi Airport)** (0 2723 0000/www.bangkok airport.org) is currently under construction about 25 kilometres (15.5 miles) from Hualumpong station. It is scheduled to be completed in 2004, with flights starting around October 2005.

It might be more welcomed were it not for the astronomical bill, the wrangle over the rail link to it and the 'plan' to keep domestic flights at Don Muang. Airlines and passengers are aghast at this nightmare prospect (it'd be easier to transfer to Phuket in Singapore), which could scupper the aim to make Bangkok the regional hub. Thailand is superbly positioned for that role and boasts a huge range of airlines and connections. Particularly if you're willing to fly indirect, long-haul journeys can be very cheap from the city's countless travel agents.

**Bangkok International Airport**
*Thanon Wiphawadi Rangsit, Outer North (0 2535 1111/ www.airportthai.or.th).*

**International terminal 1** *Arrivals*
0 2535 1149/1310. *Departures* 0 2535
1254/1123. **International terminal
2** *Arrivals* 0 2535 1301. *Departures*
0 2535 1386. **Domestic terminal**
*Arrivals* 0 2535 1253/1305. *Departures*
0 2535 1192/1277. **Thai Airways
check-in** 0 2535 2242. **Tourist
police** 0 2535 1641/1155. **Don
Muang police station** 0 2535 6222.
Bangkok's rather dowdy terminals
form a line from north to south:
international terminals 1 and 2;
domestic; cargo. In each, arrivals
are on the ground level and
departures upstairs. International
terminals 1 and 2 are conjoined and
a covered bridge links terminal 2
with the domestic terminal. A shuttle
bus (every 15mins, 5am-11pm daily)
links the domestic and international
terminals and also accesses the
car parks (0 2535 6635-7). These
are free for the first 15mins for
arriving or departing passengers,
then rates are around B20 for 1hr
up to B220 for 7-24hrs.

International arrivals offers
airport, tourist, hotel and tour
information. Phones and 24hr
banks/currency exchanges are
everywhere. At departures there are
internet terminals, a hairdressing/
massage parlour, VAT refunds (third
floor, terminal 2) and left luggage.
King Power Duty Free (0 2996
8005-7/www.kingpower.com)
operates 24hrs in arrivals/departures
at international terminals 1, 2 and
domestic departures. Choice is
minimal and the presentation tacky.
You can't even buy a newspaper in
departures (or transit), and the only
newsagent in public areas (ground
floor, southern end of terminal 2)
has few international publications.

## Airport taxis

**Public Taxi-Meter** *Outside
arrivals, all terminals (0 2535 5774/
5247).* **Open** 24hrs daily.
To help prevent scams, taxi-meter
hailing is controlled by the airport,
managed from desks *outside* arrivals.
You keep the card carrying the
driver's number in case of rip-off,
robbery, assault, complaints or lost
property, which still occasionally
happen (call 0 2535 1616 immediately).
At journey's end, you pay the meter
fare (around B150-B250 to downtown),
plus a B50 airport surcharge; en
route you pay any toll fees.

**TG Airport Limousine** *Inside
arrivals, all terminals (0 2973 3191/
www.thaiair.com/Thailand/limousine).*
**Open** 24hrs daily.
Deceptively signed as 'Airport Taxi'
*inside* arrivals, this limo service gets
you downtown by luxury Mercedes
Benz or Volvo for about B450 per hr.
Also available from downtown to the
airport (B650) and for general hire.

**Airport Associate** *International
terminals 1 & 2 (0 2982 4900/
www.airporttaxithai.com).* **Open**
24hrs daily.
Cars with driver. Rates depend on
the destination, from B450 per hr
for a Merc or B600 per hr for van to
downtown, or to Pattaya for B2,250.

## Airport Bus

*All terminals (0 2995 1252-4).*
Running every 30mins 5.30am-
12.30am daily, the airport bus is
cheap, comfortable and convenient
for those with less luggage. Flat fare
is B100. Using expressways, it
passes most hotel, shopping and
business areas on four routes: **AB1**
(to Oriental Hotel via Pratunam,
Ratchadamri and Silom), **AB2**
(Sanam Luang via Phyathai, Larn
Luang and Banglamphu), **AB3**
(Thonglor via Sukhumvit and New
Petchaburi) and **AB4** (Hualumpong
via Ploenchit and Siam).

## Airlines

**Air Andaman** *Airport 0 2535
6231/reservations 0 2229 9555/
www.airandaman.com.*
New private airline linking
Bangkok, Chumphon, Narathiwat,
Khorat, Buriram, Tak, Phrae, Loei,
Chiang Mai, Chiang Rai, Nan and
Phitsanulok.
**Bangkok Airways** *Airport 0 2535
2497/8/reservations 0 2265 5555/
www.bangkokair.com.*
Bangkok Airways' rapidly growing
network links Bangkok, Chiang Mai,
Phuket, Krabi, Hua Hin and Asian
World Heritage Sites (Luang
Prabang, Bagan, Hue, Siem Reap and
Xian), plus its own airports in Samui,
Sukhothai and Trad (due March 2003).
**PB Air** *Airport 0 2535 4843/4/
reservations 0 2261 0220-5/
www.pbair.com.*
New private airline linking Bangkok,
Lampang, Krabi, Sakhon Nakhon,
Nakhon Phanom, Roi Et, Petchaburi
and Nakhon Sri Thammarat, plus
Luang Prabang in Laos.
**Phuket Airlines** *Airport 0 2535
6695-7/reservations 0 2679 9395/
www.phuketairlines.com.*
New private airline flying from
Bangkok to Ranong and Phuket.
**Thai Airways** *Airport 0 2535
2846/7/reservations 0 2628 2000/
www.thaiairways.com.*
Flag carrier with a huge international
and domestic network.

## By car, bus or boat

Most of Thailand's border
crossings, including all those
with Burma, are locals-only
and not suitable for overland
travel by foreigners. There are
some exceptions:

## From Laos

Foot passengers from Vientiane
can use a ferry to the pier and
immigration at Nong Khai in Isaan.
Drivers and shuttle buses use the
nearby Friendship Bridge, which
also has an immigration post and
duty-free shop. Another bridge
over the Mekong river will link
Savannakhet in Laos to Mukdahan
in Isaan by the end of 2005.

## From Cambodia

Increasing numbers (particularly
expats doing visa runs) now travel
by road to and from Cambodia,
crossing to Aranya Prathet from
Poipet, which has a reasonable road
from Battambang and Phnom Penh,
or a terrible one from Siem Reap
(Angkor). Another option is by road
and boat from Sihanoukville via Ko
Kong into Trad province. Cruise
ships call usually at Laem Chabang
port near Pattaya, or at Phuket.

## From Malaysia

There are two crossings from Kota
Bharu into Narathiwat province. A
ferry from Pengalan Kubur to Ban
Taba leads towards Narathiwat
town. The main gateway is by road
or rail from Rantau Panjang into
the brothel town of Sungai Kolok
and on to Had Yai and points north.
Into Satun province, Malaysian
shared taxis drop passengers at
Bukit Kayu Hitam for the Thai
border post near the headquarters
of Thale Ban National Park. Or you
can go to Thammalang pier in Satun
by longtail boat from Kuala Perlis,
or by one of four daily ferries from
Langkawi island, ensuring you call
at Thammalang's immigration post.

## By train

Plans for a trans-Asian rail
network have resurfaced with
the opening up of Indochina
and China. Many of the
missing links are from
Thailand into formerly closed
neighbours, cutting across
Laos to Vietnam, across Burma
to China and resuscitating the
line from Phnom Penh in
Cambodia, and the 'Death
Railway' from Burma. At
present, only the train line
terminating in Singapore
crosses uninterrupted into
Thailand (from Malaysia at
Sungai Kolok), while the
railhead at Nong Khai is a
popular route to Bangkok after
crossing from Vientiane, Laos.

**Directory**

## Maps

Central Bangkok street maps are included at the back of this guide, starting on p306. Tourist offices provide so-so free streetmaps; bookshops sell better ones. A unique, hand-drawn chart of the city's quirks, shops, stalls and under-noticed attractions is *Nancy Chandler's Map of Bangkok*; it's especially useful for Chinatown and Chatuchak Market. BTS maps are free from its stations. The best of the bus route maps is no longer produced in English.

## Public transport

The **BTS SkyTrain** brought a mass transit revolution to Bangkokians, but is all the more astonishing because of Thailand's non-co-operation approach to transport integration. Only after its benefits became apparent did shopping malls connect bridges to BTS concourses. Buses jealously still haven't altered routes to feed its stations, so BTS had to institute free shuttle buses.

Not only is the **subway** (scheduled to open in August 2004) as far below ground as the SkyTrain is above it, but supposedly 'connecting' stations are about 100m apart. Even where they just about touch, as at Asoke/Sukhumvit, they couldn't agree to share a dais. Both BTS and the metro fail to connect all four corners of most junctions they straddle. So while they make crossing town amazingly fast, you'll waste gained time (and get rained on) changing trains. Combined with taxis, the BTS and subway are the best options for tourists, business people and the middle classes.

The masses have been priced out of mass transit, and suffer the gargantuan **bus network** – the only public transport to the far suburbs. Buses are cheap, but don't really cater for tourists (signs are in Thai only). Only where bus routes make short cuts (for example, north up Soi Asoke) is it quicker than by taxi.

## BTS SkyTrain

### BTS Tourist Information Centre

*0 2617 7340/www.bts.co.th.*
This elevated train – with a bird's eye view – is the fastest way to reach downtown destinations. Privately built and run by Bangkok Mass Transit System, it has two lines (which interchange at Siam station): the Sukhumvit line (dark green) from Morchit to Onnut; and the Silom line (light green) from National Stadium to Saphan Taksin. The latter is also Central Pier of the Expressboat network (*see p285*), with which BTS promotes a river sightseeing tour. The BTS will connect (sort of) with the subway at Saladaeng/Silom, Asoke/Sukhumvit and two Morchit stations.

Three-car trains operate 6am-midnight daily, every 3mins peak, every 5mins off-peak, crossing the town in a matter of minutes. Designed by Siemens, the system is efficient and clean, with bans on food, drinks and smoking, though the spacious station concourses have become littered with shops and stalls. The elegant, airy stations reach the street via staircases (or escalators at most stations, disabled lifts at some) anchored by porches shaped like a Thai dancer's hand.

### Fares

**Single-journey** tickets (B10-B40) are available from the counter and self-service machines (which don't take notes, so you may have to queue for B5 and B10 coins from the counter). There's also an array of passes, all with no distance limits: **1-Day Pass** (B100); **3-Day Tourist Pass** (B280, for 3 nights, 4 days); **30-Day Adult Pass** (10 trips B250, 15 trips B300, 30 trips B540; and **30-Day Student Pass** (10 trips B160, 15 trips B210, 30 trips B360) for students under 23, showing ID and a student card. The **Sky Card** (refillable, minimum B200 plus B30 refundable deposit) is valid for 2yrs.

## Subway

### Bangkok Metro

*0 2690 8200/*
*www.bangkokmetro.co.th.*
Scheduled to open in August 2004, the underground Chaloem Ratchamongkhon line (blue) arcs 20km (12 miles) from Hualumpong railway station via Thanon Rama IV and Thanon Ratchadaphisek to Bang Sue railway station. Trains will carry a purported 400,000 people a day from 5am-midnight, at a frequency of 2-4mins peak, 4-6mins off-peak. Fare rates are B14-B36, at B2 increments by distance, available at station offices and vending machines.

Each of the 18 stations will have escalators, lifts, toilets, shops and disabled conveniences. Entrances open a metre above the highest recorded flood level, so don't worry about riding the subway in the rain. The system will link (kind of) with BTS stations at Silom/Saladaeng, Sukhumvit/Asoke and two Morchit stations.

Run in a 25-year joint project with the state's Mass Rapid Transit Authority, the metro is planned to be extended (eventually) from Hualumpong to Bang Khae via Chinatown, Rattanakosin and Thonburi; and from Bang Sue north-west to Phra Nang Klao Bridge. A future line would run from Bang Kapi in the north-east via Dusit, Chinatown and Thonburi to Rat Burana in the south.

## Buses

### Bangkok Mass Transit Authority

*0 2246 0973/hotline 184/*
*www.bmta.moct.go.th.*
The BMTA, with more than 13,400 buses on 442 routes around Bangkok, Nonthaburi, Nakorn Pathom, Samut Sakhon and Samut Prakarn provinces. Reputedly the world's biggest bus network, it's mindbogglingly complex, with new and old buses having the same number but different colours and prices – and sometimes slightly varied routes. Return routes are often different due to loops and one-way systems. Air-con and non-air-con buses ply fairly similar routes, with many exceptions. Route signs are all in Thai. Cramped standing is usual in rush hours.

Failure of buses to cover new estates, deep *soi* or changing workplace patterns has prompted thousands of minibuses, whose staff went on strike in 2002 in defiance of bureaucrat and bus company resistance. Commuters favour them being licensed, to ensure safety.

**Air-conditioned buses** are blue with a white stripe (5am-11pm), with fares by distance: B8-B16, same for all-white articulated buses. Newer orange Euro2 buses (5am-11pm) charge by distance: B10-B18.

**Non-air conditioned buses** are red/cream (5am-11pm, B3.50), or newer blue/white ones (5am-11pm, B5). Red/cream ones running on expressways cost B5.50; running as nightbuses (11pm-5am) it's B5.

**Bus passes** (unlimited distance): 1-Day B10 non-air-con, B30 includes air-con; buy from the conductor. Buy other passes – 1-Week B50 non-air-con, B150 with air-con; 1-Month B200 non-air-con, B600 with air-con – from desks at the terminus of each route (especially Victory Monument).

**Green buses** are short, battered, non-air-con, fast and furiously driven, with conductors hanging off the door rail. Fares: B3.50 daytime, B5 after 10pm.

**Micro-buses** are air-con with TV and a guaranteed seat, run by the Land Transport Department. B25.

## Rail services

### State Railway of Thailand

*0 2621 8701/2220 4567/ www.srt.or.th.*
Most trains depart from the refurbished Italianate terminus **Hualumphong station**. Trains are long-distance only, calling at Samsen, Bang Sue, Don Muang, Makkasan and Hua Mark stations, but the service is too slow and infrequent to use for crossing Bangkok. Some trains for Nakhon Pathom, Kanchanaburi, Prachuab Khiri Khan and Chumphon depart from **Bangkok Noi station**, Thonburi (0 2411 3102), which is part-converted into a tourist centre and market. A short line from **Wong Wian Yai station** in Thonburi runs to Samut Songkram via Samut Sakhon.

### Hualumpong station

*1 Thanon Rong Muang, Chinatown (0 2225 6964/advance booking 0 2220 4444/schedule hotline 1690/ www.srt.or.th). Bus 7, 25, 29, 34, 40, 49, 73, 85, 109, 113, 159.* **Open** *Trains* 4.20am-11.25pm daily. *Advance booking (3-60 days ahead)* 8.30am-4.30pm daily. *Tour desk* 8.30am-4pm daily. **No credit cards.** **Map** p309 & p310 D/E5.

## Taxis

### Taxi-meters

Now with radios and non-tamperable digital meters, *rot taksee mee-terrrr* (air-conditioned cars running on liquid petroleum gas, aka LPG) – are plentiful and congregate most at shopping, tourist, nightlife and event locations. There are few designated ranks and they'll stop on a dime at the merest glance (but rarely pulling in from the traffic flow). A red light in the windscreen means the taxi is available. Signal by flapping your fingers, palm *down* (same with waiters; raised finger beckoning is offensive).

Taxis are coloured according to company (remember the two-tone colours in case of lost property or complaints); red/blue and yellow/green are easily the best. Don't get in if the driver refuses to use the meter, and avoid non-metered taxis. Poorly maintained vehicles nearly always imply a bad driver – hence the many amulets, garlands and monk's blessings on the dashboard, mirror and ceiling. Front seatbelts are compulsory.

It helps to give directions in Thai (especially written) rather than to show maps. Initial rate is B35 for two kilometres, then increase from B0.40-B5.50 per kilometre depending on distance covered. A surcharge of B1.25 per minute applies in traffic jams up to six kilometres (four miles) long. Keep change handy as drivers sometimes run out; tip up to ten per cent, and be generous late at night when there's no increase in rates.

For safety and convenience, 24-hour call taxis (listed below) will pick up within 15-20 minutes (B20 surcharge). They also offer full-day taxi hire for self-guided group tours (around B1,200 in Bangkok, B1,500 beyond).

**Radio Taxi** *hotline 1681*
**Siam Taxi** *hotline 1661*
**Bangkok Taxi Radio Centre** *0 2880 0888*
**Nakornchai Transportation** *0 2878 9000/www.taxithai.com*

## Tuk-tuks

Relished by tourists as 'authentic', these funky motorised rickshaws are sometimes called *samlor* (three-wheelers). Customised with flashing lights by their Kratindaeng-sauced drivers (mostly from Isaan), they come in myriad variants. The name derives from their LPG-fuelled chainsaw rasp; the quieter electric *tuk-tuk* launched in 1994 hasn't caught on. The low bench behind the central driver takes three (overlapping) *farang*, but half a dozen Thais or vast supplies of produce.

*Tuk-tuks* are open-air, so you get rain, fumes, soot and sweat en route, and even the compensating *sanuk* (fun) may fade if you haven't agreed the price beforehand. Beyond 2km (about B30), they're poorer value than taxis, combining the worst of both cars and motorbikes. Thailand got indignant when a British importer of the vehicles tried to patent the name, and there's a plan to export them. Now in decline (partly due to self-defeating attempts to tout and cheat on prices), *tuk-tuks* are getting rarer and are destined for a future as novelties.

## Songthaews

Red, open-sided, pick-up truck buses – also called *seelor* (four-wheelers) or *hoklor* (six-wheelers) – are standard transit upcountry, but in Bangkok mainly ply side *soi* for B3-B10. Just hail and hop on, paying the driver when you buzz (or bang loudly) to alight. *Songthaew* means 'two rows', which is how the bench seating is arranged.

## Motorcycle taxis

Those with appointments may take their life in their hands with a pillion ride on *rot motocy* (or *rot jakrayan yon*) from mafia-controlled ranks at the mouths of most *soi*. Mostly used for short runs into side streets for B5-B15 (never over B20; agree the rate first), they bargain for long-distance rides via main roads. Police like to fine riders for not wearing helmets, but they're rarely worn in soi and rarely strapped tight on highways. To ask for a helmet, say *ow muak garn knock* (which means literally 'hat against knocks').

Numbered *motorcy* boys (few women do this), playing Thai chess or chequers with bottle caps while waiting their turn, are notorious for wearing protective tattoos, amulets and *balad kik* (phallic belt charms), as well as inserting glass beads under their foreskins.

## Driving

With driving licences easily bought, there's little incentive to learn road rules or manners. Fines against common offences typify the easy panacea of punishment over the responsibility of teaching. The one rule is 'biggest goes first', and rich Thais in smart cars never get stopped or fined. Nor do buses, which are particularly inconsiderate and polluting. If you insist on driving despite the dangers, jams and parking problems, you'll need patience, four sets of eyes and an international driving licence (foreign licences not accepted).

**Directory**

Thais drive on the left, front seatbelts are compulsory and speed limits are 80kmh within the Bangkok area and 90kmh outside. Beware of vehicles changing lane without indicating, driving too close and overtaking stopped traffic. Expressways have tolls and many *soi* get very narrow, while one-way systems and 'no right turns' are common. Motorcycles swarm so fast and indiscriminately that Thais dub them 'flies'. Motorcycle racing is common on straight roads, particularly at night.

Illegalities are punished with a points deduction system and fines: driving without a licence (up to B1,000); driving drunk over 50mg alcohol (up to B500); running a red light (up to B1,000); speeding over 110kmh (B200-B500).

## Breakdown services

### B-Quik Service
*Lake Ratchada Office Complex, 193/144-5 Thanon Ratchadaphisek, North-east (office 0 2661 9831-9/ battery delivery 0 2661 9899/*

*www.b-quik.co.th). Asoke BTS/ Sukhumvit subway.* **Open** 8am-9pm daily.
Solves battery, tyre and breakdown woes through more than 28 branches.

### Carworld Club
*2/1 Thanon Rama IV, Sukhumvit (emergency breakdown 0 2260 1111/office & membership 0 2204 0666/www.cwc.co.th). Queen Sirikit NCC subway/bus 4, 22, 45, 46, 47, 107, 115, 116, 507.* **Open** *Office* 8.30am-5.30pm Mon-Fri. *Breakdown service* 24hrs daily. **Credit** AmEx, MC, V. **Map** p311 J7.
Full breakdown services.

## Car hire

Car rental firms, taking most major credit cards, include:

**Avis** *(0 2255 5300-4/www.avis thailand.com).***Open** 8am-8pm Mon-Sat; 8am-6pm Sun.
**Budget** *(0 2203 0250/www.budget. co.th).* **Open** 7.30am-7pm daily.
**Japan Rent** *(0 2259 8867-70/ www.japanrenthailand.com).* **Open** 8am-5pm Mon-Sat.
**Highway Car Rent** *(0 2266 9393-8/www.highway.co.th).* **Open** 8am-10pm daily.
**Tranex Services** *(0 2874 1174/ 0258/9/www.tranex.yellowpages.co.th).* **Open** 8.30am-5.30pm Mon-Sat.
**Thai Prestige Rent-A-Car** *(0 2941 1344-8/2231-3/www.thai prestige.yellowpages.co.th).* **Open** 8am-5pm Mon-Fri.

## Fuel

Petrol, now unleaded, is cheap (B12-B14 per litre) and petrol stations are plentiful on major roads. Open 24hrs daily with attendants, many have convenience stores, toilets, ATMs, car washes and air hoses.

## Parking

There are few restrictions to street parking, though it is banned 5am-10pm on some highways and bus lanes. Car parks in malls, hotels and offices charge from B40 per hr, often with a free initial period if you get the ticket stamped at a venue on site. Spaces are so hard to find that double parking is normal, even in multistorey car parks, and has a procedure. Park parallel to the road in neutral, wheels straight, handbrake off, so your car can be shunted back and forth to allow access for other vehicles. Expect dents. Attendants of street parking outside busy venues should be paid B10-B20, because you never know what might happen.

## Water transport

For boat rental and river/canal tours, see *p53*.

### Canals in Bangkok
Quick, exhilarating, but very cramped and logistically awkward covered longtail boats ply **Khlong**

---

# Jam today

Temples, silk, boxing... Bangkok is famous for many things, but it's also a byword for *rot tit* (traffic jams). Visitors imagining the problem to be lanes blocked by rickshaws are shocked by thunderous highways wide to cross and a grid of elevated expressways. These arteries feed into narrow *soi*, zigzagging round obstacles and old farm divisions, and have to carry local traffic because of a lack of cut-throughs.

All movement is subservient to the car, marginalising boats, bicycles, vendor carts and pedestrians, whose dogged persistence thus impacts at random. The weaving character of traffic flow is accentuated by swerves to avoid broken surfaces and a paucity of driving skills thanks to licensing corruption.

Thaksin Shinawatra once promised to solve traffic problems in six months, and as prime minister he tried again in 2002. Placards

caution about road courtesy, fewer officials are allowed road closures for motorcades and continued road construction helps somewhat – if only car numbers weren't increasing again after a blissful cut during the recession. There's talk (again) of more sophisticated traffic lights, except they get overridden in efforts to 'empty' roads in turn, so passing on the blockages. That's because traffic follows the laws of fluid dynamics, though ironically not when it gridlocks during floods... which is another story. After building Thanon Sri Nakharin ring road, an official admitted they 'forgot' to put in drains.

Singapore's model of restricting inner-city car use is being mooted, though it would be futile until the rail expansion materialises. And symbolising the problem, rising beside the SkyTrain's downtown interchange is... the country's biggest car park.

**Saen Saeb**, an east–west canal from Tha Saphan Phan Fah (Golden Mount, for old town) taking 15-17mins to Tha Pratunam (change boats) and 40mins to Tha Bang Kapi. Useful stops are at Bobe Market; Phyathai (for Siam); Pratunam (for markets); Ratchadamri (for World Trade Centre and other malls); Chidlom (for Central Dept Store); Witthayu (for Hilton and the British Embassy); Nana (for hotels); Asoke; Thonglor; Ekamai; and Ramkhamhaeng (for stadiums, malls and the student scene).

Services, run by Family Transport (0 2375 2369/2374 8990), operate every 2-11mins (depending on the time of day) 5.30am-7.15pm Mon-Fri, and every 5-11mins 6am-6.30pm Sat, 6am-6pm Sun. Tickets cost B5-B15, rising every four piers. Note that maps may show obsolete routes on Khlong Phadung Krung Kasem or Khlong Banglamphu.

### Canals in Thonburi

Tour touts may try to stop foreigners using these local *rua hang yao* ('longtail boat') residents' routes, which are best going one-way only because of the odd timings.

**To Tha Chang from Talad Bang Yai** via Khlong Bangkok Noi (takes 40-90mins). Runs irregularly 4-6pm daily; returns every 30mins 6am-9pm, every hr 9-11pm daily. Fare is B13-B15 Thais; B30 tourists. Contact Khun Piya on 0 6783 2623.

**To Tha Chang from Tha Thanon Wongwaen** via Khlong Bang Cheuk Nang, then Khlong Mon (takes 40-90mins). Runs every 10mins 5.30-8.15am Mon-Fri; every 20mins 6-8am Sat; returns every 15-30mins 4-9pm Mon-Fri; every 30mins 5-9pm Sat. Fare is B8-B12. Contact Khun Somchai on 0 6880 3351.

**To Tha Tien from Tha Thanon Sai Nueng** via Khlong Bang Noi, then Khlong Mon. Runs every 20mins 6.30-8.30am Mon-Fri; returns every 30mins 4.30-7pm Mon-Fri. Fare is B8-B10. Contact Khun Piwan on 0 1711 6197.

### Expressboats

*Chao Phraya Express Boat, 78/24-9 Thanon Maharaj, Phra Nakorn (0 2623 6001-3). Bus 32, 39, 53, 59, 123, 203, 506, 508.* **Open** 8am-6pm Mon-Sat. **Map** p308 A3.
The only river bus service is private, founded by the mother of the owners of Patravadi Theatre and Supatra River House restaurant. Tickets are available from the boat conductor or from counters at Tha Rama VII, Tha Bang Po, Tha Payab, Tha Kiak Kai, Tha Sang Hi, Tha Phra Pinklao, Tha Pran Nok, Tha Wang Lung, Tha Ratchawong, Tha Si Phraya

and Tha Sathorn, which has been designated as Central Pier in a tourist-friendly link with BTS Saphan Taksin. Each pier is being upgraded and renumbered with signs in English.

Carrying 40,000 passengers a day to 35 piers over 18km (11 miles) are three kinds of Expressboat, identified by a flag on the roof:

**Yellow flag (rush-hour express)**
From Tha Nonthaburi to Tha Sathon, stopping at Tha Rama VII, Tha Bang Po, Tha Thewet, Tha Phra Pin Klao, Tha Wang Lung, Tha Ratchawong and Tha Si Phraya. Runs Mon-Fri only every 10mins 6.10-6.30am, every 4mins 6.30-8.40am, every 15mins 4.30-6.20pm, Returns start at 3.45pm, then every 10mins 4-7.30pm. Route takes 45-50mins; B15 flat rate.

**Orange flag (express)**
From Tha Nonthaburi to Tha Wat Rajsingkorn, stopping at Tha Rama VII, Tha Bang Po, Tha Kiak Kai, Tha Payab, Tha Sanghi, Tha Thewet, Tha Rama VIII, Tha Phra Pinklao, Tha Wang Lung, Tha Chang, Tha Saphan Phut, Tha Ratchawong, Tha Si Phraya, Tha Oriental, Tha Sathon and Tha Wat Vorachanyawas. Runs Mon-Fri every 5mins 5.50-9.15am, every 15mins 3-5.50pm. Returns every 12mins 6.30-8.45am, every 20mins 2-4pm, every 10mins 4-6pm, every 15mins 6-7pm. On Sat every 15mins 6.45-8.40pm, 4-6.20pm; no Sun service. Route takes 1hr, and there's a flat-rate fee of B10.

**No flag (local)**
From Tha Nonthaburi to Tha Wat Ratchasingkhon. Returns Mon-Fri every 15mins 6-8am, every 20mins 8am-6.40pm. On Sat and Sun every 20-25mins 6am-6.40pm. Calls at every pier; fare B6-B10.

There are also Expressboat tourist trips to **Koh Kret** (9am-3pm every Sun, B250) and **Bang Pa-in**. The **Bangkok River Tour** (9am-12.30pm daily, B780) loops from Tha Sathorn via Wat Arun, Royal Barges, Phra Sumen fort and Grand Palace.

### River ferries

Dumpy ferries (*kham fahk*) still provide useful, if wallowing crossings for tourists and commuters over the Chao Phraya river from piers such as Tha Sathorn, Tha Si Phraya (River City), Tha Ratchawong, Tha Saphan Phut, Tha Tien, Tha Chang, Tha Phra Chan and Tha Phra Athit. Ferries cost B2 and run about every 5mins 5am-midnight (some only until 9pm) daily.

Hotels with elegant guest ferries include the Royal Orchid Sheraton, the **Marriott Bangkok Resort**

(*see p38*), the **Oriental** (*see p41*) and the **Peninsula** (*see p39*), nearly all calling at Tha Saphan Taksin, Tha Oriental and Tha Si Phraya (River City). Tha Maharat has a private ferry to Supatra River House restaurant and Patravadi Theatre.

## Cycling

Not a great option: Thai traffic and road surfaces are inconsiderate to cyclists and there are few cycle lanes.

### Probike

*231/9 Thanon Ratchadamri, Pathumwan (0 253 3384/ www.probike.co.th). Ratchadamri BTS.* **Open** 10am-7pm Mon-Fri; 8.30am-7pm Sat; 8.30-5pm Sun. **Map** p311 G6.
A shop selling bicycles and equipment. It also rents bikes for B350 per day.

## Walking

You'll see, hear, feel, smell and taste a different and more interesting Bangkok on foot – though pollution is only one of many factors making this difficult. At every turn pedestrians lose out to vehicles, a prejudice linked to Thai and Chinese perceptions that darker skin from outdoor physical activity indicates lower status. If you've got power and income to be transported in air-conditioned comfort, why walk?

Pedestrianisation is new to Thais, who embrace it as a novelty when focused on an activity like 'walking street' festivals (*see p156*), but not yet for its wider benefits. For now, *saphan loi* (footbridges) are infrequent, small *soi* often have no pavements, and vehicles push people aside, even on pavements and zebra crossings. Pavements are not only uneven obstacle courses, but shared with stalls, carts, tables, motorcycles, stray dogs, beggars on skateboards, parked cars and a lot of other people, not necessarily moving, but engaged in activities like shopping, eating or chatting – but always in the shade.

**Directory**

# Resources A-Z

## Addresses

Bangkok addresses are complicated and often vary. They typically start with a room or unit number and/or floor number (mixing UK/US systems, so you enter on either the first or ground floor), then building name and street number (which sometimes is written earlier on) with numbers following an oblique slash being a subdivision of a plot, ie 49/16. In suburbs it may be in a *moo* or *moo baan* ('estate'), which are named and/or numbered. Then comes the *thanon* ('road') name, eg Moo 2, Thanon Bangna-Trad.

If it's on a named *trok* ('lane', which are rare) or *soi* ('sidestreet'), it may be followed by a *thanon*, eg Soi Phiphat, Thanon Silom. If it's on a numbered *soi* running off a *thanon*, it drops the word *thanon*, hence Silom Soi 4. If the numbered *soi* also has an oft-used name, that may be written Sukhumvit Soi 21 (Soi Asoke) or many other permutations: Sukhumvit 21, Soi Sukhumvit 21, Soi Asoke or even Sukhumvit Road Soi 21 or Asoke Road (such English terms are used particularly in resorts, eg Beach Road, Pattaya). Long roads may use kilometre markers, eg km1 Thanon Bangna-Trad.

That's all followed by the subdistrict name (*khwaeng* in Bangkok, *tambol* in villages and upcountry towns), then district name (*khet* in Bangkok, *amphoe* upcountry) and province name (*jangwat*). There follows a five-digit postcode, roughly one for each district, starting with 1 in Bangkok (eg Lumphini, Pathumwan, Bangkok 10330 or Tambol Wat Kate, Amphoe Muang, Chiang Mai 50000). Each province shares its name with its capital whose district is always Amphoe Muang ('town district') followed by the province name.

'Thailand' is anglicised from Prathet Thai, with Muang Thai the less formal name for the country. Siam (pronounced 'See-yam'), once the kingdom's proper name, may still be used for retro effect.

## Age restrictions

You must be 18 to drive (and have an international driving licence) and to buy cigarettes and alcohol. You need to be 20 to enter a pub or nightclub, and ID is often requested of young-looking people. The age of consent, straight and gay, is 18.

## Attitude & etiquette

Thailand is known as the 'Land of Smiles' – not one beauteous grin repeated, but specific smiles according to the myriad social concepts that govern Thai behaviour and language. Here are some dos and don'ts:

● Show respect for the monarchy, members of the royal family, Buddhism and the monkhood. Criticism causes universal offence and may be heavily penalised.
● Stand for the king's anthem at the start of performances and the national anthem when played in public.
● The head is the highest part of the body spiritually and must not be touched or pointed at, particularly the feet, the lowest part of the body.
● Never use feet to move, shut or point at things; it's insulting. Don't step on Thai coins or banknotes (they bear the king's head). Sitting on the 'head' of a boat is also taboo.
● Treat Buddha images with respect. Don't point at them (especially with feet), hang anything on them or pose with them in photos.
● Inside temples, wear polite clothing (cover shoulders and knees). Sit with feet tucked back or cross-legged in front of monks/Buddha images.
● Monks are celibate and must not touch women. Females giving them something should place it down or pass it via a male. *Mae chi* (nuns) are treated like ordinary women.
● Shoes must be removed before entering rooms in temples, palaces, homes and some museums. Step over, not on, door thresholds.
● Make a symbolic effort to make your head lower than those of elderly/very senior Thais you pass in a room.
● Avoid direct criticism of anyone or anything (including Thailand).
● Don't lose your temper. Anger is viewed (and avoided) as temporary insanity and prevents resolution of problems, often swapping culprit and victim in Thais' esteem. Jollying along those from whom you need co-operation can move mountains though: Thais like to help.
● Presentable, clean clothing, footwear and hair will gain you respect and assistance, particularly from bureaucrats.
● Eat and pass things with your right hand as the left is used for cleaning after defecating, though left-handed foreigners are understood.

## Business

### Conventions & conferences

**Impact Exhibition Centre** *99 Thanon Popular, Tambon Banmai, Amphoe Pakkred, Nonthaburi Province, Outer North (0 2504 5050/www.impact.co.th).*

**Queen Sirikit National Convention Centre** *60 Thanon New Ratchadaphisek, Sukhumvit (0 2229 3000/www.qsncc.co.th).*

**BITEC (Bangkok International Trade & Exhibition Centre)** *8 Km1 Thanon Bangna Trad, East (0 2749 3939-60/www.bitec.net).*

### Couriers & shippers

**DHL Worldwide** *22nd Floor, Grand Amarin Tower, Thanon New Petchaburi, North-east (0 2658 8000/www.dhl.com).* **Open** 24hrs

---

# Travel advice

For up-to-date information on travelling to a specific country – including the latest news on safety and security, health issues, local laws and customs – contact your home country government's department of foreign affairs. Most have websites packed with useful advice.

**Australia**
www.dfat.gov.au/travel

**New Zealand**
www.mft.govt.nz/travel

**Republic of Ireland**
www.irlgov.ie/iveagh

**UK**
www.fco.gov.uk/travel

**USA**
http://travel.state.gov/travel

**South Africa**
www.dfa.gov.za

daily. **Credit** AmEx, DC, MC, V. **Map** p311 J4.

**Federal Express** *8th Floor, Green Tower, Thanon Rama IV, Sukhumvit (0 2367 3222/www.fedex.com).* **Open** 8am-5pm Mon-Fri; 8am-3pm Sat. **Credit** AmEx, V. **Map** p311 J7.

**TNT Express Worldwide** *599 Thanon Klong Chong Non See, Bangrak (0 2249 0242/www.tnt.com).* **Open** 8am-6.30pm Mon-Fri; 8.30am-5pm Sat. **Credit** AmEx. **Map** p310 F7.

## Office hire & services

### IB Your Office
*14th Floor, Two Pacific Place, 140 Thanon Sukhumvit, Sukhumvit (0 2653 5000/www.office-bangkok. com). Nana BTS.* **Open** 8am-6.30pm Mon-Fri; 8.30am-noon Sat. **Credit** AmEx, MC, V. **Map** p311 J5.
Rents office space on flexible terms with own phone and fax numbers, conference rooms and secretarial support. Business addresses provided.

### Mr Centre
*43rd Floor, United Centre Tower, 323 Thanon Silom, Bangrak (0 2631 0330). Saladaeng BTS/ Silom subway.* **Open** 8am-5.30pm Mon-Fri. **Credit** AmEx, MC, V. **Map** p310 F7.
Offices for monthly rental, plus phone, fax, mail and secretarial services up and running instantly.

### Tower Inn
*3rd & 4th Floors, Tower Inn, 533 Thanon Silom, Bangrak (0 2237 8277/www.towerinn.com). Saladaeng BTS/Silom subway.* **Open** 8.30am-5.30pm Mon-Fri. **Credit** AmEx, DC, MC, V. **Map** p310 F7.
Office space rental including direct phone lines.

### Women Secretaries' Association
*6/2 Thanon Phichai, Dusit (0 2241 5555). Bus 18, 28, 108, 125, 510, 515.* **Open** 8.30am-4.30pm Mon-Fri.
Finds secretaries according to your specifications.

## Translators & interpreters

### Bangkok Translation Services
*562 Thanon Ploenchit, Pathumwan (0 2251 5666). Ploenchit BTS.* **Open** 8am-5pm Mon-Sat. **Map** p311 H5.
Between Thai and other languages for serious documentation needs. Price and time varies by language.

## Interlanguage Translation Centre
*501 Thanon Samsen, Dusit (0 2243 2018). Bus 3, 30, 32, 33, 49, 64, 65, 66, 506.* **Open** 8.30am-5pm Mon-Sat. **Map** p308 C2.
Official standard translations between all major languages. Cost depends on subject and language.
**Branches:** 554 Thanon Phloenchit, Pathumwan (0 2252 4307); 1 Sukhumvit Soi 1, Sukhumvit (0 2252 3877); 57/3 Thanon Witthayu, Pathumwan (0 2650 7831); 89/12-3 Thanon Witthayu, Pathumwan (0 2650 7981/2).

## Useful organisations

**American Chamber of Commerce** *140 Thanon Witthayu, Pathumwan (0 2254 8748/fax 0 2253 3545/www.amchamthailand. com). Ploenchit BTS.* **Open** 9am-5pm Mon-Fri. **Map** p311 H5.
**Australian-Thai Chamber of Commerce** *Unit 203, 20th Floor, Thai Chamber of Commerce Tower, 889 Thanon Sathorn Tai, South (0 2210 0216-8/fax 0 2675 6696/ www.austchamthailand.com).* **Open** 8.30am-5pm Mon-Fri. **Map** p311 G7.
**British Chamber of Commerce** *7th Floor, 208 Thanon Witthayu, Pathumwan (0 2651 5350-3/fax 0 2651 5354/www.bccthai.com). Ploenchit BTS.* **Open** 8.30am-5.30pm Mon-Fri. **Map** p311 H5.
**Canadian Chamber of Commerce** *9th Floor, Set Thi One Building, Thanon Pan, Bangrak (0 2266 6085/6/fax 0 2266 6087/ www.thai-canadian-chamber.org). Chong Nonsi BTS.* **Open** 9am-5.30pm Mon-Fri. **Map** p310 E7.
**New Zealand-Thai Chamber of Commerce** *9th Floor, ITF Tower, 140/11 Thanon Silom, Bangrak (0 2634 3283/fax 0 2643 3004/www.nztcc.org). Saladaeng BTS/Silom subway.* **Open** 9am-noon Mon, Wed, Fri. **Map** p310 F7.
**Thai Chamber of Commerce** *150 Thanon Ratchabophit, Phra Nakorn (0 2622 1860-76/fax 0 2225 3372/www.tcc.or.th).* **Open** 8.30am-4.30pm Mon-Fri. **Map** p308 B4.

## Consumer

Some shops might refund or exchange faulty goods; this is less likely if you lose your temper. Refer any problems to the **Office of the Consumer Protection Board** (hotline 1166/0 2629 8262-4/ www.thaiconsumer.net). For complaints about food or medicines, call the **Food & Drug Administration** (hotline 1556).

## Customs

On arrival, fill in a Passenger Declaration Form (Form 211) for Customs. Duty-free import limits include 200 cigarettes or 250g of cigars/tobacco; 1 litre of spirits; 1 litre of wine; B10,000 of perfume; B10,000 of effects for personal or professional use. Prohibited imports/exports include drugs, pornography, protected wild animals or related products.
Goods requiring a permit for import/export include firearms, ammunition, explosives (**National Police Office** 0 2205 1000); Buddha images, artefacts and antiques (**Fine Arts Department** 0 2221 7811); radio transceivers/ telecom equipment (**Post & Telegraph Department** 0 2271 0151-2); plants/agricultural materials (**Agriculture Department** 0 2579 0151-7); live animals/animal products (**Live Stock Development** 0 2653 4550-2); medicines and chemical products (**Food and Drugs Administration** 0 2590 7000). You can also contact Thai **Customs** (hotline 1164/www.customs.go.th).

## Disabled

Despite the helpfulness of Thais, Bangkok has dismal provision for the disabled, who tend to be kept well hidden, partly due to karmic belief, face and prejudice about appearance, partly as wheelchairs can only progress *in the road*. Upgrades forced by hosting the 1998 Asian Games/Fespic Games, included (too steep) bevelled kerbs and bobbled paths for the blind. Some buses have wheelchair access and protests made BTS install rarely used lifts at Morchit, Siam, Asoke, Onnut and Chong Nonsi stations, plus up escalators at many more. Every subway station has escalators, lifts, WCs and shops with disabled access. Contact the **Association of the Physically Handicapped** (0 2951 0445/0447/www.flyingwheelchairs. org) for details.
Thai deaf have a subculture, running many street stalls and using the elaborate Thai sign language. Note: maimed/leprous beggars are mostly Khmer amputees press-ganged by mafia who pocket the money and keep the beggars incarcerated and their babies doped.

## Drugs

Punishment for possession – and particularly for dealing or trafficking – of illicit drugs is severe and executions of drug dealers have increased. Nightlife premises and

even schools that have been infiltrated by drugs are periodically raided and urine tests enforced on everyone, including foreigners. Ecstasy, cocaine and the psychologically damaging Burmese-produced amphetamine *ya ba* ('crazy drug') are of most current concern. Those in possession are liable to imprisonment for one to ten years and fines of B10,000-B100,000, depending on the drug's category.

## Electricity

The standard current in Thailand is 220V, 50 cycles/sec, but plugs are unearthed two-pins (round or parallel flat), so beware of shocks.

## Embassies & consulates

**American Embassy** *120-22 Thanon Witthayu, Pathumwan* (0 2205 4000/*www.usa.or.th*). Ploenchit BTS. **Open** 7am-4pm Mon-Fri. **Map** p311 H5.

**Australian Embassy** *37 Thanon Sathorn Tai, South* (0 2287 2680/ *www.austembassy.or.th*). Bus 22, 62, 67, 76, 116, 149, 530. **Open** 8am-4.30pm Mon-Fri. **Map** p311 G7.

**British Embassy** *1031 Thanon Witthayu, Pathumwan* (0 2305 8333/ *www.britishemb.or.th*). Ploenchit BTS. **Open** 8am-4.30pm Mon-Thur; 8am-1pm Fri. **Map** p311 H5.

**Canadian Embassy** *15th Floor, Abdul Rahim Place, 990 Thanon Rama IV, Bangrak* (0 2636 0540/ *www.bngkk.gc.ca*). Saladaeng BTS/ Lumphini or Silom subway. **Open** 7.30am-4pm Mon-Thur; 7.30am-1pm Fri. **Map** p311 G7.

**Delegation of the Commission of European Communities** *19th Floor, Kian Gwan Building II, 140/1 Thanon Witthayu, Pathumwan* (0 2255 9100/*www.deltha.cec.eu.int*). Ploenchit BTS. **Open** 8.30am-5.30pm Mon-Thur; 8.30am-2.30pm Fri. **Map** p311 H5.

**New Zealand Embassy** *14th Floor, M-Thailand Building, 87 Thanon Witthayu, Pathumwan* (0 2254 2530). Ploenchit BTS. **Open** 7.30am-4pm Mon-Fri. **Map** p311 H5.

## Emergencies

In case of serious problems, ring the responsive, English-speaking **Tourist Police** (24-hour hotline 1155) or **Tourist Assistance Centre** (0 2281 5051). If necessary, try the 24-hour **Police Hotline** (191) or for utilities crises the **Bangkok Metropolitan Administration Call Centre** (hotline 1555). For Bangkok hospitals, *see p289*; for

helplines, *see p290*; for police stations, *see p292*. Most embassies have duty officers outside normal working hours.

# Gay & lesbian

## Help & information

### Anjaree Group
*PO Box 322, Ratchadamnoen, Bangkok 10200* (0 2668 2185 press 0 then 3/*www.anjaree.org*). **Open** 9.30am-6pm. **Map** p308 B3. Campaigning lesbian organisation that publishes *AN Magazine* in Thai, and holds seminars and socials. The Lesline service (0 2668 2185, press 2) opens every Wed, Fri and Sat at 8-10.30pm for psychological advice.

### Long Yang Club
*PO Box 1077, Silom, Bangkok 10504* (0 2266 5479/ *www.longyangclub.org/thailand*). **Map** p310 E7. Thai chapter of the international Asiaphile social group. Members get *Typhuan* monthly bilingual newsletter, invites to activities and discounts from shops and venues.

### Bangkok Rainbow
*bangkokrainbow@yahoo.com*. Part of the Asian Rainbow network, this well reputed Thai group provides counselling for gays and their parents, plus school projects.

# Health

## Accident & emergency
Road casualties often get picked up by the Chinese 'bodysnatcher' charities such as Poh Tek Tong; many end up in the **Police Hospital** (*see p289*). **Bangkok Hospital** (*see p289*) also runs ambulances, two-wheel motorlances and aerial helilances.

### Erawan Centre
*514 Department of Medical Services, Bangkok Metropolitan Administration, Thanon Luang, Phra Nakorn* (0 2223 9401-3/ hotline 1646/1554). Bus 7, 15, 47, 48, 204, 508. **Open** 24hrs daily. **Map** p308 C4. Free emergency medical treatment and distribution of ambulances and doctors, plus health advice.

### International SOS Services Thailand
*11th Floor, Diethelm Tower, 93/1 Thanon Witthayu, Pathumwan*

(0 2256 7145-6/*www.international sos.com*). Ploenchit BTS then taxi. **Open** 24hrs daily. **Map** p311 H5. Tackles any emergency, emphasising speedy ambulances and police contact.

## Before you go
It's advisable to get vaccinations for hepatitis A (and possibly B), polio, rabies, typhoid and tuberculosis, but those for cholera are reputedly ineffective, even counter-productive. Arrivals from Africa or Latin America must be vaccinated for yellow fever. All travellers should have had tetanus and diphtheria boosters, and checked their measles, mumps and rubella immunisation is complete. High AIDS awareness means needles aren't reused, so no need to bring a syringe pack unless it's for insulin etc. Some vaccinations require shots weeks apart, so enquire at least six weeks before departure. Avoid wading in floodwater, which may be infectious from rat urine or drain overflow.

Thanks to eradication programmes, malaria is only an issue on the Burma, Laos or Cambodia borders and in remoter forested parts of Thailand. Thai tropical medicine experts often caution against malaria prophylaxis due to resistant strains of the disease and sometimes severe side effects (particularly from Larium) – if you plan to go trekking or visit border areas, consult a specialist. Not getting bitten is the best protection, so wear white and use insect repelling lotions (Jaico is reliable), sprays, coils and electric tabs. Most rooms have screens or nets.

That's also the only defence against haemorrhagic dengue fever (*kai leuad ok*), which has increased throughout the tropics, notably in cities during rainy season. Passed on by the daytime, striped-legged Aedes mosquito, dengue has similar symptoms to malaria, but no prophylaxis or cure. It is most serious in children, the elderly and repeat sufferers. Seek early diagnosis (before the rash starts).

It's also worth consulting **Travel Doctor** (*www.traveldoctor.com.au*).

## Contraception
Foreigners will be pleased that Thai condoms are now available in larger sizes too.

### Planned Parenthood Association of Thailand
*8 Thanon Wiphawadi Rangsit, North-east* (0 2941 2320). Bus 24, 69, 92, 504, 513. **Open** 8.30am-4.30pm Mon-Fri.

Under the patronage of the king, the association's clinic provides advice on contraceptives (which are also sold here), pregnancy and family planning.

## Population & Community Development Association (PDA)

*8 Sukhumvit Soi 12, Sukhumvit (0 2229 4611-28/www.pda.or.th). Asoke BTS/Sukhumvit subway.* **Open** 8.30am-5pm Mon-Fri. **Map** p311 J5.

Founded by outspoken ex-minister and social campaigner, Senator Mechai 'Mr Condom' Viravaidhya, PDA offers advice on family planning, AIDS and unplanned pregnancy; supplies morning-after pills and contraceptives; and raises rural living standards through environmentally sustainable projects. It's also the headquarters of the international Cabbages & Condoms chain of Thai restaurants and hotels.

## Dentists

**Asavanant Dental Clinic** *58/5 Sukhumvit Soi 55, Sukhumvit (0 2391 1842/www.asavanant.com). Thonglor BTS.* **Open** 9am-8pm Mon-Fri; 9am-5pm Sat, Sun. **Credit** AmEx, MC, V. **Map** p312 M5.

**Dental Hospital** *88/88 Sukhumvit Soi 49, Sukhumvit (0 2260 5000-15/ www.dentalhospitalbangkok.com). Phrom Phong BTS then taxi.* **Open** 9am-8pm Mon-Sat; 9am-4pm Sun. **Credit** AmEx, DC, MC, V. **Map** p312 L6.

**Glas Haus Dental Centre** *Glas Haus (Baan Chiang), Sukhumvit Soi 25, Sukhumvit (0 2260 6120/1/2). Asoke BTS/Sukhumvit subway.* **Open** 10am-6pm Mon-Fri; 10am-5pm Sat. **Credit** AmEx, MC, V. **Map** p312 K6.

**Siam Family Dental Clinic** *292/6 Siam Square Soi 4, Pathumwan (0 2255 6664/5/ www.siamfamilydental.com). Siam BTS.* **Open** 11am-9pm Mon-Fri; 9am-9pm Sat, Sun. **Credit** AmEx, MC, V. **Map** p309 & p310 F4.

## Complementary medicine

Thai and Chinese herbal apothecaries and traditional doctors are found in older districts like Phra Chan and Lampang. Increasingly, mainstream stores and fairs sell manufactured versions of ancient remedies, plus vitamins and Western holistic supplements. For a chiropractor, try Dr Mark Leoni's homely clinic:

## Holistic Health Systems

*438/13 Thanon Ekamai, Sukhumvit Soi 63, Sukhumvit (0 1627 0312/ 2711 5102/www.thailand chiropractor.com). Ekamai BTS then taxi.* **Open** 8am-7pm Mon-Thur; Sat, Sun; appointment required. **No credit cards. Map** p312 K6.

## Doctors & hospitals

State hospitals range from the humble to teaching institutions, and since 2001 have faced managing and financing the ambitious B30 universal healthcare policy. Private hospitals have English-speaking doctors in outpatient clinics, which also dispense medication – beware of over-prescription.

The efficient, luxurious, US-style **Bangkok, Bumrungrad, BNH** and **Samitivej Hospitals** all have travel clinics.

**Bangkok Hospital** *2 Soi Soonvijai 7, Thanon New Petchaburi, North-east (0 2310 3000/www. bangkokhospital.com). Bus 23, 60, 72, 99, 113, 512.* **Map** p312 L4.

**BNH (Bangkok Nursing Home) Hospital** *9/1 Thanon Convent, Bangrak (0 2632 0552/www. bangkoknursinghome.com). Saladaeng BTS/Silom subway.* **Map** p310 F7.

**Bumrungrad Hospital** *33 Sukhumvit Soi 3, Sukhumvit (0 2667 1000/www.bumrungrad. com). Nana BTS.* **Map** p311 J4.

**Police Hospital (state)** *492/1 Thanon Ratchadamri, Pathumwan (0 2252 8111-25/www.hospital. police.go.th). Ratchadamri BTS.* **Map** p311 G5.

**Samitivej Hospital** *133 Sukhumvit Soi 49, Sukhumvit (0 2711 8000/fax 0 2391 1290/ www.samitivej.co.th). Thonglor BTS.* **Map** p312 K6.

**Sirirat Hospital (state)** *2 Thanon Prannok, Thonburi (0 2419 7000). Bus 57, 81, 83, 91, 146, 149, 157.* **Map** p308 A3.

## Opticians

Hospitals also have eye clinics, notably the private **Samitivej Hospital** (*see above*).

## Laser Vision Lasik Centre

*9th Floor, Siam Tower, 989 Thanon Rama I, Pathumwan (0 2658 0900/ www.laservision.co.th). Siam BTS.* **Open** 8am-8pm Mon, Tue, Thur, Fri, Sat. **Credit** AmEx, DC, MC, V. **Map** p309 & p310 F4.

## Rutnin-Gimbel International Excimer Laser Eye Centre

*20th Floor, Q House Tower, 66 Sukhumvit Soi 21, Sukhumvit (0 2664 0440). Asoke BTS/Sukhumvit subway.* **Open** 8am-8pm. **Credit** AmEx, DC, MC, V. **Map** p312 K5.

## Pharmacies & prescriptions

Hospitals dispense in-house, sometimes at inflated prices and dosages. Notoriously, medicines are sold from any *kai ya* (pharmacy) without prescriptions, except ones with major physiological, mental or narcotic impact (including sleeping pills and pain relief).

## Community Pharmacy Laboratory

*22 Thanon Phayathai, Pathumwan (0 2218 8428-9). National Stadium BTS.* **Open** 8am-7pm Mon-Sat. **Map** p309 & p310 F4.

Pharmacists and trainees from Chula Uni advise on symptoms and sell drugs cheaply without prescription.

## Plastic surgery

Thai plastic surgery is world famous, particularly beautification and sexual reassignment. It's regulated by the **Society of Plastic & Reconstructive Surgeons** (0 2716 6214/www.plastic surgery.or.th).

## Yanhee General Hospital

*454 Thanon Charan Sanit Wong Soi 90, Thonburi (0 2879 0300/ www.yanhee.net).* Renowned for plastic surgery and beauty treatments (sex change $3,850, Adam's apple removal $500).

## STDs, HIV & AIDS

The **PDA** (*see above*) has been pivotal in HIV/AIDS prevention, for which Thailand's pioneering campaigns have been hailed as an international model.

## AIDS Access Foundation

*Centre Place, 48/282 Thanon Ramkhamhaeng, East (www.aids access.com). Bus 58, 113, 143, 168, 514, 519.* **Open** phone lines (0 2372 2222/3) 3-8pm daily.

Formed in 1991, Access furthers participation in AIDS prevention and patient support. Clinic bookable by phone, or will visit patient's home.

**Directory**

## Anonymous Clinic

*1871 Thanon Ratchadamri,
Pathumwan (0 2256 4107-9/
www.redcross.or.th). Ratchadamri
BTS.* **Open** noon-7pm Mon-Fri;
1-4pm Sat. **Map** p311 G5.
Thai Red Cross HIV/AIDs testing,
information, counselling and
treatment.

## Division of Venereal Disease

*Bangrak Hospital, 189 Thanon
Sathorn Tai, South (0 2286 0108/
0431/www.sti-thai.org). Bus 22, 62,
67, 76, 116, 149, 530.* **Open**
8.30am-4.30pm Mon, Wed, Fri.
**Map** p310 F7.
Information and cures for STDs.
**Branches**: Klong Toey, South
(0 2249 2141); Si Phraya, Bangrak
(0 2236 4055); Ratchadamri,
Pathumwan (0 2253 8933); Dusit
(0 2281 0651).

## Médecins Sans Frontières

*311 Lad Phrao Soi 101, North-east
(0 2375 6491). Bus 8, 22, 27, 44,
73, 92, 96, 122, 126, 502, 514, 518.*
**Open** 8.30-5pm Mon-Fri.
Worldwide charity. Nurses offer
data, advice and initial treatment for
HIV/AIDS, then patient home visits.

## Wednesday Friend Club

*104 Thanon Ratchadamri,
Pathumwan (0 2253 2666/7893/
fax 0 2255 7894). Ratchadamri
BTS.* **Open** 8.30am-4.30pm Mon-Fri.
**Map** p311 G5.
HIV/AIDS group activities, talks and
support with volunteers and officers.

# Helplines

## Alcoholics Anonymous

*Holy Redeemer Church, 123/19
Ruam Rudi Soi 5, Thanon Witthayu,
Pathumwan (0 2256 6305/6157).*
**Map** p311 H5. *Ploenchit BTS then
taxi.* **Meetings** 7-8pm Mon, Wed,
Fri, Sun; 5-6pm Tue, Thur; 4.30-
5.30pm Sat.

## Narcotics Control Board (ONCB)

*5 Thanon Din Daeng, North-east
(0 2247 0101, 0 2247 0901-19/
fax 0 2246 8526/www.oncb.go.th).
Bus 24, 69, 73, 92.* **Open** 8.30am-
4.30 Mon-Fri.
Info on all narcotics, plus advice on
quitting and treatment.

## New Community Services

*230/60 Soi Thai Chamber of
Commerce University, Thanon*

*Wiphawadi Rangsit, North-east
(0 1692 2981/0 2275 6762). Bus 24,
69, 92, 107, 504, 513.* **Open** 9am-
4pm Mon-Fri.
Thai and non-Thai counselling on any
problem (family, addiction or anxiety,
cross-cultural adjustment), group
therapy, training and seminars.

## Quit Line

*Hotline 1667.*
Service offering help coping with
mental problems and quitting tobacco.

## The Samaritans of Thailand

*PO Box 11, Klong Toey, Bangkok
10111, South (0 2249 9977/
www.samaritansthai.bethai.net).*
**Open** *Helpline* noon-10pm Mon-
Thur, Sun; noon-7am Fri, Sat.
Trained volunteers provide a friendly
ear to those with emotional and
mental problems.

## ID

If possible, always carry your
passport or photocopy, especially for
hotel check-ins, cashing travellers'
cheques or exchanging more than
$500. Store copies off your person.

## Insurance

It's advisable to bring travel
insurance, including health cover;
otherwise try **American
International Assurance** (0 2634
8888/0 2236 6452/www.aia.co.th) and
**Ayudhya Allianz CP Life** (0 2263
0333/4/www.ayudhyaallianzcp.co.th).

## Internet

Many shops stock prepaid online
packages, notably **Loxinfo** (0 2263
8222/www.loxinfo.co.th). Other
ISPs include **Inet** (0 2617 3999/
www.asiaaccess.net.th), **KSC** (0 2979
7000/www.ksc.net), **Pacificnet**
(0 2618 8888/www.pacific.net.th) and
**Qnet** (0 2377 0555/www.qnet.co.th).
Terminals are common in business
and tourist areas, most cheaply in
Banglamphu, while **CATNET** at
selected post offices costs B0.12 per
minute using CATNET cards
(B100, B300).

The following provide net access:
**AIT Internet Center** *Room 1C16-
1C17, Warner Tower, Thanon
Mahesak, Bangrak (0 2635 9039-41/
www.aitcenter.com). Surasak BTS.*
**Open** 8.30am-midnight Mon-Sat.
**Rate** B30 per hr. **Map** p310 E7.
**Amazing Cyber** *925/6-8 Thanon
Rama I, Pathumwan (0 2216 6236-7/
www.bossapparels.com). National
Stadium BTS.* **Open** 8am-10pm daily.
**Rate** B50 per hr. **Map** p309 & p310 F4.

**Olavi Internet Service** *53
Thanon Chakrabongse, Phra Nakorn
(0 2282 1178/www.olavi.com). Bus
3, 9, 19, 30, 32, 33, 43, 49, 53, 64,
65, 506.* **Rate** B40 per hr. **Open**
10am-11pm daily. **Map** p308 B3.
**Time Internet Café** *2nd Floor,
Times Square, Sukhumvit Soi 12,
Sukhumvit (0 2653 3636-9/
www.thaiit.com/time). Asoke BTS/
Sukhumvit subway.* **Rate** B1 per min.
**Open** 9am-midnight daily.
**Map** p311 J5.

## Left luggage

**Bangkok Airport** *International
Terminal 1 (arrivals/departures 0
2535 1250). International Terminal
2 (arrivals 0 2535 2102/departures
0 2535 2010).* **Open** 24hrs daily.
**Rates** B70-B140 per piece per day.
**Hualumphong Station** *Thanon
Rama IV, Chinatown.* **Open** 4am-
11pm daily. **Rates** B10-B30 per piece
per day; B100-B150 per bicycle/
motorcycle. **Map** p309 & p310 D5.

## Legal help

In legal difficulties, immediately
inform your embassy, then a lawyer.
These firms are English-speaking.
Some may not take criminal cases.

**Baker & McKenzie** *22nd-26th
Floor, Abdul Rahim Place, 990
Thanon Rama IV, Bangrak (0 2636
2000/www.bakernet.com). Saladaeng
BTS/Silom subway.* **Map** p311 G7.
**Legal & Commercial Services
International** *Suite 1704, 17th
Floor, Two Pacific Place, 140 Thanon
Sukhumvit Soi 4, Sukhumvit (0 2255
4941/www.legalcommercialservices.
com). Nana BTS.* **Map** p311 J5.
**Rehabilitation & Legal
Consultant** *Room 2103, 21st Floor,
United Centre Building, 323 Thanon
Silom, Bangrak (0 2630 4712-4/
www.rehab-legal.co.th). Saladaeng
BTS/Silom subway.* **Map** p310 F7.
**Tilleke & Gibbins** *64/1 Soi
Ton Son, Ploenchit, Pathumwan
(0 2263 7700/0 2254 2640-58/
www.tillekeandgibbins.com). Ploenchit
BTS.* **Map** p311 M5.
**Vovan & Associes** *17th Floor,
Silom Complex, 191 Thanon Silom,
Bangrak (0 2632 0180/www.vovan-
associes.com). Saladaeng BTS/Silom
subway.* **Map** p310 F7.

## Libraries

Most libraries are members-only,
but allow reading on site.
Photocopying is available at the
National Library and university
libraries; the British Council also
rents UK videos.

### Neilson Hays Library

*195 Thanon Surawong, Bangrak
(0 2233 1731/www.neilsonhays
library.com). Bus 16, 36, 93, 162.*
**Open** 9.30am-4pm Tue, Thur-Sat;
9.30am-7pm Wed; 9.30am-2pm Sun.
**Map** p310 E7.
A beautiful old building with the best
range of English reading in town,
plus exhibitions in the Rotunda.
Entry for non-members is B50.

## Lost property

Report any lost property quickly to
the police (*see p292*) in order to get
a statement for insurers.

### Airport

For lost tickets, contact the airline.
For property lost at the airport, call
**Bangkok Airport** (0 2535 1254).

### Public transport

**BMTA Bus Operation Division**
*Hotline 184/0 2246 0973/0339/
www.bmta.moct.go.th*
**BTS SkyTrain** *Hotline 0 2617
7141/7142.*
**Hualumphong railway station**
*24hr hotline 1690.*
**Subway** *0 2690 8200/
www.bangkokmetro.co.th*

### Taxis

**Jor Sor Roi (JS100) Radio
Station** *100FM (hotline 1137).*
**Ruam Duay Chuay Kun
Community Radio Station**
*96FM (hotline 1677).*
Drivers often tune into these Thai
language radio stations, which
broadcast lost items and traffic news,
co-ordinating between taxi firms,
listeners and police. Your report to
the police should note the taxi's
colour (ie company) and number
(printed inside and out).

## Media

Freedom of expression and public
access to information are enshrined
in the very progressive Thai
constitution. Despite recent disputes
between journalists and officials
being settled in the latter's favour
and some journalistic self-censorship,
reporting remains about the most
vigorous in the region. Many foreign
news agencies have bases here. For
the **Foreign Correspondents
Club of Thailand**, *see p173.*

## Newspapers & magazines

Two high-quality English daily
newspapers, *Bangkok Post* and the
*Nation*, publish local and international

news and current affairs, with event
listings supplements every Friday.
Thai and English magazines faced
more competition since the late
1990s. Listings magazines include
monthly *Metro* (akin to *Time Out*)
and two free bi-weeklies from shops
and venues: *BK* (cosmopolitan) and
*Guide of Bangkok* (less sophisticated).
Feature monthlies in English include
*The Big Chilli* (expat focus), *Living
in Thailand* (coffee table), *Thailand
Tatler* (high society) and the free
*Farang* (backpackers). There are
also free tourist magazines of
variable quality. Papers, listings
mags and free booklet *Shakers &
Movers* carry classified ads, as does
the **Villa Market** (*see p143*) expat
noticeboard. *Art Connection* is a
bilingual, pocket-sized map listing
over 70 events monthly at more than
40 venues; it's free from cultural and
tourist centres, and trendy shops/bars.

## Radio

FM and AM broadcasts in Thai and
English tend to play mainstream
music with news bulletins. They're
being liberated incrementally from
military control, though **Radio
Thailand**'s official pronouncements
continue on 95.5FM, 105FM and
918AM at 7am-8am, noon-1pm,
7-7.30pm and 8-8.30pm daily. English
language stations include:
**Chulalongkorn University**
101.5 FM. 9.35pm-midnight daily.
Classical.
**Eazy FM** 105.5 FM. 6am-midnight
daily. Easy listening.
**FMX** 95.5 FM. 5am-2am daily.
Pop dance and hits.
**Get Radio** 102.5 FM. 24hrs daily.
DJs' choice, from retro and pop rock
to indie and dance.
**Smooth** 105 FM. 5am-2am daily.
Easy listening.
**Voices of Thailand** 95.5 FM &
105 FM, 8.15am-8.30pm daily.
Features.

## Television

Of the six stations, two are
commercial: **Channels 3** and **7**
show mass market soaps, game
shows and so on. **Channels 5, 9** and
**11** are government/army-controlled
and broadcast news, documentaries
and fewer entertainment shows.
Independent Television (**ITV**) was
set up to do investigative news and
documentaries; it's majority-owned
by the prime minister's family.
Satellite/cable channel **UBC** (0 2271
7171/www.ubctv.com) offers BBC
World, CNN, CNBC, MTV Thailand,
Channel [V] and various international
movie, sport and entertainment
channels, mostly in English.

## Money

Thailand's currency is the *baht* (B).
B1 equals 100 *satang*. B1 and B5
coins are silvery; B10 coins are
copper with a silver rim; 25 and 50
*satang* coins are copperish. Bank
notes are B20 (green – the most
useful; always have several), B50
(blue), B100 (red), B500 (purple) and
B1,000 (grey). At time of writing,
£1 equals B64; $1 equals B43.

### ATMs

ATMs are plentiful at banks, malls,
petrol stations and many shops.
They're open 24 hours, and most
accept credit cards.

## Banks & bureaux de change

Banks generally open 9.30am-3.30pm
Mon-Fri, except public and bank
holidays. Some in department stores
may open 10am-8pm daily; those in
Chatuchak Weekend Market open
7.30am-8pm Sat-Sun; ones in the
airport are open 24 hours. Bureaux de
change are found in tourist areas and
major local and international banks,
usually opening 8.30am-9pm daily.

## Credit cards

Most hotels, restaurants, shops
and department stores catering to
foreigners or middle-class Thais
accept credit cards. Visa, MasterCard
and American Express are more
widely accepted than either Diners
Club or JCB.

### Lost/stolen credit cards

All are open 24 hours daily, except
JCB (open 9.30am-6pm Mon-Sat).
**American Express** 0 2273 5500.
**Diners Club** 0 2238 3660.
**JCB** 0 2631 1940.
**MasterCard** 0 2260 8573.
**Visa** 0 2256 7324-7.

## Opening hours

**Banks** 9.30am-3.30pm Mon-Fri.
**Malls** 10am-10pm daily, although
their shops and department stores
mostly close at 9pm, their cinemas
around midnight.
**Shops outside malls** variable:
10am-usually 8pm daily, some
business supply shops 9am-6pm
Mon-Fri, 9am-noon Sat.
**Restaurants** open 11am-10pm daily
(some open and close early or late).
**Bars** open 5pm-2am daily.
**Nightclubs** open 9pm-2am daily.

**Directory**

**Government offices** 8.30am-4.30pm Mon-Fri.
**Museums** state museums 8.30am-4pm Wed-Sun; private museums 9am-6pm daily (some close Sun).

## Police

The **Tourist Police** at Tourist Information, 4 Ratchadamnoen Nok Avenue, Dusit (0 2678 6801-9/national hotline 1155) are the best bet for English skills, perseverance, familiarity with non-Thai concerns, and less bureaucracy. Most other police speak little English and their approach may be convoluted, making a crisis even more stressful: get in touch with local officers/stations or the **Metropolitan Police Bureau**, 323 Wang Parus, Thanon Si Ayutthaya, Dusit (hotline 191/0 2280 5060-4/www.police.go.th).

## Police stations

**Bangrak Police Station** *50 Thanon Naret, Bangrak (0 2234 0242/2631 8014-7/2237 2601).* **Map** p310 F7.
**Chakkrawat Police Station** *324 Thanon Chakkrawat, Chinatown (0 2225 4077/8).* **Map** p309 & p310 D3.
**Chanasongkram Police Station** *74 Thanon Chakrabongse, Banglamphu (0 2281 8786/8574/2282 1374).* **Map** p308 B3.
**Dusit Police Station** *75 Thanon Rama V, Dusit (0 2241 2361-2/4399).*
**Huay Kwang Police Station** *2000 Thanon Pracha Songkhro, North-east (0 2277 2629/0630).*
**Pathumwan Police Station** *1775 Thanon Rama VI, Pathumwan (0 2215 2991-3).* **Map** p311 G5.
**Thonglor Police Station** *800 Sukhumvit Soi 55, Sukhumvit (0 2390 2240-2).* **Map** p312 M6.

## Postal services

Letters not over 20g cost B2 within Thailand; postcards and letters abroad B12; aerogrammes B15. **Post offices** (hotline 1545) have parcel packaging, express and registered mail, and CATNET terminals (*see p290*), usually opening 8.30am-4.30pm Mon-Fri, 9am-noon Sat. The GPO holds **Poste Restante** mail for up to a month (bring ID, fee payable). Stamps are sold at convenience stores and souvenir, local and stationery shops.
**General Post Office (GPO)** *Bangrak (0 2233 1050-80).*
**Open** *Packing* 8am-4.30pm Mon-Fri; 9am-noon Sat. *Post* 8am-8pm Mon-Fri; 8am-1pm Sat, Sun. *Postal orders & money services* 8am-5pm Mon-Fri; 8am-noon Sat. *Poste Restante* 8am-8pm Mon-Fri; 8am-1pm Sat, Sun.

## Prohibitions

Smoking is now prohibited in public places. The B2,000 littering fine has greatly cleaned-up Bangkok. Jaywalking on designated congested roads carries a minimum B200 fine. For information on drugs, *see p287*.

## Religion

### Anglican

**Christ Church** *11 Thanon Convent, Bangrak (0 2234 3634/2233 8525). Saladaeng BTS/Lumphini subway.* **Open** 8.30am-4.30pm Mon-Fri. **Services** 7.30am (Eng), 10am (Eng), 3pm (Thai), 5pm (Eng) Sun. **Map** p311 G7.

### Baptist

**Calvary Baptist Church** *88 Sukhumvit Soi 2, Sukhumvit (0 2251 8278/www.thai-info.net/churches/calvary). Nana BTS.* **Open** 8am-4pm daily. **Services** *English* 10am, 6.30pm Wed; 7pm Thur; 8pm Fri; 7pm Sat; 9.30am, 10.45am, noon, 1pm (Bible study, in Thai), 2pm, 4pm (in Burmese) Sun. **Map** p311 J5.

### Buddhist

Thai Therevada Buddhist temples typically open 6am-8pm daily; *bot* (ordination halls) may open 9am-5pm daily or require permission to enter. Daily services, in Thai, are generally 7pm-9pm or longer, with prayer, *dharma* sermons and meditation. Wat Suthat is a model example of devout practice.
**Wat Suthat** *146 Thanon Bamrung Muang, Phra Nakorn (0 2224 9845/2222 9632/www.watsuthat.org). Bus 2, 8, 35, 39, 44, 59, 60, 79.* **Open** 8.30am-9pm daily. **Meditation sessions** *Thai* noon-1pm, 7-9pm Mon-Fri; 1-3pm, 7-9pm Sat, Sun. **Map** p308 C4.

### Catholic

**Assumption Cathedral** *23 Trok Oriental, Charoen Krung Soi 40, Bangrak (0 2234 8556/4592). Bus 1, 35, 75.* **Open** 9am-4.30pm daily. **Services** 6am, 5.15pm Mon-Fri; 6am, 5pm Sat; 6am, 7.30am, 8.30am, 10am (Eng), 5pm Sun. **Map** p310 D7.
**Holy Redeemer Catholic Church** *123/19 Soi Ruam Rudi 5, Thanon Witthayu, Pathumwan (0 2256 6305/6422). Ploenchit BTS then taxi.* **Open** 8.30am-8.30pm daily. **Services** 6.30am (Thai), 7am (Eng), 8am (Eng), 5.30pm (Eng) Mon-Sat; 7pm (Thai) Sat; 6.30am (Thai), 7.30am (Thai), 8.30am (Eng), 9.45am (Eng), 11am (Eng), 12.30pm (Thai), 5.30pm (Eng) Sun. **Map** p311 H6.

## Safety & security

Bangkok is about as safe as metropolises get. Some foreign women urbanites choosing to live here because it's so unthreatening, even at night, with minimal hassle from Thai men. Muggings and rapes of foreigners are rare (although disproportionately publicised).

Still, it always pays to be cautious and take the following advice: be on your guard against pickpocketing, theft, scams, credit card fraud and planting of contraband in your bags. Ignore touts, gem scammers, predatory *tuk-tuk* drivers or approaches by private guides. Avoid walking in very quiet or dimly lit areas at night. Avoid involvement in narcotics, gambling, prostitution or illegal activities. Keep important documents such as passport, credit cards, insurance, air tickets or ID in separate places, with copies in other locations.

## Smoking

Prohibited in public areas and transport (fine B2,000), smoking is allowed in areas of pubs, bars and restaurants. International brands are usually available, plus local brands like Krong Thip.

## Study

Thai universities have some courses or programmes open to foreigners, with Thai language the main subject studied. Many people come to Thailand to learn skills; those covered in depth elsewhere in this guide include cooking, diving, gemology, meditation, *Muay Thai* boxing, rock climbing and Thai massage.

Tourist centres may offer courses in batik, jewellery or other crafts. For Thai and modern fusion dance, try English-speaking **Dance Centre** at Soi Klang Racquet Club (*see p207*) and **Patravadi Theatre** (*see p201*) or the predominantly Thai **House of Indies** (*see p187*), which also teaches Lanna drumming and 'indie' arts like DJing. For Thai traditional music, **Siam Dontree** (*see p152*) has English-speaking teachers. For Thai painting technique, contact **Silpakorn University** (*see p293*). For yoga, try the **Yoga Elements Studio** (*see p183*).

## Thai language classes

**Jentana Personal Tutors** *5/8 Sukhumvit Soi 31, Sukhumvit (0 2260 6138-9).* **Map** p311 K6.

# Tourist information

A travel agency sign at Ban Phe pier says 'Tourist information everywhere'. It means 'to everywhere', but it states a reality. Countless companies use the 'i' logo to lure tourists; though biased, they may have more info than some tourist offices, and may be more accessible. **BTS Tourist Information** is at Siam, Nana and Saphan Taksin stations.

**Tourist Line** (0 2714 3334) is a phone service on every imaginable topic, with messages in English.

### Bangkok Tourist Bureau

*17/1 Thanon Phra Athit, under Phra Pinklao Bridge, Phra Nakorn (0 2225 7612-5).* Bus 6, 32, 33, 43, 53, 64, 506. **Open** 9am-7pm daily. **Map** p308 B2/3. An excellent source of information on attractions and tours, plus BTB's own

rewarding tours (*see p54*). White BTB booths are numerous, found at tourist, hotel and shopping areas.

### Tourism Authority of Thailand (TAT)

*TAT Building, 1600 Thanon New Petchaburi, North-east (0 2250 5500/www.tat.or.th).* Bus 11, 23, 58, 60, 72, 93, 99, 113, 512. **Open** 8.30am-4.30pm Mon-Fri. **Map** p311 J4. TAT's head office. Publishes lots of useful information and leaflets, not always available at TAT offices nationwide; the latter often have local insights but can't recommend particular companies/hotels.
**Branches:** 4 Ratchadamnoen Nok Avenue, Dusit (0 2282 9773); Bangkok Airport: Terminal 1 (0 2504 2702), Terminal 2 (0 2504 2703).

---

**Nisa Thai Language School** *32/14-16, Thanon Yen Akat, South (0 2671 3343-4).* Bus 4, 14, 22, 45, 46, 47, 109, 115, 116 then taxi. **Open** 8am-8pm Mon-Fri. **Map** p311 H8.

**Siri-Pattana Thai Language School** *15th Floor, YWCA, 13 Thanon Sathorn Tai, South (0 2213 1206/2677 3150).* Bus 22, 62, 67, 76, 116, 149, 530. **Open** 7am-8pm Mon-Fri. **Map** p311 G7.

**Union Language School** *11th Floor, CCT Building, 109 Thanon Surawong, Bangrak (0 2233 4482).* Saladaeng BTS/Silom subway. **Open** 8am-3pm Mon-Fri. **Map** p310 F6.

## Universities

**Chulalongkorn University** *254 Thanon Phaya Thai, Pathumwan (0 2215 0871-3/students union 0 2218 7040).* Bus 16, 21, 25, 29, 34, 40, 47, 50, 93, 113, 159, 163, 502, 529. **Map** p309 & p310 F5.

**Ramkhamhaeng University** *Thanon Ramkhamkaeng, East (0 2310 8000/students union 0 2310 8079).* Bus 22, 58, 60, 71, 92, 93, 95, 99, 109, 113, 501.

**Silpakorn University** *31 Thanon Na Phra Lan, Phra Nakorn (0 2623 6115-21/students union 0 2223 3411).* Bus 1, 25, 32, 39, 44, 47, 53, 59, 123, 203, 508. **Map** p308 B3.

**Thammasat University Phrachan Campus** *2 Thanon Phrachan, Phra Nakorn (0 2221 6111-20/students union 0 2613 3965).* Bus 32, 39, 53, 59, 123, 201, 203, 508. **Map** p308 B3.

## Tax

VAT is likely to rise from 7 per cent to 9 or 10 per cent. It is added to the prices of most shop goods and restaurant meals, but not to goods sold in markets or by vendors. Hotels and top-class restaurants add it with 10 per cent service (known as 'plus plus'). At the airport, VAT can be claimed back on substantial purchases if they were bought at shops displaying the right sign and are each valued at more than B2000+VAT (and totalling at least B5,000+VAT). For details, contact the **VAT Refund of Tourist Office** (0 2272 9387-8/ www.rd.go.th/vrt) or the airport VAT Refund offices:

**Bangkok Airport** 3rd Floor, International Terminal 2 (0 2535 6577-8).
**Chiang Mai Airport** 0 5392 2207.
**Hat Yai Airport** 0 7425 0400.
**Phuket Airport** 0 7632 8267.

## Telephones

### Dialling & codes

It is always necessary to dial the full area codes in Thailand, even when calling numbers that are within the same area. So Bangkok's 7-digit numbers are prefixed with an 0 2 code, and provincial 6-digit numbers with 3-digit codes (Chiang Mai 0 53, Samui 0 77). Local calls cost B3 (unlimited time). Dialling

upcountry (that is, not 0 2 numbers) is outrageously expensive, but cheaper from mobile phones, which follow the 9-digit format, but starting 0 1, 0 6 or 0 9 (hence area codes and mobile numbers aren't easily distinguished).

To dial Thailand, dial the country code 66, then drop the 0 and dial the remaining 8 digits. To call outside Thailand, internet dialing is possible, and there are several other ways:

**International Subscriber Dialing (ISD)** Dial 001, then the country code, area code and destination number. Peak time is 7am-9pm; off-peak 5-7am, 9pm-midnight; cheapest is midnight-5am. For operator assisted calls, dial 100 and let the operator call (minimum three minutes, so you automatically enter a fourth minute).

**eFone** is an automatic international telephone service via a special network with one cheap 24-hour rate. No need to register; dial direct 001 809 (home phone) or 009 (on mobile), then dial country code, area code and phone number.

**Thaicard** is a prepaid card for calling internationally from and to anywhere in the world, charged at the ISD or IDD rate (1 unit = 6 sec). Cards costing B100, B300, B500, B1,000 or B3,000 are available at post offices, shops with the Thaicard sign or offices of the Communications Authority of Thailand (CAT; 0 2950 3712/www.cat.or.th).

**PhoneNet** (0 2252 3888) is another CAT prepaid card using Hatari technology, similarly priced and distributed.

**Directory**

## Public phones

Call boxes require B1, B5 or B10 coins and/or a phone card. Some accept credit cards for international calls. Calling within the Greater Bangkok 0 2 area, the minimum price is B1 for three minutes, from B5 for 15 minutes. Dialing a mobile costs B3 for one minute. Buy phone cards at post offices or convenience stores.

## Operator services

**Directory inquiries** *Hotline 1133 Bangkok; 183 regional.* 24hrs; free. **Talking Yellow Pages** *Hotline 1154.* 6am-midnight daily.

## Telephone directories

There are two phone directories. The **TOT Corporation** (www.tot.co.th) directory has data on people, companies and organisations; **Teleinfo Media** (www.yellowpages.co.th) focuses on business and services.

## Mobile phones

Signified by the cacophony of personalised ringtones, Thailand is addicted to *meur teur* (mobile phones), with record handset and subscriber sales in 2002, when new competitors prompted overdue liberalisation. Previously having to use global roaming or buy a local phone (from B3,500 including some calls), visitors whose phones use the same systems as Thailand (900 or 1800 GSM) can now buy a local prepaid SIM card at some convenience stores or any phone shop, especially in the MBK mall. You buy a number, incorporating free calls, on a rechargeable SIM card; most common is AIS, while rivals DTAC and Orange are improving.

Americans using 1900 GSM should consult their service provider.

## Time

Thailand is seven hours ahead of Greenwich Mean Time, 12 hours ahead of US Eastern Standard Time, and three behind Sydney. The Thai calendar is 543 years ahead of the Gregorian calendar, starting at Buddha's enlightenment; hence 2003 is 2546 BE (after Buddhist era).

## Tipping

In this hierarchical culture, service is not a professional calling, but a role (sometimes temporary; even a poor diner gets to summon a waiter as

*nong,* 'younger sibling'). Hence tips are small. Leaving a fair 10 per cent might be bashfully (ie gleefully) received, since Thais consider B20 as a ceiling (B50 as extreme). Taxi drivers might round *down* a metered fare, such is the Thai heart.

Some view big tips as 'spoiling' future expectations and inflating costs for all, though equally it might improve standards. And generosity breeds good karma to Thais. Thus a group's host slipping B100 to a waiter on seating ensures prime attention, and hotel staff will remember tips on arrival. Hotels and posh venues add 10 per cent service, but they don't always divvy that out, so leave more change.

Tips are expected for guides and maids, maybe drivers, but not hairdressers or food vendors. Always reward masseurs, who get low piece rates and rarely any salary.

Whatever the service means to you, a commensurate tip will mean more to its recipient.

## Toilets

A 2002 campaign aims to improve public *hong nam* or *suka,* which aren't widely seen, so use those in gas stations, department stores, hotels or (asking politely) pubs or restaurants where you're not a patron. You literally have to spend a penny (B2) at toilets in markets, stations and public places. Mobile toilet buses are provided for large, crowded events.

Squat pans are common, with a plastic dipper and a water trough for cleaning yourself and flushing. Flush toilets usually have a spray hose. Tissue paper is often not provided (carry some) and must go in the basket so that it doesn't block the pipes. *Hong nam* ('water rooms') are indeed often wet, yet lack hooks for bags. Gents' often have unfazed women cleaners. Fewer night venues now have attendants who massage men's shoulders while they (attempt to) pee; decline with a polite *mai ow khrap* ('no thanks') or tip B10.

## Visas & immigration

### Immigration Department

*507 Soi Suan Plu, Thanon Sathorn Tai, South (0 2287 3101-10/ www.imm.police.go.th).* Bus 22, 62, 67, 89. **Open** 8.30am-4.30pm Mon-Fri. **Map** p311 G8.

US, UK, Australasian and most European nationals can get a visa on arrival for 30 days, though this is

under review. As well as business visas, Royal Thai embassies and consulates abroad grant tourist visas for 60 days, extendable by two weeks.

## Water & hygiene

Drink more water than you're used to. If you get dehydrated, you should also take glucose and mineral salts (this is why Thai fruit and juices often come with salt/sugar as dips/ mixers). Coconut juice is a good hydrator. Tap water in Bangkok and major cities is filtered and chlorinated, but that doesn't make it good for drinking. Bottled and filtered water is everywhere (clear bottles signify more filtration than white bottles). Ice cubes (or rings) are filtered, shaved ice often not – your call.

Peel fruit, check expiry dates and in street eateries wipe plates and cutlery (as the Thais do) with those otherwise useless tiny napkins.

## Weights & measures

Metric now predominates. Distance is measured in mm, cm, m and km; food in kg or g; petrol, water, milk or beer in litres. Fabric is measured in metres (or yards), but there's a Thai measurement for land: $1 \, wa = 2$ sq m; $1 \, rai = 4 \, ngan$ or $400 \, talang \, wa$ (square *wa*); $1 \, rai = 1,600$ sq m; $1$ acre = $2.5 \, rai$; $1$ hectare = $6.25 \, rai$. Gold comes not in ounces, but non-monetary *baht* (15.2g) and *saleung* (25 *satang* = 0.25 *baht*) weights.

## What to take

Thailand is tropically humid and Bangkok is the world's hottest city (on average, since it varies so little by hour or season), so pack loose-fitting, lightweight clothes. Clothes and shoes are cheap and fashion-aware here, but not available in large sizes. Learn from the Thai jacket shirt: free-hanging tops cool by convection. It's also bright and burning, so bring hats, shades and sunscreen. White deflects glare (and deters mosquitoes). For the May-October rains an umbrella is useful (and widely sold), but raincoats become saunas. Winter nights are cool in Bangkok and really cold up north; wearing layers and one sweater/fleece and/or light jacket is wise, and carry a sleeping bag if trekking. Boots or trainers with ankle support are wise for trekking, but lace-ups are a bore as you'll have to shed shoes continually. Velcro strap-sandals are practical, but announce you're a tourist. Have one ensemble that's smart for bureaucratic or social situations as neatness (and

cleanliness) is severely judged by Thais, who despise unkempt *farang kee nok* ('birdshit Westerners').

On arrival, buy a sarong, which has myriad uses besides wearing (changing in, lying on, cushioning, wrapping, carrying things, covering dirty surfaces or burnt shoulders, being a picnic mat etc). At beaches, many visitors end up constantly wearing wrap-around *gahng-gaeng talay* (fisherman's trousers).

In urban/tourist areas, most medicines are notoriously easily obtainable without prescription (except very strong ones) at independent pharmacies, prompting indiscipline with drugs like antibiotics that reduces their effectiveness. So you only need to bring specialised personal medication.

Other essentials include door and luggage locks, a money belt, insect repellent, photocopies of documents, sunscreen (SPF 15), spare batteries and an electrical adaptor. You might also want candles, an English-Thai dictionary, a torch, a penknife (remember to pack it in your hold luggage), a teaspoon, toiletries, sanitary towels and an umbrella.

## When to go

### Climate

Thailand is tropical but has various climate zones. It stretches south to a sunny and almost equatorial, rainforested peninsula with different monsoons in each ocean causing rains intermittently year round; most severe in late Oct-Dec in the Gulf (Pacific Ocean) and June-Oct in the Andaman Sea (Indian Ocean), most pleasant in May-Oct and Nov-Mar respectively.

Bangkok sits in the hotter, humid, less breezy central plain, which, like the east coast, follows clear seasons. It's the world's hottest city since it doesn't vary hugely by hour or season from an average 27.8°C (81°F) and 77% humidity. The north-eastern plateau (Isaan) and the north get roasting hot in summer and pleasantly cool in winter thanks to winds from China, though the highlands (actually Himalayan foothills) are always cool and drop to around zero in winter. Given recent seasonal variations and occasional El Niño years, get forecasts from the **Meteorological Department** (0 2399 3031/hotline 1182/ www.tmd.go.th). The seasons are:

**Hot** mid Feb-mid May, with Apr the hottest month (hitting 40°C/104°F); Mar is windy.

**Rainy** mid May-Oct, starting with heavy, unpredictable downpours (as early as mid Apr) and after a lull, regular rain in the late afternoon or evenings, with Sept being wettest. Flood risks are worst at the first rains and the highest tides of early Oct.

**Cool** Nov-mid Feb, when days are sunny, clear and fresh, and nights are balmy. This is the tourist high season, when it's fine across most of Thailand.

### Public holidays

**New Year's Day** 1 Jan.
**Makha Bucha Day** Jan-Mar (lunar).
**Chakri Day** 6 Apr.
**Songkran** (Thai New Year) 13-15 Apr.
**National Labour Day** 1 May.
**Coronation Day** 5 May.
**Royal Ploughing Day** (officials only) 9 May.

**Visakha Bucha Day** May-June (lunar).
**Khao Phansa** (Buddhist Lent) July (lunar).
**HM The Queen's Birthday** (Mother's Day) 12 Aug.
**King Chulalongkorn Day** 23 Oct.
**Ok Phansa** (end of Buddhist Lent) Oct (lunar).
**HM The King's Birthday (Father's Day)** 5 Dec.
**Constitution Day** 10 Dec.

## Women

### National Council of Women of Thailand

*Baan Manangkasila, 514 Thanon Lan Luang, Dusit (0 2281 0081/ www.thaiwomen.net/ncwt).* Bus 2, 8, 39, 44, 59, 60, 79, 157, 503, 511, 512. **Open** 8.30am-4.30pm Mon-Fri. **Map** p309 & p310 D3.
An organisation with members nationwide that aims to improve women's status in every field, through female education, development of family institutions and co-operation with international organisations.

### Paveena Foundation for Children & Women

*Puengluang Complex Tower, 1047-9 Phahon Yothin Soi 69/1, North (hotline 1134).* Bus 34, 39, 114, 356, 185, 503, 520, 522, 523, 543. **Open** 24hrs daily.
Established by Pavena Hongsakul MP, this high-profile group tackles sexual harassment, prostitution and other children's and women's issues.

### Thai National Commission on Women's Affairs

*Government House, 1 Thanon Luk Luang, Dusit (0 2282 2690/ www.thaiwomen.net/tncwa).* Bus 16, 23, 53, 99, 110. **Open** 8.30am-4.30pm Mon-Fri. **Map** p309 D2.
Conducts policy research and data analysis, as well as co-ordinating gender equality work, protection of women's rights and furthering of female participation.

## Working in Thailand

Work permits (and tax returns) are required for those seeking paid work in occupations not restricted to Thais, and require the correct business visa and paperwork. Certain workers are eligible for the faster **One-Stop Service Centre** (0 2693 9333-9, visas ext 225, work permits ext 301/www.doe.go.th/workpermit/ onestopservice).

# Bangkok climate

| Month | Max temp | Min temp | Rainfall |
|-------|----------|----------|----------|
| Jan | 33°C/92°F | 25°C/78°F | 11mm/0.4in |
| Feb | 34°C/94°F | 25°C/78°F | 9mm/0.3in |
| Mar | 33°C/92°F | 26°C/79°F | 175mm/6.8in |
| Apr | 36°C/98°F | 28°C/82°F | 28mm/1.1in |
| May | 33°C/92°F | 26°C/79°F | 257mm/10.1in |
| June | 33°C/92°F | 26°C/79°F | 102mm/4in |
| July | 33°C/92°F | 27°C/80°F | 62mm/2.4in |
| Aug | 33°C/92°F | 26°C/79°F | 149mm/5.9in |
| Sept | 34°C/94°F | 26°C/79°F | 450mm/17.7in |
| Oct | 33°C/92°F | 25°C/78°F | 480mm/18.9in |
| Nov | 32°C/90°F | 23°C/74°F | 37mm/1.45in |
| Dec | 32°C/90°F | 23°C/74°F | 4mm/0.1in |

*Directory*

# Language

Though daunting, attempting Thai is useful and delights locals. The Thai language expresses cultural contexts of hierarchy, social obligation and the culture's multiple origins. And much of the vocabulary and many of the names proudly trace their lineage from from Indian Sanskrit and Pali. Modern nouns such as *torasap* ('telephone') are assembled from these Asian classical cousins to Latin and Greek, forming one tenuous link to European tongues; the other is a smattering of English, French and Portuguese words. Otherwise, Thai is utterly alien to Romance, Teutonic or Slavic speakers, using an Indianised script without word spaces. Hailing from Chinese are monosyllables, numbers, more words and the notorious five tones (low, falling, flat, rising and high) that turn the same sound into different words. Meanwhile, regional dialects demonstrate the inflence of Mon, Khmer, Burmese, Lao or Malay, while other minorities such as hill tribes speak Sinified, Tibeto-Burman or other languages.

Central Thai is the standard, but – just as Londoners range from 'BBC English' to dropping their Cockney Hs – Bangkokians enunciate special languages to address royalty, nobility or monks, even though many 'drop' their Rs in a slightly Sino-accented vernacular that turns Rs into Ls and Ls into Ns. Be careful who you learn from: talk *pak talad* ('market speak') and you won't get far in society.

Politeness is ingrained in different layers of personal pronouns, in closing each sentence with *kha* for females or *krub* for males (which is like saying 'please'), in opening requests with *khor* ('I would like'), and in multilevel words such as the verb 'to eat'. In everyday lingo it's *kin*, *than* is more polite, *rappathan* formal, *chan* only with monks, and *savuey* just with royalty.

## Transliteration & grammar

Many contradictory systems are used, partly because monosyllables lead to words being separated out or conglomerated, partly as there are more consonants and vowels than ways to write in them in English, with several Ks, Ts, Js, Ps, As, Ss, Us, Ts, etc. An H following a T, P, K or B softens and aspirates it, those without are harder, explosive, sounding more like DT, BP, G or P; hence Phuket is not Fookhet but Pooget. Even academic phonetic spellings require countless accents to approximate Thai, so accept the many anomalies. While wrong tones may still be understood through context (sometimes), mistaking a long or short vowel is fatal to comprehension. Grammar has no articles or tenses; adjectives follow the noun; the name of a road, canal, hotel etc follows its generic noun (eg Thanon Silom, Tha Chang, Rong Raem Sukhothai), but numbers go before the 'generic counter' of any quantity, hence *som-o song luuk* (two rounds of pomelo) or *baeb form sam bai* (three sheets of forms), with *un* (small thing) being a multi-purpose counter. Consonants often change sounds, whether at the end of a word or when put together. Thais can't pronounce most combinations of two consonants together without putting a sound in between, and some spellings reflect that: *pollamai* (fruit) is said *ponlamai*; *stang* (cent) is pronounced *satang*; *spaghetti* is rendered 'sapaa-get-tii'. Grasping such 'Thainglish' pronounciation of foreign words is a first step to spotting the key differences.

## Consonants

**bh** as in peace
**j** is like ch, often spelled ch or tch
**kh** as in camel
**k** like g in began, not George
**ll** in mid word becomes -nl-
**ng** as in sing without the 'si'
**p** like bp, as in explode
**ph** as in pine, not f
**r** is trilled, or slurred to l
**ss** in mid word becomes -ts-
**t** like dt, as in bottle
**th** as in Thai, not 'the'/'three'
**v** is like w

When ending a word or syllable: **-j**, **-ch** and **-s** becomes -t; **-r** often becomes **-orn**; **-l** becomes **-n**; **-tr** becomes **-t**; and **-se** and **-ha** are usually silent.

## Vowels

**a** as u in upon
**aa** as in barn, with no r
**ae** as in air, with no r (also used for a as in cat)
**aew** as in air-uw with no r
**ai** as in high
**ao** as in how with no w
**aw** as in awe with no w or r
**eu** as in urban, but flatter
**eua** as above with a rising a
**i** as in hit
**ii** as in teeth
**o** as in hot
**oe** as in earn with no r
**oh** as in so
**oo** or **u** as in book
**uu** as in fool
**uay** as in oo-way with no w

## Tones

There are five tones, signified thus: high (ó), falling (ô), neutral (no mark), rising (ǒ), low (ò).

## Thai names

Thais have at least three names. Formal first names are words with auspicious

meanings, followed by a family name. Every Thai person gets a nickname from birth, sometimes later; they're often descriptive like Daeng (red), Neung (one), Lek (small), Yai (big) or amusing, such as Moo (pig), Odd (tadpole), Gop (frog) or Maew (cat), even fashionable: Benz, Golf or Neon. Monks get a special name on ordination.

## Vocabulary

### Basics

hello *sawàsdee;* goodbye/see you later *la kòrn/lâew jeur kun;* good luck *chôk dee;* what's your name? *khun chêu arai (khâ/krúb);* my name is...*chán/phŏm chêu ....* I *chán (female)/phŏm (male);* Mr/Mrs/Miss/you *khun;* he/she *khǎo;* girl/boy friend *faen;* friend *puéan;* wife *mia;* husband *samee;* minor/wife *mia-nói;* monk *lûang phór;* child/boy/girl *dek/dekchai/ dekyiñg;* man *phúchai;* women *phúyiñg;* gay *gay,* ladyboy *katoey;* lesbian *tom-dée.*
yes *châi;* no *mâi châi;* can *dâi;* cannot *mâi dâi;* please *pròd, garúna;* thank you *khòb khun khâ (female)/krúb (male);* excuse me *kŏr thôd khâ/krúb;* I'm sorry *chán /phŏm sia jai (khâ/krúb);* never mind *mâi pen rai.*
ask/can I have... *chán /phŏm kŏr...;* excuse me *kŏr thôd (khâ/krúb);* please help me *dâi pròd chûay chán/phŏm noi;* wait a moment *ror sàk khrú (khâ/krúb).* what is this in Thai? *Nii ríak pen Thai wâh arai?* do you speak English? *khun phôod pasaa angìd dâi mǎi (khâ/krúb)?* sorry, I can't speak Thai *sia jái, chán/phŏm phôod pasaa Thai mâi dâi (khâ/ krúb);* I can speak Thai a bit *chán/phŏm phôod Thai dâi nid nói;* I don't understand *chán/phŏm mâi khâo jai;* speak slower, please *pròd phôod châ noi (khâ/krúb),* why? *thǎm mai?,* when? *múea rài?,* who? *krai?,* what? *arai?,* where *têe nǎi?,* how? *yàng rai?,* informal *yàng ngài?*
very *mâak;* and *láe;* or *rûe;* with *dûay;* without *mâi mee* open *pèrd;* closed *pìd;* what time does it open/close? *pèrd/pìd kèe mong?*
I want/would like... *chán/phŏm tòng karn...;* how many would you like? *khun tòng karn thâo rai?;* I like... *chán/phŏm chôrp...;* I don't like... *chán/phŏm mâi chôrp...;* OK/fine *OK;* that's enough *pôr láew.*
price *raakha;* rent, hire *châo;* free *free;* discount *lód raakha;*

how much? *thâo rai (khâ/krúb);* could you discount? *lód raakha dâi mǎi (khâ/krúb);* that's expensive/cheap *paeng mâak/tòok mâak;* the bill/check, please *chék bin (khâ/krúb);* do you have any change? *khun mee torn mǎi (khâ/krúb).*
what's that? *nán arai?,* where is...? *...yòo tée nǎi?,* I'm going to... *chán ja pai.*
good *dee;* bad *mái dee;* big *yài;* small *lék;* little *nói;* entrance *thang khǎo;* exit *thang òkk;* painful *jêb;* help *chûay;* dangerous *antarai;;* accident *ùubut hèd;* doctor *mŏr;* medicine *ya;* on one's own *khon dêe-o;* smile *yim.*

### Places

bridge *sàphan;* canal *khlong;* main road *thanŏn;* side road *soi;* alley *tròk;* expressway *thang dòuan;* river *mâe nám;* pier *thâ;* station *satǎnee;* shop *ràanká;* temple *wát;* bank *thana karn;* post office *prai sa nee;* restaurant *ráan ar-hǎrn;* ...hospital *rong phaya baan...;* ...palace *wang...;* housing estate *mòo bâan;* town *muang;* island *kò;* beach *hàad;* bay *ào;* mountain *khǎo;* forest *pà;* market *talàd;* embassy *satǎhn tôot;* province *chǎngwàt;* district *amphoe;* sub district *tambon;* country *prâthêt;* where's the toilet? *hông nám yooo nǎi (khâ/krúb).*

### Transport

bus *rót may;* boat *ruea;* express boat *ruea dòuan;* ferry *ruea khâm fâk;* long-tailed boat *ruea hǎang yáo;* taxi *tairk-sêe;* train *rót fai;* skytrain *rót fai fáh;* subway *rót fai tâi din;* pickup bus *sŏngtaew;* plane *krêuang bin;* platform *charn cha la;* ticket *tuǎ;* one way *têo dêo;* bus stop *pâi rót may.*
do you know the way to...? *khun róo thang pai...màii (khâ/krúb)?*
to the end of the street *sòod thanŏn,* sòod soi; near *klâhy;* far *klâii;* right *khwǎ;* left *sái;* stop *yuut;* stop here/there *yùut tíi-nii/tíi-nán;* return *pai klàb;* turn *lée-o;* u-turn *lée-o klàb;* opposite *trong khâm;* beside *kháng kháng;* the next stop *pâi ná.*

### Accommodation

...hotel *rong raem...;* room *hông;* with/without bathroom *mee hông nám/ mâi mee hông nám;* shower *fàk bua;* air-conditioned *hông air;* fan-cooled *hông phát lom;* double bed *tiang khòo;* breakfast included *ruam ar-hǎrn cháo;* lift *lift;* swimming pool *sà wâi nám;*

an inside/outside room *nai hông/nók hông.*
do you have a double/single room for tonight/one week? *khun mee hông khóo/hông dêow sŭmrub kheun nii/nèung athít;* we have a reservation *rão jong hŏng lâew;* where is the car park? *tíi jòrd rót yòo tíi nâi.*

## Time

morning *ton cháo;* midday *klang wan;* noon *thíang wan;* afternoon *ton bài;* evening *ton yen;* night *ton klang keun;* midnight *thiang keun;* early *cháo;* late *sǎi;* weekend *wan sòod sàb da;* now *ton nii;* later *pai lang;* today *wan nii;* yesterday *méu wan;* tomorrow *wan próong nii;* delayed *chá.*
what's the time? *kèe mong;* hour *chûamong;* in an hour *eek nèung chûamong;* last 2 hours *chái way-la sŏng chûamong;* at 8am *pàed mong cháo;* at 1pm *bài mong;* at 2pm *bài sŏng mong;* at 7pm *nuèng thûm;* at 8pm *sŏng thûm.*
day *wan;* Monday *wan jun;* Tuesday *wan ankarn;* Wednesday *wan phúd;* Thursday *wan pàréuhàssàbordi, wan pàréuhàt;* Friday *wan sùk;* Saturday *wan sǎo;* Sunday *wan athít.*
January *mòkkharakhom;* February *koomphaphan;* March *meenakhom;* April *maesǎyon;* May *prúedsaphakhom;* June *míthùnayon;* July *karákkadakhom;* August *singhǎkhom;* September *kunyayon;* October *tùlakhom;* November *prúesajikayon;* December *thanwakhom*
summer *réudoo rón;* rain *réudoo fŏn;* winter *réudoo nǎow;* year *pii.*

## Slang

handsome *lòr;* cute *nǎa-rák;* beautiful *suǎy;* delicious *aròi, sàb-e-lèe (Isaan word);* cool *jěng;* lousy *hùay tàek;* international *inter;* modern *dérn;* going out *pai têe-o;* ticklish *jàkkajèe;* exclamation sound *oô-ee.*

## Numbers

0 *sŏon;* 1 *nèung;* 2 *sŏng;* 3 *sǎm;* 4 *sìi;* 5 *hâ;* 6 *hòk;* 7 *jèd;* 8 *pàed;* 9 *kâo;* 10 *sìb;* 11 *sìb-èt;* 12 *sìb-sŏng;* 13 *sìb-sam;* 14 *sìb-sìi;* 15 *sìb-hâ;* 16 *sìb-hòk;* 17 *sìb-jèd;* 18 *sìb-pàed;* 19 *sìb-kâo;* 20 *yî-sìb;* 21 *yî-sìb-èt;* 22 *yî-sìb-sŏng;* 30 *sǎm-sìb;* 31 *sǎm-sìb-èt;* 32 *sǎm-sìb-sŏng;* 40 *sìi-sìb;* 50 *hâ-sìb;* 60 *hòk-sìb;* 70 *jèd-sìb;* 80 *pàed-sìb;* 90 *kâo-sìb;* 100 *nèung-rói;* 101 *nèung rói nèung;* 200 *sŏng rói;* 1,000 *nèung phun;* 10,000 *nèung meun;* 100,000 *nèung sǎen;* 1,000,000 *nèung lâan;* 1st *tée nèung;* 2nd *tée sŏng;* 3rd *tée sǎm.*

# Further Reference

## Books

### Fiction

**Barang, Marcel** (translator) *The 20 Best Novels of Thailand* Annotated excerpts recrafted into English.
**Needham, Jake** *The Big Mango* Asia Books' Elmore Leonard gives the usual suspects unusual panache.
**Pinkayan, Salisa** *Chalida* First novel written in English by a Thai woman, chronicling a coddled girl's discovery of *hi-so* power abuses.
**Somtow, SP** *Jasmine Nights* Bangkok coming-of-age tale, written with edge, beauty and wit.
**Srinawk, Khamsing** *The Politician & Other Stories.* Scathing progressive prose fables of modern village life.
**Sutham, Pira** *Monsoon Country* & sequel *The Force of Karma* Historical novels by an Isaan villager turned Sussex expat dissecting the roots and results of corruption.

### Non-fiction

**Bhikkhu, Buddhadasa** *Handbook for Mankind* Pertinent, non-preachy philosophy for lay people by influential late abbot.
**Eckhardt, James** *Bangkok People* Portraits of the prominent, from MPs and PRs to expats and eccentrics.
**Fellowes, Warren** *The Damage Done* Excoriating exposé of Thai prisons by a former inmate.
**Hoskin, John** *Bangkok by Design* Modern Thai architecture.
**Jackson, Peter** *Dear Uncle Go: Homosexualities in Thailand.* Letters to a Thai agony uncle analysed by trailblazing academic.
**Jotisalikorn, Chami** *Classic Thai* Traditional arts and design with contemporary insight Plus *Thai Spa Book*, the fullest guide yet to indigenous Siamese healing.
**Lees, Paul** *The Dive Sites of Thailand* The where, what and how of scuba diving.
**Mann, Niclaire & McKenzie, Eleanor** *Step-by-Step Thai Massage* Clearest pictorial lesson yet, instructed by ITM's Chongkol Setthakorn.
**Odzer, Cleo** *Patpong Sisters* Sex-positive, no-holds-barred window on Thai prostitution.
**O'Reilly, James & Habegger, Larry** (editors) *Travellers' Tales Thailand* Mostly superb compendium gets under the country's skin.
**Pannapadipo, Phra Peter** *Phra Farang.* Updated memoirs of an ordained Western monk.

**Phongpaichit, Pasuk & Phriyanarangsan, Sungsidh** *Corruption & Democracy in Thailand* and *Guns, Girls, Gambling, Ganja* Names the names, times, places and acts that made the Thai boom bust.
**Poshyananda, Apinan** *Modern Art in Thailand* By leading Thai curator.
**Pramoj, Kukrit** *Si Phaendin (Four Reigns)* Late PM, academic and noble embodiment of Thai culture's tale of times under Ramas V-VIII.
**Redmond, Mont** *Wondering into Thai Culture* Incisive ponderings on manners and conventions.
**Stewart-Cox, Belinda** *Wild Thailand* Campaigning book on animals and their threatened environments.
**Winichaikul, Thongchai** *Siam Mapped* Tracking Thailand's past shapes with resonance for today.
**Wyatt, David** *Thailand: A Short History* Leading revisionist historian's revelatory and accessible account.

## Music

### Classical/phiphat

**Bangkok Symphony Orchestra** *Mahajanaka Symphony* (BSO Foundation) The pastiche that launched an opera house. Conducted by composer (and writer) SP Somtow.
**Fong Naam** *Jakajan* Bruce Gaston's compositions and/or arrangements for *phiphat*, plus rock/jazz ensemble. *Siamese Classical Music Vols 1-5* (Marco Polo World Classics) is the only complete catalogue of five centuries of Thai classical music; played by virtuosi.
**Kangsadan** *Golden Jubilee Overture* (Pisces) Modern *phiphat* ensemble outdoing the Latin, jazz and lounge fusion of labelmates **Boy Thai**.
**Richard Harvey** *The Spirit of Suriyothai* (Asian Music International) Distillation/elaboration of his original film score.
**Thai Elephant Orchestra** (TECC) Wild chance music from a chorus of six elephants and two humans.

### Luuk thung/morlam

**Jintara Poonlarp** *Greatest Hits Vols 1 & 2* (MGA) Over 30 CDs, so pick this collection from Grammy's Nashville/Khorat division.
**Phomphuang Duangjan** *Through the Years, Vol 1 & 2* (Topline) Lovely anachronism: the Thai equivalent of Hank Williams versus modern C&W.
**Siriporn Amphipong** *Greatest Hits Vols 1-5* (MGA) Vol 3 is easiest on Western ears (feels like the blues).

## Indie/dance

**A Mosquito** *This is Asia* (Red Beat) Peculiarly Thai dance music. Too fast and pretty loopy, but sweetly funky. Irresistible phone sex hook line.
**Joey Boy** *Anthology* (Bakery Records) From funkfest 'Chinese Connection' to 'Fun Fun Fun', Thonburi is the new Brooklyn.
**Modern Dog** *Café* (Bakery) This home-grown nu-metal opened the floodgates in 1994 and still rocks.
**Orn-aree** *Peel* (Bakery) Little heard until its 1990s reissue. Beguiling fusion of Bonnie Raitt, Portishead, Hole and Phomphuang.
**Photo Sticker Machine** *Color Lab* (Hualampong Riddim) Think Stereolab, Tortoise, Cornelius… Now put this on and stop thinking.

## Pleng puer cheewit

**Ad Carabao** *Best of* (Warner) Splendid gold-covered primer.
**Caravan** *Best of: Vol 1* (UPL) Songs that sparked a revolution; James Tayloresque ballads to rootsier folk.
**Pongsit Khampee** *Best of… 2530* (ATO) Sweet-voiced, deep-thinking rebel; Thailand's Jackson Brown.
**Marijuana** *Buppha Chon* (Milestone/MGA). The mellow Deadhead side of *pleng puer cheewit.*

## T-Pop

**LOSO** *The Red Album* (Grammy) Testosterone power ballads and raunchy rock by Bangkok's Bon Jovi.
**Palmy** *Palmy* (Grammy) Hook-laden, non-stop hip-sway grooves in a hippy-dippy trip-hop-lite mode.
**Tata Young** *Amita Tata Young* (BEC Tero) Not-a-girl-but-a-hell-of-a-woman; funky dance marred only by syrupy ballads.

## World beat

**T-Bone** *Ruam Pleng Dee T-Bone* (Warner) Studio album still available, but the live sweat is a rarity.

## Websites

**www.bangkokpost.net** Online newspaper.
**www.eThailand.com** Established English language bookmark.
**www.nationmultimedia.com** Diverse media homepage.
**www.pantip.com** Oft-reported noticeboard for public opinion.
**www.tat.or.th** Official gateway. UK office runs www.thaismile.co.uk.

# Index

# Advertisers' Index

Pleas refer to the relevant pages for addresses
and telephone numbers

| Place of interest and/or entertainment | ▢ |
| Railway & bus stations | ▪ |
| Parks | ▢ |
| Hospitals/universities | ▢ |
| Neighbourhood | DUSIT |
| Subway station | Ⓤ |
| Subway route | — |
| BTS route | ═ |
| BTS station | S1 |
| Temple | ⚰ |

# Maps

# Greater Bangkok

NORTH-EAST

NORTH-EAST

NORTH-EAST

OUTER NORTH

OUTER NORTH

OUTER NORTH

OUTER NORTH

DUSIT

THONBURI

THONBURI

THONBURI

NONTHABURI

NONTHABURI

3 miles
3 km

© Copyright Time Out Group 2003

Royal Thai Air Force Academy
RTAF Museum
Don Muang Railway Station
Robinson Department Store
Amari Airport
Bangkok International Airport
THANON PHAHON YOTHIN
THANON WIPHAWADI-RANGSIT
THANON RAM INTHRA
RAM INTHRA-AT NARONG EXPRESSWAY
THANON WAT LAD PLAKHAO
THANON KASETNAWAMIN
SOI CHOK CHAI 4
Central Department Store
Army Golf Course
Sri Pathum University
THANON PHAHON YOTHIN
Exhibition Hall
Civil Court
Laksi Plaza
Rama Gardens
THANON KAMPHAENG PHET VI
RATTANA YOTRIN
RATTANA YOTRIN JUNCTION
SCB Park Plaza
Thai-Airways International Building
Lak Si Railway Station
Kasetsat University
Siam Jusco Supermarket
IMAX
Central Sofitel
Central Plaza
Sirikit Park
Chatuchak Park
OUTER NORTH
Racha Phuk Golf Course
Rajpreuk Golf Course
THANON CHAENG WATTHANA
THANON PRACHA CHUN
Dhurakit Bundit University
THANON NGAM WONG WAN
Khlong Prem Prison
Muang Thong Thani Sports Complex & Impact Arena
Golden Dragon
Banglamphu Dept. Store
Northern Bus Terminal
North Eastern Bus Terminal
THANON PRACHA CHUEN
PRACHA RAT
WONG SAWANG
RACHA RAT SAI 1
Sukhothai Thamma Thirat University
THANON SAMAKKHI
Srithanya Hospital
THANON PRACHA RAT
RAMA VII BRIDGE
Pakkret District Office
THANON TIWANON
THANON RATTANA THIBET
THANON REWADI
District Office
RAMA V BRIDGE
Wat Poramai
Mon Village
Ko Kred
Chao Phraya River
PHRA NANG KLAO BRIDGE
Wat Chaloem Prakiat
THANON NONTHA
BIRI
Khlong Om
THANON PHRA KIAT
Wat Pho Bang-O
THANON RATTANA THIBET
Khlong Om

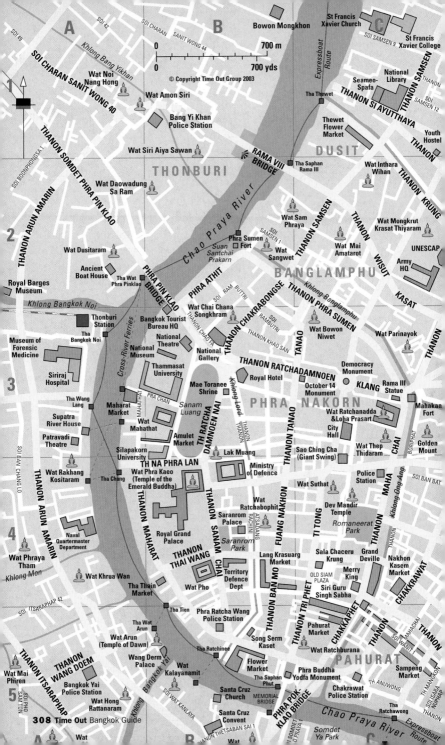

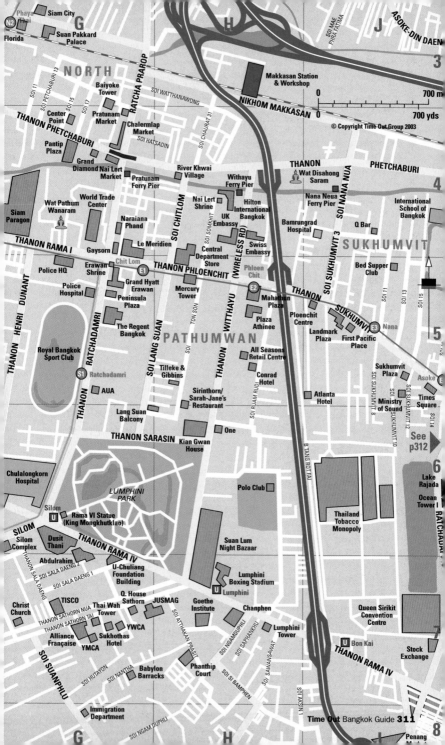

# Street Index

Aksin 1, Soi - p311 H7/8
Anuwong, Thanon - p308 C5
Ari, Soi - p312 K7
Arun Amarin, Thanon - p308 A2-5
Asoke-Din Daeng, Thanon -
p311 & p312 J3
Atsadang, Thanon - p308 B3/4
Attha Wiphat, Soi - p312 M4
Atthakan Prasit, Soi - p311 H7

B Tang Rot Fai, Thanon - p311
H5/J6/7
Bamrung Muang, Thanon - p309
& p310 D4/E4
Ban Bat, Soi - p308 C4
Ban Chang Lo, Soi - p308 A3/4
Ban Mo, Thanon - p308 B5/4
Banthat Thong, Thanon - p309 &
p310 E5/4/F4/3
Boonphongsa 1, Soi - p308 A2/1
Boriphat, Thanon - p308 C4/3
Bun Chuai, Soi - p309 F1

Chakkaphatdi Phong, Thanon -
p309 & p310 D3
Chakkaphet, Thanon - p308 C5
Chakkrawat, Thanon - p308 C5/4
Chakrabongse, Thanon - p308
B3/2
Chao Fa, Thanon - p308 B3
Charan Sanit Wong 40, Soi -
p308 A1
Charan Sanit Wong 42, Soi -
p308 A1
Charan Sanit Wong 44, Soi -
p308 A1/B1
Charan Sanit Wong 49, Soi -
p308 A1
Charoen Krung 45, Soi - p310
E7/6
Charoen Krung 51, Soi - p310
Charoen Krung, Thanon - p310
D5/6
Charoen Muang, Thanon - p309
& p310 E5
Charoen Nakhon 2, Soi - p310
D7
Charoen Nakhon 9, Soi - p310
D7
Charoen Nakhon 10, Soi - p310
D7
Charoen Nakhon 14, Soi - p310
D7
Charoen Nakhon 17, Soi - p310
D8
Charoen Nakhon 19, Soi - p310
D8
Charoen Nakhon, Thanon - p310
D6-8
Charoen Suk, Soi - p312 K7
Chatat Muang, Thanon - p309 &
p310 E5
Chaurat 31, Soi - p311 H4/3

Chitlom, Soi - p311 H4
Chulalongkorn 5, Soi - p309
E5/4
Chulalongkorn 5, Soi - p310 E6-4
Chulalongkorn 7, Soi - p309 &
p310 E5
Chulalongkorn 9, Soi - p309 &
p310 E5/F5
Chulalongkorn 12, Soi - p309 &
p310 E5/F5
Chulalongkorn 22, Soi - p309 &
p310 E5/F5
Convent, Thanon - p310 F7

Damrong Rak, Thanon - p309 &
p310 D3

Fuang Nakhon, Thanon - p308
B4
Hatsadin, Soi - p311 G4/H4
Henri Dunant, Thanon - p311 G5
Hutayon, Soi - p311 G7

Isara Nuphap, Soi - p308 C5
Itsaraphap 42, Soi - p308 A5/4
Itsaraphap, Thanon - p308 A5

Khao San, Thanon - p308 B3
Khlong Lam Pak, Soi - p309 &
p310 E3
Krung Kasem, Thanon - p308
C1/2, p309 D2-5/E3/4

Lan Luang, Thanon - p309 &
p310 D3/E3
Lang Suan, Soi - p311 G6/5/H5
Local Road - p312 L4
Luang, Thanon - p309 & p310 D4
Luk Luang, Thanon - p309 D2/3

Mae Phra Fatima, Soi - p311 J3
Maha Chai, Thanon - p308 C4/3
Maha Nakhon, Thanon - p310
E8-3
Maha Phrutharam, Thanon -
p310 D6
Mahachai, Thanon - p308 C5
Maharat, Thanon - p308 A4/B4
Mahathat, Thanon - p308 A3
Maitri Chit, Thanon - p309 &
p310 D4/5
Man Sin 4, Soi - p309 & p310
E3/F3
Mangkon, Thanon - p308 C5
Memorial Bridge - p308 B5

Na Phra Lan, Thanon - p308
A4/B4
Nakhon Sawat, Thanon - p309
D3/2
Nana Nua, Soi - p311 J4
Nantha, Soi - p311 G7/H7
Nara Thiwat Ratcha Nakharin,

Thanon - p310 F7/8
Naret, Thanon - p310 E6
Ncharoen Krung (New Rd),
Thanon - p309 & p310 D5
Ngam Duphli, Soi - p311 J5/6
Ngamduphli, Soi - p311 H7
Nikhom Makkasan, Thanon -
p311 H3/4/J4

Old Siam Plaza - p308 C4

Pan, Thanon - p310 E7
Petchaburi 11, Soi - p311 G4/3
Petchaburi 13, Soi - p311 G4/3
Petchaburi 15, Soi - p311 G4/3
Petchaburi 17, Soi - p311 G4/3
Phai Singto, Soi - p311 J7
Phaniang, Thanon - p309 D3
Phat Phong 1, Thanon - p310 F6
Phaya Nak, Soi - p309 E3/F4
Phaya Nak, Thanon - p309 E3,
p310 E3/F4
Phaya Thai, Thanon - p309 F5-3,
p310 F6-3
Phetchaburi 5, Soi - p309 &
p310 F3
Phetchaburi 7, Soi - p309 &
p310 F3
Phetchaburi 18, Soi - p309 F4
Phetchaburi, Thanon - p309 &
p310 E3/F3/4, p311
G4/H4/J4
Phiphat 1, Soi - p310 F7
Phiphat 2, Soi - p310 F7
Phiphat, Soi - p310 F7
Phitsanulok, Thanon - p308
C1/2, p309 D2/E3
Phlab, Thanon - p309 & p310
D5/4
Phloenchit, Thanon - p311 H5
Pho Pan, Soi - p312 K3
Pho Sam Ton, Soi - p308 A5
Phop Mit, Soi - p312 L5/4
Phra Athit, Thanon - p308 B2
Phra Nakharet, Soi - p310 E6
Phra Phinij 7, Soi - p310 F7
Phra Pin Klao Bridge - p308 B2
Phra Pokklao Bridge - p308
B5/C5
Phra Sumen, Thanon - p308
B2/C2/3
Phrom Chit, Soi - p312 K5/L5
Phrom Khan, Soi - p312 L5
Phrom Sri 1, Soi - p312 L5
Phrommit, Soi - p312 L6
Pikul, Soi - p310 F8
Pra Chan, Thanon - p308
A3/B3
Praditsoi 20, Soi - p310 E7
Pramuan, Thanon - p310 E7

Rachini, Thanon - p308 B3/4
Ram Buttri, Soi - p308 B2

# Bangkok by Area

2 km
2 miles

© Copyright Time Out Group 2003

THANON PRACHA
UTH-
THANON WIPHAWADI-RANGSIT

Thailand Culture Centre

NORTH-EAST

Khlong Tan Station

Bangkok Playhouse

SUKHUMVIT 55
SUKHUMVIT 63

Eastern Bus Terminal

Planetarium

UNESCO

Samitivej Hospital

E6
E7

THANON PHETCHABURI

THANON SUKHUMVIT

SUKHUMVIT

THANON RAMA IV

SUNTHON KOSA

ASOKE - RACHADAPISEK EXPRESSWAY

Khlong Saen Saeb

E5

Queen Sirikit Convention

E4
E3

CHALERM MAHANAKHON EXPRESSWAY

N5
N4

THANON PHAHON YOTHIN

NORTH

Victory Monument

N3

See page 311

World Trade

E2
E1

THANON WITTHAYU

Night Bazaar

Lumphini Park

SOUTH

S1

PHAYA THAI

RAMA IV

THANON

N2
N1

CEN

PATHUMWAN

THANON PHETCHABURI

National Stadium

Snake Farm

S2

SATHORN NUA
SATHORN TAI

THANON PHAHON YOTHIN

THANON PHETCHABURI

PHAYATHAI - BANGKHLO EXPRESSWAY

THANON RAMA VI

See page 308

Dusit Zoo

Anantasamakhom Throne Hall

THANON SRI AYUTTHAYA

DUSIT

LAN LUANG

BAMRUNG MUANG

Hualumphong Station

CHINA TOWN

SI PHRAYA

THANON SURAWONG

THANON SILOM

BANGRAK

S3
S4
S5
S6

CHAROEN KRUNG

TAKSIN BRIDGE

Bangkok Dockyard

See page 310

RAMA VIII BRIDGE

PHRA PINKLAO BRIDGE

Royal Barges Museum

Thonburi Railway Station

PHRAN NOK

Khlong Bangkok Noi

SAPHAN (KRUNG THONI) BRIDGE

THONBURI

See page 308

Democracy Monument

BANGLAMPHU

PHRA NAKORN

SANAM CHAI

Wat Phra Kaeo

PHRA POKKLAO BRIDGE

CHAROEN NAKORN

THONBURI

THANON LAT YA
THANON CHAROEN RAT

Taksin Monument

Wongwian Yai Station

THOET THAI

Khlong Bangkok Yai

THANON PHRA PIN KLAO

THANON ITSARA PHAP

THONBURI

See page 312

# Bangkok
# BTS & subway

Major Cineplex

THANON PHAHON YOTHIN

0 — 2 miles
0 — 2 km

© Copyright Time Out Group 2003

NORTH-EAST

SOI CHOK CHAI 4

PRACHA RAT
PRACHA CHUEN

PHRA RAMA VII BRIDGE

Northern Bus Terminal

Sirikit Park

Phahon Yothin

North-eastern Bus Terminal

PRACHA RAT SAI 1

DUSIT

Bangsue
Bangsue Station

THANON

Boon Rawd Brewery (Singha)

AMNUAI SONGKHRAM

Morchit/ Chatuchak Park
Chatuchak Park

Thai Airways International Building

Lad Phrao

THANON LAT PHRAO

Mochit

PRADIPHAT

Chatuchak Weekend Market

Kamphaengphet

Saphan Khwai

SUTTHISARN

WINITCHAI

Ratchada/ Ratchadaphisek

Sutthisarn

THANON PHAHON YOTHIN

NORTH

THANON RAMA VI

Ari

THANON WIPHAWADI-RANG SIT

THANON PHISEK

THANON RATCHADA

Pracharat Bumphen/ Huay Khwang

THANON PRACHA UTHIT

Dusit Zoo

Anantasamakhom Throne Hall

Sanam Pao

THANON SI

DUSIT

AYUTTHAYA

Victory Monument

Victory Monument

Tiem Ruam-mit/ Thailand Cultural Centre

Thailand Cultural Centre

NORTH-EAST

LAN LUANG

PHETCHABURI

Phaya Thai

Rama IX

CHINA TOWN

Ratchathewi

World Trade

Chit Lom

Petchaburi

THANON PHETCHABURI

Khlong Tan Station

National Stadium

Siam

Phloen Chit

Bangkok Playhouse

Hualumphong

PATHUMWAN

Nana

Hualum-phong

Samyan

Ratchadamri

Asoke

Sukhumvit

SOI 39

Phrom Phong

SUKHUMVIT 55

SUKHUMVIT 63

SUKHUMVIT 71

SI PHRAYA

THANON

Silom

SARA SIN

Lumphini Park

THANON SUKHUMVIT

SUKHUMVIT

SURAWONG

SILOM

RAMA IV

Night Bazaar

Queen Sirikit Convention Centre

Thong Lo

Eastern Bus Terminal

BANGRAK

NARA

Sala Daeng

Chong Nonsi

Lumphini

Queen Sirikit Centre

UNESCO

Ekamai

TAKSIN BRIDGE

Surasak

Bon Kai/ Khlong Toey

Planetarium

Saphan Taksin

THIWAT RATCHA NAKHARIN

NANG LINCHI

SUNTHON KOSA

THANON RAMA IV

Phra Khanong

Bangkok Dockyard

SATHU PRADIT

Port Authority of Thailand

Khlong Pujak Hanong

THANON ROT FAI KAO

On Nut

THANON CHAN

RAMA III

NUA-TAI

SOUTH

RAMA III

**SUBWAY STATIONS**
As this guide went to press, the following stations were changing their names:
Bon Kai (Khlong Toey); Tiem Ruam Mit (Thailand Cultural Centre); Pracharat Bumphen (Huay Khwang); Ratchada (Ratchadaphisek); Morchit (Chatuchak Park).